ENCYCLOPEDIA

OF

SOUTHERN

CULTURE

CHARLES REAGAN WILSON & WILLIAM FERRIS

Coeditors

ANN J. ABADIE & MARY L. HART

Associate Editors

Sponsored by
The Center for the Study of Southern Culture
at the University of Mississippi

ENCYCLOPEDIA

OF

SOUTHERN

CULTURE

VOLUME 4
Religion—Women's Life

☆ ☆ ☆ ☆ ☆ ☆ ☆ ☆ ☆ ☆ ☆ ☆ ☆ ☆ ☆ ☆ ☆ ☆ ☆

ANCHOR BOOKS

DOUBLEDAY

New York London Toronto Sydney Auckland

AN ANCHOR BOOK
PUBLISHED BY DOUBLEDAY
a division of Bantam Doubleday Dell Publishing Group, Inc.
666 Fifth Avenue, New York, New York 10103

ANCHOR BOOKS, DOUBLEDAY, and the portrayal of an anchor
are trademarks of Doubleday, a division of Bantam Doubleday
Dell Publishing Group, Inc.

Encyclopedia of Southern Culture was originally published in hardcover
in one volume by the University of North Carolina Press in 1989. The
Anchor Books edition is published by arrangement with the University
of North Carolina Press.

Both the initial research and the publication of this work were made possible in part through a grant from the Division of Research Programs of
the National Endowment for the Humanities, an independent federal
agency whose mission is to award grants to support education, scholarship, media programming, libraries, and museums, in order to bring the
results of cultural activities to a broad, general public.

Book design by Chris Welch

Library of Congress Cataloging-in-Publication Data

Encyclopedia of Southern culture / Charles Reagan Wilson & William
Ferris, coeditors; Ann J. Abadie & Mary L. Hart, associate editors.
—1st Anchor Books ed.
p.   cm.
"Originally published in hardcover in one volume by the University of
North Carolina Press in 1989"—T.p. verso.
Includes bibliographical references and index.
Contents: Vol. 1. Agriculture–Environment—v. 2.   Ethnic Life–Law—
v. 3.   Literature–Recreation—v. 4.   Religion–Women's Life.
1. Southern States—Civilization—Encyclopedias.   2. Southern States—
Encyclopedias.   I. Wilson, Charles Reagan.   II. Ferris, William R.
F209.E53   1991   975'.003   90-973
CIP

ISBN 0-385-41548-6

"Tell about the South. What's it like there. What do they do there. Why do they live there. Why do they live at all."

WILLIAM FAULKNER
Absalom, Absalom!

The *Encyclopedia of Southern Culture* was
produced through major grants from the Program
for Research Tools and Reference Works of the
National Endowment for the Humanities, the
Ford Foundation, the Atlantic-Richfield
Foundation, and the Mary Doyle Trust.

The publication of this volume
was made possible by the
Fred W. Morrison Fund of the
University of North Carolina Press.

CONTENTS

||||||||||||||||||||||||||||||||||||||||||||||||||||||||||||||

CONSULTANTS

AGRICULTURE
Thomas D. Clark
248 Tahoma Road
Lexington, Ky. 40503

ART AND ARCHITECTURE
Jessie Poesch
Department of Art
Tulane University
New Orleans, La. 70118

BLACK LIFE
Thomas C. Holt
Department of History
University of Chicago
Chicago, Ill. 60637

EDUCATION
Thomas G. Dyer
Associate Vice President for
Academic Affairs
University of Georgia
Old College
Athens, Ga. 30602

ENVIRONMENT
Martin V. Melosi
Department of History
University of Houston
Houston, Tex. 77004

ETHNIC LIFE
George E. Pozzetta
Department of History
University of Florida
Gainesville, Fla. 32611

FOLKLIFE
William Ferris

Center for the Study of
Southern Culture
University of Mississippi
University, Miss. 38677

GEOGRAPHY
Richard Pillsbury
Department of Geography
Georgia State University
Atlanta, Ga. 30303

HISTORY AND MANNERS
Charles Reagan Wilson
Center for the Study of
Southern Culture
University of Mississippi
University, Miss. 38677

INDUSTRY
James C. Cobb
Honors Program
P.O. Box 6233
University of Alabama
Tuscaloosa, Ala. 35487-6322

LANGUAGE
Michael Montgomery
Department of English
University of South Carolina
Columbia, S.C. 29208

LAW
Maxwell Bloomfield
Department of History
The Catholic University of
America
Washington, D.C. 20017

LITERATURE
M. Thomas Inge
Randolph-Macon College
Ashland, Va. 23005

MEDIA
Edward D. C. Campbell, Jr.
Virginia State Library
11th Street at Capitol Square
Richmond, Va. 23219

MUSIC
Bill C. Malone
Department of History
Tulane University
New Orleans, La. 70118

MYTHIC SOUTH
George B. Tindall
Department of History
University of North Carolina
Chapel Hill, N.C. 27599

POLITICS
Numan Bartley
Department of History
University of Georgia
Athens, Ga. 30602

RECREATION
John Shelton Reed
Department of Sociology
University of North Carolina
Chapel Hill, N.C. 27599

RELIGION
Samuel S. Hill

Department of Religion
University of Florida
Gainesville, Fla. 32611

SCIENCE AND MEDICINE
James O. Breeden
Department of History
Southern Methodist University
Dallas, Tex. 75275

SOCIAL CLASS
J. Wayne Flynt
Department of History
Auburn University
Auburn, Ala. 36830

URBANIZATION
Blaine A. Brownell
School of Social and Behavioral
Sciences
University of Alabama at
Birmingham
Birmingham, Ala. 35294

VIOLENCE
Raymond D. Gastil
48 E. 21st Street
New York, N.Y. 10010

WOMEN'S LIFE
Carol Ruth Berkin
Baruch College
City University of New York
17 Lexington Avenue
New York, N.Y. 10010

FOREWORD

||||||||||||||||||||||||||||||||||||||||||||||||||||||||||

Can you remember those southern elder men who "jes' set" on their favored chair or bench for hours, every day—and a year later they could tell you at about what time of day someone's dog had trotted by? And the counterpart elderly ladies, their hands deeply wrinkled from decades of quilting, canning, washing collective tons of clothing in black cast-iron pots, in which at other seasonal times pork fat was rendered into lard, or some of that lard into soap? These southern ancestors, black and white, have always struck me as the Foundation Timbers of our South, and I think that we who were reared and raised by them, and amongst them, are blessed that we were.

I consider this *Encyclopedia of Southern Culture* the answer to a deep need that we resuscitate and keep alive and fresh the memories of those who are now bones and dust, who during their eras and in their respective ways contributed toward the social accretion that has entered legend as "the southern way of life," which we continue today.

It is a culture resulting from the antebellum mixture of social extremes based on the chattel slavery that supported an aristocratic gentility; in between the slaves and planters a vast majority struggled for their own survival. Centuries of slavery were abolished by an indelible war whose legacies continue to haunt us. The southern memory is of generations of life, of the good and the bad, the humor and the suffering from the past. The southerner does not sentimentalize but only remembers.

Out of the historic cotton tillage sprang the involuntary field hollers, the shouts, and the moanin' low that have since produced such a cornucopia of music, played daily, on every continent, where I have been astounded at how much I heard of the evolved blues, jazz, and gospel—as well as bluegrass and country—all of them of direct southern origin.

Equally worldwide is southern literature. Writers took the oral traditions of the South—the political rhetoric, preaching, conversational wordplay, and lazy-day storytelling—and converted them into art. The latest addition to southern literature is this *Encyclopedia*, no small part of whose greatness, I think, is that it is compiled by many researchers who did not simply read books but who rubbed shoulders with those whom they interviewed and recorded and studied. They walked and talked with the sharecropper farmers, the cooks, the quiltmakers, the convicts, the merchants, the fishermen, and all the others who make these pages a volume of living memories.

The region and its people have undergone dramatic changes in the last decades, overcoming much, although not all, of the poverty of the past, and they are now sharing in the nation's prosperity. Old ways that divided the people have fallen away to be replaced by new dreams. The hard lessons from the past are not forgotten in this *Encyclopedia.* I testify that this *Encyclopedia of Southern Culture* mirrors the very best of what has lately come to be called "the new South." Never before have such volumes been pro-duced by a team so committed to distilling and presenting our southern distinctiveness.

Alex Haley

ACKNOWLEDGMENTS

These volumes could never have been completed without the assistance of countless individuals. The coeditors and associate editors wish to thank our consultants and contributors for their planning, researching, and writing of articles. We should note that Raven McDavid helped to plan the Language section before his untimely death in 1984. Clarence Mohr's work on the early design of the *Encyclopedia* provided the basic organizational structure for the volumes. Many scholars reviewed articles, made suggestions for improvements, and verified factual material. Richard H. Brown, of the Newberry Library in Chicago, advised wisely on *Encyclopedia* matters, as with other projects of the Center for the Study of Southern Culture. Howard Lamar offered sage counsel on the *Encyclopedia* from its earliest planning stages. Research assistants Elizabeth Makowski and Sharon A. Sharp supervised the review and verification of entries, assisted by numerous teaching assistants and volunteers, and also served as staff writers. Editorial assistants Ann Sumner Holmes, Ginna Parsons, and Karen McDearman Cox supervised final production of copy and served as endless sources of good advice and varied skill. Lolly Pilkington read the entire manuscript with a skilled eye. Teaching assistants in the Department of History and the Southern Studies program spent much time in the library checking and rechecking information and reading galley proof. Personnel in the John Davis Williams Library of the University of Mississippi often came to our rescue, and we are grateful to the many archivists and librarians across the nation who assisted us with obtaining illustrations. Special thanks are due the staff of the University of North Carolina Press, especially its director Matthew Hodgson, editor-in-chief Iris Tillman Hill, managing editor Sandra Eisdorfer, and Ron Maner, Pamela Upton, and Paula Wald.

The *Encyclopedia of Southern Culture* was produced with financial support from the National Endowment for the Humanities, the Ford Foundation, the Atlantic-Richfield Foundation, and the Mary Doyle Trust. The Graduate School and alumni and friends of the University of Mississippi donated required funds for a matching NEH grant in 1983, and the editors are grateful for their assistance. Donors include: The James Hand Foundation by Kathleen Hand Carter; Mrs. R. R. Morrison, Jr.; Mrs. Hester F. Faser; David L. May; James J. Brown, Jr.; Lynn Crosby Gammill; First National Bank of Vicksburg, Mississippi; The Goodman Charitable and Educational Trust, Hallie Goodman, Trustee; Dr. F. Watt Bishop; Robert Travis; Mrs. Dorothy Crosby; Christopher Keller, Jr.; Worth I. Dunn; Wiley Fairchild; Mrs. Eric Biedenharn; John S. Callon; Betty Carter; Shelby Flowers Ferris; Mary Hohenberg; Mr. & Mrs. John Kramer; Samuel McIlwain; and Prescott Sherman.

INTRODUCTION

||||||||||||||||||||||||||||||||||||||||||||||||||||||||||||||||||||||||||||||||||||

The American South has long generated powerful images and complex emotions. In the years since World War II, the region has undergone dramatic changes in race relations, political institutions, and economic life. Those changes have led some observers to forecast the eventual end of a distinctive southern region. Other scholars and popular writers point to continuities with past attitudes and behavior. The *Encyclopedia of Southern Culture* appears during a period of major transition in the life of the South and is in part a reflection of these changes. It examines both the historical and the contemporary worlds of southern culture. The *Encyclopedia*'s editors have sought to assemble authoritative, concise, thoughtful, substantive, and interesting articles that will give scholars, students, and general readers a useful perspective on the South.

SOUTHERN CULTURE

|||||||||||||||||||||||||||||||||||||||||||||||||||

The *Encyclopedia*'s definition of "the South" is a cultural one. The geographical focus is, to be sure, on the 11 states of the former Confederacy (Alabama, Arkansas, Florida, Georgia, Louisiana, Mississippi, North Carolina, South Carolina, Tennessee, Texas, and Virginia), but this tidy historical definition fails to confront the complexities of studying the region. Delaware, Kentucky, Maryland, and Missouri were slave states at the beginning of the Civil War, and many of their citizens then and after claimed

a southern identity. Social scientists today use statistical data covering the "census South," which includes Delaware, Maryland, West Virginia, Oklahoma, and the District of Columbia. The Gallup public opinion polling organization defines the South as the Confederate states plus Oklahoma and Kentucky.

Moreover, the realities of cultural areas require a broadened definition. Cultural areas have core zones, where distinctive traits are most concentrated, and margins, where the boundaries of the culture overlap with other cultural areas. The *Encyclopedia*'s articles explore the nature of both these core areas and margins in the South. The borders of the South have surely varied over time. In the colonial era Delaware was an agricultural slave state with a claim of being southern. Maryland was a southern state, sharing much with its neighbor, Virginia, in a Chesapeake subculture. Maryland did not join the Confederacy, but soldiers from the state fought in the Confederate armies and one finds Confederate monuments in Baltimore. St. Louis was a midwestern city and the gateway to the West, but southerners have also claimed it. The Mississippi River culture tied St. Louis to areas of the Lower South, and southerners have often been associated with it. John F. Kennedy once said that Washington, D.C., was known for its southern efficiency and northern charm. Carved from an area of Maryland as a concession to southerners, Washington was a slaveowning area and was once a center for slave auctions. Later, under Woodrow Wilson, a southern-born president, the nation's capital became a racially segregated bastion reflecting southern regional mores. Washington has also long been a center for southern black migration, an educational mecca for blacks, and a center for black musicians, artists, and writers. Most recently, geographical proximity to Appalachia has made Washington a center for the performance of such other expressions of southern culture as bluegrass music. Contemporary Washington, however, appears to be less and less "southern," and urban historians consequently omit it from the list of regional cities (and thus there is no separate entry on Washington in the *Encyclopedia.*

Contributors to the *Encyclopedia* at times transcend geography and history when examining questions of regional consciousness, symbolism, mythology, and sectional stereotyping. The "South" is found wherever southern culture is found, and that culture is located not only in the Deep South, the Upper South, and border cities, but also in "little Dixies" (the southern parts of Ohio, Indiana, Illinois, and parts of Missouri and Oklahoma), among black Mississippians who migrated to south Chicago, among white Appalachians and black Alabamians who migrated to Detroit, and among former Okies and Arkies who settled in and around Bakersfield, California. This diaspora of southern ethnic culture is also found in the works of expatriate southern artists and writers. Although Richard Wright and Tennessee Williams lived in Paris and New York, respectively, they continued to explore their southern roots in their writing.

The South exists as a state of mind both within and beyond its geographical boundaries. Recent studies of mythology suggest that the New York theater in the late 19th century and Hollywood in the 20th century have kept alive images, legends, and myths about the South in the national consciousness. One can view the American South and its culture as international property. The worlds of *Roots*, *Gone with the Wind*, blues, country music, rock and roll, William Faulkner, and Alice Walker are admired and closely studied throughout the world. The South has nurtured important myths, and their impact on other cultures is a vital aspect of the *Encyclopedia*'s perspective. In the end, then, the *Encyclopedia*'s definition of the South is a broad, inclusive one, based on culture.

These volumes focus specifically on exploring the culture of the South. In the 1950s anthropologists Alfred Kroeber and Clyde Kluckholn cataloged 164 definitions of culture, suggesting the problems then and now of a precise definition. To 19th-century intellectuals culture was the best of civilization's achievements. Matthew Arnold was perhaps the best-known advocate of this Victorian-era ideal, and H. L. Mencken—the South's nastiest and most entertaining critic in the early 20th century—was also a believer in it. Mencken argued in his essay "The Sahara of the Bozart" (1920) that the upper-class, aristocratic southerner of the early 19th century "liked to toy with ideas. He was hospitable and tolerant. He had the vague thing that we call culture." Mencken found the South of his era severely wanting, though, in this ideal of culture. He saw in the South "not a single picture gallery worth going into, or a single orchestra capable of playing the nine symphonies of Beethoven, or a single opera-house, or a single theater devoted to decent plays, or a single public monument (built since the war) that is worth looking at, or a single workshop devoted to the making of beautiful things." Mencken allowed that the region excelled "in the lower reaches of the gospel hymn, the phonograph and the chautauqua harangue."

The South of Mencken's day did trail the rest of the nation in the development of important cultural institutions; but today the South, the nation, and the world celebrate the "lower reaches" of southern culture. This judgment on the value of the sounds and words coming from the region reflects 20th-century understandings of culture. Anthropologists have taken the lead in exploring the theoretical aspects of cultures. Edward Burnett Tylor gave a classic definition of culture as "that complex whole which includes knowledge, belief, art, morals, law, customs, and any other capabilities and habits" acquired by the members of a society. For students of culture, the goal was to study and outline discrete cultural traits, using this definition to convey the picture of a culture. During the 20th century another major anthropological theory of culture emerged. Kroeber, Bronislaw Malinowski, and Ruth Benedict stressed the study of pattern, form, structure, and organization in a culture rather than the simple listing of observed traits. Patterns could include customs associated with food, labor, and manners as well as more complex social, political, and economic systems.

Recently culture has been viewed as an abstraction, consisting of the inherited models and ideas with which people approach their experiences. The theory of social structure, first developed by British anthropologist Alexander Reginald Radcliffe-Brown in the 1930s and 1940s, stressed that culture must include recognition of the persistence of social groups, social classes, and social roles. The structuralist theories of Claude Lévi-Strauss attempt to apply abstract mathematical formulae to society. Although social anthropologists avoid the term *culture*, they have insured that the study of culture not neglect social background.

The theoretical work of Clifford Geertz is especially significant in understanding the definition of culture developed for the *Encyclopedia of Southern Culture*. Geertz defines *culture* as "an historically transmitted pattern of meanings embodied in symbols, a system of inherited conceptions expressed in symbolic forms." Through culture, humans "communicate, perpetuate, and develop their knowledge about and attitudes toward life." This contemporary definition stresses mental culture, expressed through symbol systems, which gives human beings a framework for understanding one another, themselves, and the wider world. Culture patterns, including material, oral, mental, and social systems, are blueprints for organizing human interaction.

The *Encyclopedia of Southern Culture* is not intended as a contribution to the general study of culture theory, although awareness of theories of culture has been useful background in the conceptualization of the volumes and in the selection of topics. The volumes attempt to study within the southern context what 20th-century humanist T. S. Eliot said, in *Notes towards the Definition of Culture*, was culture—"all the characteristic activities and interests of a people." Articles in the volumes deal with regional cultural achievements in such areas as music, literature, art, and architecture. The broader goal of the volumes is to chart the cultural landscape of the South, addressing those aspects of southern life and thought that have sustained either the reality or the illusion of regional distinctiveness. The volumes detail specific cultural traits, suggest the cultural patterns that tie the region together, point out the internal diversity within the South, and explore with special attention the importance of social structure and symbolism. Above all, the volumes have been planned to carry out Eliot's belief that "culture is not merely the sum of several activities, but a *way of life*."

Eliot's definition of culture, then, can be seen as a working definition for the *Encyclopedia of Southern Culture*. In order to foster interdisciplinary communication, the editors have included the full range of social indicators, trait groupings, literary concepts, and historical evidence commonly used by students of regionalism. The criteria for the all-important selection of topics, however, have been consistently to include the characteristic traits that give the South a distinctive culture.

A special concern of the *Encyclopedia* has been to identify distinctive regional characteristics. It addresses those aspects of southern life and thought—the individuals, places, ideas, rituals, symbols, myths, values, and experiences—which have sustained either the reality or the illusion of regional distinctiveness. The comparative method has been encouraged as a way to suggest contrasts with other American regions and with other societies. One lesson of earlier regional scholarship has been the need to look at the South in the widest possible context. The editors of the *Encyclopedia* have assumed that the distinctiveness of southern culture does not lie in any one trait but rather in the peculiar combination of regional cultural characteris-

tics. The fundamental uniqueness of southern culture thus emerges from the *Encyclopedia*'s composite portrait of the South. The editors asked contributors to consider individual traits that clearly are unique to the region. Although some topics may not be uniquely southern in themselves, contributors have been asked to explore particular regional aspects of those topics. Subjects that suggest the internal diversity of the region are also treated if they contribute to the overall picture of southern distinctiveness. The Cajuns of Louisiana, the Germans of Texas, and the Jews of Savannah, for example, contribute to the distinctive flavor of southern life. Their adaptations, and resistance, to southern cultural patterns suggest much about the region's distinctiveness.

The question of continuity and change in southern culture is another central concern of the *Encyclopedia*. Contributors have examined themes and topics in an evolutionary framework. Historians represent by far the largest group of contributors to the project. The volumes do not attempt to narrate the region's history in a systematic way, a task ably achieved in the *Encyclopedia of Southern History* (1979), but contributors from all disciplines have developed material within an appropriate time perspective. As Clifford Geertz has written, culture is "historically transmitted," a fact that is especially relevant for the study of the South, where the apogee of cultural distinctiveness may well have been in an earlier period. Because the *Encyclopedia* focuses on culture rather than history, historical topics were chosen because they are relevant to the origin, development, or decline of an aspect of southern culture. Given the historical shape of southern cultural development, one would expect less material on the colonial era (before there was a self-conscious "South") and increased concentration of material in the Civil War and postbellum eras (perhaps the high points of southern cultural distinctiveness). Nearly all articles include historical material, and each overview essay systematically traces the development of a major subject area. In addition, such selected historical entries as "Colonial Heritage," "Frontier Heritage," and "Civil War" are included with a cultural focus appropriate to the volumes.

STUDY OF
SOUTHERN REGIONALISM

The *Encyclopedia of Southern Culture* reflects a broad intellectual interest in regionalism, the importance of which in the United States is far from unique when seen in a global context. The struggle to accommodate regional cultures within a larger nation is an experience common to many Western and Third World peoples. Despite the contemporary developments in transportation and communication that promise the emergence of a "global village," regionalism is an enduring reality of the modern world. The Basques in Spain, the Scots in Britain, the Kurds in the Middle East, and Armenians in the Soviet Union are only a few examples of groups that have recently reasserted their regional interests.

Although public emphasis on the United States as a cultural melting pot has sometimes obscured the nation's enduring regional heritage, the study of regionalism has long been a major field of scholarship involving leading authorities from many academic disciplines

both in the United States and abroad. The *Encyclopedia* is part of the broader field of American Studies, which has dramatically evolved in recent years from a focus on such regional types as the New England Yankees, the southern Cavaliers, and the western cowboys and Indians. Since the 1960s studies of black life, ethnic life, and women's life have significantly changed the definition of American culture. In the 1980s the study of American region, place, and community—whether it be a Brooklyn neighborhood or a county in rural Mississippi—is essential to understanding the nation. In the context of this American Studies tradition, the *Encyclopedia* focuses on the American South, a place that has influenced its people in complex and fascinating ways.

Significant bodies of research exist for all major regions of the United States, but by almost any standard the American South has received the most extensive scholarly attention. Since the 1930s virtually all aspects of southern life have come under increasingly rigorous, systematic intellectual scrutiny. The *Encyclopedia of Southern Culture* is a collaborative effort that combines intellectual perspectives that reflect the breadth of Southern Studies. Sociologists, historians, literary critics, folklorists, anthropologists, political scientists, psychologists, theologians, and other scholars have written on the region, and all of these fields are represented by contributors to the *Encyclopedia*. Journalists, lawyers, physicians, architects, and other professionals from outside the academy have also studied the South, and their contributions appear in these volumes as well.

Students of the South operate within a well-developed institutional framework. The proliferation of academic journals that focus on the South has mirrored expanding disciplinary boundaries in regional scholarship. The *Journal of Southern History*, the *Southern Review*, the *Southern Economic Journal*, *Social Forces*, the *Southern Folklore Quarterly*, the *Virginia Quarterly Review*, the *South Atlantic Quarterly*, and the *Southwestern Political Science Quarterly* are only a few of the titles that have specialized in publishing material on the region. The contemporary era has witnessed a dramatic expansion in the publication of books on the South. The University of North Carolina Press was the first southern university press to publish an extensive list of titles on the South, and by the early 1950s the press alone had produced some 200 studies. Works on the region are now published by university presses in every southern state and find a ready market with national publishers as well.

Research on the South has led to greater appreciation of the region's internal diversity, which is reflected in the study of smaller geographical areas or specialized themes. Such recent periodicals as the *Appalachian Journal*, *Mid-South Folklore*, and *South Atlantic Urban Studies* illustrate the narrowing geographical and topical focus of recent scholarship on the South. Overlapping interests and subject matter shared among regional scholars have exerted a steady pressure toward broadening disciplinary horizons. Meaningful cooperation among disciplines is complicated by differences of vocabulary and method, but students of the American South demonstrate a growing awareness that they are engaged in a common endeavor that can be furthered as much by cooperation as by specialization. Such periodicals as *Southern Quarterly*, *Southern Studies*, and *Per-*

spectives on the American South have established forums for interdisciplinary study.

In recent years regional scholarship has also influenced curriculum development in colleges and universities. Leading institutional centers for the study of the South include the Center for the Study of Southern Culture at the University of Mississippi, the Institute for Southern Studies at the University of South Carolina, the Institute for Southern Studies at Durham, N.C., and the Center for the Study of Southern History and Culture at the University of Alabama. Appalachian study centers are located at, among other places, the University of Kentucky, East Tennessee State University, Appalachian State University, Mars Hill College, and Berea College. The Institute for Texan Cultures is in San Antonio, and Baylor University launched a Texas Studies Center in 1987. The Center for Arkansas Studies is at the University of Arkansas at Little Rock, while the University of Southwestern Louisiana's Center for Louisiana Studies concentrates on Cajun and Creole folk culture. These developments are, again, part of a broader interest in regional studies programs at universities in other regions, including the Center for the Study of New England Culture at the University of Massachusetts at Amherst and the Great Plains Center at the University of Nebraska.

The *Encyclopedia of Southern Culture* grows out of the work of the University of Mississippi's Center for the Study of Southern Culture, which was established in 1977 to coordinate existing university resources and to develop multidisciplinary teaching, research, and outreach programs about the South. The center's mission is to strengthen the university's instructional program in the humanities, to promote scholarship on every aspect of southern culture, and to encourage public understanding of the South through publications, media productions, lectures, performances, and exhibitions. Center personnel administer a Southern Studies curriculum that includes both B.A. and M.A. degree programs; a Ford Foundation–funded, three-year (1986–89) project aimed at incorporating more fully the experiences of blacks and women into the teaching of Southern Studies; an annual United States Information Agency–sponsored project for international scholars interested in regional and ethnic cultures; such annual meetings as the Porter L. Fortune Chancellor's Symposium on Southern History, the Faulkner and Yoknapatawpha Conference, and the Barnard-Millington Symposium on Southern Science and Medicine; and a variety of periodicals, films, and media presentations. The center administers these programs in cooperation with the on-campus departments in the College of Liberal Arts, the Afro-American Studies program, and the Sarah Isom Center for Women's Studies. The University of Mississippi and its Center for the Study of Southern Culture provided the necessary institutional setting for coordinating the diverse needs of the *Encyclopedia*'s hundreds of participants.

Recognizing both the intellectual maturity of scholarship in the American South and the potential role of regional study in consolidating previously fragmented academic endeavors, the *Encyclopedia* planners conceived the idea of an interdisciplinary reference work to bring together and synthesize current knowledge about the South. Scholars studying the South have been served by

a number of reference works, but none of these has had the aims and perspective of the *Encyclopedia of Southern Culture*. The 13-volume series, *The South in the Building of the Nation* (1909–13), which attempted a comprehensive survey of the region's history, was the closest predecessor to this encyclopedia. Other major works include the 16-volume *Library of Southern Literature* (1908–13), Howard W. Odum's monumental *Southern Regions of the United States* (1936), W. T. Couch's edited *Culture in the South* (1936), and, more recently, the *Encyclopedia of Southern History* (1978), the *Encyclopedia of Religion in the South* (1984), and the *History of Southern Literature* (1986).

Like any major reference work, the *Encyclopedia* addresses the long-range needs and interests of a diverse reading audience. Before launching the project the editors consulted extensively with leading authorities in all areas of American Studies and Southern Studies and sought additional advice from directors of comparable projects. Planning for the original single-volume edition began in 1978 with the compilation of a working outline of subjects that had received frequent attention in major studies of regional culture. During the fall of 1979 some 270 U.S. and international scholars received copies of the preliminary topical list, together with background information about the project. Approximately 150 of these scholars, representing a variety of disciplines, responded to this mailing, commenting upon the potential value of the proposed volume and making suggestions concerning its organization and content.

In 1980 the Center for the Study of Southern Culture commissioned several

scholars to prepare detailed lists of topics for major sections of the volume, and
to write sample articles as well. The
National Endowment for the Humanities
supported the *Encyclopedia of Southern
Culture* with a 1980–81 planning grant
and grants covering 1981–83 and
1984–86. The Ford Foundation, the
Atlantic-Richfield Foundation, and the
Mary Doyle Trust also provided major
funding. Full-time work on the *Encyclopedia* began in September 1981. The
content of the volume was divided into
24 major subject areas, and the editors
selected a senior consultant to assist in
planning the topics and contributors for
each section. During the fall and winter
of 1981–82, the consultants formulated
initial lists of topics and recommended
appropriate contributors for entries. In
general, the consultants were actively
involved in the initial stages of planning
and less involved in later editorial work.
Project staff handled the paperwork for
assignments. The editors sent each contributor a packet of information on the
project, including the overall list of topics, so that contributors could see how
their articles fit into the volume as a
whole. Authors were encouraged to
make suggestions for additional entries,
and many of them did so. When contributors were unable to write for the
volume, they often suggested other
scholars, thus facilitating the reassign-
ment of articles. The editors assumed
the responsibility for editing articles for
style, clarity, and tone appropriate for
a reference book. They reviewed all entries for accuracy, and research assistants verified the factual and
bibliographical veracity of each entry.
The senior consultants, with their special expertise in each subject area, provided an additional check on the quality
of the articles.

ORGANIZATION AND CONTENT OF THE ENCYCLOPEDIA

The *Encyclopedia of Southern Culture* is
a synthesis of current scholarship and
attempts to set new directions for further
research. The *Encyclopedia*'s objectives
are fourfold: (1) The volumes provide
students and general readers with convenient access to basic facts and bibliographical data about southern cultural
patterns and their historical development. (2) By bringing together lucid
analyses of modern scholarship on
southern culture from the humanities
and the social sciences, the *Encyclopedia* is intended to facilitate communication across disciplinary lines and
help stimulate new approaches to regional study. It attempts to integrate disparate intellectual efforts and represents
an innovative organization and presentation of knowledge. (3) The volumes
can serve as a curriculum component
for multidisciplinary courses on the
American South and provide a model
for scholars wishing to assemble similar
research tools in other regions. (4)
Viewed in its totality, the *Encyclopedia*
locates the specific components of regional culture within the framework of
a larger organic whole. At this level, the
volumes attempt to illuminate the nature
and function of regionalism in American
culture.

The editors considered an alphabetical arrangement of articles but concluded that organization of information
into 24 major sections more accurately
reflects the nature of the project and
would provide a fresh perspective.
Cross-references to related articles in
other sections are essential guides to
proper use of the *Encyclopedia*, en-

abling readers to consult articles written on a common topic from different perspectives. Sections often reflect an academic field (history, geography, literature), but at times the academic division has been rejected in favor of a section organized around a cultural theme (such as social class) that has become a central scholarly concern. In general, the sections are designed to reflect the amount and quality of scholarship in particular areas of regional study. Articles within each section are arranged in three divisions. The overview essay is written by the *Encyclopedia*'s consultant in that section and provides an interpretive summary of the field. That essay is followed by alphabetically arranged thematic articles and then by alphabetically arranged, brief topical-biographical sketches.

Although the editors and consultants conceived each section as a separate unit, sections are closely connected to one another through cross-references. The titles of major sections are brief, but the editors have grouped together related material under these simple rubrics. The Agriculture section thus includes rural-life articles, the Black Life section includes articles on race relations, Social Class includes material on social structure and occupational groups, and Industry includes information on commercial activity.

Several sections deserve special comment in regard to their organization and content. The Black Life section (Vol. 1) contains most, though not all, of the separate entries on southern black culture. The editors placed Richard Wright and Ralph Ellison in Literature (Vol. 3) to honor their roles as central figures in *southern* (as well as black) literature, and most blues musicians are similarly

found in Music (Vol. 3). But the list of biographies in Black Life is intended to stand on its own, including individuals representing music, literature, religion, sports, politics, and other areas of black achievement. The *Encyclopedia* claims for southern culture such individuals as Mary McLeod Bethune, Ida Wells-Barnett, Arna Bontemps, and James Weldon Johnson, who traditionally have been seen as part of black history but not southern culture. The separate Black Life section is intended to recognize the special nature of southern black culture—both black and southern. Black culture is central to understanding the region and the *Encyclopedia*'s attempt to explore this perspective in specific, detailed topics may be the most significant contribution of these volumes toward understanding the region. Although the terms *Afro-American* and *Euro-American* are sometimes used, *black* and *white* are more often used to refer to the two major interrelated cultures of the South. These terms seem the clearest, most inclusive, and most widely accepted terms of reference.

The Women's Life section (Vol. 4) has similar aims. Many thematic articles and biographies of women of achievement appear in this section, which is designed to stand on its own. Scholars in the last 20 years have explored southern women's cultural values and issues, and their work provides a distinctive perspective on the region. Gender, like race and social class, has set parameters for cultural life in the South. The section includes articles on family life, childhood, and the elderly, reflecting the major responsibilities and concerns of women. The inclusion of these topics in this section is not meant to suggest that family responsibilities were the sole concern of women or that men were un-involved with family, children, and the elderly. The articles usually discuss both male and female activities within the family. Scholarship on family life has often focused on women's roles, and family matters traditionally have played a significant part in women's lives. Most of the Women's Life section is concentrated, however, on concerns beyond the family and household, reflecting the contemporary scholarship in this area.

The Education section (Vol. 1) presented especially difficult choices of inclusion, and again, a selective approach was adopted. The flagship state public university in each southern state is included, but beyond that, institutions have been selected that represent differing constituencies to suggest the diversity of educational activity in the region. Berea College, Commonwealth College, the University of the South, and Tuskegee Institute each reflect an important dimension of southern education. The inclusion of additional school entries would have departed from the *Encyclopedia*'s overall guidelines and made a four-volume reference work impossible.

The History and Manners section (Vol. 2) contains a mix of articles that focus on cultural and social dimensions of the South. Combining topics in history and manners reflects the editors' decision that in a reference work on cultural concerns, history entries should deal with broad socio-cultural history. There are, thus, no separate, detailed entries on Civil War battles, but, instead, long thematic articles on the cultural meaning of battlefields, monuments, and wars. The article on Robert E. Lee discusses the facts of Lee's life but also the history of his image for southerners and Americans.

Overview essays in each section are interpretive pieces that synthesize modern scholarship on major aspects of southern culture. The consultants who have written them trace historical developments and relate their broad subjects to regional cultural concerns. Many specific topics are discussed within overview essays rather than through separate entries, so readers should consult the index in order to locate such material. As one might expect, major subject areas have developed at a different pace. In such fields as literature, music, religion, folklife, and political culture, a vast body of scholarship exists. In these areas, the *Encyclopedia* overview essays provide a starting point for those users of this reference work interested in the subject. Such other fields as law, art, science, and medicine have only recently emerged as separate fields of Southern Studies. In these areas, the overview essays should help define the fields and point toward areas for further research.

Most thematic, topical, and biographical entries fall clearly within one section, but some articles were appropriate for several sections. The Scopes trial, for example, could have been placed in Religion, Law, or Science and Medicine. Consultants in Black Life, Music, and Women's Life all suggested Bessie Smith as an entry in their categories. The article on cockfighting clearly related to the Recreation section but was placed in Violence to suggest how recreational activities reflect a culture of violence. The gospel music articles could have appeared in Religion, but the editors decided that Music was the most appropriate category for them.

Much consideration and consultation with authorities in relevant fields occurred before such decisions were made on topics that did not fit perfectly into any one section. Readers should rely on the index and cross-references between sections to lead them to desired entries.

Biographies focus on the cultural significance of key individuals. The volumes do not claim to be exhaustive in their biographical entries. Rather than attempt to include all prominent people in a subject area, the editors decided to treat representative figures in terms of their contributions to, or significance for, southern culture. In selecting individuals, the goal was to include biographies of those iconic individuals associated with a particular aspect of the region's culture. Consultants identified those major figures who have immediate relevance to the region. The editors and consultants also selected individuals who illuminate major themes and exemplify southern cultural styles. Persons in this category may have made special contributions to southern distinctiveness, to cultural achievements, or to the development of a characteristic aspect of southern life. The Music and Literature categories have been given somewhat fuller biographical attention than other subject areas, a decision that is warranted by southern achievements in those areas. In addition to the separate biographical entries, many individuals are discussed in such thematic articles as "Linguists" or "Historians," which outline contributions of key persons to certain fields. Readers should consult the index in each volume to locate biographical information on southerners who appear in that volume.

The *Encyclopedia* includes biographies of living persons as well as the deceased. It is especially concerned with regional cultural issues in the contemporary South, and the inclusion of living individuals was crucial to establishing continuities between past and present. Entries on Bill Moyers and Charles Kuralt, for example, help readers to understand that the journalistic traditions of the South have been extended into the television age.

Selecting approximately 250 individuals for inclusion in the *Encyclopedia of Southern Culture* was no easy task. The list of potential individuals was widely circulated, and the choices represent the informed judgment of our consultants and contributors, leading scholars in the field of Southern Studies. The selection of biographies was made in light of the *Encyclopedia*'s overall definition of culture. The goal was not to list every cultural trait or include every prominent individual in the South but to explore *characteristic* aspects of the region's life and culture and to show their interrelationships. The biographical entries are not simply descriptive, factual statements but are instead intimately related to the broader thematic and overview essays. Biographical entries were meant to suggest how a representative individual is part of a broader pattern, a way of life, in the American South.

Interdisciplinary study has become prominent in a number of scholarly areas, but in few is it as useful as in the study of region. The interrelatedness of such specific fields as politics, religion, economics, cultural achievement, and social organization becomes especially obvious when scholars study a region. Interdisciplinary study of the South is a means of exploring humanity in all its aspects. The intellectual specialization of the modern world often makes this study difficult, but the editors of the *Encyclopedia* hope these volumes will promote that goal. Scholars exploring various aspects of the South's life now compose a distinct field of interdisciplinary Southern Studies, and the *Encyclopedia* joins those scholars in common effort to extend the present bounds of knowledge about the South.

The Editors
Center for the Study of Southern Culture
University of Mississippi

EDITORS' NOTE

The *Encyclopedia* is divided into four volumes and 24 major subject areas, arranged in alphabetical order. A table of contents listing articles in each section is found at the beginning of the section. An overview essay is followed by a series of alphabetically arranged thematic essays and then brief, alphabetically arranged topical-biographical entries. Readers are urged to consult the index, as well as the tables of contents, in locating articles.

When appropriate, articles contain cross-references to related articles in other sections. Material is cross-referenced only to similar-length or shorter material. Thematic articles, for example, are cross-referenced to thematic articles or to short topical articles in other sections but not to longer overview essays. Topical-biographical entries are cross-referenced to topical-biographical articles in other sections but not to longer overview or thematic essays. Each cross-reference to related material lists the section in small capital letters, followed by the article title. If the entry is a short topical-biographical article, the title is preceded by a slash. The following example is a cross-reference to, first, a thematic article and, then, a topical-biographical entry, both in the Folklife section:

See also FOLKLIFE: Storytelling; / Clower, Jerry

Every effort was made to update material before publication. However, changes in contributors' affiliations, in biographical data because of the death of an individual, and in the names of institutions, for example, could not be made after the book went to press.

RELIGION

SAMUEL S. HILL

University of Florida

CONSULTANT

Overleaf: River baptism in rural Kentucky

RELIGION
||||||||||||||||||||||||||||||||||||||||||||||||

The South's religious life is distinctive in ways that parallel the region's general distinctiveness. Its fervently religious people are frequently described as "born again," their religion as "fundamentalist." There is some accuracy in the use of these terms. But even they refer to complex concepts. Moreover, they do not do justice to the diversity of the South, which includes the religion of white people, the religion of black people, and the varieties of each.

Students of religious movements always do well to ask about the intentions of the religious people themselves. What do they believe? What has powerful meaning for them? What happens to them when they attend church services; what are they seeking to express when they worship and when they support church causes?

Focus on baptism and the Lord's Supper, the two Protestant sacraments, or "ordinances" as they are often called in the South, affords insight into the dynamics of regional faith. Why baptism is such a persistent and public issue tells a great deal about the religious history of the region. It also discloses much about the interaction of religion and culture there. Similarly, such topics as the character of church services, their tone and emphasis, the style of church architecture and the activity that takes place there suggest what the people believe and how their faith is expressed.

Perspectives such as these yield understanding of the humanistic dimensions of the South's religious life. They point to the metaphors in which the message is couched, the mythos on which it is founded, and the system of values that prompt characteristic behavior. They reflect the overall regional culture, in history and in the present, yet they have a life of their own and are not simply by-products of economic, political, or social forces.

Distinctiveness of Southern Religion. Three features stand out in making the religion of the South different from the patterns that prevail elsewhere. (1) The forms that are common in the region are relatively homogeneous. The range of popular options is narrow. (2) The South is the only society in Christendom where the evangelical family of Christians is dominant. Evangelicalism's dominance is decisive in making the South the "religious region" that it is and in marking off the South from patterns, practices, and perspectives prevalent in other parts of America. (3) A set of four common convictions occupies a normative southern religious position. Movements and denominations in the South are judged for authenticity in the popular mind by how well they support these beliefs: (a) the Bible is the sole reference point of belief and practice; (b) direct and dynamic access to the Lord is open to all; (c) morality is defined in individualistic and personal terms; and (d) worship is informal.

The permeation of religion throughout the southern population continues to puzzle observers imbued with the "modern mind" and a secularist outlook. To a remarkable degree for a modern Western culture, the South adheres to traditional Christianity. It believes in a supernaturalism reminiscent of medieval Europe. Religion is still treated as a vital concern. A majority accept orthodox teachings. And many who are not church members believe they should submit to conversion and expect that some day they will. Traditional faith continues to be the popular form, and its hold on the hearts and minds of people is quite firm.

The identification of Christianity with the "old-time religion" makes believing difficult for other southerners, however. To a sizable and growing segment, the South's traditional religion seems outdated and is untenable. Such people have not abandoned the faith; rather they are unable to respond to it through the typical regional forms. The South is, in Flannery O'Connor's apt phrase, "Christ-haunted." The old-fashioned faith is integral to the regional way of life. Though others resist such a worldview, they cannot give up religion or get away from it. They are so deeply indoctrinated in the orthodox faith that they cannot articulate alternative formulations of it, much as they wish they could.

Few characterizations of the South are more acute than the recognition that it has been a limited-options culture. Historically that has been true, especially in the 75 years following the Civil War. National economic development largely bypassed the region. In hardly any other aspect has the limitation of choices been more pronounced than in religion. Southerners' range of options with respect to personal faith has been narrow. Roman Catholicism has been limited.

Pulpit of Rose Hill Baptist Church, Vicksburg, Mississippi, 1974

Such classical Protestant churches as the Episcopal and Lutheran have been viewed as suited to certain classes, families, and tastes, in the former case, and to people of German stock in the latter. Other denominations such as Moravians and the Brethren have been seen as "ethnic." It is only a partial exaggeration to classify the remaining Protestant options as variations on a theme. From Presbyterian to Pentecostal, from Campbellite to Holiness, in black churches and white, there is an insistent preoccupation with the "four common convictions"—the Bible as authority, direct access to the Holy Spirit, traditional morality, and informal worship.

Notable differences in style, teaching, and emphasis differentiate the Presbyterian churches from the Assemblies of God, the Southern Baptists from the United Methodists, the Disciples of Christ from their historic kin in the Churches of Christ, black Methodists from white Methodists, the southern

Congregationalists from the independent Baptist congregations. But, all things considered, the impact of a single coherent way of understanding Christianity is extensive and tenacious in the South.

Protestantism can be classified into four major families—liturgical, classical (or Reformation), evangelical, and radical. The evangelical predominates in the South. Even Presbyterianism, which falls within the classical category, takes on features of evangelicalism. Radical Protestantism—Mennonite, Amish, Quaker—has left its stamp on regional forms but has not been prominent in its own right. Its commitment to pacifism has had very little acceptance in the South. At the same time convictions about the possibility and necessity of biblical primitivism have contributed to the popularity of restorationist thought. Prominent among Churches of Christ and Landmark Baptists (some of them members of Southern Baptist churches) especially, restorationism seeks to duplicate church life exactly as it was in New Testament times.

Other families of Protestantism do exist in the South. The Presbyterian presence represents the classical Protestant heritage, even though evangelical influence has modified it somewhat. Radical Protestantism's absence must surprise those who expect to find all kinds of conservativism in the South. A few Mennonite congregations can be found here and there, but even fewer Amish, and no Hutterite. The Episcopal church represents the liturgical family throughout the region. The Lutheran tradition, partly liturgical by classification, is present in selected small areas, sometimes in strength. Episcopalianism's influence has always exceeded its size. It

has served as home for certain kinds of regional traditionalists and as an alternative for people dissatisfied with evangelicalism.

Nevertheless, the dominance of the evangelical family is striking. The hold of the four common convictions: concerning Bible, Spirit, morality, and worship dramatizes this point. Examples of its effects are finding fault with the Episcopal church because it practices formal worship and with the Presbyterian church because of its understated adherence to the direct access of each Christian to the power of the Holy Spirit.

Black Christianity. The faith of black Christians in the South is both very similar to that of white Christians and quite distinctive from it. Nearly all of what has been discussed about "southern religion" applies to both racial groups in the region. Recent research has shown how co-implicated white religion and black religion were in the antebellum period. At one level, the same denominational traditions, the Methodist and the Baptist especially, but also the Presbyterian, the Episcopalian, and the Roman Catholic, served both groups. The evangelical approach was particularly effective in its appeal to blacks. When white Christians sought to evangelize black people (most of whom were slaves), blacks responded in great numbers and with enthusiasm. The extent of that responsiveness reinforced the white commitment to evangelicalism because (1) it attracted a black following, and (2) in church services where whites and blacks worshiped together the black presence contributed to the music, the theology, and the overall vibrancy of the gathering. Aware of the evangelical faith's power in the daily lives of blacks and in their separate religious services,

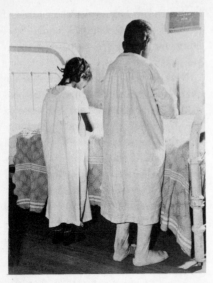

Children saying their prayers, Greene County, Georgia, 1941

white Christians had strong incentives to promote it. Also, their own views of evangelicalism were enriched, and somewhat modified, by the participation of blacks in it. The significant differences between the forms of evangelicalism among the two races came to the fore once blacks had formed independent congregations and denominations in the months and years following the end of the Civil War.

Rituals. In notable ways, the role of the two central rituals of historic Christianity, baptism and the Lord's Supper, reveal the South as a distinctive religious setting. These sacraments, or "ordinances," hold a significant place in regional life and are viewed differently by southerners than by other Christians in the world. For example, baptism outranks Communion in importance. Communion often has a limited importance and place. It is observed just as is baptism. Nevertheless, on a value scale honored by millions of southern Prot-

estants, especially those most vocal about their positions, baptism has primacy.

During most of the colonial period white southerners were practicing Anglicans, nominal Anglicans, or nothing. Few slaves embraced Christianity in any form before the 1790s. An outburst of enthusiastic faith, evangelical in theology and revivalistic in method, altered the denominational profile. The movement developed from Presbyterian beginnings in the 1740s into a "great" awakening in Baptist hands during the 1750s. Soon thereafter Methodist-leaning Anglicans took up the same cause, with the result that there were "Methodists" before the Methodist church was officially organized in 1784.

The southern evangelicals acted on conviction that faith is a relationship one claims in a very personal way. The individual is not born into it, educated into it, or even gradually nurtured into it. Instead, one experiences God's presence and saving power directly, intimately. Thus each life is divided into two periods, life before and after a person receives the gift of salvation. The transition becomes central. Entry into this new condition is life's greatest need and most decisive event.

Baptism understood as a rite of initiation is thus essential. Passage from nominal to genuine practice, from being lost to being saved, from knowing intellectually to experiencing with the heart, becomes a pivotal event. It does not follow, however, that all denominations using revivalism as the technique for introducing people to personal faith have practiced "believer's baptism." Evangelical Presbyterians and Methodists juxtaposed their views of the "new birth" with several other Christian teachings—the family as a covenantal unit, the doctrine of election, and an organic connection between entry and what followed it in a person's spiritual growth. The revivalistic Baptists were more single-minded. Even so, entry, passage, the division of life into a before and an after, came to the fore as a fundamental feature in the southern religious tradition. It was soon to hold an even more prominent position.

The Great Revival on the Kentucky-Tennessee frontier between 1799 and 1805 reinforced and enlarged the role of *entry* into the Christian life. That event assumed primacy and acquired a ritualistic character. One could know, indeed must know, when the passage from death to life occurred. So signal an event ought to be symbolized by an outward sign. These Bible-devout Christians did not have to look far to find one. Indeed, as they read their Bibles, the Lord had intended all along that only people making this transition were subjects for baptism—as the Baptist people had insisted from their English origins about 1610. And as they reproduced the pattern as it existed in the time of Christ, they followed the idea to its logical conclusion, namely, to perform the rite by submerging the new Christian in water, baptism by immersion. Of the three earliest denominations to be both evangelical and revivalistic, only the Baptists insisted upon the straight logic of the position. To their minds, only those personally assured of regeneration in a conscious, willful experience should be baptized; also, proper baptism was by immersion. Presbyterians and Methodists set conversion in a wider context, understanding several doctrines dialectically rather than hierarchically, and seeing entry as having organic continuity with what went before in a person's life and with what was to follow.

Soon the restorationist movement began to develop and take hold. These "Christians" or "Disciples of Christ," those of the Campbellite tradition, were identifiably on the scene by 1830. For them, too, entry into the Christian life was of critical significance. They sought the restoration of New Testament practices in every detail and as a test of faith. Proceeding from somewhat different perspectives, Baptists and "Christians" both seized upon the "rite of initiation" as the distinguishing doctrine in biblical Christianity. The act of entering the saving relationship with Christ and the state of being a Christian claimed first place. Baptism, the badge of entry, thus acquired a dominating significance in the region. It is no wonder that so many denominational squabbles have occurred over the mode of baptism.

Nowhere else is baptism elevated to such eminence—and Communion so deemphasized. Popular southern religion's treatment of the two classic Protestant sacraments adds up to a basic regional distinctiveness, highlighting a unique history. In viewing the place of baptism and the Lord's Supper, one sees the genuine continuity in religious patterns dating from the period 1800–1850. (By contrast, the "North" began to be metamorphosed socially, culturally, and religiously in the 1830s.) Understanding this singular arrangement underscores that the South was cut off from the historical career of the church, Protestant and Catholic, in favor of either a simple repetition of traditional patterns or a deliberately restorationist program.

That the sacraments, their nature and their place, can tell so much about the social history of a region is astonishing. Conventional wisdom would raise doubts that anything so "sacred" could make such a "secular" impact. But their impact has been great. Yet one must take pains not to stretch the truth. For many southern Protestants, Episcopalians and Presbyterians among the larger denominations and Congregationalists and Moravians among the smaller, baptism is not so dominant. Moreover, it is administered to infants by "sprinkling." In addition, Methodists stand as a special case. Some evangelical-revivalistic blood courses through Methodist veins. But the fact of entry, the moment of entry, and the mode of entry do not define Methodist sensibility and practice. That is due to the breadth of its teachings and concerns as well as to the strength of the worship component in its heritage. Within that denomination Communion is granted a large place vis-à-vis baptism.

Communion, the Holy Communion, the Eucharist, or the Lord's Supper—all terms used to refer to taking the bread and the fruit of the vine in celebration of Christ's suffering—is the foremost rite within traditional Christianity. Historically, it has been considered the central act in worship by most branches of the church. In turn, worship has been considered the fundamental act of the church. Thus, worship defines Christian living and Communion is the primary expression of worship.

In the popular religion of southern whites, worship ranks below evangelism and concern with moral uprightness. Converting lost souls, which entails training lay people to engage in that ministry, is the first priority. Not far behind is instruction in and practice of Christian ethical standards. The act of worshiping God, prizing patience and mystery as it does, comes after. In fact, much of the focus in "church services" is on converting the lost, urging members to become involved in soul-winning, and denouncing unrighteous living. Worship as an end in itself, as itself the "work of the people of God," is much less important.

It is not surprising that among Baptists, Pentecostals, Holiness people, and other highly evangelistic groups the Lord's Supper is observed because it is considered a commandment to be obeyed, but is usually observed quarterly and is seen as a departure from the congregation's ordinary rhythm. Whereas exhortation is fast-paced and bent on results, Communion is deliberate and done for its own sake. It simply follows a different cadence. Moreover, a ritual (such as the Lord's Supper) takes some time, makes no person or group of people the primary object (the minister's role being rather minor and passive), and cannot be used to other purposes than its own. It is not the occasion for exhorting or for the preacher to pursue a direction of his own choosing. The service of the Lord's Supper controls; it cannot be controlled. Therefore, following a prescribed course, as it must, it is inevitably liturgical. The cadence is radically different from "preaching service" in which everything moves with vigor and rises to crescendo in the sermon.

The instrumental nature of many white church services and their preference for evangelism over worship offers an interesting comparison with church services of black evangelicals in the South. There is nothing instrumental about black services. The "preaching service," "worship," "going to church" are ends in themselves for the South's black Christians. The gathering is a joyous one, a vital event in the course of the week. Singing is spirited, much of the music coming from the black Christian experience. The congregation actively participates in singing, responds to prayers and the sermon with vocal expressions, contributes its offering to plates that may be passed more than once, and accepts assignments in the choir or in the usher force. The preacher proclaims God's word for the comfort, challenge, and reassurance of the people. The congregation joins their utterances with his in a rhythmic call-and-response. A sermon that does not elicit their vocal participation is regarded as a failure. For the preacher's part, a congregation that does not give back its encouragement and testimony is indifferent.

Thus, what happens in a black church—whatever the denomination—on Sunday or during a revival meeting is the central activity of the church. The service does not focus exclusively on individuals in need of conversion (although they may be led to make that decision). It is an act of worship by all the people present. They praise God for daily blessings and for the forgiveness of sins. They pray to God for strength and courage, for healing, and for the power of the Holy Spirit. The other activities of the congregation, support for mission causes or colleges or appeals for help for those in need, may be mentioned but they are incidental to the singing, praying, testifying, and preaching that are the reasons for the service.

Communion rates well below baptism in the evangelical-revivalistic religion that pervades the American South. Preoccupation with introducing people to faith and the church has proven to be a legacy with staying power. A worship-related, self-contained action, which Communion is, will always have a place but does not quite fit. Nowhere else in Christendom, to repeat, does the ceremony around Christ's final meal with his disciples occupy such a small place. The rhythm is simply different from that of evangelism. What a momentous season it was when southern churches ceased alternating worship services and evangelistic services and turned nearly all into the latter.

The two ordinances are correlated in another way: the affinity between the deemphasis on Communion and the insistence that only conscious, decision-making candidates are suited to baptism. Clearly the stress in this understanding of religion falls on each person's part in the process, on everyone being an active agent. Terms such as the following are in common usage—decide, follow, commit, yield, surrender, give, sacrifice. That is the lexicon of evangelism and believer's baptism (under the conditions of revivalism). It is not the language of Communion. In the Lord's Supper one acknowledges that everything is done for him or her, affirming that grace is raw grace. The rite (and maybe even the elements themselves) suffuses the communicant. Something laden with mystery confronts the dynamic of each person's existence. Its impact cannot be measured. It is not likely to generate immediate activity. Instead its essence is more liquid. Receiving renders one quiet, submissive, reflective, consoled, nourished. A people conditioned to operate in the active voice does not readily shift into that sort of disposition. There is far more affinity between the raw grace of infant baptism and the receptive posture of Communion. (A simple glance at their historical symbiosis would seem to confirm such an interpretation.)

Religion and the Senses. What senses (or faculties) are most prominent in the evangelical-revivalistic nature of southern religion? What are the roles of seeing and tasting, for example? Viewed from a different perspective, what kinds of sense-based achievements emanate from religion of this kind? Standing in the Protestant and Puritan traditions, popular southern religion maximizes hearing and speaking. The term *Word of God* referring to the Bible is not taken metaphorically. Words are sacred, an utterly reliable guide to reality. Thus, speaking and hearing enable one to participate in reality in the most effective way. Tasting and smelling are simply not considered as potential means of divine revelation. Rites involving bread and wine (regularly grape juice) are deemphasized. The visual sense likewise is not highly cultivated because it too is not regarded as a potential link between the divine and the creation. Art and architecture accordingly do not flow from religious sensibilities. Southern religion rarely generates art, whether paintings or sculpture. One exception is baptistery wall depictions of the River Jordan. Architecture is mostly functional although some surprisingly good forms, classic and modern, sometimes appear in Baptist, Assemblies of God, Seventh-Day Adventist, and other settings.

Speaking and hearing, then, are the senses brought alive by southern religion. It has been remarked that Protestants hear entirely too much, more than they can possibly put into practice. Be that as it may, the Word, words, sermons, exhortations, testimonies, soul-winning conversations, and the like are endemic to this religious style. Relating to the Almighty through seeing, tasting, and smelling—whatever might be the specific forms of such responses—is foreign to this sensibility.

References to the oral and auditory senses suggest music. Singing has a vital place in southern Christianity. The expression of faith through this medium, especially as joy for sin's forgiveness and God's daily blessings, is a regular, natural, and indispensable part of church services, revival meetings, church socials, youth gatherings, and even Sunday school assemblies. Music has to do with the ear and the voice; that makes it a neat fit in the setting of a voice/ear religion.

In a large number of Baptist churches, the music is of diverse sorts, ranging from classical hymnody to gospel songs to choruses and spirituals. In the rest of the denominations that make up popular regional religion, classical hymnody generally disappears. Musical forms include everything from quieter, semiformal gospel songs (or popular-style hymns such as "How Great Thou Art") to simpler choruses. With church services more inclined to the revivalistic and less to worship, musical tastes are predictable. Thus, "living it up," "let's really sing, all together now," and "pulling out all the stops" are representative expressions used by the person leading the singing to arouse the congregation to robust participation.

A glance inside the auditorium—a term far more apt than "sanctuary" when listening is primary and conduct is informal—is revealing. The choir is seated behind and above the rostrum on which the pulpit stands. Its members are facing the congregation and are in the direct vision of most or all of them. The minister of music or song leader typically directs the choir in its special numbers, having turned around from facing the congregation when leading them in the singing of the hymns. In most popular churches of any size, each song is called out by name and number by the "song leader" who directs from the rostrum.

This positioning and these actions afford clues to the understanding of worship prevalent in the popular southern religious tradition. It is not altar-centered. Everything centers on the stand where the Holy Bible rests and from behind which the preacher declares its message. Additionally, in the visual line of the pulpit people seated in the congregation may see the choir and the music director. That central area in the front of the "auditorium" is the focus of attention, by theological intention. The reason for the Word, the words, the congregational and choral music, and the entire event of gathering is the improved spiritual condition of the people in the congregation. They do not move to the special area raised in the front of the building, rather the message of truth and inspiration is projected to them from there.

When this conception of the theological architecture is put into practice, the preacher becomes an exhorter or a persuader, whose aim is to convince members of the error of their ways, to point them to the path of spiritual treasures, such as conversion, power for living, perhaps the gift of tongues, or to rally their support for causes, typically evangelistic in purpose. This approach generates direct response. It takes shape as personal accountability to the Lord—for the salvation of your own soul or as the mandate of dedicated service at his bidding. Closely related is the call to personal responsibility, to follow his commandments concerning your own righteousness and what he wills you to do for others. With the individuals present pressured to respond in active ways, set liturgical forms could hardly be expected to have wide usage in church services. Subtlety and belief that religious growth occurs best at a gradual rate are not features of this approach. Instead, the pace is energetic, the mood urgent, and the manner of approach straightforward.

Seriousness of Southern Religion. The mode of much popular southern religion is rooted in the view that religious issues are enormously significant. The God who has given everything requires a total commitment in return. To fail to heed his commandments, to spurn the pardon he offers to lost humankind is grievous indeed. Behavior in that vein makes no sense; moreover, it entails the direst consequences. A religious animation of this kind instills a keen attitude of guilt, the knowledge that one has defied, disobeyed, and rejected an all-loving and all-requiring God.

Millions of the southern religious are open, even vulnerable, to the message, delivered so forthrightly, that they have fallen short and must conform their lives to God's will. On the positive side, they respond to the appeal of loyalties and causes. They really hear urgings to support their church and its projects. Accordingly, an impressive percentage are involved in the organizational life of the congregation, often attending three or more activities per week. Their generosity with money matches their dedication of time. Many tithe 10 percent of the family's gross income. Concern for the work of the church, evangelistic and mission programs, and charitable institutions runs deep and stimulates much giving.

Some scholars have argued that guilt is a natural by-product of the white southerner's treatment of black people. The convincing demonstration of that interpretation is fraught with problems.

Religious sign on roadside, north of Carthage, Mississippi, 1985

Guilt is surely much appealed to in southern religious life, and the fundamental injustice of slavery and segregation is equally evident. How they correlate, however, remains a matter of interpretation.

One is struck by the strength revivalistic evangelicalism attained during the period of slavery's tightest hold and of that ideology's rapid growth during the Jim Crow era, when segregation reached its zenith. It would take a thoroughly cynical interpretation to attribute southern religiosity *solely* to guilt. Guilt can be a constructive and appropriate reaction to a religious understanding that divine love should bear the fruits of grateful obedience. Evidence abounds that many of the southern faithful have historically drunk from a wellspring of joy and gratitude for deliverance, not one of terror accompanying visions of an eternal hell.

Black religious attitudes concerning guilt have been somewhat different from white attitudes. Through the age of slavery, the experience of dramatic conversion rooted in the acknowledgment of each sinner's guilt was as much a part of black faith as of white. But the roles of guilt and responsibility shifted somewhat, once southern black Christians had their own churches. Everything came to be seen in communal terms including personal salvation and ethics. Being a part of the worshiping congregation and seeing to the needs of others in the (segregated) black community diffused and redirected the previously more individualistic orientation. Guilt, pardon, and gratitude continue to be elements in black religious practice, but the evangelism-based program of many white churches has been significantly recast.

Church life of the sort that is informal, direct, urgent, and evangelistic remains standard for southern whites. Almost everywhere else in America such an approach to Christianity is viewed by the majority as somewhat strange, a form of faith for extremists. Southern products of this kind of religion may be referred to indiscriminately as "born again" Christians. That ascription, rarely understood in most communities, is what a great many southerners think all Christians, if serious, are. What is mainline in the South is peripheral elsewhere.

To repeat, four common convictions distinguish serious religion in the eyes of the rank-and-file southern religious: (1) the Bible as the sole reference point; (2) direct and intimate access to the Lord; (3) Christian morality defined in the terms of individualistic and personal ethics; (4) informal, spontaneous patterns for worship. The Baptist-like approach scores high on all four tests and is the most popular form of southern religious life. Catholicism, to take the opposite example, fails all four instances and is hence judged deviant. The American South perpetuates a distinctive type of religion. Although different from forms of Christianity found elsewhere only in degree, the degree is decisive. The *standard* form in the South is normative for *all* forms, and the linkage between faith and the regional culture is intimate.

The effects of social change may be seen throughout contemporary southern society. A great many disruptions of the regional culture have occurred in the past 25 years. Urbanization is one major factor making for change; the in-migration of many thousands another. The appearance of new prosperity and the South's significant role in the national economy reflects a dramatic alteration. Racial desegregation of the society is also very important. A secularization of life and thought has accompanied these changes. Many people experience a new freedom to admit that their outlook on life is secular, and far less now distinguishes the South from the rest of the country.

At the same time, fundamentalism grows. The electronic church bases some of its leading programs in the South. The marriage of conservative politics and conservative religion is in evidence and affects elections. The development of evangelicalism in old and modified forms spells a tightening of the four common convictions. Liberal instincts and concerns, and mainline denominations, have been somewhat eclipsed—for how long no one knows.

See also BLACK LIFE: Preacher, Black; Religion, Black; /Jackson, Jesse; King, Martin Luther, Jr.; Mason, Charles Harrison; Southern Christian Leadership Conference; EDUCATION: Religion and Education; / Baylor University; Bob Jones University; Christian Academies; University of the South; FOLKLIFE: Funerals; Voodoo; GEOGRAPHY: Religious Regions; LAW: Reli-

gion and Law; MUSIC: Gospel Music, Black; Gospel Music, White; / All-Day Singings; Brumley, Albert; Dixie Hummingbirds; Dorsey, Thomas; Fisk Jubilee Singers; Jackson, Mahalia; Revival Songs; Shape-Note Singing Schools; Vaughan, James; MYTHIC SOUTH: Religion and Mythology; SCIENCE AND MEDICINE: Science and Religion; SOCIAL CLASS: Religion and Social Class; WOMEN'S LIFE: Religion and Women ☆

Samuel S. Hill
University of Florida

David T. Bailey, *Shadow on the Church: Southwestern Evangelical Religion and the Issue of Slavery, 1783–1860* (1985); Kenneth K. Bailey, *Southern White Protestantism in the Twentieth Century* (1964); Tod A. Baker, Robert P. Steed, and Laurence W. Moreland, eds., *Religion and Politics in the South: Mass and Elite Perspectives* (1983); John B. Boles, *The Great Revival, 1787–1805: The Origins of the Southern Evangelical Mind* (1972), *Maryland Historical Magazine* (December 1982); Dickson D. Bruce, Jr., *And They All Sang Hallelujah: Plain-Folk Camp-Meeting Religion, 1800–1845* (1974); Will Campbell, *Brother to a Dragonfly* (1977); John R. Earle, Dean D. Knudsen, and Donald W. Shriver, Jr., *Spindles and Spires* (1975); Jean E. Friedman, *The Enclosed Garden: Women and Community in the Evangelical South, 1830–1900* (1985); David Harrell, *All Things Are Possible: The Healing and Charismatic Revivals in Modern America* (1976), ed. *Varieties of Southern Evangelicalism* (1981); Samuel S. Hill, ed., *Encyclopedia of Religion in the South* (1984), *The South and the North in American Religion* (1980), *Southern Churches in Crisis* (1967); E. Brooks Holifield, *The Gentlemen Theologians: American Theology in Southern Culture, 1795–1860* (1978); C. Eric Lincoln, ed., *The Black Experience in Religion: A Book of Readings* (1974); Anne C. Loveland, *Southern Evangelicals and the Social Order, 1800–1860* (1980); Donald Mathews, *Religion in the Old South* (1977); Robert Moats Miller, *Southern*

Humanities Review (Summer 1967); Laurence W. Moreland, Tod A. Baker, and Robert P. Steed, eds., *Contemporary Southern Political Attitudes and Behavior: Studies and Essays* (1982); Albert J. Raboteau, *Slave Religion: The "Invisible Institution" in the Antebellum South* (1978); Charles Reagan Wilson, *Baptized in Blood: The Religion of the Lost Cause, 1865–1920* (1980), ed., *Religion in the South* (1985); Norman Yance, *Religion Southern Style: Southern Baptists and Society in Historical Perspective* (1978). ☆

Appalachian Religion

||||||||||||||||||||||||||||||||||||||||||||||||||||

Using many of the ingredients that historically were part of mainstream Protestant Christianity in the United States, Appalachians imprinted on them a regional particularity. In the Virginias and Carolinas, in eastern Kentucky and Tennessee, in northeastern Alabama, northern Georgia, and western Maryland, the mountains provided a discrete and, for much of American history, isolated landscape in which distinctive religious expression could grow. The earliest contributions to this Appalachian regional religion were made by American Indians, notably the Cherokee, and probably survive in a continuing native tradition of herbal healing (although this was no doubt also influenced by European folk traditions and the "root work" of black conjure). Beginning in the 18th century, however, English, Scotch-Irish, and German immigrants brought left-wing dissenting Protestantism. The English came from Nonconformist (Puritan) roots, and the Scotch-Irish, similarly, were Presbyterians. The Germans included Reformed, Lutheran, and Moravian church members as well as radical sectarians such as Dunkers and Mennonites. By 1850 the regional religion of Appalachia could be clearly discerned; and in its majority expression it became the province of the poor.

Built on prevailing cultural attitudes of Appalachians toward nature, a God beyond nature, and one another, this regional religion was grounded in paradox. There were love and preference for the natural world and, at the same time, awe at the inscrutable and largely Calvinist (and unnatural) God who controlled life. There were strong ties of natural kinship and yet a supernaturally oriented suspicion of the evils that lurked in the human heart. Cast against this background, Presbyterian churches thrived early in the mountains, but with the 19th-century Great Revival and subsequent history, Baptists flourished. Meanwhile, a split from Presbyterian ranks produced the Cumberland Presbytery, which, with the Baptists, preached a modified Calvinism. Methodists, with their efficient network of circuit riders and class system, weakened Calvinism further. The Christian Church (Disciples of Christ) emerged with a doctrine of free grace and an intent to restore the New Testament church, and after 1870 Holiness and then Pentecostalism came. Fundamentalism grew strong (really only a reinforcement of traditional preference for the literal word of God in the Bible), and nondenominational churches made their appearance.

In recent times the traditional churches have continued as a distinctive part of Appalachian culture. Yet in keeping with the history of Appalachian religion, vast portions (probably over half) of the population are unchurched.

Thus, understanding the religiousness of this intensely religious people requires more than examining the beliefs and practices of the churches. Even today it is unusual to find a house in the mountains without its Bible—a Bible perhaps not read regularly but quoted often and also at times, in a divinatory way, opened randomly to supply inspired counsel. Folk healers still use specific biblical verses in their cures; and, along with the "root work" of herbal healing, there are shamanistic techniques that perhaps echo the laying on of hands in Holiness churches, and yet independent of it, effect cures for burns, traumatic bleeding, or the perennial children's "thrash." With their enduring nature religion, some Appalachians continue to plant their crops by the signs of the zodiac and rely on other signs for direction in everyday life. Often dismissed as collections of folk sayings or superstitions, these affirmed correspondences (cradle signs, body signs, weather signs, to name some) possess strong implicit religious coherence. All are grounded on a natural occultism that sees the (anciently celebrated) tie between microcosm and macrocosm as contemporary reality.

Meanwhile, the traditional churches, even with their differences, express a more or less identifiable Appalachian religion. At its creedal base is a doctrine of human estrangement from God through sin. Questions of predestination and free will occupy a central place and, although they are answered variously by different churches, constitute a major religious problem. In this Bible Belt territory of the South, the Bible holds the key to its resolution, but the Bible (mostly the King James version) must be unfolded both in everyday and ritual contexts.

The personal moral code formed by a religion of revival and epitomized in the Holiness churches influences the daily lives of the Appalachians. Swearing and Sabbath-breaking, drinking and gambling, cardplaying, dancing, and sexual license—all receive a stern religious rebuke, although with another bow to nature, a practical permissiveness coexists, so that illegitimate children and acts of violence, often in a family context, are accepted realities. With the individualism of mountain character, a social ethic has not been central to Appalachian moral style.

In ritual expression, again shaped by a religion of revival, the felt gap of sin and alienation is overcome in the dramatic experience of conversion. Typically involving a public liturgy of "walking the aisle" in response to an altar call, conversion draws people to the churches. The old style of rhythmic inspired preaching can be found in many of these Appalachian churches today, frequently in one-room buildings in mountain hollows or along country roads. Here men and women sit separately, while in the front, from the amen corner, old Psalms and hymns or new gospel songs are lined out. In Old Regular Baptist congregations, the inherited Anglo-Saxon singing style with its modal scales is employed, but the distinctive southern shape note singing thrives among other groups. Traditional decoration services (honoring the graves of the dead) and funeral preachings (commemorations of death and burial often long after the event) persist. Protracted meetings of annual revival are common. Meanwhile, sacred ordinances—baptism by triple immersion, foot washing, communion (with grape juice or wine and crackers usually)—are typically observed, and, in a few churches, fire and snake handling are practiced. With the awareness of nature that informs the Appalachian religious style, these ordinances take on a sacramental quality in mountain liturgies: they acquire an intensity that is felt as the power of God in people's lives. That some churches experience this power through glossolalia (speaking in tongues) and faith healing provides still further continuity for the theme.

While the Baptist-Methodist establishment dominates this distinctive Appalachian Protestantism, its establishment remains plural and fragmented. Major denominations such as the Southern Baptists and the United Methodists have made inroads, especially in the towns, and the trend for present-day Appalachian religion is to become less distinguishable from Protestantism elsewhere in the United States. Moreover, Roman Catholics now rank after Baptists, Methodists, and Presbyterians among mountain churches. A requiem, nonetheless, would be premature: Appalachian "old-time religion" has proved a tough and enduring expression of tradition in the midst of the modern world.

See also FOLKLIFE: Folk Medicine

Catherine L. Albanese
Wright State University

John C. Campbell, *The Southern Highlander and His Homeland* (1921); Eleanor Dickinson and Barbara Benziger, *Revival!* (1974); Paul F. Gillespie, ed., *Foxfire 7* (1982); Elizabeth R. Hooker, *Religion in the Highlands: Native Churches and Missionary Enterprises in the Southern Appalachian Area* (1933); Emma Bell Miles, *The Spirit of the Mountains* (1905); John D. Photiadis, ed., *Religion in Appalachia: Theological, Social, and Psychological Dimensions and Corre-*

lates (1978); Eliot Wigginton, ed., *The Foxfire Book* (1972). ☆

Architecture, Church
|||||||||||||||||||||||||||||||||||||||||||||||||||||

The earliest southern churches, Roman Catholic missions, dotted the East Coast from Florida to Virginia beginning in the 16th century. Although none of these is extant, Roman Catholic missions and chapels built in the 18th century in Texas survive in such places as San Antonio, El Paso, and Goliad. These buildings reflect the then-current styles of Spain, including the elaborate stone carving at San Jose mission, San Antonio, and the Moorish details at St. Francis Espada in San Antonio. The Roman Catholic parish churches of Louisiana, on the other hand, reflect 18th- and 19th-century French classical styles.

The earliest Anglican churches of Virginia reflect a nostalgia for English Gothic (Jamestown, 1627; St. Luke's, Smithfield, 1681). By the end of the 17th century widespread experimentation in building for Anglican worship became evident and continued in the next century. A number of existing buildings scattered throughout the Tidewater region of Virginia and Maryland testify to a willingness to seek new forms and arrangements for Anglican worship. The Anglican churches of South Carolina reflected English sophistication in the Charleston churches of St. Michael's and St. Philip's, but in the backcountry a variety of influences prevailed, including the traditions of the West Indies and Huguenot builders. St. James, Goose Creek (1711), is a marvelous Baroque building arranged around a central pulpit and altar-table.

The 18th century saw the arrival of other groups whose buildings, whether Presbyterian, Methodist, or Baptist, took exterior forms that were rather domestic in appearance. These usually had balconies on three sides and a dominant pulpit raised high on the fourth. Occasionally Congregationalists built distinctive structures as at Midway, Ga., and Lutherans as at Jerusalem, Ga. After the Revolution, new buildings were oriented so that a short side faced the road; a tower, and occasionally a portico, were sometimes added. High pulpits and horseshoe-shaped balconies continued to characterize the interiors throughout most of the 19th century.

Like the rest of the nation, the South was overrun by stylistic revivals in the 19th century. Greek Revival buildings appeared in the 1830s and continued to be popular in neoclassical forms among Methodists and Baptists up through the 1920s. The Gothic Revival appeared a decade later and found expression in such early examples as the Chapel of the Cross, Chapel Hill, N.C. This style flourished off and on until World War II, reaching its apex in the Duke Chapel at Duke University. There were two Gothic revivals—a rather primitive one in the 1840s and a more academic one in the early 20th century. The latter found favor among Methodists and Presbyterians especially. The work of Gothicist Ralph Adams Cram is represented by Trinity United Methodist, Durham, N.C. In the late 19th century the neo-Romanesque styles pioneered by H. H. Richardson gave way in time to eclectic combinations of various styles.

An important factor in 19th-century church architecture was the widespread development of Sunday schools. These led to the addition of classrooms and meeting halls so that today many church plants tend to rival the worship space in size. The scale of buildings increased in time and, by the 20th century, worship space was frequently referred to as the "auditorium."

Changes in the worship space occurred. In many churches, choirs were introduced in the 19th century, necessitating a new liturgical space for them. Revivalism popularized a platform instead of the older tub pulpit. On the platform appeared a desk pulpit plus chairs for preacher, guest preacher, and song leader. A small table for the Lord's Supper stood lower down and, for Baptists and Disciples, a baptismal pool was often built into the wall above the pulpit and hidden by a curtain. The popular Akron Plan—which was designed by an Ohio Methodist Sunday school superintendent to allow easy movement between the congregational worship area and surrounding classrooms—fitted pulpit and choir into a corner of a square building and surrounded them on three sides by semicircular seating. Overflow seating was provided by moving partitions.

The 20th century increased the variety of options. Baptists tended to build a Greek-temple form in the early years but then favored brick Georgian Revival buildings, more reminiscent of New England than the South. Methodists and Presbyterians went through a Gothic phase in the 1920s, but since World War II have favored a whole spectrum of styles. Increasingly the altar-table receives equal emphasis with the pulpit.

Modern architecture appeared slowly in the South. Frank Lloyd Wright pioneered with the chapel at Florida Southern College, Lakeland. More recent monuments have been Paul Rudolph's chapels at Tuskegee Institute and the Bishop William R. Cannon Chapel at Emory University. The Thorncrown Chapel, designed by Fay Jones, opened in a remote area of the Ozark Mountains, near Eureka Springs, in 1981. Roman Catholics and Protestants alike have found contemporary architecture congenial, especially in Florida and such urban centers as Dallas and Houston. Lutheran churches with little connection to Old South traditions have especially embraced modern styles. Important examples of innovative contemporary architecture are St. Richard's Roman Catholic, Jackson, Miss.; First Baptist, Austin, Tex.; St. Michael's and All Angels Episcopal, Dallas; and Temple Emmanual (Jewish), Dallas.

Much of the church architecture of the South is a vernacular architecture, built without the aid of an architect. Countless roadside chapels dot hills and valleys, reflecting local building traditions more than formal architectural skill. The churches of black congregations tend to resemble the white churches in each area. The typical country church is a wooden structure, painted white, often with pointed windows and a small tower. The pulpit dominates the one-room interior, which is usually filled with pews. A cemetery surrounds the building and often there

Rural Baptist church, Mississippi Delta, 1975

is a space in a grove of trees for homecomings and meals on the grounds. Occasional camp meeting grounds have space for outdoor sessions or provide wooden tabernacles. Such buildings have provided the setting for the South's vital folk religion for generations.

See also ART AND ARCHITECTURE: Gothic Revival

James F. White
University of Notre Dame

Robert C. Broderick, *Historic Churches of the United States* (1958); Charles M. Brooks, *Texas Missions: Their Romance and Architecture* (1936); Elmer T. Clark, *An Album of Methodist History* (1952); Stephen Dorsey, *Early English Churches in America, 1607–1807* (1952); Carl Julien and Daniel W. Hollis, *Look to the Rock: One Hundred Antebellum Presbyterian Churches in the South* (1961); Kenneth Murray, *Appalachia* (October–November 1974); James Patrick, *Winterthur Portfolio* (Summer 1980); James F. White, *Protestant Worship and Church Architecture: Theological and Historical Considerations* (1964). ☆

Black Religion
||||||||||||||||||||||||||||||||||||

See BLACK LIFE: Religion, Black

Broadcasting, Religious
||||||||||||||||||||||||||||||||||||||||||||||||||||

Religious broadcasting is as old as broadcasting itself. The first wireless voice transmission was an informal religious broadcast. Beamed from Brant

Rock, Mass., on Christmas Eve of 1906 to ships within a several-hundred-mile radius, the program content consisted of Bible readings, a violin solo of "O Holy Night," and a vocal recording of Handel's "Largo."

When the first regularly scheduled radio programming began at station KDKA in Pittsburgh, regularly scheduled religious programs commenced within two months. Radio broadcasting exploded in the 1920s so that by early 1925 there were over 600 stations on the air. Just over 10 percent were owned by churches or religious organizations.

In every city and town in the country with a radio station there were preachers who wanted to broadcast. And many did. But as is still true today, for every mainline church that wanted to broadcast its Sunday worship services, there were a dozen evangelicals trying to get on the air. The current feud between the evangelical and fundamentalist syndicated broadcasters, on the one hand, and the liberal denominations affiliated with the National Council of Churches, on the other, also dates to the early years of broadcasting.

The first religious telecast took place on Easter Sunday, 1940. This was the beginning of two decades of growth that would see television transformed from a laboratory experiment to a consumer commodity that was available in 90 percent of American households.

Bishop Fulton Sheen, who was the first speaker on *The Catholic Hour* presented by NBC in 1930, became the first superstar of religious broadcasting. Bishop Sheen's program, *Life Is Worth Living*, which began in 1952, remains the only regularly scheduled religious program on a network with a commercial sponsor. With an impeccable delivery, a twinkle in his eye, and an angel to clean his blackboard, Sheen attracted millions of viewers.

Sheen's success in television probably was the single most important factor in persuading evangelicals that television—far more than radio—was the medium best suited to their purposes. Television could bring back the evangelistic face-to-face meeting in which a powerful and charismatic preacher could sway audiences and enlist followers.

A few evangelical-fundamentalist preachers saw "televangelism," then, as their great opportunity to spread the Gospel; but getting on television proved to be even more difficult than getting on the radio. Air time for television was a much scarcer resource than was radio air time. Mainline Protestants and Catholics cooperated with Jews and Southern Baptists in sharing the scarce resource of free network time.

For many years evangelicals and fundamentalists believed there was a conspiracy to keep them off the air. Broadcasting stations, under the Communications Act of 1934, are not common carriers and, hence, are not obliged to sell time just because someone wants to buy it. As radio stations grew prosperous, many adopted policies of refusing to sell time for religion and giving it only to ecumenical groups. Most television broadcasters followed the same policy.

But evangelists and fundamentalists were persuaded early that the airways, both radio and television, were a special gift from God that made possible the fulfillment of the great commission to spread the Gospel to every living creature. They persisted. When radio and television stations refused to deal them in on the sharing of free public service time, they offered to buy time. When refused, they offered to pay more. Gradually, station owners recognized that they were passing up a very lucrative market. Little by little, the evangelicals inched their way onto the airwaves.

The cash the evangelists use to pay for air time is raised through audience solicitations. Many styles and gimmicks have been developed to persuade viewers to contribute to radio and television broadcasts, and they work. By the early 1980s the total revenues from religious broadcasting in the United States were estimated at $1 billion.

Technological developments contributed significantly to the expansion of religious television. The first important development was the introduction of videotapes. Lower costs and speed of production made possible wide distribution of the same program for broadcast on the same day all across the country. The number of syndicated programs (those appearing on five or more stations) increased gradually during the 1960s. A big jump occurred during the first half of the 1970s when the number of syndicated programs advanced from 38 in 1970 to 66 in 1975. After leveling off for the remainder of the 1970s, program development increased sharply in the early 1980s to nearly 100 syndicated programs.

Satellite broadcasting promoted the expansion of syndicated programs in the early 1980s. Three religious networks, Christian Broadcasting, PTL, and Trinity Broadcasting, began broadcasting 24 hours, seven days a week around the turn of the decade. Initially, they carried almost exclusively religious programs. None had the capacity to produce more than a few hours of programming daily. Hence, they were in the market for programs. For a while almost anyone who could produce a vid-

eotaped program could send it to one of these new networks and be accepted for satellite broadcast. Audiences were very small, but the broadcasts provided good exposure. And once they got on the air via satellite, many evangelists decided to go the syndication route. The quality of many of these programs was not very good, but other technological innovations significantly lowered production costs and made possible the production of technically respectable programs at a cost many preachers could afford.

Audience size, as measured by Arbitron, increased from under 10 million viewers in 1970 to over 22 million by the middle of the decade. Audience size stabilized during the second half of the 1970s and did not appear to expand much during the first half of the 1980s. Religious broadcasters dispute Arbitron and Neilsen ratings, claiming that neither organization has developed adequate methods to accurately measure broadcasts received via satellite on cable channels. There is some evidence to support their position, including various Gallup polls asking people about their viewing of religious programs.

Audience size is clearly much smaller than the claims of many individual "televangelists." Jerry Falwell, for example, has claimed as many as 50 million viewers, but Arbitron and Neilsen have consistently measured the audience for his *Old-Time Gospel Hour* at well under 2 million. Still, the total audience is a sizable minority of the American population. Together with the religious recording and publishing industries, they have forged a new counterculture in America.

Like the youth counterculture of the 1960s, the religious counterculture is hardly monolithic. When Martin Luther

King, Jr., led civil rights activists on a march in 1965 from Selma to Montgomery, Ala., Jerry Falwell boldly castigated clergy for involvement in political protest. "Preachers are not called to be politicians," he claimed, "but to be soul winners." By 1976 he had changed his mind and in 1979 he founded the Moral Majority, a conservative political organization.

In 1980 religious broadcasters were divided over whether it was proper for them to engage in partisan political activity. With the encouragement of Ronald Reagan, who addressed their professional organization, the National Religious Broadcasters, each year during his first term as president, a sizable proportion of radio and television broadcasters by 1984 were on the political bandwagon.

The amount of religious broadcasting available varies by region and metropolitan area of the country. The major "televangelists" claim that they are popular in all regions of the country and that they attract the young and the old, males and females, the educated and the uneducated, the rich and the poor to view their "electronic churches." In one sense these claims are true. Their programs are broadcast on stations across the country and there are some viewers from the various age, education, income, and sex categories.

These claims notwithstanding, the "electronic church" remains uniquely a southern phenomenon. Virtually all the major "televangelists" are from the South or have migrated to the South to establish their ministries: Billy Graham (North Carolina), Oral Roberts (Oklahoma), Rex Humbard (Arkansas), Jerry Falwell (Virginia), Pat Robertson (Virginia), Jim Bakker (North Carolina), Jimmy Swaggart (Louisiana), Richard

De Hann (Florida), James Robison (Texas), Kenneth Copeland (Texas), and D. James Kennedy (Florida). Robert Schuller is the only person with a successful television ministry who is neither from the South nor concerned with a southern ministry. Operating out of Orange County in southern California, he is also the only mainline Protestant to develop a successful television ministry.

The audiences of the "electronic church" are also drawn disproportionately from the South. Whereas the South has slightly less than one-third of the nation's population, the major television ministries draw in the range of 45 to 55 percent of their audience from this region. The Midwest, with roughly a quarter of the nation's population, provides roughly that proportion of the audiences, with the eastern and western regions of the country significantly underrepresented.

These regional figures probably underestimate the extent to which religious broadcasting, especially television, is a southern regional phenomenon. Much of its appeal outside the South is to persons who have migrated from the region. Rex Humbard and Ernest Angley (a lesser light in the "electronic church") both built large congregations in Akron, Ohio, with farm migrants from the South who came to the industrial Midwest in search of blue-collar jobs.

Present migratory patterns into the Sunbelt will reinforce the southern character of the audience. Virtually all the syndicated programs have audiences of which two-thirds to three-quarters are 50 years of age or over. Audiences are also disproportionately female. The Sunbelt movement is a disproportionately older migratory flow and, as females survive males by an average of about seven years, the proportion of females in the region will increase. Only CBN, with its *700 Club* and its soap opera, *Another Life*, seems to be making a systematic effort to attract a broader audience.

Jeffrey K. Hadden
University of Virginia

Charles E. Swann
Union Theological Seminary
Richmond, Virginia

William F. Fore, *Christian Century* (18–25 July 1985); Frye Gaillard, *Race, Rock and Religion: Profiles from a Southern Journalist* (1982); Jeffrey K. Hadden and Charles E. Swann, *Prime Time Preachers: The Rising Power of Televangelism* (1981); Peter G. Horsfield, *Religious Television: The American Experience* (1984); Stephen W. Tweedie, *Journal of Popular Culture* (Spring 1978). ☆

Calvinism
||||||||||||||||||||||||||

Calvinism designates that way of being Christian that has its roots in the life and work of John Calvin (1509–64), the Protestant reformer of Geneva. Its theology is both Catholic and Protestant. It is Catholic in that Calvin reaffirmed the ancient catholic faith, in particular the Apostles' Creed, the doctrine of the person of Jesus Christ as found in the Nicene Creed and the Chalcedonian Definition, and the doctrine of the Trinity. It is Protestant in that Calvin thought he was continuing the work of Luther. He built upon the affirmations of Luther's writings of 1520: the supreme authority of the Holy Spirit

speaking through Scripture, justification by grace through faith, the priesthood of all believers, the sanctity of the common life, and the necessity of personal decision and responsibility. This theology influenced southern religious developments and also found expression in political attitudes, literary works, and the folklore of daily living.

Calvin's greatest work was a comprehensive statement of Christian faith, *The Institutes of the Christian Religion*, which, beginning as a small book in 1536, was continually revised until Calvin found satisfaction with the final Latin edition of 1559. He also prepared a liturgy and a church order for Geneva that was influential in Calvinist churches. He directed the completion of a Psalter in 1562. As a churchman Calvin was in constant contact with Protestant leaders throughout Europe. His letters comprised almost 11 volumes of his collected works.

Calvinism is sometimes used as a synonym for Reformed Protestantism, because Calvin was the latter's dominant personality and, in later history, its most influential figure. Yet the Reformed churches in Zurich under the leadership of Zwingli and Bullinger, in Basel with Ecolampadius, and in the Rhineland all had a part in shaping Reformed Protestantism. In general, the Reformed theology of German-speaking Switzerland and the Rhineland was less passionate and more generous and humanistic, less determined to have an independent church, than Geneva; but each type shared a common perspective in theology.

(1) Calvin's work and theology were shaped by emphases that distinguish it from other forms of Protestantism. Calvin perceived God, the creator of the universe, primarily as energy, activity, power, moral purpose, intentionality.

The characteristic response to a God so conceived was not contemplation and the vision of God, but action in service of the Kingdom of God and a life that embodies the purposes of God.

Calvin's understanding of God as energy and purpose found expression in God's lordship in history, in which the sovereign God works as creator, judge, and redeemer. Hence, Calvin understood the Christian life as the embodiment of the purposes of God in history. From the beginning Calvinists were activists engaged in transforming economic, political, and cultural life according to their vision of the Kingdom of God. Calvin sought the coming into being of the holy community in Geneva. The Calvinists carried this vision of the holy community, the embodiment of the purposes of God in society, to Scotland, to Puritan England, and to Massachusetts, where they went on an "errand into the wilderness" to demonstrate the possibility of a Christian society. The Baptists and the Presbyterians embodied Calvinism's influence in the South most clearly, although in neither case so dramatically as with the New England Puritans. Calvinism has always been uneasy with a personal piety defined simply in terms of the relation of the soul to God, but that kind of piety has been the dominant religious form in the evangelical South.

Predestination, the doctrine popularly identified with Calvinism, attributed human salvation to the initiative of God. While Calvinists rejoiced in human freedom, they believed that once the human will becomes sinful it cannot by its own efforts transform itself. A self-centered person can become unself-centered only when divine grace attracts the self away from itself to God.

The Calvinists defined the chief end of life as the glory of God. Calvin, perhaps with Luther in mind, insisted that God's glory, not the salvation of one's own soul, must be the primary human concern. Later Calvinists were skeptical of revivalists who made the salvation of one's soul the center of attention. Calvinism thus represented an important counterforce to the evangelicalism dominant in the South since the early 1800s.

(2) A second characteristic of Calvinism is an emphasis upon sanctification. Luther had rediscovered the primacy of God's mercy over every form of work righteousness: salvation by human merit is beyond human power; our best deeds as well as our worst are flawed by self-interest. As a second generation Protestant, Calvin faced the criticism that this great emphasis on justification by grace undercut the Christian life. Calvin knew that justification, the fact and experience of forgiveness, is the principal hinge on which Christian life hangs, but he also knew that God's grace is power that renews as well as mercy that forgives. He conceived of the Christian life frequently in military terms as a war against the world, the flesh, and the Devil and as the obligation to obey God's command and fulfill his purposes.

(3) Calvinism has also been marked by a distinctive emphasis upon the life of the mind in the service of God and by a skepticism about feelings not subjected to rational scrutiny. Calvinists have always insisted that it is important to know what one believes and to be able to give a reason for one's faith. Catechetical instruction has been characteristic of Calvinistic churches until recent times. Southern Presbyterians and denominations that grew out of that group have especially championed this idea in the region.

(4) Closely related to the emphasis on the life of the mind was a similar emphasis on the task of the minister as

teacher and preacher. The Calvinist sermon not only proclaimed the Gospel, but also educated people in logical, coherent thought and discourse. Important southern colleges, such as Davidson and Rhodes, founded by Presbyterians reflect this strong belief in education.

(5) A fifth characteristic has been the importance of the organized church and the disciplined life. Order was a basic concept for Calvin. Salvation could be understood as the proper ordering of a life, an order that found primary expression in the church. Order was also a personal virtue. Calvinist asceticism and discipline were not based upon any depreciation of the world, which the Calvinists knew was God's good creation, but upon the need for an economical use of life's resources.

(6) An emphasis upon simplicity was pervasive in Calvin's writings and in the manner of his life. In literary expression he never used two words when one would do. In liturgy he protested against pomp and "theatrical trifle." In manner of life he insisted upon moderation. Calvin and the Calvinists abhorred the pompous, the pretentious, the ostentatious, the contrived, and the artificial. They insisted upon authenticity, clarity, directness, simplicity. The simple for Calvin was closely related to sincerity. It was open to reality. The ostentatious, the contrived, and the pompous covered up reality.

Calvinism was modified and transmitted to later generations through the "school" theology of the 17th century. Scholasticism was a necessary development. Calvin as a preacher did not write theology with care for definition. He left many theological issues poorly defined or unresolved. In addition, Calvinism had to face intellectual challenges from Roman Catholics, from other Protestants, and from later Calvinists whose internal debates had to be resolved. The scholastic theologians with great technical skills gave to Calvinism a clearly defined, logical, coherent form.

Protestant scholasticism also developed a common theological vocabulary, which was carefully defined and generally in the language of ordinary human discourse. This common theological vocabulary, which was influential in the South through the first half of the 20th century, made it possible for people with little formal training to become competent theologians.

Calvinism was mediated to the South largely through the 17th-century scholastic theology. *Institutio Theologiae Elencticae* by Francis Turretin (1623–87), a Genevan theologian, was used as a textbook at such Presbyterian seminaries as Princeton, Union Theological Seminary in Richmond, Va., Columbia Theological Seminary in Columbia, S.C., and at the Southern Seminary of the Baptists in Louisville, Ky. The Westminster Confession of Faith (1643–47) was the authoritative summary of Calvinism for American Calvinists in Presbyterian, Baptist, and Congregational churches. It was also one of the most influential books of colonial America. The Shorter Catechism, a question-and-answer summary of the Westminster theology, was until World War II the basic text for the education of Presbyterian young people.

The original work of Calvin was not only modified by Protestant scholasticism, but by many other influences as it came to the South. Among these were English Puritanism, the Scottish Common Sense philosophy, and the Scotch-Irish immigrants who constituted the main body of southern Calvinists.

The most influential expressions of Calvinism in the South are to be found in the work of James Henley Thornwell (1812–62), Robert Dabney (1820–98), and Charles Hodge (1797–1878), a Princeton theologian whose influence was widely felt among southern Presbyterians.

Scholastic theology, for all of its technical excellence, was challenged from the late 17th century on by the Enlightenment and by the cultural developments of the 19th century. Yet it maintained a pervasive influence, especially in the South through the first half of the 20th century. The task of giving a statement of Calvinist faith in light of the legacy of the Enlightenment and the social, political, and scientific developments of the 19th and 20th centuries is not yet complete. The most influential 20th-century statements have been the works of the Swiss theologians Karl Barth, *Church Dogmatics* (1932–67), and Emil Brunner, *Dogmatics* (1946–60), and the American theologian Reinhold Niebuhr, *The Nature and the Destiny of Man* (1941–43). No theology now has the pervasive influence that Calvinism did in significant segments of southern society. In a pluralistic society dominated by mass media this may no longer be possible.

Calvinism's influence, however, has extended far beyond its importance as a formal theology. It was one of the fundamental forces creating a distinctive character of the people of the region. W. J. Cash saw popularized Calvinism as part of the major dichotomy of southern psychology—the South was the world's supreme paradox of hedonism in the midst of puritanism. He believed that by the mid-19th century "the whole South, including the Methodists," had moved "toward a position of thorough-

going Calvinism in feeling if not in formal theology." Arminian free will surely also entered into the character of the region through the large Methodist influence, but the two combined in a peculiar cultural synthesis. Noting Calvinism's part in another cultural combination, James McBride Dabbs talked of "the spiritual pride of the God-selected Calvinist" combining with the pride of "the imperial Englishman" to produce the white southerner. Calvinist belief in human depravity, God's sovereignty, and an ordained universe helped to condition southern enslavement of blacks, he wrote.

Cash called southern Calvinism "puritanism," and so have others. Fred Hobson points out that "Southern 'Puritanism' was vastly different from the New England variety, less structured, less intellectual, more emotional—raw Calvinism, rather than the cerebral Puritanism of the Massachusetts Bay." This faith had a dramatic impact on the southern frontier. Calvinism early became an influence in the region through the prominence of the Scotch-Irish on the frontier. It became a particularly significant aspect of southern culture during the Civil War and its aftermath. Calvinism was one factor that led southerners to expect victory for the Confederacy. The belief in God's sovereignty and His determination of the elect led southern whites to see themselves as God's chosen engaged in holy war. As Daniel Hundley said after hearing of Confederate battle triumphs in Virginia, "When God is for us, who is against us?"

Unreconstructed southerners after the war, however, were frustrated, trying to come to terms with defeat in a holy war. They could see no explanation except for the mysterious will of God.

Their popularized Calvinism led them to believe they had sinned and God was punishing them for their sins, preparing his people for a greater destiny. Not only ministers, but teachers and journalists, generals and common soldiers came to believe that God did not fail them; they had rather been unworthy. Stonewall Jackson was the war's supreme incarnation of a Calvinist warrior, but even the aristocratic Robert E. Lee, according to his biographers, had much Calvinism in his soul.

Calvinism was used in a variety of ways by a variety of people, suggesting its pervasive influence in southern culture. Presbyterian Robert Dabney used it to justify a slave society, and others have used the belief in a God-ordained social order to argue against changes in racial customs and against the rights of labor and of women. But George W. Cable, Ralph McGill, Lillian Smith, and other liberals used Calvinism to justify change; as McGill said in *The South and the Southerner*, he became a racial liberal because his "Calvinist conscience was stirred by some of the race prejudice I saw."

Calvinism also influenced the literary development of writers such as William Faulkner. He once noted that he had used religious symbols in his works because they were all around him in north Mississippi, and Calvinism was perhaps the central religious influence he explored. Faulkner disliked what he saw as a puritanical stress on sober living, the discouragement of fleshly pleasures, and a spiritual self-righteousness, all of which he saw stemming from Calvinism. He portrayed characters made authoritarian and repressively violent by a Calvinist outlook. His Calvinists, or Puritans, as he sometimes called them, show little concern for ritual or piety,

but believe in God's justice and in human practicality and good works. Characters such as Lucas Beauchamp in *Go Down, Moses* and Mink Snopes in *The Town* believe, for example, less in a divine being of mercy and more in a God of justice. Faulkner did seem to admire especially one emphasis in Calvinism—as it was translated into human behavior in the South—that on the human will and the need for action. *Light in August, Absalom, Absalom!*, and "The Bear" in *Go Down, Moses* represent the most thorough explorations of Calvinism's influence in southern literature.

John H. Leith
Union Theological Seminary
Richmond, Virginia

Cleanth Brooks, *William Faulkner: The Yoknapatawpha Country* (1963); W. J. Cash, *The Mind of the South* (1941); James McBride Dabbs, *Who Speaks for the South?* (1964); Fred Hobson, *Tell about the South: The Southern Rage to Explain* (1983); John H. Leith, *Introduction to the Reformed Tradition: A Way of Being the Christian Community* (1977); John T. McNeill, *The History and Character of Calvinism* (1954). ☆

Civil Rights and Religion

The relation of religion and civil rights in the South is as old as southern culture. Black religious experience, forged from oppression, differs from its white counterpart in the South. The oldest black spirituals had political and civil rights overtones imbedded in their religious message. "Wade in the water . . . ," ". . . with my face to the rising sun . . . ," "shall we gather at the river . . . ," and many others had to do with meeting, planning, and escaping. Freedom singing has been a key ingredient in the modern civil rights movement, incorporating gospel music in powerful and moving ways. For instance, the nationally known Freedom Singers were formed out of the often-jailed ranks of the Student Nonviolent Coordinating Committee (SNCC), and their songs in churches greeted protesters returning from jail.

In black churches, preachers constantly compared the plight of black people with the children of Israel. The basic issue of civil rights was seen not in the first instance as legal, sociological, economic, or political, but as moral and spiritual. The black church was the organizational building block of the civil rights movement; its leadership was predominantly clergy, ministerial students, and women of strong religious backgrounds.

Black religious leadership in civil rights in the South came mainly from the clergy and seminary students. Kelley Miller Smith, C. T. Vivian, Martin Luther King, Sr., Fred Shuttlesworth, Metz Rollins, Ralph Abernathy, and Wyatt T. Walker have been key figures. Of course, Martin Luther King, Jr., symbolized most dramatically the mobilizing strength of black religious traditions.

James Lawson was a Vanderbilt Divinity School student when he helped to organize the Nashville sit-ins in 1960 with other seminary students from American Baptist Theological Seminary such as John Lewis, Bernard Lafayette, and James Bevel, all of whom played pivotal roles in SNCC. Andrew Young, a United Church of Christ minister, became Martin Luther King, Jr.'s chief assistant in the Southern Christian Leadership Conference (SCLC), along with several other ministers such as James Orange and Jesse Jackson. Charles Sherrod, a divinity student in Virginia, became a key leader in SNCC.

Strong black women with religious backgrounds were also numerous in the civil rights struggle, and their struggle was often exacerbated by the traditional male clergy leadership. Rosa Parks sat down in the front of the bus in 1955 and started the Montgomery movement that produced Martin Luther King, Jr. Ella Jo Baker wanted to be a medical missionary, and instead became the first full-time executive secretary of the SCLC and founding mother of SNCC. Sharecropper Fannie Lou Hamer joined the civil rights movement in a Mississippi church, became a field secretary for SNCC, and ran for the U.S. Congress.

A common observation is that the civil rights movement in the South lost some of its "soul," or meaning, or heart when it became more secular and popular. Some, such as John Lewis, thought that that happened because of the influx of people from the North, black and white, who had little relationship or kinship to religious foundations or to southern experience.

The white church in the South, overwhelmingly Protestant, at its best experienced guilt and practiced restraint; at its worst, it was the ideological linchpin of racism and segregation. The white southern church has mainly been a conservative, reinforcing agent for traditional values of white southern society. There have been significant exceptions, but often those instances had to do with courageous acts or stands taken by individual white Christians allying themselves to the civil rights movement because of Christian conscience and religious values. Their positions, however, were neither practiced nor condemned by the white institutional church.

Marginal, predominantly white, southern Christian organizations have had an important part in civil rights; among them are United Church Women, the YWCA and YMCA, Councils on Human Relations, the Fellowship of Southern Churchmen, and various churchwomen's and youth groups. Such religiously based organizations, although often ostracized by the southern white church and supported by northern patrons, have served as the "call to conscience" of other southern whites, and often had they not been involved, news organizations might not have paid as much attention to civil rights events. But these marginal organizations, while strategic and courageous, also inadvertently served to help mask the deep differences between black and white religious experience.

Within white southern Christianity the courageous individuals rather than organizations, institutions, or "the beloved community" stood out in support of civil rights. Many protesters had seminary training outside the South and in the 1930s and 1940s were active in farm and labor movements. They were often defrocked, fired by their own churches, and forced to seek employment outside the region. In the 1960s they might have been supported by their national church, while ostracized by the local and regional church; many times they were physically beaten and sometimes murdered.

Southern white religious leadership in civil rights was native and grounded in southern tradition, but also it was

conspicuously "against the grain," often isolated, and in danger.

The Commission on Interracial Cooperation was founded in 1919 by Methodist minister Will Alexander. Through the 1920s, 1930s, and 1940s a lineage of Christian-based activists followed, including Alva Taylor, the teacher of many southern organizers at Vanderbilt School of Religion; Don West, a Georgia minister and poet; Myles Horton, a Cumberland Presbyterian from Union Seminary and founder of the Highlander School; Presbyterian Claude Williams; Methodist ministers Ward Rogers and James Dombroski; YMCA leader and Presbyterian Howard Kester; YWCA's Lucy Mason Randolph; also Sam Franklin, Charles Jones, Winifred Chappell, and Harry and Grace Kroger. Many of these leaders worked with the farm labor movements and were in the Fellowship of Southern Churchmen.

In the 1950s and 1960s southern white religious leadership continued out of the Fellowship of Southern Churchmen and the "Y" with Will Campbell, Nelle Morton, Helen Lewis, and others. Thelma Stevens, in the Methodist church, Hayes Mizell and Connie Curry of the American Friends Service Committee, and Jane Schutt of Church Women United are just a few of the white organizational leaders that emerged in southern civil rights struggles.

Ed King, Mississippi-born chaplain at Tougaloo College, was an important activist in the Jackson Movement and the Mississippi Freedom Democratic Party in the 1960s. Bob Zellner, son of an Alabama Methodist minister, was the first white field secretary of SNCC. Jane Stembridge, a Virginian, left Union Theological Seminary to become the first office secretary of SNCC. Maurice Ouillet, a Catholic priest in Selma, Ala., was the only white person there who openly helped the civil rights movement.

Because of continuing black pressures, established religious bodies moved over time to support racial brotherhood, and some even to lend support to ministers persecuted for their stands on civil rights. Nonetheless, the vast majority of white churches in the South remained silent and apart, and many formed the institutional base for evading public school desegregation by founding private "Christian academies" and for promoting reactionary policies through the electronic church and the New Christian Right in the 1970s and 1980s.

In spite of the fundamental role that the southern black church and many southern white Christians played in the struggle for civil rights during the last 50 years, to the present day the southern black church and the southern white church stand far apart. Sunday is still the most segregated day of the week. Ministerial alliances, church boards, and agencies remain segregated, with token representation at best.

Nonetheless, black religion has not become antiwhite, acting on the belief that the liberation of the children of Israel and the teachings of Jesus are universal values. The white religion of the South in its essential Christianity knows that it has no religious basis for racism and oppression, and that the stratified southern society that it has sanctified and defended is itself making accommodations with other forces.

See also BLACK LIFE: Race Relations; Religion, Black; / Hamer, Fannie Lou; Jackson, Jesse; King, Martin Luther, Jr.; Southern Christian Leadership Conference; EDUCATION: / Christian Schools; MYTHIC

SOUTH: Racial Attitudes; POLITICS: / Young, Andrew; SOCIAL CLASS: / Highlander Folk School; WOMEN'S LIFE: / Baker, Ella Jo

James Sessions
Commission on Religion
in Appalachia
Knoxville, Tennessee

James H. Cone, *Black Theology and Black Power* (1969); James McBride Dabbs, *The Southern Heritage* (1958); Anthony P. Dunbar, *Against the Grain: Southern Radicals and Prophets, 1929–1959* (1981); Samuel S. Hill, ed., *On Jordan's Stormy Banks: Religion in the South: A Southern Exposure Profile* (1983), *Religion and the Solid South* (1972). ☆

Ethnic Protestantism

Southern Protestantism arose, almost entirely, from ethnic roots. During the 18th century nearly a million immigrants entered the southern backcountry—the majority of them of Germanic or Celtic ancestry—as well as numerous Pennsylvania Quakers who formed a special English subcultural, if not ethnic, community. Highland Scots also entered the region through Wilmington and settled the upper Cape Fear Valley in North Carolina, and Salzburgers and Huguenots did so through the ports of Savannah and Charleston respectively. Non-English immigration into the backcountry profoundly shaped the culture of the entire region. In the late 18th century, Presbyterians emerged as the elite in much of the South. Religious pacifism weakened state governments during the Revolution, and Quaker antislavery proved to be a potent witness against human bondage.

Then, suddenly, during the first three decades of the 19th century, ethnic distinctiveness rooted in European heritages became absorbed into a new, dominant southern way of life. Dunkers and many Quakers, who were victims of discrimination, migrated to Indiana, and most Lutheran, Moravian, and Reformed churches and communities adopted the English language. The older coastal aristocracy, largely Episcopalian in affiliation, and newer back-country elites, almost entirely dissenters in religious preference, tended to coalesce. The spread of evangelicalism blurred differences between denominations, even between Episcopalians and other Protestants, and the preservation of social order and communal purity took precedence over maintenance of traditional liturgy, theology, and polity—further reducing the memory of European origins and ethnic identification. Nonetheless, a handful of ethnic churches can still be found in the South. Infinitesimal in number, they reflect values absent in the dominant culture as well as the persistence of some elements of the region's historical cultural mosaic.

The earliest ethnic Protestants in the South were Huguenots in colonial South Carolina. Part of a diaspora of French Protestants following the revocation of the Edict of Nantes (in 1685), they comprised an eighth of the white population of South Carolina in 1700. Educated, energetic, commercially skilled, and soon intermarried with the English stock elite, these French Calvinists became Anglicized after 1910. Most of the 10 Huguenot churches in the province became Anglican, and when George Whitefield delivered a controversial ser-

mon in the "French Church" in Charleston in 1740 the Huguenot minister quietly dissociated himself from Whitefield's revivalism. Despite a fire that destroyed the largest French church in Charleston in 1796 and the looting of its successor building by Union troops in 1865, descendants of the early French settlers kept the church alive until 1950. Then, on 17 October 1982, the Huguenot Church of Charleston reopened with a membership that is half former Episcopalian, and the remainder Presbyterian, Baptist, and Methodist. The church continues to be Calvinist in theology and uses a Swiss Protestant liturgy. The minister of the reorganized church is Philip Charles Bryant, a Southern Baptist clergyman and an administrator of the Baptist College of Charleston.

The next oldest ethnic Protestant tradition in the South is that of the Moravians. Dating from the followers of John Hus and organized into the Unity of Brethren (Unitas Fratrum) by Count Nicholas von Zinzendorf in the early 18th century, Pennsylvania Moravians purchased a large tract of land in North Carolina from Lord Granville. There, between 1753 and 1766, they established the towns of Bethabara, Bethania, and Salem and practiced communal management of economic, family, and religious life. Although communalism ceased in the early 19th century and Moravians reluctantly became a Protestant denomination, the churches in North Carolina preserve a wide range of rituals and cultural observances dating to Zinzendorf's practices in Moravia— among them the arrangement of the cemetery into four separate "choirs" for men and women, married and unmarried, using identical flat white grave markers; an Easter sunrise service held in the Old Salem burial ground every year since 1772; lively traditions in Christmas cooking and decorating; and an important musical heritage of brass music and hymnology.

The Waldensians, a dissenting sect founded by the followers of Peter Waldo, a merchant of Lyon in the late 12th century, were among the last ethnic Protestants to reach the South. In 1893, 101 families from nine Alpine Italian towns settled in Burke County, N.C. Their patron in this migration was a Pittsburgh industrialist, Marvin F. Scaife, who owned land in Morganton, N.C. Though at first supported by the Congregationalist church, they chose to affiliate with the southern Presbyterian Church in the United States. By the early 1920s the Valdese Presbyterian Church had abandoned several distinctive Old World Waldensian practices— leaving the offering plate at the rear door of the church, receiving communion in pairs at the altar, seating men and women on opposite sides of the church, and worshiping exclusively in French. In 1941 the use of French services ended altogether.

The Lutheran Church–Missouri Synod represented the ethnic tradition of conservative German confessionalism brought to the United States by immigrants in the mid-19th century. In contrast with Lutherans who had been in America since the colonial period and had absorbed evangelical and other Protestant patterns of worship and theology, the Missouri Synod insisted on upholding the hierarchical and legalistic formalism of 17th- and 18th-century continental Lutheranism. The relative isolation of this branch of American Lutherans enabled the Missouri Synod, in a modest way, to serve as an instrument for racial justice in the South. During the late 19th century, the synod's home mission board adopted many black Lutheran churches in the South, which had been denied admission to older Lutheran synods, and in the 20th century it established schools for blacks—Emmanuel College in Greensboro, N.C., and Selma Lutheran Academy and College in Alabama. In 1966 Professor Richard Bardolph, a Missouri Synod layman in Greensboro, drafted the denomination's statement on "Civil Disobedience and the American Constitutional Order," citing biblical and historical support for defiance of law as a tool of the civil rights movement.

The North Carolina Yearly Meeting of the Religious Society of Friends (Conservative), comprising seven Monthly Meetings in North Carolina and one in Virginia, identifies closely with 17th-century English Quakerism. These Quakers broke away from the larger body of evangelical Quakers in the South in 1904. The formal Discipline of the sect (1956) emphasizes parental diligence, harmony and unity with Monthly Meetings, worship under the Holy Spirit without resort to a professional ministry, protection of children from "pernicious books" and "corrupt conversation," pacifism, wholesome diversions and opposition to alcoholic beverages and gambling, living within one's own resources and avoiding business enterprises beyond prudent risk, and care of the poor within each Monthly Meeting.

Mennonites, who settled in Virginia in the 18th century, were pacifists in both the Revolution and the Civil War. At present, they comprise two bodies in the South, the Virginia Mennonite Conference (67 churches, mainly in Virginia and North Carolina) and the Western Conservative Mennonite Fellowship (16 in North Carolina, 6 in

South Carolina, 71 in Virginia, and 11 in West Virginia). The Virginia Conference is a part of the Mennonite church and the Conservative Fellowship is an offshoot body culturally close to the Amish in practice and discipline.

The most rapidly growing ethnic Protestant group in the South today is represented by the Korean Presbyterian churches—the product of Presbyterian church (U.S.) missionary activity in Korea, an upsurge of Christianity as an indirect form of opposition to political expression since the 1950s, the migration of Korean professionals to the United States, and the existence of Korean-American families in this country. Twenty Korean Presbyterian congregations can now be found in seven southern states. Finally, there is the Chinese Presbyterian church in New Orleans. Founded in 1882 as a language school and mission for Chinese men, it was until the 1950s operated by four dedicated Presbyterian women. In 1958 Grace Yao came from Hong Kong to become director of Christian education. The service is bilingual.

See also ETHNIC LIFE articles

> Robert Calhoon
> University of North Carolina
> at Greensboro

Peter Brock, *Pacifism in the United States: From the Colonial Era to the First World War* (1968); Jon Butler, *The Huguenots in America: A Refugee People in New World Society* (1983); *Concordia Historical Institute Quarterly* (November 1969; February 1971; Summer 1975; Summer 1977; Fall 1979); Damon Douglas Hickey, "Bearing the Cross of Plainness: Conservative Quaker Culture in North Carolina" (M.A. thesis, University of North Carolina, Greensboro, 1982); Hunter James, *The Quiet People of the Land: A Story of the North Carolina Moravians in Revo-*

lutionary Times (1976); George B. Watts, *The Waldenses in the New World* (1941). ☆

Folk Religion
||||||||||||||||||||||||||||||||||||||||

A leading scholar of American folk religion, William M. Clements, defines it as "unofficial religion," the spiritual experience that exists separate from, but alongside, the theological and liturgical religion of the mainline established churches. Clements has identified 10 traits of the folk church: "general orientation toward the past, scriptural literalism, consciousness of Providence, emphasis on evangelism, informality, emotionalism, moral rigorism, sectarianism, egalitarianism, and relative isolation of physical facilities."

Folk religious events include Sunday school classes, Vacation Bible school meetings in the summer, Bible study gatherings, covered-dish suppers, singing services, devotional hours, and all-day services with dinner on the grounds. The church worship service is perhaps the central ritual of folk religion in the South. Worshipers may clap or wave their hands as they listen to spiritual songs like "Over in Glory Land." Some churches have a cappella services, but many include electric guitars, tambourines, and other instruments. Shouts of "Thank you, Jesus" and "Praise the Lord" are heard, as are extended public prayers, testimonials, and drawn-out invitations by the preacher to come forward. Faith healing and glossolalia sometimes occur. The preacher conveys a message of the need for conversion, controlling and directing the raw emotions of true believers. In the South's well-defined oral culture, the folk preacher is a prime performer of the word, and the religious service is a crucial folk event. Films such as Blaire Boyd's *Holy Ghost People*, which records Appalachian snake handlers; William Ferris's *Two Black Churches*, which shows Sunday morning worship services in rural southern and urban northern churches; and *Joy Unspeakable*, a videotape on southern Indiana Pentecostals, have become important modern tools for studying folk religion.

The relation between southern religion and folk culture is seen in the dynamic of conversion. Born sinful, the individual can be saved by conversion. He accepts the rule of Jesus and God, sometimes through a dramatic conversion experience after which he gives up aspects of folk culture that are regarded as profane. Thus, the hell-raising "good old boy" becomes the "good man," who is a pious member of the church. Drinking and dancing on Saturday night are replaced by temperance and dignified behavior, though in some Pentecostal churches addiction to spirits is transmuted into being possessed by the Spirit and dancing in the flesh to dancing in the Spirit. As one moves from the evangelical/fundamentalist end of the spectrum, which is most identified with folk religion in the South, to the established Southern Baptist, Methodist, and Presbyterian churches, the dramatic conversion syndrome becomes rare, virtually disappearing as one enters the more liturgical churches, such as the Episcopalian (which one southern minister described as "religion in its mildest form").

Some established southern churches, however, include survivals of folk religion. Methodists, for example, may not include in today's services the testimonials and shouts from the day of John Wesley at Aldersgate, but they continue to sing the old Wesleyan hymns as well as hymns from revivals and camp meetings.

After conversion, fundamentalist Christians may stop singing ballads or country music or blues and shift to hymns, spirituals, and gospel songs; or they may keep on doing the old music, but in secular contexts, such as the bluegrass festival, clearly separating that from the sacred song. Lines are thus drawn between folk and sacred music, even though similarity of form may be detected. Folktales do not normally enter the church, but tale-telling forms and the love of telling tales are apparent in southern sermons and testimonies. Religious rhetoric enters secular life through the sermon-speeches of Martin Luther King, Jr., Jesse Jackson, and others.

Folk medicine, as exemplified by the root doctor or herbalist, is rarely drawn explicitly into the church, but folk healers integrate religious symbolism into their systems. Within folk religion faith healing stands in a complementary relationship to the individual folk healers

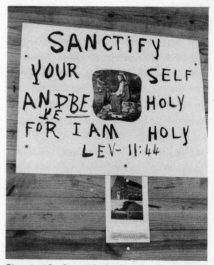

Sign inside Sanctified church, Clarksdale, Mississippi, 1968

in that faith healing is performed by groups in a church, tent, or prayer band.

Hierarchy creeps into the church as it becomes more institutionalized and mainline, but the overriding emphasis of folk religion is on friendliness, togetherness, hospitality. These qualities have been coded into greeting behaviors, for example, to a greater extent in southern churches than in some of non-southern location or sponsorship. Other values that folk churches in the South share with the wider regional culture include a love of the heroic, the theatrical, the charismatic, and the vivid. Such qualities are exhibited by the most popular southern preachers as well as politicians, by southern sermons and worship services as well as in literature. Often overlooked are the compensating senses of irony and tragedy, and, for some, a Calvinistic puritanism. Behind every Elmer Gantry is a Hazel Motes; but behind them a Cotton Mather and John Bunyan.

Southern familialism finds expression especially in the rural folk churches in family reunions, homecomings, and the decoration of graves. Excepting the family, however, southern folk religion has been remarkably reluctant to identify itself with social units. On the whole, southern folk religion works through preaching and teaching directed at the individual mind, heart, and soul rather than through social or political institutions.

See also BLACK LIFE: Preacher, Black; Religion, Black; FOLKLIFE: Folk Medicine; Folktales; Voodoo; / John the Conqueror Root

James L. Peacock
University of North Carolina
at Chapel Hill

William M. Clements, "The American Folk Church: A Characterization of American Folk Religion Based on Field Research among White Protestants in a Community in the South Central United States" (Ph.D. dissertation, Indiana University, 1974), in *Handbook of American Folklore*, ed. Richard M. Dorson (1983); Robert Coles, *Psychology Today* (January 1972); William Ferris, *Keystone Folklore Quarterly* (1970); Paula H. Anderson Green, *Tennessee Folklore Society Bulletin* (September 1977); Terry G. Jordan, *Southwestern Historical Quarterly* (Spring 1976); Charles Joyner, *Down By the Riverside: A South Carolina Slave Community* (1984); Newbell Niles Puckett, *Folk Beliefs of the Southern Negro* (1926; reprint ed. 1969); Bruce A. Rosenberg, *The Art of the American Folk Preacher* (1970). ☆

Frontier Religion

Three primary phases of southern frontier experience occurred—(1) the colonial frontier; (2) the initial trans-Appalachian frontier; and (3) the frontier created by Indian removals. In each period, the religious life of the Southwest was distinct and in certain respects unique in the nation.

After the first century of southern colonial settlement, which amounted to a frontier experience for Europeans, the southern colonial frontier consisted of the western piedmont and the Great Valley. Settlement of the valley began in earnest in the 1730s, with the massive migration of Scotch-Irish and German settlers, who were attracted by the cheap and plentiful land along the Great Philadelphia Wagon Road. Gradually, these migrants began to spread south and east, so that the westernmost sections of the southern piedmont and the extension of the valley into the Carolinas and Georgia contained perhaps 250,000 settlers by the time of the American Revolution.

These migrants received scant attention from Church of England clergy. The poorly organized established church faced a severe shortage of clergy, the physical barrier of the Blue Ridge, and the non-Anglican background of most of the settlers; it could only watch as the first southern frontier became fertile ground for dissent. Indeed, almost all of the South Carolina backcountry was in one Church of England parish; by 1750 only one Anglican church and two chapels served the upper valley.

The Presbyterian church dominated the first southern frontier, although Dunkers and Moravians found support among the German migrants. By 1768, 21 Presbyterian churches had been built on the South Carolina frontier; Presbyterians were equally successful in northern and southern frontier regions. Southern colonial governments even provided moderate support for the religious freedom of the migrants. In Georgia, the government ignored the wishes of the Privy Council and provided land for 107 Presbyterian settlers on the Great Ogeechee River. In Virginia, Governor Gooch answered a petition of the valley settlers in 1738 by guaranteeing that their religious practices would be tolerated.

These western Presbyterians received the Great Awakening with some suspicion, and most of the frontier response to the religious enthusiasm sweeping the nation took place in the western piedmont, where the settlers of the valley blended with easterners looking for cheaper land. In the piedmont, southwesterners in North Carolina listened to

the preaching of Shubal Stearns, a Boston-born Baptist, who led a movement that came to be termed the Separate Baptists. The sometimes radically democratic, highly experiential Separate movement spread north and east, and by the 1760s had influenced much of the western piedmont in Virginia as well.

By the end of the colonial period the settlement of the piedmont and the Great Valley had progressed to the extent that these sections could only very loosely be defined as frontier. Although still dominated by Presbyterians, Baptists—both Regular and Separate—had begun to make inroads, as had Quakers, Moravians, and Dunkers. This first phase of the southwestern frontier experience was unique, because of its religious diversity and the high degree of toleration afforded most faiths.

The second phase of the southern frontier experience was the trans-Appalachian West. Settlers had begun to cross the Appalachian mountain barrier by the 1770s, but the first significant wave of migration into the trans-Appalachian West came at the end of the Revolutionary War. By 1790, 110,000 people lived in these new southwestern settlements; by 1796 both Kentucky and Tennessee were members of the Union; by the first decade of the 19th century most of the best land in the two states was already densely settled.

In the earliest years of this rapidly developing frontier, the most enthusiastic promoters of religion were Baptist preachers who moved with the migrants, settled farms, and became permanent members of the communities. In one of several such instances, 500 members of the "traveling church" followed the lead of the Reverend Lewis Craig from Spotsylvania County in Virginia, to the Bluegrass country of Kentucky. Itinerant Methodist preachers, encouraged by the visits of their tireless bishop, Francis Asbury, began to develop small congregations at numerous points along their circuits. Presbyterians remained self-consciously aloof from the other denominations, concentrated as they were in Bourbon County, Ky., the eastern quarter of Tennessee, and the towns and cities springing up on the frontier. Intermingled among these three dominant denominations were scattered Quakers, Episcopalians, and even a few Roman Catholics. Ministers of the leading denominations tried to set themselves up as the moral guardians of the frontier, and some, led by Presbyterian David Rice, even went so far as to propose an end to slavery.

In spite of this religious diversity and activity, ministers in the Southwest of the 1790s complained continually about the lack of piety on the frontier. Most settlers did not attend church, and Deism had begun to be discussed in Nashville and Lexington. Increasingly, preachers began to stress watch-care within their congregations, rather than expansion and evangelism. In the face of real despair, however, a religious fervor began to emerge, first in 1799 in Logan County, Ky., and then by the next year spreading north and south throughout the region. Presbyterians probably served the most important role in the development of this Great Revival, but Methodists joined in many of the services. Although Baptists were reluctant to participate in the interdenominational services, they probably gained the most converts in the awakening.

The Great Revival exerted greatest influence upon southern and national re-ligious development in its stress upon complex revivalistic techniques. The McGee brothers, one a Methodist minister, the other a Presbyterian, served as two of the most innovative leaders of the movement, promoting in particular the concept of the camp meeting. The greatest of these, the 1801 Cane Ridge meeting in Bourbon County, Ky., may have brought 25,000 worshipers together to listen to a flock of preachers, who spoke day and night for a week. The meetings were not segregated by sex, nor in many instances by race, and several black preachers earned their initial reputations speaking at these gatherings.

In the wake of the revival came an inevitable period of reassessment and self-evaluation. In the Presbyterian church the revival had brought a series of schisms, some members following the Shakers, others forming a new denomination, the Cumberland Presbyterians, and still others, under the leadership of Barton W. Stone, taking a long theological odyssey that eventually contributed to the creation of the Disciples of Christ. As Presbyterians and, to a lesser extent, Baptists and Methodists recovered from the social earthquake of the Great Revival, the frontier spirit of the region also began to disappear. Instead, the second decade of the 19th century began to witness the development of a regional culture, a regional economy, and a regional self-consciousness.

This resulted in the third phase of frontier religious development in the Deep South. The area of the trans-Appalachian West, south of the Tennessee River, received some initial settlement by the time of the Great Revival, and sufficient migration had occurred by 1817 to allow Mississippi to enter the Union, followed by Alabama two years later. During the 1820s much of the extremely rich soil of the "Black Belt" began to be exploited with the use of large-scale slave labor. Only in the 1830s, however, with the mass expulsion of the Creek, Cherokee, Chickasaw, and Choctaw Indians, did this section begin to lose its frontier quality and develop both lasting settlement patterns and enduring religious, governmental, and economic institutions. Even as late as the end of the 1830s, according to Joseph Baldwin's account in *The Flush Times of Alabama and Mississippi*, much of the area remained wild, reckless, dangerous, uncivilized—in short, a frontier.

Because this section was at once the frontier for South Carolina and Georgia and an extension of settlement for Kentucky and Tennessee, the religious life of the Deep Southwest was an odd mixture of elements. In the first years a series of missionaries from the three major evangelical denominations visited the region, sometimes risking their lives to endure rough conditions of travel, at other times facing hostile reception from early settlers. Some frontier ministers began to adopt the swaggering, unyielding characteristics of many of the settlers, threatening unruly congregations from the pulpit, fighting when they deemed fighting appropriate. A premium was placed upon a straight-ahead preaching style, and a thundering voice helped drown out any heckling. In these ways, the pioneer preachers faced the same problems they would have found on other frontiers.

Churches of the southwestern frontier were heir to the factionalism and confusion coming out of the Great Revival period. Perhaps no frontier in American history faced so many religious choices. In addition to mainstream Presbyterians, Baptists, and Methodists, the factions, sects, and new denominations of the frontier included the Cumberland Presbyterians, the Shakers, the Stoneites, the Campbellites, the Republican Methodists, and, perhaps most important, the followers of a Baptist preacher, Daniel Parker, variously termed Hardshell, Two-Seed, or Antimission Baptists. This last group, which radically opposed missions and other benevolent actions as well as the education of clergy, disrupted the already difficult work of more conventional Baptist preachers. As a consequence, the first attempt to organize a state convention in Mississippi failed after five years of constant bickering.

Reflecting the confusion of religious life in the region, slaves remained in the white-run churches, participating in watch-care activities, long after Kentucky and Tennessee churches had begun segregating their buildings and their church services. Yet at the same time that this limited measure of equality existed in some Deep Southwest churches, others had begun to encourage the mission to the slaves with its powerful message of social control. Such confusion of purpose could be seen in other aspects of religious life on this frontier; for example, drinking preachers lived nearby those in the same denomination who viewed liquor as diabolic. This religious "split personality" from the frontier era continued to characterize the section for decades after. W. J. Cash and other commentators have even attributed paradoxical 20th-century southern characteristics to the survival of frontier ways, and this seems true in regard to religion.

See also BLACK LIFE: Religion, Black; HISTORY AND MANNERS: Frontier Heritage

David T. Bailey
Michigan State University

Joseph G. Baldwin, *The Flush Times of Alabama and Mississippi: A Series of Sketches* (1853); John B. Boles, *The Great Revival, 1787–1805: The Origins of the Southern Evangelical Mind* (1972); Catharine C. Cleveland, *The Great Revival in the West, 1797–1805* (1916); Wesley M. Gewehr, *The Great Awakening in Virginia, 1740–1790* (1930); Robert D. Mitchell, *Commercialism and Frontier: Perspectives on the Early Shenandoah Valley* (1977); Walter B. Posey, *The Baptist Church in the Lower Mississippi Valley, 1776–1845* (1957). ☆

Fundamentalism
||||||||||||||||||||||||||||||||||||||||||||||

Although much of southern religion has remained conservative into the 20th century and has been popularly characterized as "fundamentalist" in belief, the organized Fundamentalist movement penetrated the South slowly. Broadly defined, the Fundamentalist movement was a reaction of conservatives within most American Protestant churches to the rise of liberal religious beliefs and the social gospel at the beginning of the 20th century. In a narrower sense, the Fundamentalist movement was identified with the spread of dispensational premillennialism, which taught that the various historical eras or dispensations recounted in the Bible were sharply, literally separated into distinct ages, leading to the second coming of Christ before His thousand-year reign on earth. This idea was promoted by a series of prophetic conferences prior to World War I. Perhaps the most important milestones in the early development of the movement were the publication of a series of booklets, *The Fundamentals*, between 1910 and 1915 and the establishment of a number of independent organizations, the most important being the World's Christian Fundamentals Association founded in 1919.

Southerners contributed very little to these developments. The only southerner to contribute to *The Fundamentals* was President E. Y. Mullins of Baptist Theological Seminary in Louisville: his essay was so moderate that he himself was later attacked by fundamentalists. Very few of the early leaders of the Fundamentalist movement were from the South, and only one, J. Frank Norris of Fort Worth, Tex., spent his life working in the South.

In the years immediately after World War I, the fundamentalist-modernist controversy heated up, centering first on battles for control of northern Baptist and Presbyterian churches. Generally, southern churches escaped serious disruption because of their uniformly conservative nature. Militant southern fundamentalists like Norris warned against decay in the southern churches, but a separatist spirit was not strong in the pre–World War II South. On the other hand, when organized fundamentalism, under the leadership of William Jennings Bryan, expanded its attack to include banning the teaching of evolution in the public schools, the South became the movement's stronghold. Between 1921 and 1929, five states, all in the South (Florida, Tennessee, Mississippi, Arkansas, and Oklahoma) passed laws prohibiting the teaching of evolution. The Scopes Trial in Dayton,

Tenn., in July 1925, solidified two false notions: that fundamentalism was simply the baroque theology of southern hillbillies and that the movement would soon die under the weight of its own absurdity.

The preeminent southern fundamentalist in the first half of the 20th century was J. Frank Norris. Norris was one of the early leaders of the World's Christian Fundamentals Association, and in 1917 he founded a paper that later became *The Fundamentalist.* From his pulpit and in print he generated a stream of sensational attacks on liberalism, especially censuring his own denomination, the Southern Baptist Convention. Norris's career included a series of stormy confrontations that led to the expulsion of his church from the Texas Baptist Convention in 1923, his indictment and trial on charges of arson and murder, and countless bitter feuds with his closest associates. But in the long run he was the father of southern fundamentalism. In the 1930s and 1940s a generation of young, aspiring Southern Baptist preachers was exposed to the Texas Tornado's flamboyant style and premillennial, separatist teachings; some came to idolize him. In 1939 Norris established a "Bible Institute" at his Fort Worth church, where hundreds of young followers were taught his successful techniques for soul winning and church building.

Scores of other preachers roamed the South in the 1930s, fighting evolution and urging fundamentalist separatism. The most important of these evangelists was Bob Jones, Sr., one of the few Methodist ministers to take up the cause of organized fundamentalism. In 1926 Jones established an interdenominational fundamentalist college and settled permanently in Greenville, S.C., in 1947. In the 1980s Bob Jones University was the educational center of extreme fundamentalism in America. Probably the most widely circulated fundamentalist paper published since the 1930s is *The Sword of the Lord,* founded in 1934 by Independent Baptist evangelist John R. Rice of Murfreesboro, Tenn.

Since World War II, sectarianism and religious conservatism have remained strong in the South, but many southerners could hardly be considered fundamentalists. The Churches of Christ agree with many fundamentalist beliefs, but the movement is militantly anti-premillennial. Pentecostals have generally been rejected as heretics by fundamentalists. Many Southern Baptists sympathize with the Fundamentalist movement, but militant fundamentalists refuse to cooperate with them until they separate from the United Southern Baptist Convention.

On the other hand, in the 1940s and 1950s the South became the most fertile breeding ground of separatism—premillennial fundamentalism—especially among Independent Baptists. Hundreds of Independent Baptist churches were founded in the South after World War II, with many sponsoring private schools and scores supporting fundamentalist Bible institutes or colleges. Several important Independent Baptist associations were founded, including the Baptist Bible Fellowship headquartered in Springfield, Mo. Initially dominated by Norris, the movement in 1950 came under the leadership of his two close associates, Noel Smith and G. Beauchamp Vick, who broke with him. Among the generation of fundamentalist church builders trained at Bible Baptist College in Springfield since 1950 was Jerry Falwell, pastor of the Thomas Road Baptist Church in Lynchburg,

Va., and founder of Moral Majority. Another important Independent Baptist association was the Southwide Fellowship founded in 1956 and led by the huge Highland Park Baptist Church of Chattanooga, Tenn., and its pastor, Lee Roberson. The post–World War II southern fundamentalists built huge churches; in 1980 Falwell's church claimed over 15,000 members and Roberson's 50,000.

These Baptist fundamentalists once again politicized the movement in the late 1970s. Isolated and ridiculed for a half century after the Scopes Trial, southern fundamentalists had built huge empires in their isolation. By the end of the 1970s they were ready to reassert their influence. At the same time, the success of the movement has deeply divided it. Falwell's political interests have led him to cooperate on public issues not only with Southern Baptists such as James Robison and Bailey Smith but with Roman Catholics and Jews. Separatist fundamentalists, headed by the leaders of Bob Jones University, have openly denounced Falwell as a defector. One fundamentalist recently divided the movement's institutions into three camps: militant, moderate, and modified fundamentalists. These divisions are widely visible in the South in the 1980s and make it increasingly difficult to discuss fundamentalists without additional modifiers.

See also SCIENCE AND MEDICINE: Science and Religion; / Scopes Trial

David Harrell
University of Alabama
at Birmingham

George W. Dollar, *A History of Fundamentalism in America* (1973); Jerry Falwell, ed.,

The Fundamentalist Phenomenon (1981); George M. Marsden, *Fundamentalism and American Culture: The Shaping of Twentieth-Century Evangelicalism, 1870–1925* (1980); Royce Lee Measures, "Men and Movements Influenced by J. Frank Norris" (Th.D. thesis, Southwestern Baptist Theological Seminary, 1976); Clovis Gwin Morris, "He Changed Things: The Life and Thought of J. Frank Norris" (Ph.D. dissertation, Texas Tech University, 1973); Ernest Sandeen, *The Roots of Fundamentalism: British and American Millenarianism, 1800–1930* (1970); Robert Elwood Wenger, "Social Thought of American Fundamentalism 1918–1933" (Ph.D. dissertation, University of Nebraska, 1973). ☆

Jewish Religious Life

The religious life of the 785,000 Jews currently dispersed throughout the South defies generalization. It ranges from a strict ritualistic definition of Judaism to a purely cultural or philosophical interpretation of the faith. Though a number of southern Jews are not associated with any Jewish religious or philanthropic organization, thriving Jewish communities exist that vary in size and character from the 900-family Reform congregation in Dallas, Tex., to an eight-member Orthodox congregation in Vidalia, Ga. (with the smallest synagogue in the United States), to a "one-man congregation" in a small Louisiana town (he offers a scholarship to a nearby college for a Jewish student to act as a rabbi for his children).

This diversity mirrors the individual responses of Jews—in the absence of a unified higher authority—to the unexpected, widespread, but historically ignored congeniality that has usually greeted them during their more than 300-year residency in the South. As elsewhere in the United States, most Jewish immigrants to the South were from two groups—Sephardic Jews, the earliest to arrive, came from the Iberian Peninsula, whereas the Ashkenazi Jews came in the 19th century from central and eastern Europe. Although New Orleans was one destination for the huge wave of Orthodox Jewish immigrants in the late 19th and early 20th centuries, relatively few stayed there or in the region as a whole. The southern gentile religious outlook, in any event, often acted as a benevolent catalyst allowing the Jews of diverse origins and religious convictions to become far more of an integral part of the southern landscape than has been supposed.

Southern intolerance of Jews, to be sure, did appear at certain times and places. Jews were sometimes portrayed as outsiders. Critics accused them of profiteering during the Civil War and not sacrificing for the southern cause. Over 10,000 Jews, in reality, served the Confederacy, with Judah P. Benjamin, the new nation's secretary of war and secretary of state, the most famous. Some frustrated southerners, though, at the end of the war made Benjamin and Jews scapegoats for defeat. Anti-Semitism in the South seems to have increased in the late 19th century; as Jewish southerners became more prosperous than before as businessmen, commodity brokers, mill owners, and plantation landlords, bigotry toward them increased. The lynching of Leo Frank in 1915 for the alleged murder of Mary Phagan in Georgia was the worst incident of anti-Semitic southern violence. The Ku Klux Klan persecuted southern Jews along with other groups,

driving them from political participation by the 1920s.

Southern religion proved, however, a force for Jewish-gentile accommodation. Southern gentiles drew their religious fervor more from piety than from an unswerving doctrinal position. Because piety lends itself more easily to ecumenism than does doctrinalism, southerners were inclined to accept what they perceived as pious Jews. Most southern gentiles, however, did not define Jewish piety solely in the restricted terms of ritual devotion. Their broader understanding of Judaism emphasized the Jewish moral character that manifested itself as an inclination to be socially responsible and unusually charitable, which the gentiles believed was the result of the Jews' religious heritage as "God's chosen Ministers of the Book." As biblical fundamentalists, southern Protestants honored the Jewish Old Testament tradition. This respectful religious stereotype, more than any other, generally proved sufficient to quell bigoted voices and to provide Jews with credentials for acceptance.

Yet, although southern gentiles were willing to accept religious distinction, they generally refused to accept Jewish cultural separatism. Consequently, as gentiles beckoned the Jews to become a part of southern society, they exerted a pressure upon the Jews to forego their old ways and adopt southern lifestyles.

Judaism, nevertheless, developed into an ethnic religion. Its religious traditions were an integral part of a sociocultural system that Old World Jews had developed through the ages as a means of preserving their own identity while coming to terms with the persecutions of the gentile majority. Inescapably, therefore, any process of acculturation in the South automatically required a modification of religious life. Southerners, in fact, became early advocates of the Jewish Reform Movement. Beth Elohim congregation in Charleston, for example, distinguished itself in the 19th century through ritual changes such as organ music in worship, confirmation classes, and the use of family pews.

American Jews evaluated the utility of their Old World religious traditions in two ways. The first was to retain but alter those traditions that allowed them to be different, without appearing to be alien, from their gentile neighbors. Isolated individually and in small groups, the Jews wanted to retain contact with their heritage, from which they could draw a stabilizing sense of identity while shedding what some southerners termed their "outward strangeness." If there was any hesitancy about putting aside the traditions of their forefathers, many Jews overcame it with the excuse that it was impossible to be properly observant: economic and social realities forced se-

vere modifications and even abandonment of Sabbath observance; the unavailability of proper foods and ritual slaughterers seriously weakened resolve to maintain the dietary laws; proper quorums for prayer were often impossible to convene; the proper ritual accoutrements could not be secured; and holidays could not be adequately celebrated.

In those areas where Jews congregated in small communities, they sought to purchase land for a Jewish cemetery, engaged in organized charitable activities, and eventually organized a congregation, all of which were indicators of a communal commitment to their heritage and a devotion to their religion that acted to offset individual ritual laxity. Nevertheless, the form of religious practices often took on a Protestant appearance as Jews tried to minimize outward ritual difference and thereby demonstrate the common religious experience shared with the gentiles. Increasingly,

Jewish religious service, Waco, Texas, 1890s

English was substituted for the Hebrew language in the religious service; choirs and musical instruments were introduced into the service and the use of distinctive prayer caps and shawls neglected; the rabbi slowly took on the character of a Protestant clergyman; and even the architecture of later Jewish houses of worship copied Protestant prototypes.

The second criterion Jews used to evaluate the usefulness of their traditions in southern society emphasized the traditional Judaic sense of moral responsibility as a viable substitute to demanding ritual Judaism. In short, if Jews could not be punctiliously ritualistic, their ethical commitment and display of a "good heart" would place them beyond reproach. Thus, often, before congregations were formally organized, a myriad of charitable and social agencies appeared throughout the South: orphan homes, aid societies, relief societies, service clubs for widowed and disabled members, and benevolent societies. It was no accident that Reform Judaism began in the South, nor that early southern Jewry took the lead in transformations that often set the pattern for Jews in other sections of the country.

Jews in the agrarian South could not group together in sufficient numbers to enable them to resist or minimize the lure to acculturate through the creation of ghetto-like communities, as did many of their northern urban counterparts. The receptiveness of the South to the Jewish presence made such resistance less desirable. Though the forces of acculturation that were at work were not uniquely southern, the pressure imposed upon the Jews was greater in the South. The receptiveness of the South to the Jewish presence made it more difficult for the Jews not to be lured into becoming a part of their environment.

In addition, the relatively few numbers of Jews who came South imposed a greater sense of vulnerability and isolation on those who did, thereby creating a greater sense of urgency in the minds of these Jews.

The southern Jewish response to the demands of southern gentiles, however, was not uniform. The great diversity of contemporary southern Jewish religious life demonstrates that the process of acculturation has occurred at different stages because southern Jews arrived in different waves over the past 300 years, the last of which ended only in the 1920s. Moreover, the Jews came not only at different times but from different lands, carrying with them varied national, cultural, and religious experiences. Thus, their judgments about what traditions to discard, retain, and alter were not always the same as those of the previous generation of immigrants. Indeed, differing judgments regarding religious celebration, ritual performance, and form of ceremony created a sense of alienation and antagonism among Jews themselves that in some cases was greater than that existing between Jews and gentiles. Migration since World War II of American-born Jews from large northern communities, combined with the absence of any significant number of first-generation immigrants and the formation of Jewish activities into national networks, may be blurring the strong and distinctive sectional religious identities that existed, not too long ago, among southern Jews.

See also ETHNIC LIFE: / Jews

Louis E. Schmier
Valdosta State College

Myron Berman, *Richmond's Jewry, 1769–1976* (1979); Mark Elovitz, *A Century of*

Jewish Life in Dixie: The Birmingham Experience (1974); Eli Evans, *The Provincials: A Personal History of Jews in the South* (1973); Steven Hertzberg, *Strangers within the Gate City: The Jews of Atlanta, 1845–1915* (1978); Ben Kaplan, *The Eternal Stranger: A Study of Jewish Life in the Small Community* (1957); Bertram Korn, *The Early Jews of New Orleans* (1969); Louis E. Schmier, *Reflections of Southern Jewry: The Letters of Charles Wessolowsky, 1878–1879* (1982); *Southern Israelite* (1926–). ☆

Literature and Religion
||||||||||||||||||||||||||||||||||||||||||||||||||||||||

Religion has influenced the imagination of southern writers in fundamental ways. Both aesthetically and thematically, religious practice in the region has helped writers render a particular place and time as a target for their satire and as a prism through which they interpret human experience. Often southern writers' debts to the religious beliefs and practices of their region are unacknowledged, perhaps even unconscious. William Faulkner asserts such influences exist, nonetheless: "The writer must write about his background. He must write out of what he knows and the Christian legend is part of any Christian's background, especially the background of a country boy, a Southern country boy. I grew up with that, took that in without even knowing it. It's just there. It has nothing to do with how much of it I might believe or disbelieve—it's just there." Southern writers, whether or not they expressly address religious issues, engage questions that preoccupy southern culture, questions that often arise in the practice of religion.

The South historically has been more homogeneous and orthodox in its beliefs than other regions. In a recent study by John Shelton Reed, 90 percent of southerners surveyed identified themselves as Protestant as opposed to 60 percent of non-southerners. The same study found more agreement in religious beliefs among these southern Protestants than among non-southern Protestants or Catholics. Within this homogeneity, there is, however, individuality—institutionalized in the many Protestant denominations—producing colorful variants in religious behavior. This individuality within an overwhelmingly Protestant culture resulted from the particular emphasis of the southern church as it parted from the pluralistic patterns of the North. The Baptist and Methodist movements which swept across the largely rural South after 1755 often featured preachers who delivered dramatic, emotional pictures of the struggle to escape sin and achieve salvation. With common roots in the New England Calvinism of the Great Awakening, this expressive religion stressed personal piety and the preeminent importance of achieving one's salvation. Appealing to the often-isolated poor, it cared little for abstract theology or issues of ethical responsibility within the society. No church-state was envisioned. In the hospitable, fertile southern landscape, preachers taught that one must struggle inwardly with an inherent sinfulness. This sense of human frailty and limitation combined with the hedonism of a rich, frontier culture led to what Samuel S. Hill has called a pattern of "confession, purgation, and going out to sin again."

As private morality became more exclusively the domain of the church, engagement with issues of public morality became less frequent. The explanation lies with the South's commitment to slavery. Because the southern church avoided confronting the immorality of the institution of slavery, it could not validly address issues of ethical responsibility in the larger society. Instead, spokesmen of the church defended the institution as consistent with God's plan, vilifying its critics as ungodly in motivation and action and reaffirming the position that the church should concern itself only with issues of personal piety and salvation. Also, the southern church undertook elaborate missionary efforts to teach the slave community to share its outlook.

When writers of the Southern Literary Renaissance looked to the social history of the South for reasons behind its 20th-century ills, they blamed the church's preoccupation with matters of personal behavior and its carefully defended historical blindness to slavery. Writers like Faulkner, Allen Tate, Flannery O'Connor, and Erskine Caldwell created communities of self-righteous churchgoers and hypocritical preachers practicing a narrow, spiritless religion insensitive to the moral issues with which these writers were concerned. Mark Twain had earlier laid the ground for satirizing the formal practice of religion in the South as a fountain of intolerance; Faulkner tilled the same soil in his depiction of the good Baptist ladies of Jefferson who close the door to those who violate the standards of personal behavior endorsed formally by the church. Once questioned about his own religious beliefs, Faulkner said what other southern writers seemed to be implying in their portrayal of institutional religion: "I think that the trouble with Christianity is that we've never tried it yet." These writers created worlds where issues of public

morality had to be engaged; adherence to strict codes of personal piety was insufficient. As Robert Penn Warren wrote at the end of *All the King's Men*, the challenge was to immerse oneself in "the awful responsibility of time."

Yet even as they attack the self-satisfied attitudes of the southern religious establishment, many of these writers accept views basic to regional religious belief. For example, Flannery O'Connor, a writer who makes this gap between belief and practice the focus of her work, finds in the southerner's belief in the Devil, in the reality of evil, an important article of faith. From the perspective of her own orthodox Roman Catholic beliefs, O'Connor keenly perceives the fundamentalist Protestant experiences of the majority of southerners. She introduces her collection of short stories *A Good Man Is Hard to Find* with a quotation from St. Cyril of Jerusalem: "The dragon is by the side of the road, watching those who pass. Beware lest he devour you. We go to the Father of Souls, but it is necessary to pass by the dragon." O'Connor believes she addresses a modern world in which evil is dismissed as sociological or psychological aberration. In the South, particularly the rural Protestant South, this Roman Catholic writer ironically recognizes another point of view.

Episcopal Bishop Robert R. Brown writes that southerners "believe more in the reality of Satan than in the reality of God," and John Shelton Reed's recent study shows that by a significant margin (86 percent to 52 percent) southerners are more likely than non-southerners to say they believe in the Devil. Southern writers, too, insist upon the reality of evil. They present it as active, powerful, inescapable, irreducible, threatening the individual from within as well as from without. They also criticize ideas of social reform dependent upon a view of mankind as essentially good. Writers such as Faulkner, Warren, Katherine Anne Porter, Carson McCullers, and Truman Capote join O'Connor in representing evil as violence, grotesque psychological distortion, selfish pride, or despair. These storytellers find in the individual's confrontation with evil the conflict from which dramatic fiction arises.

Another common theme that reflects the debt of southern writers to their religious environment is closely allied to this acceptance of the existence of evil: humans are flawed, limited, imperfect. "Man is conceived in sin and born in corruption," says Warren's Willie Stark, "and he passeth from the stink of the didie to the stench of the shroud." The viewpoint is essentially conservative, even pessimistic if contrasted with visions of a more idealized human nature. Without explicitly referring to original sin, southern writers create characters more sinning than sinned against. Mr. Thompson of Katherine Anne Porter's "Noon Wine" or Horace Benbow of Faulkner's *Sanctuary* awaken to their own capacity for violence and evil. Individuals resist or succumb to their own selfish pride, their greed, their bestial natures. It is a mistake, however, to label such a vision of human behavior as pessimistic or deterministic. Within the context of the accepted religious beliefs of their culture, southern writers turn their attention to how one conducts life given these imperfections. The measure of the spiritually healthy individual is in his or her ability to recognize limitations and then to involve oneself with the world and its complexities.

In the emotional style of southern evangelical Protestantism lie the clear-est connections to the South's creative literature. The southern writer could have and often did turn to the preacher for models of imaginative, moving uses of language. Faulkner once speculated about the appeal of the Southern Baptist movement: "It came from times of hardship in the South where there was little or no food for the human spirit—where there were no books, no theater, no music, and life was pretty hard and a lot of it happened out in the sun, for very little reward and that was the only escape they had." The southern preacher dramatized the struggles of good and evil in vivid, concrete stories, enlivened by expressive flourishes, which allowed the congregation to forget for the moment their day-to-day fight to survive. In the competitive world of the itinerant preacher, he who could touch the imagination as well as the conscience of his congregation thrived. Every writer who grew up in the South, then, breathed in this dramatic, emotional atmosphere.

The preacher offered southern writers literary tools and visions that guided them in confronting central questions about life. Writers worked scenes of camp meetings and revivals into their stories. Johnson Jones Hooper, for example, introduces the character Captain Simon Suggs to a camp meeting, where he becomes the object-lesson sinner for the preacher. Mark Twain presents a camp meeting through Huck Finn's eyes as the duke and the king, Huck's con-artist companions, prey on the gullible there assembled. Flannery O'Connor in "The River" shows the preacher Bevel, who baptizes a small boy so that he will "count now." Recently, Lisa Alther has portrayed the modern youth revival and evangelist Brother Buck, who couches his message in extended football metaphors of Christ Jesus Thy Quarterback, the Celestial Coach, and the water boys of life. And Faulkner shows the power of the preacher to raise his audience to new levels of self-recognition in *The Sound and the Fury* with the sermon of the Reverend Shegog.

Faulkner chose to depict a black preacher when he wanted to express a redemptive quality in the religion practiced in the South. Samuel Hill has pointed out that the black church developed along lines different from those of white Protestantism, in that "the theology of black people's Christianity was shifting, not away from glorious heaven, to be sure, but away from the threats of hell. It remained a religion of salvation, but less and less from eternal punishment and more from alienation from Jesus. . . . [Black people] created an authentic folk variant of a traditional religion. It featured expressiveness, joy, fellowship, moral responsibility, pious feelings and the hope of heaven." Yet black southern writers, like their white counterparts, respond with ambivalence when portraying religious practice in the region.

Richard Wright in his autobiographical *Black Boy* depicts the women of his family as threatening him with God's punishment for his transgressions. In *Native Son* religion weakens black rebellion with promises that suffering in this life will be rewarded in the next. But in the short story "Fire and Cloud," Wright presents the Reverend Taylor as a man who lives his religious commitment as social action. In his picture of the Reverend Homer Barbee in *Invisible Man*, Ralph Ellison illustrates the rhetorical power of the black preacher even as he suggests it is used to misdirect the attention of the congregation from their exploitation. Alice Walker, however, seems to capture the spirit of what Hill

called the joyful folk variant of traditional southern religion in *The Color Purple*. Shug Avery celebrates a personal religion, independent from any formal church, which asks only that one express love for God's creation. It is one of the most positive, albeit unconventional, expressions of religious feeling in southern literature.

H. L. Mencken once characterized the South as the "bunghole of the United States, a cesspool of Baptists, a miasma of Methodism, snake-charmers, phony real-estate operators, and syphilitic evangelists." Southern writers have populated their work with hypocritical preachers, self-righteous congregations, rigid Calvinists, and spiritually twisted fanatics. They have, nevertheless, drawn their vision of human limitation and a world in which good and evil contend from the most basic beliefs of southern religion. Perhaps as the distinctions between the South and other regions fade, the southern writer will become more indistinguishable in his response to his community. In the work of Walker Percy, a southerner and a Catholic, there is attention to philosophical and theological issues that cannot be said to be strictly southern. As long as religion remains a focus within the southern community, it cannot be disregarded by those whose imagination feeds on the southern experience. The ambivalence that has marked writers' responses to the religious beliefs and practices in the South is unlikely to change. Southern religious beliefs will continue to influence the writers' vision.

See also LITERATURE articles

Robert R. Moore
State University of New York
at Oswego

Samuel S. Hill, *The South and the North in American Religion* (1980); C. Hugh Holman, *The Immoderate Past: The Southern Writer and History* (1977); Charles Lippy, ed., *Bibliography of Religion in the South* (1985); Ralph Luker, *Southern Studies* (Summer 1983); Rosemary Magee and Robert Detweiler, in *Encyclopedia of Religion in the South*, ed. Samuel S. Hill (1984); Perry Miller, *Errand into the Wilderness* (1956); John Shelton Reed, *The Enduring South: Subcultural Persistence in Mass Society* (1972); Louis D. Rubin, Jr., in *The Added Dimension: The Art and Mind of Flannery O'Connor*, ed. Melvin J. Friedman and Lewis A. Lawson (1977); Lewis Simpson, in *The Cry of Home: Cultural Nationalism and the Modern Writer*, ed. H. Ernest Lewald (1972); Thomas Daniel Young, in *The American South: Portrait of a Culture*, ed. Louis D. Rubin, Jr. (1980). ☆

Missionary Activities

Religious revivalism swept the South in the early days of the Republic and brought with it an intense belief in the millennium—the thousand-year reign of Christ on earth that would commence when all peoples of the world had been given a chance to accept Christ. By natural extension foreign missions joined domestic missions to Indians in the effort to carry out the great commission: "Go ye therefore, and teach all nations, baptizing them . . . ; [and] teaching them to observe all things whatsoever I have commanded you." (Matthew 28:19–20). Richard Furman, pastor of the First Baptist Church of Charleston, S.C., adjoined nationalism to religion in 1802 when he asserted that the United States would "participate, largely, in the fulfillment of those sacred prophecies

which have foretold the glory of Messiah's kingdom. . . . Hence God has prepared this land for a great mission, to lead the world into the millennium." Nationalism thus reinforced religious belief and determined the religiocultural nature of American foreign missions.

The formal organization of at least one major denomination in the United States resulted from the missionary impulse. Baptists believed so strongly in the autonomy of the individual congregation that they had resisted all efforts to form even statewide organizations. Yet they established a national body when confronted with the need to support foreign missionaries. Adoniram Judson and his wife and Luther Rice, Congregationalists, had been sent to India by the American Board of Commissioners for Foreign Missions (ABCFM) in 1812. During their voyage they became convinced that baptism of believers was scripturally correct, so they requested and received baptism by immersion from a British Baptist upon their arrival. Luther Rice returned to the United States to inform the ABCFM of their actions, whereupon the board severed its connection with them. Rice toured Baptist churches, North and South, requesting support for the Judsons. The need to sustain these missionaries already in the field led to the organization, in 1814, of the General Missionary Convention of the Baptist Denomination in the United States of America for Foreign Missions. Richard Furman, long an advocate of this effort, was elected its first president, and other Baptists from southern states who supported both foreign missions and a national organization for Baptists also served in positions of responsibility.

Frontier Baptists were not as enthusiastic about foreign missions as their eastern brethren. Indeed, in the early 19th century there were more differences between rural and urban Baptists than there were between northern and southern Baptists who lived in cities, and this was most likely true of other denominations as well. Until American sectional issues caused divisions in three Protestant bodies—Methodists in 1844, Baptists in 1845, and Presbyterians in 1861—southerners were among the early missionary volunteers and worked alongside their colleagues from the North. The three new southern denominations quickly established foreign missions as a major part of their program, with China as one of the first fields to be manned. Each had experienced missionaries who had worked there before the separation, and China loomed large in the millennial view. Here were more people than in any other country; they had to be reached before the millennium could begin.

Several circumstances retarded the southern missionary effort in China. Before the Peking Treaties of 1860 missionaries had been confined to a few treaty ports. Access to the interior, even when obtained, could not be exploited until the financial strains of the Civil War and Reconstruction ended. By that time missionary efforts in India and the Near East, without imperial restrictions on the free movement and activities of foreigners, had become well established and drew heavily on mission budgets. Throughout the 19th century, American support for foreign missions—in expenditure, manpower, and capital construction—went for the most part to the Near East and to the Indian subcontinent.

Qualitatively, if not quantitatively, southern missionaries of the last century made significant contributions to China

in particular and to the missionary enterprise in general. A southern Methodist from Georgia, Young J. Allen, arrived in Shanghai in 1860. During his long tenure in China he became one of the most influential American missionaries through his magazine, *The Globe.* Written in Chinese, it became a vehicle to inform readers, non-Christian as well as Christian, of the Western scientific knowledge so many of them sought beginning with the Self-Strengthening Movement of the 1860s and particularly after China's humiliating defeat by Japan in 1895. A young woman from Virginia, Charlotte "Lottie" Moon, served as a missionary to China and became the inspiration for extensive fund-raising activity by the Women's Missionary Union of the Southern Baptist Convention. The Lottie Moon Christmas Offering annually collects millions of dollars, which the Foreign Mission Board uses to maintain the largest number of American Protestant missionaries now in the field.

Perhaps the most influential missionary activity of the late 1800s occurred in the southern United States. In 1880 an American ship's captain, Charles Jones, discovered a young Chinese stowaway on his vessel, and when he docked in Wilmington, N.C., he entrusted the boy to the care of the pastor of the Fifth Avenue Methodist Church there. The lad, named Soong, was converted and took as his Christian name that of the captain. He remained in the United States to receive an undergraduate and ministerial education. In 1886 Charlie Jones Soong returned to China an ordained Methodist minister and became involved in the revolutionary movement of Sun Yat-sen. One of his sons, T. V. Soong, and three of his daughters, Ai-ling, Ching-ling, and

Mei-ling Soong, were educated in the United States and became internationally known figures in Chinese political life.

Southern missionaries in the first half of this century generally were indistinguishable from those of other regions of the United States. They volunteered for the same mission fields—Latin America, Africa, the Middle East, South and East Asia—and engaged in the same kinds of activities: evangelization, education, medical missions, and social work. Independence granted to former colonies and the establishment of Socialist governments in the Third World from about 1950 created a divergence between the missionary emphases of southern and northern denominations. The latter mainly joined the National Council of Churches and the World Council of Churches, which stressed the social gospel, with cultural and technological aid projects predominating. Southern denominations have retained a more evangelical focus in their missions overseas. These lines, however, should not be too sharply drawn. As of the early 1980s the evangelical bodies supported more than three times as many foreign missionaries as the "liberal" churches and American Catholics combined. As governments sensitive to foreign presence have discouraged if not forbidden foreign missionary activity, many of today's missionaries seek out the 16,000 tribal groups in remote areas around the world who have not heretofore been reached with the gospel. This may be the greatest change in Protestant missionary strategy of the last decade.

George B. Pruden, Jr.
Armstrong State College

Ecumenical Missionary Conference: New York, 1900, 2 vols. (1900); John K. Fairbank, ed., *The Missionary Enterprise in China and America* (1974); Kenneth Scott Latourette, *A History of the Expansion of Christianity*, vol. 6, *The Great Century in Northern Africa and Asia A.D. 1800–A.D. 1914* (1945); *Time* (27 December 1982). ☆

Modernism and Religion
||||||||||||||||||||||||||||||||||||||||||||||||||||||||||||

In American religious studies the term *modernism* describes a style of Christian theology that attempted to adjust traditional religious doctrines to the intellectual demands of the modern world, especially to biological evolution and historical-critical study of Scripture. Although the term is often used to describe the beliefs of all who make such adjustments, it is usually reserved for the liberal theology of the early 20th century (1920–40).

Modernism has not been a significant position among southern theologians. The predominant southern orientation has been theological orthodoxy. Even before the Civil War, southern theologians, especially in the culturally influential Presbyterian church, tended to adopt more traditional theological positions than their northern counterparts. This was partly because of the conviction that the Bible, if interpreted literally, supported the institution of slavery. The Civil War reinforced this pre-existent conservatism in two ways. First, the revivals that periodically swept the Confederate armies solidified the evangelical churches as the expression of southern piety. These revivals, often led by lay preachers, stressed biblicism as a key element in religion. Second, the defeat of the South and the subsequent forcible reunion of the country forced the former Confederates to find new ways to express their loyalty to the Lost Cause. An amalgamation of sentimentality, conservatism, and southern identity took place—a southern civil religion—that inhibited intellectual change and adventure.

James Woodrow (1828–1907), Professor of Natural Science in Connection with Revelation at Columbia Presbyterian Seminary in South Carolina from 1861 to 1886, was one of the first southerners to approach the question of the relationship between the new biology and Christian theology. As a result of the publication of his position, controversy arose over the issue from 1884 to 1886, which, although not leading to his conviction for heresy, resulted in his dismissal from the school. Crawford Howell Toy (1836–1919), Professor of Old Testament at Southern Baptist Seminary in Louisville, Ky., had been trained as a biblical critic at the University of Berlin. While teaching the Bible at Southern, he referred to the views current in Europe on such matters as the authorship of the Pentateuch and Isaiah. Fearful of controversy, his colleagues asked for his resignation before the trustees could force the issue by dismissing him. William Whitsitt (1841–1911), president of Southern from 1895 to 1899 was, likewise, persuaded to resign after he applied modern historical techniques to Baptist history.

Among Methodists, a migration of students from Randolph-Macon, Wofford, and other colleges to Germany after the Civil War and to Johns Hopkins after its founding in 1876 created a noticeably larger contingent of progressive thinkers in that denomination than among Presbyterians or Baptists. In 1875 Alexander Winchell was brought to the new Vanderbilt University and within four years came to advocate pub-

licly Darwin's theories. He was dismissed in 1879 after a prolonged controversy. Nonetheless, Vanderbilt became a center for advanced biblical study as well as for the Christian interpretation of evolution. The struggle that separated Vanderbilt from the Methodist church was technically over the issue of who had the right to govern the school, but theological factors were also involved. The elevation of Emory to university status and the establishment of its Candler School of Theology as a response to the Methodist loss of Vanderbilt were also partially antimodernist developments.

During the 1920s the nation as a whole witnessed a battle between modernists and fundamentalists. On the one hand, it was a struggle within various denominations for control of each church's teaching and government. Although these struggles took place primarily in the North, they influenced those southern churches that had miniature fundamentalist-modernist controversies.

In southern Methodism, Bishops Candler, Denny, and DuBose were continually critical of liberal theology, which they saw as a threat to historic Methodist belief, and they were in contact with Harold Paul Slvan, a New Jersey pastor who led the conservative wing in the northern church. In the Southern Baptist Convention, the issue of whether evolution should be taught in the denomination's schools was hotly debated in the twenties, and in 1925 a new confession of faith—*The Baptist Faith and Message*—was adopted to guard against liberal ideas in the church.

The controversy was even more marked in the Presbyterian Church in the United States. This southern denomination had a series of trials in the early 20th century that prepared the way for the major controversy in the 1920s. The Reverend William Caldwell, who moved to Fort Worth from Baltimore, was at the center of a debate on biblical inerrancy that lasted from 1900 to 1909, and F. E. Maddox was suspended from the ministry in 1909 for heresy. Darwinism was continually denounced in the church press, and evolution was an issue before the 1920s made antievolutionism a popular crusade. The internal Presbyterian controversy in the 1920s revolved around The Bible Union of China, which charged that modernism had infected the mission field. Much of the controversy concerned Nanking Theological Seminary, a joint enterprise of the northern and southern churches. In addition, the question of whether a candidate needed to affirm his acceptance of biblical inerrancy was also hotly discussed. Feelings on this issue were so high that Walter Moore, president of Union (Richmond), withdrew his nomination of Harris Kirk, a Baltimore pastor, for a faculty position at the denomination's seminaries. By 1930, however, the debate was quieted, although it reemerged from 1938 to 1940 in a controversy over the theology of Ernest Trice Thompson of Union Seminary. When the general assembly declined to investigate the doctrinal views of the faculty of the church's seminaries in 1940, the battle ended.

The other side of the debate in the 1920s was over the teaching of evolution in the public schools. In North Carolina, this debate was particularly hard fought. The presidents of Wake Forest College (Baptist) and Duke University, William Louis Poteat and William Preston Few, took the position that freedom of inquiry was essential to education and resisted the passage of a law preventing the teaching of evolution. For many Baptists

and Methodists, their advocacy of academic freedom branded them as modernists and brought them much criticism in the church press. Their alliance, however, helped to block the passage of the act. The issue was fought more dramatically in the neighboring state of Tennessee, whose law prohibiting the teaching of evolution in the public schools resulted in the Scopes Trial in 1925.

The comparatively small number of modernists in the southern churches did not prevent "modernism" from becoming symbolically important in southern religion. The denunciation of modernists became a stock element in much southern preaching, and Bible colleges and similar institutions used the fear of modernism as a way of promoting their own cause. For many southerners, resistance to modernism was a central element of their faith. As part of the system of symbols by which southerners have ordered their religious lives, modernism—real or imagined—has been one of the dominant forces in the 20th century.

See also EDUCATION: / Duke University; Emory University; Vanderbilt University; SCIENCE AND MEDICINE: Science and Religion

Glenn T. Miller
Southeastern Baptist
Theological Seminary

Kenneth K. Bailey, *Southern White Protestantism in the Twentieth Century* (1964); Norman F. Furniss, *The Fundamentalist Controversy, 1918–1931* (1954); Willard B. Gatewood, Jr., ed., *Controversy in the Twenties: Fundamentalism, Modernism, and Evolution* (1969); Robert T. Handy, *Religion in Life* (Summer 1955); William R. Hutchison, *The Modernist Impulse in American*

Protestantism (1976); George M. Marsden, *Fundamentalism and American Culture: The Shaping of Twentieth-Century Evangelicalism, 1870–1925* (1980). ☆

Pentecostalism
||||||||||||||||||||||||||||||||||||||

American Pentecostalism comprises many diverse organizations, some of which are predominantly southern in both membership and influence. Much of the drama of early Pentecostal history occurred in the South, among the socially disinherited whose yearnings for spiritual perfection and otherworldly ecstasy had made them participants in the Holiness movements that had swept the region intermittently for decades.

Pentecostalism became a definable movement after 1901 when a consensus on the evidence of the baptism with the Holy Spirit emerged among the followers of Charles Parham, a Kansas Holiness preacher. The simple assertion that glossolalia (or speaking in tongues) was always the initial evidence of a crisis experience indicating a baptism of the Holy Spirit separated Pentecostals from others who shared the same concern for vital spiritual experience.

For five years this doctrine was preached primarily in Kansas, Oklahoma, and Texas, until in 1906 William Seymour took the message to California. From a warehouse on Azusa Street in Los Angeles the distinctive Pentecostal assertion spread and shaped a movement that would have long-term significance for American religion across the nation, and especially in the South.

Out of the fluid religious culture of the late 19th century came several currents that would converge in 20th-century Pentecostalism. The conviction of some individuals about the imminence of the second advent made them yearn for both "enduement with power for service" and holiness. The focus on restoration that had been a creative force throughout the American religious experience motivated others to desire the contemporary realization of the charismatic experiences of the New Testament church. Others were led through the healing revivalism of people like John Alexander Dowie and Mary Woodworth-Etter to stress the present manifestation of the spiritual gifts cited in I Corinthians 12–14. Another group, influenced by the loosely organized Wesleyan Holiness movement, stressed a "second blessing" of encounter with the Spirit resulting in holiness of heart and life. All these emphases became significant for Pentecostalism. Each stressed intangible blessings and otherworldly benefits and consciously discounted material possessions. Each had a consequent appeal to those who were "dispossessed" in this life.

These approaches to spirituality stressed the Holy Spirit and had some conception of a crisis encounter with the Spirit. There was no consensus among believers, however, as to incontrovertible evidence of the Spirit's special gifts, and those who responded to Parham's assertion of such evidence and thus became Pentecostal were thereby alienated from others in the religious culture whose concerns and heritage most closely resembled their own.

In the South, restorationist and Holiness thinking created a setting favorable to the Pentecostal message. Holiness teaching stressed the necessity of a work of grace, subsequent to the conversion experience, in which the individual would be sanctified. It focused on the Holy Spirit and on a definite religious experience subsequent to conversion. By 1906 outspoken southern Holiness advocates had largely left their original base in the Methodist Episcopal Church, South, to form independent groups, many of which had precise understanding not only of valid spiritual experience but also of appropriate Christian general behavior. Prohibitions against pork, coffee, colas, chewing gum, tobacco, alcohol, dancing, "spectator sports," and mixed bathing were common, as were directives regarding jewelry, short hair for women, and many types of clothing. "Holiness" came to be associated with specific external evidences. Across the South, small Holiness groups, local in character and different in emphasis, struggled to survive. Among these who already claimed a "second blessing" of sanctification were some to whom a "third blessing" of enduement with spiritual power seemed plausible.

Among the hundreds who visited Los Angeles in 1906 to observe the Pentecostal movement were two whose importance to southern Pentecostalism would be central—G. B. Cashwell of the Pentecostal Holiness Church, a Holiness group based in Falcon, N.C., and Charles Harrison Mason of Memphis, Tenn., who shared leadership with Charles Price Jones in the predominantly black Church of God in Christ. Both claimed an experience of Spirit baptism, and returned to the South as advocates of the Pentecostal message. Southern Holiness preachers had already been advised of the Los Angeles Pentecostal revival through articles and letters in such widely circulated Holiness periodicals as *The Way of Faith*,

and many responded with interest to the teaching. Cashwell traveled widely, primarily among rural southeastern Holiness groups, with some ministry in urban centers like Memphis and Birmingham. One result of his ministry was the coalescence of several small southern Holiness groups to form the Pentecostal Holiness Church in 1911. Another would be the uniting with the Pentecostalism of Ambrose J. Tomlinson and the restorationist Church of God that he led. Ultimately, at least three important Pentecostal groups would result from this connection—the Church of God; the Church of God of Prophecy (both with headquarters in Cleveland, Tenn.); and the Church of God, World Headquarters with offices in Huntsville, Ala.

Mason's acceptance of the Pentecostal message divided the Church of God in Christ. Mason assumed leadership of the Pentecostal majority; Jones renamed his Holiness followers the Church of Christ (Holiness) U.S.A. and moved his headquarters to Jackson, Miss.

The earliest division among Pentecostals centered around their understanding of sanctification. Initially Pentecostal leaders had insisted that sanctification was a discreet experience, a "second work," which always preceded the baptism with the Holy Spirit. After 1910 increasing numbers accepted teaching associated with William Durham, a Chicago pastor who understood sanctification as progressive, and perfection as impossible, and who developed his ideas under the heading "the finished work of grace." For several years controversy raged between "two-work" and "one-work" Pentecostals. Southern Pentecostal groups accepted the older "two-work" understanding of sanctification, and the "finished work of grace" became associated with the newer Assemblies of God.

Organized in 1914, the Assemblies of God drew together into a loose association some of the many independent Pentecostal missions across the country. Two important centers of its early strength were Alabama and Texas, but its constituency was always broader than any single geographic region. About 35 percent of its current membership is in the South. The Pentecostal Holiness Church and the several Pentecostal Churches of God, on the other hand, are overwhelmingly southern in membership, essential Holiness in doctrine, and centralized in polity. These southern Pentecostal groups were scarcely touched by the second dividing crisis in Pentecostal history—the oneness controversy.

Oneness Pentecostalism stresses the name of Jesus, claiming that Jesus is the name of Father, Son, and Spirit. This insistence, with its variant conception of the Trinity, as well as several other doctrinal traits, split the Assemblies of God and gave rise to an array of new Pentecostal groups, none of which has a strong southern base.

One distinct segment of Pentecostalism, then, is an integral part of the southern experience. Wesleyan in theology and centralized in structure, it remains largely confined to the South. The Church of God (Cleveland) and its several offshoots also incorporate a strong restorationist motif that Pentecostalism in other parts of the country does not include. The Church of God in Christ remains predominantly black and maintains its headquarters in Memphis. Its initial southern base has been extended to include outreach in major metropolitan black communities across the nation.

Although Pentecostalism is not exclusively a southern religion, some of its institutions have been shaped by their southern roots and continue to have their principal outreach in the South. Southern Pentecostalism incorporates theology and polity that set it apart, at least to some extent, from the movement at large. It has validity in the culture while perceiving itself as part of a force that transcends culture to provide spiritual vitality to the church.

See also BLACK LIFE: / Mason, Charles Harrison

Edith L. Blumhofer
Evangel College

Cross atop Sanctified church, Clarksdale, Mississippi, 1968

Robert Mapes Anderson, *Vision of the Disinherited: The Making of American Pentecostalism* (1979); Charles Conn, *Like a Mighty Army Moves the Church of God* (1977); William Menzies, *Anointed to Serve: The Story of the Assemblies of God* (1971); John T. Nichol, *Pentecostalism* (1966); Vinson Synan, *The Holiness-Pentecostal Movement in the United States* (1971). ✩

Politics and Religion

||||||||||||||||||||||||||||||||||||||||||||||||||

Scholars who have examined the relationship between religion and politics in the South generally agree that the region has identifiable religious patterns that have influenced the conservative political and social attitudes of southerners and promoted cultural beliefs, values, and institutions that can be thought of as distinctively "southern." Religious historian Samuel S. Hill has pointed out that the South, dominated by Baptist and Methodist denominations, remains a distinct religious region, characterized by evangelical, fundamentalist Protestantism. Geographer James R. Shortridge has asserted that the South should be considered a religious region, arguing that "a religious regionalization is as close to an objective cultural regionalization as we are likely to get in the foreseeable future." Sociologists Joseph Fichter and George Maddox have written that "almost every observer of the South has, sooner or later, recorded impressions about the pervasiveness and peculiarity of religious behavior and institutions in the region." Finally, sociologist John Shelton Reed has analyzed the elements of southern religious beliefs and practices, including overwhelming Protestant dominance, with Baptist-Methodist hegemony; a relatively high level of church attendance for members of all social classes; a greater tendency to "attend" church services conducted by electronic preachers; and adherence to concrete, literal, and orthodox beliefs.

The early history of southern religion gave little indication of these future patterns. The first settlers at Jamestown, to be sure, brought their Anglicanism with them, and a pervasive religious-moral tone, nurtured by government, existed in Virginia's early years, although to a lesser degree than in the Puritan colonies in New England. The first religious-political establishment in the South, then, was Anglican, but it was institutionally weak and grew even more so when colonists moved into the backcountry. With the American Revolution, the Church of England in the new United States became the Episcopal church, and its privileged status ended, replaced by a system of religious freedom and voluntary denominational competition. Evangelical Protestant groups such as the Baptists and Methodists, who had begun as dissenting sects, emerged from recurrent frontier revivals to become the dominant religious groups in the South by the Civil War.

Despite their doctrine of "the spirituality of the church"—which taught that religious institutions should concentrate on purely church matters and stay removed from politics—southern churches in the antebellum period forged close church-state ties. Ministers articulated a biblical defense of slavery, and the southern Baptists, Methodists, and Presbyterians split off from their northern brethren to form distinctly sectional religious bodies, which survived long after the Civil War. Religious leaders justified the Confederacy as a holy war and played a key role in maintaining morale for the war effort. After defeat, the southern churches created a "religion of the Lost Cause," which saw religious meaning in the southern historical experience and discouraged any criticisms of the regional way of life.

Ministers and churches in the late 19th century launched a series of moral crusades, using the power of the state to establish laws to prevent gambling (including the end of the popular Louisiana lottery and prevention of horse racing), to honor the Sabbath with blue laws, and, above all, to prohibit the sale of alcoholic beverages. Some ministers were actively involved in the Fundamentalist movement and worked to pass laws regulating textbooks and preventing the teaching of evolution in the schools.

Most of these campaigns were attempts by conservative religious leaders and institutions to shape the South into a moralistic evangelical empire. But religion was also used to promote liberal reform. The Populists of the 1890s used religious rhetoric to justify their call for fundamental reforms in the American economy, although ultimately their efforts proved to be a new "lost cause." In the 20th century, and especially during the Great Depression, reform-minded Christians formed organizations such as the Southern Christian Tenant Farmers' Union, the Fellowship of Southern Churchmen, the Commission on Interracial Cooperation, the Association of Southern Women for the Prevention of Lynching, and the Southern Christian Leadership Conference. Many of those were organized efforts to bring economic reforms in the spirit of a Christian Socialist society, whereas others have aimed at the related goal of racial justice. Southern church women, in particular, launched numerous progressive moral campaigns, including efforts to improve the life of prisoners, the poor, immigrants, industrial workers, and blacks, as well as to end discrimination against women.

Southern religion, nonetheless, has been predominantly a conservative, tradition-oriented influence. Francis Butler Simkins once asserted that "Orthodox Protestantism . . . is a likely explanation of why the section . . . has kept its identity as the most conservative portion of the United States." Charles Roland, in his study of the post–World War II South, noted that in the postwar era southern churches have come out against guaranteed annual income proposals, have denounced the northern churches that promoted such matters as family planning and urban renewal, and have supported American participation in the Vietnam War. And Ted Jelen, in an analysis of National Opinion Research Center data, found that southern fundamentalists tended to be less tolerant of Communists, homosexuals, and atheists than was the case for their non-southern counterparts. In a somewhat broader analysis, published in the early 1960s, W. Seward Salisbury compared religiously orthodox and unorthodox college students in the South and non-South on a number of points. Whereas a rather sharp orthodox-unorthodox distinction existed regardless of region, orthodox students from the South tended to be considerably more opposed to interracial marriage, much more supportive of segregated schools, significantly less willing to extend full pastoral rights to women, and more likely to find some good resulting from war than was the case for their orthodox brethren outside the South.

Scholars agree that southern churches have been closely tied to their culture. I. A. Newby has noted that religious beliefs in the South have tended to reflect secular values rather than to mold them; Fichter and Maddox have pointed out that "the churches seem to employ God to maintain and retain the Old South"; and Reed has stated that "most Southern churches are . . . so much a part of the community as to be indistinguishable from it." Hill has emphasized that "the overall impact of the church leadership has been priestly in that secular traditions and values have been 'baptized' and accorded legitimacy." An important function of religion, thereby, has been to support orthodox and distinctively southern beliefs and values.

Recent research has compared southern whites with non-southern whites as well as southern whites and southern blacks, and again supported the notion that, religiously, the South does indeed constitute a distinct region. Michael L. Mezey, for example, in assessing the importance of religious beliefs for southern distinctiveness found that religious attitudes divided southerners from those outside the South; however, those differences were not as great as the differences on a number of other issues, such as race, tolerance of deviants, military issues, moral issues, and women's rights issues. Furthermore, considerable variation was found on religious issues, with attitudes toward school prayer showing a great deal of southern distinctiveness and confidence toward the clergy showing none. He concluded, therefore, that religious beliefs tended to have a moderate and mixed effect in distinguishing southerners from people in the rest of the country.

Other research has reaffirmed the religious distinction of the South. Corwin Smidt, who compared the political attitudes and behavior of white evangelicals in the South with those outside the South, found a considerably higher percentage of southerners met the definition for evangelical. A recent study by Robert P. Steed, Laurence W. Moreland, and Tod A. Baker reached much the same conclusion with regard to members of the southern political elite, arguing that the impact of fundamentalism on southern political life was due mainly to the South having more fundamentalists, rather than to qualitative differences between southern and non-southern fundamentalism.

Other research studying the linkages between religion and specific political attitudes has shown, however, that religious beliefs tended *not* to have a *general* conservative effect on political values. Instead, the linkage tended to be limited to social issues, or, perhaps even more specifically, to issues with a moral content. Smidt, for example, found that economic issues divided the respondents in his study along regional lines. However, social issues—including the role of women in society, busing, prayer in schools, and abortion—divided respondents along religious lines, with evangelicals tending to take the more conservative positions. Similarly, Jerry Perkins, Donald Fairchild, and Murray Havens found that, on 8 of the 15 issues they examined, racial differences were greater than religious ones; but on three social issues they examined—abortion, school prayer, and the place of women in society—religious differences were greater. Reaching much the same conclusion, Kenneth Wald and Michael Lupfer sought to determine the causal role of religious beliefs; in their Memphis study, they found that religious orthodoxy was most powerful once again in explaining the effect of moral conservatism on issues such as abortion, women's rights, and drugs.

Research on political activists has also sought to determine the relationship between fundamentalist beliefs and distinctively southern political and social attitudes. In their research on party convention delegates in Virginia and South Carolina, Baker, Steed, and Moreland measured the effects on this relationship of the development of party competition and the movement of blacks into the Democratic elite. They found that on issues such as the Equal Rights Amendment, the SALT II treaty, affirmative action, and increased defense spending, party identification and race divided the party elite much more sharply than religion. However, religious beliefs (along with race) were important in separating their respondents on abortion issues. In short, except for issues with a moral content, changes in the nature of the party system and in the status of blacks seem to have undermined religious beliefs as a principal foundation of southern distinctiveness.

In summary, the most recent research cited above tends to demonstrate the following: first, much of the contemporary impact of religion on the South (as compared with the rest of the nation) is accounted for by the much larger portion of the southern population that considers itself to be fundamentalist; and, second, southern religion's direct impact on political attitudes is greatest on moral and social issues for both the mass public and the political elite.

Inasmuch as the impact of religious beliefs on political and social attitudes must be qualified, as noted above, the research potential of this topic might seem rather limited. Yet, some areas do appear to offer promise. For example, the emergence of blacks in political life could have a profound effect on the nature of evangelicalism in the South and its relation to political life. The white church in the South has historically reflected dominant, orthodox viewpoints in the region and, hence, has been la-

beled as conservative and as a major support to southern distinctiveness. On the other hand, the black church, also largely evangelical and fundamentalist, has struck a much more progressive note, beginning long before the civil rights movement of the post–World War II period. The black church has a long history of commitment to change and, as a result, could be thought of as constituting a principal mechanism through which blacks have sought to bring about changes in southern mores.

The political attitudes and behavior of black ministers will be of growing interest, just as studies of southern white ministers have contributed to our understanding of religion and politics in the region. For example, James Guth's analysis of data from a survey of white Southern Baptist ministers revealed an association between political ideology and political activism with the politically most conservative being significantly more likely to be politically active. Inasmuch as blacks have now moved into the mainstream of southern political life, comparable studies of black ministers should prove equally useful.

The possibility of evangelical coalitions across racial lines is another potential research focus even though the probability of such a development appears to be low. Perkins and associates concluded that among southern voters race is a considerably more important cleavage than religion; and Baker and associates, in their study of state party activists, found that the cleavages created by party identification and race were more important than the one created by religion. Yet the possibility remains that on the state or local level issues may arise that mobilize people on the basis of religious beliefs. As the

South continues its transformation from a rural, small-town society, social issues such as liquor, gambling, and pornography could prompt religious coalitions across racial lines.

The development of party competition could also affect the relationship between religion and politics, particularly with regard to the composition of party elites. Because evangelicalism and fundamentalism are conservative creeds and because members of the political elite tend to be more ideological than the mass of the citizenry, white evangelicals and fundamentalists would likely gravitate to the more conservative party. Steed and associates found that 70 percent of the white fundamentalist party activists in South Carolina and Virginia identified with the Republican party. On the other hand, blacks—both fundamentalist and nonfundamentalist—are overwhelmingly Democratic. Thus, it seems that the Republican party is developing a rather strong white fundamentalist wing whereas the Democratic party is developing a black fundamentalist one. If this is indeed occurring, black fundamentalists within the Democratic elite will tend to take strong conservative positions on moral issues and strong liberal positions on others, with black nonfundamentalists taking more consistently liberal positions. Further, within the Democratic party white nonfundamentalists will tend to take—relative to black Democrats—liberal positions on moral issues and relatively conservative positions on others. Within the Republican party fundamentalists will tend to take strong conservative positions on all issues, with nonfundamentalists taking slightly more liberal positions on moral ones.

Finally, additional research on the role of fundamentalists among political elites may also be useful. Alan Abramowitz, John McGlennon, and Ronald Rapoport have shown that on some occasions fundamentalists have fitted comfortably into southern party organizations, but at other times they found themselves largely isolated and, to a large extent, uncomfortable in the party in which they were active.

See also POLITICS articles; SOCIAL CLASS: Religion and Social Class

Tod A. Baker
Robert P. Steed
Laurence W. Moreland
The Citadel

Tod A. Baker, Robert P. Steed, and Laurence W. Moreland, eds., *Religion and Politics in the South: Mass and Elite Perspectives* (1983); Joseph Fichter and George Maddox, in *The South in Continuity and Change*, ed. John C. McKinney and Edgar T. Thompson (1965); Samuel S. Hill, *Religion and the Solid South* (1972), *Southern Churches in Crisis* (1966), in *Religion in the South*, ed., Charles Reagan Wilson (1985); Laurence W. Moreland, Tod A. Baker, and Robert P. Steed, eds., *Contemporary Southern Political Attitudes and Behavior: Studies and Essays* (1982); Hart M. Nelson and Anne Kusener Nelson, *Black Church in America* (1975); Liston Pope, *Review of Religious Research* (Spring 1963); John Shelton Reed, *The Enduring South: Subcultural Persistence in Mass Society* (1972); Charles Roland, *The Improbable Era: The South since World War II* (1975); W. Seward Salisbury, *Journal for Scientific Study of Religion* (October 1962); James R. Shortridge, *Journal for the Scientific Study of Religion* (June 1977); Joseph R. Washington, *Black Religion: The Negro and Christianity in the United States* (1964). ☆

Preacher, White
||||||||||||||||||||||||||||||||||||||

White southern religion, once considered a monolithic, unidimensional structure, is now recognized as diverse and filled with ambiguities. Previously accepted stereotypes have been challenged by recent scholarship, which points out the diversity of southern culture in general and of southern religion in particular. Accordingly, the tendency to categorize all southern preachers as over-zealous evangelists espousing a fiery brand of fundamentalism must be called into question as well. Ministers of southern white Protestant churches have been represented among the ranks of the theological elite, multimedia practitioners of the Gospel, and country parsons alike. There are as many images as there are preachers, and the effort to discuss *the* image of the southern white preacher seems, at least initially, a futile one. Yet one quality distinguishes the southern white preacher from his neighbors and also from his northern colleagues—and that is precisely his image. Whatever his social situation or professed beliefs, wherever he may live and work, awe and reverence accompany him. His is a powerful image; it is one of authority.

Certainly this distinctiveness is a matter of degree rather than of kind. Protestants in America, Robert S. Michaelsen has pointed out, "have looked to their ministers as the defenders of morality and the representatives of spirituality. They have expected them to stand out as examples of what people ought to be morally and spiritually." If this depiction is accurate in the country as a whole, then it is even more apt as a description of conditions in the South.

The centrality of Protestantism in southern culture gives the preacher his legitimacy as an articulator of truths, and he in turn provides religion with its shape and power. For people who are devout believers in God, as large numbers of southerners profess to be, his earthly representative is an awesome figure. Although the preacher's image has consistently been one of authority, his role in southern culture has not been static. Indeed, it is possible to trace certain trends in southern history by examining the unfolding of the image of authority.

During the early days of the South, this sparsely populated region with its scattered outposts demanded a preacher who was an itinerant man of God. As he traveled from place to place, he served as a cultural bonding force. Although southern religion had not yet developed a distinct and separate identity, the region's faith and its self-understanding were gradually becoming inextricably interwoven. Simplicity ruled in those hard times: the minister was one called by God. Educational or professional preparation was incidental to his activities. Peter Cartwright, an early Methodist minister, once explained that when a man went into the ministry he did not seek a seminary; rather he "hunted up a hardy pony of a horse . . . and with his library always at hand, namely Bible, Hymn-Book and Discipline, he started, and with a text that never wore out or grew stale, he cried 'Behold the Lamb of God.' " The sacred works identified him wherever he roamed.

The preacher's image was enhanced as the revivals swept through the South in the early 19th century. Now he had to be a skilled exhorter who could bring sinners into the fold in large numbers and with rapid precision. Although all southerners did not by any means participate in these massive spectacles, the revivals exerted a significant force on southern society. The growth in church membership was impressive, and, though a variety of denominations emerged, within and among the churches there was a strong sense of shared values and beliefs. The feeling of community that evolved contributed to the prestige of the minister in the South; he was the official exponent of religious and regional beliefs. His sphere of power extended beyond the domain of the church steeple. In the words of John Holt Rice, an early 19th-century Presbyterian minister, the preacher's work "embraces every duty, in every situation."

Increasing population density resulted in churches that were established permanently in a particular place, with a wide influence over the inhabitants there. The popular Methodist and Baptist denominations became part of the status quo: the clergy became more educated, church members more affluent, and the churches' attitude toward the world more accepting. As a consequence, the minister of a church with prestigious community members exercised considerable influence over local and regional affairs. His presence at group meetings and political gatherings was not merely perfunctory; he represented the forces of the divine.

With the emergence of the issue of slavery and the subsequent Civil War, the white minister in the South articulated a solid defense of his region's way of life. In so doing he gained even greater prestige and visibility. Although controversies over proper education and appropriate qualifications erupted from time to time, the white preacher—no matter what his background—was an important regional spokesman. At times, however, as villages grew into cities and towns in the antebellum period, his image became fragmented. On the one hand, he was to converse with other professional members of his community and maintain a rational and sophisticated demeanor; on the other hand, he was to represent the simple way of life and belief of the rural past. The result was often a dwindling sense of inner assuredness for individual preachers. All the same, in the days of Reconstruction, the preacher's power expanded significantly as large numbers of southerners turned to churches for a rationale to explain defeat. In 1885 a noted Methodist editor claimed that "there is no part of the world in which ministers of the Gospel are more respected than in the Southern states."

In the first half of the 20th century the white Protestant preacher continued to exercise considerable influence in the South. Erskine Caldwell, the popular southern novelist whose father was a minister, asserted that "in the 'twenties and 'thirties . . . a Protestant minister was frequently called upon to act as a social welfare worker, a marriage counselor, a financial adviser, an arbitrator between feuding families, a psychiatric

Fundamentalist minister, Red Banks, Mississippi, 1968

consultant, and as a judge to decide what was and what was not moral conduct." In many small towns such expectations continue. But more and more psychologists, college professors, physicians, and other professionals fulfill the tasks traditionally performed by the local minister. The preacher's public role in the South, then, has diminished substantially. Although the national media have brought them increased attention, charismatic exhorters are by no means peculiar to this region. Moreover, in the South, as in the rest of the country, the preacher has repudiated many of the traits that clearly distinguished him in earlier times. Nonetheless, the image of the white preacher as an authority figure, a moral, upright person who represents the divine and speaks the language of the Gospel, still prevails in the South.

See also BLACK LIFE: Preacher, Black

Rosemary M. Magee
Emory University

Erskine Caldwell, *Deep South: Memory and Observation* (1972); Peter Cartwright, *The Autobiography of Peter Cartwright: The Backwoods Preacher* (1856); *Christian Advocate* (17 October 1885); Samuel S. Hill, *Southern Churches in Crisis* (1967); E. Brooks Holifield, *The Gentlemen Theologians: American Theology in Southern Culture, 1795–1860* (1978); Robert S. Michaelsen, in *The Ministry in Historical Perspectives*, ed. H. Richard Niebuhr and Daniel D. Williams (1956). ☆

Protestantism
||||||||||||||||||||||||||||||||||||

Southern Protestantism and southern culture are as inseparable as bourbon and fruitcake. The South stands out both as a discernible cultural entity and as an equally unique religious region. Indeed it is the most religious and Protestant area of an extraordinarily religious nation. Southerners tend to be more active in religious organizations and more orthodox in measurable belief than any of their fellow citizens. Evangelical Protestants often make up 80 to 90 percent of the "churched" population, and most call themselves Baptists and Methodists. Yet there is also great diversity—independent churches, all the major organized denominations, and numerous small, proudly independent associations and congregations, which are properly denominations unto themselves.

The South has given rise to distinctively American and even regional styles of religion. This pattern results from a combination of geography (America's early and hence formative frontier), economic conditions (extremes of plantation wealth, slavery, and rural poverty), great mobility (geographic and economic), and a fierce individualism. Protestantism in the South is also nostalgic, smoldering, and languorous. It has an ethos haunted by guilt, defiance, a deep attachment to sacred places and heroes, a strong positive sense of mission, and a painful memory of the bitter combination of chosenness and inexplicable defeat.

The southern Protestant ethos decisively began with the extended period of revivalism that swept in waves over the South from 1799 until 1820. Baptists and Methodists, far more adaptive to frontier conditions than their Presbyterian and Episcopalian competitors, quickly became the dominant organizations and remain so today. The influence of revivalism is everywhere in southern religion. Emotive, rhetorically persuasive preaching designed to produce personal crisis and conversion is central. There are, consequently, traditions of great preaching and great preachers—charismatic leaders whose personalities often serve as the bonding agent of their personal churches. Worship focuses upon the production of palpable religious experiences for congregation-audiences. Christianity tends to be reduced to the simplicity of sin, guilt, conversion, and forgiveness, always centered around individual salvation. An individual's religious life is intensely focused upon the conversion experience. It is an event continually recalled and even relived through revivalistic rededication, the evangelical equivalent to the Catholic sacrament of penance. Additionally there are presumptions of perfectability or at least thorough transformation. One "gets saved" or is "born again" or "gets right with God."

The shadows of slavery and segregation have fallen heavily across the social gospel, limiting but not eliminating social responsibility. For over 150 years voluntary societies as well as churches have fought for temperance, printed and distributed literature and Bibles, and built settlement houses and educational institutions; yet they were always reluctant to confront the fundamental structure of a society based upon a system of racial oppression. Revivalism insists one attend to the immediate demands of piety; it "verticalizes" one's religion from God above to humans below, enclosing it in what James McBride Dabbs calls "a limited, private world" free from the complexities of social and political life. Additionally, because the revivalistic style takes people out of their normal context and places them as individuals before the righteous God, it has had the power to suspend their usual

social rules, including those of hierarchy. This creation of "liminality" (a state "in between" classifications) allowed slaves to instruct their masters in religious matters, urge their conversion, and assume, for the duration of the liminal period, a position of superiority. The "limited world" made possible the experience of socially sage bonds of affection and even friendship between slave and master, black and white. Such a limitation of the ethical dimensions of Christianity required a moralistic ethical style—the connection of specific biblical "principles" to specific individual moral choices, often in an ad hoc and surprisingly legalistic way.

A final and defining characteristic deeply embedded in the evangelical tradition is assurance. This involves a certainty of salvation arising from the varied sources of conversion, Scripture, and experiences of God's presence. It appears almost as an evangelical personality style or perhaps a state of being—warm, confident, immediately and openly religious, intensely yet comfortably intimate with a somewhat domesticated deity, but also quite unquestioning and rather unteachable.

For many white Protestants the line between Christian religion and Christian civilization has often been too fine to discern. Ironically, during the periods of slavery and legal segregation, southerners were in the forefront of those celebrating America's Christian identity and even claiming the achievement of a high degree of social perfection. From this perspective the Civil War was a noble and tragic effort undertaken in defense of a last bastion of Christendom. After the war southern Protestantism became a "suffering servant," a moral and religious preservative with a mission of national salvation.

World War I, fought against the German originators of academic biblical criticism and liberal religion, was seen as a triumph of American, Protestant, southern, and Baptist values. This evangelical civil religion continues to inform and motivate numerous southerners and their churches.

For blacks, too, the entwinement of religion and culture has run deep. Slave religion and later the black churches have always served social and political purposes, often providing black people with their primary source for social cohesion and political mobilization. Black churches have given leadership, continuity, and organization to the black community ever since Emancipation. They launched the civil rights movement of the 1950s and 1960s, and a presidential candidacy in 1984, permanently changing southern society at its most basic levels. The enthusiasm of the South's black population for the white vision of a Christian America has been understandably limited. Slaves took the evangelical Protestantism handed them by their captors and adapted it to their own special needs and circumstances. Unlike southern whites, blacks attended to the prophetic dimensions of Christianity, finding the self-esteem and strength necessary to withstand the dehumanization of slavery and segregation in the knowledge that Jesus, too, had felt the oppressor's lash. Christianity confirmed for slaves what they had always known—that slavery was wrong—and what they had always hoped—that it was not permanent. Slaves quickly determined that they were considerably closer to the example established by Jesus than were their owners, and they soon found their own version of Christianity superior to that of the whites. Out of their suffering the slaves created a form of evangelicalism considerably more celebratory than that of white society. Much remained the same—the intensity, experience, simplicity, and informality—but there were crucial differences. Whereas white Protestantism consistently appealed to authority, particularly that of the Scriptures, black religion tended to allow authority to remain tacit while celebrating God's love and deliverance. In the words of Eugene D. Genovese, whites sought forgiveness from Jesus and blacks sought recognition.

As America enters the final decades of the 20th century, southern evangelicalism again stands at the center of action, emerging as the most modern and energetic American religion. In the face of the rather contradictory currents of disintegrating regionalism, growing cultural uniformity, and an ever-increasing social diversity, proponents of Christian civilization have reemerged, creating new voluntary societies aiming to save America for Christendom and the world. This in itself represents a significant secularization of southern evangelicalism as it focuses itself on political questions and mixes hefty amounts of civil religion with its traditional worldview. In related developments, southern evangelicals have discovered that their religious style with its emphasis on ministerial action and congregational consumption translates easily to television, making possible the dawn of evangelical media empires. A growing worldliness, and even a materialistic spirit, is evident in television ministries, which commonly promise tangible transformation—healing or financial success guaranteed for those supporting the ministries. Prophetic voices on the evangelical left warn that idolatry is inherent in the very idea of Christian civilization. Moderates seek areas of compatibility between Christianity and secular republican virtue. Clearly Protestantism in the South is becoming less regional. Geographical and cultural isolation have become impossible to maintain. Rapid population growth, diversification, and continued social and economic mobility promise an immediate future of conflict and realignment. What will emerge is surely in doubt, but it seems likely that the distinctiveness of southern Protestantism and culture will become increasingly difficult to preserve.

See also BLACK LIFE: Religion, Black

Dennis E. Owen
University of Florida

Kenneth K. Bailey, *Southern White Protestantism in the Twentieth Century* (1964); John B. Boles, *The Great Revival, 1787–1805: The Origins of the Southern Evangelical Mind* (1972); John Lee Eighmy, *Churches in Cultural Captivity: A History of the Social Attitudes of Southern Baptists* (1972); Samuel S. Hill, ed., *Encyclopedia of Religion in the South* (1984), *Religion and the Solid South* (1972), *Southern Churches in Crisis* (1967); C. Eric Lincoln, ed., *The Black Experience in Religion: A Book of Readings* (1974); Donald Mathews, *Religion in the Old South* (1977); John Shelton Reed, *The Enduring South: Subcultural Persistence in Mass Society* (1972); Charles Reagan Wilson, *Baptized in Blood: The Religion of the Lost Cause, 1865–1920* (1980). ☆

Restorationist Christianity

‖‖‖‖‖‖‖‖‖‖‖‖‖‖‖‖‖‖‖‖‖‖‖‖‖‖‖‖‖‖‖

Restorationist Christianity, which self-consciously seeks to ignore historic Christian forms and traditions and to reproduce primitive Christianity, has flourished in the American South, but it is not unique to the South. This style of Christianity has deep roots in British Protestantism and appeared with particular vitality in the left wing of that heritage, especially among the Puritans, Baptists, and Quakers, and later among the early Methodists. Thus, restorationist traditions that persist in America today—in addition to the modern heirs of the Swiss and German Anabaptists—include Mormons, various types of Baptists, various Holiness and Pentecostal groups, Christian Churches, and Churches of Christ.

At least two factors influenced the openness of southern Christianity to the restorationist impulse in the 19th century. First, the Baptist and Methodist domination of southern religion created a climate of deference both to the Scriptures and to Christian antiquity. Second, the stubborn persistence of the southern frontier until well into the 20th century in some regions (e.g., Appalachia and the Ozarks) created a cultural situation particularly resistant to modernity and especially amenable to various types of primitivism. When Baptists and Methodists with a primitivist theological orientation settled in large numbers on the southern frontier, it was perhaps inevitable that this potent religious/cultural mix would spawn numerous restorationist movements, some of which would coalesce into lasting denominations.

Four major movements, all with a self-conscious restorationist orientation, emerged in the South after 1800: the Churches of Christ; the Primitive or Antimission Baptists; the Landmark Baptists; and southern Pentecostalists, especially the Church of God (Cleveland, Tenn.) and the snake handlers of southern Appalachia. Interestingly, all these traditions have roots in middle or eastern Tennessee and western North Carolina.

Churches of Christ emerged in Tennessee, Kentucky, and southern Ohio under the leadership of Barton W. Stone in the first decade of the 19th century and by 1825 had made headway into northern Alabama. Reflecting in many ways the quest for liberty that characterized the American Revolution, participants in this movement threw off the yoke of history and bondage to historical traditions, rejected the authority of creeds and clerics, used the primitive church as portrayed in Scripture as a model for their individual and ecclesiastical behavior, and styled themselves simply "Christians" and their congregations "Churches of Christ." Ardently optimistic and utopian, they argued that a universal emulation of the primitive church would bring Christian unity and then the millennium.

Although Stone and some of his "Christian" colleagues had Presbyterian roots, the vast majority of both members and leaders in the new movement came from the ranks of Separate and Regular Baptists, whose allegiance both to Scripture and to the primitive church made them restorationists in their own right. This was particularly true of the Separate Baptists, who determined to follow the Bible as their only confession of faith in the mid-18th century. They followed Shubal Stearns to North Carolina and Virginia in 1755 and later in the century migrated to Kentucky and Tennessee, where they increased the ranks of the Christian movement. According to one observer in 1812, the Christians in the West had by that time over 13,000 members and at least 117 preachers.

By 1823 Alexander Campbell began to influence both Baptists and the

"Christians" of Kentucky and Tennessee, largely through his new periodical, the *Christian Baptist*. Campbell's contribution in this region was essentially twofold. To begin, he was by then a significant link in the growing, nationwide resistance to the new missionary societies of the North and East, viewed by many as flagrant attempts to extend the power of the New England Standing Order throughout the nation in the wake of disestablishment. Campbell's opposition to ecclesiastical societies, clerics, and creeds, and his affirmation of the primitive church as the alternative to modern innovations, greatly strengthened both the restorationist and the antimissionist sentiments already present among both Baptists and Christians. In addition, Campbell superimposed on the primitivist piety of the Stone movement a hard-headed, rational, common sense approach to the restoration ideal that has characterized Churches of Christ ever since. By 1860 the Churches of Christ flourished in middle Tennessee under the leadership of Tolbert Fanning and David Lipscomb.

Due to post–Civil War migration patterns, Churches of Christ are today concentrated not only in southern Kentucky, middle Tennessee, and northern Alabama, but also in other portions of Tennessee, Arkansas, Oklahoma, and Texas, with significant strength in southern California as well.

The Primitive or Antimission Baptists arose out of the same ideological matrix that provided such a fertile field for the growth of Churches of Christ: a passion for liberty, an expectation of the millennium, a rejection of the power of the older ecclesiastical establishments and of their missionary societies, and a consequent affirmation of the freedom and simplicity of the primitive church as a model for Baptists of the 19th century.

The antimission agitation, based on a fear of eastern ecclesiastical power and of state-church resurgence, was a nationwide, interdenominational phenomenon in the 1810s and especially the 1820s, led by Deists like Elihu Palmer, Christians like Elias Smith and Alexander Campbell, Baptists like John Leland, Methodists like Peter Cartwright and Lorenzo Dow, and interdenominational figures such as Theophilus Ransom Gates whose *Reformer* (1820–35) was a veritable clearinghouse for antimission sentiment from a wide variety of sources. Antimission arguments from these and other leaders typically contrasted the elaborate extraecclesiastical and interdenominational agencies and societies of that age with the simple, congregational autonomy of the early Christians. The restorationist thrust of this agitation could even be seen in the titles of some of the periodicals, for example, *The Evangelical Restorationist* (Troy, N.Y., 1825) and *Priestcraft Exposed and Primitive Christianity Defended* (Lockport, N.Y., 1828–29).

Although opposition to eastern ecclesiastical power was nationwide, it was especially strong in the Jacksonian South, where rural religionists resented the efforts of eastern missionaries and "dandies" to save the frontier from barbarism. Further, among some Regular Baptists in the South, opposition to missions was buttressed by a rigid predestinarianism: after all, why organize mission societies if the eternal fate of mankind is already determined? These Baptists appealed both to the structure (no societies) and to the theology (predestination) of the primitive church to legitimize their positions, and throughout the 1820s these questions were debated in Regular Baptist churches and associations throughout America and especially in the South.

The key early leaders of Baptist antimissionism were John Leland, Daniel Parker, and John Taylor. By 1820 most Baptist churches in Tennessee and northern Alabama apparently had adopted the primitivist, antimission posture, and the Kehukee Association of North Carolina followed suit in 1827. By 1832 the primitive antimissionists began the process of separating into a distinct denomination. Their greatest early success was in Tennessee and northern Alabama, but they also experienced significant growth in Georgia, Virginia, North Carolina, Kentucky, and Texas.

It is ironic that the Primitive Baptists drank so deeply from the well of optimistic postmillennialism that sustained the early antimission agitation nationwide, for when these Baptists blended their opposition to mission societies with their rigid predestinarianism, they emerged as stridently pessimistic and premillennial—a perspective reflected in their first widely circulated periodical, *Signs of the Times* (1832–35). Their pessimistic and isolationist worldview perhaps accounts for their speedy decline from at least 68,000 members in 1844 to only 45,000 in 1890.

Although Primitive Baptists began as a white denomination, they eventually had even greater strength among blacks than among whites. By 1900 the black church had become more progressive than the white church, employing both Sunday schools and conventions, and by 1936 the black church had considerable strength in Alabama, Florida, Tennessee, Georgia, Texas, and North Carolina. By 1975 the black National Primitive Baptist Convention of the U.S.A. claimed over 1.5 million members. The white church, on the other hand, enjoyed its greatest early success in Tennessee and northern Alabama but also experienced significant growth in Georgia, Virginia, North Carolina, Kentucky, and Texas before experiencing decline.

A third restorationist tradition emerged in 1851 in Tennessee—the Landmark Baptists. Like the Churches of Christ, this tradition drew its greatest strength from the revivalistic Separate Baptists and focused almost exclusively on questions of ecclesiology and particularly on the identity of the "true church." The Landmark leader, James Robinson Graves of Nashville, argued that the true church had existed in an unbroken chain throughout Christian history and had always borne the marks of congregational autonomy, ecclesiastical democracy, and baptism by immersion. Any religious body organized since apostolic days was no church whatsoever, and the true church could be traced by the "trail of blood"—those martyrs who have refused throughout Christian history to be seduced by modernity.

The term *Landmark* was taken from a tract by James Madison Pendleton, "An Old Landmark Reset," which raised and answered negatively the question of whether Baptists should invite pedobaptists to preach in their pulpits. A third significant leader was Amos Cooper Dayton, who articulated fundamental Landmark themes in a two-volume novel, *Theodosia Ernest* (1857). Though Landmarkism had gathered significant strength in Tennessee and parts of the Old Southwest by 1880, it was not organized into a formal denomination until 1905, when Ben M. Bogard and others led in establishing the General Association of Landmark Baptists in Texarkana, Ark., renamed in 1924 the American Baptist Association. By 1980 the American Baptist Association claimed its greatest strength in Arkan-

sas and Texas, with lesser strengths in Oklahoma, Louisiana, and Florida.

Not until the late 19th century would the restoration sentiment again incarnate itself in lasting and major institutional forms and structures in the South. This later development was the Holiness/Pentecostal phenomenon that grew largely, though not exclusively, from Methodist soil and was, like the earlier antimission agitation, a national phenomenon. The restorationist underpinnings of the Holiness revival, which preceded the Pentecostal phase of the movement, were implicit in the Holiness rejection of modern trends in established denominations. But some Holiness denominations, such as the Church of God, Anderson, Ind. (1880), made the restorationist appeal to the primitive church both explicit and fundamental.

During the last two decades of the 19th century, a more radical phase of the Holiness movement was developing—a phase that appealed especially to the poor and disinherited and that emphasized the baptism of the Holy Ghost as a third work of grace (following justification and sanctification), physical healing, and premillennialism. By 1906 and thereafter, most of these more radical churches also accepted glossolalia (speaking in tongues) and emerged as Pentecostalist, separate from the more moderate Holiness movement.

Although Pentecostalism, like the Holiness movement, was a nationwide phenomenon, it is significant that many of the Holiness churches in the South became Pentecostal. A clue to why this occurred lies in the otherwordly rejection of history that was implicit in early Pentecostalism and that appealed powerfully to the disinherited of a still alienated and impoverished South. This otherworldly dimension was evident in two central themes of early Pentecostal theology. First, whereas the Holiness phenomenon had been rooted early in an optimistic postmillennial perspective, Pentecostalism embraced a more pessimistic premillennial theology anticipating an imminent second coming of Christ. Second, implicit in Pentecostalism's emphasis on the baptism of the Holy Ghost and glossolalia was a restorationist perspective that looked beyond the present age to the primitive church and made the power of Pentecost available to disinherited southerners some 19 centuries later. This was true of the four major southern Pentecostal traditions in the early 20th century: the Church of God (Tennessee), the Pentecostal Holiness Church, the Fire-Baptized Holiness Church, and the predominantly black Church of God in Christ.

Although the restoration sentiment was merely implicit in much of Pentecostalism, it was explicitly acknowledged in some of the movement's early literature such as B. F. Lawrence's *The Apostolic Faith Restored* (1916). And it came to full flower especially in the Church of God, Cleveland, Tenn., a major Pentecostal denomination that emerged at the turn of the century in the mountains of southwestern North Carolina. By 1903 the acknowledged leader of the embryonic Church of God was an Indiana Bible salesman, A. J. Tomlinson, who stamped the young church with the conviction that the true church had disappeared in the Dark Ages but was now being recovered in the mountains of Tennessee and North Carolina. The Church of God, Tomlinson taught, had no man-made creed, was not a denomination, and took the Bible as "our only rule of faith and practice." Further, in due time Christ would organize his millennial kingdom at

Burger Mountain (North Carolina) and Christians from all denominations would flow into the true Church of God. By 1980 the various factions of the Church of God had particular strength in Georgia, Florida, North and South Carolina, Tennessee, and Alabama, with lesser strength in Texas, Mississippi, Kentucky, Virginia, and West Virginia.

A more radical form of Pentecostalism, but no less restorationist, is the snake-handling tradition that arose in the mountains of southern Tennessee in 1909, under the leadership of George Went Hensley, and then spread throughout southern Appalachia, into other parts of the rural South, and later into industrial centers of Michigan, Ohio, and Indiana where Appalachian folk sought work. Snake handling could be construed as a logical extension of Pentecostal restorationism, which contends that gifts of the primitive church have been restored in these latter days. Most Pentecostals limit these gifts to glossolalia and healing, but snake handlers include "taking up serpents" and drinking poison, according to their reading of Mark 16: 17–18, and many snake handlers self-consciously regard their activities as a restoration of primitive Christianity. Steven Kane cities a Tennessee snake handler: "Some people believe that miracles and signs ended with the Apostles. But if I got the same Holy Ghost as John and Peter, then I ought to be able to do the same things they did. Like heal the sick and cast out devils and handle serpents."

The forms of restorationism that have flourished in the South range from the rational and cognitive Churches of Christ to the charismatic and experiential Pentecostals, but all share in common the goal of transcending history and restoring primitive Christianity. Middle and eastern Tennessee and western North Carolina have been a seedbed where all these forms of restorationist Christianity either have germinated or have taken root to an extraordinary degree.

Richard T. Hughes
Abilene Christian University

Robert Mapes Anderson, *Vision of the Disinherited: The Making of American Pentecostalism (1979)*; David Harrell, *Journal of Southern History* (August 1964); Steven Kane, "Snake Handlers of Southern Appalachia" (Ph.D. dissertation, Princeton University, 1979); Byron Cecil Lambert, *The Rise of the Anti-Mission Baptists: Sources and Leaders, 1800–1840* (1980); Vinson Synan, *The Holiness-Pentecostal Movement in the United States* (1971); Robert G. Torbet, *A History of Southern Baptist Landmarkism in the Light of Historical Baptist Ecclesiology* (1980); Earl Irvin West, *The Search for the Ancient Order* (1949, 1950, and 1979). ☆

Revivalism

||||||||||||||||||||||||||||||||

Revivalism is characterized by an emphasis in religion on a renewal of interest in belief and practice, marked by the conversion of new members and the rededication of existing members to the church. In the South revivalism has set the dominant tone for Protestant Christianity since the early 19th century, informing the main religious concerns of mainstream denominations and smaller organizations alike.

Southern revivalism has occurred at two levels. One is comprised of the spectacular general awakenings of society, which at several periods of the region's history have brought significant numbers of people into connection with various southern denominations. These awakenings have provided the foundation for revivalism at a much less spectacular but more profound level, consisting of an ongoing effort by southern religious organizations to maintain their goal of bringing new members into the church and taking shape most clearly in gatherings called "revival meetings," which are held regularly throughout the South.

Four major periods of general revival have occurred in the South. The first, throughout what were then the English colonies of North America in the mid-18th century, was known as the Great Awakening. It was followed by the Second Awakening, or Great Revival, which centered on the southern frontier between about 1795 and 1805. A third, beginning in the latter part of the 19th century, was also national in scope and involved such noted evangelists as Dwight Moody and Billy Sunday. A fourth began in the mid-20th century and has been strongly identified with the southern evangelist Billy Graham.

The revivalism that is an ongoing phenomenon of southern religion involves a tendency on the part of southern religious organizations to view evangelism as their primary activity, with other aspects of the religious life interpreted in terms of the evangelistic impulse. To a great extent, revivalism at this level has become the religion of the South, for it crosses denominational lines to unite in sympathies and purposes members of most religious organizations, particularly those of the region's dominant communions, the Methodist and Baptist churches.

This revivalistic thrust of southern religion has had major implications for the specific content of religious ideas and practices in the region. Because southerners have understood such a thrust to involve, above all, the conversion and salvation of individual souls, their religion has had an extremely individualistic orientation. Questions of faith, belief, and sinfulness have all been interpreted in terms of the individual's religious state, and the church itself has been considered more a gathering of converted individuals than a community that, as such, has important relationships with God.

The roots of this religious individualism are theological, and may be traced not only to the traditional Protestant concern for salvation, but, more specifically, to the triumph in the Second Awakening of an Arminian theology of free and universal grace. According to this theology, God has called everyone to salvation, but each individual must heed and follow God's call. The mission of the church, given this, is to make each individual aware of this call and its significance. Thus, theology not only demands an evangelical focus in religion but also insures that evangelism will be directed toward the individual and individual salvation rather than toward any religious collectivity. Supplanting the older Calvinist notions of predestination and irresistible grace, Arminianism would, by the early 19th century, underlie the practical religion of even such nominally Calvinist bodies as the Presbyterian and Baptist churches and, because of its popularity, would contribute greatly to the growth of the Methodist church, which had embraced it wholeheartedly. Arminianism has, since that time, been the theology of southern Protestantism, the underpinning of its evangelical efforts.

Accompanying a theology that defines the church's duty as reaching individual souls has been an emphasis on personal experience as the most significant element in the religious life. This, too, has its roots in the Second Awakening, when revivalistic denominations made the direct experience of conversion a test for church membership and even sought evidences for such experience in the spectacular physical "exercises" that often accompanied conversion. Although such exercises have become rare in mainstream churches since the middle of the 19th century, the stress on personal experience remains important, and the talented revivalist still tries to bring even the most affluent mainstream congregation to tears. Strong feeling is a significant element in southern revivalistic religion.

This stress on personal experience can be seen in one of revivalism's most important contributions to southern religious practice, the gospel hymns. Composed, for the most part, during the late 19th-century revival, these songs have entered into all the mainstream denominational hymnals, having virtually replaced more traditional hymns for use even in Sunday morning services. Simple in message and stressing God's love for every individual, these gospel hymns evoke a highly personal and emotional sense of the nature of faith. More spectacularly, the stress on personal experience has contributed to a mid-20th-century charismatic revival. A development in the larger Pentecostal movement, which had its American beginnings around 1905, this revival has adopted traditional techniques and emphases from the southern revival heritage but has elaborated on them through an emphasis on such charismata as divine healing and speaking in tongues. Although most mainstream Protestants tend to desire more decorous forms of experience, the charismatic movement's main concerns are well within the southern revival traditions of evangelism and an individualistic, personal faith.

Southern revivalism has led the region's churches, in general, to adopt a stance toward society that differs markedly from that of religious organizations outside the South. Whereas American religion has been dominated, since the antebellum period, by a liberal Protestantism that has sought to respond to social issues and problems—from temperance and antislavery in the antebellum period to modern problems of race and war—southern churches and religious leaders have tended to avoid questions having deep social roots and to deal mainly with problems that can be addressed from the standpoint of the sinfulness of individuals and their need for conversion and salvation. Thus, southern churches have generally not participated in efforts for social change, even when they have been politically active, as with the conservative efforts of the Virginia-based Moral Majority, but have continued to focus on evangelism as their primary mission in the world.

See also MUSIC: / Revival Songs

Dickson D. Bruce, Jr.
University of California
at Irvine

John B. Boles, *The Great Revival, 1787–1805: The Origins of the Southern Evangelical Mind* (1972); Dickson D. Bruce, Jr., *And They All Sang Hallelujah: Plain-Folk Camp-Meeting Religion, 1800–1845* (1974); David Harrell, *All Things Are Possible: The Healing and Charismatic Revivals in Modern America* (1975); Samuel S. Hill, *Southern Churches in Crisis* (1967); Anne C. Loveland, *Southern Evangelicals and the Social Order, 1800–1860* (1980); William G. McLoughlin, Jr., *Modern Revivalism: Charles Grandison Finney to Billy Graham* (1959); Donald Mathews, *Religion in the Old South* (1977). ☆

Roman Catholicism

From the first Catholic settlers in colonial Maryland to the recent influx of Spanish-speaking and Asian Catholics, "southern" Catholics have traditionally occupied an ambivalent place in the region as they struggled to balance a universal faith with their own peculiar ethno-religious differences in a social environment that often has been hostile toward them. After the American Revolution the American Catholic church, composed of roughly 35,000 native Catholics located largely in Maryland, Kentucky, and Pennsylvania and under the leadership of John Carroll, the first American bishop (1790), had sought social and cultural assimilation into American life. By the mid-19th century, however, the American Catholic church had veered away from the genteel Anglo-American Catholicism of John Carroll's generation. The annexation of "Latin" Louisiana and the Gulf areas and, more importantly, massive European immigration, chiefly Irish and German, beginning in the 1830s, fixed the multiethnic character of American Catholicism thereafter. Ethnic disputes over liturgical rites, ecclesiastical jurisdictions, and customs came with immigration. They racked Norfolk, Charleston, Richmond, and New Orleans congregations in the early 19th century and prefigured more serious divisions within the American church throughout the century.

With force of numbers and an English-speaking advantage, the Irish gained control of the American church hierarchy. Coming during the devotional revolution underway in Ireland at mid-century, which stressed piety through regular devotions and worship and respect for clerical authority, the Irish had the energy and discipline to impose their ways on the church. Indeed, they largely subdued German elements in Baltimore and New Orleans during the 19th century. In lower Louisiana, however, the European immigrants confronted an entrenched French Catholic population heavily tinged with Continental French liberalism and with Spanish and African cultural strains. The French Creoles lost the contest for control over the church, but enough Creole customs survived in the increasingly austere American church to give Louisiana Catholicism a Mediterranean flavor that exists even today.

Without endorsing ethnic pluralism, the American church muted cultural tensions by establishing nationality parishes, in effect conceding a measure of cultural diversity in parish life while it insisted on greater uniformity in formal church practices and pushed Americanization through education. The cultural development of the church in the South, however, diverged from the national pattern when immigration to the South virtually ceased after the Civil War. A period of relative internal stability in the southern church followed the end of the war and lasted through World War II. Overall, the southern church escaped

the cultural and social tremors of the "new immigration" wrenching Catholicism in northern communities, except in Louisiana, where the arrival of southern Italians to work in the sugar fields in the 1890s created fresh cultural tensions in the local church for a generation. By moderating its internal ethnic and ecclesiastical stresses, the southern church slipped into a respectable obscurity in the region until the 1960s.

Catholics remained a religious minority everywhere in the South outside of Louisiana, while Catholicism became the majority religion in the North. Conscious of its minority status in the overwhelmingly evangelical Protestant South, the church assumed a low political and social profile. The Catholic emphasis on personal salvation through the sacramental system tended to deflect Catholic concern from social action, and from John Carroll until Vatican II (1962–65) church leaders preached social and political accommodation with the host society—as much to focus their resources on building a church establishment as to fend off nativism and anti-Catholic prejudices. Southern church leaders provided scriptural justifications for slavery and a conservative social order in the antebellum period, supported secession and the Confederacy, inveighed against Republican rule during Reconstruction, and instituted their own form of Jim Crowism in the 1890s—all in conformity with the dominant regional values and practices. Such actions did not wholly dispel Protestant suspicions concerning Catholic loyalties, however, for nativism and anti-Catholicism flared in the Populist movement in the 1890s and lingered through the 1930s as a political factor in southern life. Effective lay Catholic political resistance—the creation of the

Georgia Laymen's League to combat the Ku Klux Klan, for example—and the church's accommodationist policies on race and social issues countered such external threats, but the persistent, if often only latent, anti-Catholic temperament of evangelical Protestantism in the region inclined the Catholic church toward a policy of social enclosure. Concerned about the corrupting influence of the Protestant Bible, hymns, and teaching in public schools, for example, Catholic bishops in the late 19th century began to build a parochial system in their dioceses. Church-sponsored devotional societies, religious and recreational organizations, and the recruitment and training of native-born southerners for religious vocations solidified the southern Catholic culture, although the church's effort to match secular society in social services and schooling led to a proliferation of institutions that sapped the meager financial endowments of an always-poor southern church.

In the 20th century the ideology of southern Agrarianism reduced differences between Protestants and Catholics in the South and, thereby, increased the acceptance of Catholics in southern society. The conservative social views of Catholics increasingly assumed an important place in the region's general critique of modernism. Southern Catholic writers—especially Kate Chopin, Flannery O'Connor, William Alexander Percy, Katherine Anne Porter, and Allen Tate—shared a framework of values that was both Catholic and southern. They distrusted abstraction and modern liberalism, particularly its celebration of the rootless individual in search of the American dream; evidenced a strong sense of place; and praised organic, communal society. Like so many non-Catholic southern writers, they idealized a simpler southern past and decried the insidious secularism of industrial, urban America.

Catholicism, which taught the sanctity of marriage and family, also easily allied with the host society in attacking divorce and abortion—moral positions that contributed to the thawing of relations between Catholics and evangelical Protestant groups. During the 1970s, for example, several regional Southern Baptist/Roman Catholic conferences were held in a mutual effort both to undo generations of stereotypes and mistrust that had separated the two churches and, secondarily, to build a consensus for social action. The improved position of Catholics in the region's public life in recent years further testified to Protestant tolerance of Catholics and to Catholic integration into southern life. If Catholics did not quite belong in the Protestant South, they were no longer universally condemned as wholly antithetical to it.

Yet, even as Catholicism gained acceptance in the South, liberal forces swept into the church and the region to loosen the anchors of social conservatism and political accommodationism. More than anything else, the church's social posture shifted in response to Vatican II, which, among other influences, modified church hierarchical authority by calling for greater lay initiative in devotions and discipline. It also altered the ritual foundation of Catholic conservatism and cultural consensus by modernizing liturgical practices. Tradition gave way to change, and often confusion, in worship and social vision. Catholics reared in a tradition of docility groped to separate new truths from old errors in belief.

In the South, papal denunciation of

racism in 1958 and insistence on social justice after Vatican II posed immediate challenges to local Catholic and southern habits. Catholic segregationist policy had begun to crumble in the late 1940s and early 1950s because of the actions of individual prelates in Washington, St. Louis, Raleigh, and Nashville in desegregating parochial schools, but the rush came in the 1960s when Catholic school desegregation moved at a pace faster than that in the public sector. Desegregation of other Catholic institutions soon followed. Desegregation, imposed as it was from above, met stiff resistance from white Catholic laity, particularly in the Deep South where many persons defied church orders. The continued practice of segregated worship virtually everywhere in the South revealed the fragmented nature of the new Catholic church and the tug between church authority and social norms among southern Catholics. The involvement of Catholic religious leaders in the civil rights movement further alienated southern communicants from the official church, even though many southern bishops opposed civil rights activity.

Similarly, the church's grip on lay thinking weakened as parochial schools became battlegrounds of social change. With fewer nuns, brothers, and priests in teaching positions the influence of lay instructors, who did not always share common social values, increased. The creeping secularism in Catholic education led some pastors to question openly the necessity of parochial schools at all. The floodtide of Spanish-speaking migrants and immigrants in the last few decades, combined with the migration of northern-born and often better-educated Catholics into the southern Sunbelt, introduced new cultural stresses into the church while pulling it toward new, non-southern definitions of social concern. As sections of the South have become "northernized" by industrialization and ethnic pluralism, so too has the southern Catholic church.

On the face of it, the Catholic imprint on the South has been negligible. A small, scattered Catholic population has not developed a regional influence. Within areas of Catholic concentration, however (particularly Louisiana, the lower Gulf region, Florida, Texas, and parts of Maryland and Kentucky), Catholicism continues to inform local cultural and social life. In lower Louisiana, especially, where well over one-third of the population is Catholic, Catholic religious symbols abound in the practice of regular nightly prayers, and in more public, if secularized, expressions such as the annual rice and sugarcane festivals, the Yambilee, the blessing of the shrimp fleets, and even Mardi Gras, which is not without religious overtones.

The contribution of diverse, immigrant Catholic cultures to southern character remains incalculable because it is so elusive and fluid. Catholics have always existed as both outsiders and insiders in southern culture, and the tension between their public and private roles has produced subregional permutations wherever Catholics have lived in significant numbers. On the negative side, cultural differences between Catholic and Protestant reinforced or forged stereotypes and rivalries that have threatened the region's social harmony. The accommodation of the Catholic church and its people to southern social and political norms, in addition to the higher religiosity of southern Catholics compared to their northern counterparts, paradoxically reaffirms the evangelical Protestant core of southern culture with its stress on personal religious accountability and conservative social values.

See also ETHNIC LIFE: Nativism; / French; Germans; Irish; Italians; Mexicans; Spanish; LITERATURE: / O'Connor, Flannery; Porter, Katherine Anne; Tate, Allen; WOMEN'S LIFE: / Chopin, Kate

Randall M. Miller
Saint Joseph's University

John Tracy Ellis, *American Catholicism* (1969); Joseph Fichter, *Southern Parish: Dynamics of A City Church* (1951); John C. McKinney and Edgar T. Thompson, eds., *The South in Continuity and Change* (1965); James Hennesey, *American Catholics: A History of the Roman Catholic Community* (1982); Samuel S. Hill, ed., *Encyclopedia of Religion in the South* (1984); Randall M. Miller and Jon L. Wakelyn, eds., *Catholics in the Old South: Essays on Church and Culture* (1983); William A. Osborne, *The Segregated Covenant: Race Relations and American Catholics* (1967). ☆

Theological Orthodoxy

The theological orthodoxy that permeated the 19th-century South was one expression of a broader pattern of conservative European religious thought then prevailing throughout the United States. It was an eclectic innovation consisting of biblical literalism, 17th-century scholasticism, 18th-century British apologetics and Scottish philosophy, and 19th-century science. It attempted, above all, to confront the Enlightenment on its own terms. The more solicitous the orthodox theologians

were about biblical revelation, the more they sought rational proof and explanation. To be orthodox was to assume the unity of truth and therefore to affirm a "natural theology" based on human reason as the corollary of scriptural revelation.

Such a "rational orthodoxy" flourished throughout the region, but its articulate exponents were the pastors of town and city churches and the professors in colleges and seminaries. They were especially attuned to the planter aristocracy and an urban constituency who sought respectability by distancing themselves from the religious and social ineptitude of the unwashed. Almost every college had a required course on "the evidences of Christianity," and between 1795 and 1860 well over 150 ministers from every denomination published treatises and articles exhibiting the logic of rational orthodoxy.

That logic invariably exhibited a threefold pattern: the theologians argued that reason served as a means of preparation, validation, and interpretation of the biblical revelation. To prepare the mind to accept revealed truth, the theologian could assemble all the traditional rational arguments for the existence of God based on the harmony of the natural order, the mutual adaptation of its parts, its complexity, the necessity of a sufficient cause for its existence, and the universality of religious belief. The insights thus garnered constituted a natural knowledge of God, independent of the biblical revelation but clearly congruent with biblical claims. The theologians, therefore, found it necessary to confirm the trustworthiness of rational knowledge; hence they turned to the Scottish philosophy of Thomas Reid and Dugald Stewart, who had seemingly refuted David Hume's skepticism. And they found it equally necessary to maintain a close and optimistic watch over the natural sciences, which, they thought, could become one more weapon in the apologetic armory of Christendom. They admired and tried to emulate the inductive methods favored by Sir Francis Bacon. Scottish philosophy and Baconian method became mainstays of orthodox religious thought.

Having prepared the mind through natural theology to recognize the elementary truths of religion, reason, they thought, could then validate the higher biblical revelation. Therefore, they elaborated endlessly the traditional "evidences of Christianity," which demonstrated that the Bible was the unique word of God. From such English opponents of Deism as Richard Watson and William Paley, they derived the so-called external arguments, designed to show that the validation of the biblical miracles and the fulfillment of its prophecies demonstrated the divine status of the biblical message. From other opponents of Deism—especially Bishop Joseph Butler in England—they took the "internal arguments," which were claims about consistency. The Bible, they hoped to show, was internally consistent: it was consistent with human need and thus capable of transforming the heart; it was consistent with the highest ethical ideals of the race; it was consistent with science. Reason, in short, could determine that the Bible was the authentic word of God; in that sense reason was the criterion for revelation. But the theologians also agreed that reason, having confirmed the Bible, was then to submit itself to Christian truth.

The third task assigned to reason was the interpretation of revelation. The theologians acknowledged that the exegesis

of Scripture required the exercise of human understanding. Most interpreters tried to adhere strictly to the "grammatical-historical" methods of interpretation, but their allegiance to the notion of the unity of truth also compelled them to harmonize Scripture with true philosophy and science. They normally argued, for instance, that the Creation account in Genesis referred to seven geological eras rather than seven literal days, or they contended that the Creation in Genesis was but the culmination of aeons of divine creative activity. Such rationalist readings of the biblical text became common among both liberals and conservatives in the South well into the 20th century.

Theological orthodoxy thus reflected the spirit of 17th-century European scholasticism, with its confidence that revelation was above reason though never contrary to it. Southern theologians appealed often, in fact, to such earlier scholastics as Francis Turretin and Jacobus Arminius, and they conducted their quarrels about such doctrines as atonement, predestination, and the sacraments within the conceptual environment formed by the scholastic heritage.

In their adherence to rational orthodoxy, the southern theologians diverged in no significant way from their counterparts in the North, except insofar as they explicitly used theological conclusions to defend the region and its slave economy. Rational orthodoxy dominated the churches, colleges, and seminaries of 19th-century America. It was a commonplace in the nation's churches—as the Methodist Thomas Ralston wrote—that God had "never enjoined upon man the duty of faith, without first presenting before him a reasonable foundation for the same." In their confidence that a rational ortho-doxy was compatible both with emo-tional revivalism and with modern science, the southerners shared in a na-tional consensus.

Rational orthodoxy maintained its hegemony in many southern churches, colleges, and seminaries until late in the 19th century. Theological conservatives have held to its tenets even throughout the 20th century. Indeed, the older or-thodoxy stood in the background of both religious modernism and fundamental-ism in the South. The later fundamen-talists, who merely duplicated the earlier scholasticism within a narrower, more defensive vision, viewed the Bible itself as a rational system of divinely inspired propositions. The modernists still sought to prove the reasonable-ness of faith. The era of revivalism was also an age of reason in southern reli-gion, and in some respects the rational-ism has proved to be as durable as the fervor.

See also SCIENCE AND MEDICINE: Science and Religion

E. Brooks Holifield
Emory University

Theodore Dwight Bozeman, *Protestants in an Age of Science: The Baconian Ideal and An-tebellum Religious Thought* (1977); John L. Dagg, *Manual of Theology* (1857); E. Brooks Holifield, *The Gentlemen Theologians: American Theology in Southern Culture, 1795–1860* (1978); George M. Marsden, *Fundamentalism and American Culture: The Shaping of Twentieth-Century Evangelical-ism, 1870–1925* (1980); Thomas Ral-ston, *Elements of Divinity* (1871); James Henley Thornwell, *The Collected Writings of James Henley Thornwell*, ed. John Adger (1971). ☆

Women and Religion

See WOMEN'S LIFE: Religion and Women

Zion, South as

The 17th century saw the crumbling of the old feudal and manorial systems that dominated the geographic and economic landscape of Europe and had held the landless peasant in virtual bondage, but the modern systems that replaced them did little to elevate the least elements of the general populace. Capitalism was more beneficial to the neophyte capi-talists than to the laborers; population pressures, worn-out soil, and prob-lems associated with displacement abounded; unsatisfactory religious con-ditions paralleled economic woes. Princes in central Europe demanded that their subjects adhere to the religion of their political leaders and religious dissent was not countenanced. When England's King James I promised to "harry them out of the land," he was refering to dissenters to the Church of England who were experiencing both economic hardship and religious intol-erance.

Given these Old World conditions, the New World attracted people from the British Isles and mainland Europe. Ex-plorers reported the wonders of the Western Hemisphere, painting America as a land of milk and honey. Dissatis-faction with conditions in Europe com-bined with the advantages of America—both real and fancied—attracted count-less people to the New World. The first Englishmen to settle in Virginia came for multiple reasons: a higher standard of living, a permanent home, a place to worship. These men viewed Virginia and the colonies to the south as a paradise, a utopia, a new Zion. They thought of themselves as descendants of God's chosen people and of America as the new Promised Land.

The Puritans who settled New England attempted to establish a "city upon a hill," but New Englanders did not have a monopoly on religious idealism. It inspired the southern colonists as well. As historian Perry Miller pointed out, southern settlers come out of an English culture that reflected a religious worldview. The Great Awakening, at a later time, affected all the colonies. As English and other Europeans swarmed into the southern colonies, they worked to reap the fruits of the boundless land, at the same time thanking God for their harvests and for the freedom they enjoyed.

As people along the seaboard moved westward, religion and religious ideas permeated southern colonial culture. Geographic and demographic conditions kept early southerners from joining churches in large numbers, but this fact did not negate the religiosity of the South. The Second Awakening of the early 19th century both grew out of and reinforced this religiosity. It also increased church membership statistics, especially those of the Baptists, Methodists, and Presbyterians. By the mid-19th century, southerners had begun to identify religion and culture so closely that they could not be separated.

The southern religious experience became intertwined with the South's political ideology, both essential elements in what became the southern way of life. Throughout the middle period of American history, when economics,

states' rights views, westward expansion, the abolition movement, and a host of other tangible conditions and intangible forces drove wedges between North and South, southerners took umbrage at those who criticized their regions and its institutions. The South's intellectual and emotional defense of itself and its ideals, its myths and its realities were to some extent an outgrowth of the impact of religious zeal. When the great sectional crisis reached its climax, the South defended its way of life with fervor imbued with religious convictions. From the southern point of view, the Civil War was a fight between right and wrong, a religious crusade, a holy war, a defense of a beloved Zion. Southerners who died for the cause saw themselves as being like the religious warriors of an earlier era who had defended the Holy Land from the attack of the infidels.

Once the Civil War was over, southerners surrounded themselves with both old and new myths, as they idealized a society "gone with the wind" and orated about the glories of the "Lost Cause." In the latter years of the 19th century and into the 20th, when powerful social and economic forces racked American society, southerners turned to religion for solace. The church in both hamlet and city was a "solid rock" in an unstable world. Religious revivals stemming from the frontier camp meeting tradition reaped a great harvest of souls. Baptists and Methodists together constituted as much as 90 percent of the church-going population in some states within a region recognized as the most religious in the nation. Religion continued to infiltrate politics, society, and culture, and—despite the Baptists' belief in the doctrine of separation of church and state—the two largest Protestant denominations in the South became essentially the "established" churches of the region. In the 20th century, when denominations like the Southern Baptists and Methodists epitomized and defended the status quo, much of the southern religious commitment continued to be the result of firmly held beliefs (rightly or wrongly) that the South contained the most desirable conditions in the nation. Whatever its shortcomings, for southerners the South continued to be the American Zion.

See also MYSTIC SOUTH: / Lost Cause Myth

Monroe Billington
New Mexico State University

Kenneth K. Bailey, *Southern White Protestantism in the Twentieth Century* (1964); Hunter D. Farish, *The Circuit Rider Dismounts: A Social History of Southern Methodism, 1865–1900* (1938); Samuel S. Hill and Robert G. Torbet, *Baptists: North and South* (1964); Charles A. Johnson, *The Frontier Camp Meeting: Religion's Harvest Time* (1955); Walter B. Posey, *The Baptist Church in the Lower Mississippi Valley, 1776–1845* (1957), *The Development of Methodism in the Old Southwest, 1783–1824* (1933); Rufus B. Spain, *At Ease in Zion: Social History of the Southern Baptists, 1865–1900* (1967); Ernest T. Thompson, *The Presbyterians in the South, 1607–1861* (1963). ☆

AFRICAN METHODIST EPISCOPAL CHURCHES

The African Methodist Episcopal (AME) church and the African Methodist Episcopal Zion (AME Zion) church have never been distinctively "southern" churches, but they have been two of the most popular and powerful religious denominations among southern blacks.

Both groups originated in northern cities—Philadelphia and New York City, respectively—in the late 18th century. Blacks were among early converts to Methodism in North America, but segregated church services and discrimination in the ritual of communion led to the withdrawal of black Methodists. Richard Allen, Absalom Jones, and William White were early founders of the AME church, while William Brown, Francis Jacobs, and Peter Williams had incorporated the precursor of the AME Zion church in New York City by 1801. Before the Civil War, the two denominations had established congregations in such border South cities as Louisville, Washington, and Baltimore, and the AME church had even appeared in New Orleans. Both denominations opposed slavery and were therefore closely watched in these locations. Daniel Payne and Morris Brown, both born and reared in Charleston, S.C., became the most prominent antebellum southerners in either denomination, serving as AME church bishops.

The AME churches assumed a new significance in the South with the Civil War and emancipation. Membership expanded as ministers and missionaries came south to work with the freedmen. At the end of the war, the AME Zion church, led by Bishop J. J. Clinton of the Southern Conference, worked vigorously in Alabama, Florida, Lousiana, and, perhaps most effectively, North Carolina. Such colleges and schools of theology as Fayetteville State, Winston-Salem State, and Hood Theological Seminary were formed in this era. Leaders of the AME church organized a state conference in 1865 in South Carolina, and from there ministers expanded throughout the Deep South and into the Southwest. South Carolinian Henry

McNeal Turner was among the prominent leaders of the postbellum AME church. He served as bishop of the Georgian Conference from 1880 to 1892 and played a key role in introducing Methodism to Africa. Both AME denominations are currently active in Africa and the Caribbean as well as the United States.

Charles Reagan Wilson
University of Mississippi

David M. Bradley, *A History of the A.M.E. Zion Church*, 2 vols. (1956–70); Harry V. Richardson, *Dark Salvation: The Story of Methodism as It Developed among Blacks in America* (1976); Clarence E. Walker, *A Rock in a Weary Land: The African Methodist Episcopal Church during the Civil War and Reconstruction* (1982); William J. Walls, *The African Methodist Episcopal Zion Church: Reality of the Black Church* (1974). ☆

ASBURY, FRANCIS

(1745–1816) Minister.

Francis Asbury was born four miles from Birmingham, England, 20 or 21 August 1745. As early as age 15, he began to preach, and in 1766 he became one of John Wesley's traveling ministers in the "Methodist" connection. Five years later he volunteered to become a Wesleyan missionary to the colonies. There the greatest interest in the evangelical movement existed in the South, where Asbury took charge of the Baltimore district in 1773. As the only missionary to remain during the Revolution, he became superintendent of the evangelical enterprise throughout the nation. In the first years of the Revolution he began to attract the suspicion of the authorities, who questioned his loyalty to the Rev-

olutionary cause, and he found himself restricted to preaching in Delaware. Such suspicions declined, and by 1779 Asbury had begun to resume control of the American evangelical movement.

Asbury attempted to maintain discipline among the lay preachers, especially the increasingly rebellious southerners, and at the same time he implored Wesley to provide greater support for the American enterprise. Finally, in 1784, Wesley sent representatives who met with Asbury and most of the lay ministers at the "Christmas Conference" in Baltimore, at that point the center of evangelical Anglicanism. Although Thomas Coke, Wesley's main representative, was officially in charge of the meeting, Asbury in fact controlled the events. The members voted to create a new denomination, the Methodist Episcopal church, and, at Asbury's insistence, they voted to invest him with the office of superintendent, a position Wesley had intended to give him without the advice or consent of the American clergy. Again showing his conscious independence of Wesley, Asbury began to call himself "bishop."

As leader of the new denomination, Asbury traveled great distances on horseback and focused most of his attention upon the South and Southwest, where the greatest numbers of Methodists remained during his lifetime. He continually fought minor bureaucratic battles and often ran the denomination with a strong, some said dictatorial, style. He weathered the great crisis of the early years of the denomination, James O'Kelley's movement to democratize Methodism, and only in the last years of his life yielded power to his hand-chosen successor, William McKendree. Never in particularly robust health, Asbury nevertheless continued to travel until his death on 31 March 1816.

Francis Asbury never received acclaim as a great preacher, nor was he a scholarly man. Strongly committed to the necessity of sinless behavior, he vigorously opposed slavery during much of his life, yielding only toward the end of his travels to moderation on the issue. Asbury's greatest strength, and the one that made him one of the most exceptional men in American religious history, was organizational. He had a keen instinct for church politics, managed church expansion with intelligence and remarkable intuition, and built a denomination that became central to 19th-century southern religion.

David T. Bailey
Michigan State University

Herbert Asbury, *A Methodist Saint: The Life of Bishop Asbury* (1927); Elmer T. Clark, ed., *The Journal and Letters of Francis Asbury* (1958). ☆

BIBLE BELT
||||||||||||||||||||||||||||||||||

Bible Belt is a term coined by H. L. Mencken in the 1920s to describe areas of the nation dominated by belief in the literal authenticity of the Bible and accompanying puritanical mores. He did not give the term a specific location, but he did associate it with rural areas of the Midwest and, especially, the "Baptist back-waters of the South." He used the term as one of derision, referring, for example, to "the Bible and Hookworm Belt" and calling Jackson, Miss., "the heart of the Bible and Lynching Belt."

The term has been used by scholars

as well. In mapping the geographical range of the Churches of Christ, Edwin Gaustad commented that the denomination's influence represented "perhaps more a Bible Belt than any other region can offer." A 1952 survey by John L. Thomas in *Religion and the American People* (1963), concluded that, based on the prevalence of Bible reading, the Bible Belt was primarily in the West South Central, East South Central, and South Atlantic census areas. Cultural geographer James R. Shortridge analyzed 1971 denominational membership figures and mapped a Bible Belt region of "conservative churches" extending in influence from the Atlantic seaboard through Texas and eastern New Mexico; its northern boundary was the upper state lines of Virginia, Kentucky, Missouri, and Oklahoma, extending into southern Illinois. "Jackson, Mississippi, could perhaps be called the 'buckle' of the Bible Belt, but Oklahoma City is definitely marginal, and Kansas is not in it," he wrote. Stephen W. Tweedie's study, "Viewing the Bible Belt," analyzed the viewership of evangelical, fundamentalist religious television programming, and concluded that "the Baptist South certainly is a major part of this Bible Belt, but areas of strength also include parts of the Methodist dominated Midwest as well as portions of the predominantly Lutheran Dakotas." These modern studies seem, then, to confirm Mencken's use of the term, although now it is used proudly by those in the Bible Belt to describe their commitments.

Bible Belt is a particularly useful term to describe the importance of the Scriptures in the South. When Hazel Motes in Flannery O'Connor's *Wise Blood* left his hometown of Eastrod, Tenn., he took with him only a black

Bible and a pair of glasses belonging to his mother. At his little country school, he "had learned to read and write but that it was wiser not to: the Bible was the only book he read." He was perhaps typical of many southern true believers. On the early frontier and in rural areas throughout southern history, the Bible has been a main source of reading material and intellectual stimulation. Preachers took it as their only text for preaching. Politicians used a campaign language spiced with references to biblical stories and quotes to illustrate their political points, and two favorite southern pastimes—storytelling and conversation—were often filled with biblical references. Writers such as O'Connor and Faulkner used biblical symbols and motifs, artists painted biblical heroes and heroines in their works, and quilters even stitched the stories as themes for their works. Historian Kenneth K. Bailey noted of the South in 1900 that "few Southerners doubted the literal authenticity of the Scriptures or the ever-presence of God in man's affairs," and sociologist John Shelton Reed's studies of southern attitudes in contemporary times suggest the Bible Belt is still literally that.

See also MYTHIC SOUTH: Mencken's South

Charles Reagan Wilson
University of Mississippi

Kenneth K. Bailey, *Southern White Protestantism in the Twentieth Century* (1964); H. L. Mencken, *Prejudices: Sixth Series* (1927); John Shelton Reed, *The Enduring South: Subcultural Persistence in Mass Society* (1972); James R. Shortridge, *The Geographical Review* (October 1976); Stephen W. Tweedie, *Journal of Popular Culture* (Spring 1978). ☆

BLUE LAWS

Considered reverential by some, overly puritanical by others, blue laws, or Sunday closing laws, exist in most of the southern states. Based on an English statute passed in 1678 during the reign of Charles II and carried piously into the colonies, blue laws prohibit worldly business and diversion—except when deemed necessary or charitable—on the traditional day of rest.

The term *blue laws* comes from the blue paper used in binding the Massachusetts statutes on moral behavior in the 1600s. The first American colonial law regulating Sabbath activities was passed in Virginia in 1610, requiring Sunday church attendance, and other southern colonies followed suit. In the 19th century Sabbath laws did not require church attendance but did regulate public activities on that day.

Fearing growing secularization after the Civil War, religious groups such as the Baptists, Methodists, and Presbyterians urged their members to refrain from participating in public entertainment, social activities, and recreational travel on Sundays, and eventually they successfully pressured for greater enforcement of blue laws, especially in small towns and rural communities.

Today, stores are closed or merchandising is restricted in honor of holy observance. Realistically, the laws assure merchants of at least one noncompetitive day a week.

The result of such laws, passed by state and local governments, is a chaotic canon of "do's" and "don't's." Hence, the merit of the legislation is challenged constantly. For example, Arkansas's blue law—which permitted the sale on Sunday of film and flashbulbs but not cameras—was deemed unconstitutional in 1982.

In Louisiana there are only a handful of businesses—including ice houses, book stores, funeral parlors, and steamboats—which can operate legally on Sundays. In South Carolina most commercial endeavors are illegal on Sunday. Exceptions include sanctioned steeplechases, annual harness races, and the sale of fish bait, seeds, swimwear, and ice cream. These anomalous statutes appear on many a code of ordinances, but most communities wink at the law. Enforcement is haphazard and sporadic.

Though probably an endangered species, blue laws linger on most local lawbooks. The one sabbatical restriction that most southern officials insist upon is the prohibition of the sale of alcohol—except in large cities, resort areas, and at private clubs. Because of the irreconcilable differences between whiskey and worship, Sundays in the rural South will be dry for a long time to come.

Linton Weeks
Arkansas Times
Little Rock, Arkansas

Neil J. Dilloff, *Maryland Law Review* (No. 4, 1980); Warren L. Johns, *Dateline Sunday, USA: The Story of Three and a Half Centuries of Sunday-Law Battles in America* (1967); Richard E. Morgan, *The Supreme Court and Religion* (1972). ☆

CAMPBELL, ALEXANDER
(1788–1866) Minister.

Campbell was a major figure in a religious movement that came into being on the American frontier in the early 19th century and continues to thrive in the modern South. Its purpose was to restore the unity of the church on the basis of the Scriptures. Campbell, Thomas Campbell (his father), Barton W. Stone, and Walter Scott were the founders of a movement whose congregations today call themselves Churches of Christ, Christian Churches, and Christian Church (Disciples of Christ). The movement had great appeal to individuals in Virginia, North and South Carolina, Georgia, Tennessee, and Kentucky.

Campbell was born in northern Ireland. His father was a minister in the Anti-Burgher Seceder Presbyterian Church. Accepting the teachings of the Scottish school of Common Sense philosophy, the Campbells were influenced by the evangelical movement led by such men as James and Alexander Haldane, Roland Hill, and John Walker.

Disturbed by the conflict between Protestants and Catholics in northern Ireland, the father in 1807 came to America. His wife and family, led by young Alexander, followed in 1809. When the family reunited in America both father and son had broken with the Presbyterian tradition. Practicing believer's baptism by immersion, the Campbells were in fellowship with the Baptists of western Pennsylvania and northern Virginia between 1815 and 1830, but they soon parted over doctrinal questions.

Alexander Campbell was giving leadership to a growing group of followers, generated in part by a series of debates with such figures as Robert Owen, Bishop John Purcell, and Nathan Rice and William Maccalla of Kentucky. By means of his publications, the *Christian Baptist* and its successor, *The Millennial Harbinger*, Campbell's views were spread throughout the South. In 1829 Campbell served as a delegate to the Virginia Constitutional Convention.

To prepare young men for the ministry, Campbell founded Bethany College in 1840. Located in Brooke County, Va. (now West Virginia), the college was unique in that it was the first college to teach the Bible as a subject along with other studies. Students came to Bethany from most of the southern states but especially from Alabama, Georgia, and Mississippi.

As the slavery controversy grew more heated in the 1850s, Campbell was called upon to take a stand. Always popular with southern audiences, he temporized saying "slavery is a matter of opinion," meaning that it was not central to Christian faith. This position satisfied neither those of the North nor of the South.

Campbell lived near the college, serving as president and teaching several generations of preachers until his death in 1866.

Lester G. McAllister
Christian Theological Seminary

Lester G. McAllister, *Thomas Campbell: Man of the Book* (1954), with William Tucker, *Journey in Faith: A History of the Christian Church* (1975); Robert Richardson, *Memoirs of Alexander Campbell* (1897). ☆

CAMPBELL, WILL
||||||||||||||||||||||||||||||||||||||||||||||||
(b. 1924) Minister and social activist.

Will Davis Campbell was born 18 July 1924 near Liberty, Miss., a small community in the pine belt of southern Mississippi, which also produced comedian and storyteller Jerry Clower. Educated

in local schools at East Fork and ordained a Southern Baptist preacher at the age of 17, he then enrolled in Louisiana College at Pineville (1941–43), intending to be a rural Baptist minister. Campbell was among the several million southerners who migrated during World War II to army camps, munitions factories, and shipyards outside the South. Campbell's own service in the U.S. Army Medical Corps during campaigns in the South Pacific was crucial to his life's work. He became more aware of the injustices suffered by blacks and was strengthened in his new interest in social justice by a reading of Howard Fast's *Freedom Road*.

Returning to the South accompanied by his wife, Brenda, he studied at Wake Forest College (A.B., 1948). After further study at Tulane University, Campbell enrolled at Yale University and received the Bachelor of Divinity degree in 1952. Campbell's first—and only— assignment to the formal ministry paralleled his untraditional training. In his brief 18-month stay as a minister in Taylor, La., Campbell became involved in several human rights issues, an experience that convinced him that his calling was not to assume the role of a traditional minister.

In 1954 he became director of religious life at the University of Mississippi and, after two years, left that post to become head of the Southern Office of the Department of Racial and Cultural Relations for the National Council of Churches.

In 1957 Campbell was among those who escorted black children through jeering mobs during the crisis at Little Rock, Ark. Later, Campbell was the only white man allowed to participate in the organization of the Southern Christian Leadership Conference. He served

Will Campbell, a leader of the Committee of Southern Churchmen, 1980s

for white southern views of black people.

A change in Campbell's style was evident in his first book, *Race and Renewal of the Church* (1962). Here Campbell first publicly stated his now-celebrated view that institutions had failed to bring true social change in the South. Campbell suggested it would have been better had the Supreme Court not ruled favorably in 1954 on the segregation issue, because individual Christians would have been forced to resolve the issue. This book was the initial statement of Campbell's continuing belief that the real enemies of human rights in the South were formal institutions, such as government and the business community, which divided downtrodden whites and blacks.

From his farm in Mt. Juliet, Tenn., near Nashville, Campbell devotes himself to writing, speaking engagements, truck farming, and his duties as a leader in the liberal Committee of Southern Churchmen. Campbell became publisher of the group's journal, *Katallagete*, and published a novel, *The Glad River*, in 1982. His concern for southern betterment has become an individualistic guerrilla ministry, which appeals to one's individual conscience rather than to collective action.

as a coordinator, troubleshooter, and observer during demonstrations in Clinton and Nashville, Tenn., Greensboro, N.C., Birmingham, Ala., and Albany, Ga. Will Campbell's resignation in 1963 from his post with the National Council of Churches involved a change in his attitudes toward social reform. The tragic decline and death of his brother, a central theme of the celebrated *Brother to a Dragonfly* (1977), brought Will Campbell back to his Amite County poor white heritage and an awareness that suffering knew no color lines. His association with a liberal Mississippi newspaperman, P. D. East, editor of *The Petal Paper*, influenced Campbell to become aware that he had not allowed southern poor whites the same measure of Christian charity that he had shown to black people. Finally, Campbell became disillusioned with the hostility expressed by some civil rights activists toward southern whites—attitudes he had assumed would have been reserved

Thomas L. Connelly
University of South Carolina

Orley B. Caudill, ed., "An Oral History with Will Davis Campbell, Christian Preacher," vol. 157 of The Mississippi Oral History Program of the University of Southern Mississippi (1980); Thomas L. Connelly, *Will Campbell and the Soul of the South* (1982); Marshall Frady, *Southerners: A Journalist's Odyssey* (1980); Frye Gaillard, *Race, Rock and Religion: Profiles from a Southern Journalist* (1982). ☆

CANNON, JAMES, JR.

‖‖

(1864–1944) Minister

Born in Salisbury, Md., James Cannon, Jr., entered the ministry of the Methodist Episcopal Church, South after a religious conversion experienced while attending Randolph-Macon College. He received training at Princeton Theological Seminary and was given his first charge in 1888 in the Virginia Conference.

Cannon's multifaceted career included educational, editorial, and interdenominational work. He twice served as principal of Blackstone Female Institute in Virginia, substantially adding to that school's funding and enrollment. As the first superintendent of the Junaluska Methodist Assembly in North Carolina, he further demonstrated his administrative talents.

From the beginning of his ministry Cannon was active in ecclesiastical affairs and participated in the annual state and general conferences of his denomination. Cannon's work outside the confines of his church included semiautonomous editorial positions with church newspapers in Virginia and organizational activity with the Federal Council of Churches and Near East Relief. Like many other southern progressives, he adopted prohibition as his primary reform ideal. Helping organize the Virginia Anti-Saloon League in 1901, he also founded a dry publication, the *Richmond Virginian*. Cannon fought against the wet Democratic machine in Virginia, got a wet-dry referendum on the ballot, and then led the state's prohibition forces to victory in 1916. As chairman of the legislative committee of the Anti-Saloon League, he successfully lobbied in Washington for passage of prohibition legislation culminating in the Eighteenth Amendment.

In 1918 the General Conference elected Cannon bishop, a position he held for the next 20 years. His original district included most of the Southwest and part of the Deep South. He also accepted responsibility for Methodist mission fields and made extensive inspection tours of the Belgian Congo, Mexico, and South American countries.

During the 1920s Cannon became chief spokesman for prohibition enforcement. In the tumultuous presidential campaign of 1928, he broke with the Democratic party for the first time and organized the Anti-Smith Democrats. Always a combative personality in both speech and print, Cannon continuously had to answer charges of anti-Catholicism.

Not long after the defeat of Al Smith, Cannon came under relentless attack from the Hearst press and other enemies he had accumulated over the years. The charges against him included wartime hoarding, stock market gambling, misappropriation of campaign funds, and adultery. Much of the early 1930s he spent in seemingly endless legal battles and investigations. On one occasion he shocked the nation by walking out of a congressional hearing. Although never found guilty of any wrongdoing by either court or church tribunal, his image suffered irreparable damage. He spent the remainder of his life after 1938 in retirement, but never relinquished his passion for prohibition.

Perhaps no one in public life exemplified southern mores in the 1920s better than did Cannon. The fall of national Prohibition in 1933 was a watershed for the type of leadership he provided. No southern minister would be as influential until Martin Luther King, Jr., emerged as a civil rights leader in the mid-1950s.

William E. Ellis
Eastern Kentucky University

Virginius Dabney, *Dry Messiah: The Life of Bishop Cannon* (1949); Richard L. Watson, Jr., ed., *Bishop Cannon's Own Story: Life as I Have Seen It* (1955). ☆

CHRISTIAN BROADCASTING NETWORK
||||||||||||||||||||||||||||||||||||||||

The Christian Broadcasting Network (CBN) was founded in 1960 by M. G. (Pat) Robertson and began broadcasting from one-kilowatt station WYAH-TV in Portsmouth, Va., on 1 October 1961. From this modest beginning, CBN grew by the early 1980s to become the largest religious broadcaster and the fourth largest cable network in the United States. In 1984 its programs appeared by syndication on approximately 200 television stations in the United States and on CBN cable network transmitted via satellite to more than 4,000 cable systems. CBN owns and operates television stations in three major markets and has 80 radio affiliates.

Satellite delivery systems permit 24-hour global transmitting capability, and CBN programs are seen or heard in approximately 50 nations. A CBN owned and operated television station in Lebanon transmits to much of the Middle East.

The flagship program of CBN is the *700 Club*, a 90-minute talk, news, and political commentary show, hosted by Robertson. The program took its name from a telethon in 1967 during which participants pleaded for 700 persons to pledge $10 a month to meet the network's budget. From this inauspicious start, the total annual budget for CBN operations by the mid-1980s had reached approximately $100 million.

CBN has initiated a number of religious programs. The most successful to date has been *Another Life*, a soap opera with a Christian outlook. CBN conducts a counseling ministry, which is tied to the *700 Club*. In 1983 the network had 79 domestic and 40 international counseling centers. These centers also administer a program called "Operation Blessing," which provides material assistance for persons in need.

CBN's headquarters are in Virginia Beach, Va., on a 700-acre site that also includes CBN University, which opened in 1978 with 77 students. Focusing on graduate education, student enrollment grew to 570 in 1984. A $13.2 million library was dedicated in October of that year. The CBN master plan calls for 14 schools eventually and projects a student body of 6,000.

Born in Lexington, Va., in 1930, Robertson is the son of the late U.S. Senator A. Willis Robertson. Pat Robertson earned a degree in law at Yale University (1955) and is an ordained Southern Baptist clergyman (1961). He has used the *700 Club* as a platform for his conservative political, as well as religious, views before becoming a Republican presidential candidate during the 1988 campaign.

Jeffrey K. Hadden
University of Virginia

Dick Dabney, *Harper's* (August 1980); Jeffrey K. Hadden and Charles E. Swann, *Prime Time Preachers: The Rising Power of Televangelism* (1981). ☆

DABBS, JAMES McBRIDE

|||||||||||||||||||||||||||||||||||||||||||||||||||||||||||

(1896–1970) Minister, writer, and reformer.

Dabbs was born in 1896 in Sumter County, S.C. He died there in 1970. In the course of his life he was a teacher, a farmer, a poet and essayist, and a symbol of both the past and future. Educated at the University of South Carolina, Clark University (Massachusetts), and Columbia University, he taught English at the University of South Carolina (1921–24) and Coker College (1925–37). In 1937 he returned to the family home where he farmed with an intensity unknown to the academics of the time who extolled the virtues of the agrarian way but remained in the scholarly world.

As a poet, Dabbs was often published, but his mark was made as an essayist. He addressed issues of agrarianism, industrialism, and change in the South. His themes were often similar to those of the Vanderbilt Agrarians, but while he knew the personalities and their work, his relationship to them was not intimate. More significantly, his writing began to address religious issues in the 1940s, and he had become by 1950 a dissenting voice in South Carolina. He tended his garden while the postwar world convulsed. Eventually the convulsions reached Sumter County; the black citizens there and across the South began to march. Dabbs's learning and resulting worldview, his religious insights and commitment to the Presbyterian church, but most importantly his love for the South, made him a formidable spokesman for change. He found his voice in journals such as *The Christian Century* and in organizations like the South Carolina Council on Human Relations and eventually the Southern Regional Council. As president of the Southern Regional Council (1957–63), Dabbs was a spokesman for the view that the South of the future would be integrated.

In his books he reworked themes addressed in his most widely read book, *The Southern Heritage* (1958). He argued that those standing in the mainstream of southern history were the blacks demanding recognition and a place in the body politic. His influence was subtle and far-reaching. He spoke to a generation of young southerners who felt caught between their love of the region and the reality of the postcolonial world. As historian-folklorist Charles Joyner noted, "He was not so much a liberalizing force, but he was a means of reconciling the alienation from the South which I then felt as a result of my hostility to racism. Earlier I had drawn a circle leaving the black folks out, later replacing it with a circle replacing the blacks with the red-necks. Dabbs opened the circle." Representing as he did the revered influences of the region, the church, the university, and the land, Dabbs prepared the way for an era of reconciliation. His other books included *The Road Home* (1960), *Who Speaks for the South?* (1964), *Civil Rights in Recent Southern Fiction* (1969), and *Haunted by God* (1972).

Robert M. Randolph
Massachusetts Institute
of Technology

John Egerton, *New South* (Winter 1969); Richard H. King, in *Perspectives on the American South*, vol. 2, eds. Merle Black and John Shelton Reed (1984); Robert M. Randolph, in *From the Old South to the New: Essays on the Transitional South*, eds. Walter J. Fraser, Jr., and Winifred B. Moore, Jr., (1981). ☆

ENGLAND, JOHN
(1786–1842) Roman Catholic bishop.

Born in Cork, Ireland, John England won fame there as a preacher, writer, editor, and political agitator against the proposal to allow the British king a veto in the selection of Catholic bishops. When he came to the United States in 1820, he found in his diocese 5,000 Catholics scattered over 140,000 square miles. Most were Irish immigrants or refugees from revolution in Santo Domingo. He had responsibility for Catholics in Georgia and the Carolinas from 1820 to 1842.

England was an active bishop, establishing congregations headed by catechists in the three southern states, where priests visited periodically to say mass. Religious education was his major concern. He wrote a catechism and translated the Roman missal into English for lay use. In 1822 he founded the first Catholic newspaper in the United States, the *United States Catholic Miscellany*, and in 1825 opened the first Roman Catholic seminary in the South. By 1842, 20 priests had been ordained. He founded an orphanage and organized two communities of teaching sisters for the education of whites and free blacks and for the religious instruction of slaves. His effort to establish a school for blacks was blocked. In 1833 he became the first American to serve in the papal diplomatic corps as apostolic delegate to Haiti.

On the national church scene, he was instrumental in persuading Catholic bishops to meet in the series of national councils that began at Baltimore in 1829. A similar collegial sense of the need for shared responsibility in church affairs led him to frame a diocesan constitution and to organize in each parish a lay vestry to share in management of temporal affairs. Organizations representing clergy and laity met in each state and in a general convention of the diocese. In shaping diocesan government he paid explicit attention to the polity of other Christian churches and to the democratic atmosphere of the country, which he tried to integrate with traditional Roman Catholic structures. He opposed John C. Calhoun's nullification doctrine—an extreme version of states' rights—but had an ambivalent approach to slavery. He was "not friendly to the existence or continuation of slavery," but was hostile to abolitionists and in an 1840 exchange with Secretary of State John Forsyth stated that Pope Gregory XVI's condemnation of the slave trade the previous year did not apply to American domestic slavery. In American Roman Catholic annals, John England stands as one of the two or three greatest bishops.

James Hennesey
Boston College

Peter Guilday, *The Life and Times of John England, First Bishop of Charleston, 1786–1842*, 2 vols. (1927, 1969); Sebastian G. Messmer, et al., eds., *The Works of the Right Reverend John England*, 7 vols. (1908); Ignatius A. Reynolds, ed., *The Works of the Right Reverend John England, First Bishop of Charleston*, 5 vols. (1849, 1978). ☆

FALWELL, JERRY
(b. 1933) Minister.

Born on 11 August 1933 in Lynchburg, Va., Jerry Falwell is the son of a successful businessman and a pious Baptist mother. Falwell did not regularly attend church as a youth, but on Sunday mornings his mother turned on a radio broadcast called the *Old Fashioned Revival*

Hour, a pioneering religious broadcast from southern California. His born-again conversion occurred at a Lynchburg Baptist church on 20 January 1952. Two months later, after intensive study of the Bible, he decided to become a minister. Falwell entered Lynchburg College in 1950 as an engineering student, but after his conversion experience he transferred to Baptist Bible College in Springfield, Mo., earning a Th.G. degree in 1956. He returned to Lynchburg that year and founded the Thomas Road Baptist Church. His ministry soon included a daily radio program, and in late 1956 he launched the *Old-Time Gospel Hour*, a weekly television broadcast of the Sunday morning worship services at his Lynchburg church, which is still on the air.

In 1971 Falwell began Lynchburg Baptist College, now called Liberty University, and a new campus was built in 1977. During the U.S. Bicentennial of 1976, Falwell staged a series of "I Love America" rallies throughout the nation, after which he became increasingly involved in conservative politics. He held "Clean Up America" campaigns in 1978 and 1979 and in the latter year founded

Jerry Falwell, founder of Moral Majority, 1980s

the Moral Majority, a group that advocated a political agenda focusing on such issues as prayer in school, abortion, homosexuality, and pornography. His 1980 book, *Listen, America!*, urged that "a coalition of God-fearing moral Americans" reform society. Moral Majority was credited with helping to defeat several liberal senators and to elect Ronald Reagan in the election of 1980. Falwell called that November election "my finest hour," and since 1980 he has been an influential spokesman in New Right politics.

Falwell is the epitome of a middle-class, business-oriented fundamentalist minister in the contemporary South. Dressed in his three-piece suit, Falwell substitutes upbeat lectures for the traditional fire-and-brimstone sermons, even when talking about the coming judgment of the Lord. Like other "televangelists," though, Falwell has been accused of financial mismanagement. In 1973 the Securities and Exchange Commission, for example, filed charges against his church for "fraud and deceit" and "gross insolvency," but a federal judge later dismissed the charges. The increasing competition of other electronic churches in the 1980s has taken its toll, and the average viewing audience for his television broadcast has declined from 889,000 households in 1977 to 438,000 in November 1986. *Gospel Hour* contributions fell from $52.6 million in 1983 to $44.3 million in 1986. In early 1987 Falwell replaced Jim Bakker as director of the PTL television network following Bakker's admission of a sexual indiscretion. By 1988, though, Falwell had given up leadership positions in both Moral Majority and PTL.

Charles Reagan Wilson
University of Mississippi

Frances FitzGerald, *Cities on a Hill: Journeys through Contemporary American Cultures* (1986); Julie B. Hairston, *Southline* (6 May 1987); Charles Moritz, ed., *Current Biography* (1981); Jerry Strober and Ruth Tomczak, *Jerry Falwell: Aflame for God* (1979). ☆

FATALISM

In an outlook distinctive to the South, history is viewed as having a predestined outcome. This dark outlook has shaped southern social institutions, literature, and politics, and it has inhibited social reform. In such a view, time and history are not the arena of grand visions and idealistic reconstruction *à la* Thoreau and Emerson. Rather, as Faulkner had Quentin Compson's grandfather say while giving him his pocket watch in *The Sound and the Fury*, time is "the mausoleum of all hope and desire." The battles with time "are not even fought. The field only reveals to man his own folly and despair, and victory is an illusion of philosophers and fools."

Fatalism is manifest in the Stoic romanticism that W. J. Cash saw rooted in the "neo-Catholicism" and "neo-medievalism" of both William Alexander Percy and the Vanderbilt Agrarians. It is evident in Faulkner's sense of doom as the sins of the fathers are visited on the third and fourth generations in *Absalom, Absalom!* It is present in the Calvinistic ordaining of blacks, women, and laborers to their place in the social order (W. J. Cash said the God of the southern mind was "a Calvinist Jehovah"). It is a part of the populist rage, down to George Wallace, that sees the courts and the national media consign the South to a loser status. Journalist

Gerald W. Johnson saw a positive side to this outlook in the "sober realism" of southern politics; indeed, Senators Sam Ervin and J. W. Fulbright were good examples of this impulse to resist grand schemes of political salvation.

Stoic fatalism was very much a part of Robert E. Lee's consciousness—as it was for William Alexander Percy. It accented resignation before the forces of fate and death, rather than a struggle with guilt and social responsibility. Percy's melancholy Stoicism led him to write his "Sideshow Gotterdammerung" in 1941 (*Lanterns on the Levee*): "A tarnish has fallen over the bright world . . . my own strong people are turned lotus-eaters: defeat is here again, the last, the most abhorrent."

The Stoic notion of "harmony" was often invoked during the civil rights struggle as a counter to the call for "justice." A deep and continuing conflict abides in the soul of the South between Stoic resignation to fate and death and Christian reconciliation to sin and guilt. The struggle is seen in the fiction of Walker Percy and Flannery O'Connor and is at its height in Faulkner's *Absalom, Absalom!* where Sutpen plays out his tragic role while "behind him Fate, destiny, retribution, irony—the stage manager—was already striking the set." Faulkner portrays the failure of the Stoic tradition in Sutpen. For Faulkner, the human problem is seen as guilt, and when things go wrong, the responsibility is humankind's.

In addition to the Stoic and Calvinist contributions to the sense of fatalism in the South, there is the compounding imprint of history. The Great Defeat, restrictive freight rates, punitive federal legislation, the caricatures portrayed through the media—all hung over the South like "a promissory note" in which everyone had to pay for his past and "fate or luck or chance, can foreclose on you without warning" (Faulkner, *Requiem for a Nun*).

The primary forces working in southern history to counter this sense of fatalism have been Christian affirmations of reconciling hope, liberal idealism that argued history could be bent in more humane and realizable directions, and, more recently, the forces of technological development and capital formation, which suggest the Sunbelt may be the land of fateful promise, rather than defeat and guilt.

See also HISTORY AND MANNERS: Stoicism

Robert L. Johnson
Cornell University

William Faulkner, *Absalom, Absalom!* (1936); John W. Hunt, *William Faulkner: Art in Theological Tension* (1965); William Alexander Percy, *Lanterns on the Levee* (1941). ☆

GRAHAM, BILLY

(b. 1918) Evangelist.

Born 7 November 1918 near Charlotte, N.C., William Franklin Graham, Jr., was the firstborn of a fundamentalist Presbyterian couple. His rise to national fame as an evangelist came during the prime of McCarthyism and the early fear of atomic warfare. Graham exploited these two sensations by proclaiming a brand of Christian Americanism that promised to give the United States victory over both internal subversion and external Soviet threat. He perceived the United States as the chosen nation after the order of ancient Israel, with himself as Jehovah's prophet to help save America from spiritual, military, and economic ruin. His favorite Old Testament personality was Daniel, a prophet involved with politicians and politics. Graham befriended presidents and saw himself as their spiritual advisor. He encouraged both Eisenhower and Nixon to run for office, and during the Nixon and Kennedy presidential campaign of 1960, he wrote a magazine article portraying Nixon as a Christian, moral leader. At the last minute, Graham withdrew the article from publication.

The Billy Graham Evangelistic Association represents one of the earliest phases of entrepreneurial religion of the modern South. Despite his rural, small-town upbringing, Graham quickly utilized the most advanced technology and organizational sophistication in transforming the Billy Graham Evangelistic Association into an efficient corporation for exporting southern fundamentalism. Paradoxically, long-range, this-worldly planning for this soul-winning corporation was mingled with the typically southern preoccupation with the apocalypse macabre. His 1983 book *Approaching Hoofbeats: The Four Horsemen of the Apocalypse* represents a throwback to southern revivalism's characteristic preoccupation with "prophecy," including sensational, if not obscene, scenarios of the fate of those outside the circle of the saved. Throughout his ministry Graham struggled to balance his lurid and explicit premillennial apocalyptic vision with his implicit postmillennial drive to transform the United States into a latter-day Christocracy.

In the early 1950s Graham and his fellow southerners in the organization were faced with a consistency crisis. Could they preach to integrated audiences north of the Mason-Dixon line and to segregated audiences in the South and Southwest? In 1953, a year before the U.S. Supreme Court struck its monumental blow against segregation, in *Brown* v. *Board of Education*, Graham had elected to preach only to integrated audiences in the South, beginning with the crusade to Chattanooga, a city made infamous by an earlier race riot. Graham chose, however, to make a weak witness against segregation, which he regarded as much less wicked than either sexual lust or failure to regard Jesus as the Messiah.

The seeds of the New Religious Right of the 1980s are found in Graham's early preaching. He denounced the Supreme Court for removing God from the public schools and called for an American "Christocracy." To date, no other Christian in the world has preached to more people than has Billy Graham. His 1982 trip to preach in the Soviet Union drew considerable fire and misinterpretation from both civil libertarians and funda-

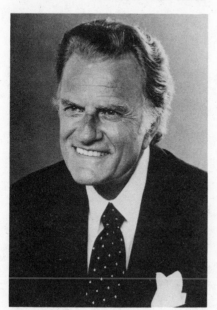

Billy Graham, the modern South's best-known evangelist, 1980s

mentalists. Captured by the vision of proclaiming his evangelical gospel inside the Soviet Union (where communism was the official religion), Graham took the risk of criticism, knowing in advance that he would be falsely accused of becoming a tool of Soviet propaganda regarding religious liberty there.

In the early 1980s Graham modified his premillennial apocalyptic views sufficiently to entertain plans of nuclear disarmament. Finally, despite the complexity of the Billy Graham Evangelistic Association, it has remained on the whole a model of financial integrity.

Joe E. Barnhart
North Texas State University

Joe E. Barnhart, *The Billy Graham Religion* (1972); Marshal Frady, *Billy Graham: A Parable of American Righteousness* (1979); John C. Pollock, *Billy Graham: The Authorized Biography* (1966). ☆

GREAT REVIVAL

The series of religious revivals that swept across the southern states between 1800 and 1805 is sometimes called the Second Great Awakening in the South. The movement was more accurately the South's first *great* awakening. It changed the religious landscape of the region, ensuring a Protestant evangelical dominance that continues today.

Small outbreaks of intense religious activity had occurred previously in the South, but these earlier small revivals had been confined to specific locales and to one denomination. Examples of these were the Presbyterian revival centered in Hanover County, Va., in the 1740s, the Separate Baptist revival beginning in North Carolina in 1755 and soon spreading to Virginia, and the Methodist awakening beginning in Virginia and North Carolina in the 1760s. These smaller awakenings slowly built up a popular evangelical belief system and a network of churches and ministers. Although these are prerequisites for a larger revival, a sense of cultural-religious crisis was required to weld the separate denominations together into common concern and action.

Westward migration in the late 1780s and 1790s, political controversies, and the worrisome news about the radical, deistic tendencies of the French Revolution contributed to a widespread perception of religious crisis in the 1790s. As clerics tried to understand their dilemma, they began to believe that it was a punishment sent by God for their preoccupation with wordly affairs. Recognition of this cause and a willingness to ask God for "deliverance" would, it was argued, end the religious "declension." Through such a religious defense the depressed clergy of the 1790s found reason to expect a miraculous recovery of religious vitality. This sense of expectancy led them to interpret an intensely emotional religious service led by James McGready in Logan County, Ky., in June 1800 as visible evidence that God was ushering in a new season of religious vitality, a second Pentecost. This feeling of heady optimism quickly spread across the South, facilitated by the adoption of camp meetings—huge, outdoor revivals.

In area after area church membership increased markedly, new churches were established, and many young male converts decided to enter the ministry as

thousands of laypersons either joined churches for the first time or revived their dormant faith. The resulting religious energy greatly strengthened the popular denominations (especially the Baptists and Methodists) and led to almost a complete dominance in the South by 1830 of evangelical Protestantism, a dominance that included blacks as well as whites.

John B. Boles
Rice University

John B. Boles, *The Great Revival, 1787–1805: The Origins of the Southern Evangelical Mind* (1972), in *Religion in the South*, ed. Charles Reagan Wilson (1985); Dickson D. Bruce, Jr., *And They All Sang Hallelujah: Plain-Folk Camp-Meeting Religion, 1800–1845* (1974). ☆

HAYS, BROOKS

(1898–1981) Politician and religious leader.

Brooks Hays personified, during his more than 50 years in public service, the Christian layman in politics. Born 9 August 1898 near Russellville, Ark., to Sallie Butler and Steele Hays, he graduated from the University of Arkansas (B.A. 1919) and George Washington University (LL.D. 1922). After serving in World War I, he married in 1922, the year he was admitted to the bar.

Hays was an assistant attorney general of Arkansas, twice an unsuccessful reform candidate for governor of that state and once for Congress, before he went to Washington as an attorney for the U.S. Department of Agriculture in 1935. A prominent member of the Southern Baptist Convention, he became an influential religious leader during his years as a member of Congress from Arkansas (1943–59). Washington, D.C., ministers chose him as their Layman of the Year in 1951, and he was later named Churchman of the Year by the Religious Heritage Foundation. He served on the Southern Baptist Christian Life Commission for 15 years and was its chairman in 1957 and 1958. He was president of the Southern Baptist Convention, 1957 through 1959.

His long-standing and widely publicized support of civil rights for southern blacks involved him in his congressional district's 1957 controversy over the integration of Little Rock Central High School. Attempting to moderate the passions on all sides, he was the victim of what was most likely an illegal write-in vote that stripped him of his seat in Congress at the height of the passionate battle in 1958.

The following year, as his prestige grew through what was considered a "political martyrdom," Hays became a director of the Tennessee Valley Authority. With the return of Democrats to the White House in 1961, he became special assistant to President Kennedy and then to President Johnson for "congressional relations, international relations, federal-state relations, and church-state relations." In this capacity he carried his appeal for Christian brotherhood throughout the nation and around the world from 1961 to 1964.

Between 1964 and 1974 Hays taught government at Rutgers and the University of Massachusetts, ran unsuccessfully for governor of Arkansas, directed the first Baptist Ecumenical Institute at North Carolina's Wake Forest University, and ran unsuccessfully for Congress from North Carolina. He died at his home in Chevy Chase, Md., 12 October 1981.

James T. Baker
Western Kentucky University

Brooks Hays, *A Hotbed of Tranquility* (1968), *Politics Is My Parish* (1981), *A Southern Moderate Speaks* (1959), *This World: A Christian's Workshop* (1958). ☆

KING, MARTIN LUTHER, JR.

See BLACK LIFE: King, Martin Luther, Jr.

MERTON, THOMAS

(1915–1968) Religious figure and writer.

Born in Prades, France, Thomas Merton was the son of Owen Merton, a painter from New Zealand, and Ruth Merton, an American. Thomas Merton settled in the United States in 1935 to attend Columbia University after a tumultuous youth on the Continent and in England where he had attended school after the death of his parents. Converted to the Roman Catholic church while at Columbia, Merton entered the Cistercian (Trappist) monastery at Gethsemani, Ky., in 1941. His spiritual autobiography *The Seven Storey Mountain* (1948) was an immense success. He soon followed this work with a torrent of books, essays, reviews, and articles on subjects that ranged from theology and spirituality to the history of monasticism, belles lettres, and social commentary. He died in 1968. His best known books include *Seeds of Contemplation* (1949), *The Sign of Jonas* (1952), *Conjectures of a Guilty Bystander* (1966), and *Zen and the Birds of Appetite* (1968). Two post-humous collections are important— *Collected Poems* (1977) and *The Literary Essays of Thomas Merton* (1981).

Merton rarely left his monastery home in Kentucky, but through his writings he became one of the most celebrated Roman Catholic writers of this century. Merton's connection with the South was more than geographical. He was a long-time contributor to the *Sewanee Review* and in the last year of his life edited a little magazine at Gethsemani called *Monk's Pond*. He published widely on the fiction of William Faulkner, Flannery O'Connor, and other southern writers. From his days at Columbia University, Merton had a keen interest in the race question, and, with his admiration for Gandhi, it is no surprise that he was a fervent admirer of Martin Luther King, Jr. In the early days of the civil rights movement, fueled partly by his reading of James Baldwin and his friendship with John Howard Griffin, he championed the movement to a then somewhat skeptical and hostile church public. This interest in racial justice and his long stand as a pacifist made him a natural ally of southern church people of a similar mind. He was a contributor to Will Campbell's *Katallagate*, and through Campbell's association came to know Walker Percy.

Merton lived his life in the comparative solitude of Kentucky's knob country, but his immense intelligence and compassion led him to both love and criticize his fellow southerners from the peculiar angle of the contemplative monk.

Lawrence S. Cunningham
Florida State University

Monica Furlong, *Merton: A Biography* (1980); Patrick Hart, ed., *Thomas Merton:* *Monk* (1974); Elena Malits, *The Solitary Explorer: Thomas Merton's Transforming Journey* (1980); Michael Mott, *The Seven Mountains of Thomas Merton* (1984); Paul Wilkes, ed., *Merton: By Those Who Knew Him Best* (1984). ☆

METHODIST EPISCOPAL CHURCH, SOUTH

Methodists first entered the South in the 1760s, and by the 1780s most American Methodists were concentrated there. The movement grew dramatically after the revivals of the early 1800s. The Methodist Episcopal Church, South, existed from 1845 until 1939, with most of its membership in the southern states, but with a few churches in the border states and in the West. The precipitating cause of its formation was the slave ownership of one of the bishops of the Methodist Episcopal Church, James O. Andrews, an involvement that led to the division of the church into predominantly northern and southern parts. The church enthusiastically supported the Confederacy, providing chaplains and missionaries and distributing Bibles and religious literature. Methodist leaders such as Atticus G. Haygood later became advocates of a New South.

The Methodist Episcopal Church, South, whose membership was almost 3 million in 1939, reflected a distinctive kind of Methodism. It accepted the Methodist quadrilateral of the Bible, but tended to emphasize the Bible and religious experience more than its northern counterpart. Both branches of Methodism were led by bishops; but, following the southern paternalistic tradition, southern Methodists gave their bishops virtually unlimited power, so that the 58 men who filled the episcopal chairs dominated the life of the southern church, appointing the preachers, presiding over various conferences, and serving as leaders of most of the important boards and agencies.

Southern Methodists limited the mission of the church to the saving of souls, steering clear of most social issues. Bishop James Cannon, Jr., however, led many Methodists in support of Prohibition. Entering vigorously into missionary work in Africa, Latin America, and the Far East, they confined their work in these areas, as at home, to evangelism, education, and medical care. A notable exception to this understanding of the mission of the church was the women's home and foreign missionary movement, which, catching a vision of a social gospel, worked to improve the lot of blacks, immigrants, and women and sought to secure world peace.

In many ways, the southern church lagged behind the northern branch of Methodism, not establishing a theological seminary until the 1870s, more than 30 years after northern Methodists had taken the same step, and not admitting women to the General Conference until the 1920s, 20 years after this had been done in the North. Southern Methodists were busy, like northern Methodists, maintaining schools, colleges, and universities, but the southern institutions often lacked both support and academic distinction and generally served as bastions of the white southern way of life. The church established Vanderbilt University in 1873 but withdrew support in 1914. Southern Methodist, Emory, and Duke became prominent Methodist universities.

Having begun its existence with a large number of black members, the Methodist Episcopal Church, South, after the Civil War, pushed most of these free blacks into their own ecclesiastical organization and became an institition devoted primarily to the welfare of white southerners.

Thus, the Methodist Episcopal Church, South, represented an almost perfect example of Richard Niebuhr's "Christ of Culture" Christianity—usually not just following its proclaimed

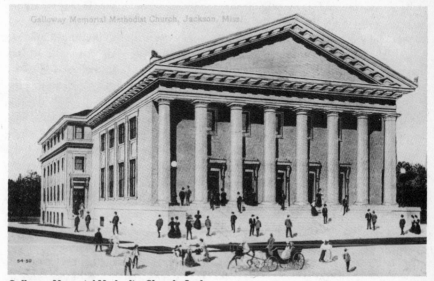

Galloway Memorial Methodist Church, Jackson, Mississippi, postcard, early 20th century

Lord, Jesus Christ, but taking its values from the white South that had helped create it and that it in turn sustained.

See also EDUCATION: / Emory University; Duke University; Vanderbilt University

F. Joseph Mitchell
Troy State University

John Patrick McDowell, *The Social Gospel in the South: The Woman's Home Mission Movement in the Methodist Episcopal Church, South, 1886–1939* (1982); Frederick A. Norwood, *The Story of American Methodism: A History of the United Methodists and Their Relations* (1974). ☆

MOON, CHARLOTTE DIGGES "LOTTIE"

(1840–1912) Southern Baptist missionary.

For four decades Lottie Moon was a pioneer China missionary of the Southern Baptist Convention (SBC). Her life is skillfully celebrated by denominational literature, which declares her the most famous individual in Southern Baptist history, as well as the human symbol of her church's ongoing commitment to overseas missionary work.

Growing up on a plantation near Charlottesville, Va., Lottie Moon developed marked interests in religion and in the study of foreign languages and cultures. Following the Civil War she taught school in Kentucky and Georgia until 1873, when deepening spiritual concerns led her to enter missionary service. From that point until her death 40 years later Moon worked as an evangelist and teacher at Tengchow and at other Southern Baptist stations in Shantung province, northeast China. In ad-

dition to demonstrating compassion for the Chinese and skill in adapting to their culture, she displayed considerable courage and professional resourcefulness. All these qualities were particularly evident in her life during the late 1880s at P'ingtu, an isolated city in the Shantung interior. Working alone under difficult circumstances, Moon initiated at P'ingtu a successful mission at a time when Baptist efforts in north China were otherwise near collapse.

Moon's unique reputation among Southern Baptists, however, is a product chiefly of the Lottie Moon Christmas Offering for Foreign Missions. Inspired by an 1888 effort to raise money in the United States to help her work at P'ingtu, the Christmas Offering became a churchwide institution and in 1918 was named specifically for her. An extensive promotional literature has developed, idealizing Moon in books, poems, pamphlets, motion pictures and film strips, portraits, photo albums, tape cassettes, dramatic scripts, greeting cards, and even a Lottie Moon Cookbook. The Christmas Offering, with a 1984 goal of $66,000,000, currently accounts for about half the annual funding of the SBC's Foreign Mission Board and is indispensable to American Protestantism's largest foreign missionary program.

Any explanation of Lottie Moon's stature among Southern Baptists is inevitably subjective and arguable. Her story as promoted by the SBC, however, contains at least two themes interesting in terms of southern culture. One is the traditional theme that W. J. Cash called southern gyneolatry or the "pitiful Mother of God" image, centering on white women of intelligence, courage, and high capacity for self-sacrifice. The other theme, also strongly present, is of

Lottie Moon as an undeclared feminist—single, self-reliant, wiser and stronger than male associates, pushing in "her own way" (the title of one of her SBC biographies) to advance the Kingdom of God and the status of women both in China and within the Southern Baptist Convention. Rather than being mutually exclusive, these contrasting themes seem instead significantly to have extended Lottie Moon's symbolic range and enduring influence.

Irwin T. Hyatt, Jr.
Emory University

Catherine B. Allen, *The New Lottie Moon Story* (1980); Irwin T. Hyatt, Jr., *Our Ordered Lives Confess: Three Nineteenth Century American Missionaries in East Shantung* (1976); Una Roberts Lawrence, *Lottie Moon* (1927). ☆

MORAL MAJORITY

Moral Majority is an educational, lobbying, and fund-raising organization dedicated to conservative Christian causes. Founded in 1979 with the assistance of "New Right" leaders, the Moral Majority has been led by Jerry Falwell, pastor of the 18,000-member Thomas Road Baptist Church in Lynchburg, Va.

Nationally, Moral Majority maintains a legislative office near the Capitol in Washington, D.C., monitors legislation, issues regular appeals to its members for political action through letter-writing, lobbies Congress on behalf of specific legislation, and publishes the *Moral Majority Report*, a small monthly newspaper. Legally, Moral Majority is comprised of three separate organizations: Moral Majority, a lobby; the Moral Majority Foundation, an educational foundation; the Moral Majority Legal Defense Foundation, an organization offering legal assistance and funds to various conservative religious groups such as Christian schools that regularly do battle with secular authorities.

Moral Majority operated a "Political Action Committee" during the 1980 national campaign but abandoned it after spending only $20,000. The national organization is loosely replicated at state and local levels by Moral Majority chapters variously centered in election districts, counties, or major population centers. Lobbying, publication of voting records and newsletters, and organized action are also undertaken at the local level. The national Moral Majority has been active in establishing local chapters and in training their leaders, often by sponsoring regional training programs in conjunction with The Committee for the Survival of a Free Congress. Voter registration, involving participation of local churches, has also been a major concern at all levels.

Although the basic source of support for Moral Majority has been from independent fundamentalist churches, often Baptist, the organization sees its agenda as moral, not religious. It welcomes and cooperates with all who share its views regardless of their religious orientation. Moral Majority seeks to "return the nation to moral sanity," to revitalize those values "which made America great." It opposes abortion, homosexuality, pornography, the exclusive teaching of evolution, feminism, the welfare state, and secularism in general. Issues supported include prayer in public schools, state support for private (particularly religious) education, recognition of parents' and churches' rights to educate children without outside interference, a strong national defense coupled with an aggressively anticommunist foreign policy, and a laissez-faire capitalism at home that subordinates itself to the national interest abroad.

Geographically, Moral Majority has drawn its major support from the South and Midwest and its most effective leadership from the South. It represents a "going public" and an attainment of national influence on the part of southern religion. Moral Majority's political activism constitutes a significant revision of the traditionally separatist and nonworldly tendencies of its supporting churches, but not necessarily a reversal or a sharp break. Moral Majority perpetuates a southern Protestant tradition of selective social activism on a narrow range of issues centered upon personal morality. In so doing, it reflects fundamentalism's holiness roots and the conviction that social well-being is born of individual purity. The call for national repentance as a cure for impending disaster (God's rejection of America) coupled with its Manichaean sense of rigid good and evil in all matters, religious, social, or political, reflects a tradition of revivalism that has moved its converts from total depravity to thorough regeneration.

Moral Majority represents a wedding of fundamentalist religion with a "chosen people" style of civil religion, which represents a major tie between religion and mythology in the region. It is convinced that America's success as a nation depends upon its people rendering obedience to God's law as understood in a fundamentalist reading of the Bible. Moral Majority supporters regard themselves as a saving remnant, calling the nation back to faithfulness, to its covenant with the biblical God who, although once so near to rightfully

forsaking America, awaited a sign of repentance that would again allow him to bless that bastion of true religion and return it to its rightful, dominant place in world affairs.

Jerry Falwell's two books, *How You Can Help Clean Up America* (1978) and *Listen, America!* (1980), give a summary of the Moral Majority's aims and its "action programs for decency" in the nation.

Dennis E. Owen
University of Florida

Gabriel Fackre, *The Religious Right and the Christian Faith* (1982); Samuel S. Hill and Dennis E. Owen, *The New Religious Political Right in America* (1982); Peggy Shriver, *The Bible Vote: Religion and the New Right* (1981). ☆

MORAVIANS

The Moravians are a Protestant religious group, known also as the *Unitas Fratrum*, that was founded in the 15th century by followers of John Hus, a Bohemian reformer and martyr. The movement spread to America, and today the headquarters of the Southern Province of the Moravian Church in America are located in Winston-Salem, N.C. Although not representative of predominant southern religious evangelicalism, the Moravians have contributed a distinctive history and aesthetic tradition to the South's culture.

To serve as missionaries to the Indians, as well as to escape German intolerance of their beliefs, a small group of Moravians left Europe and settled in Georgia in 1735. Their settlement was brief, for in 1740, when pressured to fight the Spanish, they moved to Pennsylvania. After the church purchased a

98,985-acre tract of land in the Piedmont of North Carolina, members of the sect again traveled to the South to settle. They called the tract *Wachau* (Wachovia) and settled the villages of Bethabara (1753) and Bethania (1759) before founding, in 1766, Salem, the town that became the governmental and economic center of the settlement.

The ambitious settlers established in a wilderness a carefully planned, organized community—a theocracy, in which the church was the governing body and their religion a way of life. To ensure the survival of the community and its ideals, the church kept strict control during those early years. Residents did not buy land but leased it from the church, until the lease system was abolished in 1856. Church members were divided according to age, gender, and marital status into choirs, each group having its own officers, living quarters, and burial sites in the congregation cemetery. Trade competition was restricted in favor of a system of monopolies so that each member had opportunity to earn a living.

As a self-sufficient commercial center, Salem, along with the smaller Moravian communities, had skilled craftsmen, trained doctors, fine musicians, and dedicated schoolteachers. The Moravians stressed education and their female academy at Salem, opened to non-Moravians in 1802, quickly gained prominence and operates today as Salem Academy and College. Moravian aesthetic tastes became well known, too, as Moravian craftsmen often produced distinctive work that dominated their cultural region. Fine pottery, needlework, furniture, paintings, metal work, and architecture remain as evidence of their talents.

Believing that they should, in all endeavors, serve the Lord, early Moravians worked and lived to that end, and in the process they made significant contributions to the ethnic, material, and religious culture of the South. Their unique music is central to church programs, love feasts, and Easter sunrise services that are celebrated by Moravians and non-Moravians alike. The rigid structure of the early Moravian communities dissolved years ago but the church remains active and dedicated to its missionary efforts.

Jessica Foy
Cooperstown Graduate Programs
Cooperstown, New York

John Bivins and Paula Welshimer, *Moravian Decorative Arts in North Carolina* (1981); Adelaide Fries, K. G. Hamilton, D. L. Rights, M. J. Smith, eds., *The Records of the Moravians in North Carolina*, 11 vols. (1922–69); Kenneth G. Hamilton, *North Carolina Historical Review* (April 1967); Samuel S. Hill, ed., *Religion in the Southern States* (1983). ☆

NATIONAL BAPTISTS

The National Baptist Convention, U.S.A., Inc., the unincorporated National Baptist Convention, U.S.A., and the Progressive National Baptist Convention have a combined membership of 12 million people in over 50,000 congregations and together form a historic tradition that has dominated southern black Baptist life since the late 19th century. Black Baptists had worshiped in independent congregations and as part of biracial churches before the Civil War, but emancipation quickly brought the establishment of separate black denominations.

From 1865 to 1895 black Baptists worked to achieve a separate religious identity. The Consolidated American Baptist Missionary Convention tried unsuccessfully to unify black Baptists, but it collapsed from internal social divisions in 1879. Black unity received a boost in 1895 with the formation in Atlanta of the National Baptist Convention, U.S.A. The year 1915 brought division, however, as a dispute over control of the National Baptists' publishing house led to the withdrawal of supporters of Robert H. Boyd, the corresponding secretary of the publication board, and establishment of the unincorporated National Baptist Convention, U.S.A. The Progressive National Baptist Convention, Inc., led by L. Venchael Booth, split off from the "incorporated" National Baptists in 1961 as the result of a controversy concerning the process of electing church leaders.

Black Baptist churches represent a vital social, as well as religious, force in the South. The mainstream has been dominated by the ideals of, in James M. Washington's typology, "bourgeois black Baptists." The middle-class ethos of the mainstream has been supplemented by "prophetic black Baptists" who have sought progressive political change. "Black Baptist folk culture" is still a third representation of the faith, stressing the distinctive use of music, prayers, oral testifying, and African rhythms in worship.

Charles Reagan Wilson
University of Mississippi

William D. Booth, *The Progressive Story: New Baptist Roots* (1981); Joseph H. Jackson, *A Story of Christian Activism: The History of the National Baptist Convention, U.S.A., Inc.* (1980); Owen D. Pelt and Ralph Lee Smith, *The Story of the National Baptists*

(1960); James M. Washington, *Frustrated Fellowship: The Black Baptist Quest for Social Power* (1986). ☆

O'CONNOR AND RELIGION

Flannery O'Connor's contribution to the literature of the English-speaking world is widely known. Equally important is her contribution to the knowledge of religion in the South and to contemporary understanding of the Christian faith grounded in southern experience. As a native of Georgia, she knew intimately the dominant Protestant faith of the area and was especially fascinated by the untutored practices and convictions of backwoods religious folk. She often found their religious convictions skewed and desperate and their practice crude; yet she found among them, by her own accounting, a surprising pattern of true Christianity that encompassed the pattern of her own Catholic faith. A Hazel Motes (*Wise Blood*) and a Tarwater (*The Violent Bear It Away*) are eccentric, but through their rough circuitous route they find and claim the Christian God missed by countless reasonable and progressive people.

At an artistic level, O'Connor investigates the concrete, regional scene (a possessed evangelist, a manipulative grandmother, a Bible salesman) in order to touch a deeper, wider reality. The plot of each story therefore climactically focuses on some revealing action or gesture (a blinding of oneself, a reaching out toward one's killer, the theft of an artificial limb) that penetrates the essentials of character and circumstance.

The religious level of her work follows readily upon the artistic because of her sensitivity to the region: "While the South is hardly Christ-centered, it is most certainly Christ-haunted," she stated in a 1960 lecture. Yet a theologically discerning southern writer can disclose, through Christ-haunted chaos, moments that *are* surprisingly Christ-centered. True revelation occurs even amid distortion. The result is pointedly ecumenical: the author's Catholic doctrine comes alive in the actions of back-country Protestants. Her stories are thereby full of irony and humor, the ultimate comedy of the one true God, who uses outlandish servants in order to reveal himself. As Christian evangel, O'Connor therefore jolts her readers with cultural and Christian reality, sharply distinguished in her work from the conventional and benign Christianity of custom.

See also LITERATURE: / O'Connor, Flannery

William Mallard
Emory University

Robert Bain, Joseph M. Flora, and Louis D. Rubin, Jr., eds., *Southern Writers: A Biographical Dictionary* (1979); Jeffrey Helterman and Richard Layman, eds., *Dictionary of Literary Biography*, vol. 2 (1978); Linn Mainiero and Langdon L. Faust, eds., *American Women Writers: A Critical Reference Guide* (1982). ☆

PRESBYTERIAN CHURCH IN THE UNITED STATES (PCUS)

Initially known as the Presbyterian Church in the Confederate States of America (PCCSA), the denomination originated as a result of the Civil War. It was organized at Augusta, Ga., in 1861, and it remained separated from the Presbyterian Church in the United States of America (PCUSA)—until 1983 when it reunited with the parent body, which had become the United Presbyterian Church in the United States of America (UPCUSA). The PCUS thus no longer has a separate existence, but it was an institutional embodiment of a distinctly regional religious identity. The PCCSA supported slavery and secession, and it continued to exist after the war because of southern concern about an unbiblical and unnatural involvement in political life by the PCUSA, a concern aggravated by the bitterness of the war and Reconstruction. The PCUS established itself in border states, the Southeast, and Texas.

Theologically, the PCUS affirmed with Protestant Christians the belief that the Bible of the Old and New Testaments is the only "rule of faith and practice," and it endorsed the trinitarian and christological decrees of the early Christian councils. In addition the denomination adopted and its officials subscribed to the *Westminster Confession of Faith* (1646) and the Larger and Shorter Catechisms of the 17th century as subordinate standards to the Scriptures. Nineteenth-century theologians James Henley Thornwell (1812–62) and Robert Lewis Dabney (1820–98) shaped a southern Presbyterian mind, and James Woodrow (1828–1907), although disciplined by the denomination, nevertheless helped the South adjust to the evolution hypothesis. Church historian Ernest Trice Thompson (1894–1985) and biblical critic John Bright (b. 1908) led the denomination in facing recent intellectual ferment. Some leaders attempted to modify the theological stand in recent years, with the writing of "A Declaration of Faith." This attempt was defeated by the presbyteries of the church, but the "Declaration" was widely used throughout the church.

Presbyterians believe themselves part of the "one holy catholic and apostolic church." Structurally, however, the PCUS is presbyterian, governed by a representative system with a graded court structure, provisions for the form and discipline of which are found in the *Book of Church Order*. Congregations elect pastors, in cooperation with the presbytery, and also elders and deacons, all ordained in the name of the Trinity by the laying on of hands. Pastors are ordained to the ministry of word and sacrament; elders, to assist in governance; and deacons, to assist in service. Congregations form presbyteries of pastors and elders, and presbyteries are organized in synods and a General Assembly. At first the PCUS controlled its various programs through committees of the various courts and then in 1949 organized education and publishing, domestic and foreign missions, and the pension system under boards. Pastors Stuart Robinson (1814–81), Benjamin M. Palmer (1818–1902), and Moses Drury Hoge (1818–99) and laymen John J. Eagan (1870–1924) and Francis Pickens Miller (1895–1978) gave unusual leadership to the church. Since 1963 women have been ordained to all the offices of the church. Rachel Henderlite (b. 1905) was the first woman ordained.

Liturgically, members of the PCUS have used the *Directory of Worship* of the Westminster Assembly, modified through the centuries, which provided a guide for the public and family worship of God. They have been suspicious of fixed forms, a suspicion reinforced by the revivalist spirit prevalent in the South. They have placed an emphasis on worship (biblically sound, simple, intelligible, and spiritually satisfying) with a focus on reading and interpreting the Bible and the administration of the two sacraments—baptism of children and adults in the name of the Trinity and by sprinkling—and the Lord's Supper, celebrated at least four times a year, and recently, more often. In 1932 the PCUS followed the PCUSA in allowing the "voluntary use" of the *Book of Common Worship* (adopted by the PCUSA in 1903), a collection of services and prayer designed to enrich the worship of congregations. Although Presbyterians were at first Psalms singers only, throughout the years they have broadened their use of hymns of "human composure." *The Hymnbook* (1955) is now the most widely used hymnal.

From the beginning the PCUS engaged in the support of education, missions, domestic and foreign, and also showed its social concerns. Four seminaries (Union, Richmond, Va., 1812; Columbia, Decatur, Ga., 1828; Louisville, 1901; Austin, 1902), numerous liberal arts colleges (such as Hampden-Sydney, 1776, Davidson, 1836, Stillman, 1876, and Agnes Scott, 1889, and the Presbyterian School of Christian Education, 1914) serve the church, as do the *Presbyterian Survey* (1911) and the John Knox Press. Presbyterians adopted the Sunday school movement, and in 1963 experimented with a graded Covenant Life Curriculum in cooperation with other denominations and under the leadership of educator Lewis Sherrill (1882–1957). Since the Civil War the PCUS has developed mission work among blacks and Indians, and mission fields in China, Japan, Korea, Colombia, Brazil, Mexico, Africa, Greece, and Italy. Although the denomination thought it had a special mission to preserve the "spirituality" of the church, with the prodding of such persons as Walter L. Lingle (1868–1956), president of Davidson College, and E. T. Thompson, Presbyterians have taken more responsibility for dealing with social, racial, economic, and international problems. A Committee on Moral and Social Welfare was organized in 1934 to care for the moral nurture of Christians and in various forms and ways has continued its mission.

Although at first not ecumenically inclined, gradually the PCUS emerged from its regionalism to participate in the World Alliance of Reformed Churches (1876–77), the Federal Council of Churches (1912), the National Council of Churches (1950), and the World Council of Churches (1948). In 1982 before the reunion with the UPCUSA, the PCUS embraced in its constituency 821,008 communicant members, 4,250 churches, and 6,077 ministers.

James H. Smylie
Union Theological Seminary
in Virginia

A Digest of the Acts and Proceedings of the General Assembly of the Presbyterian Church in the United States, 1861–1965 (1966); Ernest Trice Thompson, *Presbyterians in the South,* 3 vols. (1963–73). ☆

PROHIBITION

Although closely identified with the southern ethos in the 20th century, the movement to limit the sale and use of alcoholic beverages has never been an exclusively southern endeavor. The areas first touched by this effort were in the East and Midwest in the antebellum period. Prohibition, as an ideal, originated in the voluntarism of the early temperance movement. After the Civil War more advocates adopted the policy of abstinence, or "teetotalism," and followed the legislative example of the state of Maine. Such groups as the Woman's Christian Temperance Union and the Anti-Saloon League of America organized for the fight.

In the first decade of this century dry sentiment gained momentum in the South as Georgia enacted statewide prohibition. By 1910 over two-thirds of southern counties were dry. Nationally, the economic exigencies of World War I combined with the denouement of Progressivism to bring about passage of the Eighteenth Amendment and the start of the Prohibition period (1920–33), during which the manufacture and sale of alcoholic beverages were forbidden.

Various interpretations have been offered for this monumental struggle against liquor. Until the early 1970s liberal historiography scorned prohibitionists in general, and the southern variety in particular, as misguided provincials who eschewed genuine reform, advocating prohibition instead, as a panacea for their fears about a changing America.

Recent scholarship has been more sympathetic to the prohibitionist cause, finding a greater degree of diversity among its adherents. For example, not all members of the liturgical churches opposed prohibition. Patrick Henry Callahan, a leading southern Catholic layman, actively supported prohibition. Moreover, studies of individual psychological crises of the late 19th and early 20th centuries indicate that alcohol abuse did, indeed, cause severe economic and social distress. Alcoholism particularly attacked the prevalent middle-class ideal of family autonomy. In effect, the methods now used to study the drug subculture are being applied to alcoholism, past and present.

The presidential election of 1928 solidified the southern consensus favoring prohibition. Many southerners voted against Al Smith because of his lack of support for prohibition, though their votes were read as anti-Catholic. After the repeal of national prohibition in 1933, the South became the bastion of dry support in the nation. While Mississippi opted for statewide prohibition, other southern states adopted some form of local option and allowed municipalities and counties, even precincts, to decide the issue. Will Rogers once commented that "southerners will vote dry as long as they can stagger to the polls." Into the present decade, more southerners live in areas of strict alcohol control than any other region of the United States.

Consequently, the bootlegger and moonshiner have continued to ply their trades, often with the full cooperation of local authorities. Most southern communities have legends about the classic confrontations between moonshiner and revenue agent.

With the development of the Sunbelt South and urbanization, legalization of liquor without restriction has become more common. However, conservative and fundamentalist Christian groups oppose such change in southern mores and often still muster enough votes to win local wet-dry elections.

See also INDUSTRY: / Liquor Industry; SCIENCE AND MEDICINE: Alcohol and Alcoholism

William E. Ellis
Eastern Kentucky University

Paul A. Carter, *Another Part of the Twenties* (1977); Norman H. Clark, *Deliver Us from Evil: An Interpretation of American Prohibition* (1976); James H. Timberlake, *Prohibition and the Progressive Movement, 1900–1920* (1963). ☆

PROTESTANT EPISCOPAL CHURCH

The earliest English settlers at Jamestown brought their Anglican religion with them. With the American Revolution, though, the Church of England became the Episcopal church and lost its position as the established church of the South. The recovery of the Episcopal church in the South from its near extinction after the Revolution was brought about through the work of strong leaders, many of them southerners, such as Richard Channing Moore, the second biship of Virginia, who was a New Yorker, and the second and third bishops of South Carolina, Theodore Dehon and Nathanial Bowen, who were New Englanders. Stark Ravenscroft, the first bishop of North Carolina, was born in Virginia but educated in Scotland and England.

The degree to which Episcopalians in the South felt isolated from their northern brethren by cultural factors before the late 1830s is difficult to discern. The American Colonization Society, whose aim was to colonize parts of West Africa with freed black slaves, received active support from such Episcopalians as William Meade, later third bishop of Virginia. The existence of slavery was recognized as a factor of southern culture that the church, per se, was unable to eliminate. The church thus aimed to convert blacks and to influence owners and other whites to treat slaves humanely.

Many southern Episcopalians sent their sons to eastern colleges in the antebellum era but became irritated about the prevalence of antislavery sentiments there. This strengthened the felt need for a first-class collegiate institution under the control of the Episcopal church. Leonidas Polk, bishop of Louisiana, took the lead in promoting the founding of such a college. The site chosen was on Sewanee Mountain in Tennessee, and the name chosen was the "University of the South." Some temporary buildings were erected and the cornerstone of the proposed main building was laid just before the outbreak of the Civil War, which brought all activity to a close.

St. Mark's Episcopal Church, Mississippi City, Mississippi, postcard, early 20th century

Southern Episcopalians were not of one mind regarding secession. Polk so strongly supported secession that he accepted a commission as a Confederate general. Bishop Nicholas H. Cobbs of Alabama was strongly opposed, as was Bishop James Hervey Otey of Tennessee, the first chancellor of the university. Some of the clergy strongly opposed to secession left the South, but others stayed. The Protestant Episcopal Church in the Confederate States was organized after the outbreak of hostilities on the principle that the church follows nationality. No desire was expressed to end relations with the church in the North. There was little friction between the churches, and after the surrender of the Confederate forces the church in the South resumed affiliation with the church in the North, beginning with the appearance of southern representatives at the General Convention of 1865. There were problems encountered in this reunion, but resolutions condemning the actions of

southern Episcopalians were defeated and the fellowship of the church was restored. Sewanee was revived and became an important resource for the southern dioceses.

One of the urgent problems of the Episcopal church in the postbellum South was the situation of its black membership. After Emancipation, many blacks left the church. The need for clergy of their own race was acute. Undergraduate study was afforded in several schools supported by the church's Freedman's Commission, including St. Augustine College, St. Paul's Industrial School, and Voorhees College. In Virginia the Bishop Payne Divinity School was established at Petersburg and for many years provided theological instruction to black candidates. The commission later became the American Church Institute for Negroes and gained backing nationwide. Separate convocations for the black churches were established under the jurisdiction of the diocesan bishop, and the creation of a racial episcopate was proposed but rejected by General Convention several times.

Several dioceses founded missions in

outlying areas, attracting children of working-class families lacking transportation to the mother church. Galveston, Dallas, San Antonio, and Houston in Texas furnish examples of such missions. Growing numbers of churches demanded more supervision than bishops of the older dioceses could give, so new jurisdictions were created. The Eastern Shore of Maryland was the first, in 1868; Northern Texas and Western Texas were set apart as missionary jurisdictions in 1874. Later divisions had added 11 new jurisdictions in the South by 1900. In 1985 there were 22 more dioceses in the South than there were in 1865. Along with multiplication of dioceses came increasing differences in social, cultural, theological, and ritualistic emphases, and a diminution of consultation and agreement about them. Migrants from the great urban centers of the North and East have diluted the southern mindset, so that the sense of southern identity in the southern Episcopal church has been muted.

Lawrence L. Brown
Episcopal Theological Seminary
of the Southwest

Lawrence L. Brown, *Historical Magazine of the Protestant Episcopal Church* (March 1966); Arthur Benjamin Chitty, *Reconstruction at Sewanee: The Founding of the University of the South and Its First Administration, 1857–1872* (1954); William Wilson Manross, *A History of the American Episcopal Church* (1935); Joseph H. Parks, *General Leonidas Polk, C.S.A.: The Fighting Bishop* (1962); Charles S. Sydnor, *The Development of Southern Sectionalism, 1819–1848* (1948). ☆

ROBERTS, ORAL

(b. 1918) Evangelist.

Born 24 January 1918 in Pontotoc County, Okla., Granville Oral Roberts was the fifth child of Ellis and Claudius Roberts. His father was a minister in the Pentecostal Holiness church, one of the small Pentecostal sects born in the early 20th century. Like many Pentecostal youngsters, Roberts rebelled against the restraints of his religious upbringing, but a series of crises in his life in 1935, culminating in what he believed was a divine healing from a severe case of tuberculosis, led him to decide to become a minister in the Pentecostal Holiness church.

Roberts served his denomination for 12 years both as a pastor and as an itinerant revivalist. In 1938 he married Evelyn Lutman; they had four children, Rebecca Ann, Ronald David, Richard Lee, and Roberta Jean. Roberts was extremely successful as a young preacher, but he nonetheless chafed under the restraints of denominational control and the poverty and social disrepute he shared with other Pentecostal ministers.

In 1947 Roberts made the bold decision to begin an independent healing ministry. A part of a larger revival that brought fame and fortune to numerous other Pentecostal preachers after World War II, he became the ablest and most successful of the tent revivalists who for two decades preached divine healing throughout the country. Roberts became the preeminent spokesman for the Pentecostal message—the availability of God's miracle-working power and a renewed emphasis on the gifts of the Holy Spirit. In 1954 he took this message on television and greatly expanded his national visibility.

The importance of Oral Roberts rests

largely on the skill with which he expanded and preserved his ministry when interest in healing revivalism began to wane in the 1960s. In 1965 he opened Oral Roberts University in Tulsa; in 1968 he joined the Methodist church and the following year he returned to television in a modern entertainment format, which had a lasting impact on religious programming. In 1975 Roberts announced the addition of a number of graduate programs at his university, including a medical school, and in 1978 began the construction of a huge hospital and medical research center called the City of Faith. In the mid-1980s the value of the Roberts empire in Tulsa—increasingly managed by Richard Roberts, his son—approached a billion dollars.

While Oral Roberts constantly changed his methods, he insisted that his central call from God, to bring healing to his generation, had remained constant throughout his life. Roberts's grandiose plans, his controversial fund-

Oral Roberts, Pentecostal and Methodist minister, 1980s

raising techniques, and his claims of direct divine guidance made him the subject of much attention and criticism in the press. He is, however, probably the most widely known and respected figure in the burgeoning charismatic revival of the late 20th century.

David Harrell
University of Alabama
at Birmingham

David Harrell, *All Things Are Possible: The Healing and Charismatic Revivals in Modern America* (1976), *Oral Roberts: An American Life* (1985); Oral Roberts, *The Call* (1971). ☆

SACRED PLACES

Does the religious life of the South, centering in evangelical Protestantism, really acknowledge specific sites to which some kind of sacred significance is attached? Not so, of course, if the question assumes a classic Catholic frame of reference. In several other respects, however, it does. In the South, the dominance of center to left-wing Protestantism dictates the particular terms on which certain places are recognized as very special, even sacred.

Four sets of terms exist. The first is places where denominations had their American start, or where momentous events have occurred in their history. The second is locales where indigenous denominations or movements originated. The third is religious "capital cities," that is, headquarters of denominations or clusters of religious institutions. The fourth is major conference or retreat centers. There are many other notable places in the image-life and actual practice of the southern faithful, not least among them churches, rural and urban, to which people return for annual homecomings, and the cemeteries that sometimes adjoin them.

(1) Jamestown, Va., is a notable place to Episcopalians, because of the Church of England's placement there in 1607; Sewanee, Tenn., home of the University of the South, is its modern "capital." Similarly, Bardstown, Ky., for Roman Catholics reflects on their forebears' settlement in the West, and of course St. Augustine, Fla., dates back to 1565. Methodists point with pride to Lovely Lane Chapel in Baltimore, where their church in the United States was officially launched in 1784, and to Frederica and Savannah in Georgia, the initial stopping point for John Wesley in the colonial South. Several groups claim Savannah and Charleston, including Jews who established early settlements in both places, Unitarians in the latter case, and black Catholics in the former. Black Baptists revere Silver Bluff Church near Augusta, the first black church in North America, founded around 1773, and Gillfield Church in Petersburg, Va., which dates to the 18th century and was notable for controlling its internal affairs throughout the slavery era.

(2) The Campbellite Tradition (Disciples of Christ, Churches of Christ), which is a part of Restorationist Christianity, celebrates Bethany, W. Va., and Cane Ridge near Paris, Ky., cooriginating places for that movement. Pentecostalists, a rather diverse family, all take pleasure in memories of Dunn, N.C., Franklin Springs, Ga., and Hot Springs, Ark.

(3) Nashville outranks all other religious "capital cities." Baptists and Methodists have major installations there, especially in the publishing industry. Probably more church people visit Nashville than any other sacred place. Springfield, Mo., in the border South, is a headquarters for Fundamentalist Baptists and Pentecostalists.

(4) In western North Carolina, Presbyterians summer at Montreat, Methodists confer at Lake Junaluska, and Southern Baptists throng to Ridgecrest. Most denominations sponsor regional and state conference and retreat centers across the region.

Pilgrimages, shrines, and holy places as such are not part of southern evangelicalism's outlook. The general religious climate does not provoke their creation or acknowledgement. Yet in ways that accord with the culture, the South has its share of "sacred places."

Samuel S. Hill
University of Florida

Samuel S. Hill, ed., *Encyclopedia of Religion in the South* (1984). ☆

SHAKERS

The people who took the name of United Society of Believers in Christ's Second Appearing began as a dissenting group among English Quakers. Mother Ann Lee and her followers came to America and founded a settlement in New York in 1774. The Shakers—short for "shaking Quakers"—received their name from the spiritually ecstatic, frenetic whirling and dancing of their religious meetings. They founded the agricultural community of Pleasant Hill in the bluegrass country of Kentucky in 1805 and the South Union community soon after near the Tennessee border with Kentucky. Shaker settlements believed in equality among blacks and whites, women and men; cooperative living; celibacy; nonviolence; and simplicity in living. They depended for continuity on recruiting new members and on raising orphans who one day would become adult members of the group. Members lived in groups of 30 to 100 people called families, each with its own residence, barns, workshops, and industries.

The Shaker communities were the most successful utopian settlements of the antebellum South. They ran well-operated farms. Pleasant Hill pioneered in establishing nurseries and orchards in Kentucky, new crops, the silk industry, experimentation with new seed varieties, and the importation of new breeds of sheep and hogs. They were inventive and not afraid of new technology. They made distinctive pottery, quilts, rugs, bonnets, silk scarves, brooms, cedar pails, and churns. They were noted for an aesthetic tradition favoring simplicity and functionality in design. Shaker furniture was of clean, wooden construction. Northeastern Shakers used pine, but those in Kentucky primarily worked with cherry, walnut, and, to a lesser degree, oak. Architecture stressed solid buildings, of brick and stone, with little embellishment and arranged in symmetrical patterns. Shaker music was an important part of their culture. Hymns were passed along from member to member by letter until the first hymnal appeared in 1813.

The Shaker communities of the South suffered physical and financial damage during the Civil War, as these pacifists cared for both Union and Confederate soldiers. After the war their decline continued, as the Shakers were increasingly unable to recruit new members. Pleas-ant Hill closed in 1910 and South Union in 1922. Restoration efforts at Pleasant Hill began in 1961, and the restored farm reopened for public tours in 1968.

Charles Reagan Wilson
University of Mississippi

Thomas D. Clark and Gerald Ham, *Pleasant Hill and Its Shakers* (1968); Julia Neal, *The Kentucky Shakers* (1982); Mary Richmond, *Shaker Literature: A Bibliography*, 2 vols. (1976). ☆

SNAKE HANDLERS

These religious people are members of various independent Pentecostal Holiness churches who interpret Mark 16:18 ("They shall take up serpents") as an injunction to use poisonous snakes in religious services. At least two nights every week they gather in their one-room frame houses of worship and, to the accompaniment of loud rhythmic music, handle rattlesnakes, copperheads, and other venomous snakes with complete abandon. Sometimes they place the snakes on top of their heads, wrap them around their necks, tread on them with bare feet, or toss them to other worshipers. Bites are surprisingly infrequent and are generally seen as evidence that the victim experienced a wavering of faith or failed to follow the Holy Ghost. Most devotees refuse to consider medical treatment for a bite, preferring to trust the Lord for their healing. Since the start of the snake-handling movement in 1913, at least 63 men and women have died from snakebites suffered in religious meetings. The movement's early leader was George W. Hensley, an illiterate preacher from eastern Tennessee. It began in the coal-mining areas of the Appalachians, at a time when the region was beginning the process of economic modernization.

The great majority of snake handlers live in the southern highlands, in ordinary towns, hamlets, and hollows scattered throughout the region. With very few exceptions they are whites, descendants of English and Scotch-Irish pioneers who settled in the mountains in the period between 1780 and 1840. Their daily lives differ in no essential respects from those of neighboring unbelievers. The men work in the mines, mills, and factories, while the women attend to domestic chores. Snake handlers are people of limited formal education. Some of the older members can neither read nor write.

It would be an error to see the snake-handling religion as a gross aberration in southern religious life. The roots of the snake-handling movement lie deep in the religious heritage of the South—in the Methodism of John Wesley and the frontier revivals and backwoods camp meetings of the early 19th century. Moreover, with the exception of the practices of snake handling, fire handling, and strychnine drinking,

there is no element of ritual or belief in the snake-handling religion that is not found in conventional Pentecostal Holiness churches throughout the South. And even these dangerous ritual practices are, after all, based on a literal interpretation of Scripture and on the idea (common to Pentecostal people in the South and everywhere else) that the spirit of God can "move upon" believers and empower them to perform extraordinary and unusual acts.

Despite state and municipal laws prohibiting handling of poisonous snakes, and despite the ever-increasing number of snakebite fatalities, snake handlers remain firm in the conviction that they are "doing the will of the Lord." Their religion continues to draw new adherents even today. Most of these persons are sons and daughters of veteran followers of the movement.

Steven Kane
Connecticut College

Steven Kane, *Appalachian Journal* (Spring 1974), in *Encyclopedia of Religion in the South*, ed. Samuel S. Hill (1984), *Journal of American Folklore* (October–December 1974), *Ethos* 10 (1982). ☆

Snake handlers of eastern Kentucky, September 1946

SOUTHERN BAPTIST CONVENTION
|||||||||||||||||||||||||||||||||||||||||||||||||||||||||||

No other major denomination has shaped white southern religion and culture as powerfully or as long as has the Southern Baptist Convention (SBC). Organized in 1845 due to disagreement with northern Baptists over slavery and sectionalism, the SBC became the official "established" church of the South and America's largest Protestant denomination. While retaining a traditional Baptist emphasis on local church autonomy, freedom of conscience, and individualistic conversion, the SBC united a fiercely independent constituency around southern culture, denominational programs, and missional zeal. White southern culture provided a core of values, myths, and symbols that enhanced denominational stability; the denomination itself reinforced them. By sanctioning the southern white way of life—economics, politics, morality, race—Southern Baptists helped preserve regional unity among whites following the Civil War and validated their own continued existence as a distinct Baptist denomination.

The denomination was the means by which a defeated people sought to reclaim their region and to distinguish themselves from their northern counterparts and other "independent" Baptists in the South. Southerners rejected the northern Baptist "society" approach to denominational endeavors for a more centralized "convention" system, which coordinated activities of all agencies. Autonomous local churches united in order to accomplish broader evangelical tasks than their individual resources could facilitate.

While general theological consensus prevails, Southern Baptist churches are heirs of diverse theological traditions. Some represent a Regular Baptist tradition incorporating Calvinism, orderly worship, and a strong commitment to education. Others reflect a Separate Baptist heritage of modified Calvinism, revivalistic worship, and an antieducational bias. Still other segments reveal fundamentalist, Arminian, sectarian, and moderately liberal perspectives. Denominational solidarity and southern cultural stability long provided a sense of "Southern-Baptistness" that held theological diversity in check.

Southern Baptist evangelical zeal has focused primarily on individual conversion and personal morality, often ignoring the corporate sins of southern society. In so doing, the denomination has witnessed significant numerical growth while perpetuating the prevailing mores of white southern culture. Preachers utilized the rhetoric of southern populism and evangelical revivalism to awaken sinners to Christian and white southern values. The denomination sought to dominate southern culture, often without changing it.

This unity of culture and denomination protected the SBC from the doctrinal schisms that divided many Protestant denominations during the 20th century. As pluralism has overtaken their culture and their denomination, Southern Baptists have experienced a significant identity crisis. Unity and diversity, once protected by cultural and denominational uniformity, have become increasingly difficult to maintain.

Bill J. Leonard
Southern Baptist
Theological Seminary
Louisville, Kentucky

John Lee Eighmy, *Churches in Cultural Captivity: A History of the Social Attitudes of Southern Baptists* (1972); Bill J. Leonard, *Baptist Quarterly* (June 1985); Rufus B. Spain, *At Ease in Zion: A Social History of Southern Baptists* (1961). ☆

THORNWELL, JAMES HENLEY

(1812–1862) Minister and theologian.

Religious educator, editor, and author, James Henley Thornwell was born in Marlboro District, S.C., graduated from South Carolina College in 1831, studied at Andover Theological Seminary, Harvard, and Presbyterian Theological Seminary (Columbia, S.C.), and was licensed to preach in 1834. He served several churches for short periods of time and took part in the affairs of the Presbyterian Church in the United States of America (Old School) beginning in 1837 when he attended his first General Assembly, being elected moderator in 1847. He was elected professor of metaphysics at South Carolina College in 1837 and taught at that institution until 1855, serving as president after 1851. In 1855 he became professor of didactic and polemic theology at the Presbyterian Theological Seminary, a position he held until his death.

Thornwell was known as a careful logician, for his biblicism, and for his Calvinist orthodoxy because of his defense of the Westminster Confession of Faith with ideas of Francis Bacon and the aid of the Scottish philosophy of the 18th-century Enlightenment. As churchman, he held to a strict interpretation of doctrine and structure. He opposed, for example, the development of boards for furthering the church's work because they did not conform to biblical or doctrinal standards of ecclesiastical accountability. As educator he supported the teaching of new scientific knowledge, confident of the harmony of Christian faith and God's created order. He also supported public education in the state of South Carolina. He edited the *Southern Quarterly Review* and the *Southern Presbyterian Review* for a time.

Referred to as the Calhoun of the church, Thornwell used his skills as an author to support the institution of slavery on biblical and natural grounds, calling not for the condemnation of the master-slave relationship, but for its regulation. When the Civil War erupted, he defended the South and accused the General Assembly of the PCUSA of unbiblical and unnatural meddling in the affairs of state, and of thus violating the true "spiritual" character of the church. He encouraged the Synod of South Carolina to endorse political as well as ecclesiastical secession and took part in the organization of the Presbyterian Church in the Confederate States of America, which became the Presbyterian Church in the United States after the war. His pamphlet *The State of the Country* was widely circulated, and he was the principal author of the new denomination's "Address to All the Churches of Jesus Christ throughout the Earth" in 1861. Although he did not write or publish a systematic theology, *The Collected Writings of J. H. Thornwell* (4 vols., 1871–73) were edited and published by J. B. Adger and J. L. Gireadeau, assuring his continued influence among Presbyterians and in the South.

James H. Smylie
Union Theological Seminary
Richmond, Virginia

Theodore Dwight Bozeman, "A Nineteenth Century Baconian Theology: James Henley Thornwell an Enlightenment Theologian" (Th.M. thesis, Union Theological Seminary, Richmond, Va., 1970), *Journal of Presbyterian History* (Winter 1972); James O. Farmer, Jr., *The Metaphysical Confederacy: James Henley Thornwell and the Synthesis of Southern Values* (1986); E. Brooks Holifield, *The Gentlemen Theologians: American Theology in Southern Culture, 1795–1860* (1978); Benjamin M. Palmer, *The Life and Letters of J. H. Thornwell* (1875). ☆

SCIENCE
AND MEDICINE

JAMES O. BREEDEN

Southern Methodist University

CONSULTANT

☆ ☆ ☆ ☆ ☆ ☆ ☆ ☆ ☆ ☆

Overleaf: Physician visiting a patient and her family in a needlework scene by Ethel Mohamed, photographed in 1978

SCIENCE
AND MEDICINE
||||||||||||||||||||||||||||||||||||||||||||||||||||||||

Although little noticed by the myriad students of the South, science and medicine have been important and instructive components of southern culture. On one level, they have contributed to social progress. On another, they have been barometers for gauging intellectual life. The South's experience in these areas also sheds valuable light on the question of southern distinctiveness, providing additional support for the contention that regional separateness has had a retarding effect on cultural development.

Colonial South. An interest in science was part of the cultural baggage that the first colonists brought to the South. This interest was fed and intensified by the seemingly insatiable curiosity of Europeans regarding the natural life and products of the New World. Consequently, from the earliest days of colonization the pursuit of science was a prominent feature of southern life.

Throughout the colonial period and into the 19th century, science was generally divided into two broad categories—natural philosophy (the physical sciences) and natural history (the natural sciences). The former was concerned largely with the verification of existing scientific principles and the latter with the observation, collection, and classification of the phenomena of the natural world. Because of the physical and intellectual limitations of their frontier setting, colonial Americans

were ill prepared to do much in natural philosophy, but they were ideally situated to excel in natural history. Their research in natural history set a pattern of activity that dominated American science for three centuries.

Motivated by the irresistible appeal of the lush, often exotic, natural world that surrounded them as well as by requests for assistance from English and European students of nature anxious for New World botanical, zoological, and mineral specimens for their research and personal collections, hundreds of early southerners became actively involved in natural history. Most of them served as field collectors for Europeans. By the late colonial period a few became highly competent scientists and as respected members of the international circle of natural historians made contributions to scientific advancement. The most important figures in southern natural history in the 17th century were John Clayton I and John Banister, and in the 18th, Mark Catesby, John Clayton II, John Mitchell, and Alexander Garden. Garden, a Charleston physician, was perhaps the most accomplished and best known of the group.

The activities and accomplishments of the early South's natural historians were highly significant: they made the region, along with the middle colonies, the colonial leader in the study of the American natural world; they played an indispensable role in filling in the New World book of nature; they contributed to the advancement of Western science;

and they helped lay the foundation for American science.

The medical story of the early South was not nearly so bright or promising. It was in fact tragic. Disease and death were constant companions of colonists everywhere, but especially in the South. Here health hazards, ranging from endemic "ague" (chills and fever) and "flux" (dysentery) to epidemic outbreaks of smallpox and yellow fever, were at their worst. It is easy to see why the southern colonists were less healthy. "Seasoning," or becoming acclimated to the region's semitropical climate, was the source of extreme morbidity and mortality. Moreover, because of an environment that encouraged insect life, a general disregard for the draining of swamps, and the steady influx of black carriers with the rise of slavery, malaria—early America's most dangerous endemic disorder—tightened its hold on the South in the 18th century as it began to disappear from New England. Southern forms of the disease were more debilitating and deadly than those that prevailed elsewhere in the colonies. Finally, the medical reforms of the late colonial period that improved health— more and better-trained physicians, therapeutic advancements (the use of variolation to prevent smallpox and Cinchona bark to control malaria, for example), and the gradual appearance of regional medical institutions such as schools, societies, and licensing— made less headway in the South than elsewhere.

As the health picture of the South suggests, the American colonies exhibited regional distinctions quite early, because of the diversity of colonizing experiences and New World conditions. But while New England and the middle colonies became recognizable colonial divisions, the southern colonies showed the greatest cultural diversity. Indeed, during the century-and-a-half between the settlement of Jamestown and the outbreak of the Revolution the seeds of southern distinctiveness were planted and the first shoots sent up. A number of influences encouraged a separate southern identity. The region's first European settlers transplanted the social model of the English country gentleman to the New World and tried to follow it. They found favorable climatic and geographic conditions and established a plantation economy based on slavery and a staple-crop system.

Sectional identity had little immediate meaning for the principal areas of regional life, but in the cases of science and medicine the factors that underpinned it boded ill. Agrarianism and the plantation system, for example, fostered ruralism and a sparse pattern of settlement that discouraged and retarded urbanization, with its greater opportunities for intellectual contact and its nurturing environment for societies, journals, and other institutions for the promotion of science. The poor health of the South was in large measure attributable to the social consequences of the region's unswerving devotion to a way of life based on slavery and the plantation economy.

Old South. Southern colonists on the eve of the Revolution were no more devoted to sectionalism than those in New England and the middle colonies. Moreover, following the break with England, they were among the most strident cultural nationalists and celebrated America's special destiny. Independence and nationhood, however, provided the impetus for the transformation of the embryonic South into the sectional South.

This unintended, and largely unconscious, historical process was the result of growing inconsistencies between the southern way of life and emerging national patterns that became increasingly obvious after independence. None was more glaring than the South's slave-based economic system and its underlying racism, which stood in contradiction to the philosophy of the Revolution and the idealism of the early Republic. Forced to choose, southerners rejected freedom and equality in favor of slavery and racism. Such unsettling experiences led, by the end of the 18th century, to the emergence of a southern sectional consciousness—the First South. After 1820 a sense of grievance and feelings of defensiveness united southerners as never before and pushed them further out of the national mainstream. This was the Old South, the supreme expression of southern distinctiveness. Science and medicine, like all of southern life, bore the imprint of the South's sectional philosophy.

Reflecting the cultural nationalism of the era, science in the early national period was characterized by the establishment and shaping of institutions and attitudes aimed at ending America's intellectual subservience to Europe. Among the achievements of the period were the establishment of new schools and the improvement of existing ones, the founding of scientific societies and journals, and the building of museums and herbaria. As the result of these steps, the United States by 1830 had become a junior partner with Europe in science and had started down the path that would lead to eventual leadership in the scientific world. The South's leaders of science supported and contributed to the drive for national scientific independence. In fact, Thomas Jefferson, the region's best-known scientist of the early national period, was crucial to the quest for a first-rate American science. Although Jefferson was not a great scientist, his influence permeated the pursuit of science nationwide, and he was a tower of strength to all interested in science.

America's striving for scientific respectability coincided with the maturing of Western science. Indeed, the 19th century was a golden age for science. During this century science came of age and established its utility for social progress. The result was a veritable cult of science that affected every aspect of life. The United States, while overshadowed by the scientific leaders in Europe, was actively involved in the modernization of science.

Between 1820 and 1860, the four decades that are generally associated with the Old South, all parts of the country did not participate equally in the advancement of American science: the Northeast was the clear leader; the West contributed the least; and the South occupied an intermediate position. After performing splendidly in the colonial period, the South fell behind the Northeast in science after the Revolution. The South's comparative lag in science was evident in a variety of ways, including the production of fewer scientists than the northern and middle states, a slower pace of institutional development for the support of science, a lower level of scientific activity, and a less progressive attitude toward science.

Reasons for the region's declining national position ranged from agrarianism to the capitulation of the South to evangelical Protestantism and the defensiveness that accompanied mounting sectional tensions. These forces retarded the growth of institutions for the pursuit of science and created a climate of opinion that inhibited the free inquiry crucial to scientific advancement.

For all its problems, limitations, and comparative lag, science occupied a prominent place in antebellum southern culture. Natural history continued to be the dominant type of scientific activity. Although leadership in this area had shifted to the North by the advent of the Old South, southern contributions to the advancement of natural history were extensive and important. Students of the natural world were to be found throughout the region. Among those of note were William B. Rogers in Virginia, Elisha Mitchell and Moses A. Curtis in North Carolina, Gerard Troost in Tennessee, Charles W. Short in Kentucky, Alvan W. Chapman in Florida, John L. Riddell in Louisiana, and Gideon Lincecum on the Texas frontier.

The greatest activity in natural history was concentrated in the Charleston area. Long the chief center of southern science, this city and its environs were home to some of the most outstanding scientific figures of the Old South, such as Stephen Elliott, John Bachman, John E. Holbrook, and Henry William Ravenel. Its large number of active students of science made Charleston the Old South's most important scientific community. This remarkable group's pursuit of science was nurtured by the Charleston Museum, one of the nation's oldest and most important collections of natural history specimens, and the Elliott Society of Natural History, one of two noteworthy scientific societies in the Old South, the other being the New Orleans Academy of Sciences.

When compared with its outstanding performance in natural history, the Old South's showing in the pure sciences was strikingly lackluster. This situation was the result of a combination of factors: the absence of a tradition of important activity and accomplishment in pure science, the low level of professionalization and institutional development that characterized southern science, and cultural considerations. The cumulative effect of these things was the perpetuation of the South's preoccupation with the collection, description, and classification of natural phenomena and the relegation of experimental research to the periphery of scholarship.

Like Americans everywhere, antebellum southerners were keenly interested in the practical applications of science. Applied science in the Old South largely involved attempts to bring science to bear on the region's mounting agricultural problems toward the end of the era. The highly acclaimed research of Edmund Ruffin in soil chemistry is a case in point.

Like science, medicine in the antebellum South exhibited unmistakable regional characteristics. By the time the Old South emerged, a distinctive southern health picture was evident. It was the worst in the nation. So poor was the state of health in the region that northern life insurance companies charged their southern policyholders higher premiums. Malaria remained endemic and was the principal cause of disability and death. Residents of the southern port cities and the surrounding countryside lived in fear of yellow fever, which became a southern disease in the 19th century. New Orleans, the Old South's largest city, was popularly known as "the graveyard of the Southwest" because of its frightful mortality rate (nearly three times that of Philadelphia and New York). Infant mortality rates in the South were the highest in the nation. In addition, it is estimated that as many as half of all southern children suffered from hookworm infection, a condition not diagnosed until the opening years of the 20th century. Finally, inadequate diets, poor housing, unhealthy quarters, and hazardous working conditions exacted a heavy toll on the health of the South's large slave population.

The Old South's health problems were the result of environmental and cultural factors. Climate and frontier conditions in the developing region, in conjunction with slavery, combined to account for the continued presence of malaria. The insect vectors of yellow fever and typhoid fever also thrived. In addition to fostering insect life, the long, hot summers made the preservation of food difficult, increased sanitary problems, and encouraged going barefoot, a habit associated with the spread of hookworm.

The growing cultural lag that increasingly set the South apart from the more progressive North contributed to regional health problems in a variety of ways. The low level of southern education, the lowest in the nation, clearly complicated the health picture. Nationwide, the "heroic" procedures of physicians were questioned during the first half of the 19th century, a development that encouraged the reliance on traditional healers and self-dosage with patent medicines. The rural and undereducated southerners were particularly prone to resort to these health-threatening practices. The absence of a social conscience on the part of the dominant planter class also had an adverse effect on health. Finally, institutions for the advancement of medicine, such as schools and journals, were, like those in science, slow to appear in the overwhelmingly rural South, and those that were founded faced a difficult struggle

for survival. The few that survived were inferior to those in the North. The rise of southern medical nationalism, or states' rights medicine, did little, despite its rhetoric, to change this situation. The product of regional patterns of disease and sectional tensions, states' rights medicine stressed the uniqueness of the South's medical problems and the subsequent need for southern-trained physicians and a southern medical literature. Although the desire to improve the practice of medicine in the region was indisputably one of its goals, southern medical nationalism, like the scientific racism of Josiah C. Nott and others, was primarily a defense of the civilization of the Old South. Consequently, it contributed more to sectionalism than to medical reform.

Although easily overlooked because of the health problems of the region, the antebellum South's strides in surgery contributed significantly to the rise of modern medicine. Two southerners—Ephraim McDowell and J. Marion Sims—achieved international acclaim in operative obstetrics and gynecology. The former, while practicing on the Kentucky frontier in 1808, performed the first successful ovariotomy, pioneering abdominal surgery. The latter, an Alabama surgeon, used slave women as subjects to perfect, in the 1840s, the initial procedure for the treatment of vesicovaginal fistula, a major breakthrough in gynecology. The third southerner who contributed to the birth of American surgery was Crawford W. Long, a small-town Georgia physician who was the first to use ether as a surgical anesthesia in 1842, helping to launch a new age of painless surgery.

Civil War. The culture of the Old South was inhospitable to scientific inquiry and threatening to health, but the region's scientists and physicians closed ranks with their countrymen to defend it against all perceived enemies. In 1861, when the South withdrew from the Union, they pledged their lives and fortunes to the new Confederate nation.

The Civil War was not a scientific war. Neither the North nor the South used scientific talent in ways that led to new or drastically improved weapons that altered tactics and strategy on the battlefield. Still, each side made extensive use of scientists. The North did considerably better than the South in this area. Prominent scientists were consciously incorporated into the northern war effort in an advisory capacity. In the South, they were engaged as problem solvers. The Confederacy's failure to devise a science policy is attributable to the many and pressing problems to be overcome in order to wage war and to the popular perception in the South of scientists as problem solvers.

Scientists in the southern war effort worked in the government-run munitions industry, and the War Department's Ordnance Bureau most especially. Headed by Josiah Gorgas, this agency was responsible for the Confederacy's supply of war materiel. Gorgas and his assistants accomplished the near impossible, building a munitions industry from scratch. It was largely through their efforts that the South was able to keep its armies in the field for four years against a vastly superior enemy. Indeed, the Confederacy ran out of men before it did arms.

Disease, disability, and death stalked the Civil War soldier and made this the costliest conflict in American history. A major reason for the unequaled carnage was the state of contemporary medicine. Indeed, the nation's doctors were

plunged without warning into a modern war with its unprecedented medical problems at a critical turning point in American medical history. Out of this era of transition, which saw established beliefs and practices come under attack, was to emerge the beginning of modern American laboratory medicine. In the meantime, a majority of the standard therapeutic measures—puking, purging, bleeding, and giving large doses of potentially dangerous drugs in particular—met with little success in the day-to-day struggle against common complaints and failed miserably when confronted by yellow fever, cholera, and typhoid fever, the great killer epidemics of 19th-century America.

The cruelest blow of all to the Civil War soldier was that the lifesaving antiseptic management of wounds, growing out of the research of Pasteur and Lister, came too late to be of help. Consequently, any serious injury to a limb meant amputation and the distinct possibility of death from one of the so-called surgical fevers—gangrene, erysipelas, or pyemia. Abdominal wounds were especially feared and constituted an almost certain death sentence.

The Civil War's toll of misery and death was most evident in the Confederate army. Like Gorgas and the manufacture of the tools of war, Samuel P. Moore, the southern surgeon general, had to build a medical service from scratch. He also was successful in meeting this challenge. But the efforts of the Confederate medical officers were hampered by an inadequate supply of trained physicians, near-crippling shortages of medicines and medical stores, and a steadily worsening military situation. Still, they faithfully kept at their tasks and provided valiant and commendable service. Few medical lessons, however, emerged from the carnage. For the South, the chief gain was the experience that the war provided in the treatment of the sick and injured and most especially the sharpening of surgical skills.

New South. The civilization of the Old South perished on the battlefields of the Civil War. The legacy of the South's failed bid for independence was frustration, poverty, and obsession with the past. These things supplanted in significance such long-standing cultural determinants as agrarianism and ruralism. Their immediate and lasting effect was to blight life in the region. Indeed, passing time seemed only to worsen matters. Even the much ballyhooed New South movement, with its promise of progress and prosperity based on the northern industrial model, did little to relieve the plight of the southern people. Consequently, as the New South era drew to a close in the opening years of the 20th century, the South was mired in backwardness and misery. Nowhere is this better seen than in science and medicine.

In the North, the Civil War was a catalyst for scientific progress, and American science matured rapidly during the last years of the 19th century, paving the way for domination in the century ahead. In the South, the war produced intellectual stagnation. Consequently, southern scientific leaders were largely sideline observers of Gilded Age and early 20th-century advances in science. The comparative gap separating southern and national science was probably greater at the end of the New South period than ever before.

With life in the South reduced to a scramble for survival and with spiritual malaise rampant in the dark days after Appomattox, there was little opportunity or desire to pursue science. So unbear-

able were conditions to some scientists, like John and Joseph LeConte, two of the New South's emerging scientific leaders, that they joined the postwar exodus from the region. Yet the beginnings of the revival of southern science date from the immediate postwar period. As the initial shock and agony of defeat began to abate, southern scientists reestablished contact with northern friends, who generously assisted them in rekindling their scientific interests, providing, for example, news of wartime developments in science and copies of recent works.

The first tangible signs of the revival of southern science were predictably found in natural history. The principal figures, men like Henry William Ravenel, Moses A. Curtis, and Alvan W. Chapman, were holdovers from the antebellum period. Natural history would continue to dominate science in the South, but its heyday was at an end. It was giving way to the modern science of botany, and the evolving professional scientist was supplanting the amateur collector.

As before, the southern record in the pure sciences was meager and undistinguished. The fate of this branch of science was inextricably bound up with that of higher education. At the beginning of the period, the South's colleges and universities were paralyzed by the effects of the Civil War and the political turmoil of Reconstruction. By its end, the best of them had made the transition to multipurpose institutions. But the region's continuing poverty, conservative social philosophy, and religious fundamentalism prevented them from becoming true centers for the advancement of learning.

The prospects of applied science in the South were as encouraging as those of abstract science were unpromising.

Economic necessity made this the case. A long list of southern scientists sought to bring science to bear in the effort to restore the region's prosperity. In agriculture, the traditional but troubled source of southern wealth, George Washington Carver exemplifies the renewed emphasis on scientific farming and farm management. In industry, Charles Holmes Herty's research on forest products is illustrative of the attempt to use science to create new economic opportunities.

The Civil War and its aftermath had a disastrous effect on health in the South. On the one hand, the hostilities left untold thousands of southerners in precarious or weakened health. On the other, the conflict's legacy of poverty exacerbated the region's tradition of poor health. As a result, old diseases increased in incidence and virulence, and new health problems arose. Malaria, the leading cause of debility and loss of efficiency in the antebellum South, had showed signs of decline in the decade preceding the Civil War. In the postwar period, however, it soared to record levels and reappeared in areas where it had previously been brought under control. Yellow fever, another old and distinctively southern disease, was a recurrent source of terror, death, and economic blight. Tuberculosis was more prevalent in the South than elsewhere. Blacks were especially hard hit. But a higher incidence of tuberculosis was only one indication of the deteriorating health of the former slaves. Left to fend for themselves after the collapse of Reconstruction, freedmen experienced excessively high rates of sickness and death.

Black health problems, as well as those of a growing number of whites, were in large part the result of the rise and spread of tenancy, the cruel backbone of postwar southern agriculture. The proliferation of the mill town, the chief symbol of the New South, further eroded the health of the poor whites. The principal diseases of poverty were hookworm and pellagra. The former, although undetected, was an old health hazard. In the antebellum period, however, it had been limited to slaves and the relatively small class of poor whites. Postwar poverty exposed growing numbers of southerners to hookworm infection, making it a major threat to regional health. Pellagra was the most spectacular and deadly of a number of disorders caused by dietary deficiency that plagued the swelling ranks of the southern poor. Almost exclusively southern in incidence, hookworm and pellagra were widespread by the time they were diagnosed at the turn of the century.

Urbanization in the South was largely a postbellum phenomenon, and New South cities were notoriously unhealthy. Chief among the health hazards were unpaved and poorly drained streets, inadequate or nonexistent sewage arrangements, public garbage heaps, and contaminated water supplies. Conditions were the worst in the segregated quarters into which urban blacks were crowded. With their growth came the multiplication of health problems. Health administrations were virtually nonexistent before the last two decades of the century, so little was done to improve conditions.

The threat of disease did not go unnoticed in the South. But poverty and the inability of the medical profession to combat the principal causes of morbidity and mortality stymied would-be reformers. Toward the end of the century, however, improvement in the southern economy and the acceptance of the new germ theory of disease provided the opportunity for health reform. The result was the genesis of the southern public health movement. Boards of health were established and empowered to investigate and combat health problems. Although the effectiveness of these agencies was limited by inadequate budgets, legislative interference, suspicion and hostility on the part of businessmen, and the ignorance of the masses, they pushed health reform on a broad front. The state boards of health uncovered and attacked a host of health hazards, inspected water supplies, sought to impose quarantines during outbreaks of epidemic disease, supervised vaccines, published reports, and strove to educate the public on health matters.

20th-century South. Still suffering from the physical and emotional effects of the Civil War, the South entered the 20th century with an uncertain future. The years ahead, however, brought slowly improving prospects, the result of the slow transformation of southern society during the interwar years. Indeed, change became the major theme of southern history. The Progressive movement, which flowered after 1910, marked a turning point in the region's reaction to change by making it palatable, indeed desirable, to many southerners. Following World War I, change resumed, stronger than ever.

To the region's traditionalists, however, the prospects of change were not only subversive to the southern way of life but actually threatened to destroy it. The result was social controversy that set southerner against southerner. The struggle for control of the South's destiny was long and often bitter, but the outcome was inevitable—ever so slowly

there was an erosion of the South as a distinctive social and cultural entity. Put another way, the South was closing the circle, gradually moving back into the national mainstream, which it had left during the era of the Old South. The consequences of the Americanization of the South were to be immensely beneficial for science and medicine, although they were not to be realized until after World War II. In the meantime, both disciplines faced continued rough sledding.

The maturation of American science accelerated during the interwar years, and by the outbreak of World War II, the United States was poised for world scientific leadership. Owing to its physical, cultural, and intellectual poverty, the South contributed only marginally to national greatness in science.

The state of science during this transitional period in the South's history is best seen through an examination of academic science, for scientific inquiry nationwide was largely university centered. Building on the beginnings from the Progressive era, southern education, from bottom to top, underwent progressive change after 1920. By the outbreak of World War II, the South had experienced a veritable revolution in education. The prospects for the region's colleges and universities, however, were not as bright as the foregoing might seem to indicate. The gap to be closed was great and progress was slow and uneven. Indeed, the perennial problems facing southern schools were numerous and weighty. They included inadequate financial resources, overworked and underpaid faculties, mediocre students, and the desire of communities to control their schools. Such factors severely limited the capacity of the southern schools for intellectual attainment.

The South's institutions of higher learning, however, were not devoid of scholarship. As a matter of fact, there was a general reawakening of the southern intellect in the 1920s. But science fared less well than the social sciences and humanities in the southern intellectual renaissance. To be sure, the South had dedicated scientists. They worked to keep up with developments in their fields of interest, and some engaged in research, the results of which were occasionally noteworthy. Moreover, with the gradual upgrading of student bodies, faculties, and facilities as the 20th century wore on, the general state of science in the region improved. Still, when viewed comparatively, science in the South's institutions of higher learning was undistinguished.

As before, the realities of southern life shed informative light on the reasons for the state of science in the region. The interwar years were the era of the Benighted South. This popular image was the product of the South's long-standing social and economic problems and the unprecedented attention that the raging controversy between the proponents of change and the traditionalists drew to them. Benightedness influenced science in two major ways. First, the region's continuing economic problems, which worsened in the 1920s, meant modest expenditures on education, thereby limiting what could be done in science. Science also found itself embroiled in a conflict with the forces of social and religious fundamentalism. Such a confrontation was perhaps inevitable, for the vital interests of the two were diametrically opposed—free inquiry on the one hand and intellectual conformity on the other. The battleground was evolution, and the celebrated Scopes Trial of 1925 was only the best known of a host of violations of freedom of thought by the crusading fundamentalists. But the proponents of progress refused to yield to the traditionalist onslaught and tenaciously resisted. Their most powerful weapon, however, was time, for try as they might, the traditionalists could not quarantine the South from the formidable and unrelenting winds of change that were buffeting the region.

Owing to a series of medical discoveries around the turn of the century that propelled the southern public health movement into a new stage of activity and accomplishment, medicine made greater progress than science in the South after 1900. Between 1898 and 1906 the insect carriers of malaria (1898) and yellow fever (1899) were identified, and hookworm (1902) and pellagra (1906) were diagnosed as endemic among the southern poor. On the one hand, these developments vividly underscored the South's unique and stigmatizing health problems and focused national attention on them. On the other, they paved the way for the eventual control of the region's principal causes of sickness and death and promoted increased interest in public health reform.

The campaigns against malaria, yellow fever, hookworm, and pellagra, although hindered by regional poverty and the resistance of business and political leaders who were outraged over the embarrassing exposure of the South's myriad and frightful health problems, were landmark victories for southern health. By the end of World War II these scourges had been eradicated (or controlled in the case of pellagra), in large part as the result of the national discovery of the South's health plight after 1900. While publicity about the shocking state of southern health reinforced the stigma of regional backwardness, it also led to crucial assistance from northern philanthropies and the federal government. The indispensable role of the Rockefeller Foundation in the control of hookworm and the U.S. Public Health Service in the fight against pellagra are cases in point.

The nascent southern public health movement was a major beneficiary of the late 19th- and early 20th-century medical advances that stripped the region's principal diseases of their mystery. As increasing numbers of southerners became aware of the modern concept of disease and the lifesaving potential of laboratory medicine, the long-standing belief that an unhealthy climate was the cause of disease was toppled, the importance of sanitation and drainage was recognized, and a lessening of opposition to the recognition of regional health problems and a greater willingness to confront them evolved. These developments coincided with and were influenced by the southern Progressive movement. Chagrined by the South's backward image, the Progressives sought to rid the region of the principal causes of backwardness. Health reform was high on their agenda.

Disease was attacked on a broadening front. Crusades against malaria, yellow fever, hookworm, and pellagra touched off similar campaigns against tuberculosis and syphilis. Sanitaria and hospitals were built. Boards of health were set up in those states that had not already established them. Responding to the stimulus of the Rockefeller Sanitary Commission for the Eradication of Hookworm Disease, which combated this disease at the local level, county health departments mushroomed, propelling the South into the lead in this

area. And health department expenditures increased, despite the region's ongoing economic woes. Additional funding for health reform came from philanthropic organizations and federal agencies. The Frontier Nursing Service, established in 1925 by Mary Breckinridge in the mountains of Kentucky, typified the growing concern for the health of the isolated people of southern Appalachia. Finally, southern senators and congressmen began to take a greater interest in health legislation. The cumulative effect of these developments was the gradual improvement of southern health. The narrowing of differences in mortality rates between the regions attests to the gains made.

But as revolutionary as the progress in health reform was, the South remained the nation's sickliest section at the onset of the Depression. Familiar disease forms continued to plague the region. For example, malaria had not been brought under control, and the plummeting of cotton prices in the 1920s led to a resurgence of pellagra. And southern cities remained unhealthy.

The first attempts at a national health program were made during the New Deal, and the South was a major beneficiary of the New Dealers' concern for health. Funds for medical care were provided by the Federal Emergency Relief Administration. Civilian Conservation Corps members received medical attention. The draining of 2 million acres of swamp by the Civil Works Administration, the Federal Emergency Relief Administration, and the Works Progress Administration and studies of the breeding habits of mosquitoes by the Tennessee Valley Authority expedited efforts to eradicate malaria. The control of typhoid fever and dysentery was advanced through the federally sponsored construction of 2.3 million sanitary privies by 1939. New crusades against tuberculosis and venereal disease were launched. The Works Progress Administration built hospitals and sewage plants. The Federal Housing Administration's slum-clearance programs, half of which were in the South, promoted urban health reform. Of far-reaching significance was the Social Security Act of 1935. This historic piece of social welfare legislation provided federal funds for health purposes and created permanent machinery for distributing them.

World War II had major uplifting effects on southern health. The stationing of large numbers of troops in the region brought the resources of the federal government to bear in the fight against disease on an unprecedented scale. As the conquest of malaria illustrates, public health was greatly advanced. The health screenings and medical attention that accompanied military service led to vastly improved health for thousands of southerners. And military instruction in hygiene inculcated in them the importance of good health and taught them how to achieve it. The wartime appearance of enriched flour and bread, containing synthetic vitamins, considerably curtailed the threat of pellagra and other disorders resulting from dietary deficiencies.

Recent South. World War II was a landmark in southern history: it reinvigorated the region's long-troubled economy and swung the battle between the modernists and traditionalists in favor of progressive change, greatly accelerating the Americanization of the South. Indeed, no other period in the South's past has witnessed as much fundamental change as have the years since World War II. The changes in southern life extended across a broad front. Prominent among them were the triumph of industry, the transformation of agriculture, burgeoning urbanization, the breaking of the hold of ruralism, the ending of physical and cultural isolation, the dismantling of the Jim Crow system, the disintegration of the political Solid South, and a revitalized role in national politics. The result, as one historian put it, has been the demise of the "sectional South" and the rebirth of the "American South." Although accomplished at the expense of regional distinctiveness and at times, as in the case of race relations, vigorously opposed, the Americanization of the South has led to unprecedented prosperity, dramatic improvements in the quality of life, growing opportunities for southerners, and renewed respect for the region. Science and medicine have been major beneficiaries of the postwar changes in southern life.

The Americanization of the South has sparked a veritable revolution in the pursuit of science in the region. At the outbreak of World War II, the South was little more than an outpost of American science. At the present, it has risen, at the least, to the status of junior partner in the national scientific establishment. This amazing turnabout is easily demonstrated. The South is producing and using scientists at greater rates than ever before in its history. Institutions of every type for the support of science are unprecedented in quantity and quality. Levels of scientific achievement have soared. Finally, the region's attitude toward science has become increasingly progressive and supportive. The great distance that science in the South has traveled since World War II is clearly seen in the reversal of the South's "brain drain"; the region is now a magnet for scientific talent. To be sure, parity with the national leaders in science, such as the Northeast and the West Coast, has not been achieved, but the prospects for science in the South, especially if the Sunbelt phenomenon is perpetuated, are promising indeed.

With the postwar transformation of the South have also come unparalleled improvements in health. Indeed, the "sickly South" is rapidly becoming a thing of the past as the region moves toward national patterns and norms in health matters. Problems, however, remain to be overcome before it can be said that southerners as a people enjoy good health. These problems include an elevated rate of postnatal mortality, a high incidence of poverty-related diseases, and substandard health care in rural areas. As before, ethnic minorities and the poor are the least healthy southerners.

In retrospect, southern science and medicine have closed the circle. They began on a roughly equal footing with the rest of British North America. With the rise of a distinctive southern culture after the Revolution, they became sectional and second rate. The Civil War and its lingering aftermath perpetuated the South's scientific lag and poor health well into the 20th century. But since World War II national patterns and norms have increasingly prevailed. Indeed, it is appropriate to speak not of southern science and medicine but of science and medicine in the South.

See also BLACK LIFE: Health, Black; ED-UCATION: Academic Freedom; Learned Societies; ENVIRONMENT: Naturalists; HISTORY AND MANNERS: Philanthropy, Northern; MYTHIC SOUTH: New South Myth; SOCIAL CLASS: Health, Worker; WOMEN'S LIFE: Healers, Women

James O. Breeden
Southern Methodist University

Wyndham B. Blanton, *Medicine in Virginia in the Eighteenth Century*, 3 vols. (1930–33); James O. Breeden, *Joseph Jones, M.D.: Scientist of the Old South* (1975); Clark R. Cahow, *People, Patients, and Politics: A History of North Carolina Mental Hospitals, 1848–1960* (1982); J. H. Cassedy, *Journal of History of Medicine and Allied Sciences* (April 1973); James X. Corgan, ed., *The Geological Sciences in the Antebellum South* (1982); Horace H. Cunningham, *Doctors in Gray: The Confederate Medical Service* (1958); George Daniels, *American Science in the Age of Jackson* (1968); Richard Beale Davis, *Intellectual Life in the Colonial South, 1585–1763*, 3 vols. (1978); William H. Deaderick and Lloyd Thompson, *Endemic Diseases of the Southern States* (1916); John Duffy, *Epidemics in Colonial America* (1953), *The Healers: A History of American Medicine* (1976), *Journal of Southern History* (May 1968), ed., *The Rudolph Matas History of Medicine in Louisiana*, 2 vols. (1958–62); Clement Eaton, *The Mind of the Old South* (1964); Clark A. Elliott, *Biographical Dictionary of American Science: The Seventeenth through the Nineteenth Centuries* (1979); Elizabeth W. Etheridge, *The Butterfly Caste: A Social History of Pellagra in the South* (1972); John Ettling, *The Germ of Laziness: Rockefeller Philanthropy and Public Health in the New South* (1981); Gaines M. Foster, *Journal of Southern History* (August 1982); Brooke Hindle, *The Pursuit of Science in Revolutionary America, 1735–1789* (1956); Howard L. Holley, *A History of Medicine in Alabama* (1982); Thomas Cary Johnson, Jr., *Scientific Interests in the Old South* (1936); Leo J. Klosterman, Loyd S. Swenson, and Sylvia Rose, eds., *100 Years of Science and Technology in Texas* (1986); Dorothy Long, ed., *Medicine in North Carolina: Essays in the History of Medical Science and Medical Service, 1524–1960*,

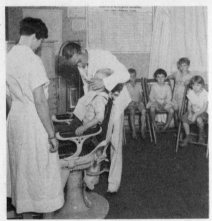

A Red Cross dental clinic in Kentucky, c. 1932

2 vols. (1972); Edward T. Martin, *Thomas Jefferson, Scientist* (1952); Nancy Smith Midgette, "The Role of the State Academies of Science in the Emergence of the Scientific Profession in the South, 1883–1983" (Ph.D. dissertation, University of Georgia, 1984); Ronald L. Numbers and Janet Numbers, *Journal of Southern History* (February 1982); Nathan Reingold and Marc Rothenberg, eds., *Scientific Colonialism, 1800–1930: A Cross-Cultural Comparison* (1986); Todd L. Savitt, *Journal of Southern History* (August 1982), *Medicine and Slavery: Diseases and Health Care of Blacks in Antebellum Virginia* (1978); Richard H. Shyrock, *South Atlantic Quarterly* (April 1930); Raymond Phineas Stearns, *Science in the British Colonies of North America* (1970); Joseph I. Waring, *A History of Medicine in South Carolina*, 3 vols. (1964–71). ☆

Aerospace

||||||||||||||||||||||||||||||

The term *aerospace* gained currency during the 1950s and was a product of U.S. Air Force nomenclature. It evolved in response to the growing interest of aviation manufacturers and the government in space exploration as well as in traditional aeronautics. From the first flight of the Wright brothers at Kitty Hawk, N.C., to the launch of America's first astronauts from Cape Canaveral, Fla., the South has played an active role in aerospace developments.

On 17 December 1903 the Wrights made the world's first flights in a powered airplane. During the years prior to World War I, planes were generally viewed as carnival curiosities, although a number of events in the South gave a hint of future trends and made southerners aware of the coming "air age." In 1911 Cal Rodgers completed the first transcontinental flight, which lasted three months. His route took him across Texas, where good weather and level terrain promised an easier course around the Rocky Mountains. Three years later in Florida promoters launched the country's first commercial airline—a flying boat service across the bay between Tampa and St. Petersburg.

After 1917, when America entered World War I, the attributes of sunny weather and open spaces made the South a center of flight training, a pattern that has persisted across the region. During the 1920s commercial aviation began to expand, especially after the Air Mail Act of 1925, which transferred post office airmail routes to private contractors. Numerous companies launched services, but much consolidation eventually thinned their ranks. On the eve of World War II major airlines with a southern heritage included National and Eastern (in Florida), Delta (in Georgia), and Braniff (in Texas). Also, Pan American had major routes from Florida into the Caribbean and from Brownsville, Tex., into Latin America.

As southern farmers continued their

perennial campaign against the cotton boll weevil, aerial crop dusting grew rapidly during the 1920s. Agricultural aviation owed much to pioneering work conducted by Dr. B. R. Coad and the U.S. Bureau of Entomology in Louisiana. Among the many commercial crop-dusting companies, Huff-Daland of Monroe, La., was one of the most successful and grew into Delta Airlines. Aerial crop treatment became even more widespread after World War II; a research and development project at Texas A&M during the 1950s produced a unique design for a crop duster with special safety features that became standard for the industry.

During World War II its even terrain and good flying weather again made the South a major center of flight training; U.S. Army and U.S. Navy facilities turned out thousands of pilots, navigators, and bombardiers. In the postwar era, many of these training fields continued to serve as operational air bases and as centers of flight training. Similarly, aviation manufacturers moved south during the war to take advantage of climate, available land, and a plentiful supply of labor. The Dallas-Fort Worth area continued as a major producer of bombers, fighters, and helicopters; plants in Atlanta, Ga., turned out huge transports and other aerospace hardware. Many cities developed facilities for producing electronics and a variety of aerospace products. Following the creation of the National Aeronautics and Space Administration (NASA) in 1958, the South became known worldwide for its role in America's space program. The John F. Kennedy Space Center in Florida became NASA's principal launch site; the George C. Marshall Space Flight Center in Alabama played a major role in developing

Alan L. Bean, astronaut from Texas, 1969

launch vehicles and in handling manned operations; and the Lyndon B. Johnson Space Center near Houston, Tex., was the focal point for astronaut training, mission control, and other tasks. As one historian noted, these centers represented a "fertile crescent" of advanced technology in the South. The spin-off of their presence was seen in the science-technology activities of neighboring schools, universities, and businesses; they also became major tourist attractions.

Air travel expanded in the postwar years, especially after the introduction of jets in the late 1950s. Certain cities became major hubs of national and international significance. Atlanta's airport (currently handling about 40 million passengers annually) became the second busiest in the nation, trailing only Chicago. The Dallas-Fort Worth regional airport ranked fourth in the United States and was a significant factor in attracting so many national corporations that the Dallas-Fort Worth area ranked third behind New York and Chicago as a location of corporate headquarters. Major southern airports also offered nonstop flights to major cities in Europe, Latin America, and the Pacific, bringing new dimensions of business and vacation travel to southerners. By the 1980s mergers and deregulation left four major airlines in the South—Eastern (Miami), Delta (Atlanta), American (Dallas), and Continental (Houston).

See also AGRICULTURE: / Pest Control; IN-DUSTRY: Military and Economy; / Delta Airlines

> Roger E. Bilstein
> University of Houston
> at Clear Lake City

Roger E. Bilstein, *Flight in America, 1900–1983: From the Wrights to the Astronauts* (1984); R. E. G. Davies, *Airlines of the United States since 1914* (1972); W. David Lewis and Wesley P. Newton, *Delta: The History of an Airline* (1979); Loyd S. Swenson *Southwestern Historical Quarterly* (January 1968). ☆

Agriculture, Scientific

||||||||||||||||||||||||||||||||||||||||||||||||||||

Although southerners made remarkable agricultural progress between 1800 and 1860, science contributed comparatively little until the 1870s. Before the Civil War, American agriculturists using empirical methods developed the essentials of modern farming. In the 20th century science and technology built upon this foundation to make American agriculture the most productive in the world.

In the South planters started in the 1790s to cultivate new crops of Sea Island cotton, upland cotton, and sugar with slave labor and primitive farming methods based on spades, hoes, and ox-drawn turning plows. Within the span of a single lifetime they created advanced systems for producing those crops on a vast scale. During the period from 1830 to 1860 they mechanized their farming operations with mule-drawn implements and even used steam engines to power their gins, mills, and presses. By 1850 cotton growers had bred the modern type of upland cotton by crossing varieties imported from the Caribbean Islands, Mexico, and Siam and then refining the resultant cotton with selective breeding. During the 1840s planters adopted horizontal culture of row crops, crop rotation, and elaborate drainage systems in order to preserve the fertility of their farmlands. Finally, they devised effective methods of managing slaves in which rewards replaced threats of punishment. By 1860 southern agriculturists employed almost all the implements and farming methods still in vogue during the 1920s.

In the prewar era chemistry made several useful contributions to southern agriculture. Edmund Ruffin of Virginia demonstrated that marl could renovate worn-out soils by reducing acidity, and Justus Liebig, the German chemist, analyzed soils to discover that cultivation of crops removed important elements from the soil. From him, southerners learned to plow under the stalks of their cotton and corn. Liebig's research also pointed the way to improving soil fertility by adding missing elements.

Many of the South's agricultural achievements were lost as a result of the Civil War. Plantations were subdivided into family-sized farms worked by unsupervised sharecroppers. In the process the economies of large-scale farming disappeared, and the improved management techniques of the 1850s became inapplicable. The prewar trend toward farm mechanization ended and soil-conservation systems were abandoned. Inevitably, the productivity of farmlands and agricultural workers diminished. Had it not been for two contributions made at this time by chemistry, the South's agricultural economy would have declined still further. Newly introduced commercial chemical fertilizers partially offset the loss of soil fertility characteristic of sharecropping, and the first arsenic-based insecticides reduced crop losses.

Around the turn of the 20th century state and federal governments established experiment stations employing chemists, botanists, and entomologists to seek solutions for agricultural problems. In the private sector of the economy, commercial plant breeders who earlier had relied on selective breeding now began to apply the science of botany with noticeable effect.

Between the two world wars gasoline tractors benefited southern agriculture even more than improvements made in chemical fertilizers and insecticides. Early models assumed the heavy labor of breaking land for planting, and later tricycle types increasingly performed much of the cultivation formerly done with mule-drawn implements. With the coming of tractor-drawn, multirow mechanical implements, landowners regained much authority over farm workers that had been lost with the collapse of slavery. A new system of day labor began slowly to replace sharecropping. By 1940 mechanization had progressed so far that crops of cotton could be planted and cultivated almost entirely with machines. Manual labor was required only for a small amount of hoeing and for harvesting the crop.

Between 1945 and 1950 the mechanization of southern agriculture was completed. Mechanical cotton strippers and cotton pickers now harvested the South's principal crop, and flame-throwing devices and chemical herbicides replaced the last of the hoes. With the advent of these revolutionary machines, the system of sharecropping became obsolete and by 1960 was virtually dead. In the place of sharecropping arose a new system of large landholdings worked as single units, not unlike the old slave plantations, with diesel- and gasoline-powered machines taking the places of slaves and mules.

With the emergence of consolidated mechanized plantations in the 1960s, the age of scientific agriculture finally dawned in the South, decades later than in other sections of the nation. Landowners who had gained full control over their farming operations began effectively to apply modern techniques of management, introducing the new products of science and technology into their system of agriculture. Machines distributed a new generation of chemical fertilizers, insecticides, fungicides, and herbicides with scientific accuracy. Scientific plant breeders supplied farmers with prolific new plants tailored for disease resistance and ease of harvesting by machine. In all major crops yields per acre increased dramatically.

In the post–World War II era, southern agriculturists acquired a new versatility from science and technology. They were able to contend with changes in the market by shifting from cotton to supplementary crops of soybeans or small grains. In some areas cotton was entirely abandoned for rice, corn, or peanuts.

Scientific and technological progress in southern agriculture brought new problems as well as benefits. Millions of farm workers lost their employment, and rural populations declined. With mechanization, the South became dangerously dependent upon the international oil industry for fuel and agricultural chemicals. Insect pests demonstrated a dismaying capability of developing resistance to insecticides, and hybrid plants proved vulnerable to epidemic viral plant diseases. Thus far chemists have overcome insect resistance with new toxic substances, but the future of this approach is clouded because the number of suitable chemical combinations is limited. Agricultural scientists therefore are turning to the control of insects through both natural enemies and sterilization with radiation. In the future southern farmers will undoubtedly find their most serious problem to be obtaining adequate supplies of fertilizers, without which modern scientific agriculture cannot be carried on.

See also AGRICULTURE: Mechanization; / Agricultural Experiment Stations; Fertilizer; Pest Control

John Hebron Moore
Florida State University

Gilbert C. Fite, *Agricultural History* (January 1979, January 1980); John L. Fulmer, *Agricultural Progress in the Cotton Belt since 1920* (1950); Paul W. Gates, *The Farmer's Age: Agriculture, 1815–1860* (1960); Douglas Helms, *Agricultural History* (January 1979, January 1980); Williard Range, *A Century of Georgia Agriculture, 1850–1950* (1954); Charles R. Sayre, *Agricultural History* (January 1979); Richard C. Sheridan, *Agricultural History* (January 1979). ☆

Alcohol and Alcoholism

||||||||||||||||||||||||||||||||||||||||||||||||||||||||

Anthropologists who describe American drinking practices often use the word "ambivalent" to describe conflicting attitudes toward alcohol. For the South, however, ambivalence is too mild a label; "schizoid" comes closer to the mark. Extremes of opinion and practice can be found in practically any southern community, ranging from teetotalers who condemn all drink to heavy drinkers who swill it in manly ritual. As Will Rogers pointed out, some southerners will "vote dry as long as they can stagger to the polls."

It was not always so. Southern colonists and their descendants in the early years of the Republic had few qualms about alcohol; they drank hard and often. The Virginia Company was plagued by planters who crowded aboard floating taverns in the James River, bartering their tobacco for spirits

Paul Newman and Elizabeth Taylor as Brick and Maggie in Cat on a Hot Tin Roof *(1958), in which alcoholism was a prominent theme*

and sack. They, like later frontiersmen, caroused to escape the loneliness and hardship of wilderness life. Even in well-established towns and plantations, however, drinking was nearly universal among adult white males. Men drank upon arising and retiring; during and between meals; and while celebrating holidays, recuperating from illness, conducting business, and soliciting or pledging votes.

Variety, as well as quantity, characterized southern drinking. Brandies were made from apples, peaches, pears, and other local fruit; cider was also popular, although not as universal as in the North. Imported wines, especially Madeira and claret, graced wealthy planters' tables. All classes drank rum, which was obtained in exchange for southern commodities. Rum fortified most strong drinks of the 18th century, including punch, flip, toddy, grog, and blackstrap.

When the Revolution disrupted trade, making supplies of West Indian molasses expensive and uncertain, rum consumption declined. Its place was taken by whiskey, a drink already familiar to Scottish, Irish, and Scotch-Irish immigrants. Their knowledge of making whiskey, combined with improved stills and ample grain, water, and fuel, assured an abundant supply. Distilling was especially important in the corn-growing areas of the Upper South—the word *bourbon* derives from Bourbon County, Ky. Those who were alarmed by the deluge of cheap spirits, such as Thomas Jefferson, proposed viticulture and brewing as more salubrious alternatives, but domestic wines and beer failed to make significant inroads against whiskey in the South, at least until the mid-20th century.

Southerners paid dearly for their indulgence: heavy drinking led to widespread alcoholism and heightened violence. The latter danger arose not only from drinking but from drinking in an environment where weapons were ubiquitous and men shared a homicidal sensitivity about honor. Slaves suffered as well, for there was little they could do to protect themselves from a master turned brutal by drink. Harriet Beecher Stowe capitalized on their plight in *Uncle Tom's Cabin* (1852), which contains several pointed references to Simon Legree's drinking.

The temperance movement in the antebellum South was relatively weak. Although it had 44 percent of the population, the South accounted for only 8 percent of the nation's temperance pledges in 1811; no slave state, save Delaware, had adopted prohibition by the 1850s. A perceived link with antislavery hurt the temperance cause in the South, as did the economic circumstances of isolated farmers, who depended on distilling to retard spoilage, reduce bulk, and enhance the marketability of their crops. Some of the more substantial farmers and aspiring middle-class townsfolk joined temperance societies, but their influence was outweighed by the planter elite, who remained aloof—and conspicuously wet.

The Civil War had mixed consequences for southern drinking. The short-term effects were largely negative: temperance societies were disrupted during the war, and defeat gave many demoralized southerners added cause to resort to the bottle. Yet, in other ways, the war paved the way for the eventual triumph of the drys. First, it set a precedent for prohibition; during 1862 Confederate legislatures sought to preserve grain by outlawing its distillation. As a result, whiskey prices rose sharply. They fell again after 1865, but not to antebellum levels, due to the retention of federal excise taxes on beer and liquor. Bootleggers, of course, did not pay taxes, but trouble and risk necessarily inflated the cost of their product. The net, long-term effect of higher prices was to discourage consumption, at least among nonalcoholics.

In destroying planter hegemony the war also made possible the rise of a new leadership group, the middle class, whose members were much more hostile toward drink. Middle-class reformers were quick to climb aboard the prohibition bandwagon, denouncing alcohol in the name of economy, discipline, and other progressive virtues. They were not alone. Populists also hated the liquor dealers, whom they accused of exploiting the people and (not without evidence) of manipulating their representatives. Ironically, they were joined on this issue by many New South industrialists, who saw liquor as undermining productivity. To this diverse alliance were added the evangelicals, whose numbers and influence were growing rapidly during the postbellum decades. Evangelical ministers admonished their flocks, chided backsliders, and vocally supported antiliquor legislation.

The drys were opposed by conservatives who thought that what a man drank was his own business, as well as by urban machines and the formidable liquor interests. But the wet coalition was fighting, at best, a delaying action. Local-option elections and special legislation dried up more and more territory; 825 of the 994 ex-Confederate counties had some form of prohibition by 1907. Part of the wets' problem was demographic: most of the immigrants with cultural backgrounds favorable to drinking had settled outside of the South during the 19th century. Native-born,

lower-class voters of both races were courted as an alternative source of support, but when disfranchisement thinned their ranks, southern drys could no longer be contained. From 1907 to 1909 there was a burst of statewide prohibition victories in Georgia, Oklahoma, Alabama, Mississippi, North Carolina, and Tennessee.

A recurring theme in the southern prohibition debates was control of the lower classes, especially blacks. Before the Civil War, law and custom confined plantation slaves to an occasional holiday spree, but these restraints were loosened by emancipation. Prohibitionists exploited this situation by alleging that atrocities were committed by drunken blacks; "nigger gin" joined "demon rum" as a favored epithet. D. W. Griffith's *Birth of a Nation* (1915) gave cinematic expression to these fears. Drawing upon two earlier novels by Thomas Dixon, Jr., Griffith portrayed freedmen who were drunken, arrogant, and lecherous, in contrast to their sober, docile, and hardworking slave forebears. Not to be outdone, some wets played up stories of cocaine rampages— the implication being that if blacks could not drink, they would turn to more dangerous drugs.

Dry propaganda notwithstanding, postbellum blacks did not have a serious alcohol problem. On the contrary, they drank less than poor whites, especially in rural areas. But as uprooted blacks began drifting to cities, where morals were looser and liquor more abundant, the situation changed. With little prospect of steady employment, many of them settled into a life of drinking and idling; predictably, their alcoholism rate worsened. Today poor black males living in cities (southern or otherwise) are more likely to develop drinking problems, and to develop them sooner, than either the general population or their country relations. In 1974, for example, the District of Columbia, with its large black underclass, had the highest adult alcoholism rate in the nation; however, Alabama and Mississippi, states with large numbers of rural blacks, ranked lowest.

Urban blacks are not the only afflicted group. Alcoholics can be found throughout the South, from Appalachian hollows to the streets of the Vieux Carré. Nevertheless, studies undertaken since World War II have consistently shown that the South, as a region, has the lowest rate of alcoholism and the highest percentage of abstainers in the country. That the South remains disproportionately Protestant, rural, and dry (many areas retaining prohibition long after national repeal) largely accounts for the difference. This may be changing, however, as the sprawling Sunbelt cities attract millions of immigrants with more permissive attitudes toward drink.

See also HISTORY AND MANNERS: / Moonshine; Whiskey; INDUSTRY: / Liquor Industry

David T. Courtwright
University of Hartford

C. C. Pearson and J. Edwin Hendricks, *Liquor and Anti-Liquor in Virginia, 1619–1919* (1967); W. J. Rorabaugh, *The Alcoholic Republic: An American Tradition* (1979); James B. Sellers, *The Prohibition Movement in Alabama, 1702–1943* (1943); Muriel W. Sterne, in *Alcoholism*, ed. David J. Pittman (1967); Joe Gray Taylor, *Eating, Drinking, and Visiting in the South* (1982); Ian R. Tyrell, *Journal of Southern History* (November 1982); Daniel Jay Whitener, *Prohibition in North Carolina, 1715–1945* (1945). ☆

Black Health

See BLACK LIFE: Health, Black

Drug Use

The use of drugs, especially the opiates, cocaine, and marijuana, has deep roots in southern culture. In fact, during the late 19th and early 20th centuries, drug use was more common in the South than in virtually any other region of the country.

The opiates (including opium, laudanum, paregoric, and morphine) comprised the largest part of the problem. These drugs were valued for relieving pain, alleviating anxiety, and checking diarrhea. Widely prescribed by physicians, opiates were also taken as home remedies. "Came home disheartened and miserable," Mary Chesnut confided in her journal. "Was so ill I had to take morphine." Later she wrote, "After several weeks' illness—dawdling on, kept alive by Dr. T's opium—once more I was on my feet."

The trouble with such medication was that it might, if continued for a sufficiently long time, lead to addiction. In this southerners were hardly unique: medical opiate addicts could be found on both sides of the Mason-Dixon line. But what set southerners apart was their higher rate of opiate addiction—perhaps 60 or 70 percent higher than the rest of the country. This in turn reflected the greater prevalence of certain diseases in the South, notably diarrhea, dysentery, and malaria. Simply stated, southerners were ill longer and more frequently than northerners; hence, they resorted to opiates more often. Southerners also suffered, on a per-capita basis, more Civil War casualties; no less than one-fifth of Mississippi's entire 1866 revenue was required to purchase artificial limbs for crippled soldiers. Wounded and shell-shocked veterans, grieving parents and widows, and those afflicted with chronic diseases endemic to the region combined to make up a disproportionately large pool of candidates for addiction. The use of opiates was thus both a manifestation and a symbol of the postbellum South's profound physical and spiritual malaise.

The situation gradually changed during the early 20th century. As addicted veterans and older addicts died off, as the medical profession became more conservative in prescribing, and as opiates were subjected to more stringent legal controls, a new group of users began to emerge. They were typically younger men who began using opiates as a means of sobering up after alcoholic sprees or as a source of pleasure. Although some addicts continued to be created through the treatment of chronic diseases or injuries, their importance was declining relative to the nonmedical type.

Similar changes were observed in other parts of the country. But what set the new breed of southern addicts apart was their continued use of morphine. Even though northern addicts had largely switched to black-market heroin, their southern counterparts injected morphine well into the 1930s. This reflected regional variations in the pattern of drug trafficking, as well as the greater willingness of southern physicians to maintain addicts quietly. When a doctor "wrote scrip" for an addict he prescribed morphine, heroin being illegal after 1924.

In addition to the tendency to use morphine, there was another continuity between 19th- and early 20th-century southern opiate addicts: they were disproportionately white. Studies from states as diverse as Tennessee, Texas, and Florida consistently showed blacks to be underrepresented among known users. This was partly because impoverished blacks often lacked access to doctors. They were thus less likely to receive opiates, especially in the dangerous and tempting form of a hypodermic injection.

This is not to say that southern blacks were without drug problems. Rather than using opiates, they showed a preference for cocaine. Sometime in the late 1880s or 1890s black stevedores in New Orleans began using cocaine as a pick-me-up during long stretches of loading or unloading steamboats. The practice spread to other black laborers scattered across the South; cocaine could be found on cotton plantations, in railroad work camps, and at levee construction sites. Cocaine was also a popular recreational drug among blacks, especially those who lived in or on the fringes of the urban underworld. The drug was generally taken by sniffing or in a patent medicine or a soft drink; cocaine injection was largely confined to those who were also morphine addicts.

Blacks' cocaine use was controversial. "Many of the horrible crimes committed in the Southern States by the colored people can be traced to the cocaine habit," charged Colonel J. W. Watson of Georgia in 1903—an allegation that was repeated by a number of white authorities over the next decade. More recently, scholars have denied these charges, dismissing them as politically or racially motivated. Alternately, it is possible that a handful of

of medical inquiry in their region. Their defensive sense of inferiority stemmed from both the profession's failure to cultivate the region's natural medical resources and its educational dependence on northern schools, textbooks, and journals. The institutions of medical education offered physicians a concrete context within which their commitment to southern medical distinctiveness could be objectified, and they were thereby a means of energizing the medical community and satisfying the physician-intellectual's social and cognitive needs.

Both the reform objectives and theoretical underpinnings of the argument for a distinctive southern medical education were expressed in the flourish of new southern medical schools and journals in the 1840s and especially the 1850s. Editorials in journals and inaugural addresses at schools routinely promoted the South's medical distinctiveness as an imperative to professional vigor. The sensitivity of curricula to the South's peculiar medical needs was clearly expressed in the 1850s when a New Orleans school created a separate professorship of the diseases of blacks. Southern medical schools self-consciously stressed that portion of medical education—clinical knowledge—that was specific to region, thereby legitimizing their distinctive regional identity.

More destructive than the Civil War itself to the case for distinctive southern medical education were changes in the structure of medical thought. From the 1870s the gradual ascendance of a new medical epistemology grounded upon experimental science carried with it a commitment to the universalism, not specificity, of medical knowledge. By denying the principle of specificity, this posture undermined the theoretical justification for a distinctive southern medicine, the core of the argument for regional education. Regional differences in practices, other than incidental ones, were no longer legitimate engines of professional improvement, but rather stigmata of inferior practice.

The founding of separate medical schools in the South to educate black physicians, beginning with Howard in 1867 and Meharry in 1876, gave southern medical education what was from that time through the present virtually its only unique feature. The creation of black medical schools was not informed by an allegiance to specificity, but was instead premised on sociopolitically defined racial differences among physicians and driven by white pietism, paternalism, and separatism.

The most pervasive characteristic of medical education in the postbellum South taken as a whole was its inferiority. Persistent poverty made prospects of parity with northern schools unlikely, and through the early 20th century southern physicians attributed a perceived deterioration of the profession's status in the region to its educational deprivations. When the Southern Medical College Association was organized in 1892, the underlying objective of the improvements it endorsed was to make medical education in the South conform to the superior standards of northern schools. Reformation of southern medicine was to be effected not by celebrating its individuality but by effacing it.

In 1910 Abraham Flexner published his influential report on medical education in the United States, and he left no doubt that medical education in the South was inferior to that in any other region. Endowments and organic university affiliations such as that at Tulane, he held, were essential elements of a proper medical school; however, most of the South's schools were proprietary and impoverished. In subsequent years, private endowments at such schools as Baylor, Duke, Emory, and Vanderbilt were principally responsible for elevating standards at a few institutions and forcing the closure of proprietary schools. By the mid-20th century southern medical education was no longer inferior. Moreover, the substance and underlying ideology of medical education in the South and North did not differ in any fundamental way, and through the present such geographically southern schools as Duke, Emory, and Vanderbilt teach virtually the same medicine as Harvard, Michigan, or San Francisco. As of 1982 in the 13 southern states there were 60 medical schools, 37 of which were approved by the American Medical Association.

See also BLACK LIFE: Health, Black

John Harley Warner
Harvard University

AMA *Directory of Physicians in the U.S.* (1982); John Duffy, *Journal of Southern History* (August 1957); Abraham Flexner, *Medical Education in the United States and Canada: A Report to the Carnegie Foundation for the Advancement of Teaching* (1910); Herbert M. Morais, *The History of the Negro in Medicine* (1968); Ronald L. Numbers, ed., *The Education of American Physicians: Historical Essays* (1980); Ronald L. Numbers and John Harley Warner, in *Scientific Colonialism, 1800–1930: A Cross-Cultural Comparison*, ed. Nathan Reingold and Marc Rothenberg (1986). ☆

Health, Mental

||||||||||||||||||||||||||||||||||||||

Before the mid-19th century there was little publicly supported mental health treatment in the South. By 1825 Virginia, which made the first public attempt to treat the insane before the Revolution, was the only southern state to have a hospital for the insane. The South lagged behind the rest of the nation in this regard: eight other asylums existed in states outside the South. The sufferings of the insane in the South, as elsewhere in the nation, were looked upon as the natural consequences of a stern, unbending Providence, meting out judgment to the wicked and the innately inferior. The shame brought on by such a concept bred an attitude of contempt for, and lack of interest in, the needs of the insane. The families that could afford special accommodations provided strong rooms in attics and barns to shut away the family shame, or they sent the insane member to a neighboring state where institutional care could be purchased. The dependent insane who were not considered violent were allowed to wander through the town begging for food and becoming the butts of children's ridicule. Only those who were considered dangerous to the public welfare or who were a nuisance to the community received any public attention. Motivated by fear, communities used the local jail or almshouse as the common solution to the problem of public protection from the violent.

The South's concern for the insane was awakened by the reform movement of 1825 to 1860. In that period South Carolina, Georgia, Alabama, Louisiana, Tennessee, Missouri, North Carolina, Mississippi, and Texas opened the doors of mental health care to the indigent insane, radically altering the character of the mental hospital movement in the South and bringing it up to par with the rest of the nation. In the early stages of development, moral therapy was employed as the accepted mode of treatment in the new state hospitals. Moral treatment involved removing the patient from the community to an asylum, where therapy of kindness and consideration for physical and emotional needs would lead to a cure. The assumption was that the insane could be cured in institutions removed from local conditions that prompted the onset of insanity. Before the growth of large public mental institutions the insane had been embarrassments to their families, but they had been curiosities to the public. Now removed from the community, the mentally disturbed no longer posed a public embarrassment or a threat to the community, but they were still a public spectacle. For instance, the transfer of patients to the new North Carolina Western Insane Asylum at Morganton created a circus atmosphere in the town when the residents lined the road to watch patients being marched from the train station to the hospital. Likewise, the constant urging by the superintendent at Dorothea Dix Insane Asylum for construction of a fence around the Raleigh, N.C., facility was not for the purpose of protecting the citizens of the town, but rather to control the townspeople who came to the hospital grounds to watch and generally excite the patients.

Although widely heralded in the United States as an effective and successful therapeutic method during the first half of the 19th century, moral therapy fell into disrepute before the end of the century. The failure of moral therapy can be attributed, in large measure, to the exuberance of superintendents who issued reports of high recovery rates to stimulate the founding of new mental institutions and the expansion of existing ones. Superintendents willingly squeezed every patient they could into the hospital. Overcrowding and inadequate financial support made moral treatment impossible to practice. Nevertheless, outside pressures continued to exist to transfer mental patients away from the local community to the central state hospitals. The result of overcrowding and the absence of adequate medical treatment was the creation of warehousing facilities where patients were put out of sight and, therefore, out of mind. No one found it necessary to deal with the profoundly negative attitudes toward mental illness that permeated society.

As the state became increasingly responsible, local government and, more importantly, individual families began to assume that mental illness was not their responsibility alone. Unfortunately, those operating local hospitals were not attuned to the dangers of relegating responsibility for the mentally ill to a central state hospital. A relatively secure and simple hospital routine provided for a patient enabled him or her to avoid facing the more complex problem of life "on the outside" and created, more often than not, a pathological dependence on the institution. Recognition of this particular problem prompted the movement toward community clinics and local mental health programs.

Community responsibility was encouraged after World War II when three major factors combined to reverse the pressures on large state hospitals: (1) the introduction of psychotropic drugs growing out of wartime research, (2) federal support for research and mental health centers prompted by the reports of various presidential and congressional commissions in the 1960s, and (3) civil rights legislation and Supreme Court decisions on behalf of mental patients between 1961 and 1975 that dramatically changed state hospital census patterns. Between 1955 and 1977 patient enrollment in mental hospitals declined from over one-half million to less than 200,000. In the same period over 800 community mental health centers were established. The psychiatric patient has been returned from the large state hospital to his home community. Between 1955 and 1975 psychiatric patient care in state hospitals declined by 50 percent. Outpatient care in community clinics increased 70 percent in the same period.

The South has played a leading role in this movement. No southern state, though, has established a smooth transition from institutional care to community care. Meeting existing needs of the mentally disturbed at the community level rests on three factors: proper distribution of state resources, continuing public support of research and local community acceptance of mental health centers, and establishment of halfway houses and outpatient services. Every southern state has experienced a rapid growth in community mental health centers and comparative declines in state-hospital populations, yet a commensurate shift in the allocation of funds to support local clinics has not occurred. The situation in Texas is typical of the resource distribution of all the states in the South. Between 1965 and 1977 Texas established 28 community centers serving 82 percent of the population of the state. Yet only 9 percent of the state's support for mental

health went to community mental health centers. Although the situation has improved since 1959 in the area of research funding, when only four southern states (Florida, Louisiana, Tennessee, and Texas) were allocating more than $25,000 annually for research, every southern state commission cites the shortage of research funds as a deterrent to providing an adequate mental health system.

The return of the mental patient to the local community does not necessarily bode well for the individual. The "Proceedings of the First Robert Lee Sutherland Seminar on Mental Health" held at the University of Texas in 1978 noted that the movement of chronically ill mental patients away from state hospitals to local communities has "exacerbated the problems faced by the people who most need help." Mental patients and those labeled as mentally ill are still considered to be relatively worthless, dangerous, frightening, and disruptive—all terms that have been used to describe the mentally ill during 100 years of institutional psychiatric care.

Significant studies completed by independent researchers in Virginia, North Carolina, and Louisiana and by state agencies in Texas, Florida, and Georgia have concluded, in the words of the Sutherland seminar proceedings, that "mentally ill persons discharged from hospitals or state institutions face difficulties in being accepted by people in their own community because of the communities' insensitivity, ignorance, fear of mental illness, discrimination and social banishment." Surveys in these states indicate that society ranks the mentally ill below the convicted felon and the alcoholic on the scale of social acceptance. The studies in North

Carolina and Virginia during the late 1960s and early 1970s (William C. Butz and J. Edgerton, *Social Psychiatry*, 1971) suggest that "the mentally ill are heavily stigmatized, that [community] educational programs have had only a minor effect, and people still respond with the fear, dislike and aversion that traditionally have been manifested toward mental patients in American society." In a 1930s study in Louisiana Charles D. Whatley notes the tendency of the community to "shun or restrict interaction with ex-patients in personal relationships but to generally accept them in relatively impersonal situations."

In this changing pattern of patient care, the fear of being labeled mentally ill may be the reason that the majority of people who receive treatment for mental disorders seek out primary-care facilities and non–mental health professionals in order to avoid being labeled mentally ill. Hence, even mental health services offered by modern community-structured programs are failing to meet existing needs, in large measure because of public apathy toward or opposition to community clinics and the presence of mentally disturbed people in the community.

In spite of the difficulties that the medical profession has experienced in securing research funds or effecting the reallocation of state funds for better support of community mental health centers, significant progress has been made in the South in these areas. Unfortunately, an understanding of the problem of mental illness does not appear to have produced much progress in changing cultural values that affect communities' acceptance or rejection of chronically disturbed people in their midst. Improved clinical services at the commu-

nity level have not produced a better life for most mentally ill people. Significant research and educational efforts are needed to improve cultural attitudes toward mental illness. Until the social norms that shun the mentally disturbed can be reversed through the joint effort of the medical profession and community leadership, mentally ill people in the South will continue to suffer the same stigma of fear, distrust, and dislike that has persisted for more than a century.

Clark R. Cahow
Duke University

Leopold Bellak, ed., *A Concise Handbook of Community Psychiatry and Community Mental Health* (1974); Clark R. Cahow, *People, Patients, and Politics: A History of North Carolina Mental Hospitals, 1848–1960* (1982); Norman Dain, *Concepts of Insanity in the United States, 1789–1865* (1964); Gerald N. Grob, *Mental Institutions in America* (1973); Jim C. Nunnally, *Popular Concepts of Mental Health: Their Development and Change* (1961); Judith Rabkin, *Schizophrenia Bulletin* (Fall 1974); R. D. Scott, *Schizophrenia Bulletin* (Fall 1974), Charles D. Whatley, *Social Problems* (1958). ☆

Health, Public

The public health experience of the South, at least until the mid-20th century, was in many respects unique in the nation. Perceived as distinctive by northerners—and some southerners—for more than a century, the region's poor health record served as one more defining characteristic, one more peculiar burden added to southern history's extensive list. Although sharing many disease problems with the rest of the country, the South at various times exhibited maladies largely peculiar to itself—yellow fever in the 19th century and hookworm and pellagra in the early 20th century. Furthermore, certain infectious diseases that had afflicted the nation at large (malaria, typhoid fever, and tuberculosis, for example) persisted at serious levels in the South until the 1930s and 1940s, years after having been brought under control elsewhere.

The "Sickly South" was an important facet of the region's image in the 19th century when yellow fever epidemics repeatedly ravaged the Gulf states and lower Mississippi Valley. This "scourge of the South" attracted much negative attention, drained financial and human resources, deterred capital investment and urban population growth, and disrupted commerce and transportation. For much of the 19th century state and local health measures concentrated on epidemic emergencies. With limited knowledge of the nature of diseases and modes of transmission, efforts at control through commercial quarantine and sporadic urban cleanup campaigns had little effect.

A turning point came in the 1870s and 1880s when germ theory and other medical advances brought increased understanding of disease processes. About the same time, the widespread yellow fever epidemic of 1878 led southern urban business interests to support increased public expenditures for such health-promoting, image-improving measures as public water supplies, drainage and sewerage systems, street paving, and garbage collection. These efforts clearly paid off in the improved state of health among whites in the urban South, although blacks showed only slight improvements, as the new urban services rarely extended to poor neighborhoods.

The threat of yellow fever was finally brought under control through discovery of its transmission by the mosquito and the dramatic campaign against New Orleans's last epidemic in 1905. This demonstration of the power of "modern science" applied through the combined efforts of federal, state, and local health authorities, widely viewed as another turning point in southern health history, ended the long reign of "Yellow Jack" and removed what many called the last great obstacle to southern progress.

New obstacles soon appeared, however, as hookworm and pellagra were identified as prevalent ailments in the rural South. These peculiar debilitating disorders together with malaria, a persistent and widespread old malady, served to explain other longstanding features of the stereotyped South—its laziness, its backwardness—at least to the satisfaction of some "progressive" southerners and other Americans who sought in public health improvement a panacea for all the region's problems and a pathway to the modern world. State and local health authorities, assisted by the U.S. Public Health Service, the Red Cross, the Rockefeller Foundation, and other northern philanthropies, set forth to spread the gospel of health and bring modern medicine to the rural South during the next few decades.

Despite substantial achievements in developing health education and institutions, these efforts could provide only a palliative as long as basic conditions remained unchanged. Black and white southerners in the 1930s continued to manifest a remarkably high incidence of malaria, tuberculosis, typhoid fever, diphtheria, smallpox, venereal disease, hookworm, and pellagra, as well as high maternal and infant mortality rates.

Southern public health problems would not be solved by medical knowledge and health crusades alone; lasting solutions required broad social and economic change. Massive federal expenditures and changes associated with the Great Depression and World War II would finally transform the socioeconomic system, ending one-crop agriculture, stimulating urbanization and industrialization, and bringing about a higher standard of living for most of the southern population. With material improvement came the virtual disappearance in the postwar era of many diseases long sustained by the region's poverty. With the decline of nutritional-deficiency and infectious diseases, southern state and local health departments could devote more attention to chronic disorders, environmental and occupational health and safety, and other services. Nonetheless, prevention of communicable diseases remains a central part of public health vigilance.

Southerners now suffer and die from

Unidentified physician with child, Kentucky, 1950s

the same major causes as the rest of the country—heart disease, cancer, stroke, and accidents—and they are served by similar state and local agencies. Some parts of the South still show the nation's highest death rates, infant mortality in particular, and a continuing high incidence of certain diseases—problems closely correlated with poverty and minority populations. Climate and the continued presence of appropriate mosquito vectors make the southern states still receptive to the threat of imported dengue, an infectious tropical disease, and yellow fever. Hence, while southern distinctiveness in health has been substantially diminished, it has not yet been eliminated altogether.

Because of their severity, southern health problems have brought about the establishment of new public health institutions, local, state, and national. Louisiana created the first state board of health in the country in 1855 as a response to several widespread yellow fever epidemics. The epidemic of 1878, affecting the South and the Mississippi Valley interior and threatening the commerce of the nation at large, influenced Congress to establish a National Board of Health, and, after that experiment failed, to assign an expanded federal role in quarantine and inspection service to the U.S. Marine Hospital Service, which became the Public Health Service by 1912. Another distinctive health agency with a southern connection is the National Leprosarium in Carville, La., a state institution in the 1890s that became national in the 1920s. The earliest and most extensive development of county health departments relying heavily on public health nurses occurred in the South in the early decades of the 20th century, funded in part by the U.S. Public Health Service and the Rockefeller Foundation. Finally, the Centers for Disease Control are located in Atlanta because of their origins in the Office for Malarial Control in War Areas. Established in 1942, in the center of the region where malaria was still most prevalent, the office sought to protect troops being concentrated and trained in the South, as well as the war industries labor force. The agency's success in coordinating federal and state action led to its postwar continuation and expansion as the Contagious Disease Center, now the Centers for Disease Control.

See also BLACK LIFE: Health, Black; SOCIAL CLASS: Health, Worker; Poverty

> Jo Ann Carrigan
> University of Nebraska at Omaha

CDC, *Morbidity and Mortality Weekly Report* (22 February 1980); Charles V. Chapin, *Report on State Public Health Work [1915]* (1977); John H. Ellis, *Bulletin of the History of Medicine* (May, August 1970); Elizabeth W. Etheridge, *The Butterfly Caste: A Social History of Pellagra in the South* (1972); Dennis N. Tunnell, "Regional History of Southern Branch, American Public Health Association" (Ed.D. dissertation, University of Alabama, 1977); Margaret Warner, *Journal of Southern History* (August 1984). ☆

Health, Rural
||||||||||||||||||||||||||||||||||||

Historically, the southern countryside and the city have differed in almost every way, including health. Although a national homogenization process has changed much of rural culture and social structure, unique qualities still flourish. Low incomes, poor diets,

inadequate housing, impure water supplies, poor transportation and communication, and limited medical resources remain key factors in explaining the overall health status of southern rural areas. A particularly important factor in understanding rural health is the problem of access, including the distribution of health services. Throughout rural areas there are shortages of physicians, dentists, and other health care providers. Approximately 49 million people reside in "medically underserved areas" in the nation, with 60 percent being rural.

Until the past decade, public health activities provided the major health services in the rural South unless there happened to be a private doctor in an area. The Rural Sanitation Act of 1916 provided funds to improve such aspects of rural health as disposal of human waste, the protection of water supplies, and the control of insects. In the following years, public health services continued to focus their efforts on malaria control, community sanitation, construction of sanitary privies, and sealing abandoned mines.

In 1935 the Public Health Service began to attack what it deemed the major problem facing rural families— the lack of adequate medical care. As a consequence, new programs for rural rehabilitation provided active medical care personnel to reach more rural residents. After World War II, programs developed in the area of environmental health with a focus on communicable diseases. Increased institutional services were offered by newly constructed hospitals.

More recently, in the 1970s a program called the Rural Health Initiative Projects was begun, administered by the U.S. Public Health Service. Its purpose is to develop and systematize the delivery of health care in rural areas. The several projects included under this act are (1) National Health Service Corps, (2) Community Health Centers, (3) Migrant Health Program, (4) Health Underserved Rural Areas Program, and (5) Appalachian Health Programs. These policies seek to provide primary health care for rural areas, and they have resulted in the construction of small clinics in small towns throughout the South.

Whatever is used to measure the health status of rural peoples, one fact is clear: they remain worse off than any other population. Indeed, scholars have identified several predominantly rural groups that have disproportionately severe health needs. They include southern rural blacks, Chicanos, Appalachian and Ozark whites, aged migrant workers, illegal aliens, and residents of environmentally polluted areas. All these groups share several characteristics—they are poor, powerless, and discriminated against because of race, culture, or lifestyle. Many of them live in the South and, as with other rural peoples, have an accident rate four times the national average, infant mortality rates that are 20 percent higher than the urban poor and 50 percent higher than the national average, and limited access to health resources.

The epidemiological patterns of blacks and whites in the rural South reflect serious health problems. The mortality rates are substantially higher than in other regions of the country. Within the South the death rates are significantly higher in the nonmetropolitan South than in the cities. With regard to ethnic differences, infant mortality rates among rural southern blacks are 65 percent higher than among rural southern whites. In addition, the morbidity and disability rates are higher in rural areas, with more dis-

ability involving bed confinement among the elderly in rural areas. Although children have a lower incidence of respiratory and infectious disease, adults have a higher rate of acute conditions, especially injury rates. National levels are lower, but the incidence of most chronic conditions (hypertensive heart disease, cerebrovascular heart disease, ulcers, emphysema, arthritis, and rheumatism) is greater in the South.

Most people in rural areas have inadequate water and sewer systems or rely on wells and/or outdoor bathrooms. Consequently, dental problems stemming from the lack of properly fluoridated water are a major problem, as are bacteria and parasitic diseases. Likewise, lack of solid-waste disposal creates a higher risk for injuries and contaminated water supplies. Most rural areas are limited in their economic opportunities and their cultural and recreational resources and, as a consequence, have a high rate of mental health problems such as alcoholism and depression. Furthermore, there are fewer patient-care physicians per capita in the rural areas of the South than elsewhere, and rural southerners obviously receive fewer physician services and incur more hospital stays. Dental visits are 65 percent lower than in the urban South. In general, the health care services in rural areas are inadequate and the health status is poor compared to urban areas in the South.

In 1970, 41.2 percent of southerners were rural. Excluding Florida, more than 47 percent of the South was rural, with the states of Mississippi, North Carolina, and South Carolina having over 50 percent rural population. Poverty is a crucial cause of poor rural health. Over 40 percent of rural people are poor, a factor that contributes substantially to health problems in the

South especially. In 1977, 20.7 percent of all households in the rural South had incomes under $5,000, with the average income for all households being $11,591. The median income for the region was $12,562, while the average individual income was $3,765. Furthermore, the percentage of poor families headed by females was higher. Although, in absolute terms, more poor families are headed by white males, the incidence of poverty was highest among black families headed by women. In fact, two out of three of the latter are poor, while 1 out of 10 white male-headed families are poor. Overall, 50 percent of blacks in rural areas are poor, and about 17 percent of whites are poor in the rural South. As Perry B. Rogers states, "the level of family income in a population group is the most influential characteristic which determines whether a population will have health services which are appropriate and accessible."

The rural southern poor, both black and white, use folk medicine and share information about how to alleviate health problems. Middle-class whites often use folk remedies but do not use folk healers as frequently as poor people do. Because of limited access to health services, a unique rural southern culture has developed that not only tries to explain illness but also offers ways to heal the sick. These ideas complement the scientific medical system, and they do not preclude the use of medical services. The poor in rural areas share a sense of community, a worldview that is reflected in their health ideas, many of which are inextricably bound to religious beliefs. Many southern rural people depend on their kin and their friends to help them in times of illness and misfortune. Changes are occurring in rural areas, but traditional ideas of health remain in the face of policy changes that have increased services in the past decade.

See also BLACK LIFE: Health, Black; FOLKLIFE: Folk Medicine; Voodoo; GEOGRAPHY: Population; WOMEN'S LIFE: Healers, Women

Carole E. Hill
Georgia State University

M. C. Ahearn, U.S. Department of Agriculture, *Agriculture Information Bulletin No. 428* (1979); C. L. Beal and Glenn V. Fuguitt, in *Social Demography*, ed. K. L. Taeuber, Larry L. Bumpass, and James A. Sweet (1978); James H. Copp, *Rural Sociology* (December 1972); Karen Davis and Rau Marshall, *Research in Health Economics* (1979); J. Lynn England, Eugene Gibbons, and Barry Johnson, *Rural Sociology* (Spring 1979); Dorothy M. Gilford, *Rural America in Passage* (1981); Carole E. Hill, *Current Anthropology* (June 1977); Olaf F. Larson, in *Rural U. S. A.: Persistence and Change*, ed. Thomas R. Ford (1977); Holly Mathews and Carole E. Hill, *Perspectives on the American South*, vol. 1, ed. Merle Black and John Shelton Reed (1981); Peter A. Morrison and Judith P. Wheeler, *Population Bulletin* (October 1976). ☆

Health, Worker

See SOCIAL CLASS: Health, Worker

Medicine, States' Rights

As slavery came under increasing attack in the 30 years before the Civil

War, southerners in all fields closed ranks. The professions, as might be expected, sought to provide the intellectual justification for the South's peculiar institution—lawyers argued on constitutional grounds, ministers cited the Bible, and physicians, as natural scientists, endeavored to demonstrate that blacks were an inferior race and that southern medicine was distinct from northern medicine. The first southern physician to argue the inferiority of the black race was Dr. Josiah C. Nott, a prominent physician in Mobile, Ala., who had learned his medicine in the best northern and European medical schools. In the early 1840s he published an article maintaining that blacks had less endurance, had shorter lives, and were less prolific than whites, and that intermarriage could only result in the destruction of both races. By 1850 he was arguing that "an immutable law of nature" made it impossible for blacks to become civilized. Following his argument to its logical conclusion, he asserted that blacks were "better off in slavery [in] the South than in freedom elsewhere."

Because Nott argued that blacks were an entirely separate race from whites, his views, by conflicting with the biblical account that humans descended from Adam and Eve, ran counter to the religious fundamentalism of the South. Much more to the liking of southerners in general were the ideas of the physiological school, represented by physicians who accepted the biblical view of creation but still maintained that striking anatomical and physiological differences separated whites and blacks. The leading exponent of this school was Dr. Samuel A. Cartwright of Natchez, Miss., and New Orleans. Like Nott, Cartwright was well trained and was widely recognized for his scientific work. He was also a born controversialist who loved to express his views. Beginning in the 1840s he wrote a stream of articles on blacks and southern medicine. In 1850 he was appointed chairman of a committee of the Medical Association of Louisiana to investigate the diseases and physical peculiarities of blacks. His report declared that the "shade of pervading darkness" was present not only in the skin but throughout all parts of the body—even including the "fluids and secretions." The skeletal structure of blacks was distinct from whites, the brain 10 or 11 percent smaller, the vascular system much less developed, and the lungs smaller. Moreover, their brains were so constituted as to produce an excess of "nervous matter," which would have made blacks unmanageable had it not been for the "deficiency of red blood" due to the inefficiency of their lungs.

Cartwright's studies also revealed two new diseases among slaves—one was *drapetomania*, a disorder that caused them to run away, and the other was *dyasthesia Aethiopis*, generally known to overseers as rascality. As his studies continued, Dr. Cartwright was led inexorably to the conclusion that the fundamental differences between the two races meant "that the same medical treatment which would benefit or cure a white man, would often injure or kill a Negro." The ideas of Nott, Cartwright, and other medical writers confirmed what many southern physicians had been thinking, and in the ensuing years a flood of articles in southern medical journals cited more and more "scientific" evidence of black inferiority.

Cartwright's argument for a distinctive form of southern medical practice also had a receptive audience. In the quest for causes of disease, physicians had constantly studied the role of climate, meteorology, and topography; southerners believed these factors affected their health. Cartwright insisted not only that the diseases of blacks and their treatment were distinct from those of whites but that southern diseases in general were different from those in the North. Like the anatomical argument, the thesis about southern diseases contained a modicum of truth. Yellow fever was essentially a southern problem at that time, malaria and enteric disorders did tend to be more acute in the South than in the North, and southern blacks did have a greater degree of immunity to certain disorders.

If southern medicine was distinct, it was logical that southern practitioners should be trained in the South. Although American medicine, with some exceptions, generally lagged behind that of Western Europe, medical education in the South was not even up to the level provided by the better northern schools; consequently, southern medical students seeking the best training went first to the North and then to Europe. The South in the antebellum years was trying to gain economic independence from the North, and keeping its medical students at home was financially advantageous. Southern businessmen were acutely conscious of the considerable economic loss entailed by training over half of all southern medical students in the North.

Added to this was the self-interest of southern medical schools. Nearly all medical schools in the United States were proprietary institutions dependent upon student fees for revenue; hence, there was keen competition for students. Southern medical journals and newspapers beginning in the early 1850s constantly emphasized the distinctiveness of southern medicine and the need for southern practitioners to be trained in the South. As the idea of separate southern medicine gained credence, enrollment in southern schools steadily increased and a number of new medical schools appeared on the scene. The campaign to keep southern medical students at home culminated in the mass resignation in the 1859–60 academic year of some 200 students from Jefferson Medical College in Philadelphia and another 100 from the University of Pennsylvania.

By 1860 only a few skeptics in the South questioned the concept of a specific southern medicine. The vast majority of southern physicians never doubted that the diseases they treated and the methods they used differed from those in the North.

See also BLACK LIFE: Health, Black

John Duffy
University of Maryland

James O. Breeden, *Bulletin of the New York Academy of Medicine* (1976); John Duffy, *Journal of Southern History* (May 1968), ed., *The Rudolph Matas History of Medicine* (1962); Mary Louise Marshall, *New Orleans Medical and Surgical Journal* (1940–41). ☆

Professionalization of Science

Although hardly an ordinary man, Andrew Jackson, with his election to the White House in 1828, signaled the "Age of the Common Man" in America.

Hard work, determination, and self-improvement were the catchwords of the day, and elitism was out of fashion. Public insistence that knowledge be immediately understandable and useful aroused concern among a growing number of scientists. Scientists resented their need to supplement their meager incomes, usually derived from college professorships, by traveling the popular lecture circuit to which Americans flocked. The root of their discomfort lay in their awareness that rapidly expanding scientific knowledge, and the means by which this knowledge was acquired, could no longer be communicated to a general audience.

As scientific inquiry, fueled by the growth of experimentation, expanded knowledge beyond the realm of the layman's understanding, fields that once belonged in the public domain came to be dominated by small, select groups of scholars with specialized educations. Pleading the necessity of basic research, these scientists maintained that their efforts to advance man's knowledge of his world could proceed only as the result of careful observation and experimentation, free of the financier's watchful eye and the public's preference for utility. These men gained a growing respect for one another as professionals and were anxious that the general public afford them the same professional status as that enjoyed by physicians, lawyers, and clergymen. They struggled to disassociate themselves from technical inventors and, more importantly, from quacks and charlatans who touted miracle cures and regaled the public with outrageous "corrections" of accepted scientific principles.

To foster a spirit of professionalism, American scientists needed contact among themselves. The American Association for the Advancement of Science (AAAS) was founded in 1848 to encourage scientific research, arbitrate scientific disputes, and weed out "pretenders" to the profession. By the end of the century more specialized societies emerged, including the American Chemical Society, the Geological Society of America, and the American Mathematical Society. All of these organizations defined their profession to include a specialized graduate degree, employment as a scientist, and evidence of scholarly research.

Most antebellum southern scientists remained on the periphery of this movement. Although some of them maintained membership in the AAAS, they seldom attended national meetings, usually held in the northeastern region of the nation, because of the distance involved, inadequate transportation, and financial pressures. However, the long-perpetuated notion of the antebellum South as "essentially unscientific" simply is not true. Planters such as Henry William Ravenel, James Hamilton Couper, and Benjamin L. C. Wailes maintained an active correspondence with scientists throughout the world and enjoyed enviable reputations for the specimens, drawings, and descriptions of southern flora and fauna that they provided.

Scientists in the emerging professional sense also inhabited the cotton kingdom. Thomas Cooper, John and Joseph LeConte, Frederick A. P. Barnard, and Elisha Mitchell, all college professors, earned the respect of their colleagues nationwide. Other professionals included Denison Olmsted and Michael Tuomey, who headed the state-sponsored geological surveys of North Carolina and Alabama. Charleston, S.C., the region's major metropolitan area, boasted the greatest concentration of scientific talent. With its relatively large, stable, and wealthy population and intellectual centers such as the Charleston Museum and the College of Charleston, the city sustained such notables as John Bachman, Lewis R. Gibbes, John McCrady, Edmund Ravenel, and Francis S. Holmes.

The move toward professionalization in the South, hardly begun by 1860, suffered in the years following the Civil War. Colleges throughout the region, the primary employers of scientists, closed their doors for a varying number of years during Reconstruction. Some, such as the University of Alabama, lay in smoldering ruins. Libraries and laboratories, ravaged by neglect as much as by war, had to be rebuilt from scratch. Faculty members were scattered. Some chose alternative careers; others, such as John and Joseph Le-Conte, grew discouraged with Reconstruction politics and moved elsewhere. Young men seeking a science education attended northern or German universities, and many of those who thus imbibed the spirit of research sought positions in schools that would support such work. Southern institutions of higher education, slowly reopening during the 1870s, could scarcely scrape together sufficient funds to pay their faculty members; they provided little in the way of compensated time or financial incentive for research.

Nonetheless, a few well-trained men of science did serve in the postbellum South's colleges, among them Eugene Allen Smith of the University of Alabama, Francis Preston Venable of the University of North Carolina, and William Louis Jones of the University of Georgia. Although pleased that southern colleges were reopening and even

expanding their curricula, these men, all products of a graduate education that emphasized the spirit of scientific inquiry through research, suffered from isolation, restricted budgets, and poor communication and transportation facilities. Hoping to "ward off the deadening effect that isolation was bound to have upon our scientific work," Venable and three of his colleagues at the University of North Carolina in 1883 organized the Elisha Mitchell Scientific Society. It met monthly during the academic year to provide North Carolina scientists contact with one another and an opportunity to share research efforts; in addition the society published quarterly the *Journal of the Elisha Mitchell Scientific Society*. However, neither the Mitchell Society nor a similar group in Alabama, the Alabama Industrial and Scientific Society, was able to serve the needs of the relatively few and scattered southern scientists of the late 19th century. Attracting little popular support and receiving almost no institutional financial aid, the societies could not continue their activities. The Alabama organization collapsed completely, and the Mitchell Society survived only as a local university forum.

The pool of southern scientists continued to increase, however, with the growth of southern colleges and universities under the leadership of progressive educators who witnessed the expansion of northern and midwestern universities and coveted for their own region similar educational advantages. The best indicator of the professionalism of this growing body of pre-World War II southern scientists lies once again in their organizations. Still isolated from colleagues in other regions of the nation, they formed state academies of science to provide contact with one another, to foster the spirit of research, and to offer at least a modest outlet for publication. By the mid-1930s every southern state boasted a state academy of science; by 1940 approximately 3,500 scientists throughout Dixie, over 90 percent of whom were college and university faculty members, belonged to these academies. An ever-increasing number of these persons held the doctoral degree, and, if only a handful of them were on the cutting edge of scientific research, many others remained informed and conducted research of local interest and benefit.

Prior to World War II, very few scientists were employed by industry or independent research laboratories. Most southern industry was either extractive, as in the case of the copper mines of Tennessee and the iron-ore mining operations of north Alabama, or labor-intensive, as with the tobacco factories, textile mills, and fertilizer plants that dotted the landscape. With profits more dependent on a labor force willing to work for low wages than on increased efficiency through research and development, management saw no reason to employ professional scientists. Research laboratories such as those at United States Steel and Bell Telephone, an integral part of northern industry by World War I, would not appear in the South for another generation.

World War II and the accompanying financial boom changed the South drastically and permanently. Rapid industrial development brought research-oriented corporations into the region as southern states competed for their attention with such incentives as low taxes and prime locations. Independent research laboratories emerged, as well. Areas such as the Research Triangle Park near Raleigh, N.C., now rival any

other region of the nation for productive, scholarly, scientific research. Universities blossomed, too, thanks to greatly increased financial support. Graduate schools attracted highly qualified professors; increasingly, southerners not only chose to remain at "home" for their education but often accepted permanent employment in the region. Modern transportation and communication, coupled with institutional funding for travel and research, meant that these scientists were no longer isolated as they had been earlier. By the 1970s and 1980s black and women scientists represented a growing, previously excluded human resource for the South. Southern scientists have earned the respect of their colleagues, both personally and for the institutions that now support their endeavors.

See also EDUCATION articles

Nancy Smith Midgette
Elon College

George Daniels, *American Science in the Age of Jackson* (1968); John C. Greene, *American Science in the Age of Jefferson* (1984); Brooke Hindle, *The Pursuit of Science in Revolutionary America, 1735–1789* (1956); Thomas Cary Johnson, Jr., *Scientific Interests in the Old South* (1936); Sally Gregory Kohlstedt, *The Formation of the American Scientific Community: The American Association for the Advancement of Science, 1848–1860* (1976); Nancy Smith Midgette, "The Role of the State Academies of Science in the Emergence of the Scientific Profession in the South, 1883–1983" (Ph.D. dissertation, University of Georgia, 1984); Alexander Oleson and Sanborn C. Brown, eds., *The Pursuit of Knowledge in the Early American Republic: American Scientific and Learned Societies from Colonial Times to the Civil War* (1976); Margaret W. Rossiter,

Women Scientists in America: Struggles and Strategies to 1940 (1982). ☆

Racism, Scientific

||||||||||||||||||||||||||||||||||||||||||||

The history of "scientific racism" before the 20th century is synonymous with the development of the modern scientific study of race. Scientific racism was not "pseudoscience" but an integral part of the intellectual worldview that nurtured the rise of modern biology and anthropology. In the 20th century the paradigm of racial hierarchy based on comparative anatomy came under withering attack from the American anthropologist Franz Boas and his students, but, in the history of race science before the emergence of the Boasian school, almost all the participants were racists, and the insights into human diversity provided by the "culture concept" were not available.

Southerners have always had a strong interest in the scientific discourse on race because the fate of their region has been inextricably tied to questions about the role and capacity of Afro-Americans. According to historian Winthrop D. Jordan, Thomas Jefferson's *Notes on the State of Virginia* (1786) was the strongest formal argument for black inferiority published by any native American before the 19th century. Jefferson's work appeared during the period when prejudice against people of color first became a topic of conscious concern among American intellectuals. Jefferson's description of his native habitat was representative of the international effort by natural philosophers to study systematically the bewildering diversity of plants, animals, and peoples revealed by European expansion. Since Aristotle, Western thinkers had found the metaphor of a hierarchical "great chain of being" useful, and many 18th-century natural philosophers expressed their ethnocentric condescension toward Africans by charting pyramids in which Europeans stood at the apex and blacks below, close to the ape. Jefferson's argument for black inferiority differed from the hardened racism of the 19th century in his regretful and equivocal tone, but *Notes* is one of the documents that marks the general abandonment of the Enlightenment hope that all peoples could achieve "civilization."

By later standards Jefferson's evidence was "soft." He claimed that blacks were less beautiful than whites, judged their emotional life less complex, and compared them unfavorably with Roman slaves, among whom he found many leaders in the arts and sciences despite harsh conditions that he imagined exceeded those endured by Afro-Americans.

Jefferson argued from history and personal experience, but the major 19th-century American contributions to scientific racism depended on advances in classification and morphology. The taxonomic methods that were serving the botanist well might also be used to explain why Cherokees, Mexicans, and Negroes were fated to serve the "Anglo-Saxon race" or disappear. Assuming that human diversity resulted from differences in heredity, a new generation of natural philosophers found great differences in the skulls of white people and black or red people and turned the abstraction of racial type into a fact of nature.

The reification of race through the taxonomic method is well illustrated in the work of the "American School" of anthropology, whose founder, the Quaker physician Samuel G. Morton (1799–1851), developed the first extensive quantitative data in support of "polygenism"—the theory that human races were separate biological species, the descendants of different Adams. Drawing on a collection of over 1,000 human craniums supplied by a vast network of correspondents, Morton published a series of works between 1839 and 1849 that were distinguished by brilliant lithographs of skulls and ingenious measurements of their cavities. He argued that a ranking of races could be established objectively through anthropometric measures, particularly brain size, and, unlike Jefferson, he found the Indian as well as the African absolutely inferior to the white in cranial capacity. In 1981 the Harvard scientist Stephen Jay Gould demonstrated that Morton's statistics were a "patchwork of fudging and finagling" but found "no evidence of conscious fraud."

During Morton's lifetime his work was accepted as a model of methodological sophistication and won an international audience. Morton converted Harvard's Louis Agassiz, the dominant figure in American natural science, to the doctrine that races were separate creations but found his most effective disciple in the Alabama physician Josiah C. Nott (1804–73). Nott's *Types of Mankind* (1854; written with George R. Gliddon) provided the authoritative American text on racial differences until Darwin's work necessitated revision of the racist typology. Nott's argument that races were fixed types "permanent through all recorded time" was intended as a rebuttal of abolitionists and racial equalitarians. With the help of his friend and publisher James D. B. De Bow, Nott

enjoyed great notoriety and success, despite the hostility of some southern leaders because of his anticlericalism and the incompatability of polygenism with religious orthodoxy.

Before the Civil War, leadership in scientific racism had passed to Europe, where Paul Broca (1824–80), the French surgeon best known for his discovery of cortical localization in the brain, established himself as Morton's chief scientific heir through painstaking comparative studies of brain weights. By Broca's death in 1880, scientific racism had a well-developed paradigm based on the reification of ideal types and a formidable data base drawn not only from skulls and brains but from the cranial measurements of 25 million living Europeans as well. Although the experts were unable to agree on exactly how many races there were or to produce a living example of any pure type, the faith that these types existed shaped such influential popularizations as William Z. Ripley's *The Races of Europe* (1899) and Madison Grant's *The Passing of the Great Race* (1916).

Thus, white southerners had little need to conduct basic research to justify the competitive racial caste system that emerged after the abolition of slavery. The major southern contributors to the scientific literature on race were physicians who described blacks as a diseased and debauched population that would probably be unable to survive without the paternalism of slavery. The medical claims that liberty would lead to black genocide echoed the antebellum myth of a relentless "Anglo-Saxon race" as the agent of the westward march of civilization, bound to exterminate all other breeds that it did not enslave; but the physical degradation of blacks also fit well with the varieties of Social Darwinism that were becoming fashionable.

Although Charles Darwin was a monogenist, the theory of evolution through natural selection proved compatible with the racial typology established by polygenists. Instead of advocating a series of separate acts of creation, late-19th-century scientific racists artlessly worked the established racial types into explanations of human variation that required longer time and gradual change but still assumed that racial types were the ancient determinants of human history. By the end of the century southern physicians had produced a torrent of abuse in the guise of biomedical studies and had attributed malnutrition, infection, and insanity to a lack of black "fitness" in the struggle for existence. The confidence of white America that the black problem would be solved through extinction of the inferior race was exemplified in the work of Frederick L. Hoffman, a statistician for the Prudential Insurance Company of America, whose *Race Traits and Tendencies of the American Negro* (1896) helped convince most insurance companies that blacks were unacceptable risks.

With white supremacy firmly established in the South by the turn of the century, America's racial anxieties were expressed in campaigns against mass migration from southeastern Europe, and the southern "Negro problem" got relatively little attention. The major development in 20th-century scientific racism in the English-speaking world was the rise of the eugenics movement and its campaigns for sterilization of "defectives," racially discriminatory immigration policies, and tracked school curricula based on intelligence tests. Because most of the immigrants settled in the North and the South's schools were already segregated, the

South contributed relatively little to eugenics except for illiterates, dirt eaters, pellagrins, and syphilitics, who served as objects of northern science and philanthropy.

The great public health campaigns that made dramatic contributions to the health of the region were sometimes influenced by scientific racism, most notably in the refusal of many southern physicians to admit that poverty was a better explanation for pellagra than hereditary defect. Many Americans were shocked in 1972 by newspaper headlines describing a U.S. Public Health Service experiment in which over 400 Macon County, Ala., black men were denied treatment for syphilis as part of an experiment to compare the effects of the disease on Negroes and Caucasians. The nightmare that became known as the Tuskegee Syphilis Experiment had its origins in the effort of northern philanthropists to develop model health programs during the 1920s. When the Great Depression erased the funds for a syphilis-treatment project among blacks in Macon County, government scientists decided to salvage something by charting the natural history of syphilis among sharecroppers who were told that they were being treated for "bad blood." The experiment continued until 1972, when public exposure forced the government to reexamine its policies concerning experimentation with humans. In 1974 the United States agreed to pay approximately $10 million to the victims, but there was no public contrition from the scientists involved. Historian James H. Jones concluded: "Had they been given an opportunity to retrace their steps, there is little doubt they would have conducted the experiment again."

The history of scientific racism exemplifies the powerful influence of social values on the development of biomedical science. Southerners have justified their social institutions in the idioms available to them. When revealed religion provided the primary explanation for the social order, southern leaders looked to their Bibles; in the 19th century, when science emerged as an important source of authority, southerners provided an eager audience and offered empirical studies for the new racist science. Long after it had been discredited by the advance of knowledge, racist science influenced medical opinion and helped to legitimate racial injustice. In the case of the Tuskegee Syphilis Experiment, a measure of justice was achieved not through the initiative of the scientific community but as the result of a lawsuit instituted by Fred Gray, a black attorney and native of Alabama, who first gained prominence in 1955 by defending Rosa Parks for refusing to relinquish her bus seat to a white man. Racism had become a liability for the scientist because those alleged to be inferior had endured long enough to command justice.

See also BLACK LIFE: Race Relations; HISTORY AND MANNERS: Philanthropy, Northern; / Jefferson, Thomas; MYTHIC SOUTH: Racial Attitudes

James Reed
Rutgers University

George M. Fredrickson, *The Black Image in the White Mind: The Debate on Afro-American Character and Destiny, 1817–1914* (1971); Stephen Jay Gould, *The Mismeasure of Man* (1981); John S. Haller, Jr., *Outcasts from Evolution: Scientific Attitudes of Racial Inferiority, 1859–1900* (1971); James H. Jones, *Bad Blood: The Tuskegee Syphilis Experiment* (1981); Winthrop D. Jordan, *White over Black: American Attitudes toward the Negro, 1550–1812* (1968); William Stanton, *The Leopard's Spots: Scientific Attitudes toward Race in America, 1815–1859* (1960); Nancy Stepan, *The Idea of Race in Science: Great Britain, 1800–1960* (1982); George W. Stocking, Jr., *Race, Culture, and Evolution: Essays in the History of Anthropology* (1968). ☆

Science and Religion

At the beginning of the 19th century southern theologians and the region's educated clergy entertained optimistic hopes for an alliance between science and religion. They believed that scientific discovery would confirm theological orthodoxy and even improve the methods of theology itself. By the beginning of the 20th century that earlier confidence had eroded, and religious conservatives led a series of statewide crusades against the teaching of evolutionary theory in the public schools. In large part the change resulted from the growing popular awareness of Darwinism, but it also reflected continuing preconceptions formed during the antebellum period.

When John Holt Rice became in 1824 the first professor of theology in the Presbyterian Seminary at Hampden-Sydney, Va., he was officially charged with the task of raising up a generation of scientifically minded clergymen: "that branch of knowledge should form a part of that fund of information, which every minister of the Gospel should possess." The charge embodied a consensus among the educated clergy of the Old South, who were convinced that the scientific investigation of the created order disclosed the existence and nature of the Creator and that the theologian who knew something about natural science could, in the words of Thomas Ralston, "see God . . . mirrored in his works."

The confidence in natural science was an extension of an ancient tradition of natural theology. The antebellum southern theologians—like their northern counterparts—argued that scientific investigation, properly conducted, provided a vast and grand amplification of the traditional argument that design and order in nature demonstrated the reality and trustworthiness of God, and they admired such naturalists as Hugh Miller in Scotland, who had argued that nature was filled with pattern and regularity and therefore with divine intelligence. Some presbyteries and synods required that prospective clergy take examinations on scientific subjects. The southern theological journals carried scores of articles throughout the antebellum period designed to show the harmony of science and religious faith. And the denominational colleges developed courses in chemistry, natural philosophy, geology, and astronomy, confident that they were promoting "the cause of science and religion." For the clerical elite, to become an amateur scientist was to extend and enrich the ministerial calling, and few professional groups in the South exhibited greater enthusiasm for the program of natural science than did the educated antebellum southern clergy.

The clergy did insist, though, that scientists remain within the confines of true scientific method, which they associated with the inductive restraint of Sir Francis Bacon. They opposed scientific materialism, they disliked developmental theories, and they worried about the harmony between scientific conclusions and the book of Genesis. Hence they criticized such scientific skeptics as Thomas Cooper in South Carolina. But most antebellum scientists were themselves pious Christians, and a small number of clergymen—like the Lutheran John Bachman—were respected scientists or amateur naturalists. Few of the educated clergy had much difficulty reconciling Genesis and geology. They simply argued that the seven days in the biblical creation narrative were geological periods, or they assumed that the creation account in Genesis merely described the final stage of a longer creation. So enthusiastic were they, in fact, that a number of southern theologians, including James H. Thornwell in South Carolina, hoped to model theology after the image of the natural sciences.

By the 1850s there were signs of strain. The increased interest in developmental hypotheses after the publication in England in 1844 of the *Vestiges of the Natural History of Creation* troubled some clergymen. When the Tombecbee Presbytery in Mississippi recommended the establishment of chairs in theological seminaries to refute infidel naturalists and to evince the harmony of science and scripture, some ministers favored the plan because they felt defensive about the sciences. But others favored it because they had every expectation of maintaining cordial relations between the disciplines. The leader of the drive for such chairs, James Lyon of Columbus, Miss., felt confident that God's revelation in nature, deciphered by science, was fully as authoritative and inspired as the Bible itself. When a member of Lyon's congregation, Judge John Perkins, donated $50,000 in 1859, the denomination promptly called James Woodrow to the Perkins Professorship at Columbia Seminary. His inaugural address spoke of the "harmony" of science and scripture.

Woodrow soon shifted his language, however, to refer simply to the absence of contradiction between science and religion, and in 1886 he was the defendant in a heresy trial occasioned by his acceptance of evolutionary theory. By that time the churches were increasingly edgy about the new biology: the Methodists had removed Alexander Winchell from a post at Vanderbilt in 1878, partly because of his defense of Darwin. But when the statewide struggles over the teaching of evolutionary theory in the public schools erupted in the 1920s, the churches lined up on both sides of the issue.

The opponents of evolutionary theory were noisy, but only in the Southern Baptist Convention did they succeed, in 1926, in securing an official condemnation of developmental theories of human origins. They also had mixed success in the state legislatures and statewide referenda, passing restrictive laws in Florida, Tennessee, Mississippi, and Arkansas. William Jennings Bryan's appearance at the trial of John Scopes in 1925 strengthened the antievolutionary sentiment in the rural South, but by the end of the 1920s the issue seemed to fade away. A number of prominent religious leaders—men like the Baptist E. Y. Mullins, the Methodist bishops E. D. Mouzon and John M. Moore, and the Presbyterian Hays Watson Smith—had openly opposed the antievolutionary movement, and the opponents of Darwin had failed with the voters and legislatures in all but four states.

Some of the religious opposition to Darwinism reflected a broader opposition to science itself, but many of the fundamentalist opponents of Darwin claimed to be friends of science. They contended only that Darwinism had transcended the bounds of scientific method propounded by Francis Bacon: the evolutionists, they claimed, were insufficiently inductive. Hence with the resurgence of scientific creationism in the 1960s—stimulated in part by the writings of Henry M. Morris of Virginia Polytechnic Institute—southern religious conservatives again tried to compel the schools to teach a biblical science, and only a federal judicial decision in 1982 thwarted them in Arkansas.

Both the 19th-century proponents of natural theology and the later conservative opponents of Darwin usually insisted that the Bible was itself a scientific text and that religious and scientific assertions were therefore equivalent in logical status. The 20th-century southern conservatives have simply held on to the quasi-rationalistic presuppositions of the older 19th-century theological orthodoxy.

See also RELIGION: Fundamentalism; Modernism and Religion; / Thornwell, James Henley

E. Brooks Holifield
Emory University

Theodore Dwight Bozeman, *Protestants in an Age of Science: The Baconian Ideal and Antebellum Religious Thought* (1977); Norman Furniss, *The Fundamentalist Controversy, 1918–31* (1954); Willard B. Gatewood, Jr., *Preachers, Pedagogues and Politicians: The Evolution Controversy in North Carolina, 1920–1927* (1966); E. Brooks Holifield, *The Gentlemen Theologians: American Theology in Southern Culture* (1978); George Marsden, *Fundamentalism and American Culture: The Shaping of Twentieth-Century Evangelicalism, 1870–1925* (1980); James R. Moore, *The Post-Darwinian Controversies: A Study of the Protestant Struggle to Come to Terms with Darwin in Great Britain and America, 1870–1900* (1979); Ronald L. Numbers, *Science* (5 November 1982). ☆

Self-dosage

||||||||||||||||||||||||||||||

Self-dosage has traditionally been the first line of prevention and of therapy by which people seek to combat illness; it is rooted in both the natural and the magical-religious facets of folk medicine as conveyed through oral tradition. Popular health guidebooks, reflecting input from both folk and developing scientific medicine, have influenced self-dosage patterns, as has advertising for patented drugs. The most significant distinguishing features of southern self-dosage have arisen from the higher proportion of blacks in the South than elsewhere in the nation and from the region's enduring rural atmosphere.

Immigrant groups brought their respective folk legacies to America, elements of which survived intact or with only minor adjustments. Antecedents and analogues in earlier European experience can be found for many health rituals and herb remedies still used in the South, as recorded in such collections as the Frank C. Brown Collection of North Carolina Folklore at Duke University and the John Q. Anderson Folklore Archives at the University of Houston. An example is a wart cure by magical transference: rub the wart with a stolen dishrag; bury the rag; when the rag rots, the wart disappears. Garlic, one of the most ancient folk medicines, continues to be used.

Local conditions in the New World modified inherited traditions, introducing indigenous flora and fauna learned from the Indians or discovered empirically. In Texas, prickly pear, mesquite, and the roadrunner were used as medical remedies. New amulets—alligator teeth, for instance—might join or replace old cures. Once introduced, newcomers tended to persist. A 1967 study in the environs of Jacksonville, Fla., found several very old remedies still flourishing: a cure-all made with nine rusty nails in a pint of whiskey, clay eating for worms, starch eating for easy pregnancy.

Slaves brought folk traditions from Africa, but it is impossible to tell what parts of black self-treatment represented African survivals and what parts were European modifications. Black folk medicine, in any event, became richly complex, partly because slaves and exslaves possessed few other sources of power and lacked basic medical care. These factors helped folk medical practices retain vitality among blacks after such traditions weakened in white culture. Black folk medicine survived in fullest form, still somewhat linked to its religious roots, in southern Louisiana, because of both Haitian influences and rural isolation. A renaissance of voodoo traditions has occurred in recent years. Voodoo articles are sold in drugstores and through mail-order catalogs. These black practices also penetrated white self-help approaches.

Throughout the 19th century the health manual supplemented oral tradition in guiding self-treatment. Several of the most influential volumes came from southern presses, especially J. C.

Gunn's *Domestic Medicine, or Poor Man's Friend,* published in Knoxville in 1830 and going through 100 editions by 1870. Lambasting orthodox physicians and their imported drugs, Gunn praised God for having "stored our mountains, fields and meadows with simples [medicinal plants] for healing our diseases." Despite his condemnation of the regulars, Gunn tended to imitate their heroic prescriptions. Samuel Thomson's botanical school of irregular medicine proved popular in the South, as expounded in his *New Guide to Health* and in southern derivatives like Simon Abbott's *The Southern Botanic Physician* (1844). The popularity of such works declined as patent-medicine advertising expanded.

In colonial days the old English patent medicines were advertised from Baltimore to Savannah. Some of them still survive in a generic form in the rural South. Made-in-America proprietaries, rare until independence, boomed under the impact of cultural nationalism. A few southern entrepreneurs entered the cure-all field, but their wares had a merely local sale. The titans of the trade well through the 19th century came from the North, their bilious pills and worm-destroying lozenges dominating the southern market. During the Civil War, trade interruption and Confederate nationalism combined to stimulate southern brands. In 1862 Augusta, the maker of Broom's Anti-Hydropic Tincture, proclaimed in bold type: "DROPSY CURED! NO YANKEE HUMBUG!" But at war's end, northern proprietors sought quickly to recapture their southern markets. Before 1865 was over, a Charleston druggist was shipping southern botanicals to Massachusetts in payment for the packaged remedies of J. C. Ayer. A Columbia, S.C., editor complained that southern newspapers again sold ad-

vertising at cut rates to Yankee "patent blood-suckers." Such Yankee bottles far outdistanced southern brands tossed into the moat at Fort Pulaski near Savannah, and Yankee direct-mail ads in a Georgia farm family's papers, filed along with letters from cousins in Arkansas, outnumbered southern nostrum ads.

The New South witnessed a burgeoning of proprietary medicine production. Purgatives were easier to fabricate than cotton textiles, and in this field the South sought to end its colonial subservience. In 1890 Atlanta derived a higher proportion of its gross municipal product from patented drugs than did any other city in the nation, such funds fueling the city's rise to New South leadership. Venturesome pharmacists like John Pemberton and Joseph Jacobs devised, purchased, and promoted a wide variety of brands. Pemberton's Coca-Cola began as a headache remedy and pick-me-up; Asa Candler shrewdly converted the nostrum into a beverage. Other Atlanta brands included Botanic Blood Balm, Swift's Sure Specific, Bradfield's Female Regulator, and Tanlac. Other cities saw similar developments. In Chattanooga, two Union army veterans sought antebellum southern formulas and parlayed Black Draught and

Advertisements for patented wonder drugs, South Carolina, 1938

Wine of Cardui into fortunes, aided by such salesmen as Huey P. Long.

In antebellum days northern merchandisers promoted patent medicines as of special value for slaves. Many slaves must have brought the medicine habit with them into freedom. Black entrepreneurs came to share in this market, although whites dominated it. Well into the 20th century, black newspapers—even W. E. B. Du Bois's the *Crisis*—while promoting racial pride in news and editorial columns, were forced, to stay solvent, into accepting advertisements for "skin whiteners" and hair straighteners as well as for purported cures for serious ailments.

Hadacol, the tonic devised by the Louisiana politician Dudley LeBlanc in the early 1950s, demonstrated once again the South's receptivity to patent-medicine appeals. The medicine was promoted with a popular song, the "Hadacol Boogie." A tremendous success within the region, the Hadacol boom collapsed when LeBlanc sought to promote it outside the South.

See also ENVIRONMENT: Plant Uses; ETHNIC LIFE: Indian Cultural Contributions; FOLKLIFE: Folk Medicine; Voodoo; INDUSTRY: / Coca-Cola; WOMEN'S LIFE: Healers, Women

James Harvey Young
Emory University

John Q. Anderson, Elizabeth Brandon, and Bruce Jackson, in *American Folk Medicine: A Symposium*, ed. Wayland D. Hand (1976); John B. Blake, James H. Cassedy, and Ronald L. Numbers, in *Medicine without Doctors: Home Health Care in American History*, ed. Guenter B. Risse et al. (1977); Floyd Martin Clay, *Coozan Dudley LeBlanc: From Huey Long to Hadacol* (1973); Wayland D. Hand, ed., *Popular Beliefs and Superstitions*

from North Carolina (1961, 1964, 1981); James Harvey Young, *The Toadstool Millionaires: A Social History of Patent Medicines in America before Federal Regulations* (1961). ☆

Technology

||||||||||||||||||||||||||||||

Southern industry has traditionally included the processing of lumber, coal, and agricultural commodities. Enterprises like these tended to perpetuate low wages and minimal skills. In fact, the agrarian tradition encouraged movement of the work force in and out of these industries on a seasonal basis. Early societal patterns seemed little affected by technology, although Eli Whitney's invention of the cotton gin in 1793 provided a technological foundation for the South's development. Most southerners could easily identify with the position of ardent agriculturalists like Edmund Ruffin, a staunch advocate of the superiority of southern agrarian society in the antebellum era. Rural life was generally believed to be the most wholesome, moral, and virtuous form of existence. At the same time, technological enterprises like the iron industry, dating from the early colonial era, slowly advanced with the western and southern frontiers; by 1860 furnaces, forges, and rolling mills could be found from Delaware south to Georgia and as far west as Texas. Although the Civil War stimulated the growth of iron production in the South, even that industry lay in ruins by 1865.

In the late 19th century many farsighted southern leaders argued that the region needed to industrialize or forever remain a backwater of rural poverty. The agrarian past would not be totally rejected; rather, a New South would have diversified, multicrop agriculture along with diversified manufacturing, lively commerce, and busy citizens. The best-remembered spokesman for the bold new departure was Henry W. Grady, editor of the Atlanta *Constitution*. Grady had watched a revitalized Atlanta emerge from the rubble of the Civil War. Commerce, industry, and urbanization, having worked wonders in Atlanta, could do the same for the Deep South. "The Old South rested everything on slavery and agriculture, unconscious that these could neither give nor maintain healthy growth," he argued in his famous New York address of 1886. The New South, he continued, represented a healthy democracy, "a hundred farms for every plantation, fifty homes for every palace—and a diversified industry that meets the complex need of this complex age." If the realities fell short of this generous ideal, and if overt racism and a patrician style of government still persisted, Grady's vigorous acceptance of urbanism and technology represented a significant shift away from the traditional patterns of culture.

The South's iron industry slowly recovered in the 1880s, especially in areas around Chattanooga, Tenn., and Birmingham, Ala. During World War I and World War II modern techniques for steel production developed, resulting in new plants in Texas; in the postwar era smaller, specialized facilities appeared throughout the South.

Factories and cities became more numerous in the South in the early 20th century, growing even more visible as a result of World War I and its urgent production requirements. Living patterns consistent with a technological society became more commonplace. During World War I and through the mid-1920s, lumbering made a considerable impact. Without completely disrupting rural social patterns, lumbering brought weekly paydays and tended to lessen the uncertainties of sharecropping. When the momentum of the timber industry declined, southern sawmill workers did not return to the farm but moved to newly resurgent southern cities or industrial centers in the North. In order to retain year-round farm labor, farmers in industrial areas were forced to enter into new arrangements. Wages had to come closer to industrial levels, and a day's work came to mean 8 hours, not 16. In many older farming areas, technological society, as represented by industry, encountered stubborn hostility.

The process of industrialization became the catalyst for another technological phenomenon, the automobile. For years, the lack of adequate highways was seen as a serious shortcoming in attracting new industries and expanding existing ones. Just before World War I, surfaced roads were so rare that textbooks in southern elementary schools included pictures of them as wonderful examples of the future. Aggressive highway commissions flourished in the 1920s, with gasoline taxes providing necessary revenues for road construction. Passable in every season, surfaced roads permitted large and small industries to spread throughout the rural South where railroads and rivers were nonexistent. For farmers, trucking brought new economic possibilities in marketing crops and livestock. After 1945 highways carried a flood of northern tourists in search of shrewdly marketed southern charm and a frost-free climate. Collectively, roads, cars, and trucks have helped end rural isolation.

The automobile shielded individual poverty from the public eye. On foot or astride a mule, poverty could be seen in ragged clothes and bare feet, but a car offered a technological cloak. Automobiles provided mobility, opening new horizons of change and opportunity. For poor southerners, the automobile became as significant as medicine or clothing. Following World War II, southerners bought more cars than any other regional market group in the United States. Autos were an expression of individuality, as the prewar novels of William Faulkner and Robert Penn Warren show. In the postwar era, the role of the auto as a popular icon was evident in the huge throngs attracted to stock car races in places such as Darlington, S.C., and Daytona Beach, Fla.

During the 1920s, as the South followed the seemingly irresistible patterns of commerce and industry "up North," there were still dissenters. The most celebrated example was the Agrarian movement at Vanderbilt University in Nashville, Tenn. Although the Agrarian critique was rooted in southern values and directed toward the southern scene, literary critic Louis D. Rubin, Jr., has noted that it was consonant with other contemporary attacks on the materialism and depersonalization of 20th-century industrial society. In general, the Agrarians appealed to the younger generation to resist the onslaught of modern technology and harked back to an earlier era of southern agriculture as more harmonious and reasonable. Their manifesto, *I'll Take My Stand: The South and the Agrarian Tradition* (1930), seems not to have been taken seriously as an antitechnological tract by the great majority of southerners. In truth, the Agrarians did not intend to do away with

technology but wanted to keep it within the bounds of a humanistic society. Stark Young, a contributor to *I'll Take My Stand*, asserted that "we can accept the machine, but create our own attitude toward it."

In some respects, the Great Depression of the 1930s was an interlude, a time when industrialization, city building, and technological changes subsided; but only on the surface. The advent of highways and automobiles, the creation of the TVA, the spread of rural electrification, and the onset of World War II set in motion a series of changes of fundamental significance.

In the postwar era inexpensive electricity supported the spread of air-conditioning to rural homes and urban offices alike, and the technology of the military-industrial complex left a pervasive imprint on southern culture. Army, navy, and air force installations dotted the region; Maryland, Georgia, and Texas became major centers of aerospace research and development and of manufacturing. As the nation's space program accelerated during the 1960s, the South achieved international attention due to the location of several key installations of the National Aeronautics and Space Administration in Texas, Alabama, and Florida—a new "fertile crescent." The wartime stimulus of petroleum production and the refining industry was followed by increasing sophistication of the petrochemical industry, electronics, and medical research. These and other commercial/industrial trends have profoundly influenced educational patterns and career choices within an urbanized, industrial society.

The South's fierce attachment to the soil has been altered by an array of interrelated technological factors. Mechanization has changed the pastoral rhythms set by mules and plow horses;

ancient landmarks such as boulder-strewn hummocks and fern-lined gullies have been leveled and filled for maximum farm production or for shopping malls. Although postwar industries have often provided the principal income necessary to allow rural families to stay on the "old place," while feeding a few cows and tilling a few acres on the side, much of the rural population has moved into burgeoning urban centers like Atlanta and Houston or to northern cities. More than ever, regional economics became tied to global vagaries of prices for oil, steel, pulpwood, and other commodities.

The spread of technology has contributed to some notable shifts in traditional cultural patterns. Attuned to the realities of the technological world, southern governors within the last few years banded together to urge Congress to raise certain tariffs to protect regional industry, a position that would have outraged southern Populists in the 1890s. The new realities also prompted southern civic leaders to renew criticism of the Ku Klux Klan and other racist groups because such organizations discouraged new industry from moving south.

In past decades, chambers of commerce relied on stock identifications like "Dixie" and "Sunny South," terms that promised pastoral grace of a bygone era, to advertise the region. By the 1970s the preferred term was "Sunbelt," an appellation that, although not excluding the agrarian past, identified a region of commercial opportunity, cosmopolitan services and entertainment, and a hi-tech culture.

See also AGRICULTURE: Mechanization; Rural Electrification Administration; ENVIRONMENT: Air-Conditioning; Tennessee Valley Authority; HISTORY AND MANNERS: Automobile; Railroads; INDUSTRY articles; LITERATURE: Agrarianism in Literature; MYTHIC SOUTH: New South Myth; / Agrarians, Vanderbilt; RECREATION: Tourism, Automobile

Roger E. Bilstein
University of Houston
at Clear Lake City

Richard M. Bernard and Bradley R. Rice, eds., *Sunbelt Cities: Politics and Growth since World War II* (1983); Blaine A. Brownell and David R. Goldfield, eds., *The City in Southern History: The Growth of Urban Civilization in the South* (1977); Thomas D. Clark, *The Emerging South* (1961); Louis D. Rubin, Jr., ed., *The American South: Portrait of a Culture* (1980); Loyd S. Swenson, *Southwestern Historical Quarterly* (January 1968). ☆

BRECKINRIDGE, MARY
(1881–1965) Nurse.

"If you take the unborn child as a focal point," Mary Breckinridge once said, "you will soon be led to a broad program of public health." In this succinct fashion she summarized over five decades of ongoing medical service with a unique health organization, the Frontier Nursing Service (FNS), in the isolated mountains of southeastern Kentucky.

Born in Memphis, Tenn., to a prominent southern family and educated at finishing schools in Switzerland and Connecticut, Breckinridge took a nursing degree from St. Luke's Hospital in New York. Her placid existence as an upper-class southern woman was disrupted by a series of personal tragedies. Twice married (widowed in 1906, divorced in 1920, after which she resumed use of her maiden name), she lost two children in infancy. These misfortunes coupled with a strong family sense of noblesse oblige prompted her to devote the remainder of her life to the cause of child welfare. After service in Europe with the American Committee for Devastated France, she took graduate courses in midwifery at London's British Mothers and Babies Hospital and became a certified midwife.

In 1925, at the age of 44, Mary Breckinridge brought the concept of the professional nurse-midwife to the United States when she established the FNS at Hyden, Leslie County, Ky. She chose the mountains of her family's native region because she could draw on the prestige of the Breckinridge name and the support of numerous relatives. Riding on horseback, "Mrs. Breckinridge's nurses" provided midwifery and general nursing care to some 10,000 people in a 300-square-mile area, where there were few roads and no licensed doctors, telephones, or electricity. World War II brought the departure of most of the British staff and soon prevented American travel abroad for training; Breckinridge then established a graduate school of midwifery at Hyden, which expanded in 1970 to include a family nursing program to train students in primary-care nursing.

Breckinridge's concept of rural southern health care proved prophetic. An early exponent of community involvement, she recognized that the local people themselves should participate in decisions affecting their own welfare. Furthermore, she applied the concept of the family nurse practitioner in Appalachia long before many in the medical profession became cognizant of the idea. She also demonstrated that the health of mothers and babies could be significantly improved through midwifery services. In 1980, after 55 years of operation, the FNS had supervised 18,885 maternity cases with a loss of 11 mothers in childbirth. There have been no maternal deaths since 1952.

Carol Crowe-Carraco
Western Kentucky University

Mary Breckinridge, *Wide Neighborhoods: A Story of the Frontier Nursing Service* (1952); Breckinridge Family Papers, University of Kentucky; Carol Crowe-Carraco, *Register of Kentucky Historical Society* (July 1978). ☆

CARVER, GEORGE WASHINGTON
(c. 1864–1943) Scientist.

Born in the final days of slavery in southwest Missouri, George Washington Carver was raised by his former owners, left home before his teenage years, and wandered until he was almost 30 years old seeking the elusive goal of many black contemporaries—a good education. After a brief career as an art major at Simpson College, he entered Iowa State, where his impressive abilities in botany earned him an invitation to pursue postgraduate studies. He received his master's degree in agriculture in 1896 and immediately accepted the position of director of agricultural studies at Booker T. Washington's Tuskegee Institute in Macon County, Ala. Although he intended to stay only long enough to establish a viable program, Carver remained at Tuskegee until his death in 1943.

For the first 20 years there he labored under the shadow of Washington, endeavoring to improve the conditions of the poor and often landless black farmers of the South. He tried to provide inexpensive alternatives to costly commercial products at the experiment sta-

George Washington Carver, botanist and agricultural researcher, 1906

tion he founded. His research and varied extension activities placed him in the mainstream, and sometimes the forefront, of agricultural education, but his idea of small-scale technology based on available and renewable resources was increasingly out of tune with the current trends. His efforts therefore brought limited recognition, but they did aid thousands of individuals who were struggling under crushing burdens of debt within the sharecropping and tenancy systems of southern agriculture.

His international fame came after Washington's death in 1915, when much of Carver's most useful work was over. His renown resulted mainly from his symbolic importance to a myriad of causes and was largely based on his essentially unsuccessful attempts to find commercial uses for such southern crops as peanuts and sweet potatoes. The eccentricities of his personality and the romance of his life story provided good copy for the press, and he was adopted as an exemplar by numerous groups—

some with contradictory goals. He represented both the beneficence of slavery and segregation and the ability of Afro-Americans. He was also used by the peanut industry, various religious groups, and New South editors preaching agricultural diversification and industrialization.

Although a growing mythology accompanied his rise to prominence, Carver continued to play an important role in the South. His warm, compelling personality led to numerous friendships with southern whites and provided a liberalizing influence on some newspapermen and many students whom he met during his lectures at white colleges. He also remained an inspiration to southern blacks as he was repeatedly hailed as one of Dixie's leading citizens.

Linda O. McMurry
North Carolina State University

George Washington Carver Papers, Tuskegee Institute Archives, Tuskegee, Ala.; Linda O. McMurry, *George Washington Carver: Scientist and Symbol* (1981). ☆

CHARLESTON MUSEUM

Founded in 1670 through land grants to wealthy planters from Barbados, the city of Charles Town, now Charleston, S.C., rapidly became one of the leading cultural centers in British colonial America. A keen interest in the "natural curiosities" of the region soon developed, and in 1773 the Charles Town Library Society "fitted up a Museum for the Reception and Preservation of Specimens of these . . . natural Productions." With those intentions, the first museum in America was established.

In 1778 a disastrous fire destroyed

most of its holdings, but the society began anew in temporary quarters and in 1785 moved its collections into the present courthouse. Records of specimens received by the museum from 1798 to 1808 include items from around the globe, reflecting Charleston's importance as a port of call for the growing American merchant fleet.

In 1815 the Library Society gave its collections to the newly formed Literary and Philosophical Society of South Carolina, and by 1825 the museum had made great strides under the leadership of botanist Stephen Elliott. At that time it was located in Chalmers Street and was known as the Museum of South Carolina. In 1828 the museum was moved to the Medical College but made little progress after Elliott's death in 1830.

At the urging of the celebrated naturalist Louis Agassiz, the museum collections were given to the College of Charleston in 1850 and were provided with larger quarters and a full-time curator in the person of Francis S. Holmes, a pioneer in local paleontological studies. Numerous contributions to the collections were made by the Elliott Society of Natural History, formed in 1853 by members of the Charleston scientific community, which included Holmes, John Bachman, Lewis Gibbes, John Holbrook, Edmund and Henry Ravenel, and John McCrady, all of whom published important works in their fields. With men like these, and with the only museum south of Philadelphia, Charleston was the major center of scientific activities in the South prior to the Civil War. But the ruinous defeat of the South in that conflict dealt a devastating blow to scientific progress in South Carolina, the museum's collections being among the only surviving evidence of Charleston's antebellum eminence.

The museum remained at the College of Charleston until its removal to the vacant Thompson Auditorium building on Rutledge Avenue in 1907. In 1915 it became an independent organization administered by a director and a board of trustees and was officially chartered as the Charleston Museum. After more than 70 years in the badly deteriorating Rutledge Avenue building the museum was moved to a modern new building on the corner of John and Meeting streets in 1980. One of the largest museums in the South, its extensive collections in cultural and natural history are used by scholars throughout the nation. Its holdings also include the historically significant Heyward-Washington House, Joseph Manigault House, and William Aiken House.

See also URBANIZATION: / Charleston

Albert E. Sanders
Charleston Museum

Caroline M. Borowsky, *Museum News* (February 1963); Laura M. Bragg, *Charleston Museum Quarterly* (1923); William G. Mazyck, *Charleston Museum Bulletin* (1907); David Ramsay, *The History of South Carolina from its Original Settlement in 1670 to the Year 1808* (1809); *South Carolina Gazette* (22 March 1773). ☆

COUNTRY DOCTOR
‖‖

Rural doctors have long been viewed as different from their urban counterparts. Although the distinctions well known in Britain between physicians, surgeons, and apothecaries applied occasionally in the colonial South, such distinctions were mostly absent from the later southern rural scene. During the first half of the 19th century a sense of identity among country doctors emerged. Many country doctors wrote to the growing number of medical journals in the 1840s and 1850s. One such Virginia physician commented that "the life of a physician in the country is very different from that of his professional brother who ministers to the ills of humanity in our towns and cities. Whilst the latter can recline at ease in his carriage, during the performance of his daily routine of visits, enjoying all the luxury of practice . . . his country 'confrere' has to undergo a life of constant, frequently *excessive* labor, often riding for hours during the most inclement weather, braving the frost and snows of winter."

While the general fortunes of country doctors throughout the United States were many and varied in the second half of the 19th century, the famous painting *The Doctor* (1891), by British artist Luke Fildes, conveyed an image of benevolence and trust that captured the imagination of physicians and laypersons alike throughout America. More than 1,000,000 engravings of it were to be found in parlors and physicians' waiting rooms.

How accurate is this image for the 19th-century South? The distinctive aura of the country doctor surely owed much to the practitioners' professional concerns, tinged with a negative attitude toward rural life and people. A fear of becoming outdated while living in areas without intellectual stimulation emerges time and time again in country doctors' correspondence and journals from the second half of the 19th century and into the 20th. These attitudes, coupled with the modern transformation of American medicine through rampant specialization and the relentless growth of institutions, contributed to the virtual

disappearance of the country doctor by the 1950s.

In many ways the declining numbers encouraged a sense of nostalgia for the "good old country doc" depicted in Luke Fildes's picture. On the other hand, oral testimony can still be gathered—to be added to 19th-century correspondence—that indicates many country doctors provided medical treatment within the context of community needs. They maintained congenial relations with midwives; set flexible arrangements for payment (either in coin or in kind); and prescribed both well-known botanical remedies, which were sometimes collected locally by or for the doctor, and new drugs advertised by pharmaceutical companies.

Once frequently found in the South and elsewhere, such characteristics have become the essence of a romantic stereotype. The rural South provided an ideal location for those doctors who traveled endless miles to carry out their duties.

Paul I. Crellin
Country Doctor Museum
Bailey, North Carolina

Aubrey D. Gates, in *This Is the South*, ed. Robert W. Howard (1959); Arthur E. Hertzler, *Horse and Buggy Doctor* (1970); Paul Starr, *The Social Transformation of American Medicine: The Rise of a Sovereign Profession and the Making of a Vast Industry* (1982). ☆

CREATION SCIENCE

Creation science, or scientific creationism, supports the biblical story that man and earth were created suddenly by the Supreme Being. Identified with fundamentalist religion in the United States, creation science holds that scientific evidence supports the biblical refutation of Darwinian evolution as an explanation for human existence. In the 1980s the creationism controversy has centered around the argument that creation science should be taught in the public schools as a scientific alternative to evolution.

This argument between religious fundamentalism and public education has repeatedly surfaced in the South, where conservatives and fundamentalists have organized and pressured local and state school districts and legislators. In response to such pressures, the Louisiana Legislature in 1981 passed its Balanced Treatment Act requiring teachers to teach the theory of scientific creationism if they mention evolution. The case challenging the law's constitutionality was brought by the Louisiana Board of Education and the American Civil Liberties Union and supported by some teachers, scientists, and religious groups. It was struck down by the U.S. Supreme Court in 1986. Opponents of the law contended that it was an effort to inject religion into the public schools. The Louisiana Department of Justice and scientific creationists supporting the law, however, argued that creation science is not a religion but a valid scientific theory. On these grounds, they held, the First Amendment requires the presentation of scientific creationism along with evolution.

In a similar case, which has been compared to the Scopes Trial of 1925, a group of Hawkins County, Tenn., families won a court decision against the Tennessee Board of Education for refusing to provide alternative readers for their children. The parents disagreed with several passages in the elementary readers on grounds that they conflicted with their religious views. As in the Louisiana case, fundamentalists cited the First Amendment, arguing that it guarantees their right to free exercise of religion, a right that was being hindered by the state's school system. Powerful national lobbying groups became involved in the case as it attracted attention outside the South.

The recent controversy over scientific creationism differs significantly from the post–World War I battle to outlaw the teaching of evolution of which the Scopes Trial was a part. In the 1920s, also, the South led the fight to take the theory of evolution out of public schools. Four southern states—Arkansas, Florida, Mississippi, and Tennessee—passed restrictive legislation on the issue. The antievolutionists responsible for these laws, led by William Jennings Bryan, openly defended their views as biblically based.

In the 1970s the creationism movement was revived with an entirely different focus, influenced by the efforts of Henry M. Morris, a Texas engineer. Morris, raised a Southern Baptist, argued in *The Genesis Flood* (1961) for a return to the belief in a literal six-day creation and a worldwide flood as described in the Bible. His strict creationism was hotly debated within the scientific community. Morris's book generated arguments that are significant because they appeared to be legitimate scientific ones, rather than judgments of faith based on biblical passages.

In the 1970s Morris joined with fundamentalists outside the scientific world in a renewed effort to propagate creationist ideas. The new fight stressed the scientific aspect of creationism, offered evidence for a worldwide catastrophe, and focused on arguments against evolution. Creationists in the latter part of this century have turned away from attempting to outlaw evolution and have argued that creationism deserves "equal time." The main goal of recent creationists has been to give their ideas scientific legitimacy and to establish intellectual equality with evolutionist theories. Their tactics have included portraying the withholding of alternatives to evolution as "censorship" that violates First Amendment rights.

Karen M. McDearman
University of Mississippi

Melinda Beck, *Newsweek* (28 July 1986); John Hill, Jackson *Clarion-Ledger* (5 October 1986); Ronald L. Numbers, *Science* (5 November 1982). ☆

Micheal DeBakey, pioneering heart surgeon, 1970s

DeBAKEY, MICHAEL
(b. 1908) Surgeon.

Dr. Michael Ellis DeBakey, chancellor of the Baylor University College of Medicine in Houston, Tex., ranks among the world's leading authorities in the field of cardiovascular research.

Born 7 September 1908 in Lake Charles, La., the son of a Lebanese immigrant, DeBakey received his M.D. degree from Tulane University, worked for some time under the well-known New Orleans surgeon Dr. Alton Ochsner, then served with the surgeon general during World War II. In 1948 he moved to Baylor and quickly began to earn laurels for himself and the school.

DeBakey's achievements in the world of medical science are legion. In the area of technology he made improvements in the heart-lung machine, developed an artificial ventricle to be used on a temporary basis by heart-surgery patients, and participated in the attempt to design an artificial heart to replace the human organ. A skilled surgeon, he operated successfully on thousands of patients and was a pioneer in heart-transplant surgery. He published hundreds of scholarly articles to report on the results of his research and was granted many scientific and humanitarian awards as well as a number of honorary degrees, both in the United States and abroad.

In addition to his scientific achievements DeBakey also distinguished himself as an outspoken advocate of government support for various facets of American medicine. He was appointed by Presidents John F. Kennedy and Lyndon B. Johnson to serve on advisory councils that, despite the opposition of organized medicine, recommended that federal funds be used for regional programs to improve patient care for victims of heart disease, cancer, and stroke. He also stressed the need for government sponsorship of pure research and medical education.

During the nearly four decades of his association with Baylor, DeBakey has served in a number of leadership capacities. Moreover, he was also largely responsible for the development of two of the world's leading centers of heart surgery—Methodist Hospital and the Texas Heart Institute, both in Houston. With his work receiving worldwide acclaim and his organizational skill building these lasting institutions, DeBakey has been a significant factor in transforming this southern city into a major international medical center.

Lucie R. Bridgforth
Memphis State University

Saturday Review (16 October 1971); *Time* (28 May 1965). ☆

DIRT EATING (GEOPHAGY)

Geophagy (geophagia), or the conscious consumption of soils, has been observed worldwide for centuries. References to the practice of consuming soils dates back as far as 40 B.C., when Greeks consumed specific clays to combat a variety of illnesses. Wherever the practice has been observed, its specific content has varied according to the local culture.

The practice of geophagy in the United States is decidedly associated with the South. Geophagy was first observed among blacks during slavery. References to clay eating by both black and white females and young children were frequently made in scientific and popular literature of the 1800s. The consumption of soils is not a haphazard practice but a clearly defined one, as only specific clays are extracted and at times prepared (baked) for eating. Although some physiological mechanisms may be involved, clays are consumed mainly because they are identified by the local culture as a food. No overall detrimental health effects from consuming clays have been documented.

The practice of geophagy became more widespread as a result of the mass migration of southern blacks out of the region from 1920 to 1940. However, southern culture and traditions still dominate the practice today. Because many clay eaters prefer southern clays, it is not unusual for these substances to be shipped to the urban North from the rural South. Geophagy today is on the wane with many clay eaters either stopping altogether or switching to commercial products such as laundry starch and baking soda, which have textures similar to clay.

Dennis A. Frate
University of Mississippi

Francis B. Bradley, *North Carolina Folklore* (December 1964); Dennis A. Frate, *Sciences* (November–December 1984); Robert W. Twyman, *Journal of Southern History* (August 1971); Donald E. Vermeer and Dennis A. Frate, *American Journal of Clinical Nutrition* (October 1979). ☆

DISEASE, ENDEMIC

During the height of southern nationalism (1830–60) some physicians, led by Samuel A. Cartwright of New Orleans, argued for a belief in uniquely southern diseases. In addition to the clear social and political utility of such opinions, epidemiological observations at the time strongly supported the idea. During the 18th century malarial fevers were common in the northern colonies and yellow fever struck northern ports, but, for reasons not fully understood, malaria and yellow fever almost disappeared from the northern states in the 19th century. The latitude of southern ports, and commercial ties with the tropics, gave the South semitropical diseases uncommon in other regions. Most dramatically, during the 19th century the great epidemics of yellow fever were phenomena of southern ports, but three endemic diseases—hookworm, pellagra, and, most importantly, malaria—probably had a more profound, if more difficult to evaluate, role in the shaping of southern life.

Hookworm disease, or uncinariasis, is the result of infestation with the hookworm, *Necator americanus*, identified by Charles Stiles in 1902. Hookworms thrive in areas without snow cover and in sandy soil, conditions common to most of the South. Reports in the 19th-century medical literature frequently show people with symptoms of anemia and physical and mental retardation compatible with the diagnosis of hookworm disease, but only the identification of the parasite made possible precise diagnosis. By 1911 hookworm infections had been scientifically proven by local health authorities in 719 of 884 southern counties. This level of parasitism supported, if it did not largely explain, the characteristic malaise associated with southerners; and, in fact, early in the 20th century the hookworm was widely identified as the southern "germ of laziness." One of the earliest diseases targeted for eradication by sci-

entific public health campaigns, hookworm was the first public health focus of the Rockefeller philanthropies (1909–13). Since World War II, hookworm infection has been controlled by economic improvement, case treatment, and improved public health and sanitation.

Pellagra is a disease that results from an inadequacy of niacin, one of the B vitamins. It is traditionally associated with corn diets because corn is low in niacin and in tryptophan, a metabolic precursor of niacin. Although reported in 39 states, pellagra was a southern disease because of the traditional southern diet. The early symptoms of pellagra are diverse and nonspecific, but the disease is associated with lassitude and weakness followed by anxiety and irritability. Once quite prevalent—by one estimate, 25,000 cases in 1915—pellagra has declined dramatically with improved nutrition.

Despite the importance of hookworms

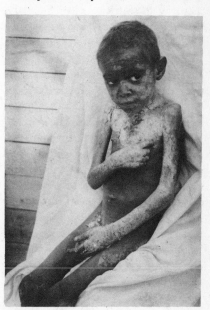

Young boy with pellagra, early 20th-century rural South

and pellagra in the New South and probably at other times, the disease that has had the greatest impact on southern culture and life is clearly malaria. Malaria is an infectious disease that classically presents a fever pattern of regular remission and exacerbation with intermittent, remittent, or periodic fever. The disease is spread from person to person via the mosquito and so does not usually appear to be contagious. Its transmission by mosquito also causes a seasonal prevalence of the disease in temperate zones; it is more widespread in the summer and fall when mosquitoes are plentiful. This pattern strongly influenced the pattern of life in the Old South, for planter families would flee the plantations for high country, coastal islands, or northern cities during the sickly season. Although malaria was common in northern Europe and was brought to America by early colonists, a particularly malignant form of the disease was probably introduced into the South by the African slave trade; its widespread incidence made southern fevers much more deadly than the similar fevers of other regions. Furthermore, malaria disappeared with lengthy settlement in the North—during the 18th century in New England and by late in the 19th century in the Midwest. In general, malaria, preeminently a disease of rural poverty, exacerbates the other effects of poverty by physically weakening its victims while making them more susceptible to other diseases.

Numerous other diseases were and are common in the American South, but these three—all diseases of poverty, but all now controlled by public health measures—have exerted a severe physical, mental, and emotional burden on the people of the region. By accidents of geography and history, all were in a very real sense "southern diseases."

Dale C. Smith
Uniformed Services University
of the Health Sciences
Bethesda, Maryland

Daniel Drake, *Malaria in the Interior Valley of North America* (1964); Elizabeth W. Etheridge, *The Butterfly Caste: A Social History of Pellagra in the South* (1972); John Ettling, *The Germ of Laziness: Rockefeller Philanthropy and Public Health in the New South* (1981); Harry Frank Farmer, "The Hookworm Eradication Program in the South, 1900–1925" (Ph.D. dissertation, University of Georgia, 1970); Rockefeller Foundation International Health Board, *Bibliography of Hookworm Disease*, Publication No. 11 (1922); Rockefeller Foundation Sanitary Commission for Eradication of Hookworm, *Annual Reports* (1910–15); Todd L. Savitt, *Medicine and Slavery: The Diseases and Health Care of Blacks in Antebellum Virginia* (1978); Allen Tullos, *Southern Exposure* (Summer 1978). ☆

DISEASE, EPIDEMIC

Historians of medicine in the South today agree that disease is a central theme in the history of southern culture, a theme at one time punctuated by epidemics related closely to forces that shaped the region. Perhaps the most important force throughout the colonial period and beyond was climate. The rigors of adaptation were much greater in southern than in northern colonies for European immigrants. Among the major epidemic afflictions, malaria (especially in its pernicious or malignant form) and dysentery took a proportionately greater toll of lives in a region where warm weather over a long season fostered the survival of insects that carry disease as well as the transmission of water- and food-borne diseases. Also, the ostensibly greater hardiness of blacks in swampy areas, due to immunological factors including the sickle-cell trait, served in part to support the rationalization of slavery and, thus, the beginnings of a culture of poverty. To some degree epidemics of respiratory diseases, diphtheria, scarlet fever, whooping cough (pertussis), and measles were moderated by relative dispersion of the region's rural population. Colonial Charleston was repeatedly ravaged by violent epidemics of yellow fever and smallpox. And there can be no question that the white man's most potent weapon in warring with southern Indian tribes was smallpox.

During 19th-century regional expansion, a rising agricultural economy, developments in transportation, and urban growth made southern cities and river towns particularly vulnerable to epidemic disease. Cholera and yellow fever were especially significant. Like other parts of the country, southern towns and their nearby countryside were devastated by cholera epidemics in the years following 1832, 1849, and 1866, but in 1873 only communities in the lower Mississippi Valley were stricken. Unlike cholera, whose ancestral home is India, yellow fever came to the Western Hemisphere by way of the African slave trade. By the 1850s, as a result of almost annually recurring epidemics of violent intensity, the name of New Orleans had become virtually synonymous in the North and abroad with sickness and death. However, it was the disastrous Mississippi Valley yellow fever epidemic in 1878, together with postwar poverty, that generated the growth of a widespread and not wholly inaccurate

perception of the South as a diseased region, which eventually brought it into the mainstream of the 20th-century American public health movement. Epidemic disease has played a historically continuous and significant role in shaping contemporary southern culture.

John H. Ellis
Lehigh University

Jo Ann Carrigan, *Journal of Southern History* (November 1970); John Duffy, *Epidemics in Colonial America* (1953); John H. Ellis, *Bulletin of the History of Medicine* (May–June, July–August 1970). ☆

GARDEN, ALEXANDER

(1730–1791) Physician and naturalist.

Alexander Garden was born at Birse, Scotland, near Aberdeen, where his father was a Church of Scotland minister. He attended Marischal College and began the study of medicine as an apprentice to an Aberdeen physician. He served two years in the Royal Navy as a surgeon's mate. After study at the University of Edinburgh, in 1752 he immigrated to South Carolina, becoming one of the leading physicians of Charleston. Although Garden was highly regarded there, his loyalty to Great Britain necessitated that he leave when Loyalists were expelled following the Revolution. He spent the remainder of his life in London.

Although he has sometimes been called the most famous physician of colonial times, Garden made even greater contributions as an untiring student of natural history. Very shortly after his arrival in South Carolina he established himself as one of the small group of men who were eagerly helping European scientists to understand the natural history of North America. He was ambitious for recognition as a scientist of importance. His interests were broad, including plants, animals, medical problems, the health of slaves, climate, minerals, and other aspects of the environment. He sent plant specimens to Charles Alston in Edinburgh, John Ellis in London, and Carolus Linnaeus in Sweden. Amphibians, fish, insects, and reptiles went to Linnaeus and to John F. Gronovius in Holland. Birds were supplied to Thomas Pennant in England. Garden contributed to the local scene as well, being a stimulus to, and an active participant in, the intellectual and cultural life of Charleston.

His importance was well recognized in his own time. He was elected to membership in the most prestigious scientific societies in both America and Europe, including the American Philosophical Society, the Royal Society of Arts and Science of Upsala, the Royal Society of London, the Royal Society of Arts (London), and the Royal Society of Edinburgh. Linnaeus named the *Gardenia* in his honor.

Garden's publications were few, largely journal articles describing plants and animals. Many of his letters survive and testify to his facility as a writer. His correspondents included all of those persons mentioned above and also John Bartram, Cadwallader Colden, John Clayton, and Benjamin Franklin.

Edmund Berkeley
Dorothy Smith Berkeley
Charlottesville, Virginia

Edmund Berkeley and Dorothy Smith Berkeley, *Dr. Alexander Garden of Charles Town* (1969). ☆

GORGAS, JOSIAH
|||||||||||||||||||||||||||||||||||||||||
(1818–1883) Confederate ordnance officer.

Josiah Gorgas was born 1 July 1818 at Running Pumps, Pa. Graduating sixth in his West Point class in 1841, Gorgas chose the ordnance service and later served in the Mexican War, mostly in depot duty at Vera Cruz. After the war, Gorgas was assigned to duty at a series of arsenals from Maine to Alabama. Ironically, during this period Gorgas strengthened the defenses of Fort Pickens in Pensacola Harbor so effectively that Confederate forces were unable to destroy it during the Civil War.

Upon the organization of the Confederacy Gorgas was offered the post of chief of ordnance. He hesitated, but after receiving word that he had been given an unsatisfactory new assignment in the U.S. Army service he accepted his new Confederate post. That such an important position had been offered to, and accepted by, a "Pennsylvania Yankee" indicates the powerful influence of southern culture, especially in the American military establishment. Gorgas was married to Amelia Gayle of Alabama and through her politically powerful family was drawn into association with prominent southerners. In the army Gorgas had become friends with many military leaders from the South, including P. G. T. Beauregard, who recognized that Gorgas's talents in ordnance administration outshone those of most southerners and persuaded Jefferson Davis to offer him the appointment.

During the Civil War Gorgas supervised one of the most effective technological operations in southern history. By midwar, despite a chronic shortage of skilled workmen, Gorgas's organization was manufacturing most of the ordnance supplies that were not secured through battlefield captures and blockade running. Gorgas was a notable technological innovator, but his strength was a knack for planning ahead. He was also able to find and hold the loyalty of talented specialists, while at the same time staying in the good graces of the secretary of war and the president. By early 1864 Gorgas could survey a vast empire east of the Mississippi: 11 arsenals, a superb powder mill at Augusta, four cannon foundries, rifle and pistol production at four armories, a leather-processing plant, a shot-and-shell foundry, and a research laboratory. Even at the Confederacy's collapse in 1865, Gorgas's bureau was able to supply the ordnance needs of the Confederate armies.

After the war Gorgas formed a company to buy an ironworks at Brierfield, Ala., but the business failed. In 1868 he became master of the junior department and later vice-chancellor of the University of the South. In 1878 he became the president of the University of Alabama, but in 1879 his health began to fail and he was forced to resign the presidency. He lingered in ill health and died on 15 May 1883. His son William entered the medical service of the U.S. Army and became the man chiefly responsible for eradicating yellow fever in Cuba and Panama, making the Panama Canal possible.

Richard D. Goff
Eastern Michigan University

Richard D. Goff, *Confederate Supply* (1969); Frank E. Vandiver, *Ploughshares into Swords: Josiah Gorgas and Confederate Ordnance* (1952), ed., *The Civil War Diary of General Josiah Gorgas* (1947). ☆

HERTY, CHARLES HOLMES
(1867–1938) Chemist.

Charles Holmes Herty was a southern chemist whose career as a teacher, researcher, and publicist contributed significantly to the economic development of the South and the growth of chemistry and the organic chemical industry in the United States. Born in Milledgeville, Ga., and educated at Johns Hopkins (Ph.D. 1890), Herty taught at the universities of Georgia and North Carolina from 1891 to 1901 and 1905 to 1916, respectively. Associated with the Bureau of Forestry in the U.S. Department of Agriculture between 1902 and 1904, he patented the Herty Cup and Gutter System of turpentining, which, by supplanting the destructive system of "boxing," then universally practiced in the American South, helped to save the threatened naval stores industry.

Twice elected president of the American Chemical Society (1915–16), Herty attained a national reputation as an expert in wood chemistry and his articulate advocacy of corporate, academic, and governmental cooperation in the establishment of chemical independence from Europe made him a natural for the editorship of the American Chemical Society's *Journal of Industrial and Engineering Chemistry*. He served in that capacity for four years (1917–21), with time out for trips to Europe to advise the American peace commissioners at Versailles on matters regarding German dyestuffs and German patents seized during the war. In 1921 he became president of the Synthetic Organic Chemical Manufacturers' Association, continuing his close relationship with Francis P. Garvan, alien property custodian in the Wilson Administration and president of the

Chemical Foundation created in 1919 to administer the development by private American firms of the seized German patents. In 1926 Herty left the manufacturers' association, became a consultant to the Chemical Foundation, and for two years worked closely with Garvan, using foundation funds to promote research in chemotherapy. He also ran his own consulting firm in New York.

Finally, still interested in southern pine trees, conservation, and diversification of the South's stagnant economy, Herty attracted enough funds from the Chemical Foundation, the state of Georgia, and the citizenry of Savannah to establish an experimental pulp and paper laboratory there in 1932. His goal was to prove that sulphite pulp, suitable for the manufacture of fine white newsprint, could be economically made from young southern pines, thereby encouraging reforestation and freeing the U.S. newspaper industry of its dependence on the more expensive and slow-growing spruce pulp imported largely from Canada. At the same time the poor southern farmer, plagued with worn-out fields or no market for his cotton, would be provided with an alternative cash crop. Most important, new industry would be attracted to the region. Herty's papermaking demonstration, conducted under commercial conditions in a Canadian newsprint factory with pulp shipped from the Savannah lab, was a thorough success. Nine southern dailies printed their 20 November 1933 editions on the first run. As a direct result of Herty's efforts, although he did not live to see it, the first southern newspaper plant was erected near Lufkin, Tex. By 1955 an expanded plant at Lufkin, together with two more firms established in Alabama and Tennes-

see, accounted for 29 percent of all newsprint produced in the United States.

See also AGRICULTURE: / Naval Stores; URBANIZATION: / Savannah

> Germaine M. Reed
> Georgia Institute of Technology

Charles Holmes Herty Papers, Special Collections, Robert Woodruff Library, Emory University; Jack P. Oden, *Journal of Forest History* (April 1977); Gerry Reed, *Journal of Forest History* (October 1982). ☆

LeCONTE, JOHN
(1818–1891) Scientist.

LeCONTE, JOSEPH
(1823–1901) Scientist.

Natives of Liberty County, Ga., John LeConte and his brother, Joseph, were sons of Lewis and Ann Quarterman LeConte. Descended from a French Huguenot, Lewis operated a large plantation and became an able amateur scientist.

Both John and Joseph graduated from the University of Georgia and earned the M.D. degree from the College of Physicians and Surgeons in New York. After the death of their father, each inherited land and slaves. The brothers operated their plantations through overseers until the end of the Civil War. John practiced medicine in Savannah, Ga., from 1843 until 1846, when he was appointed professor of physics and chemistry at the University of Georgia. Joseph established a medical practice in Macon, Ga., in 1847, but three years later he abandoned it in order to study under Louis Agassiz at the Lawrence Scientific School of Harvard University. Upon completing his studies in 1851, he returned to Georgia and accepted the professorship of science at Oglethorpe University. In 1853 he was appointed professor of natural history at the University of Georgia.

As a result of a dispute with the university president, John resigned in 1855, and Joseph left for the same reason a year later. After serving for one year as a lecturer at the College of Physicians and Surgeons, John, in 1857, accepted a post at South Carolina College, where he was joined by his brother at the same time. Held in high regard, the LeConte brothers gained national recognition as scientists during the antebellum period, but they were severely set back by the Civil War.

Devoted defenders of the South, the LeConte brothers deplored the views of the Radical Republicans, and in 1869 they accepted posts at the newly established University of California, where John served as acting president in the 1869–70 academic year and as president from 1875 to 1881. At the time of his death John was a member of several scientific organizations and had published over 80 articles on medicine and physics. Joseph continued to write and eventually published over 190 articles and nine books. A universalist, he wrote on numerous topics, including education, philosophy, religion, evolution, geology, and physiological optics. His books on vision, geology, and evolution and religion received international notice. Both LeContes were elected to membership in the National Academy of Sciences, and Joseph later served as president of the American Association for the Advancement of Science (1892) and the Geological Society of America

(1896). A devoted camper, he was a charter member of the Sierra Club.

Lester D. Stephens
University of Georgia

Joseph LeConte, *Autobiography*, ed. William Dallam Armes (1903); John Samuel Lupold, "From Physician to Physicist: The Scientific Career of John LeConte, 1818–1891" (Ph.D. dissertation, University of South Carolina, 1970); Lester D. Stephens, *Joseph LeConte: Gentle Prophet of Evolution* (1982). ☆

LONG, CRAWFORD W.
||||||||||||||||||||||||||||||||||||||||||||||||||||||||
(1815–1878) Physician.

A general practitioner in the village of Jefferson, Ga., Crawford Williamson Long in March 1842 first used ether to anesthetize a patient, James Venable, prior to the removal of an encysted tumor from the back of his neck. He was thus one of the earliest southern physicians to make a major contribution to medicine.

Born in Danielsville and raised in Jefferson, Long graduated from Franklin College (University of Georgia). After reading medicine with a Jefferson doctor, Long studied at Transylvania, then transferred to the University of Pennsylvania medical school, receiving his M.D. degree in 1839. He gained surgical experience in New York hospitals before returning to Jefferson in 1841. Long thus acquired as sound a medical education as America could offer.

Late in 1841 Jefferson's young set, hearing of antics brought on by nitrous oxide administered to volunteers by an itinerant showman then crisscrossing the country, besought Long to make this gas for their own use. As a student in Philadelphia, Long had seen a showman use sulfuric ether, after which he had joined fellow students in private ether parties. Long superintended such entertainments for the pleasure of his Jefferson friends. His observations led him to use ether as an anesthetic.

The operation, with witnesses present, proved successful. Five times more Long used ether for surgery before publishing his results. In one case Long amputated two injured fingers of a slave boy, employing ether for one operation but not the other. Long explained his delay in publishing by saying he wanted to prove that ether and not the impact of imagination negated pain. Long also had heard a Philadelphia professor condemn premature publication based on isolated experiments.

Long's article in the *Southern Medical and Surgical Journal* (1849) asserted his priority in using anesthesia against the quickly published claims of Harvard surgeon John Collins Warren and Boston dentist William T. G. Morton, who administered his Letheon in 1846. Later, Long also competed with New England claimants for recognition and possible recompense from Congress for discovering anesthesia. Confusing claims and sectional tension kept such a bill from becoming law.

Anesthesia is a classic example of multiple discovery. Long's tardy publication hurt his claim to priority, but he never lacked southern defenders, including J. Marion Sims and his own apprentice, Joseph Jacobs, whose efforts eventually placed Long's statue in the national Capitol. Long made no further discoveries, practicing medicine and operating a pharmacy in Athens for the last 28 years of his life.

James Harvey Young
Emory University

Frank K. Boland, *The First Anesthetic: The Story of Crawford Long* (1950); Crawford W. Long, *Southern Medical and Surgical Journal* (December 1849); Frances Long Taylor, *Crawford W. Long and the Discovery of Ether Anesthesia* (1928); James Harvey Young, *Bulletin of the New York Academy of Medicine* (March 1974). ✫

McDOWELL, EPHRAIM
||||||||||||||||||||||||||||||||||||||||||||||||||||||
(1771–1830) Physician.

Of Scotch-Irish descent, Ephraim McDowell was born in Rockbridge County, Va., the ninth of 11 children of Samuel and Mary (McClung) McDowell. In 1784 the elder McDowell, a former revolutionary army officer and member of the Virginia Legislature, moved his family to the small community of Danville in the Kentucky district where he served as land commissioner and magistrate. After completing his preliminary education, young Ephraim was apprenticed to Dr. Alexander Humphreys of Staunton, Va., an eminent physician and teacher. Then in 1793 and 1794 he attended medical lectures in Edinburgh, where he was influenced especially by the famous Scottish surgeon-anatomist, John Bell. Returning to Danville in 1795 without a degree (the University of Maryland awarded him an honorary M.D. in 1823), McDowell soon established an extensive practice in the surrounding area. In 1802 the successful young doctor married Sarah Shelby, the daughter of Kentucky's first governor.

In a time before the development of anesthesia and detailed knowledge of the causes of infection, the name of Ephraim McDowell became associated with that of Jane Todd Crawford in one of the most celebrated cases in the annals of surgery. In December 1809 McDowell was called to a village 60 miles from Danville to consult with physicians whose 47-year-old patient appeared to present a complicated pregnancy. Upon examining Jane Todd Crawford, he determined she was not pregnant and that the swelling in her abdomen was a huge ovarian tumor. He advised her of the gravity of the circumstances, explaining that surgery was unprecedented and likely to be fatal; he offered to operate if she would come to Danville. On Christmas Day 1809, assisted by his nephew, McDowell performed the first ovariotomy in his home, removing a 20-pound tumor in the 25-minute operation during which Crawford recited the Psalms. She recovered fully and lived to the age of 78. A delayed report of this first case and two others was received initially by the medical profession with incredulity and harsh criticism, but McDowell's reputation was subsequently vindicated. Ironically, this famous pioneer in abdominal surgery is believed to have died of acute appendicitis. The McDowell house and apothecary in Danville, a national historic site, are owned and maintained by the Kentucky Medical Association.

John H. Ellis
Lehigh University

John Duffy, *The Healers: A History of American Medicine* (1979); J. N. McCormack, ed., *Some of the Medical Pioneers of Kentucky* (1917). ☆

MAURY, MATTHEW FONTAINE

(1806–1873) Confederate general and oceanographer.

Born 14 January 1806 near Fredericksburg, Va., and reared on a plantation at Franklin, Tenn., Matthew Fontaine Maury was appointed a U.S. Navy midshipman in 1825. He sailed on three cruises, one being around the world, and rose to the rank of lieutenant before being permanently disabled in a stagecoach accident in 1839.

Maury attended Harpeth Academy, and his mastery of mathematics through calculus is evidenced in *A New Theoretical and Practical Treatise on Navigation*, published in 1836 and adopted by the navy for the instruction of midshipmen. In 1842 he was appointed superintendent of the navy's Depot of Charts and Instruments, and later, upon the completion of the U.S. Naval Observatory in Washington in 1844, he became its head as well.

Lieutenant Maury laid down an agenda for his new bureau and named it the Observatory and Hydrographical Office; soon he called for an astronomical survey of the southern heavens and a scientific study of the twin oceans of water and air. Specifically, he proposed a systematic analysis of wind and current patterns by ships to find "tracks," or the most seaworthy routes. His "abstract logs" required the collection of empirical information about 22 different meteorological and oceanographic conditions such as direction and rate of current, barometric readings, temperature of air and water, and the nature of winds and weather. As Maury explained in the *Southern Literary Messenger* in 1843, "every new fact, however trifling it may seem, that is gathered from nature or her works, is a clue placed in our hands, which assists to guide us into her labyrinth of knowledge." After an international agreement at Brussels in 1853, over 124,000 vessels, constituting over 95 percent of the world's shipping, cooperated in Maury's scientific undertaking.

As millions of daily logs came to Maury's office, his findings were published in the *Wind and Current Charts* with their accompanying *Explanations and Sailing Instructions*. As a result, clipper voyages to Australia, Brazil, and California were shortened by a quarter.

Maury early turned his research toward problems of interest to southern mariners and farmers, including the Isthmian canal, the Tehuantepec railroad, Mississippi River flood lands, and hurricanes. In attendance at various southern commercial conventions, he supported the establishment of direct trade with Europe through the use of steam packets. He found that, due to adverse winds and the Gulf Stream, vessels sailing to the South Atlantic ports made only 133 miles a day while northern ones averaged 162 miles. Nevertheless, he laid out a track for Savannah vessels that required 39 days for European passage, a saving of 20 days over normal time but still longer than the passage from New York.

Although Maury pursued practical problems of weather and navigation, he also probed the basic mechanics of the sphere. His investigations of the dynamics of the Gulf Stream emphasized the effect of temperature and demolished John Herschel's theories on the trade winds. Maury was the first to chart the Atlantic seabed and to bring up samples of soil for microsopic examination of life forms. These data facilitated the laying of the first transatlantic cable in 1858. In the area of meteorology he concluded that heated air currents and trade winds created hurricanes, and he projected such phenomena as the jet stream.

In 1855 Maury published the first modern work on oceanography, *The Physical Geography of the Sea*, with chapters on the Gulf Stream and Ant-

arctic climatology, among others. Although not all contemporaries accepted his bold interpretations, this book was translated into most European languages and appeared in 20 English editions alone before the turn of the century. After the Civil War, in which Maury served the Confederacy as a technical expert on submarine mines and as a naval purchasing agent in Europe, he continued his writing. He spoke often on science and religion, with emphasis on the earth and its systems as a giant mechanism. In 1867 Maury made a profession of faith and joined the Protestant Episcopal church. He died in 1873, while teaching at Virginia Military Institute.

Harold S. Wilson
Old Dominion University

Matthew Fontaine Maury, *Explanation and Sailing Directions to Accompany the Wind and Current Charts* (1858–59), Papers, Library of Congress, Washington, D.C., *The Physical Geography of the Sea* (1855), *Southern Literary Messenger* (August 1843); Frances Leigh Williams, *Matthew Fontaine Maury: Scientist of the Sea* (1963). ☆

MOORE, SAMUEL P.
(1813–1889) Confederate surgeon.

Samuel Preston Moore, surgeon general of the Confederate army, is among the least appreciated personages of the Civil War.

Born in 1813 in Charleston, S.C., he received his early education in his native state and graduated from the Medical College of South Carolina 8 March 1834. One year later he was commissioned assistant surgeon (with the rank of captain) in the U.S. Army, beginning a 26-year stint of service at military posts in various areas of the country. After serving in the Mexican War, he was made full surgeon in 1849. On 25 February 1861 Moore resigned from the army to avoid fighting against his native state. He entered medical practice in Little Rock, Ark., but on 30 July 1861 Confederate President Jefferson Davis appointed Moore acting surgeon general.

Moore faced an almost insurmountable task—the establishment of a medical department. Physicians, drugs, supplies, and hospitals had to be provided. Starting with only 24 physicians who had resigned from federal service, Moore, during the course of the war, recruited some 3,000 physicians for Confederate service. The medical department cared for 600,000 Confederate soldiers, 270,000 prisoners, and over 3,000,000 wounded or sick persons. Moore soon established an extensive hospital system, ranging from general hospitals to convalescent facilities. He is credited with the introduction of hospital "huts," the forerunner of the pavilion hospital. To replace medical supplies blockaded by the enemy, Moore was responsible for the preparation of drug substitutes from indigenous plants. Moore required regular sick calls, sanitary inspections, and regular reports of all medical activities.

To advance training of his medical officers, Moore encouraged educational meetings, refresher courses, and the publication of practical manuals on military medicine. He was instrumental in organizing in August 1863 the Association of Army and Navy Surgeons of the Confederate States and in the publication of the *Confederate States Medical and Surgical Journal*.

From the outset Moore was a strict disciplinarian, and his rigid enforcement of regulations often seemed to men fresh from civilian life little short of tyranny. Complaints were not wanting, but it was widely agreed that the medical department was among the most efficient in the Confederacy. President Davis accorded the highest praise to Moore and his department.

After the war, Moore remained in Richmond and devoted most of his time to the advancement of precollege education and agriculture. His contributions in both fields were significant.

He died suddenly on 31 May 1889 and is buried in Hollywood cemetery in Richmond.

Harris D. Riley, Jr.
Health Sciences Center
University of Oklahoma

H. R. McIlwane, *Surgery, Gynecology, and Obstetrics* (November 1924). ☆

REED, WALTER
(1851–1902) Physician.

Major Walter Reed, who was one of the foremost bacteriologists and epidemiologists in the nation during the formative years of modern medicine, is best known for his work as chairman of the U.S. Yellow Fever Commission and discoverer of the mode of propagation of the disease.

Reed was born near Gloucester, Va., on 13 September 1851 and spent his childhood moving around the countryside of Virginia and North Carolina with his father, a Methodist minister. He received an M.D. degree from the University of Virginia in 1869 and went on to work for several years in New York hospitals. In 1874 he became a lieutenant in the U.S. Army Medical Corps.

Though he was able to study pathology under William H. Welch at Johns Hopkins for a while, he spent most of his army career at isolated and dreary outposts.

He first began to demonstrate his skill as a medical investigator in Washington, D.C., during a virulent outbreak of malaria in 1896. When the Spanish-American War broke out in 1898, Reed was appointed to direct an investigation of typhoid. His findings made it possible to end the deadly epidemic of that disease in army camps.

In 1900 Reed became the head of an army board assigned to investigate the cause of yellow fever, which was rampant in Cuba at that time and also paid regular and deadly visits to the United States, especially the Gulf states and the Mississippi River Valley. Reed and his colleagues traveled to Cuba to search for the origins of the dread disease. Their experiments there led Reed to ascertain that yellow fever was carried by the *Aedes aegypti* mosquito. Once the cause was identified, steps were taken to eradicate the mosquito and thus the disease. The implications of Reed's work for the American South, where yellow fever took devastating tolls in life and productivity throughout the 19th century, were enormous.

Reed died following surgery for a ruptured appendix on 23 November 1902.

Lucie R. Bridgforth
Memphis State University

Century Magazine (October 1903); *New York Times* (2 November 1902); Albert E. Truby, *Memoir of Walter Reed: The Yellow Fever Episode* (1943); Laura N. Wood, *Walter Reed: Doctor in Uniform* (1943). ☆

RUFFIN, EDMUND
||||||||||||||||||||||||||||||||||||||||||||||
(1794–1865) Agricultural reformer.

The preeminent scientific agriculturist of the Old South and a dedicated southern nationalist, Ruffin was born in Prince George County, Va., the son of a prosperous James River planter. He attended the College of William and Mary, served briefly in the War of 1812, and then embarked upon a nearly half-century career as a gentleman-farmer. Plagued initially by lands impoverished by two centuries of tobacco culture, he set out to improve them. By means of an elaborate series of experiments conducted over the course of 15 years on his Coggin's Point estate, Ruffin demonstrated the useful properties of marl, a shell-like deposit consisting primarily of clay mixed with calcium carbonate, which neutralized soil acidity and rendered sterile soils productive. He published his findings in 1832 under the title *An Essay on Calcarous Manures* and during the following decade spearheaded an agricultural renaissance in the Upper South through his distinguished journal, the *Farmers' Register*. In subsequent years he conducted an agricultural survey of South Carolina, proved the efficacy of his theories by converting his two Virginia farms, Beechwood and Marlbourne, into model estates, and served four terms as president of the Virginia State Agricultural Society.

Although his lasting fame derives from his contributions as an agricultural reformer, Ruffin is significant too as a representative of the planter elite of the slave South. Like others of that class, he exhibited a cultural and intellectual versatility. Thus, quite apart from his pragmatic interest in soil chemistry, he manifested a natural curiosity about sci-

Edmund Ruffin, agricultural reformer and southern nationalist from Virginia, near the end of his career

entific phenomena ranging from geology to ethnology. Cultured and well-read—he had read all of Shakespeare's plays before he was 11 years old—he was in many respects a true renaissance man. Also typical was Ruffin's consuming interest in politics. Too opinionated and too much a party maverick to stand for elective office—he served only a partial term in the Virginia state senate—Ruffin, nevertheless, immersed himself completely in the secession movement following his retirement from farming. When his labors bore fruit in 1861, he was accorded the honor of firing the first shot at Fort Sumter. Four years later, broken in spirit and fortune by the demise of his beloved Confederacy, the embittered Ruffin, in a gesture that symbolized not only his personal tragedy but that of his region, took his own life rather than submit to the anticipated indignities of Reconstruction.

William K. Scarborough
University of Southern Mississippi

Avery O. Craven, *Edmund Ruffin, Southerner* (1932); Betty L. Mitchell, *Edmund Ruffin: A Biography* (1981); William K. Scarborough, ed., *Diary of Edmund Ruffin* (3 vols. projected; 1972–   ). ☆

SCOPES TRIAL

No event of the 1920s captured the imagination of the public and the press as did the spectacle of the Scopes Trial. Held in a little Tennessee town, Dayton, during the sweltering month of July 1925, the case of the *People of the State of Tennessee* v. *John Thomas Scopes* is the best-known trial in American history.

With passage of the Butler bill by the Tennessee Legislature—a statute outlawing the teaching of evolution—several Dayton civic boosters accepted the offer of the American Civil Liberties Union to defend any teacher held in violation of the new law. Scopes, having just completed his first year as a science teacher at the local high school, agreed to act as the defendant. Ironically, Scopes probably did not, in fact, teach the theory of evolution.

The main actors in the drama came from outside Dayton. Clarence Darrow, the most famous lawyer of the day, defended Scopes with a staff including Dudley Field Malone and Arthur Garfield Hays. William Jennings Bryan, the three-time presidential hopeful and former secretary of state, led the prosecution team. H. L. Mencken, dubbing the developing spectacle the "Monkey Trial," led a horde of news personnel who descended on Dayton from around the nation and the world.

The trial opened on 10 July 1925 to the whirring of movie cameras and live radio coverage on Chicago station WGN.

The courtroom crowd spilled over onto the lawn, and eventually Judge John T. Raulston moved the proceedings to the cooler temperatures outside.

The personalities and objectives of Darrow and Bryan did not, however, allow the trial to lessen its fever pitch. Bryan characterized the trial as a "duel to the death" between unbelievers and Christians. The agnostic Darrow, on the other hand, fully intended to prove that the Butler law was unfair and unconstitutional. The initial subject of all this furor, Scopes himself, became a secondary figure. Judge Raulston did not allow scientific and technical testimony, and the trial degenerated into a personal battle between Darrow and Bryan, a conflict encouraged by an aggressive press corps.

A Darrow challenge to Bryan brought the Great Commoner to the witness stand near the end of the trial. Bryan proved to be conservative in his religious views but not a consistent fundamentalist. For example, he did not espouse a literal meaning for the Creation as taking place in a series of six 24-hour days. Actually Bryan was consistent with his old populist leanings against monopoly, in this instance control of educational processes by educators and scientists. Moreover, his belief in a conservative social gospel scored natural selection as antithetical to reform. Darrow, one of the most clever courtroom orators in American history, was not as consistent in his reasonings. In the case of Leopold and Loeb he defended the young men by arguing that they had been corrupted by naturalistic teachings; at Dayton he defended just such instruction as proper.

The results of the trial proved inconclusive. Some liberals self-righteously believed the immediate posttrial death

of Bryan to be fitting justice. The Rhea County jury found Scopes guilty and fined him $100. However, the Tennessee Supreme Court reversed the decision on a technicality, thereby removing the possibility of a test case before the U.S. Supreme Court. Scopes left teaching and entered the oil business as a geologist. His sister was later dismissed from the Paducah, Ky., school system for teaching evolution.

Although only Arkansas and Mississippi followed Tennessee in passage of antievolution statutes, the Scopes Trial undoubtedly led to suppression of evolution instruction across the nation. Most science textbook publishers bowed to the apparent public will and deleted or deemphasized sections on evolution. This trend lasted into the early 1960s. After publication of the Biological Sciences Curriculum Study materials by the American Institute of Biological Scientists in the mid-1960s, a new round of antievolutionist activity began. Self-styled "creationists," who were usually fundamentalists, proposed equal-time statutes. Court decisions in 1982 and 1985 in Arkansas and Louisiana overturned state laws mandating that creation science, which is based on the Genesis account of creation, be given equal time in the classroom if evolution were taught. A study of high school biology instruction in Kentucky, Tennessee, and Indiana in the early 1980s indicated that most instructors placed a "moderate" stress on evolution, a conclusion suggesting that a balance or equilibrium has been reached on the subject of evolution instruction across the nation.

Since the Scopes Trial a plethora of materials has both documented and interpreted this episode in Dayton. Perhaps the most famous of these, *Inherit the Wind*, a McCarthy-era adaptation of the Scopes Trial in play and movie forms, presented a version of the episode distorted by contemporary politics.

William E. Ellis
Eastern Kentucky University

Judith V. Grabiner and Peter D. Miller, *Science* (6 September 1974); Lawrence W. Levine, *Defender of the Faith: William Jennings Bryan; the Last Decade, 1915–1925* (1965); John T. Scopes with James Presley, *Center of the Storm: Memoirs of John T. Scopes* (1967); Ferenc Morton Szasz, *The Divided Mind of Protestant America, 1880–1930* (1982). ☆

SOCIAL CLASS

J. WAYNE FLYNT

Auburn University

CONSULTANT

☆ ☆ ☆ ☆ ☆ ☆ ☆ ☆ ☆ ☆

*Overleaf: A Mississippi Delta plantation
owner (foreground), 1930s*

SOCIAL CLASS
||||||||||||||||||||||||||||||||||||||||||||||||||||||||||||

One of America's most cherished ideals is the notion that any person who strives hard can be successful. The possibility of social and economic mobility attracted millions of immigrants and sustained the "American Dream." In no region is this idea more widely believed than in the South, and no section more thoroughly scorns Marxist notions of a society rigidly divided into hostile classes based on economic relationships.

In reality the South exists somewhere between its own idealistic myth of free and easy access to opportunity and the Marxist perception of an impenetrable class structure. Whether phrased in terms of a harsh concept such as "class" or a more acceptable one such as "status," the reality of social differentiation has contradicted the noble ideals of social equality and equal access to opportunity.

Class identification involves a great deal more than one's rank in the economic order. It is related to the entire social structure, although the nature of that relationship is hotly debated. One's status may depend on family, occupation, or self-perception, and it may be expressed in one's education, place of residence, political identification, church, or even depiction in literature.

Interpretations of Social Structure. Attempts to apply class interpretations to the South's social structure may be divided into three categories. The most

familiar was expounded by Karl Marx and divided society into two classes engaged in mortal conflict. The prevailing system of economic production created a struggle between those engaged in the production of wealth and those who profited the most from its inequitable distribution. Economic struggle between classes determined all social relationships and political roles. Although some have attempted to apply rigid Marxist interpretations to the South, the more influential studies derive from a modification of Marx that deemphasizes economic determinism in favor of the cultural domination of one ruling elite over all others.

Max Weber, though influenced heavily by Marx, added two elements to the economic notions implicit in "class." "Status," as a concept of social honor or prestige, recognized that one's standing is partly determined by the consciousness of individuals, both of their own position and that of others. "Party" added the idea of political or legal power as a component because Weber observed that social stratification was a manifestation of the unequal distribution of power. Position in society was not determined solely by which economic group one belonged to but by the power that group could command compared to the power held by other groups.

Finally, an American, W. Lloyd Warner, expanded the concept of "status" and applied it specifically to American society. The social position one held depended not so much on economic criteria as on how a person lived, who his family was, and how people in the community judged, interpreted, weighed, and compared these factors. America contained not Marx's simple two-class structure, but a complex six-layer system existing not in mutual hostility and conflict, but in relative harmony.

Complicating all these considerations was the presence of large numbers of blacks in the South. Constituting a caste rigidly divided first by slavery and later by segregation, blacks developed a separate class system sometimes paralleling and at other times conflicting with the white structure.

Colonial Era. The colonial South produced conflicting patterns of landownership and class tension. Earlier historians attributed such conflicts as Bacon's Rebellion in Virginia to class tensions between wealthy seaboard aristocrats and poorer backcountry farmers, although such explanations appear now to be excessively simplistic. Actually the colonial patterns varied from one southern colony to another. For instance, the trustees who established Georgia banned slavery and prohibited ownership of more than 500 acres of land in an attempt to create a democratic region for the "worthy poor." But ambitious Georgia settlers thwarted such noble intentions, pointing to the greater prosperity of South Carolina and Virginia as precedent for introducing slavery and the plantation system. The success of plantation agriculture widened the chasm between classes and created strong antiroyalist sentiments among the upland farmers who would soon earn the title of "crackers." But land policy in Georgia remained generous throughout the colonial period; almost any male head of household could

qualify for virtually free land. Although the Revolutionary War had a leveling effect in some ways, it also reflected class tensions. Officers in the state militias came from aristocratic stock. They commanded southern units often composed of unpropertied, poor recruits. South Carolina units contained sharp distinctions in dress, lodging, and food that led to desertions, neglect of duty, insolence toward officers, and general misbehavior.

Antebellum Era. Applying class theories to the antebellum years has produced exciting new interpretations and furious arguments. White society was divided into at least three major groups: planters, yeoman farmers, and poor whites. What united these three classes was a common commitment to the racial superiority of Caucasians, common kinship ties that often existed between planters and yeomen, and belief in the possibility of movement into the upper class if one sought good land, worked hard, and subscribed to community values. Each group also contained substantial variety. Among planters the range extended from small farmers with less than five slaves who lived more like yeomen than feudal lords to legendary barons with thousands of acres who constructed Greek Revival mansions, acquired extensive libraries, and ruled their domains with paternalistic concern for their hundreds of subjects. To those of Marxist persuasion, the planter class appears not to have been so much a capitalist class as precapitalist or even anticapitalist. Planters were hostile to all manufacturing except industry that complemented agriculture, such as the textile industry. They feared the rise of cities because both the urban bourgeoisie and the white working class that would develop there were quite beyond planter control. Moreover, their wealth was concentrated in land and slaves, and credit served their agrarian interests, leaving little money for speculative industries. Their values—honor, gentility, a highly ordered social structure, and an easygoing, relaxed society— were contrary to the capitalist values of northern businessmen and explain the South's inability to sustain manufacturing on any extensive scale. Planters typically belonged to Episcopal churches and were conservative in politics, often supporting the Whig party.

The yeoman class was by far the largest of the three major social groups. Unlike the planter who grew commercially marketable products such as cotton and tobacco, the yeoman was a self-sustaining farmer who worked in his own fields, produced extensive crops of corn and wheat, and maintained herds of livestock that roamed free in woodlands adjacent to his fields. He obtained rudimentary education in one of the hundreds of academies, cast his vote for Jacksonian Democrats, especially the ones who advocated easier access to public lands, and typically belonged to emotional religious sects such as the Baptists or the Methodists. Yeomen were often related to planter families by either kinship or marriage, aspired to enter that class, and were often successful when cotton prices were high and their lands fertile. When unsuccessful, they were a highly mobile group, moving westward in search of better land. Slavery provided them a means of controlling social and economic competition with blacks and a sense of class identification with other whites.

Even poor whites, the most elusive and enigmatic of the classes, generally accepted the plantation ideal, though they participated only peripherally in the economic system. Producing neither commercially marketable staples nor extensive food crops and livestock, they barely existed by hunting, fishing, harvesting sparse crops on poor land that usually did not belong to them, or working for minimal wages as farm laborers or in the cotton mills and urban industrial jobs that began to develop in the late antebellum years. Illiterate, transient, sickly, they were often despised by blacks and other whites alike, stereotyped by the comic southwestern humorists, and dismissed as "po' white trash." Actually poor whites varied from wretched ne'er-do-wells to substantial but landless farmers with stable families. Few of the economic benefits of the plantation system leaked through to them, and their only pride was the color of their skin, praised publicly by planter and yeoman alike, but of little practical value.

The notion that racial solidarity prevented internal dissension between white classes is not supported by the historical facts. Conflict occurred at many points within the social order. There was sectional strife between upcountry farmers, living on small farms with few slaves, and low-country planters. Economically the classes differed about free and easy access to land, taxation, and education. Politically they divided between Whig and Democrat.

Religious divergence according to class inspired a famous description of denominationalism more concerned with social status than theology: a Methodist was a Baptist who wore shoes; a Presbyterian was a Methodist with a bank account; an Episcopalian was a Presbyterian who lived off his investments. Such good-humored stereotyping obscured more fundamental conflicts. During the years immediately following the American Revolution, religious strife developed in the Virginia Tidewater. Separate Baptists held mass gatherings where itinerant preachers proclaimed the depravity of man, the terrors of hell, and the glories of redemption. They denounced finery of dress, cockfighting and gambling, fiddling and dancing—the very values by which the aristocracy demonstrated its superior status. Worse than that, they opposed taxation to support a state church and demanded separation of church and state. Drawn from the lower economic groups, the Separate Baptists created a popular, nonhierarchical, participatory system of association and authority, an "egalitarian world of humble men seeking their own ultimate meaning according to their own lights." In the following years Separate Baptists moderated their fierce Calvinism, but other disputes within the religious community replaced this one. The rise of new sects, such as the Disciples of Christ and the Cumberland Presbyterians, and the bitter struggle between missionary and antimission Baptists had distinctive class aspects.

Literature also reflected the differences in social status. Most southern writers were drawn from the gentry or professional classes, and they created a substantial literary tradition by describing the foibles, eccentricities, shrewdness, and humor of poor whites. Characters such as Augustus Baldwin Longstreet's "Ransy Sniffle" or Johnson J. Hooper's "Yellow-legs" satirized and stereotyped the white lower class.

Daniel R. Hundley, born into the Alabama planter elite, was one of the first southerners to describe systematically the region's class structure. His 1860 volume, *Social Relations in Our Southern States*, devoted chapters to "The Southern Gentleman," "The Middle Classes," "Cotton Snobs," "The Southern Yankee," "The Southern Yeoman," "Poor White Trash," and "The Negro Slaves." His description of poor whites was particularly harsh. Attempting to refute abolitionist charges that poor whites were the inevitable residue of a slave society, Hundley traced the class to paupers, convicts, and indentured servants, people explained by bad blood, not economic environment. Such "lazy vagabonds" preferred to live in rude log cabins on sterile soil where their yellow-faced women dipped snuff, smoked pipes, and raised large broods of "dirty, squalling, white-headed little brats" amid squalor, superstition, and slavish adherence to the Democratic party. Their only redeeming quality was support of slavery and even that was the result of ignoble motives—"downright envy" of the planter and "hatred of the black man."

Although the world of blacks was fundamentally different from that of poor whites, internal variations occurred there also. Standing at the top of the social ladder were free blacks, who in 1860 numbered 262,000 and comprised 12.8 percent of the black population in the Upper South and 1.5 percent in the Lower South. Often of mixed racial ancestry and frequently residing in towns or cities, they developed job skills and relatively independent churches, schools, and fraternal societies. In 1860 one-sixth of Richmond's bricklayers and blacksmiths and half its plasterers and barbers were black. Protected from white competition by the stigma of "nigger work," some free blacks became substantial property holders. In the years following the Civil War many leaders came from this class, including nearly half of the 22 blacks who served in Congress between 1869 and 1900.

Differentiation by class is harder to measure among slaves. Whatever their advantages over their fellows in job skill, skin color, or literacy, free blacks remained bound to the slaves by the "peculiar institution." Nonetheless, a hierarchy did exist, with house servants, ministers, and skilled artisans at the top and field hands at the bottom. Adaptation to white culture also varied, with some slaves maintaining strong African elements and others quickly adopting American forms.

Impact of the Civil War. All class arrangements were affected by the Civil War, but no consensus exists concerning the extent of change. Class tensions—which had been somewhat confined during the antebellum years by common kinship and folkways, the ideology of white supremacy, the availability of land, rapid economic mobility, and the nonelite origins of the planter class—underwent subtle change during the Civil War. In the initial phase of conflict, yeomen and poor whites rallied to the Confederate cause despite frequent hill-country opposition to secession. Most military units contained a cross section of economic classes and elected their own officers, a process considerably more democratic than in the Revolutionary War. But as the war progressed, yeomen and poor whites bore the worst effects. Drought, draft, and taxes-in-kind fell heavily on common whites in hill counties and piney woods. The families soldiers left behind faced grievous problems by 1862–63, causing southern states to levy taxes on wealthy planters in order to distribute food to the poor. But for this relief, un-

rest would have been even greater. As it was, desertion by yeomen and poor whites increased dramatically by 1863, and southern hill counties experienced growing anarchy. Poverty, desertion, resistance to Confederate policy, and growing peace sentiment were closely related.

The appearance of discontinuity after the Civil War was certainly greater than the reality. Although planters lost their slave work force, they retained control of economic and political life and in some states adjusted quickly to the New South drive for industrialization. In Alabama and North Carolina planters apparently not only survived but participated actively in the manufacturing enterprises that flourished in the Piedmont and in bustling industrial towns such as Birmingham and Anniston. In other states, leaders in the rapidly growing textile industry were urban professionals and businessmen, with planters and farmers playing little role. In South Carolina the rise of upcountry towns had more to do with the development of manufacturing than did the survival of the plantation system.

The New Industrial Order. Whatever the origin of the new industrial order, several elements are clear. The planter class retained a major share of influence and power, although it had to compromise its opposition to towns and factories. Secondly, the promise of emancipation, which offered blacks such bright hope in 1865, dimmed amidst agricultural poverty. Nor was the black dream the only casualty of the last years of the century. New South exponents could proclaim the dawn of a different world, but economic reality defied their pronouncements. In 1900 the South remained the poorest, most technologically backward, most rural, least industrialized region of America.

Because their expectations were so great, blacks were the most disappointed of southerners. As a symbol of their emancipation, tens of thousands of former slaves temporarily left the land, filling towns to overflowing with their tent cities. Wartime devastation not only prevented them from obtaining work but necessitated the Freedmen's Bureau's providing rations to them and to poor whites in order to prevent mass starvation. Gradually most freedmen drifted back to the land, some to purchase their own farms but most to work as day laborers or as tenants. For blacks accustomed to slavery even the sharecropper system represented a step toward freedom. Though often cheated, they could negotiate their own contracts, function at least theoretically as equals, and operate their farms without the constant supervision of owners. But in terms of health, diet, and general economic well-being the status of many black sharecroppers declined even from that of slave.

For whites who had barely survived on the periphery of the antebellum economy, tenancy added social insult to economic injury. Thousands of poor whites left their remote pine barrens and mountain hollows for small plots on former plantations only to discover that falling cotton prices, advancing boll weevils, and sometimes unscrupulous owners and merchants provided no better life. Out of preference or under pressure, tenants often grew cotton because it was one of the few crops that could be marketed for cash. In this way their lot declined from that of the subsistence food producers of the antebellum years. As agricultural conditions worsened, ever larger numbers of yeoman farmers fell

through the land tenure system into some form of tenancy: 36.2 percent of all southern farms were operated by tenants in 1880, 49.2 percent in 1920, 55.5 percent in 1930. Poor diet, ill health, and illiteracy doomed one generation after another to sharecropping.

The landless poor searching for a better life were often seduced by the allurements of the industrial South. Although white tenant farmers were vaguely aware that they shared their economic bondage with blacks, some of the new industrial jobs reinforced that knowledge. Many of the industries—notably lumber, iron and steel, and mining—employed a biracial work force in which the major distinction was the white man's pride of race.

Although the intent of employers was not necessarily to exploit workers or create rigid class distinctions, that was the effect of industrialization. Workers of both races lived in company houses, sent their children to company schools, purchased goods from company commissaries, and worshipped in company-built and company-subsidized churches. Newly arrived rural families placed little value on education, barely survived economically, and pressured their children into mines or mills where they often grew up stunted and illiterate. When supplies of free labor lagged, owners contracted with sympathetic state officials to lease convicts.

The notable exception to this new biracial world of lower-class workers was the textile industry. Although blacks held menial jobs as loaders or janitors, cotton mill operatives generally were white. Attracted by the advantages of lower transportation costs, cheap, nonunion labor, and abundant water and steam power, the textile industry moved rapidly south from New England between 1880 and 1930. In 1860 the South contained only 10,152 mill workers, but by 1890 there were 36,415, and by 1900, 110,015. Salaries in the 1890s in North Carolina averaged only 50 cents a day, and 70–hour work weeks were common. By 1900 the industry employed 25,000 children below the age of 15, most of them working in the states of Georgia, Alabama, and the Carolinas.

Child labor owed its existence to pressures both from the family and from industrial society. Farm parents relied heavily on child labor and often put little stock in formal education. Hence, when parents left the land for the mill village, they seldom hesitated to allow young children who chafed under the discipline of the local schoolteacher to enter mill employment. Although 90 percent of working children under 15 were employed in textile mills in 1900, increasing numbers worked in coal mines, glass factories, as Western Union boys, and in various other occupations. Their numbers had tripled in the decade between 1890 and 1900. Other regions shared the problem but none to the extent of the South, and from that region came early organization to abolish child labor. Unfortunately, many of the South's industrialists, though by no means all of them, opposed reform. They had become accustomed to the "family wage," a salary for the male head of family that was so low it required all family members to work. During the textile boom between 1900 and 1915 expansion of the industry required an enormous increase in labor, and much of this addition came from children under the age of 16. Industrialists claimed that children learned factory routine more easily, and their hands were quicker and more agile. Furthermore, idle children were troublesome

children, and work at an early age bred habits of thrift and industry. The results frequently were illiteracy and cyclical poverty.

At first the urban middle class felt little threatened by the growth of this large white working class, even praising the conservative religious and family values that made rural Caucasians preferable to either newly arrived European immigrants or recently emancipated blacks. But as industrial conditions worsened and labor unrest increased, they began to view workers as a dangerous and disruptive element.

Organized Labor and Populism. Even though labor unions existed in the urban antebellum South, unionization had made little headway until after the Civil War. The first glimmer of the new direction of labor came in the years from 1873 to 1877 when freedmen, stereotyped as submissive, conducted a series of strikes. The Greenback-Labor party provided the framework for biracial unionization and political action. This early labor activity in the postbellum South was fundamentally different from such disruptions in other regions, not only because it involved a coalition of blacks and whites, which exposed the movement to charges of racial iconoclasm, but also because it was often sustained by a deeply religious perception that cast the conflict more in terms of striving for human justice and right than in Marxist-style confrontation of economic classes.

The failure of the Greenback-Labor party effort in the 1870s was the prelude to a long succession of disappointments for labor. Organizing efforts by the Knights of Labor beginning in 1885 recruited 45,000 members of both races and succeeded in controlling city governments in some southern cities, but these gains were wiped out by the depression of the 1890s.

Organization of farmers proved more immediately successful as the national depression multiplied agricultural problems in the 1880s and 1890s. The Farmers' Alliance at first sought to unite middle-class farmers into marketing collectives. However, rapidly escalating rural poverty carried many farmers further into radical agrarian politics. Primarily a movement of small farmers and rural professionals alarmed by their downward mobility and declining social status, the Populist party also attracted support from lower-class tenants and industrial workers. At the other end of the economic spectrum, prosperous farmers often deserted the Alliance when it moved into the political stage of Populism, frightened by its biracial political appeals and its quasi-socialistic demand for public ownership of railroads. Like the southern labor movement, Populism drew its vision of the impending apocalypse more from the Bible than from Marx or Proudhon. This was a distinctly southern brand of radicalism in which religion played a central role, even furnishing the vocabulary for public debates; Populists seldom used class terms, preferring instead words with moral connotations such as "robbed," "stolen," "injustice," and "evils." Religious imagery and Christian metaphors abounded.

Although Populism ultimately foundered upon a sea of criticism, white and black Populists seldom exceeded the prescribed limits of southern society. White Populists were willing to include blacks in common political efforts, but they were as opposed to racial equality as Democrats. Nonetheless, Populism was a landmark in southern history because it vigorously advocated economic justice for the lower middle class and for poor people of both races.

The demise of Populism forced many whites back into the Democratic party. Together with the return of middle-class farmers, who had left the Alliance earlier, these forces were strong enough to change the Democratic party, which previously had been dominated by large farmers and industrialists. Reform of party rules allowed a direct role for ordinary white voters but also restricted the franchise through the imposition of poll taxes and other strictures.

As a result of these changes, southern politics became democratized whether or not it became more liberal. The Socialist party briefly thrived in the remote farmlands of Oklahoma and Texas and in the cigar factories of Tampa and Key West. Within the increasingly class-conscious populations of mill towns and mining camps, angry voters joined poor rural farmers to elect racial demagogues who promised far more reform than they enacted. Except for the psychic good it did them to abuse the "better classes" symbolically by electing such men as Cole Blease, Sidney Catts, and Theodore Bilbo, they realized few improvements in their lives.

The poor established more enduring patterns in their efforts at unionization. The United Mine Workers conducted organizing drives that resulted in a number of strikes between 1900 and 1921. The Brotherhood of Timber Workers united some 35,000 white and black lumbermen and poor farmers in Louisiana and Texas during the same years. Most strikes were defeated by better organized and financed companies that usually had the support of the state press, the governor and state militia, farmers, and the urban middle class.

Frustrated by their defeats, most whites left both unions.

The violence of these strikes alarmed the thriving middle class. Already aware of abuses and injustices thanks to the educational efforts of ministers, social workers, and reform-minded journalists, urban professionals and businessmen sought to slow class polarization. Winning allies from among enlightened businessmen who saw reform to be in their own best interest, this coalition backed political candidates who favored moderate reforms that did not substantially threaten existing class arrangements. Supported by a middle class acting from a variety of motives—economic self-interest, genuine religious and humanitarian concern for economic and social justice, desire for social control of the lower classes—these progressive politicians challenged the more demagogic representatives of poor whites as well as the conservative Bour-

Sally Field in the title role in **Norma Rae** *(1978)*

bons who had dominated the years after Reconstruction. The most advanced reformers endorsed women's suffrage, built settlement houses, favored labor reform, and even organized an interracial movement designed to reduce racial tensions. Their hegemony temporarily broken, conservative landowners and industrialists waited for the reform mood to pass. Their wait was not long.

Progressive-era reforms were moderate and often assisted businessmen as much as or more than workers. Disillusioned by the betrayal of politicians whom they elected, by the impotence of their labor unions, and by worsening agricultural and manufacturing conditions in the 1920s, poor whites often directed their frustrations at helpless blacks. The very reform mood that had brought modest progress for whites resulted in worsened conditions for blacks. The American Federation of Labor acquiesced in the exclusion of blacks for skilled jobs. Black workers, abandoned by organized labor and by their white coworkers, became understandably cynical. They desperately sought any jobs available, even if the work involved acting as strike breakers. Natural economic hostility between workers competing for the same jobs was compounded by racial animosity, making the years from 1880 to 1930 the most racially violent in American history. Lynchings, labor violence between strikers and "scabs," and pitched battles between whites and blacks spread across the region. The ideal of working-class solidarity became a mockery in a world where color of skin obscured all other considerations.

Impact of the Great Depression and the New Deal. The maelstrom of the Depression both heightened class divisions and introduced important new elements into southern life. The steady deterioration of agricultural conditions during the 1920s drove many blacks off the land and more and more whites into tenancy. During the 15 years from 1920 to 1935, the number of white tenant families increased by 300,000 while the number of black families in similar circumstances declined by 70,000. Of the South's 1,831,000 tenant families in 1935, nearly two-thirds were white. In Mississippi nearly half the state's total population lived as tenants. Layoffs, wage reductions, and stretchouts propelled textile workers and coal miners into a wave of strikes beginning in 1929. The most famous of these disruptions, the textile strike in Gastonia, N.C., and the miners' strike in Harlan County, Ky., involved Communist organizers and unions, to which workers turned when more conservative unions either deserted them or proved ineffectual. Such actions by white workers who were often among the most religious and traditional people in their communities constituted less a proletarian uprising than a desperate outburst against a society that neither understood nor very much cared for the plight of its lower class.

Although it made few converts, the Communist party established a southern headquarters in Birmingham and even published the *Southern Worker*. It dared to challenge the South's racial taboos by defending nine black boys unjustly accused of raping two white women on a train near Scottsboro, Ala. It also organized a small Sharecroppers Union among black tenants south of Birmingham and gained a foothold in the Mine, Mill, and Smelter Workers Union, which organized Birmingham area iron ore miners of both races.

In the Arkansas Delta H. L. Mitchell,

J. R. Butler, and E. B. McKinney began the Southern Tenant Farmers' Union in 1934. A biracial union that enrolled both former white Klansmen and blacks, the STFU attracted national attention and challenged New Deal agricultural policies. Although New Deal reforms were well intentioned, powerful forces in the Farm Bureau, the state agricultural extension agencies, and the U.S. Department of Agriculture administered policies in such a way that most benefits went to landowners who were encouraged to reduce acreage and thereby dislocate thousands of tenants. The extent of such dislocation is uncertain, but early Roosevelt policies obviously did little to improve agricultural conditions among tenant farmers.

Rural rehabilitation through the Resettlement Administration provided temporary assistance, as did state relief administrations that created jobs for the unemployed. Some workers were hired to build new subsistence communities where hard-hit industrial workers could farm small plots and live in decent housing.

The boldest New Deal initiative came in 1937 with the passage of the Bankhead-Jones Farm Tenancy Act. Delayed for two years by Roosevelt's ambivalence and emasculated by intensive conservative opposition, the act provided modest loans to tenants for equipment and seeds. Unfortunately, the most visionary element, federal loans to tenants so they could purchase their own land, was so underfunded and selectively administered that only the most successful, responsible, and promising tenants received loans. Among the millions of southern tenants, only a tiny fraction received land purchase loans, and in the 1940s even this modest effort was destroyed by a conservative Congress.

Other attempts to help were more successful. An internal division within the labor movement and a national administration sympathetic to organized labor created new opportunities for workers. Already aided by New Deal minimum wage legislation, southern workers drew the attention of the Congress of Industrial Organizations (CIO). The CIO attempted to organize all workers within an industry rather than dividing them according to crafts or skills. Its commitment to biracial unions and flirtation with left-wing politics caused middle- and upper-class southerners to brand it a Communist threat to southern institutions. It sent organizers south and trained southern workers, especially at the Highlander Folk School in Tennessee. The result was fierce and often violent struggles to organize Birmingham iron and steel workers, rubber workers in Gadsden, Ala., and textile operatives across the South. Thanks to national publicity and timely help from the federal government, some of these efforts were successful, though the attempt to organize the textile industry was a notable exception.

The descent of many middle-class people into poverty provided tenant farmers and industrial workers with welcome allies. People who had never before faced real want suddenly found themselves quite as helpless as the poorest sharecropper, without job, food, or home. The New Deal provided employment, and frightened middle-class folk joined their impoverished neighbors to elect New Deal congressmen. Conservatives retained enough power to make southern congressmen the least loyal of Democrats to the New Deal, but FDR found the general population of no other region of America more receptive to his programs. Downplaying race and emphasizing economic reforms for all, Roosevelt won the South's affection.

Support for Roosevelt and the New Deal brought together liberals from throughout the region. Liberals, including CIO organizers, state Democratic leaders, social workers, ministers, college professors, and reform journalists, tried to solidify their gains through organizations such as the Southern Conference on Human Welfare. New Democratic leaders, often with strong religious backgrounds, such as Olin Johnson in South Carolina, Brooks Hays in Arkansas and Hugo Black in Alabama, combined white and black, middle- and lower-class support to win office. Unlike earlier candidates elected by poor whites, these men actually advocated significant reform programs in state houses and in Congress.

Impact of World War II. Due both to reforms and to the location of military bases and war industry in the South between 1940 and 1945, unprecedented changes swept through the region. The rate of tenancy, especially among whites, declined as industrial jobs lured tenants off the land. Union strength and federal law raised industrial wages to the point that coal miners and steel workers earned more than schoolteachers and could no longer be categorized as poor whites. Increasingly comfortable in lower-middle-class suburbs or in their own houses newly purchased from mine or mill, they soon forgot about the people left behind. When black outrage erupted among returning Negro servicemen encountering the old racial barriers, such people often became the worst and most violent opponents of change. Shrewd conservative leaders from affluent backgrounds did nothing to prevent such conflict and often fueled it, dividing unions along racial lines and defeating liberal politicians by shac-

Mechanic at work, Knoxville, Tennessee, 1943

kling them with charges of "nigger lovers" or "communists."

Turmoil also occurred within the black community. Older, traditional black elites had coexisted with racism in uneasy but practical compromise. Conservative, upper-class whites had tried to restrain lower-class violence, and blacks had sought economic opportunity without threatening to disturb social inequality. But the small black middle class of teachers, ministers, businessmen, and small-farm owners was swept aside by angry urban residents. The most liberal of the older professional classes, especially ministers, teachers, and labor leaders, provided articulate and courageous leadership, and the modern civil rights movement was born.

Threatened as it was by the aspirations of blacks, the white lower middle class reacted stridently. Rallying to the leadership of conservative politicians who threatened to close integrated public schools or interpose the state between white citizens and unpopular Supreme Court rulings, it posed a primary barrier to implementation of de-

segregation. As the years passed and black boycotts of businesses and passive disobedience disrupted one community after another, many merchants, newspaper publishers, and business leaders bowed to the inevitable and accepted black demands. But this only unleashed some poor and lower-middle-class whites to a frenzy of violence.

They accepted the leadership of conservative business people when it was available, but angry white workers found their favorite spokesman in the self-proclaimed populist, George C. Wallace of Alabama. Combining a frankly racist rhetoric with a prounion advocacy of the "little man," Wallace proved to be the shrewdest and most enduring southern politician since Louisiana's Huey Long. Although repudiated by AFL-CIO leadership, Wallace remained popular among the white rank and file, especially in the building trades. Capable of changing positions according to altered circumstances, he even survived the racist politics of the 1960s and 1970s, and won the governorship of Alabama in 1982 by class appeals to a biracial constituency of black and white workers and farmers in a state with the nation's second highest rate of unemployment.

Nearly forgotten in the giddy affluence of the war years and after was another South that profited little from the currents of change sweeping south of the Potomac. The mountains of Appalachia proved too stout and high a barrier. Of course changes did occur, particularly in the valleys of the Tennessee River watershed where government dams and cheap power fueled an economic miracle. But higher in the mountains and up the remote hollows poverty persisted. Among a people of immense pride, independence, fierce family loyalty, fatalism, and rich cultural heritage, the new era intensified problems. Technological change in the coal mining industry cost the region 265,000 jobs in just nine years between 1950 and 1959. In some eastern Kentucky counties three of every four miners lost their jobs. In the entire Appalachian region more than 600,000 jobs were lost in mining and farming during this one decade. Internal migration seemed the only solution, and more than 2 million people left the southern highlands for industrial cities between 1940 and 1970. There they carved out ethnic enclaves, established their own storefront churches, and retained their distinctive culture. Stereotyped by local media and citizens, they suffered as badly at the hands of blatant bigots or misguided reformers as blacks had before them. Cynical and bitter, longing for old places and ways, they persisted in their subculture with rare tenacity.

Whatever their woes, migrants were better off than the folks they left behind. Within 340 Appalachian counties in 1960, one of every three families lived on an annual income of less than $3,000; of those over 25 years of age, only 32 of 100 had finished high school. In Kentucky 20 percent of the population was eligible for surplus federal food.

The Appalachian Development Program, the Job Corps, and President Lyndon B. Johnson's War on Poverty made some progress toward resolving the South's enduring poverty. At first middle-class southerners provided lukewarm support for such initiatives, though even this reservoir of good will began to run thin as escalating expenditures and black participation cost the Kennedy-Johnson programs many white allies.

Paradoxically, the success of federal programs and private economic investment swelled the middle and upper classes and reduced concern for the people who remained behind. Even status-conscious, upwardly mobile blacks tended to desert old neighborhoods, churches, and institutions in search of newer and more prestigious environments. For those trapped down the lonely dirt roads or in the urban shacks, life still seemed hard indeed.

See also AGRICULTURE: Sharecropping and Tenancy; / Communal Farms; BLACK LIFE: / Commission on Interracial Cooperation; EDUCATION: Politics of Education; / Berea College; Commonwealth College; HISTORY AND MANNERS: Great Depression; New Deal; Populism; / Byrd, William, II; INDUSTRY: Industrialization and Change; LAW: / Black, Hugo; LITERATURE: / Longstreet, Augustus Baldwin; MUSIC: Protest; MYTHIC SOUTH: Plantation Myth; / "Moonlight-and-Magnolias" Myth; Poor Whites; POLITICS articles; RELIGION: / Hays, Brooks; URBANIZATION: Urban Poor; VIOLENCE: Harlan County, Kentucky; Industrial Violence

J. Wayne Flynt
Auburn University

Fred A. Bailey, *Class and Tennessee's Confederate Generation* (1987); F. N. Boney, *Southerners All* (1984); James C. Cobb, *Industrialization and Southern Society, 1877–1984* (1984); Robert Coles, *Migrants, Sharecroppers, Mountaineers* (1971); Allison Davis, Burleigh Gardner, and Mary Gardner, *Deep South: A Social Anthropological Study of Caste and Class* (1941); John Dollard, *Caste and Class in a Southern Town* (1937); Anthony P. Dunbar, *Against the Grain: Southern Radicals and Prophets, 1929–1959* (1981); J. Wayne Flynt, *Dixie's Forgotten People: The South's Poor Whites* (1979); Eugene D. Genovese, *The Political*

Economy of Slavery: Studies in the Economy and Society of the Slave South (1965); Margaret J. Hagood, *Mothers of the South: Portraiture of the White Tenant Farm Woman* (1939); Daniel R. Hundley, *Social Relations in Our Southern States* (1860); Edward Magdol and Jon L. Wakelyn, *The Southern Common People: Studies in Nineteenth-Century Social History* (1980); Jay Mandle, *The Roots of Black Poverty: The Southern Plantation after the Civil War* (1978); F. Ray Marshall, *Labor in the South* (1967); Marc Miller, ed., *Working Lives: The Southern Exposure History of Labor in the South* (1980); Roger L. Ransom and E. Richard Sutch, *One Kind of Freedom: The Economic Consequences of Emancipation* (1977); John Shelton Reed, *Southern Folk, Plain and Fancy: Native White Social Types* (1986); Leonard Reissman, *Class in American Society* (1959); Robert E. Shalhope, *Journal of Southern History* (November 1971); Tom E. Terrill and Jerrold Hirsch, eds., *Such As Us: Southern Voices of the Thirties* (1978); Jonathan M. Wiener, *American Historical Review* (October 1979), *Social Origins of the New South: Alabama, 1860–1885* (1978). ☆

Appalachia, Exploitation of

In 1884 the West Virginia Tax Commission warned that outside capitalists were rapidly acquiring the state's land. If the process was not halted, the commission charged, West Virginia would "pass into the hands of persons who do not live here and care nothing for our State except to pocket the treasures which lie buried in our hills," and with the state "despoiled of her wealth," the people would be left "poor, helpless, and destitute."

The process was not stopped. By 1900 absentee landowners controlled 90 percent of Mingo, Logan, and Wayne counties in West Virginia. By 1923 nonresidents of West Virginia owned more than half of the state and controlled four-fifths of its total value.

What happened in West Virginia was symptomatic of the Appalachian region. A 1982 survey of 80 Appalachian counties revealed that three-fourths of the surface areas and four-fifths of the region's minerals are absentee-owned. Fifty-three percent of the land and 70 percent of the mineral rights are held by the federal government and by corporations—mostly timber, coal, and other energy companies.

Absentee landownership has spelled a century of exploitation of Appalachia. The monopolization of the land and resources, for example, has weakened the material basis upon which farmers and independent commodity producers operated. By excluding other industries from the area, monopolies have prevented economic diversification, thus rendering the local economies and people liable to the pitfalls of a single industry. The economies of the coal regions of Appalachia fluctuate according to a rise or fall in the coal market; from the rise of petroleum and natural gas industries in the 1920s to the energy shortage of the 1970s, the coal market was one protracted bust, which meant massive unemployment and poverty for large segments of Appalachia. The tourist industry in western Virginia and North Carolina has produced underemployment, low wages, and seasonal employment.

Absentee ownership has polarized the people of Appalachia into those who own the land and those who labor in the logging or mining industries. Having little stake or interest in the land other than the wealth it contains, absentee coal companies have strip-mined it, laying waste to farmland, homes, and hills. In western North Carolina and Virginia tourism has led to a decline in land available for farming; consequently small farms, once of cultural as well as economic importance to Appalachia, have given way to national parks and the damming and flooding of rivers for recreational spots. In Alabama, some lumber companies gained land during Depression-era court-ordered sales, cut down the trees, and then moved to the Northwest, leaving behind ghost towns, exhausted forests, and devastated environments.

Colonial exploitation deprives Appalachians of the wealth that their land contains and that they produce, thus creating the irony of poverty amidst the region's riches. By use of the company-town system and later by establishing a political hegemony over the region (especially in the states of Kentucky and West Virginia), coal owners have maintained a colonial rule. Coal companies have used political clout to prevent the states from imposing much-needed severence taxes (a few states have token ones) and to ensure low property tax rates. Consequently, although Appalachian states are wealthy in resources, they lack locally available capital, adequate infrastructure, and access to the best lands; and there is a lack of income for goods and services. Quality health care, for example, is absent in Appalachia, as is quality education. Kentucky, one of the wealthiest states in the nation in minerals, has the highest high school dropout rate in the nation, a fact largely attributable to its inferior educational facilities. Walker County, Ala., the largest coal-producing county in the state, is periodically forced to borrow money to open its schools.

To be sure, the exploitation of the region has involved local elites working in conjunction with absentee landowners. The building of Shenandoah National Park (dedicated in 1936) pitted the desires of local but nonresident middle- and upper-class entrepreneurs and politicians anxious to promote tourism in the area against the cultural and subsistent needs of a resident, rural population that held the land in private domain. The landowners lost as the elite persuaded the federal government to issue a blanket condemnation and forcibly remove the residents; the Park Service and Civilian Conservation Corps razed their houses.

Americans have responded to the Appalachians' plight with neglect or humor. Television has derided Appalachians in programs such as *The Beverly Hillbillies*. Americans, in general, have dehumanized them with pejorative labels like "hillbillies" and "yesterday's people." In more benevolent yet still condescending moods Americans have attempted to "uplift" Appalachians with missionaries, VISTA workers, and other social redeemers.

In the 1960s the federal government established the Appalachian Regional Commission to solve the region's woes. The commission, however, ignored the absentee-landowner problem as it embarked upon a "prodevelopment" strategy of building roads, supposedly to encourage tourism and industry in Appalachia. Instead, the commission's road building helped depopulate the region, leaving it more open to corporate exploitation.

Appalachians have responded in various ways to colonial exploitation. Some acquiesced with a numbing sense of powerlessness. From the 1920s through the 1940s thousands migrated to Midwest urban-industrial centers such as Chicago, Dayton, Detroit, and Akron. Other Appalachians resisted in a century-long struggle. Labor-management relations in Appalachian coalfields have produced the most intense industrial warfare in American history. "Bloody Harlan," "Bloody Mingo," the "Matewan Massacre," the "Armed March on Logan," the "Black Lung Rebellion" are coalfield struggles that should forever haunt the memories of Americans. The willingness of Appalachian miners to deprive the nation of its energy even during wartime, as in the World War II coal strike, and for lengthy periods as in the 111-day 1977–78 coal strike, which severely disrupted the nation's economy, have caused even non-Marxists to ponder the existence of a class struggle in the Appalachian coalfields.

The miners' struggles are dramatic and visible, but they are not the only episodes of Appalachian militancy. The region's textile and lumber towns have witnessed a century of intense labor strife. Appalachian poor organized and protested their plight, and in November 1971 poverty and welfare rights organizations staged a "March for Survival" in Washington, D.C. During the 1960s and 1970s the so-called anti-strip-mining guerillas took direct action to prevent their land and homes from being bulldozed. In one year alone more than $2 million worth of strip-mining equipment was dynamited.

In recent decades writers, scholars, and others have added an intellectual dimension to the struggle. Pushing aside the old-time mountain patriarchs who accepted both the plight of Appalachia and the stereotypes of Appalachians, the new Appalachian intellectuals are helping to transform the occupational class consciousness of the workers into a regional identity. Regional publications such as *Mountain Life and Work* and *Mountain Eagle* have exposed corporate abuse of the region's land and people. Educational and cultural institutions such as the Highlander Center in Tennessee, the Appalachian Folklife Center in West Virginia, Appalshop in Kentucky, and the Appalachian centers in the region's colleges and universities are researching the Appalachian past and present, writing about its rich history and culture, and thus promoting pride and confidence in being Appalachian.

See also BLACK LIFE: Appalachians, Black; EDUCATION: / *Foxfire;* ENVIRONMENT: / Appalachian Coal Region; Appalachian Mountains; ETHNIC LIFE: / Appalachians; FOLKLIFE: "Hillbilly" Image; INDUSTRY: / Mining; Timber Industry; MYTHIC SOUTH: Appalachian Culture; / Appalachian Myth; RELIGION: Appalachian Religion; VIOLENCE: Harlan County, Kentucky; WOMEN'S LIFE: Appalachian Women

David A. Corbin
Washington, D.C.

Appalachian Land Ownership Task Force, *Who Owns Appalachia? Landownership and Its Impact* (1983); David A. Corbin, *Life, Work, and Rebellion in the Coal Fields: Southern West Virginia Miners, 1880–1922* (1981); Ronald D. Eller, *Miners, Millhands, and Mountaineers: The Modernization of the Appalachian South, 1880–1930* (1982); John Gaventa, *Power and Powerlessness: Quiescence and Rebellion in an Appalachian Valley* (1980); Helen Lewis, L. Johnson, and D. Askins, *Colonialism in Modern America: The Appalachian Case* (1978); Charles Perdue and Nancy Martia-Perdue, *Appalachian Journal* (Winter 1979–80); David E. Whisnant, *All That Is Native and Fine: The Politics of Culture in an American Region* (1983), *Modernizing the Mountaineer: Peo-*

ple, Power, and Planning in Appalachia (1980). ☆

Aristocracy
||||||||||||||||||||||||||||||

Throughout the American experience no group has retained a more unique or enduring image than the southern aristocracy. Still powerful is the *Gone with the Wind* view of dashing gentlemen and spirited ladies—the nation's first "beautiful people"—rushing bravely but foolishly into the holocaust of the Civil War. In recent times a gothic, even grotesque, image surfaces persistently, too. Its roots run back to the abolition crusade, but modern works like *Mandingo* further dramatize a world of miscegenation, incest, violence, and general degeneracy. For three centuries the southern aristocrat has stood tall. Different, and seldom dull, he is often admired as a maverick within an increasingly uniform, middle-class, capitalistic culture.

Southern aristocrats evolved among the Tidewater settlements in Maryland, Virginia, and the Carolinas early in the colonial period. Generally they were a homegrown lot unrelated to the old aristocracy of Europe. Among this early elite were merchants as well as planters, but gradually, when white settlement rolled westward, men of wealth concentrated on staple crop agriculture, especially cotton in the Deep South. Other Americans made money in agriculture, too, and some of the southern elite pursued commercial and industrial profits in the antebellum period—for example, Mary Ann Todd, the southern belle wife of Abraham Lincoln, came from an aris-

tocratic Kentucky family that made its money mainly in banking.

But the South remained predominantly agricultural as the Civil War approached while the North developed a more diversified economy with much industry. The Old South's emphasis—many said overemphasis—on market crops like cotton, rice, tobacco, hemp, and sugar made a difference, but what really set apart the South and its upper class from the rest of the nation was slavery.

While slavery was fading away in most of the rest of the Western world as the 19th century unfolded, it became an increasingly essential part of the Old South. Slave workers produced the profits of the southern aristocracy, and even the masses of southern whites who owned no slaves at all supported the "peculiar institution" as a means of keeping blacks subordinate.

The southern system based on slavery seemed increasingly "peculiar" to the North, and the Civil War loomed on the horizon. Yet in many ways leading southerners, great planters with 50 or even 100 or more slaves, were not as different as they seemed. Dueling faded away more slowly among them than among the northern elite, but such phenomena as race and class consciousness and conspicuous consumption were similar in both upper classes. Like their northern counterparts, elite southerners operated in a very competitive economy based upon bourgeois concepts of private property and free enterprise. As in the North, able, industrious (and lucky) southerners prospered, and in both sections wealth could vanish as rapidly as it had appeared. Bright, aggressive young men like Andrew Jackson, John C. Calhoun, or Henry Clay could work or marry their way into the upper class as readily in the South as in the North; nouveaux riches popped up fairly often in both sections.

Southern aristocrats moved about freely in the North. They often visited the best spots like Saratoga Springs, and they frequently sent their sons to northern schools like Princeton, Yale, and Harvard. Harvard dutifully memorialized her 136 sons who died to preserve the Union, but to this day she has never acknowledged her 64 sons who died for the southern Confederacy.

Slavery made the difference that led to war in 1861. The Confederacy chose Jefferson Davis to lead the great crusade, but, like many other southern aristocrats, he was the son of a dirt farmer. Indeed, the Davises and the Lincolns had lived less than 100 miles apart in frontier Kentucky, and both families were deeply rooted in the southern yeomanry. The Davises moved south to Mississippi and made a fortune in cotton; the Lincolns drifted north to a very different destiny.

The Civil War raged for four years before the South finally crumbled, yet out of this hideous slaughter the southern aristocracy's image emerged grander than ever. The rebel elite had fought well enough, but the real backbone of the Confederacy had been its redneck infantry (farmers like earlier generations of the Davises and the Lincolns) who slugged it out with a numerically superior enemy who were also farmers. Out of the agony of war and defeat rose the aristocratic figure of Robert E. Lee. No matter that his family had been on the economic skids for a generation, that he had no significant stake in slavery until he married into the wealthy Custis family, and that he had never been a planter but rather an officer in the American (Union) army for 32 years; Lee gave the South the hero it needed. More than a century after his death, the somber chapel at Washington and Lee University where he rests still transports the visitor back to a medieval world that never really existed in his native South.

The usual movement into and out of the elite class accelerated considerably after the Civil War, but many wealthy families managed to hold on to their money and status. Despite the optimism of New South spokesmen, the region remained mainly agrarian well into the 20th century, and various sharecropping systems kept many blacks and quite a few whites under the control of postbellum planters. Later, textile mill owners and operators exercised a similar hegemony and paternalism in regard to their employees. The southern aristocracy survived and continued to operate freely and confidently, subtly affecting American society. Through famous sons like Theodore Roosevelt and Douglas MacArthur, a few southern ladies influenced the highest levels of American life long before the nation was prepared to accept southern white male leadership again.

Even in recent decades, as the South has become more and more "Americanized," the influence of the southern aristocracy continues. Wealthy southerners today may sell Chevrolets (or Toyotas) instead of cotton, but they still rule the social roost. Family connections can still be helpful, but, as always, money is the deciding factor. Like many wealthy northerners who either settled in the South or built vacation retreats there, southern aristocrats enjoy great landed estates. Clearly, as long as America maintains a wealthy, visible elite, the southern aristocracy is secure.

F. N. Boney
University of Georgia

F. N. Boney, *Journal of Popular Culture* (Fall 1976), *Midwest Quarterly* (Spring 1974), *Southerners All* (1984); W. J. Cash, *The Mind of the South* (1941); Clement Eaton, *The Growth of Southern Civilization, 1790–1860* (1961); Jack Temple Kirby, *Media-Made Dixie: The South in the American Imagination* (1978); John Shelton Reed, *Southern Folk, Plain and Fancy: Native White Social Types* (1986); William R. Taylor, *Cavalier and Yankee: The Old South and American National Character* (1957). ☆

Communism

||||||||||||||||||||||||||||||||

Most scholars agree that the Communist party of the United States, despite inspiring much heated controversy, achieved at best only a minor impact on American political and social life. Because the American South lacked both a sizable foreign-born population and large concentrations of industrial workers, from whose ranks the party originally drew most of its members, it is not surprising that the Communist party gained fewer members and exerted less influence in the South than in other regions. Yet it would be an oversimplification to dismiss Communist influence entirely. During the 1930s and 1940s Communists were often in the vanguard of the fight against racism, and they occasionally provided assistance to the struggles of southern workers. A few native southerners even rose to positions of national influence within the party— Benjamin J. Davis of Georgia, Robert Minor of Texas, and James Jackson of Alabama, for example—but only after leaving the South. Eventually the Red Scare and government repression of the late 1940s and 1950s destroyed the par-

ty's modest gains in Dixie, just as they did elsewhere in the United States.

Founded in 1919, the Communist party appealed during its first decade mainly to residents of the industrial Northeast and Midwest. With the coming of the Great Depression and the accompanying crisis of American capitalism, Communists expanded their activities into the South. The first major incident announcing this Communist presence was the famous 1929 textile strike in Gastonia, N.C. During an outbreak of anti-Communist hysteria and violence there, Fred Beal, an organizer for the Communist-dominated National Textile Workers Union, and several strike leaders were arrested and unjustly convicted, in an infamous trial, of the murder of the local police chief. In 1930 the party began publishing the *Southern Worker* and attempted to organize workers in Atlanta, Birmingham, Chattanooga, Tampa, and other industrial centers. In eastern Kentucky in 1931, the Communist-dominated National Miners Union briefly assisted miners in Harlan County, where brutal repression also destroyed the union. These growing activities, as well as the formation of Unemployed Councils in several cities, alerted southern conservatives to an alleged Communist "invasion" of the South and helped link communism and radical ideas with unions in the minds of many southerners.

Even more frightening than Communist overtures to miners and industrial workers, who were mostly white, were the party's attempts after 1929 to recruit black members. The party's Marxist slogans did not inspire much enthusiasm. Communists found instead that what earned respect from blacks were well-organized local protests against specific discriminatory treatment and uncompromising stands against injustice. Still, only a few black (or white) southerners formally joined the party in the 1930s, although many more were affiliated with so-called Communist front organizations. Thus the party's influence was more extensive than membership figures alone would suggest. The new developments that eventually made communism appear a frightening specter in the eyes of white southerners were primarily the activities and aggressive tactics used by the International Labor Defense, a Communist-front legal defense group. In Alabama's famous Scottsboro case in 1931, the ILD vigorously defended the nine black youths accused of raping two white women on a freight train in north Alabama and, along with Communist and non-Communist allies, soon gained international notoriety for the case, thereby dramatizing racism in the South. In 1932 the ILD also represented Angelo Herndon, a young black Communist accused of attempting "to incite insurrection" against the state of Georgia. These and other ILD defense campaigns temporarily gained access to black churches and community institutions for Communists, but the Communist party's extreme left orientation at the time and its rigid Marxist theory nullified these opportunities.

The Communist party also made several efforts to enlist rural workers, especially blacks. In east central Alabama, Communists helped establish the Sharecroppers Union, which attempted to defend the rights of black day laborers, sharecroppers, and tenants against white landlords. Violent clashes in 1931 and again in 1933 resulted in massive repression of the union, but it continued to function underground until later merging with the National Farmers Union.

Communists participated in most Congress of Industrial Organizations (CIO) labor organizing drives, and the party developed a small following in the Birmingham area within the United Steel Workers Union and the Mine, Mill, and Smelter Workers Union, primarily among black workers. In the late 1930s and early 1940s chapters of the National Negro Congress and the Southern Negro Youth Congress contained a few black Communists and additional sympathizers, for the party's aggressive attacks on white supremacy particularly appealed to many young black intellectuals. Although a handful of white Communists joined the Southern Conference for Human Welfare, they did not exert any significant influence in the group after 1941.

Following a brief hiatus during World War II, Communists renewed their overtures to industrial workers, blacks, and also veterans. Yet the new climate of opinion shaped by the Red Scare, Cold War, and government repression proved most inhospitable and in time shattered the party. The CIO's purge of left-wing unions and almost anyone accused of Communist sympathies destroyed the limited Communist influence in southern unions. For a few years the Civil Rights Congress, postwar heir to the ILD, generated considerable interest in several legal proceedings dramatizing continued injustice toward blacks, the most prominent of which were the cases of Willie McGee in Mississippi, Rosa Lee Ingram in Georgia, and the so-called Martinsville Seven in Virginia. Many black southerners and occasionally a few whites were concerned about these prosecutions and the apparent racial bias in the application of the death penalty, but the anti-Communist hysteria soon frightened them away from taking direct action.

Despite the virtual collapse of the

Communist party in the South and the rest of the nation during the 1950s, a few tiny pockets of interest remained, primarily in Birmingham and Atlanta. In Greensboro, N.C., in 1979, five members of a small splinter group, the Communist Worker's party, which was active in the black community, were killed by alleged Klansmen and neo-Nazis, who were acquitted in 1984 of murder charges. Because of the elimination of the more obvious forms of racial discrimination in the South, the increased opportunities for venting black dissatisfaction through the political system, and the continued conservatism of many white workers, it seems unlikely that the future will bring any serious revival of interest in communism in the South.

See also LAW: / Herndon, Angelo; Scottsboro Case; VIOLENCE: Harlan County, Kentucky

Charles H. Martin
University of Texas at El Paso

Dan T. Carter, *Scottsboro: A Tragedy of the American South* (1969); Angelo Herndon, *Let Me Live* (1937); Charles H. Martin, *The Angelo Herndon Case and Southern Justice* (1976); Nell Irvin Painter, *The Narrative of Hosea Hudson: His Life as a Negro Communist in the South* (1979); Theodore Rosengarten, *All God's Dangers: The Life of Nate Shaw* (1975). ☆

Health, Worker

||||||||||||||||||||||||||||||||||||||

No concept of occupational health existed in the South or elsewhere in America until after 1910. "It is well known that there is no industrial hygiene in the United States," a Belgian labor expert told the International Congress on Occupational Accidents and Diseases in Brussels that year. In the next decade, however, widespread interest in social justice bore fruit in the recognition of hazards in the workplace. The U.S. Public Health Service was particularly active, and the South was the site of one of its early efforts.

The first disease associated with southern industry was pellagra, a dietary deficiency disease that affected not only southern mill workers but tenant farmers, sharecroppers, and the poor wherever they lived. It was a peculiar and often fatal malady, marking victims with a distinctive rash and sometimes leaving them insane. The disease lost much of its mystery when Dr. Joseph Goldberger of the U.S. Public Health Service proved that pellagra was caused by an inadequate diet, a product of both the peculiar dietary habits of the region and the poor economic conditions under which many southerners lived. The fatback, corn bread, and syrup diet consumed three times a day by tenant farmers and mill workers was a vestige of the frontier past when settlers depended on corn, pork, and cane for their food. Gripped by tradition, many southerners clung to this diet long after the frontier was gone. Their choice was reinforced by economic considerations. Wages, traditionally low in the southern mills, fell even lower in the fall of 1920, and Goldberger predicted a pellagra epidemic. In a brilliant epidemiological study of seven mill villages in South Carolina, Goldberger and his associates had already conclusively linked the incidence of pellagra to poor economic conditions. Irate defenders of the South denounced him and the PHS and refused all offers of aid. Despite their protests pellagra did increase throughout the 1920s and did not vanish until a quarter century later when scientists identified niacin as the missing factor in the diet. A greatly changed economy and an agricultural revolution made southern workers more prosperous and their diets more balanced.

The immediate hazards of the workplace were brought dramatically to the public's attention in the early 1930s by an incident at Gauley Bridge, W.Va. White and black laborers from mountain districts of the South were brought to West Virginia to dig a water-power tunnel through pure sandstone and quartz. The work began in 1929, and by the time it was completed three years later, 500 men had died of silicosis, pneumonia, and tuberculosis. Some dropped dead on the job and were buried within hours, sometimes two or three men in a single grave. Sensational compensation cases were tried in the courts, and Gauley Bridge became a symbol of danger on the job, particularly from dust.

As a result of this tragedy many commissions were formed to study the relationship of dust to health, though some of them may have been more concerned with forestalling massive claims than with improving working conditions. A survey of Virginia industries in 1938 showed that industrial officials believed that if their factories were free of silica dust, they were free of all occupational disease hazards, but as the Virginia study showed, more than a quarter million workers, or one-tenth of the population of the state, were employed in industries where occupational diseases were known to exist. The greatest number were exposed to dust of one sort or another, prolonged exposure to which caused trouble in the upper respiratory tract.

The number of southern workers who became ill as a result of industrial hazards was difficult to ascertain. By 1944 at least six southern states required physicians to report occupational diseases—Alabama, Arkansas, Georgia, Louisiana, Mississippi, and South Carolina—but this requirement did not provide a satisfactory method of getting statistics. The laws were not standardized nor was there any one agency in each state to whom physicians reported. In 1951, when four southern states participated in a pilot study to report occupational diseases, South Carolina found no cases of disease caused by dust in spite of its large textile industry. Nearly all states limited workmen's compensation claims to personal injury by accident, excluding occupational diseases altogether.

The first such disease to attract public attention was black lung, or pneumoconiosis, in the mid-1960s. A prevalence study showed that 1 of 10 miners working in the bituminous coal mines of Appalachia showed radiographic evidence of black lung, a disease marked by black spots on the lungs and greatly impaired breathing. One in five nonworking miners was affected. The study included miners in the southern states of Virginia, Tennessee, and Alabama and refuted the assumption that only miners of anthracite coal were subject to black lung. The disease probably had existed for many years before it became an issue. The danger that dust posed to health was increased with the introduction of mechanical loading equipment in the 1930s. These "man killers" greatly increased the dust level.

For 20 years the United Mine Workers promoted mechanization of the mines, believing that this would lead to higher wages and economic security, but the work force shrank steadily, and the dust, noise, and other hazards increased. The black lung revolt of 1968 was triggered by the refusal of the West Virginia Legislature to make the disease compensable under state law. A strike took 40,000 miners off the job, and a violent explosion in a Farmington, W.Va., mine killed 78 men, setting off a national political debate on black lung disease and resulting in the passage of the Coal Mine Health and Safety Act of 1969. This bill detailed mandatory work practices in the industry and provided compensation for victims of black lung and the widows of those who died from the disease. Activists among the miners contended that the ultimate cause of the disease was economic: mine owners did not spend enough to keep down the dust.

The increasing role of the federal government in protecting workers' health climaxed in the passage of the Occupational Safety and Health Act of 1970. A year later the first health standard was set, a temporary one for asbestos. This standard grew out of a long-range study of asbestos workers in Tyler, Tex., which showed that 39 percent of workers with more than 10 years employment in the company had asbestosis and that 30 percent of those workers who had massive exposure to asbestos fibers would develop cancer. The disclosures were so sensational that the Pittsburgh Corning Corporation, which owned the factory, closed it and buried most of the equipment.

Before the enactment of OSHA, the textile industry was barely aware of problems with cotton dust. Industrial air-conditioning improved the mill environment in the 1950s, but in the next decade speculation grew that raw cotton dust endangered workers' health. It was found to cause byssinosis, or brown lung disease, which is marked by chest tightness, shortness of breath, coughing, and wheezing. The disease begins with "Monday fever," when workers with long-term exposure to cotton dust fall ill every Monday. Later, symptoms last over several days, and finally the disease becomes chronic—the worker is disabled and the effects are irreversible. Industries responded to public pressure and stepped up the installation of dust-cleaning equipment in the 1970s. OSHA set standards for cotton dust exposure in 1978 that were upheld by the U.S. Supreme Court in 1981.

The manufacture of any new product may threaten workers' health. Viscose rayon plants in Virginia, North Carolina, and Tennessee were among those that changed their methods of manufacture in 1937 after it was found that workers were dangerously exposed to carbon disulphide, a poison that affects the central nervous system, causing paralysis in the legs or manic-depressive insanity. More recently, the increase in the number of available chemical compounds has multiplied the danger to workers. The kepone case in Hopewell, Va., in 1976 is illustrative. Workers making insecticides from kepone developed nervous disorders, bodily shakes, and sterility after exposure to the product. Waste from the plant, emptied into the James River, poisoned all the river valley and wiped out fishing there for years.

Labor unions have been important in the struggle for a safer workplace. The textile workers union forced OSHA to establish standards for cotton dust and called for programs of medical surveillance and wage retention for workers too sick to work in dusty areas. Their emphasis has been on forcing industry to modernize, not only to improve working conditions for labor but to make the companies economically viable in a competitive world.

The one constant in the effort to improve working conditions in the South and thus the health of the workers has been economics. From the fight against pellagra to the campaign against brown lung disease more than a half century later, economic factors have been primary. Workers pushed first for higher wages and later pressured industry to spend what was necessary to make the workplace safe.

See also SCIENCE AND MEDICINE: / Disease, Endemic

Elizabeth W. Etheridge
Longwood College

Daniel M. Berman, *Death on the Job: Occupational Health and Safety Struggles in the United States* (1978); Paul Brodeur, *Expendable Americans* (1974); Elizabeth W. Etheridge, *The Butterfly Caste: A Social History of Pellagra in the South* (1972); Joseph Goldberger, George A. Wheeler, Edgar Sydenstricker, and W. I. King, *A Study of Endemic Pellagra in Some Cotton-Mill Villages of South Carolina*, Hygienic Laboratory Bulletin No. 153 (1929); Joseph G. Montalvo, Jr., ed., *Cotton Dust: Controlling an Occupational Health Hazard*, American Chemical Society Symposium Series no. 189 (1982); George Rosin, *Preventive Medicine in the United States, 1900–1975: Trends and Interpretations* (1975); Barbara Ellen Smith, in *Health and Work under Capitalism: An International Perspective*, ed. Vincent Navarro and Daniel M. Berman (1983). ☆

Labor, Organized

||||||||||||||||||||||||||||||||||||||||||

Despite the general belief that southern unions are either almost nonexistent or recent arrivals, labor organizations have a long history in the South (defined here as the Confederate states plus Kentucky and Oklahoma). They emerged here about as early as they did elsewhere in the country. Southerners played a major role in the founding of the International Typographical Union, the nation's oldest national union. Indeed, some of the country's strong international unions—like the International Association of Machinists, organized in Atlanta in 1888—were formed in the South. Southerners have played and continue to play important roles in the American labor movement, especially as international union presidents, vice presidents, and international representatives. AFL-CIO president Lane Kirkland, from South Carolina, leads the nation's largest labor federation.

The image of union weakness in the South is due to the well-publicized difficulties unions have had organizing noncraft workers, especially in the textile industry in the Piedmont. These experiences are not typical of the rest of the South, where unions have made more progress and are stronger. The relative weakness of unions among nonagricultural workers in the South, as compared with other areas of the country, is largely attributable to the nature and location of southern industries. Even so, during the 1960s and 1970s unions grew much faster in the South than they did in the rest of the country.

Traditional southern institutions—e.g., the government, the economic structure—have also impeded union growth. Although these institutions could accept the emergence of a non-political craft-oriented movement of skilled white workers (or skilled blacks in segregated locals), they opposed the emergence of a more egalitarian political and economic movement among noncraft workers. This opposition was demonstrated during the late 19th century when efforts to unite black and white workers and farmers in the Knights of Labor failed because of the political and economic powerlessness of blacks and the economic powerlessness of low-income whites. With that failure, racial divisions and disfranchisement of blacks made it difficult for black and white low-income workers to unite before the 1930s.

Since World War II the South has undergone rapid industrialization and what some refer to as "the Americanization of Dixie." South/non-South per capita incomes started converging in the late 19th century with the onset of industrialization. The historical gap between the South's real per capita income and the rest of the country has almost been eliminated, especially for urban white southerners. These trends have eroded the political as well as the economic differences between the South and the rest of the nation. The South is even lumped in with the Southwest as the new "Sunbelt."

The changing character of labor and labor unions has followed this diminishing uniqueness of the South. Most industrial unions either entered the South for the first time or established their present bases during the New Deal period. The most successful was the United Mine Workers, which had support in the South during the 19th century, grew during World War I, was nearly eliminated in the antiunion period of the 1920s, but by 1935 had almost completely organized the southern coalfields. Tobacco, clothing, rubber, oil, automobile, and steel unions also revitalized or expanded their southern bases during this time, and efforts were even made by the Southern Tenant Farmers' Union to establish collective bargaining among the region's sharecroppers.

The greatest growth of southern union membership came during World War II, due to relatively full employment, rapid and stable economic growth, and the activities of the War Labor Board (WLB). The war not only increased total manufacturing in the South, but also changed its composition from the less unionized nondurables (which was two-thirds of total manufacturing before the war) to the more heavily unionized durables group—which made up 46 percent of total manufacturing employment in 1946.

The WLB's influence was due mainly to emergency conditions, which put a premium on the peaceful settlement of labor disputes. The National Labor Relations Board (NLRB), for example, has no power to compel companies to sign contracts after workers vote for the union. The WLB, by contrast, was backed by the armed forces—which took over and operated companies throughout the South when they defied the board's orders to sign contracts with unions. The WLB was especially important in strengthening unions in some industries such as oil, textiles, clothing, and food processing, which had started organizing before the war. Some unions, such as the oil and garment workers, were able to hold their memberships after the war, but the textile unions (in the South's leading industry) had greater difficulty when they had to win strikes to get contracts with intransigent companies. Increased union strength during the war energized antiunion political and business forces, and many southern states countered with antiunion legislation. Southerners were prominent in the passage of the Taft-Hartley Act (1947), which greatly restricted union activity.

Both the American Federation of Labor and the Congress of Industrial Organizations sought to counteract antiunion laws, hold their wartime gains, and organize the South's unorganized workers through campaigns launched in 1946. However, these campaigns were disappointments to both the AFL and the CIO, and labor subsequently suffered a number of important reverses in the South. These were not restricted to the weaker unions, but extended also to such union strongholds as construction, trucking, and coal mining.

An assessment of the sources of union strength and weakness in the South provides some insight into their future prospects. One of the most important forces affecting unions in the South is the strength of the American labor movement, which, except for cyclical fluctuations, has continued to grow absolutely since World War II but has declined relative to the total work force from about 35 percent in the 1950s and 1960s to about 25 percent in 1980.

There are many reasons for this relative decline in union strength: employment has been shifting away from the heavily unionized areas of the Midwest and East into the less unionized Sunbelt; away from more heavily unionized black, male, blue-collar workers to less unionized white, female, service, and professional-technical jobs; and away from large, more heavily unionized urban plants into smaller, nonmetropolitan workplaces. Major forces behind these employment shifts have been technological changes, especially the information revolution, and the internationalization of the American economy.

Industrial union strength is closely related to oligopolies in the basic industries, which have been rendered obsolete by intensified international competition from the newly industrialized countries, especially Japan and other nations adopting the highly competitive Japanese management system and export-oriented industrial policies.

Congress of Industrial Organizations pickets in Greensboro, Georgia, 1941

Unions in the clothing industry became better organized during the 1930s and 1940s because they had highly concentrated geographic bases in the Northeast. Intensified competition from Third World countries and decentralization into the Sunbelt have eroded the strength of these unions. Indeed, a major problem for unions is their inability to match economic strength with multinational corporations (MNC). The mobility of capital, and high and rising worldwide joblessness, give the MNCs tremendous bargaining advantages. Their superior information bases give the MNCs an important advantage in an internationalized information world.

Although unions probably have reflected their environments more than they have changed them, labor organizations have much more influence on southern political, social, and economic institutions today than they did in the 1950s. Unions as a whole did very little to change race relations in the South before World War II, but in the social ferment of the 1950s and 1960s, the AFL-CIO, the state federations, and some national industrial unions openly supported the more moderate civil rights leaders.

The unions also have challenged conservative domination of southern politics and have provided significant, and sometimes decisive, support for more progressive political candidates, as well as economic and protective legislation favorable to workers. Unions cannot be termed a decisive political force in the South generally, but their influence is very important in a number of states and has increased in all of them. When unions were relatively weak, they tended to reflect their environment; as they gain strength they will do more to change it.

Future union growth in the South will be determined primarily by the changing patterns of industry, and some expected employment changes are generally favorable for union growth. The composition of manufacturing employment is becoming increasingly diversified as the region industrializes. A smaller percentage of southern employment is concentrated in the older textile, tobacco, and lumber and wood products and a larger percentage in newer, better-organized industries. The main exceptions to these trends are the apparel and other finished textile products industries, which have increased rapidly in the South and are not very well organized.

Of the white-collar groups that are expected to continue to grow, the most likely to be organized are clerical and sales groups. The increasing political power of unions in the South has been and should continue to be beneficial to unions among teachers and state, county, and municipal workers. However, the reduction in government employment in the 1970s and 1980s has limited the growth of government employee unions.

Other trends favoring union growth include the following: (1) The migration of workers out of agriculture will help unions by reducing the supply of unskilled labor, and mechanization of farm work and improvement in the farm worker's income will reduce the tendency for farm workers to cross picket lines. (2) The prevailing ideology of the South may be changed with industrialization and become increasingly supportive of collective bargaining, though the prevailing attitude in most states today is still antiunion. (3) The unions' political power probably will grow because of increasing cooperation between unions and blacks (whose political power has increased greatly since the Civil Rights Act and the voter registration drives of 1965), reapportionment in favor of urban areas (where most blacks and most union members are located), the growth of a two-party system in the South, and the growing recognition by unions and workers that they cannot solve their problems in an internationalized information world through collective bargaining alone. (4) The attitudes of southern workers toward unions probably will change also as the region industrializes and their agricultural background recedes into history. In the long run workers probably will turn increasingly to labor organizations to represent their political and economic interests. (5) Pressures within the labor movement may strengthen southern organizing efforts. The unions' main motive will be the growing industrialization of the South and the consequent necessity to protect union conditions elsewhere. (6) Although the trend is very slow, increasing unionization is occurring among important white-collar workers, particularly government employees, and this trend will be accelerated by the unions' growing political power. (7) Inflation impedes union growth by lessening public support for unions and collective bargaining, but, by reducing real wages, inflation strengthens workers' desire to organize in order to catch up with rising inflation.

The trends that will make it more difficult for unions to organize include: (1) Plants tend to be located in smaller communities and rural areas. (2) Workers' homes are dispersed from areas near the plant gates, making it more difficult for union organizers to contact them. (3) Living standards are rising and patterns of living changing, which make the worker more responsive to family, community, and neighborhood influences. Other obstacles to organizing stem from rising educational levels, which make workers more questioning of both management and unions, requiring the latter to change their organizing techniques; technological changes, which increase employment in nonunion areas, small plants, and professional-technical occupations, increasing management's relative bargaining power and its ability to operate during strikes; and management's growing sophistication in avoiding unions when it wishes to.

The most important determinants of union memberships are likely to be those dramatic events, like wars and economic catastrophes, which cannot be predicted but could cause general increases in union membership throughout the region. Projections of membership trends relative to industries suggest that, although union membership in the South probably will continue to increase both absolutely and relative to the rest of the country, unions will have great difficulty bringing their membership up to the proportion of nonagricultural employment (29.4 percent in 1976) outside the region. To do this would require a doubling in southern membership, which would be very difficult in the near future. To do this would also require significant breakthroughs in the unionization of the textile, garment, and other low-wage manufacturing activities, and the service industries.

See also BLACK LIFE: Workers, Black

F. Ray Marshall
University of Texas at Austin

F. Ray Marshall, *Labor in the South* (1967), *The Negro Worker* (1967), *The Negro and*

Organized Labor (1965); Marc Miller, ed., *Working Lives: The Southern Exposure History of Labor in the South* (1980); National War Labor Board, *Reports of the Fourth Regional War Labor Board* (1945); George D. Stamer, *Monthly Labor Review* (June 1981); U.S. Congress, Joint Economic Committee, *Impact of the Federal Policies on the South*, 81st Congress, 1st Session (1949); U.S. Department of Labor, Bureau of Labor Statistics, *Labor in the South* (1946). ☆

Lower Class, Literary

|||||||||||||||||||||||||||||||||||||||||||||||||||||

When aristocratic William Byrd II wrote his *History of the Dividing Line* in 1728, he described "the world where the inhabitants live . . . in North Carolina" as a "Lubberland." Proud of both his Virginia home and his affluent lifestyle, Byrd cataloged the deficiencies of North Carolinians, who would soon be known widely as "Tarheels." The characteristics Byrd listed would become the predictable ingredients in one of the most enduring and productive of all American literary stereotypes—the southern "poor white trash."

From the perspective of his Virginia home, Byrd blamed most North Carolina vices on the "felicity of the climate," which made growing food and finding meat too easy. He did notice that the "poor women" did all the work and therefore conceded in passing that there was a good deal of work to do. But generally, he revealed, the people were slothful; the men slept late, and then, upon rising, stretched and yawned for half an hour, after which they smoked their pipes and leaned upon their shabby fences. "Thus they loiter away their lives," Byrd concluded, "through

aversion to labor." He dismissed them by assuming they had an inherent and ineradicable "disposition to laziness." The lazy lowlife everywhere meeting William Byrd's eye included widespread drunkenness, lawlessness, bad manners, incivility, and disrespect.

Once disseminated, Byrd's verbal portrait had the most profound effect on the American imagination and on southern literature in particular. Byrd portrayed a class of southern gentlemen who were unmistakably nonresidents of Lubberland. He also established the southern poor white man as a stock character in southern literature. Mark Twain, almost 150 years later, described him exactly as Byrd had, in the comic opening of *The Gilded Age*.

Out of this character developed the first literature that Americans felt was unique and indigenous. Although lowlife characters were described in the 19th century from Maine to California, the comic poor white tended to be placed in a southern locale. Thus, from the 1830s through the 1860s a body of comic stories and anecdotes came to be written and relished, capitalizing on some variety of southern clown. The most popular settings in which the comic poor were located in this southwestern frontier humor tradition were Deep South states: Georgia, Alabama, and Mississippi. These states could always be described as frontiers or backwoods, when tone demanded, because they could always be said to have backwoods, poor white characters populating them.

Even in the aftermath of Jacksonian democracy, writers creating such characters were encouraged because of the amusingly egalitarian outlook of the poor, the very air of underbred familiarity with which they treated their unrecognized superiors. Before the Civil War the most important writers creating lowlife southern rascals were Augustus Baldwin Longstreet, Johnson Jones Hooper, Thomas Bangs Thorpe, Henry Clay Lewis, Alexander G. McNutt, and George Washington Harris. Hooper's Simon Suggs, McNutt's Chunkey, and Harris's Sut Lovingood represented the southern lower-class mischief maker who lived lustily beyond the pale of social convention. He was never required to obey the rules and existed to explore the improprieties and their laughable consequences.

Thus, in the 19th century the southern lower-class clown became a national literary treasure: he allowed the release of the repressed; laughing at him exploded tensions and restored psychic balance. In the more defensive period of southern literature, after the Civil War and Reconstruction, his economic status was elevated slightly and his antics toned down a little. But as a poor but resilient farmer, he still furnished humor and allowed southern writers to imagine comic characters who were permitted to do and say more than most. His literary progeny thus evolved into several species of nationally recognized stereotypes: Mary Murfree's Tennessee mountaineer; Joel Chandler Harris's or Richard Malcolm Johnston's Georgia cracker; George Washington Cable's Louisiana Cajun. In this late 19th-century period, when such stereotypes were being differentiated under the standard of local color or regionalist writing, poor blacks were also described frequently and stereotypically. But they were separate. "Southern lowlife" was understood to mean either poor white trash or poor white, struggling upward.

With so much vitality embodied in one kind of literary character, 20th-century writers could not ignore the type. William Faulkner, Flannery O'Connor, Eudora Welty—the great southern comic talents of a more recent period—derive much of their most compelling humor from characters descended from 19th-century southern fiction. Faulkner's Anse Bundren and the Snopeses, Welty's Bonnie Dee Peacock and her robber bridegroom, O'Connor's Mr. Shortley and her lewd Bible salesman—all can be related directly to 19th-century, lower-class comic figures.

In the 20th century, however, fiction writers became more sympathetic to the proletariat. After the Gastonia textile mill strike in 1929, at least 10 different novelists based fiction on the plight of the poor southern textile worker. The most popular writer aiming for a political statement, Erskine Caldwell, seemed, however, to dwell most memorably on the sexual irregularities of which such poor were capable. Writers with other political axes to grind described the southern lower class sympathetically. Marjorie Kinnan Rawlings, for example, wrote warmly of Florida backwoods life. Shirley Ann Grau used the Cajuns of the Louisiana bayous and coastal islands. Reynolds Price has explored the emotional intricacies of lower-class life in North Carolina. But perhaps the most impassioned and poetic treatment of this class ever written remains James Agee and Walker Evans's masterful *Let Us Now Praise Famous Men*.

See also ETHNIC LIFE: Mountain Culture; FOLKLIFE: / "Hillbilly" Image; LITERATURE articles; MYTHIC SOUTH: / "Crackers"; Poor Whites

Merrill M. Skaggs
Drew University

John Q. Anderson, ed., *With the Bark On: Popular Humor of the Old South* (1967); Hennig Cohen and William B. Dillingham, eds., *Humor of the Old Southwest* (1964); Sylvia Jenkins Cook, *From Tobacco Road to Route 66: The Southern Poor White in Fiction* (1976); Shields McIlwaine, *The Southern Poor-White from Lubberland to Tobacco Road* (1939); Merrill M. Skaggs, *The Folk of Southern Fiction* (1972). ☆

Marxist History
||||||||||||||||||||||||||||||||||||||||||

As a political and social ideology, Marxism has numbered fewer adherents in the South than in the rest of America. Only a handful of white or black southerners ever joined Marxist movements. But in recent years various scholars—historians, economists, sociologists—have used Marxian concepts in an interpretative framework designed to explain the southern past and present.

Few of the scholars who apply Marxist theory to the South could be called "orthodox" Marxists. The fundamental importance that classical Marxism applies to economic (material) forces, and the accompanying class struggle, has been modified or refined in various ways by those social scientists who have examined southern history from a Marxian perspective.

Marxist interpreters of the South have tended to focus on the 19th century. Herbert Aptheker, Eugene Genovese, and Raimondo Luraghi use Marxist theory to analyze the antebellum South and its labor system of racial slavery. Luraghi focuses his research on the Confederate South. W. E. B. Du Bois's pioneering book on Reconstruction (1935) interprets the period as a time of

class as well as racial struggle. Recent books by Jay Mandle, Dwight Billings, and Jonathan Wiener use Marxist perspectives to examine economics and class relationships in the South during Reconstruction and beyond. Of these, only Mandle's work extends into the 20th century.

For their analysis of the antebellum plantation South, Luraghi and Genovese were influenced by the Italian Marxist theoretician Antonio Gramsci, who downplayed economic determinism and emphasized the role of cultural domination, or hegemony, by the ruling elite over the underclasses. Luraghi calls the planters a "seigneurial class" and describes the civilization of the Old South as patrician, paternalistic, and precapitalist—indeed, anticapitalist. Luraghi, however, says virtually nothing about the nonslaveholding white majority in southern society. Genovese would agree with some of Luraghi's assumptions, but he views "paternalism" in a more balanced way and devotes less attention to the planter's style of life. In an *Agricultural History* article (1975) Genovese wrestles with the problem of why the southern yeomanry (the nonslaveholding white majority) went against "its own apparent collective interests" by accepting planter hegemony. That question is also briefly dealt with in *Roll, Jordan, Roll*. Genovese asserts that although slavery as a system oppressed nonslaveowners, it did so in a disguised way, whereas the paternalistic spirit that animated the planter's world was extended toward poorer whites in such adroit ways as to minimize class conflict. The slaves responded to paternalism, Genovese suggests, by simultaneous accommodation and resistance; in order to keep peace, slaveowners made informal concessions that allowed slaves some measure of human dignity. But as a Marxist, Genovese maintains that paternalism, wherever it exists, "undermines solidarity among the oppressed" by linking them to their oppressors. Presumably this would apply to the poor whites as well as blacks. Emancipation, however, "meant the end of paternalism as the reigning Southern ideal of social relations," although Genovese adds that paternalism did not totally disappear in the South after 1865.

The most explicitly Marxist analysis of the postwar South is that of Jay Mandle (1978). Mandle asks "what in the historical experience of the black population of the United States is responsible for the deprivation which currently exists?" He seeks the answer in examining "the mode of production," by which he means not only the technology and labor force of the southern economy, but also the power relationships that are established between employers and workers. Mandle concludes that through the devices of sharecropping and tenancy the plantation system was able to survive emancipation; indirect means of labor control replaced the more rigid system of slavery. For blacks, poverty remained the norm, landownership was virtually impossible, and occupational mobility minimal. The grip of the plantation system did not really loosen in the South until World War II. Although the old plantation mode of production has now virtually disappeared, its legacy of poverty for blacks largely remains.

Dwight Billings (1979) deals with North Carolina from 1865 to 1900, and Jonathan Wiener (1978) focuses upon Alabama from 1860 to 1885; yet both their books have implications for the entire South in the late 19th century.

Billings concludes that although conservative Democrats controlled North Carolina politics after Reconstruction, their domination was never secure until 1900. He questions North Carolina's reputation as the most progressive of southern states, asserting that the state's leadership continued to work toward reactionary objectives during the late 1800s. The old planter elite simply became the new planter-industrial elite, with the same repressive attitudes toward the labor force.

Wiener's book on Alabama forcefully argues that the old planter elite kept control of the state's economy even during Reconstruction, making fewer concessions to business or industry than was the case in North Carolina. After emancipation, planters and exslaves worked out a reluctant compromise: the blacks, who wanted landownership, had to settle for sharecropping as a better alternative to the gang labor system preferred by planters. But this fragmentation of productive units, Wiener concludes, represented a move away from efficient, cost-intensive agriculture, which would have raised production through improved technology. Instead, planters obtained their profits by passing state laws that gradually (through debt peonage) squeezed more from the laborers. Using a phrase of Barrington Moore's, Wiener concludes that Alabama planters used "the Prussian Road" to modern society. Wiener defines this as "economic development that preserves and intensifies the authoritarian and repressive elements of traditional social relations." But Wiener adds that planter hegemony began to fade toward the end of the 19th century; in Alabama, as elsewhere, the system was increasingly anachronistic in a nation being transformed by bourgeois capitalism.

See also INDUSTRY: Industrialization and Change

William I. Hair
Georgia College

Herbert Aptheker, *American Negro Slave Revolts* (1943); Dwight B. Billings, *Planters and the Making of a "New South": Class, Politics, and Development in North Carolina, 1865–1900* (1979); W. E. B. Du Bois, *Black Reconstruction in America* (1935); Eugene D. Genovese, *Agricultural History* (April 1975), *In Red and Black: Marxist Explorations in Southern and Afro-American History* (1971), *Roll, Jordan, Roll: The World the Slaves Made* (1974); Raimondo Luraghi, *Rise and Fall of the Plantation South* (1978); Jay Mandle, *The Roots of Black Poverty: The Southern Plantation Economy after the Civil War* (1978); Jonathan M. Wiener, *Social Origins of the New South: Alabama, 1860–1885* (1978). ☆

Middle Class

||||||||||||||||||||||||||||||||||

A large, fluid middle class has long dominated America, and the South has shared in this trend, which developed so much more powerfully than in Europe. Southern colonists came mostly from the lower orders of British society with a strong dash of middle-class types, but the New World along the North American coast offered something really new—cheap land weakly held by aboriginal tribes. America was truly the land of opportunity for ordinary emigrants from Europe.

The fertile soil and long growing season in the South gave a special boost to the average farmer who could own his own land, raise subsistence and money crops, and generally do well for himself and his family by hard work—and a little luck with the weather and the market prices of his crops. In many respects he was far better off than his counterpart in Europe. By the time of the American Revolution such farmers, North and South, were relentlessly driving the Indians westward.

The successful rebellion against the British Empire ushered in the world's most exuberant bourgeois democracy, and in the South herrenvolk democracy (for whites and males only) flourished as an integral part of this new order. By the 1840s the new nation had reached the Pacific Ocean, and the increasingly restive South stretched all the way from Virginia to Texas. The southern lower classes were composed of masses of black slaves (owned by a minority of whites) and a much smaller conglomeration of poor whites. At the top of the heap stood the wealthy planters with their gangs of slave laborers, but this agrarian elite composed only a tiny proportion of the white population. In the broad middle was the same sprawling, fluid middle class that dominated the North.

The majority of the southern bourgeoisie owned no slaves at all, and the minority who did owned only a few—generally a white family owning and working alongside a black family. By the eve of the Civil War southern society had matured, and the middle class had become quite complex and diversified. Though many scholars see the middle class as limited in any society to commercial, industrial, and professional people, the antebellum southern middle class was composed primarily of farmers.

Trying to explain his native Southland to a rather puzzled North in the 1860s,

Daniel R. Hundley noted that, "the middle classes of the South constitute the greater proportion of her citizens, and are likewise the most useful members of her society. . . . There are among them farmers, planters, traders, storekeepers, artisans, mechanics, a few manufacturers, a goodly number of country school-teachers, and a host of half-fledged country lawyers and doctors, parsons, and the like." Significantly, Hundley included "planters," for most of them, even the so-called aristocrats, had bourgeois attitudes about striving and succeeding in a competitive, capitalistic economy. Hundley felt that planters with some slaves bore "a striking similarity" to prosperous New England farmers and that southern village storekeepers differed "but little" from their northern counterparts. He was especially impressed with middle-class southern women, who generally practiced the old-fashioned art of being the wife and mother, and, as he put it, lived "only to make home happy." Overall, he saw the southern middle class as proud, hospitable, generous, and straightforward; but he decried limited formal education, provincialism, religious bigotry, a pronounced lack of deference, and an abundance of self-confidence. In his view too many southern bourgeois types acted as if they carried "the world in a little private sling" and had all the answers. Grudgingly, Hundley conceded that "intermarriage" with the middle class had diluted his own elite class.

Despite his biases, Hundley drew a basically accurate picture of the dominant southern bourgeoisie. Hard-working, family-oriented folk, they led respectable lives. Generally they obeyed the law, owned property, paid taxes, and attended church (usually an evangelical sect that championed the traditional American work ethic). They remained mobile in order to exploit land that was incredibly cheap by world standards, and a steady trickle continued to filter up into the planter class (and down into the poor white ranks) within a flexible white socioeconomic system. They supported extensive educational efforts that brought functional literacy to a high percentage of citizens (higher than in Britain or France) and firmly held to their belief in progress.

The Civil War brought disaster to the Confederate South. Amidst the chaos of defeat, slavery vanished forever, but the middle-class white society that formed so powerfully in the antebellum era survived the holocaust. Indeed, blacks had felt its influence even as debased slaves, and now as freedmen they sought its fruits: property ("forty acres and a mule"), education, and equality. Leaders like Frederick Douglass and Booker T. Washington who had been shaped in slavery championed the old-fashioned American work ethic and counseled their people to strive and to succeed within the traditional middle-class system. Some blacks, playing by the old rules, made progress. White America, however, was not ready to concede full black equality: in the North, where few blacks lived, whites lost interest in the great crusade called Reconstruction; and in the South, where blacks remained concentrated, whites actively undermined it. Soon most southern blacks found themselves trapped in the sharecropping system or other forms of manual labor, condemned to more generations of discrimination and poverty. Many whites slipped into sharecropping, too, as southern agriculture suffered a long slump after the Civil War.

The southern middle class shrank in

A middle-class Tennessee couple on vacation, c. 1960

these prolonged hard times, but it did not disintegrate. Just as important, its optimistic, industrious spirit survived, just waiting for better times to return. Since the post–World War II era the southern middle class has expanded rapidly. The civil rights crusade of the 1960s, a renewal of the first great crusade called Reconstruction, brought many blacks into the southern and American middle class at last. Many women, black and white, have independently achieved middle-class status through educational attainment and pursuit of careers. The old southern bourgeoisie Hundley described in the 1860s has become much more complex and diversified and has generally moved from the country into the growing cities and suburbs and from the farm into office buildings and stores.

Southern cultural imagery in earlier times did not do justice to the middle class. The region's mythology portrayed the white population of the South as either wealthy planters or poor white trash. Middle-class southerners now appear, though, as representatives of the new cultural ideal. They work in white-collar jobs; the South added over 300,000 professional and managerial positions to the middle class each year in the early 1980s. This upper middle class is prosperous, well educated, and well traveled; it is conservative on economic and political issues but increasingly liberal on social issues; and it seems to have a well developed sense of its southern identity. This transformation has been an extension and expansion of that middle-class system that emerged in the South and the rest of the nation before the Civil War. But in the contemporary South the middle class increasingly sets the tone for society and provides cultural models. The southern bourgeoisie has a long history—and a promising future.

F. N. Boney
University of Georgia

F. N. Boney, *Southerners All* (1984); James C. Cobb, *Industrialization and Southern Society, 1877–1984* (1984); Daniel R. Hundley, *Social Relations in Our Southern States* (1860); Frank L. Owsley, *Plain Folk of the Old South* (1949); John Shelton Reed, *One South: An Ethnic Approach to Regional Culture* (1984), *Southern Folk, Plain and Fancy: Native White Social Types* (1986). ☆

Migrant Workers

Poorer than other sections of the United States, the South has historically exported its people by the millions. Whether crossing the Ohio River to flee slavery, following cotton or tobacco away from worn-out soil, or seeking employment in northern industry, the southerner has frequently sought greater opportunity elsewhere.

The "migrant worker," or "migratory laborer," moves from his southern home northward, each year repeating the pattern until he can find permanent work. His domination by his employer, usually a crew leader who furnishes transportation and subsistence, typically of low quality and high price, seems in the 1980s to be reminiscent of the authoritarian standards of earlier times. Even more clearly, the migrant's labor market is nearly as chaotically "free" as it was before World War II. There once were comprehensive planning schemes for consecutive employment in successive harvests, but only vestiges of these remain. Very few migrants follow an entire "stream," working in every state from Texas to Wisconsin or from Florida to New England; more typically, their crew boss haphazardly chooses a few employers for them in one or two other states.

In the 20th century two major southern migratory streams originate in Texas and Florida. The Texas-based movement usually includes about twice as many individuals as the Florida-based pattern; the latter is as completely black as the southwestern one is Mexican and Mexican American. Ethnicity is a key to understanding the lack of access to better employment. The migrant streams, since their origins, have been fed by excess labor from dying peonage and sharecropping systems in Mexico, the Caribbean, and the Deep South. Mechanization, irrigation or drainage, chemical and biological discoveries,

and faster refrigerated transport of fruits and vegetables have produced a large-scale agriculture that needs few workers except at peak seasons, such as the harvest period. At that time, however, from the standpoint of the employer who pays by the piece and not the hour, there can never be too much labor on hand: an oversupply guarantees the picking of fruits and vegetables at the peak of perfection, and hand picking is preferable to machine harvesting, except when taste has been sacrificed to toughness in the breeding of new hybrids.

Both southern migrant routes appeared before the turn of the century. The roots of the southwestern stream are the deeper of the two. Mexicans have long traveled north into the Rocky Mountains and Great Plains with cattle drives and at the busier sheepherding seasons. Cotton in Oklahoma and in Texas, sugar beets in the Rockies, vegetables in the upper Midwest, and the wide variety of California crops gradually became major lures out of the South. So huge was Texas that many workers established a migratory pattern within that state alone.

The development of truck farming in New Jersey in the 1890s drew in black harvest workers from Maryland and Virginia, and during World War I Middle Atlantic areas outgrew their local labor supply and attracted Carolina and Old Dominion blacks. During the 1920s, with Upper South agriculture becoming a labor-demand rather than a labor-supply industry, and with corporate agriculture reclaiming Florida swampland so that America could enjoy winter vegetables, the Atlantic Coast stream developed fully. For most of the century, there were four to five times more workers per farm employed in Florida than in other Atlantic Seaboard states, freeing thousands at the end of each winter season. Most went north along the coast, often as far as New England, though a few traveled inland to Ohio and Indiana.

The worldwide Great Depression forced poor Mexicans as well as poor whites onto the highways in a desperate search for jobs. It, and the New Deal programs designed to counteract it, also drove thousands of sharecroppers off cotton plantations into the migrant streams. In this cauldron of misery the only hopeful element was the creation in 1937 of the Farm Security Administration (FSA), which built decent housing for migrants in a few areas and attempted to establish health standards.

World War II brought the first governmental importation of foreign migrant workers. In 1942, to offset the wartime labor shortage, Caribbean workers were imported to the Atlantic states and the first Mexican *braceros*—

literally, arm workers—arrived in the Southwest. This program long outlasted the emergency and continued to bring in wage-depressing foreign migrants more than a decade after the war's conclusion. The termination of the program in 1964, once hailed as a victory for American workers, proved to have little if any impact. Immigration laws still permitted thousands of "green-carders" to enter the United States legally, but wages were undoubtedly retarded even more by the incalculably greater number who arrived outside the law. Once known as "wetbacks," later called "illegals," this uncountable army spread from the Southwest to the entire nation, from farm labor to virtually all unskilled and semiskilled work.

At the end of World War II, the Farm Placement Service appeared in the Department of Labor and offered hope that farm workers' as well as farm employers' interests might again be well served.

A migrant labor camp in Florida, 1930s

The Farm Placement Service had been a labor-supportive part of the War Manpower Commission until the American Farm Bureau Federation (AFBF) succeeded in placing it under the War Foods Administration and the state extension services, which were generally more sympathetic to employers. The AFBF had also helped kill the FSA during the war, but afterwards the FSA migrant camps were permitted to continue under public as well as private operation.

The President's Commission on Migratory Labor, established by Harry Truman in 1951, and Edward R. Murrow's 1960 television documentary, *Harvest of Shame*, highlighted the decades of greatest public sympathy toward migrant workers. In the Atlantic Coast stream their numbers dropped from a postwar peak in 1949 of well over 50,000 in any one state at a given time to under 30,000 in the 1960s. Social Security coverage was won for some migrants in 1954 and 1956, and most states markedly improved their enforcement of health and housing standards. From World War II to the 1960s, annual migrant wages rose from the $500–$1,000 range to $1,500–$3,000, if the entire family worked, and before the crew chief made his deductions.

The rise and fall of the Annual Worker Plan accompanied, and in some ways explained, the decline of migratory labor conditions after the 1960s. This plan, developed by the Farm Placement Service in 1954, sought to stabilize the harvest labor force, for the benefit of all concerned, by scheduling work crews for consecutive jobs, and by monitoring performance so that substandard workers and employers would not be supplied labor. Participation in the system peaked in about 1967. By the late 1970s the harvest labor market was virtually "free" again, due partially to bureaucratic mismanagement and crew boss chicanery, but largely, however, to employer preference for illegal immigrants and for domestic workers kept cheap and docile by competition with the illegals.

Statistics on such a disorganized labor force range from unreliable to nonexistent, but it appears that tuberculosis, malnutrition, alcoholism, and crew boss dictatorship are rising among 1980s migrants as the degree of law enforcement declines, a development that offsets the drift toward ending agricultural exemptions from labor law. Typical of the trend away from federal enforcement of federal regulations, at a time when state budgets are usually too tight to permit expanded attention to these extremely poor people who are seldom able to vote, was the decision of President Reagan's Environmental Protection Agency to let the individual states enforce pesticide control standards. The historic southern belief in states' rights and minimal government, now at least given lip service at the highest levels of American power, would appear to control the migrant worker's fate for the foreseeable future.

Zora Neale Hurston's novel *Their Eyes Were Watching God* (1937) tells of life among the "eastern stream" of migrant workers in Florida, while John Steinbeck's *The Grapes of Wrath* (1939) is the definitive account of the Depression-era migrants who moved west. Public health physician Earl L. Koos offers a unique perspective on eastern migrants in a 1957 volume entitled *They Follow the Sun* produced for the Florida State Board of Health.

Donald H. Grubbs
University of the Pacific

George O. Coalson, *Migrant Farm Labor System in Texas* (1977); Robert Coles, *Migrants, Sharecroppers, Mountaineers* (1971); Truman E. Moore, *Slaves We Rent* (1965). ☆

Politics and Social Class

||||||||||||||||||||||||||||||||||||||||||||||||||||||||||||

Class patterns imported from England took root in the South back in the colonial era. The earliest settlers included few members of the British aristocracy or large landed proprietor class; the organizers of these expeditions were for the most part adventurous, ambitious, talented people from the middle ranks of British society who sought opportunities not open to them at home in 17th-century Britain. A combination of circumstances made large-scale agriculture—or the plantation economy—not only possible, but highly desirable. The planter "aristocrat" (later designated "cavalier") became the southern upper class and was the natural source of political leadership. A pattern of rural-based, planter-dominated politics was established and then extended as the South expanded into the areas south and west of the Chesapeake Bay area. This pattern was not completely broken (despite all the vicissitudes of the region's history) until the 20th century.

At the opposite end of the social scale, of course, was the black slave. Introduced into Virginia by a Dutch trader in 1619 as long-term indentured servants, blacks provided a permanent source of agricultural labor that served the expanding plantation cash-crop system. The enslavement of blacks soon followed, and by the middle of the 17th century the practice was made legal in Virginia. From there slavery moved to other areas, seemed in decline during the relative stagnation of the Tidewater plantations from soil depletion in the late 18th century, and developed and expanded again after 1795 with the invention of the cotton gin and the growth of the Deep South states. Slavery thus provided the plantation system a labor supply that was locked into a permanent state of economic and social immobility, rendered totally dependent, and excluded from the possibility of citizenship and participation in politics. It was ironic that upper-class slaveowners like Thomas Jefferson would, in the 18th century, revolt (in the name of individual freedom and a new order of republican government) against the feudal remnants of inherited privilege. A further irony was the democratization of that republican form of government in the following century, as the South was beginning its self-conscious defense of slavery.

One other social class more or less formally identified as such well before the American revolutionary era and continuously recognized as part of the social structure ever since was the southern "poor white." In 1728 William Byrd II headed a commission to establish the boundary between North Carolina and Virginia. Among other extensive descriptions of places and events in his *History of the Dividing Line* (not published until 1841, but circulated soon after it was produced) Byrd included a graphic account of a singularly unprepossessing group of people in the border backwoods who were referred to as "lubbers." Undernourished and unhealthy, indolent and dirt poor, ignorant and unskilled to the point of surviving only through low native cunning, the "lubber" became the prototype for what, under various derogatory ascriptions, was in effect a declassed, poverty-stricken, rural southern white. Though not clearly fixed by sociological definition, and relatively small in number even when extended to include economically marginal hill farmers, "poor whites" became such a literary convention that many people outside the South (and some inside it) think stereotypically that the South is composed of only three social classes—the planter aristocrat, the poor white, and the black.

In point of fact, through much of southern history the middle class was numerically dominant, because it included the yeoman farmer as well as the small-town merchant and professional person. The planter became both an idealized type and a real wielder of economic, social, and political power, and the economic importance and potential in democratic politics of the middle class was not effectively recognized until the 20th century.

Throughout the colonial period the planter aristocratic tradition continued to hold sway in politics (most notably in Virginia and South Carolina), and public service was considered a part of the continuing obligation of that class. In the more prominent families males prepared for this role by joining a classical education to the study of law. The tradition produced a remarkable collection of early political leaders whose contributions to the American Revolution, the framing and adoption of the Constitution, and the early experience in making the Republic work are incalculable. Out of this class Virginia alone furnished the draftsman of the Declaration of Independence (Jefferson), the chief military commander of the Revolution who was later the presiding officer of the Constitutional Convention (Washington), that convention's most effective recorder and interpreter (Madison), four of the

first five presidents of the United States (Washington, Jefferson, Madison, and Monroe), and the chief justice of the U.S. Supreme Court (Marshall) who did most to shape that branch of the national government into the powerful instrument it became. Prominent figures from the South were leaders in developing the Federalist party, and Jefferson and Madison were the founders of the opposition Republican party, which later became the Democratic party. Jefferson's ideas had as much influence on the transition of the American Republic into a constitutional democracy as those of any other single person.

But if it was aristocrats such as Jefferson who provided much of the impetus for American democracy, it was left for the descendants of the "plain folk" settlers of the first American frontier (what are now the states of the Upper South) to make the practical transition in the form of Jacksonian democracy. From roughly the time of Jackson's election to the presidency in 1828 until the breakup of the party system in 1860, the South was part of national two-party politics in which the competition between the Democrats and Whigs was close, and the division in party adherence tended to be along social class lines that are still familiar. The Jacksonian Democrats found support in an expanding electorate moving toward universal white manhood suffrage, and the bulk of its supporters were farmers and laborers. The traditions of Jeffersonian agrarianism and decentralization of political power by way of geographically based pluralism also kept many planters in the Democratic fold. The Whigs, who displaced the moribund Federalists, tended to reflect the growth of the middle class business and professional classes that were part of the incipient industrial development. Early in this period the New England reform movement, of which antislavery was simply one part, combined with the rapid growth of commercial and manufacturing interests in the Northeast to produce increasing sectional tensions in which the issues often turned on the way the North-South political and economic balance was to be maintained in the face of the slave-state, free-state issue.

On the eve of the Civil War, an Alabama lawyer-planter and sometime Chicago businessman, Daniel R. Hundley, published a book entitled *Social Relations in Our Southern States* (1860). The study may well be the first attempt at a systematic analysis of the structure of social classes in the South. Hundley goes beyond the use of basic demographic characteristics in developing his taxonomy, identifying traits of character that affect political behavior and the social types he perceived. Although the southern gentleman is his ideal type, being a planter at a certain economic level is not enough to place one in this category. Two other types may be economically successful, yet never attain the nobility of character, the appropriate sense of honor, and the other virtues that would qualify them as gentlemen. These "cotton snobs" and "southern Yankees" in their respective ways were interested more in getting and spending wealth than in the conduct of individual and social life according to the higher standards of the gentleman. Similarly, Hundley analyzes the middle classes, the primary categories being those in the towns (merchants, et al.) and the yeoman farmer, with considerable ranges in each category in terms of social and economic functions and moral considerations as well. Two other categories that rank low on Hundley's scale of

character traits are the "southern bully" (who may range widely in economic status) and "poor white trash"—the extended lubber image. Hundley also includes the "Negro slaves" in his discussion, but mainly for purposes of comparing the social condition of the slaves in the South favorably with the exploited "free" laborers elsewhere.

Hundley's book provided a solid sense of the complexity of the social structure of the pre–Civil War South and revealed the extent to which the South remained traditionally status-based in its social hierarchy rather than moving toward a social structure comparable to that in the northeastern states. The South held to the plantation-agrarian ideal as opposed to contractual foundations of social, economic, and political relations. *Social Relations in Our Southern States* anticipated the restoration in the post-Reconstruction South of something as close to the social structure of the antebellum South as the emerging planter-lawyer-doctor-merchant-banker ruling elite could manage.

The South's "politics as usual" after Reconstruction was a one-party politics in which blacks were, by the end of the 19th century, removed from direct participation. Blacks were used as a symbolic threat to keep white voters in line when economic or other issues that generated divisions along class lines produced electoral challenges to the dominant structures of political power. Voter participation in elections at all levels declined as large numbers of poor whites (as well as virtually all blacks) were disqualified, and a large portion of those who were qualified did not bother to turn out for elections. Intraparty competition was carried on through various types of factional alignments, with the primary elections for nomination of candidates the point at which the real competition (if any) took place.

From time to time various political movements threatened to break the long-standing pattern of control by the Bourbon-planter class. In the 1890s the "farmer's revolt" made some headway in the South (as it did in the Midwest) when the Populist party challenged the Bourbon-planter hegemony. Although Populism's main source of support was the small farmer and labor classes, it was never able to generate a voter coalition strong enough to sustain the few successes it had at the polls, partly at least because the possibility of uniting blacks and whites in the common effort was diverted by appeals to white racial unity within the Democratic party. Vestiges of Populism appeared in factional form from time to time after 1900, most notably in the case of the Long faction in Louisiana, where economic issues overrode racial ones for a considerable period of time. Southern Progressivism, more of an urban middle-class phenomenon, also constituted reformist challenges to the dominant forces on occasion, but the voter divisions here tended to be less identifiable along class lines than in the case of Populism.

In the 20th century the South began to concentrate more on its economic development, which was interrupted by the Depression but stimulated by the New Deal reforms and by World War II. A new generation of southern political leaders emerged after the war, and the national Democratic party began to take some initiative in advancing both party and national governmental programs against racial segregation.

The actions along these lines in the 1948 Democratic convention led to a walkout on the part of some of the southern states that was the beginning of the breakup of the "old" southern one-party politics and of the social practices that had such an important role in its long perpetuation. The subsequent civil rights movement, the rapid urban-industrial growth in the South, the centralization of governmental power, and all of the related changes have gradually produced political alignments among voters in the South that are more congruent with "normal" American tendencies to vote along economic and social class interest lines than was the case during the era of the solid Democratic South. The nearest thing to a complete political mobilization of a socially identifiable group is the steady support of 90 percent and upwards of the black vote for Democratic candidates in straight contests between regular party candidates. A steady growth has occurred in middle-class, urban-suburban southern Republicanism. It remains to be seen whether the "new" politics will mean continuing movement toward convergence in the social class patterns of support for parties, factions, individual candidates, and issues in the southern and non-southern states or whether new, but still distinctive, ones will emerge.

See also HISTORY AND MANNERS: Populism; Progressivism; POLITICS articles

William C. Havard
Vanderbilt University

Daniel R. Hundley, *Social Relations in Our Southern States* (1860); V. O. Key, Jr., *Southern Politics in State and Nation* (1949); J. Morgan Kousser, *The Shaping of Southern Politics: Suffrage Restriction and the Establishment of the Old-Party South, 1880–1920* (1974); Paul Lewinson, *Race, Class, and Party: A History of Negro Suffrage and White Politics in the South* (1932); Rupert B. Vance and Nalia Danilevsku, *All These Peo-*

programs to train personnel in public health, special education for the handicapped, adult education, and social work. By the post–World War II years, there were both programs and schools in social welfare, and financing for them gradually improved. Nonetheless, the average welfare payment in the southern states has consistently remained lower than elsewhere in the nation. Most states have financed aid for the blind, relief for children and the elderly, and general assistance to the destitute, but even as late as the 1920s most relief for the poor in the South was through such private agencies as churches, benevolent groups, and the community chest.

The Depression hit the South hard because many aspects of the region's economy were depressed even before 1929. Bluesman Lonnie Johnson sang in "Hard Times Ain't Gone Nowhere": "Hard times don't worry me, I was broke when it first started out." The New Deal, though, represented a landmark in efforts to help the southern poor. President Franklin D. Roosevelt identified the South as the "Nation's No. 1 economic problem," noting the large number of its poor. Congress initiated national programs such as the National Youth Administration, Civilian Conservation Corps, Public Works Administration, and Works Progress Administration that had a dramatic effect on the region. Many programs worked specifically to help the rural poor. New Deal relief programs ran into the opposition of southern white administrators desiring to maintain racial segregation, but the laws insisted on including the black poor as well as the white. The Social Security Act was a watershed because for the first time the federal government agreed to send money to the states for distribution to

the old, the infirm, and dependent children. This led to the appearance of local public welfare boards to oversee the effort. New Deal "welfare giveaways" became a symbol for conservative southerners who criticized welfare for encouraging laziness, dependency, and the development of a permanent underclass of people living on relief and passing that status on to their children. Eligibility qualification standards and amounts of payments vary from state to state, creating a national problem of fairness and distribution.

Will D. Campbell in his memoir, *Brother to a Dragonfly* (1977), spoke for many on welfare by pointing out the insensitivity of the programs. He said the system was "inefficient, senseless, and began at the wrong end of need." Welfare recipients in 1930s rural Mississippi, where Campbell grew up, had to accept whatever commodities were available for distribution before they could receive needed cash vouchers. Thus, the Campbell family was given massive amounts of grapefruit, a food they had never seen before and would not use. Scientists who came to young Campbell's school to help fight hookworm were arrogant paternalists who treated the students and their families as backward people. "Country people were not impoverished," Campbell notes. "They were simply poor." He reminds one of the relativity of the symbols of poverty, recalling that his schooltime lunch was fried ham on a biscuit. At the time this was a lunch of the poor, eaten while the well-off consumed their bologna sandwiches on white bread.

Scholars began seriously studying the southern poor in the 1920s and 1930s, and their findings gradually replaced the stereotypes created by earlier observers.

James Agee and Walker Evans's *Let Us Now Praise Famous Men* (1941) conveys the sensory feeling of living in poverty with a tenant family. Evans and Agee provide extraordinary detail on the material culture of southern rural poverty, describing the unpainted pine houses, smokehouses, barns, and chicken coops; the furniture, fireplace, mantel, and closets; the clothes, eating utensils, the sanitation and lighting; the odors, sights, and smells; the daily rhythms of the rural poor. Walker Evans's photographs made art of this life and reminded viewers that though the rural southern poor have been materially impoverished, they are not spiritually poor.

Novels such as Erskine Caldwell's *Tobacco Road* (1932), through the character of Jeeter Lester, suggested the psychology of white poverty; Dorothy Scarborough's *In the Land of Cotton* (1923) dealt with tenant farmers; Theodore Rosengarten's *All God's Dangers* (1974) was a memoir of an Alabama black sharecropper; and *These Are Our Lives* (1939) and *Such As Us* (1978) were collections of life histories of the southern poor assembled by the Federal Writers' Project during the Depression. Horace Kephart's *Our Southern Highlanders* (1922) explored the lives of southern highland mountaineers, and psychologist Robert Coles studied *Migrants, Sharecroppers, Mountaineers* (1971). John Dollard's *Caste and Class in a Southern Town* (1937), Hortense Powdermaker's *After Freedom* (1939), John Dollard and Allison Davis's *Children of Bondage* (1964), Allison Davis, Burleigh Gardner, and Mary Gardner's *Deep South* (1944), Charles S. Johnson's *Shadow of the Plantation* (1934), Arthur F. Raper's *Tenants of the Almighty* (1943), Herbert J. Lahne's *The Cotton Mill Worker* (1944), and Margaret Hagood's *Mothers of the South* (1939) are classic explorations of the life of different groups of the poor. Howard W. Odum, Rupert B. Vance, Guy Johnson, and other social scientists associated with the University of North Carolina constantly looked at poverty as a part of their broader studies of southern regionalism.

The 1950s and 1960s witnessed a rediscovery of southern poverty. John Kenneth Galbraith's *The Affluent Society* (1958) identified two categories of the poor—"case poverty," those who were poor because of such circumstances as bad health or lack of education; and "insular poverty," those living in pockets of poverty, including rural Appalachia, the Ozarks, the rural South, and urban slums, amidst national prosperity. John F. Kennedy campaigned in the 1960 West Virginia primary, discovering and publicizing poverty. Michael Harrington's *The Other America: Poverty in the United States* (1962) and Dwight Macdonald's article, "Our Invisible Poor," (*New Yorker*, January 1963), both prominently discussed southern poverty and became influential documents for those in the Kennedy administration. Kennedy made fighting poverty a central concern of his New Frontier. The National Advisory Commission on Rural Poverty succinctly explained that "most of the rural South is one vast poverty area." The president launched the first poverty program of the decade in 1961, the Area Redevelopment Administration, to stop the economic decline and social disorganization in Appalachia. It relied on the private business community to design economic programs.

Lyndon B. Johnson launched his War on Poverty in 1964. His Council of Economic Advisers in January of that year had announced that 20 percent of the American population was under the "poverty line," a new classification for a family of four earning less than $3,000 annually. Congress passed the Economic Opportunity Act that set up an administrative agency, the Office of Economic Opportunity (OEO); a Job Corps to provide youth training; job training projects for adults; a work study program for those in school; aid to rural farmers and small businesses; loans for businesses to hire the unemployed; Volunteers in Service to America (VISTA), a program of skilled volunteers to assist the poor; and the Community Action Program, which encouraged the poor to plan and direct programs for their own development.

In May of 1964 Johnson announced that his aim in this was to build a Great Society of "abundance and liberty for all." The goal of this southern-born president would be the end of poverty in the United States. Later programs, such as the Appalachian Regional Development Act (1966), which appropriated $1.1 billion to fight poverty in isolated mountain areas, also assisted the effort, as did programs such as food stamps, medicaid (health insurance for indigents), medicare (health insurance for the elderly), aid for education (especially the Head Start program to help preschoolers), and housing programs.

The War on Poverty represented the national perception that poverty in the South was now part of a broader problem, and the effort had dramatic results in many ways. Between 1960 and 1968 some 14 million people moved above the poverty line. But the War on Poverty did not solve the problem. In 1968 about 25 million people in the nation were still below the poverty line. Southern congressmen had insisted that states be al-

lowed to administer the federal assistance programs, so the system of eligibility and payment standards continued to vary by state. The southern states remained on the low end of payments. Even before the Ronald Reagan-inspired cuts in federal spending, a Mississippi family of four on welfare received only $120 a month. Studies such as David Whisnant's *Modernizing the Mountaineer: People, Power, and Planning in Appalachia* (1981) and Michael Harrington's *The New American Poverty* (1984) studied poverty in the contemporary period and documented the persisting problem.

Many rural poor refused to participate in the federal programs. Bureaucrats who came from outside the South or the rural areas to administer the programs frequently looked at the poor simply in terms of their economic problems and ignored the cultural dimensions of their lives. Many poor whites, for example, would not acknowledge they were poor. They valued their self-respect, which partly came from how others in their communities viewed them. The charge that welfare was socialism prevented many poor from accepting it. The abiding problem of race also worked toward the same end. The admission of blacks to OEO programs led to a loss of support and interest from some poor whites. The attitude of the white working poor was summed up in a line from Merle Haggard's "Working Man Blues," which considers the option of welfare and dismisses it, saying, "that's one place I won't be."

By the 1970s, though, income transfer payments such as welfare and social security were a vital source of economic income in the South. Wealth remained more maldistributed in the region than in the rest of the nation. In 1970 the poorest 20 percent of families in the South received 4.8 percent of the regional income, whereas the top 20 percent got 43.3. A 1968 survey of malnutrition identified 220 counties in the South with authentic hunger out of 256 in the nation. A 1984 study by the Southern Regional Council revealed that 18.2 percent of the 1983 residents in the 11 former Confederate states were below the poverty line, which the Census Bureau now defines as an annual income of $10,178 for a family of four. The South's poverty rate reached a low of 15.6 percent in 1979, but 1984 findings revealed a reversal of a 20-year decline in poverty in the region. The problem, as always, was worse for blacks than whites. The poverty rate among southern blacks in 1983 was 39 percent, and over 60 percent of families headed by a black woman were in poverty.

Oscar Lewis coined the term *culture of poverty* in his studies of the poor of Central America, outlining the traits of physical and spiritual impoverishment. The southern poor surely exemplified the concept, leading lives of unceasing toil in a wearying farm or mill routine. Many southern poor, black and white, lived and continue to live in dilapidated shacks they neither own nor care for. Their yards and surroundings lack any aesthetic touches. There is a general lack of material goods, and there is little sense of the future. A lack of stability and security leads to frequent restlessness and moving about. They give up hope and live drab, unfulfilled lives with few comforts. Nicholas Lemann ("The Origins of the Underclass," *Atlantic Monthly*, June 1986) argued that the hopelessness and welfare dependency found in northern cities should be traced to the culture of poverty ex-

isting in the sharecropper South of the post–Civil War period.

The totality of the culture of poverty in the South was especially seen in the way poverty was related to the health of the poor. Joseph Goldberger, a physician with the United States Public Health Service, concluded in 1927 after studying pellagra that it was a poor person's disease. Its development correlated with the cycles of poverty in rural cotton-growing areas. The lack of proper nutrition was partly a cultural matter of food preferences (dating back to a frontier diet), but it was also an economic one. Goldberger blamed the pellagra problem on the "three M Diet" of meat, meal, and molasses—the poor person's menu in the South. Lack of proper nutrition, inadequate sanitation, exposure to the elements because of poor clothing and housing—all promoted disease and ill health and sapped the poor of energy. Health problems of the working poor included black and brown lung and tuberculosis. Inability to afford medical care resulted in lingering health problems that could eventually kill. St. Louis Jimmy's blues song "Bad Condition" captured the slow suffering of the southern poor: "I'm in a bad condition, and I'm still going down slow."

In spite of all this, the southern poor

Mississippi roadhouse, 1970s

developed their own culture that transcended the material impoverishment they faced. Much of the culture was created by the working poor, by people who were destitute only in worldly goods. It must be remembered that the southern poor, black and white, were not a hopeless people. Most maintained self-respect and had creative outlets. They shared much with the culture of the yeoman, the subsistence farmer. Theirs was an oral culture of tall tales and drawn-out humorous stories; of fiddle, banjo, and later guitar music; of quilts providing physical warmth and aesthetic beauty; of houses of simple design well adapted to the southern environment. The poor were on the cutting edge of the cultural integration that blended the contributions of the American Indians, Africans, Anglo-Saxons, and Celts into a "southern" culture.

Religion is especially important in understanding southern poverty. The religion of the southern poor is an expressive, emotional, cathartic religion. The unpredictability of life for the economically insecure may have encouraged the fatalism in popular southern religion. The conscious act of conversion in the South's evangelical religion brought the assurance of salvation and relief from the terrors of poverty in this life. Southern theology was otherworldly, appealing to those who sometimes lived truly in a "vale of tears." Religion gave the poor a sense of community, encouraged moral discipline, and provided a sense of purpose to people who might not otherwise have it.

Southern music has documented the cultural significance of poverty. It is a traditional theme of the blues. Lazy Slim Jim sang "Money Blues," Blind Lemon Jefferson did "Broke and Hungry Blues," Ramblin' Thomas recorded "Poor Boy Blues," and Bob Campbell did "Starvation Farm Blues." White country music songs about poverty tend to be of the "poor but proud" type. They provide realistic detail of hard lives, yet frequently are also sentimental. Typical songs of this genre are Dolly Parton's "Coat of Many Colors," Loretta Lynn's "Coal Miner's Daughter," Johnny Cash's "I'm Busted," and Bill Anderson's "Po' Folks." (Anderson has even marketed the "poor but proud" idea in a franchised restaurant chain called Po' Folks that serves southern cooking; in the New South southerners have learned to market poverty.)

These white and black songs show that southerners are aware they are tainted by their background of poverty. They reveal searing incidents of humiliation, of people "looking down at us" because of poverty. But the image of humiliation is counterbalanced frequently by images of the warmth of caring, loving parents, nearby kin, and the shared plight of neighbors.

See also AGRICULTURE: Sharecropping and Tenancy; FOLKLIFE articles; HISTORY AND MANNERS articles; MYTHIC SOUTH: / "Crackers"; Poor Whites; Rednecks; URBANIZATION: Urban Poor

Charles Reagan Wilson
University of Mississippi

James E. Anderson, *Journal of Politics* (February 1967); Lee S. Balliet, "Anglo Poverty in the Rural South" (Ph.D. dissertation, University of Texas at Austin, 1974); J. Wayne Flynt, *Dixie's Forgotten People: The South's Poor Whites* (1979); Gretchen MacLachlan, *The Other Twenty Percent: A Statistical Analysis of Poverty in the South* (1974), *Health Care in the South: A Statistical Profile* (1974); Paul E. Mertz, *New Deal Policy and Southern Rural Poverty* (1978);

Dudley L. Poston, Jr., and Robert H. Weller, *The Population of the South* (1981); President's National Advisory Committee on Rural Poverty, *The People Left Behind* (1967); Elizabeth Wisner, *Social Welfare in the South: From Colonial Times to World War I* (1970). ☆

Religion and Social Class

||||||||||||||||||||||||||||||||||||||||||||||||||||||||||||||

Religion and social class have been intimately related throughout the history of the South. During the early 1700s religious activity was centered in the landed gentry who were Church of England (Anglican). With the movement of Scotch-Irish settlers into parts of the South during the middle 1700s the Presbyterian church began to grow in numbers. The Anglican and Presbyterian churches had limited appeal to the masses, and not until the revival fires of the Baptists and the Methodists began during the early 1800s did the people of the South become noted for their religious enthusiasm. As a general rule the religious group that settled first in a region held a class advantage there. By the beginning of the 1800s religion in the South was stratified along class lines, with the upper classes attending Anglican or Presbyterian churches and the lower classes attending Baptist and Methodist churches.

The relationship between religion and class in the Old South was clearly seen in the emergence of higher education. Unlike settlers in New England, who established the prestigious religious colleges and universities, planters in the southern legislatures established state universities for their sons. The Baptists and Methodists led the way in founding private religious colleges, largely because access to the state universities was denied to them. As an example, in Georgia during the 1840s there was an attempt on the part of Baptists and Methodists to set fire to the University of Georgia because the Anglicans and Presbyterians on the Board of Regents were believed to be discriminating against them. Important exceptions to this pattern were Davidson College, founded in North Carolina by Presbyterians in 1836, and the University of the South at Sewanee, Tenn., founded by Episcopalians in the 1850s.

Questions of social class have also been closely related to sectarian movements. In his classic study of religion and social class in the South, *Millhands and Preachers* (1942), Liston Pope argued that any denomination that did not meet the special needs of the mill workers would soon lose these members to the "ignorant and disreputable" preachers of the newer sects. The growth of sects (the term here is used in a sociological rather than a theological sense), which began in the South during the 1930s, has continued up to the present day, with recruits drawn largely from the "disinherited" lower-class members of society. Through the years, however, many of these sectarian religious groups have achieved middle-class "social respectability." This is especially true of many of the Pentecostal and Holiness groups, of which Oral Roberts and the university that he established in 1965 are the most visible. Many former sects, like the Churches of Christ, Church of God, Foursquare, and Assemblies of God, have become denominations. Even so, continued pockets of poverty in the South are a fertile ground for the emergence of new sectarian movements.

The overwhelming dominance of Protestants in the South has had social class ramifications for non-Protestants. Jews and Roman Catholics occupy a clear religious minority status. Because of their small numbers in most southern communities, Jews and Roman Catholics of all social classes must worship together in the one synagogue or church available to them in the community.

Jews have been excluded from many of the prestigious social organizations (country clubs, lodges, clubs, etc.) found in southern communities. It would not be accurate to say, however, that Jews as a group occupy a lower social class position than Christians in the South. Although discriminated against socially, Jews in the South rank quite high in terms of the traditional criteria of social class—income, education, and occupational prestige.

Race is the most important factor by which religious membership is determined in the South. Except for a few slaves who were baptized into white churches during the colonial period, few blacks were Christians—only 3 percent of their population were church members in 1795. When blacks did convert to Christianity in great numbers, it was into black churches largely Methodist and Baptist in orientation. Segregation in southern churches lasted until the civil rights movement of the 1960s. Even now, however, very few whites or blacks are members of racially integrated local churches.

Black church membership does not seem to be based on social class differences to the same extent as that of whites. This may be in part because stratification within the black community has not been as great as in the white. Since the civil rights movement, certain denominations, most notably the United Methodists, have attempted to place both white and black churches under the same denominational governing body. It is unclear whether blacks who are part of racially integrated denominations, such as the United Methodists, differ significantly in regard to class from those who remain in exclusively black denominations, such as the African Methodist Episcopal church.

The majority of people living in the South belong to either of two denominations. The combined Baptist-Methodist membership in the Deep South states of Mississippi, Alabama, and Georgia is 88 percent, 87 percent, and 87 percent respectively of total church membership. In the five additional states of Texas, Arkansas, Tennessee, South Carolina, and North Carolina, the combined total Baptist-Methodist membership surpasses 70 percent. Such numerical dominance by two denominations suggests that class differentiation exists not only between denominations, but also between local congregations within denominations. This is especially true within the largest southern Protestant denominations. The First Baptist in the typical southern community is made up of members who occupy higher social positions than those in more recently established Southern Baptist Convention churches in the community. Although this pattern also holds true for Methodist churches in the South, the lines of social demarcation are not as clear cut.

See also BLACK LIFE: Religion, Black; LAW: Civil Rights Movement; RELIGION articles

Jack Balswick
Fuller Theological Seminary

David Harrell, *White Sects and Black Men in the Present South* (1971); Samuel S. Hill, *Religion and the Solid South* (1972), *Southern Churches in Crisis* (1966); Thomas Daniel Young, in *The American South: Portrait of a Culture*, ed. Louis D. Rubin, Jr. (1980). ☆

Socialism

|||||||||||||||||||||||||

Socialism in the South may be appreciated best by considering not only vote tallies and membership lists of historical political parties, but by a look at the influence of Socialist thought and action. In the South, as in the nation, a nominal Socialist presence in electoral politics must be acknowledged. Considered simply in terms of the numbers of votes won by the Socialist Party of America, socialism in the South might be seen as a sentimental, slow fade-out dating from the presidential campaign of Eugene Debs in 1912. If seen, however, as a continually dissenting and engaging critique of social justice in capitalist society, the Socialist vision, Socialist-influenced participants, and full-fledged Socialists of several varieties can be found in every recent and ongoing movement that seeks to eliminate social relations based upon domination.

Certainly, the "foreignness" of socialism to the South has been a consistent and hampering pattern in its history. Throughout the 19th century European immigrants most responsible for bringing socialist views and organizations to other sections of the United States largely avoided the South. Plantation slavery in the antebellum era stifled the prospects for such immigrants

not only to Deep South farms, but also to the South's few cities, limiting occupations in the crafts, industry, and trade. From the end of the Civil War until well into the 20th century, the South remained a section characterized by few decent opportunities for newcomers, by ethnic prejudice, and by the cheap wages paid to its overwhelmingly native-born, black and white work force.

Throughout most of the South's history, suspicion of outsiders and particularly of "Yankee" and "foreign" ideas regarding movements for unionization, racial equality, and women's rights has fed a popular phobia eager to label as socialistic or communistic any striving for democratic social change. The intensity of this reaction reveals an important association of socialism in the South. Abolitionists, Knights of Labor, Populists, feminists, and voting rights and civil rights organizers have all been widely and intensely hated in the South and identified collectively (and for the most part mistakenly) as "Reds."

A stanza of a song written and sung in the 1930s by the Kentucky coalfield Socialist Aunt Molly Jackson reveals the way in which Red-baiting has worked again and again to shift public outrage away from historical scenes of injustice and redirect it against Socialist "agitators":

I was raised in old Kentucky
In Kentucky borned and bred,
And when I joined the union
They called me a Russian Red.

Among the earliest self-proclaimed Socialists in the South were a number of immigrant Germans who during the 1840s and 1850s published antislavery newspapers in New Orleans and in

Texas. A close kin, if not always part of the immediate family of socialism in the South, the communitarian impulse found expression in the antebellum-era Shakers of Pleasant Hill, Ky., the short-lived Owenite Nashoba community near Memphis, the late 19th-century town of Ruskin, Tenn., the mid-1920s colony of New Llano, La., and the current Koinonia Farm in Georgia.

In the late 19th-century South, small numbers of Socialists emerged in the urban industries of New Orleans, Atlanta, and Richmond, and in the mining districts from Birmingham through Tennessee into Kentucky and West Virginia. With the defeat of the Populists in the mid-1890s and the founding of the Socialist Party of America in 1901, Socialists were recruited in the South from the ranks of small farmers, tenants, farm laborers, industrial workers, miners, and immigrant trade unionists. Turn-of-the-century Socialist locals were formed in San Antonio, Houston, Dallas, Bessemer (Ala.), Oklahoma City, and New Orleans.

Despite strong rhetoric and resolutions, such as the one passed in its 1901 founding convention at Indianapolis, and despite the urging of a minority of its members, the Socialist party (until the 1930s) generally backed away from embracing black members in integrated locals. This fear of, and resistance to, racial "social equality" had an especially strong hold in the South. During a tour of the South in 1900, Eugene Debs, who had slowly broken with many of the views of conventional racial prejudice in his own life, confronted white Georgia and Alabama Socialists over the issue of race, often refusing to speak to segregated audiences. Less than eagerly sought by white organizers, southern blacks saw little reason to join segre-

gated Socialist locals. A few blacks did feel the influence of a more indigenous Christian socialism as expounded for a time in the 1890s through publications such as *The Christian Recorder* and the *AME Church Review*, both produced by the African Methodist Episcopal Church.

Although white Socialists' ranks increased with the decline of the Populist party, the movement remained marginal to the experience of most of the South's workers and farmers. An especially effective recruiting technique was the use of the Socialist encampment, which began in Texas in the late summer of 1904 and spread into Oklahoma and the rest of the Southwest. These gatherings joined the traditional southern evangelical camp meeting's emotional style with the urgencies of agrarian revolt. Between 1909 and 1911 Socialist organizers in Oklahoma and Texas began a tenant farmers' Renters Union (or Land League). Building upon an indigenous discontent, they continued the camp meetings and published newspapers that reached tens of thousands of readers. In 1910 the Socialist Party of America counted its largest state membership (almost 10,000) among the cotton farmers in the southernmost part of Oklahoma.

Socialist party opposition to World War I and to U.S. involvement in the war led to a decline in the movement both in the nation and in the South. In 1919 Communists, Socialists, and other American radicals faced severe repression and censorship. Jailed for sedition, Debs ran for the U.S. presidency in 1920 from Atlanta's federal prison.

The 1920s and 1930s saw increasing labor unrest in the textile towns of the Piedmont South and in the Kentucky coal-mining districts. In a few sensational instances, such as those of Gastonia, N.C., and Harlan County, Ky., industrial violence came to be associated in the public mind with the very place names themselves and with Socialist and Communist unionization efforts. In most mill and mining towns, however, workers had little chance to hear any Socialist message except as interpreted by local newspaper editors and industrialists. From the mid-1930s organized Socialist activity faced a general decline due to state, municipal, and business hostility, internal factionalism, the broad appeal of Franklin Roosevelt on one hand, and the attraction of the Communist party on the other.

On the advice of Norman Thomas, the Southern Tenant Farmers' Union (STFU) was begun in the Arkansas Delta in 1934. A year later the new union was carrying out a strike of some 5,000 cotton pickers. Although largely confined to Oklahoma, Arkansas, and eastern Missouri, the STFU, writes scholar James Green, "was the most important organizing project of the Socialist party sponsored anywhere in the country after World War I." The STFU was important not only because of the numbers of grass-roots members involved and the national attention it drew to the plight of sharecroppers, but also for its inclusion of small farm owners together with tenants and farm laborers, its interracial organization, and its recruitment of women members. The STFU gave new life to the southern Socialist tradition.

The Socialist stirrings of the 1930s revealed the significance of a Christian Socialist tradition in the South. A few score renegade preachers and devout church members (ranging from Presbyterian to Holiness) viewed the human devastation of the Depression years and insisted that the biblical gospel be ap-

plied in its most egalitarian manner. Among the best known of these Christian radicals were Claude and Joyce Williams, Alice and Howard Kester, Ward Rogers, Don West, Myles Horton, and James Dombrowski.

In 1934 Horton and West began the Highlander Folk School in Grundy County, Tenn.—at that time one of the 10 poorest counties in the United States. Since its founding, Highlander has devoted itself to educational and organizational support for the southern labor movement (in the 1930s and 1940s), the civil rights movement (in the 1950s and 1960s), and the struggle for Appalachian self-determination (during the 1970s and 1980s).

Another route of Socialist influence in the South has come, at least since the mid-1920s, through the presence of a Socialist professor or two, on campus in such places as Chapel Hill, Atlanta, Charlottesville, and Tuscaloosa. Indeed, the late 1970s and early 1980s have seen most major universities in the South hire a number of young scholars—from inside and outside Dixie—intent upon bringing Socialist or Marxist interpretations to the fields of history, political science, literature, and women's studies.

The currents of feminism in the South, emerging from the civil rights and antiwar movements of the 1960s, have been affected by, and have in turn altered, Socialist views. In her 1972 "Open Letter to Southern White Women," Socialist writer and activist Anne Braden called on white women, "for their own liberation," to refuse complicity with white men in perpetuating the institutions and acts of a racist society.

From their critical but taken-for-granted roles in the 1960s struggles, a number of southern activist women came to question and ultimately resist what historian Sara Evans has described as "the discrepancy between the movement's egalitarian ideology and the oppression [women] continued to experience within it." Out of this contradiction a wave of feminism was born in the South, as well as a feminist critique of socialism capable of producing a more complex and compelling interpretation of culture and society than one limited by a singular preoccupation with class.

See also AGRICULTURE: / Communal Farms; BLACK LIFE: Freedom Movement, Black; HISTORY AND MANNERS: Populism; LAW: Civil Rights Movement; RELIGION: / Shakers; VIOLENCE: Harlan County, Kentucky; Industrial Violence; WOMEN'S LIFE: Feminism and Antifeminism; / Jackson, Aunt Molly

Allen Tullos
Emory University

Anthony P. Dunbar, *Against the Grain: Southern Radicals and Prophets, 1929–1959* (1981); Sara Evans, *Personal Politics: The Roots of Women's Liberation in the Civil Rights Movement and the New Left* (1979); James R. Green, *Grass-roots Socialism: Radical Movements in the Southwest, 1895–1943* (1978); Sue Thrasher, *Southern Changes* (November–December 1982). ☆

Tenant Farmers

The Jeffersonian dream of an America of independent, freeholding farmers never existed in the South. Before the Civil War there was slavery, and afterward the farm tenancy system replaced it as the basis for the southern economic and social order. The system created a new and growing class of permanently poor and suppressed agricultural workers. To call these people a peasantry is to upgrade them, for, unlike the peasants of medieval Europe, they had no guarantees to the land and no rights that the landlord or the government was bound to observe.

When the tenancy system was at its peak in the first three decades of the 20th century it actually resembled slavery, especially on the "tenant plantations" in rich agricultural areas of the South. The tenants there lived in shacks provided by the planter, received their supplies on credit from the plantation commissary, went into the fields each morning at dawn when the plantation bell rang, and came out again at dark when the bell rang again. Their labors were supervised by a riding boss, who was usually a sheriff's deputy and therefore armed and able to inflict physical punishment.

On such plantations women worked in the fields until it was time to prepare the evening meal. Children worked after the age of six and attended school only sporadically. Public schools in rural areas were customarily closed for weeks in the fall so that children might pick cotton.

The upper levels of tenancy, the cash tenants and share tenants, lived better lives and were less under the control of their landlords, but the sad truth is that the system worked to drive more and more people into the lower levels of tenancy. Many different factors could convert an independent farmer into a tenant or a share tenant into a cropper: floods, drought, hail, storms, the boll weevil, soil exhaustion, mechanization, sickness, laziness, injury, ignorance, low prices, or being cheated by the landlord or storekeeper.

Tenancy began in the South as a way of getting former slaves, the freedmen, back to work on the land. But by the end of the 19th century, the system had become the last refuge for the growing class of southern poor whites who had been unable to compete with the cheap labor of black tenancy or who, for other reasons, had lost their farms and equipment. By 1930 there were 1,475,325 white tenant and cropper families in the South. They made up 60 percent of all southern tenants, and their numbers were growing, as was black tenancy, which stood at 1,091,736 families. The situation was so critical that 79 percent of southern farmers owned no land.

Once southern farmers had fallen into the trap of tenancy, they were kept there by ignorance, lack of economic opportunity, disease, social pressures, debt, and state and local law. Their ignorance was a product of poor schools and the inability to attend schools. Also, there was a general distrust of book learning throughout the rural South. Many tenants could not comprehend simple mathematics and had no idea what was coming to them at the end of the crop year on settlement day.

Most tenants were given small tracts to farm, often less than 40 acres and sometimes as little as 10. Clearly, no one, no matter how good a farmer, could make enough money to escape tenancy on such small pieces of land.

Tenants were considered "shiftless and lazy" by other southerners, but often their lack of vigor was caused by pellagra, trichinosis, malaria, venereal disease, tuberculosis, and all the other diseases that went with crowded and unsanitary living conditions and poor diets. Large families of tenants lived in

one- and two-room shacks without plumbing, electricity, or much heat. Outhouses were considered a luxury. The staple diet provided by the commissary consisted of corn bread and fatback.

Most tenants not on plantations had their own chickens and pigs, and some had cows and their own vegetable gardens. Their diets were better, but for the lowliest, the sharecroppers, there was little chance to produce food. They were forced by the riding bosses to plant cotton up to the very doorsteps of their shacks, and they were too tired after long days in the fields and too debilitated by disease to tend animals and gardens.

The social pressures on tenant farmers were also a terrible burden. Southerners viewed tenant farmers as a permanent class of lazy, ignorant, immoral subhumans, unfit for a place in normal human society. When the tenants were black, racism added further degradation, but southern social disdain was not confined to blacks. White tenants were often considered "poor white trash," a social status little higher than that of the lowliest blacks. The big difference was that white tenants were not segregated by law in public places.

Debt was a way of life for tenant farmers. When settlement day came in the fall of the year, the tenant had to pay what he owed to the landlord or storekeeper for the "furnish" he had received all year. Often the settlement left the tenant with only a few hundred dollars and he would soon be living on credit again. When they got their hands on any money, the tenants and their families, who had gone without the simplest luxuries for so long, often spent their few dollars on such things as new silk dresses and phonographs.

Most landlords understood clearly

that the best way to make profits was through their commissary. Prices there were always higher than in town, and tenants had to pay high interest rates for credit. If it appeared that a landlord might lose money in a given year, he could avoid it by raising prices at the commissary or by cheating the tenants in the settlement. Some of the landlords rationalized their actions by the argument that keeping the tenants in debt was the only way to control them properly. Some even argued that tenants would not work if they were not on the edge of hunger and did not feel that they must go into the fields in order to eat that day.

Faced with such exploitation, tenants had nowhere to turn for justice. State and local law in the South favored the landowner against the tenant. These laws prevented tenants from leaving the landlord as long as they were indebted to him and allowed money owed to tenants to be paid first to the landlord so he might collect what they owed him. In some counties, sheriffs arrested vagrants and placed them in work camps. An unwritten code of civil behavior dictated that a black man never questioned the word of a white man, so black tenants dared not confront a cheating landlord or storekeeper. White tenants could challenge the landlord but the usual result was eviction, which meant being homeless and without credit.

The only escape, if it can be called that, was to move on. Every year after settlement day, the roads and byways of the South were clogged with tenant families on the move, their meager belongings and underfed children piled on wagons and old cars. Southern tenants moved with astounding frequency, especially in hard times. A government study in the 1930s showed that a considerable percentage of tenants had

moved six or seven times since they started farming, and a few had been tenants on as many as 15 different farms. They moved because they were evicted or to find a bigger piece of land to work, a kinder landlord, or a better arrangement. But they seldom found what they sought. The tenancy system was the same everywhere and there was no escape.

During the 1930s the plight of the southern tenant farmers came to national attention because of the writings of liberals who used the miserable conditions of the southern tenants to prove that poverty existed in America. John Steinbeck, in *The Grapes of Wrath*, told the tragic story of tenants driven from their farms in Oklahoma by drought, government programs, and mechanization. Erskine Caldwell shocked readers and well-dressed Broadway theater audiences with *God's Little Acre* and *Tobacco Road*, graphic pictures of the ignorance, immorality, and hopelessness of tenancy. James Agee and Walker Evans, in *Let Us Now Praise Famous Men*, told of the wretched lives of three tenant families in Alabama.

The cause of the tenant farmer was taken up by political reformers such as Norman Thomas, the Socialist leader. The Socialists helped in 1934 to form the Southern Tenant Farmers' Union, a biracial labor union that began in Arkansas and spread into neighboring states. In Alabama the Sharecroppers Union, a Communist-backed organization of mostly blacks, got started.

Awareness of the problems of tenancy had its effect on the New Deal. The programs of the Agricultural Adjustment Administration (AAA) were designed to benefit cotton farmers by reducing cotton acreage and raising cotton prices artificially, but these programs necessarily centered on those who owned the land. A small group of liberals in the AAA made an effort to protect the rights of tenants to stay on the land even though they were needed less because of acreage reduction, but the effort failed and most of the liberals were purged from the AAA for their trouble. Rexford Tugwell, a leading brain truster, conceived the idea of relocating tenant farmers to better land, which the government would buy for them. President Franklin Roosevelt bought the idea and set up the Resettlement Administration, which organized dozens of communal and experimental farms for tenants throughout the South. President Roosevelt also appointed a Commission on Farm Tenancy to study the problem. Its work led to the Bankhead-Jones Farm Tenancy Act, which created the Farm Security Administration and set in motion a program to assist worthy tenant farmers in buying their own farms.

None of these actions had a profound effect on tenancy except the AAA acreage reductions. Because of this program, hundreds of thousands of tenants were displaced from the land and the government was helpless to prevent it. The big break for tenants came during World War II when there were jobs in war plants in industrial centers outside the South. Seeking these jobs, southern tenant farmers began a mass exodus that lasted through the war years and continued in the decades that followed. In the South, work that had been done by millions of tenant farmers was taken over by heavy equipment, especially the mechanical cotton picker. Today, only vestiges of the old tenancy system survive, under the combined pressures of economics, changing social values, and the modernization of agriculture.

See also AGRICULTURE: Sharecropping

David E. Conrad
Southern Illinois University
at Carbondale

Sidney Baldwin, *Poverty and Politics: The Rise and Decline of the Farm Security Administration* (1968); David E. Conrad, *The Forgotten Farmers: The Story of Sharecroppers in the New Deal* (1965); Paul V. Maris, in *Yearbook of Agriculture, 1940* (1940); Paul Mertz, *New Deal Policy and Southern Rural Poverty* (1968); H. L. Mitchell, *Mean Things Happening in This Land: The Life and Times of H. L. Mitchell* (1979); Van L. Perkins, *Crisis in Agriculture: The Agricultural Adjustment Administration 1933* (1969); Arthur F. Raper, *Preface to Peasantry: A Tale of Two Black Belt Counties* (1936); Rupert B. Vance and Nalia Danilevsku, *All These People: The Nation's Human Resources in the South* (1945). ☆

AMERICAN FEDERATION OF LABOR (AFL)

The American Federation of Labor, from its 19th-century origins, has always found the South its Achilles' heel. The southern heritage of slavery and peonage, racial divisions within the work force, and the social control exercised by the established governing elite combined to create an inhospitable environment for a working class movement, such as the AFL, which challenged the prevailing socioeconomic order. As a result, the southern ruling elite used its considerable resources—control of local and state police power, the pulpit, and courthouses and statehouses—to contain and, when it was felt necessary, to halt encroachments by the AFL.

Despite the hostile climate, AFL organizers have made significant inroads among skilled workers, particularly building-trades workers, railroad workers, printers, and dock workers. By the early 20th century, central labor unions had been organized in most southern cities and, prior to World War I, state federations of labor had been organized in all of the states in the region. Moreover, a number of the Federation's affiliated unions had first organized in the South, including the Brotherhood of Maintenance of Way Employees (Demopolis, Ala., 1887); the Brotherhood of Painters, Decorators, and Paperhangers of America (Baltimore, 1887); the International Brotherhood of Boilermakers, Iron Shipbuilders, and Helpers (Atlanta, 1888); the International Association of Machinists (Atlanta, 1889); and the International Brotherhood of Blacksmiths, Drop Forgers, and Helpers (Atlanta, 1889).

The limited successes that the AFL had among southern skilled workers, however, were not repeated among the unskilled. Efforts to organize the large southern textile force, for example, were continually frustrated. During the 1930s, the Congress of Industrial Organizations did make some breakthroughs among industrial workers, especially in coal and steel, but these advances came primarily in industries where the union movement could use its power in the North to force concessions in the South. Such leverage was particularly obvious in the organization of the employees of the Tennessee Coal and Iron Company, the southern subsidiary of United States Steel. Meanwhile, the predominant industrial unit in the South, the single plant firm, remained highly resistant to union organization by either the AFL, the CIO, or, after 1955, the AFL-CIO. If, by the fourth quarter of the 20th century, the South has ceased to be, as it had been labeled in

the 1930s, "the Nation's No. 1 economic problem," it nevertheless remains the labor movement's "No. 1" organizing problem.

Gary M. Fink
Georgia State University

Gary M. Fink and Merl E. Reed, eds., *Essays in Southern Labor History: Selected Papers, Southern Labor History Conference, 1976* (1977); F. Ray Marshall, *Labor in the South* (1967); Merl E. Reed, Leslie S. Hough, and Gary M. Fink, eds., *Southern Workers and Their Unions, 1880–1975: Selected Papers, the Second Southern Labor History Conference* (1981). ✩

BOURBON/REDEEMER SOUTH

The Bourbon/Redeemer South refers to the period from the late 1870s until about 1900 when the Democrats returned to power and governed the South after overthrowing Reconstruction. Claiming that they were restoring home rule and good government after the extravagance and corruption of the northern-imposed Republican rule, the Democrats undermined most of the Republicans' innovations, though rarely eliminating them altogether. First, they rewrote the state constitutions that had been created in 1867–68 at the beginning of Reconstruction, thereby reducing drastically the size, scope, and cost of government. Then they rearranged public finance by scaling down or repudiating about $200 million of the state debts incurred during Reconstruction and by reducing state taxation significantly. In the economic sphere, they tightened the control of landlords over their tenants and sharecroppers; they oversaw the creation of a southern textile industry; and they ended state aid to internal improvements and instead encouraged northern capital to develop, and ultimately dominate, the region's burgeoning railroad system as well as most of its iron and steel industry. Finally, by using partisan electoral laws and reapportionment as well as the rallying cry of white supremacy, they consolidated their political hold on the region so that by the end of the century they had successfully implemented wide-scale disfranchisement, primarily of blacks; introduced the white primary; and created a narrowly based, racially exclusive one-party political system.

The terms *Bourbon* and *Redeemer* describe two contrasting interpretations of the men who dominated the post-Reconstruction Democratic party and the regimes they established. Those who at the time and during the early 20th century depicted them as Bourbons believed they were a conservative, even reactionary, element consisting of the planter class and die-hard proponents of the Confederate "Lost Cause" who wanted to restore the values and priorities of the antebellum South. By contrast, those who employ C. Vann Woodward's term and refer to them as Redeemers argue that they represented rather different interests and constituted a rising class of businessmen eager to develop the South's railroads and its manufacturing potential. Their emergence marked a major break, not only with the politics of Reconstruction, but also with the economics of the antebellum South. Despite their claims to be introducing a New South that was economically self-sufficient and diversified, they saddled the region with a dependent, almost colonial, economy and failed to release the grip on the South of the old agrarian and paternalistic values. The Redeemers' limitations

were most evident, so these historians argue, in their neglecting the small farmers who finally rose up against them in the Populist revolt of the 1890s and in their allowing the racial gains of Reconstruction to be eroded until a legalized system of segregation arose at the turn of the century. More recently, historians have reemphasized the continuities between the post-Reconstruction era and the antebellum South. They have suggested that the planters and more traditional elements were not replaced by New South businessmen; rather, they persisted and continued to play a major role in the political and economic life of the region.

Michael Perman
University of Illinois at Chicago

Michael Perman, *The Road to Redemption: Southern Politics, 1869–1879* (1984); George B. Tindall, in *The Persistent Tradition in New South Politics* (1975); Jonathan M. Wiener, *Social Origins of the New South: Alabama, 1860–1885* (1975); C. Vann Woodward, *Origins of the New South, 1877–1913* (1951). ☆

COAL MINERS
‖‖‖‖‖‖‖‖‖‖‖‖‖‖‖‖‖‖‖‖‖‖‖‖‖‖‖‖‖‖‖‖‖‖‖‖‖

From the beginnings of large-scale commercial coal mining in the South in the 1880s until the 1940s when mechanization of the mines disproportionately displaced blacks, southern coal miners were a polyglot work force. Blacks constituted 50 to 70 percent of the labor force in Alabama while West Virginia coal mines employed roughly one-third native Appalachian white, one-third black, and one-third immigrant. But, despite this diversity, ethnic and racial conflicts have been relatively rare, especially when compared to the interracial turmoil among northern miners and other workers from 1890 to 1945. This has been attributed to the egalitarian policies of the United Mine Workers of America, common occupational hazards, and, most importantly, the predominance of the company town in the southern coalfields. Although oppressive, the standardized and rigidly controlled aspects of these settlements served as a coercive melting pot.

The history of southern miners has been one of struggle and protest. Between 1887 and 1894, for example, one-third of the strikes in the South took place in the coalfields. For 50 years southern miners struggled to unionize in order to end abuses like company stores, payment in scrip, low wages, convict labor, and the mine guard system, which turned company towns into armed camps. In August 1933 the miners got their union, only to begin a 40-year struggle against the autocracy and corruption of the UMWA hierarchy. That effort culminated in 1972 when the Miners for Democracy movement successfully ousted W. A. "Tony" Boyle and elected West Virginia miner Arnold Miller president of the union. Seven years later the miners used the democratic reforms that Miller instituted to throw him out of office.

Southern miners have always shown an independent streak that has made company and union leadership difficult. Often led by legendary figures like John L. Lewis and Mother Jones, whom they allegedly adored, the miners nonetheless continuously rejected the advice of Mother Jones and fought Lewis as tenaciously as they respected him.

In their struggles against both the coal companies and their unions, southern miners developed an intense occupational consciousness that had elements of class tied to it, which par-

tially accounts for the violence that marks their history. The "Coal Creek Rebellion," the Paint Creek-Cabin Creek Strike (1912–13), the "Matewan Massacre" (1920), the "Armed March on Logan" (1921), and the "Bloody Harlan" strikes (1930s) are but a few examples. But, with the exception of Harlan County where the National Miners Union made inroads during the 1930s, southern miners eschewed radical ideologies in favor of a grass-roots brand of "Americanism" that they felt promised life, liberty, and equality regardless of condition of servitude.

The life of the southern miner has been one of resilience amid deprivation, disaster, and tragedy. The protracted depression in the coalfields from the 1920s to the 1970s and the mechanization of the mines in the 1940s produced massive unemployment and poverty. Disasters have always haunted miners in the southern coalfields: 361 died at Monogah, W.Va., in 1907; 90 at Palos, Ala., in 1910; 128 at Littleton, Ala., in 1911; 84 at Cross Mountain, Tenn., in the same year; 181 at Eccles, W.Va., in 1914, and the next year, 112 at Leland, W.Va.; and 119 at Benwood, W.Va., in 1924. During World War I West Virginia miners had a higher casualty rate than the American Expeditionary Force in Europe. Nor have the disasters ended; witness the collapse of a slag dam at Buffalo Creek, W.Va., in 1973 that killed 175 people. Yet the folklore of the coalfields suggests the miners' commitment to their work and life. "Miners' Strawberries" and other humorous songs, for example, are as much a part of miners' culture as are militant songs like "Which Side Are You On?"

A final irony stems from the common perception of the miners' culture as "macho" culture in which women have been subordinate and passive. Women have traditionally played a major role in southern coalfield history and culture, especially as union advocates and activists. The ease with which women entered the mines as miners beginning in 1973 pointed to a long history of womens' significance in the southern coalfields.

See also ENVIRONMENT: / Appalachian Coal Region; INDUSTRY: / Mining

David A. Corbin
Washington, D.C.

Harry M. Caudill, *Night Comes to the Cumberlands: A Biograhpy of a Depressed Area* (1963); David A. Corbin, *Life, Work, and Rebellion in the Coal Fields: Southern West Virginia Coal Miners, 1880–1922* (1981); Kai T. Erikson, *Everything in Its Path* (1967); Archie Green, *Only a Miner: Studies in Recorded Coal-Mining Songs* (1972); John W. Hevener, *Which Side Are You On?: The Harlan County Coal Miners, 1931–1939* (1978); George Korson, *Coal Dust on the Fiddle* (1943); F. Ray Marshall, *Labor in the South* (1967). ☆

COMPANY TOWNS
||||||||||||||||||||||||||||||||||||||||||||||||

A company town is a camp, village, or town, usually unincorporated, in which the employer owns the land and houses occupied by the employees. As the South industrialized in the late 19th and early 20th centuries, company towns proliferated, particularly in conjunction with the textile, coal-mining, and lumber industries.

Located adjacent to mineral resources or near water power, industries were often geographically isolated, necessitating the involvement of employ-

ers in providing housing and other services. But the company town also gave management greater opportunity for control over the workers. The right to occupancy was dependent upon employment. If out on strike, or ill, or injured, a worker and his family could be evicted on short notice. House leases often contained clauses used to deny union organizers access to the camp: "Lessor may forbid . . . ingress and egress . . . to any and all persons other than Lessee" (Tennessee Coal, Iron and Railroad Co., Birmingham, Alabama). A company deputy, rather than municipal or county law enforcement, provided law and order. Because the company usually furnished a schoolhouse (often subsidizing the teacher's salary) and a church building, opportunity existed for control of the school curriculum and the message from the pulpit.

Housing consisted of double twos (duplex, two rooms each side), double threes, square tops (four rooms), and shotguns, frequently without running water and almost always unsewered. Although textile towns were typically all-white, segregated housing patterns for black and white workers existed in most coal and iron ore camps.

Isolation and lack of transportation made company stores (commissaries) a necessity. In contrast to the low-rental housing, the store often made a profit for the company; however, recent research questions the stereotype of the "pluck me" store. But even if prices were in line with independent merchants and merchandise was of good quality, workers could easily "owe their souls to the company store" because of credit or advances drawn as scrip, a currency redeemable only at the commissary.

Characterizations of exploitation and subservience are an oversimplification. Great variety existed among company towns. A shortage of laborers or the desire to hold a skilled, stable work force could mitigate conditions or the degree of control a company exercised. Some industries (West Point Manufacturing, Tennessee Coal and Iron, Avondale Mills) instituted paternalistic health, welfare, and recreation programs to hold workers and lessen the attraction of unionism. Despite low wages and some loss of personal independence, many southern workers compared their lifestyle in a company town favorably with their former sharecropping existence. They often found, however, that "lintheads" or coal miners were socially ostracized by those residing outside the company town.

For many southerners the company town was a way stop in their rural to urban migration—not quite country, not quite city. Higher wages, unionization, and the automobile have all but eliminated the company town from the South. Industries began selling houses to employees in the 1940s and 1950s. But in some isolated, mountainous regions of West Virginia and Kentucky the company town still survives; in other communities the architectural style of now privately owned homes reveals their lineage as company towns.

Marlene Rikard
Samford University

Ruth A. Allen, *East Texas Lumber Workers: An Economic and Social Picture, 1870–1950* (1961); Harriet L. Herring, *Welfare Work in Mill Villages: The Story of Extra-Mill Activities in North Carolina* (1929); George B. Tindall, *The Emergence of the New South, 1913–1945* (1967). ✩

CONGRESS OF INDUSTRIAL ORGANIZATIONS (CIO)

After breaking with the American Federation of Labor (AFL) in 1937, the Congress of Industrial Organizations (CIO) quickly moved into the South, the nation's staunchest antiunion section. The CIO faced not only intransigent communities and businessmen, but also widespread racism on the part of white industrial workers and their employers. The CIO generated more controversy than the American Federation of Labor because it was determined to organize black as well as white workers and because it did not recoil from the use of Communist organizers, who worked in the most dangerous situations. Although southern workers proved on many occasions that they could behave militantly and form unions as strong as those elsewhere, the CIO encountered much more paternalism, individualism, and apathy in the southern work force than among workers in other regions.

Although they were the most downtrodden workers in the nation, southern tenant farmers and related agricultural hands were offered a glimmer of hope by the CIO, but it was dashed by the depths of their poverty and by other economic, social, and political impediments to effective strikes. Hundreds of thousands of textile workers had been beaten badly in strikes earlier in the 1930s, but the CIO mounted major organizing drives in 1937 and 1940. They won innumerable elections, but few contracts outside the Tri-Cities area of North Carolina. Coal miners and steelworkers were more successful in the late 1930s, and they coped with racism by emphasizing the necessity for economic cooperation and by electing black as well as white officers. The textile, steel, auto, rubber, clothing, packinghouse, and oil workers made their greatest gains during World War II, under the protection of the War Labor Board and a tight labor market. Board policies had some effect on easing racial and North-South wage differentials.

In 1946 the CIO launched a massive organization effort dubbed "Operation Dixie." Perhaps the most celebrated organizer was Lucy Randolph Mason. She utilized her illustrious southern ancestry and her presence as a "little old lady" to explain the requirements of fair treatment provided labor by various New Deal laws. The drive was a disappointment, and by 1953, on the eve of merger with the AFL, the 362,000 CIO members in the South were less than a third of the AFL membership. The social values of union membership in the 1930s and 1940s were almost as important as the economic rewards, and the CIO was undoubtedly among the most vital of the private agencies supporting fair play and justice for black southerners.

George N. Green
University of Texas
at Arlington

C.I.O. News, 1937–55; F. Ray Marshall, *Labor in the South* (1967); Lucy Randolph Mason, *To Win These Rights: A Personal Story of the CIO in the South* (1952). ☆

FARMERS' ALLIANCE
||||||||||||||||||||||||||||||||||||||||||||||||||||||

The southern Farmers' Alliance evolved from local farm organizations established in the 1870s in Texas. In 1886–88 the Alliance spread across the South and into the Great Plains. At its high point in 1891 it had over 1.5 million members. Admission to the organization, officially known by then as the National Farmers' Alliance and Industrial Union, was restricted to whites. However, it maintained ties with a parallel black group, the Colored Farmers' National Alliance.

The Alliance borrowed from the Grange the trappings of a secret society and from Protestant churches techniques for mobilizing rural people into community organizations. The Alliance promised relief for hard-pressed farmers through programs of economic cooperation and political advocacy. Alliance cooperative initiatives ranged from local schemes to buy or sell in bulk (thus bypassing the "middleman") to statewide purchasing and marketing exchanges.

As a political pressure group, the Alliance demanded legal recognition of trade unions and cooperatives, safeguards against land monopolies, federal ownership of railroads, reform of the banking and currency system, and creation of a federal subtreasury system. The subtreasury, conceived by Alliance leader C. W. Macune, would provide for the establishment of commodity storage facilities in rural counties. Farmers could receive legal tender notes with their stored crop as collateral. For southern farmers, the subtreasury plan held promise of breaking the annual cycle of indebtedness to the "furnishing merchant."

In 1890 southern Alliancemen demanded that Democratic candidates for office support the Alliance platform, including the subtreasury. Some prominent officeholders refused, and others reneged on backing the more controversial planks of the platform. Consequently, many Alliancemen bolted the Democratic party and joined their midwestern counterparts in forming the People's (or Populist) party. Southern leaders of this insurgent movement included Leonidas L. Polk of North Carolina, national president of the Farmers' Alliance, and Georgia lawyer Thomas E. Watson. In 1892 the Farmers' Alliance provided the organizational and ideological base for Populism in the South. The Alliance itself quickly faded.

The Farmers' Alliance was not simply absorbed into the People's party. By 1891 membership was declining because Alliance cooperatives could not resolve the massive credit and marketing problems facing southern farmers. Furthermore, the Farmers' Alliance had recruited from a broad spectrum of the rural white southern population, and many of its members had strong ties to the Democratic party. When the Alliance moved from political advocacy to insurgency under the Populist banner, many of its members dropped out.

Some portions of the Alliance platform were later enacted into law, including a form of the subtreasury plan. Additionally, the "movement culture" of the Alliance provided a way of thinking about community organizing and self-determination that lived on in movements ranging from the socialism of the 1910s to the civil rights movement of the 1960s.

Robert C. McMath, Jr.
Georgia Institute of Technology

Lawrence Goodwyn, *Democratic Promise: The Populist Moment in America* (1976); Robert C. McMath, Jr., *Populist Vanguard: A History of the Southern Farmers' Alliance* (1975). ☆

HIGHLANDER FOLK SCHOOL
||||||||||||||||||||||||||||||||||||||||||||||||||

The Highlander Folk School, founded at Monteagle, Tenn., in 1932 by fellow southerners Myles Horton and Don West, has worked for 50 years to develop leadership for democracy in labor unions and community organizations struggling for justice and social change.

The early Highlander staff, working in the poverty and despair of Depression-era Grundy County, were deeply affected by a hard-fought coal miners' strike in nearby Wilder, Tenn. Inspired as much by the determination of the strikers as by the injustices the miners fought, Highlander over the next 15 years became the principal Congress of Industrial Organizations (CIO) training center in the South. Hundreds of shop stewards, organizers, and rank-and-file union members went to Highlander to study labor history, economics, and other topics. More importantly, they learned about union democracy by practicing democracy, taking part in all decisions affecting the program.

The postwar CIO, responding to Cold War pressures, attempted to force Highlander to abandon its work with alleged leftist unions. Highlander resisted the CIO pressure, insisting on its independence. As a result, by the late 1940s Highlander's definition as primarily a labor school came to an end.

Along with the strident anticommunism of the period, it became increasingly clear to the Highlander staff that the principal obstacle to union organizing and union democracy was racism. Asserting that institutionalized racism must be met head-on, the school turned its energies to helping blacks gain full civil rights. In 1953, for example, Highlander sponsored a series of integrated workshops to discuss the anticipated Supreme Court ruling outlawing public school segregation.

Immeasurably aided by two courageous black leaders from the South Carolina Sea Islands, Septima P. Clark and Esau Jenkins, Highlander helped establish "Citizenship Schools" where black adults learned to read in order to register to vote. From a modest beginning on Johns Island with Bernice Robinson, a beautician and seamstress, as the first teacher, the Citizenship Schools spread across the South. Ultimately, tens of thousands of blacks learned to read and registered to vote, profoundly altering the southern political landscape.

As a principal meeting place of the civil rights movement, Highlander became a target and a victim of official repression. After a 1959 raid on the school and protracted legal proceedings, the state of Tennessee in 1961 revoked Highlander's charter and confiscated its Monteagle property. Highlander chose not to contest the seizure, moving instead to Knoxville with a new charter and a new name, the Highlander Research and Education Center, and continued its civil rights work.

The leadership and focus of the civil rights movement changed in the late 1960s and Highlander changed its focus in response, working since that time with the poor and disadvantaged people of Appalachia. At recent workshops, mountain people have addressed such concerns as mining and flood disasters, community-based health clinics, occupational and environmental health, and the economic issues surrounding the control of land and energy resources.

Myles Horton
Lawrence L. Bostian
The Highlander Center

Frank Adams with Myles Horton, *Unearthing Seeds of Fire: The Idea of Highlander* (1975); Dorothy Cotton and Myles Horton, in *Roots of Open Education in America*, ed. Ruth Dropkin and Arthur Tobier (1976); Aimee Horton, "The Highlander Folk School: A History of the Development of Its Major Programs Related to Social Movements in the South, 1932–1961" (Ph.D. dissertation, University of Chicago, 1971). ☆

KESTER, HOWARD ANDERSON

(1904–1977) Christian activist and educator.

Kester was born in Martinsville, Va. While a student at Lynchburg College and Vanderbilt University's School of Religion, "Buck" Kester became active in the work of the intercollegiate YMCA and the Fellowship of Reconciliation (FOR), serving as youth secretary of the latter organization from 1927 to 1929. As a result of this YMCA and FOR work, he became deeply involved in the nascent interracial student movement in the South. His work as southern secretary of the FOR from 1929 to 1934 was broader in scope than that in which he had engaged earlier, encompassing not only the South's racial but also its economic problems.

Although Kester's initial efforts were largely educational, the Depression, and capitalism's apparent inability to cope with it, persuaded him that political action was necessary. He therefore joined the Socialist party in 1931 and the following year ran unsuccessfully for Congress on the party's Tennessee ticket. In 1933 a dispute developed within the FOR over the role of violence in the class struggle. Kester deplored violence but believed it a likely consequence of the quest for social justice. The pacifist majority of FOR members considered his position too radical and dismissed him from his post as southern secretary. Reinhold Niebuhr and other disaffected Fellowship members who believed that Kester was rendering useful service in the South organized the Committee on Economic and Racial Justice, which supported his work in the region from 1934 until 1941, when the Fellowship of Southern Churchmen assumed responsibility for his activities. During these years Kester investigated lynchings and racial unrest for the NAACP, ACLU, and Workers Defense League; organized and publicized the Southern Tenant Farmers' Union; and, through the Fellowship of Southern Churchmen, sought to awaken southern Protestantism to an awareness of the social dimension of Christianity.

In 1943 he resigned as secretary of the FSC to accept a position as director of the Penn Normal, Industrial and Agricultural School in South Carolina, where he remained until 1948. He then worked for a brief period with the displaced persons program of the Congregational church and the John C. Campbell Folk School in North Carolina. In 1952 he returned to the Fellowship of Southern Churchmen, serving as its secretary from 1952 to 1957. He concluded his career as a teacher and administrator at Eureka College in Illinois and at Christmount Assembly and Montreat-Anderson College in western North Carolina. By the time of his death Kester's work had been largely overshadowed by that of a later generation of reformers, but during the second quarter of the century he was a leading figure among the small band of Christian activists in the South.

Robert F. Martin
University of Northern Iowa

John S. Bellamy, "If Christ Came to Dixie: The Southern Prophetic Vision of Howard Anderson Kester, 1904–1941" (M.A. thesis, University of Virginia, 1977); Anthony P. Dunbar, *Against the Grain: Southern Radicals and Prophets, 1929–1959* (1981); John Egerton, *A Mind to Stay Here: Profiles from the South* (1970). ☆

KNIGHTS OF LABOR

Organized in 1869 by a group of Philadelphia tailors, the Noble Order of the Knights of Labor within a decade had become the nation's largest labor union. Open to all laborers regardless of craft, the Knights stressed education, arbitration, and the development of worker-owned cooperatives rather than direct conflict with management. Shaken by the tumultuous strikes of 1877, the Knights held their first general assembly the following year and adopted a constitution, thus establishing a national organizational structure. Immediately thereafter the Knights began their efforts to organize the South, appointing organizers in Alabama, Georgia, and Florida.

Between 1878 and 1885 the Knights grew slowly in the South, their numbers concentrated in the urban centers, especially Richmond, Atlanta, Birmingham, and New Orleans. The Order experienced rapid growth in 1885, prompted by a visit of the Master Workman, Terence V. Powderly, to the region early in that year and, more significantly, by a successful strike against Jay Gould's southwestern railway system. Southern laborers, black and white, clamored to join the Knights, and organizers could not keep up with the demand. By 1886 the Knights had established district assemblies composed of several locals in Richmond,

Nashville, New Orleans, Atlanta, Norfolk, Knoxville, Memphis, Birmingham, Savannah, Augusta, Columbus, Petersburg, Chattanooga, and Key West. Large locals unaffiliated with a district organization existed in several other urban areas. By early 1887 state assemblies had been formed in Florida, Arkansas, Mississippi, and North Carolina. In other states the large district assemblies remained the dominant organizations. Local assemblies were racially segregated, but both white and black locals sent representatives to district and state assemblies.

Although most southern locals contained members representing a variety of occupations, until 1887 membership was concentrated in the mining, textile, lumber, and construction industries. Southern rank-and-file Knights proved as strike prone as members in other sections of the nation. Thousands of workers participated in strikes initiated by the Knights against the cotton mills of Augusta, Ga., in 1886 and the sugarcane growers of Louisiana in 1887. Other strikes involved coal miners, stevedores, typographers, and foundry workers. Inadequate planning, lack of funds, fierce resistance from management, and at best lukewarm support from the Order's national leadership doomed all such actions to failure.

In politics, however, the Knights experienced success, if but briefly. Southern Knights rushed into the political fray in 1886, electing members to city councils, state legislatures, and, in North Carolina and Virginia, to the House of Representatives. Within the year, however, the Order's political influence began to wane as its membership declined. Racial discord, the Order's failure to respond effectively to the membership's needs, failed strikes, and

an ineffective national leadership resulted in a swift downfall. By the end of 1888 most urban members had deserted the Knights. Those who remained represented the poorest of the region's yeoman and tenant farmers and day laborers, many of whom were blacks. A few such locals continued to exist into the 20th century.

> Melton A. McLaurin
> University of North Carolina
> at Wilmington

John Abernathy, "The Knights of Labor in Alabama" (M.A. thesis, University of Alabama, 1960); Leon Fink, *Labor History* (Summer 1978); Melton A. McLaurin, *The Knights of Labor in the South* (1978). ☆

LONGSHOREMEN
||||||||||||||||||||||||||||||||||||||||||||||

Dockworkers were vital to the port cities of the antebellum South, and they often organized to protect their interests. The New Orleans Screwmen's Benevolent Association (NOSBA), formed in 1850, probably became the South's first longshoremen's union. NOSBA, whose skilled members pressed cotton bales while others loaded ships, immediately began bargaining collectively. During the decade, NOSBA members—600 strong by 1860—waged three successful strikes. After the war, New Orleans longshoremen, with numbers greatly augmented by blacks, endured interracial strife incited by both employers and politicians. Yet, black and white screwmen in 1875 agreed to equalized wages and a quota system that survived into the 20th century.

Elsewhere, southern longshoremen formed unions in Galveston, Pensacola, Jacksonville, and Charleston. Racial friction also characterized their activities. In 1883, when Galveston's whites tried to drive off Afro-Americans, the blacks broke a strike in return for a company promise henceforth to provide them with steady work. Southern blacks, usually unionized, survived under the quota system and sometimes broke it. When the new port of Houston opened in 1917, blacks and whites, in a 99-year compact, agreed to share the work equally.

Many longshoremen's jobs, although avidly sought, provided only sporadic, backbreaking work with low pay. In New Orleans as many as 600 fruithandlers lined up for tickets to unload the banana boats. They earned 75 cents on a good day, but only 25 if just one ship arrived. According to the Marine Transport Workers Union (Industrial Workers of the World), which tried to organize the fruithandlers in 1913, dock bosses usually dispensed the tickets to favorites, and United Fruit Company paymasters cheated the men out of part of their wages.

By World War I the position of the elite screwmen also eroded as technological changes accelerated ship loading and as the high-density cotton press, operable by the unskilled, weakened the screwmen's bargaining power. With labor in ample supply, employers in 1923 easily defeated the International Longshoremen's Association (ILA) in a disastrous New Orleans strike. By 1931 the ILA had been eliminated from New Orleans and seriously crippled in the Texas Gulf ports.

The passage of the National Industrial Recovery Act strengthened the longshoremen, and in 1935 the ILA struck the Gulf ports west of Pensacola for equal wages and union recognition. Blood flowed as employers armed strikebreakers. A union threat to close all U.S. ports brought representation elections, most of which the ILA won. In 1937, amidst charges by New Orleans longshoremen of corruption and collusion with employers, the ILA-AFL was challenged by a left-wing splinter group, the International Longshoremen and Warehousemen's Union (ILWU-CIO), which advocated racial equality and industrial unionism. In a bitter election, amidst charges of "communism," the ILA won. By 1939 it claimed about 16,611 southern longshoremen.

The ILA was expelled from the AFL in 1959 for gangsterism but continued to dominate southern ports in alliance with the Teamsters. National bargaining, pressed by the ILA but opposed by southern employers and longshoremen, proceeded very slowly. As containerization replaced break-bulk cargoes, however, southern wages and benefits tended to follow trends set by the ILA's master agreement in the Northeast. By 1971 longshoremen in all the southern ports received a standard guaranteed annual income.

Merl E. Reed
Georgia State University

Joseph P. Goldberg, *International Labor Review* (March 1973); F. Ray Marshall, *Labor in the South* (1967); Merl E. Reed, *Labor History* (Winter 1972); Jerrell H. Shofner, *Labor History* (Fall 1972); Philip Taft, *Industrial and Labor Relations Review* (April 1956). ☆

MINE, MILL, AND SMELTER WORKERS

The Mine Mill union was initially known as the Western Federation of Miners. In

1916 its name was changed to the International Union of Mine, Mill, and Smelter Workers. The union met with little success in organizing workers before 1933. With the passage of the New Deal legislation, Mine Mill successfully organized in the copper, lead, zinc, iron ore, and precious metal mines of the western, midwestern, eastern, and southern states. Its center of strength in the South was in Alabama.

In Alabama chief support for the organizational efforts of Mine Mill came from the iron ore mines of Red Mountain in Jefferson County. The first local was chartered in July 1933 and eventually led to the union becoming a force to be reckoned with. This power was not realized until the workers had experienced two strikes, prolonged layoffs, harassment, and loss of many jobs. Nonetheless, concrete benefits were won by Mine Mill, for prior to the union coming to Alabama there had been no effective grievance procedures, no seniority clause, few health and safety regulations, no vacation with pay, and no portal to portal pay. In short, prior to Mine Mill arrival there had been no effective mechanism through which the workers could negotiate with management on an equitable basis.

Locally, the International Union of Mine, Mill, and Smelter Workers was termed the "Nigger Union" because it espoused racial equality during a time and in a place where segregation was the law. Its constitution stipulated a 50/50 racial mixture in the locals' leadership. This policy led many white workers to refuse to support the union. In the 1930s Mine Mill gained respectability because of a National Labor Relations Board ruling that awarded back pay to 159 workers who had been fired as a result of their participation in a strike. The union also gained company recognition as sole bargaining agent in the Tennessee Coal, Iron and Railroad Company (TCI) mines.

Prior to 1938 the work force in the iron ore mines was predominately black and the union was also. After 1938 TCI changed its hiring policy and more white workers were employed. Between 1938 and 1948 the complexion of the mines and Mine Mill would change considerably. This would lead to a conflict between the old Mine Mill members and the new members who would be mostly white.

In late 1948 certain white members of the Alabama Mine Mill locals contacted the United Steelworkers of America (USWA) about possible affiliation. This marked the beginning of the successful secessionists' struggle on Red Mountain. Between January and mid-March 1949, the secessionists mounted an intense campaign against the Mine Mill union, and the USWA challenged Mine Mill by calling for a consent election. Mine Mill accused the Steelworkers Union of raiding, and a hotly contested election drive for the loyalty of Red Mountain iron ore miners ensued. Black workers predominated in the effort to retain Mine Mill as sole representative at the workplace, although a few white workers were supportive as well. It appears that only white workers were in support of the USWA. The Steelworkers won the election and replaced Mine Mill as the sole bargaining agent in the TCI mines.

Black miners continually showed strong preference for Mine Mill rather than the USWA. As one miner suggested, "We looked upon Mine Mill not just as another labor union but as a way of life." Nevertheless, the final attempt of Mine Mill to wrest control from the Steelworkers Union was in 1952. This effort failed, and the union continued to decrease in importance on Red Mountain.

What combination made it possible for Mine Mill to organize and sustain itself on Red Mountain for nearly 15 years? First, the federal government and various pieces of labor legislation, including the National Industrial Recovery Act of 1933, the Wagner Act of 1935, and the Fair Labor Standards Act of 1938, enabled the union to achieve victories that would have been otherwise impossible. Second, the international office of Mine Mill was alert enough to recognize the necessity of organization in the iron ore mines, perceptive enough to realize the importance of black workers, and militant enough to organize interracially. Third, the white workers who remained loyal to Mine Mill before and after 1938 were a courageous group, because they and their families were under constant attack by opponents of the "Nigger Union." The fourth ingredient in the success of the Alabama Mine Mill locals was persevering black workers, without whose tenacity Mine Mill would not have survived. The black majority who set the tone and charted the direction of the locals worked heroically from Mine Mill's inception, when it was most unpopular to be a union man on Red Mountain. Eventually the same men would use their knowledge in the wider arena of black protest movements.

Horace Huntley
University of Alabama
at Birmingham

H. H. Chapman, *Iron and Steel Industries of the South* (1953); F. Ray Marshall, *Labor in the South* (1967); Philip Taft, in *Organizing Dixie: Alabama Workers in the Industrial Era*, ed. Gary M. Fink (1981). ☆

MITCHELL, H. L.
(b. 1906) Reformer.

A champion of the rights of southern tenant farmers and sharecroppers, Harry Leland Mitchell devoted much of his life to promoting and assisting their cause, mostly under the auspices of the Southern Tenant Farmers' Union (STFU). He was instrumental in founding the union, which he believed would help attract government aid and give poor farmers bargaining power with their landlords.

Mitchell was born near Halls, Tenn., and, with his family, lived his first few years in the home of his grandfather, a Baptist preacher. Mitchell did not conform to his grandfather's religious ideals, sympathizing instead with Darwinists and Socialists. In 1933 Mitchell attended a speech by Socialist party leader Norman Thomas, who condemned segregation. The notion had never before occurred to Mitchell, but he agreed and afterward worked for blacks and whites throughout his career. He became the state secretary for the Arkansas Socialist party but turned his allegiance to the Democratic party in 1936.

Having sharecropped with little success, Mitchell moved from Tennessee to Tyronza, Ark., in 1927 to open a drycleaning business. He became acquainted with many of the poor farmers in the region and helped unemployed blacks who wanted public work jobs to organize in protest of their situation. In 1934, when plantation owner Hiram Norcross evicted 23 tenant families, Mitchell and Clay East cofounded the STFU. He served as the union's executive secretary from then until 1939, when the STFU withdrew from the Congress of Industrial Organizations (CIO).

Mitchell had favored the withdrawal, believing that the STFU should protect itself from the CIO's Communist influence. The issue had been controversial within the STFU, and Mitchell escaped the furor by accepting a job with the National Youth Administration. He also worked with the International Ladies' Garment Workers' Union before he rejoined the STFU in 1941, promptly being reelected to his former position.

Mitchell served as president of the union from 1944 until 1960, during which time the union became the National Farm Labor Union and later, the National Agricultural Workers Union. Until his retirement in 1972, he continued to help organize workers ranging from dairy farmers to sugar mill workers to menhaden fishermen. His greatest influence was in advancing the cause of struggling southern tenant farmers and sharecroppers. Through his efforts for the STFU, he became an important force in the southern labor movement, leading strikes, publicizing agricultural problems in the South, and proving that blacks and whites could indeed work together to protect their rights as laborers.

Jessica Foy
Cooperstown Graduate Programs
Cooperstown, New York

Anthony P. Dunbar, *Against the Grain: Southern Radicals and Prophets, 1929–1959* (1981); Gary M. Fink, ed., *Biographical Dictionary of American Labor Leaders* (1974); H. L. Mitchell, *Mean Things Happening in This Land: The Life and Times of H. L. Mitchell* (1979); Southern Tenant Farmers' Union Papers, University of North Carolina, Chapel Hill. ☆

MURPHY, EDGAR GARDNER

(1869–1913) Clergyman and social reformer.

Murphy was born near Fort Smith, Ark., to Samuel W. and Janie Gardner Murphy. When her husband abandoned the family in 1874, Janie Murphy moved with the children to San Antonio, Tex., where young Murphy received his early formal education. In 1885 he entered the University of the South, where he was heavily influenced by Sewanee's theologian, William Porcher DuBose. After graduating four years later, Murphy studied at New York's General Theological Seminary, married Maud King, and was ordained as a priest in the Protestant Episcopal church.

In 1893 Murphy was called to a parish in Laredo, Tex., where he organized the community's protest of the burning of a black man accused of rape and murder. Although he served parishes in Chillicothe, Ohio, and Kingston, N.Y., Murphy longed to return to the South, and in 1898 the young priest moved to St. John's Episcopal Church in Montgomery, Ala. Thereafter, his liberal theological perspective, largely learned from DuBose and reflected in his own *The Larger Life* (1897), was brought to bear upon the New South's social problems—child labor, public education, and race relations—in two other works, *Problems of the Present South* (1904) and *The Basis of Ascendancy* (1910).

Murphy was instrumental in the formation of the Alabama Child Labor Committee in 1901 and two years later the National Child Labor Committee. Although his commitment to local regulatory initiatives led him to oppose national legislation against child labor, he helped to spark statewide initiatives throughout the South and saw Alabama adopt the strongest regulatory legislation within the region in his lifetime. He resigned from St. John's in 1901 and two years later withdrew from the ministry altogether to serve as executive secretary of the Southern Education Board. In that capacity, Murphy directed public relations campaigns throughout the South, which substantially succeeded in massing public support to strengthen the region's weak public school systems. From 1900, when he organized the Southern Society for the Promotion of the Study of Race Conditions and Problems in the South, until his death, he was a sophisticated spokesman for white racial paternalism. Equally opposed to radical white racists and to black or white racial egalitarians or assimilationists, Edgar Gardner Murphy was a subtle apologist for segregation, but one who gave racism a benign expression.

Ralph E. Luker
Wilmington, Delaware

Hugh C. Bailey, *Edgar Gardner Murphy: Gentle Progressive* (1968); Daniel Levine, *Varieties of Reform Thought* (1964); Ralph E. Luker, *A Southern Tradition in Theology and Social Criticism, 1830–1930: The Religious Liberalism and Social Conservatism of James Warley Miles, William Porcher DuBose, and Edgar Gardner Murphy* (1984). ☆

OIL WORKERS

Southern oil workers first acted in concert in 1905, when the Guffey Company, predecessor of Gulf, arbitrarily slashed wages. The strike saved the $3 scale, but the men soon allowed their

union to disappear. The wage remained at $3 until 1917 while the price of oil increased a hundredfold. Nonunion oil workers thus sacrificed millions of dollars in merited wage increases. Unionism bloomed again during World War I, as the wages and the primitive company camps became intolerable. Ten thousand strikers walked out after the owners of the fields in Texas and Louisiana refused even to meet with their representatives. The major companies utilized martial law and private armies to break the strike, and soon they virtually destroyed the union.

Under the protection of the National Recovery Act (1933–34) oil unionism revived. Dozens of locals were formed and a national agreement was signed with Sinclair. The demise of the NRA, rising company resistance to unions, and relatively high pay scales in the refineries drastically hindered the growth of the oil workers' union. During their renewed organizing efforts of the late 1930s and the war years, members of the Oil Workers International (Congress of Industrial Organizations) were continually labeled as a Communist front by southeast Texas Congressman Martin Dies. And the refineries established company unions, deliberately hired minorities in order to stir racial tensions, and jacked up wages just before organizing drives. Still, the union doubled its membership during the war, winning significant victories at the Texas Company and Gulf in Port Arthur. It failed to crack the nation's largest refinery, Esso at Baton Rouge, or the big Humble plant at Baytown, both of which were Standard Oil operations. In 1944 so many oil workers registered to vote that it was a major factor in convincing Martin Dies not to run for reelection. Despite CIO policy, blacks and whites maintained separate locals in Beaumont and Port Arthur for years, until the Oil Workers International forced them to integrate. The Texas-Louisiana district became the largest branch of the union and took the lead in the 1945 nationwide strike that established oil workers as the highest paid manufacturing hands in the country.

Unlike other CIO unions that "invaded" the South, the Oil Workers International for over 30 years was the only union that maintained its headquarters south of the Mason-Dixon line (in Fort Worth). It did more than any other Texas or Louisiana union in the 1940s and 1950s to obliterate wage differentials among the races.

See also INDUSTRY: / Oil Industry

George N. Green
University of Texas at Arlington

Ruth A. Allen, *Chapters in the History of Organized Labor in Texas* (1941); Clyde Johnson, in *Essays in Southern Labor History: Selected Papers, Southern Labor History Conference, 1976*, ed. Gary M. Fink and Merl E. Reed (1977); James C. Maroney, in *Essays in Southern Labor History: Selected Papers, Southern Labor History Conference, 1976*, ed. Gary M. Fink and Merl E. Reed (1977); Harvey O'Connor, *History of Oil Workers International Union* (1950). ☆

OWSLEY THESIS

The Owsley thesis is the work of Frank Lawrence Owsley (1890–1956), an Alabama-born historian who spent most of his academic career at Vanderbilt University. Disagreeing with interpretations that portrayed the Old South as a society totally dominated by the planter class, Owsley and his students, most notably

Herbert Weaver and Blanche Henry Clark, focused on the role of the southern plain folk. The Owsley thesis, based largely on data from the U.S. census returns for Alabama, Mississippi, Louisiana, and Tennessee, contended that the majority of antebellum southerners were middle-class farmers, that these yeomen (who were often nonslaveholders) owned their fair share of land comparable in quality to that held by planters, and that this middle class prospered and grew during the late antebellum years. Owsley's views were summarized most importantly in *Plain Folk of the Old South*, published in 1949.

The Owsley thesis has always had critics. Even as it was being elaborated, Fabian Linden argued in the *Journal of Negro History* (1946) that Owsley's data and methodology were open to question and that the mere existence of a large middle class did not prove that its members stood on any sort of an equal footing with the planters. Did the plain folk, Linden asked, have a share of southern agricultural wealth and production proportionate to their numbers in the population as a whole? He thought not. Other historians have pointed out that Owsley offered no precise definition of the plain folk, making them nearly indistinguishable from the planters. And the general tendency in the writing of southern history since the 1950s has been a continued, and even greater, emphasis on planter dominance rather than yeoman democracy. Nevertheless, the Owsley thesis constituted a minor revolution in historical interpretation of the Old South. Due primarily to the work of Owsley and his students, it is clear that antebellum society was not a simple three-tiered arrangement of planters, poor whites, and black slaves, and every modern account must at least consider the place and role of the plain folk majority.

Randolph B. Campbell
North Texas State University

Fabian Linden, *Journal of Negro History* (April 1946); Frank L. Owsley, *Plain Folk of the Old South* (1949), with Harriet C. Owsley, *Journal of Southern History* (February 1940). ☆

RAILROAD WORKERS
llllllllllllllllllllllllllllllllllllllllllllllllllll

The railroad has been important in the economic and geographic expansion of the United States and certainly so in the South, whose railroad network was rebuilt after the Civil War. Until recently most attention has been paid to the history of railroads as corporate institutions (or to their entrepreneurs) and not to the lives of the individual workers so important to the railroad's development. Particularly through the use of oral history, recent studies have illuminated the lives of railroad workers and illustrated the relationship of the southern railroader to railroaders elsewhere.

Among the common characteristics of railroad life is the counterpoint of hard work and danger and a romantic attachment to railroading. This latter phenomenon bridges the work force from management to labor and contributes to a sense of worker community, a form of corporate family. Railroad workers almost uniformly bemoan the transformation from steam to diesel power and admit a preference for passenger traffic over freight. They share a common store of tales, songs, and poems, which treat the pleasures and problems of railroading, undoubtedly as a means of dealing with the pressures of their occupation. Some of these are staples of folk cul-

ture, such as the story of Casey Jones, the "brave engineer" of the late 19th century who was immortalized in a Tin Pan Alley version of this railroad tale. And there are similar stories passed on by individual railroaders about the brave engineer (the "old hogger") who carried heavy loads at high speeds around dangerous curves and up steep hills, often with the reward being a trip to the "promised land."

Another well-known hero was John Henry, the giant who supposedly weighed 44 pounds at birth and later worked for the Chesapeake & Ohio Railroad laying track and driving tunnels. Legend holds that for a $100 bet he was matched against a steam drill. He won the contest but died the following night from his exertion. Such railroad songs, poems, and fables mix myth and reality. The hard work and danger faced by the railroader often resulted in death or injury, although the folk versions obviously exaggerate the magnitude of the experience.

The role of the union in dealing with management in order to improve working conditions and settle labor disputes weighs heavily on the railroader. Two other topics (which also concern the role of the union) are the status of women in the railroad work group and the treatment of blacks. While these matters are part of a national concern, they also illuminate the more general attitudes of southern society.

Women had to fight for jobs other than the most menial. Even traditional "woman's work"—such as secretarial posts—often went to men on the railroad, for rail secretaries had to travel overnight with their superiors, who were, of course, male.

In the antebellum South black railroad employees dominated most jobs except for managerial and clerical positions and those of conductor. They even drove trains, in violation of state laws. After the Civil War they were relegated to low-level positions such as porters and laborers, a trend that changed (in both North and South) only with late 20th-century fair employment practices. For example, of 136,065 black rail workers in 1924, 115,937 were laborers or porters. (Of these, 86,262 were in the South.)

The black rail worker retained a loyalty to the profession, but also a deep bitterness over the racial attitudes that resulted in crude jokes, separate (and inferior) dining and sleeping conditions on the trains themselves, and the inability to secure food or lodging outside the train yard when runs took a crew away overnight.

Although the Knights of Labor tried unsuccessfully to organize southern railroaders during the 19th century, the American Federation of Labor finally brought unionization to these railroads. Southern locals of the four major operating unions—the Brotherhood of Locomotive Engineers, Order of Railroad Conductors, Brotherhood of Locomotive Firemen and Enginemen, and Brotherhood of Railroad Trainmen—were organized shortly after the creation of their national unions. In addition, some national unions that enrolled many railroaders—Machinists, Blacksmiths, Boilermakers, Telegraphers, and Maintenance of Way—started in the South.

By 1900 most skilled southern railroaders were unionized, and after World War I—due to federal policies—virtually all southern rail employees were union members. But the unsuccessful national shopmen's strike in 1922 caused a decline in nonoperating unions in the South. (In 1925, the operating unions had 6,295 members in Georgia,

down from 6,440 in 1920.) The failure to organize blacks after this time was a weakness that also promised an opportunity for potential strikebreaking. Certainly an exception was the Brotherhood of Sleeping Car Porters, a union of black workers whose membership increased (particularly during the late New Deal, under the leadership of A. Philip Randolph).

As the nature of railroading changed—from steam to diesel, passenger to freight, local control to national (often northern)—the railroader retained a sense of nostalgia, but perhaps at the expense of the concept of community.

See also FOLKLIFE: / Henry, John; Jones, Casey; HISTORY AND MANNERS: Railroads; INDUSTRY: / Railroad Industry

Carl Ryant
University of Louisville

Stuart Leuthner, *The Railroaders* (1983); Walter Licht, *Working for the Railroad: The Organization of Work in the Nineteenth Century* (1983); F. Ray Marshall, *Labor in the South* (1967); Carl Ryant, *Register of the Kentucky Historical Society* (Winter 1984). ☆

SHARECROPPERS UNION

In the spring of 1931 the *Southern Worker*, a Communist-party newspaper based in Chattanooga, published letters from "farmer correspondents" in Camp Hill, Ala., stating that landlords and merchants in the area had cut off food advances and reduced day wages for field work. In response to calls for help, the party sent an organizer to form a farm union local. At a first meeting, tenant farmers and sharecroppers drew up a list of demands: food advances through "settlement" time with landowners; the right to sell their own crops and to plant small gardens for home use; cash wages for picking cotton; a three-hour midday rest for day workers; a nine-month school year for black children and a free school bus.

But in 1931 black farmers—and white farmers—had to struggle simply to remain on the land. A confrontation at Camp Hill was characteristic of the Sharecroppers Union's (SCU) early history from 1931 to 1933. Camp Hill farmers had not yet planned how to implement their demands when, on 15 July 1931, their meeting was raided by the high sheriff and his posse. The raid touched off several days of violence. One farmer was killed and his house burned, and 35 black men were jailed on charges ranging from carrying concealed weapons to conspiracy and assault with intent to murder. They were never brought to trial, but their local was effectively suppressed.

In the fall of 1932 the party sent another organizer to Tallapoosa County, this time to Reeltown, 15 miles southwest of Camp Hill. Following a shootout in December between a sheriff's posse and farmers attempting to stop a foreclosure, legal prosecution and vigilante violence curtailed union activity there, too.

Starting in 1933, the SCU concentrated its efforts in Black Belt counties west of Tallapoosa, where the majority of farmers were landless black farm workers whose economic position was suited to industrial-type organizing. In 1935 union-led strikes succeeded in raising wages. But repression was severe, especially in Lowndes County, where white landowners defended their

supremacy with armed force. Seeking protection and additional resources, the SCU turned to the New Deal for relief. The union moved its headquarters to New Orleans, where it could maintain an office and publish its newspaper openly. When, in 1936, the Communist party called for a "United Front" of Communist and other "progressive forces," SCU organizers were already preparing to affiliate with national unions. By late 1938 SCU tenants and sharecroppers had transferred to the Farmers Union, an organization modeled on the Grange and the Farmers' Alliance of the 1880s and 1890s. Wageworkers merged into the Agricultural Workers Union, which was chartered by the American Federation of Labor in 1937 as the Farm Laborers and Cotton Field Workers Union.

Affiliation signaled the SCU's shift from a strategy of "national liberation" of the Black Belt to positions squarely in the tradition of American agrarian protest. The union's struggle to secure a livelihood for poor farmers was resolved, in part, by the general "solutions" to the Depression. By the outbreak of World War II, war industries had begun to absorb black and white farmers displaced in the economic crisis, and public agencies were maintaining others who could not or would not leave the land.

Theodore Rosengarten
McClellanville, South Carolina

David E. Conrad, *The Forgotten Farmers: The Story of Sharecroppers in the New Deal* (1965); Donald H. Grubbs, *Cry from the Cotton: The Southern Tenant Farmers' Union and the New Deal* (1971); Theodore Saloutos, *Farmer Movements in the South, 1865–1933* (1960). ☆

SOUTHERN CONFERENCE FOR HUMAN WELFARE

The Southern Conference for Human Welfare (SCHW) was a controversial liberal organization that advocated sweeping social, economic, and political change in the South from 1938 to 1948. Inspired by President Franklin D. Roosevelt and his New Deal, some 1,200 enthusiastic delegates gathered in Birmingham, Ala., in November 1938 to form the Southern Conference. Hoping to modernize the South and liberalize its Democratic party, the group supported labor's right to organize, endorsed liberal economic policies, advocated repeal of poll tax laws, and criticized racial discrimination.

Frank P. Graham of the University of North Carolina served as the organization's first chairman until 1940, when the Reverend John Thompson, a left-wing Oklahoma minister, succeeded him. Clark Foreman, a New Deal administrator, replaced Thompson and headed the group from 1942 until 1948. Other southern liberals active in SCHW included Lucy Randolph Mason, H. C. Nixon, Virginia Durr, Aubrey Williams, Benjamin Mays, Lillian Smith, James Dombrowski, and the radical activist Joseph Gelders.

During SCHW's early years members sponsored several educational campaigns concerning social problems, devoted special attention to efforts to repeal poll tax laws, and, after World War II, organized numerous voter registration drives. The group's leadership eventually endorsed such liberal congressional legislation as an anti-lynching law, federal aid to education, and the creation of a Fair Employment Practices Committee.

This controversial support for federal intervention in southern race relations outraged many conservative whites and led to fierce attacks on the organization. Critics also repeatedly charged that SCHW was Communist dominated. Actually, only a handful of Communists ever joined the conference, but the group's leaders stubbornly refused to expel them. This principled but unpopular stand proved quite damaging to the conference during the early years of the Cold War.

The ideological split within American liberalism in the late 1940s between Cold War liberals and Popular Front liberals further divided SCHW, especially when Foreman, Durr, and several others joined Henry Wallace's ill-fated presidential campaign. The communism issue, internal factionalism, and mounting attacks from segregationists eventually combined to destroy the conference, which disbanded in late November 1948. Yet the group's tax-exempt subsidiary, the Southern Conference Education Fund, survived its parent's death and continued to support southern desegregation during the 1950s. Although SCHW failed during its lifetime, its vision was ultimately vindicated in the 1960s when Congress passed extensive civil rights legislation and the Twenty-Fourth Amendment outlawed the poll tax.

Charles H. Martin
University of Texas at El Paso

Clark Foreman, *Phylon* (June 1951); Thomas A. Krueger, *And Promises to Keep: The Southern Conference for Human Welfare* (1967); Charles H. Martin, in *Perspectives on the American South*, vol. 3, ed. James C. Cobb and Charles Reagan Wilson (1985). ✩

SOUTHERN REGIONAL COUNCIL (SRC)
||||||||||||||||||||||||||||||||||||||||||||||||||||

An Atlanta-based reform agency, the Southern Regional Council (SRC) balances a commitment to social justice with a devotion to rigorous policy analysis. Proud of its native roots yet financially dependent on non-southern foundations, dedicated to the fight against discrimination yet wary of direct action, SRC is unique among southern protest organizations. In contrast to groups like the Southern Organizing Committee for Social and Economic Justice, the council shuns political activity, demonstrations, and radical economic theory. Instead SRC works for equality of opportunity through interracial dialogue, research and publications programs, and the timely influence of "southerners of good will." At times, SRC has taken a more direct approach, notably during the 1960s when it coordinated the black registration drive known as the Voter Education Project. The council prefers, however, to serve as an information clearinghouse, providing community leaders with the knowledge and technical expertise necessary to counter prejudice and promote voluntary change.

Founded in 1944, the SRC grew out of dissatisfaction among moderate blacks and liberal whites with the Commission on Interracial Cooperation (CIC), a race relations betterment group active during the interwar years. During World War II, with racial tensions on the rise, southern blacks like Gordon Hancock and P. B. Young charged the CIC's white leadership with timidity and paternalism. In response, CIC secretary Jessie Daniel Ames convinced white liberals to support a new regional planning agency (an idea advanced by Howard W. Odum as early as 1936), which would appeal to northern foundations, revitalize southern liberalism, and check the growing independence of native blacks. The SRC's white charter members pledged constructive responses to black grievances and assured black leaders of a full partnership in the organization. Yet council leaders were equally committed to winning the support of moderate white professionals and businessmen. Under Executive Director Guy Benton Johnson the SRC avoided a stand on the segregation issue, choosing instead to work for racial progress within the separate-but-equal doctrine. SRC programs, like those of the CIC, reflected a deep respect for regional folkways, especially the white South's antipathy for "racial agitation" and "outside interference."

Critics like Lillian Smith and J. Saunders Redding soon branded the SRC "a defensive holding action" against genuine change. By early 1947, however, as the hope of attracting prominent whites dimmed, the council began to modify its policies in response to the changing racial climate. In 1948, under the leadership of former New Dealer George Mitchell, SRC endorsed the more active federal role proposed by President Harry Truman's Committee on Civil Rights. In 1951, despite an acute financial crisis, SRC renounced segregation as "a cruel and needless penalty on the human spirit." SRC's respected monthly, *New South*, closely monitored the progress of federal desegregation suits. In early 1954, in anticipation of the *Brown* decision and with the help of the first in a series of major Ford Foundation grants, SRC committed itself to the development of a network of state human relations councils. When *Brown* came, SRC officials promptly embraced it, predicting that "the South will go along." By 1956 virulent white resistance forced SRC to place the faltering state councils "on their own mettle" and to refocus on regionwide programs run out of the Atlanta office. Segregationists constantly charged that SRC was a "Communist front" and a threat to the "southern way of life." Yet the council stepped up its analysis of segregationist tactics and even launched new programs, including a race relations consultant service, which sent SRC staff members into racially troubled communities.

In 1960, soon after the Greensboro sit-ins, SRC leaders like Leslie Dunbar and James McBride Dabbs recognized the legitimacy and staying power of the new student activism. In 1961 a report on *The Federal Executive and Civil Rights* caught the attention of the John F. Kennedy Administration. At the suggestion of Martin Luther King, Jr., SRC became the coordinating agent for five major civil rights groups involved in the Kennedy-endorsed but foundation-financed Voter Education Project. Using registration data gathered in the project, SRC threw itself into the fight for the Voting Rights Act of 1965. The council also denounced black separatism and rejected the confrontational tactics some activists thought essential. Tensions between black staff members and white administrators in the Atlanta office threatened SRC's central program. Critics complained that the council had become little more than the voice of an elite white progressivism.

Such charges were symptomatic of the disintegation of the civil rights movement in the late 1960s. SRC's response was to reemphasize its traditional fact-finding role and broaden its range of concern. While SRC research-

ers documented southern noncompliance with federal civil rights laws, the council published scores of influential reports on such pressing social problems as housing, hunger, public health, prison conditions, and migrant labor. In the 1970s, SRC's "government monitoring project" weighed the social impact of the "new federalism" and a new information service aided southern legislators sympathetic to minorities and the poor. During the 1980s, when SRC became a persistent critic of Reagan Administration policy on voting rights and social welfare issues, the council continued to search for indigenous financial support. Yet SRC had earned a national reputation as an interpreter and advocate of southern change and had become a rallying point for southerners inspired by the council's vision of a "humane and democratic South."

See also BLACK LIFE: / Commission on Interracial Cooperation; Hancock, Gordon Blaine; King, Martin Luther, Jr.; LAW: / *Brown* v. *Board of Education*; MEDIA: / Young, P. B.; WOMEN'S LIFE: / Ames, Jessie Daniel; Smith, Lillian

Anthony Newberry
Jefferson Community College

William C. Allred, Jr., "The Southern Regional Council, 1943–1961" (M.A. thesis, Emory University, 1966); Edwin Lee Plowman, "Analysis of Selective Strategies Used by the Southern Regional Council in Effecting Social Change in the South" (Ph.D. dissertation, Boston University, 1976); The Southern Regional Council Papers, Robert W. Woodruff Library, Atlanta University Center. ☆

SOUTHERN STUDENT ORGANIZING COMMITTEE

The Southern Student Organizing Committee (SSOC) was a predominantly white organization that encouraged and coordinated student activism on southern campuses from 1964 to 1969. At first the group represented an updated version of liberal interracialism, but eventually many of its members became associated with the New Left. In 1969 the organization disbanded after an internal split resulting from its repudiation on ideological grounds by Students for a Democratic Society (SDS).

In April 1964 some 45 representatives from 15 southern colleges met in Nashville to form SSOC. The organization's major goals, stated in a declaration of principles entitled "We'll Take Our Stand," were to educate well-intentioned but somewhat sheltered southern students at predominantly white schools concerning civil rights, poverty, and other vital national issues, and to sponsor various community and campus projects. The delegates also endorsed such activities as fighting segregation, combating poverty, expanding social services, encouraging peace and disarmament, and ending "man's inhumanity to man."

Elected as officers were Gene Guerrero, Jr., chairman, Sue Thrasher, executive secretary, and Ron Parker, treasurer. As its distinctive symbol the group selected a Confederate flag on which clasped black and white hands had been superimposed. SSOC published several newspapers including *New South Student* and the *Phoenix* and distributed numerous pamphlets on such topics as civil rights, the Vietnam War, and women's liberation.

At first the organization worked closely with the Student Nonviolent Coordinating Committee (SNCC), and the group was even briefly viewed as SNCC's white counterpart. At the same time, SSOC also received recognition as a "fraternal organization" from SDS, and in effect became SDS's southern agent. As ties to SNCC weakened, SSOC leaders moved closer to SDS and its evolving New Left ideology. Meanwhile, SSOC did not seek a mass membership but instead attempted to coordinate local groups' diverse activities while relying on grants from national foundations for its financing. This led to wide variations in local programs and a feeling that the organization lacked direction.

Despite cooperation with SDS, SSOC leaders continued to display a "southern consciousness" and insisted that the unique historical development of the South warranted a special organizing perspective that avoided taking unnecessarily controversial stands. For example, SSOC sponsored various peace activities including antiwar workshops, yet it never adopted a formal resolution condemning the Vietnam War for fear of harming its image. This emphasis on southernness and moderation eventually brought criticism to the group from the New Left.

In March 1969 SDS, racked with bitter internal divisions, unexpectedly condemned these liberal tendencies in SSOC and severed all connections with the group. Taken aback, SSOC activists gathered in Edwards, Miss., in June to discuss the organization's future. Although one faction favored reorganizing and continuing SSOC, pro-SDS members carried the day and voted to disband the group and destroy all records and correspondence.

Charles H. Martin
University of Texas at El Paso

Clayborne Carson, *In Struggle: SNCC and the Black Awakening of the 1960s* (1981). ☆

SOUTHERN TENANT FARMERS' UNION
|||||||||||||||||||||||||||||||||||||||||||||||||||||

The Southern Tenant Farmers' Union was founded in Tyronza, Ark., in April 1934 by a handful of black and white sharecroppers, tenants, and small businessmen. Prominent among the latter were cofounders H. L. Mitchell and Clay East, native southerners whose beliefs derived from southwestern Populist, Socialist, and other radical traditions. Responding to growing misery as the Great Depression deepened, Mitchell and East noted that the New Deal's Agricultural Adjustment Administration (AAA) not only created a cotton scarcity but thereby gave planters both the means and the incentive to drive labor off the land. The AAA offered a federal subsidy that could be used to mechanize; the incentive was the easily circumvented requirement to share the subsidy with tenants but not wage laborers. Roosevelt had already explained away his creation of scarcity as a necessary evil, but for the creation of unemployment there could be little justification. With the purge of liberal sharecropper supporters from the AAA and the outbreak of violence against STFU members and leaders, both during the first months of 1935, financial aid began to appear from outside the South. A radical but anti-Communist Virginia clergyman, Howard Kester, and a railroad heir purged from AAA, Gardner Jackson, led a nationwide "sharecropper consciousness" movement that helped produce the LaFollette Civil Liberties Committee, a fact-finding com-

mission on farm tenancy, and generated a degree of visibility that may have saved the STFU from as violent a fate as some other radical, racially mixed organizations. Its membership reached about 35,000 in Arkansas, Oklahoma, and Texas.

Racial integration was common at the larger STFU meetings, although in a few places segregated locals were permitted. The fundamentalist religion of the members furnished inspiration and ritual. Such men as A. B. Brookins and John Handcox, both black, changed gospel music into protest songs, such as "We Shall Not Be Moved," that endured into the 1960s and beyond.

The STFU broke away from a more leftist agricultural union in 1939, exaggerating disagreements over dues and STFU autonomy into one of America's first "Communist rule-or-ruin" controversies. The ruined STFU furnished a base after World War II for cofounder Mitchell's continued efforts to aid farm workers in California and Louisiana.

Donald H. Grubbs
University of the Pacific

Anthony P. Dunbar, *Against the Grain: Southern Radicals and Prophets, 1929–1959* (1981); Donald H. Grubbs, *Cry from the Cotton: The Southern Tenant Farmers' Union and the New Deal* (1971); H. L. Mitchell, *Mean Things Happening in This Land: The Life and Times of H. L. Mitchell* (1979); Southern Tenant Farmers' Union Papers, University of North Carolina and microfilm. ☆

TEXTILE WORKERS
|||||||||||||||||||||||||||||||||||||||||||||||||||||

Southern textile workers, often called "lintheads," have been categorized as a subspecies of "poor whites." Their numbers alone command attention, reaching nearly 600,000 in 1950 and far outnumbering any other group of workers in industrial manufacturing in the South. Nowhere in the United States, save for New England and parts of the Middle Atlantic states, have textile workers had such numerical weight. Southern textile workers lived and worked in the southern Piedmont from southern Virginia to northern Alabama and Mississippi with clusters in Tennessee and into the midlands of the Carolinas and Georgia.

Child laborer in a textile mill, North Carolina, early 1900s

The antebellum southern textile industry worked whites, free blacks, and slaves, sometimes in racially mixed factories. But a shift to using only white workers began before 1865 and became a hallmark of the industry. Although other southern manufacturers, like those in tobacco, iron and steel, or forest products, employed blacks extensively, southern textiles remained a white bastion for more than 100 years.

Textile factories in the Northeast and the Middle Atlantic states also had predominantly white work forces, but that was more the product of demographic factors than overt discrimination. Moreover, these northern factories relied heavily upon immigrant labor from Europe and Canada. By contrast, southern companies used an overwhelmingly white, Anglo-Saxon, Protestant work force drawn from where the industry was located and from southern Appalachia. Employers found that in the economically underdeveloped South, textiles attracted an adequate supply of labor despite its low pay, its characteristic machine tending, and its slim prospects for promotion and upward mobility.

Southern mills used the "Slater system" of family labor for many years. The heavy reliance upon children under 16 for workers persisted in southern mills longer than elsewhere in the nation. Women always formed a large part of the work force in southern textiles, at times a majority. In fact, textiles probably is unique among manufacturing industries in the United States for employing males and females in nearly equal parts.

Until the selling of most of the company-owned mill villages after the mid-1930s, textile workers lived in company-owned houses. That, plus the power of the companies in local churches, schools, and even stores, gave management great power but not complete control over their labor. Management struggled with high rates of turnover and absenteeism and dealt with workers who often struck even if they were not union builders. Southern textile workers struck as early as the 1870s, and they precipitated the largest strike in American history, the Great Textile Strike of 1934. Southern textile workers even forced management not to reduce its low labor costs further by drawing upon the vast pool of black labor in the South. Management, on the other hand, used the threat of black labor as an effective means for setting limits to worker power, in particular defeating most efforts to unionize.

Individual homeownership, post–World War II economic growth, and the spread of the automobile and of television broke the bounds of the southern textile village. Once virtually the only alternative to farming, the textile industry and the life associated with it began to lose their hold after 1940. Southern textile workers began seeking jobs and futures elsewhere for themselves and their children. Government pressures and economic forces opened the textile industry to blacks after 1960. Once among the most racially segregated of southern laborers, textile workers became some of the most racially integrated, and the transformation occurred largely without violence.

Recent developments suggest that southern textiles will offer fewer jobs for blacks or whites and will play a diminishing role in the regional economy. As in many other manufacturing industries, southern textiles have become less labor-intensive, more capital-intensive, and more dependent upon overseas operations. Textiles and textile workers, the foot soldiers of the New South, are being displaced as a result of the growth of the New South.

See also INDUSTRY: / Textile Industry

> Tom E. Terrill
> University of South Carolina
> at Columbia

Mimi Conway, *Rise, Gonna Rise: A Portrait of Southern Textile Workers* (1979); Herbert J. Lahne, *The Cotton Mill Worker* (1944); J. Kenneth Morland, *Millways of Kent* (1958). ☆

TIMBER WORKERS

Laborers from England, Europe, and Africa were the first to exploit colonial southern forests for fuel, building materials, ship timber, and lumber for export. They also cleared trees and tapped and burned stately longleaf pines along the Atlantic and Gulf coasts for naval stores such as pitch, tar, and turpentine. The arduous forest work was done by hand. Originally, the chief tool was the cumbersome European felling ax, unimproved until the 18th century. Woodsmen sawed the felled trees on the spot, dragged the logs with draft animals, or floated them in streams to the sawmills. There others squared logs, and two men, one on the log and the other in a pit, sawed them. When waterpower was available, this hard work could be done by European up-and-down saws until steam-powered mills with circular saws appeared in the 19th century. Working in naval stores was also difficult. Making tar, a sideline to agriculture, occurred in wintertime after

Hauling logs in Heard County, Georgia, 1941

summer crops were harvested, but turpentine workers toiled the year round, chopping boxes into the pines, "chipping" the bark so the gum flowed, "dipping" the gum into barrels, and hauling it to the still. This work, performed mostly by blacks, was the least desirable.

After the Civil War, improved technology made some work easier. The woodsman got the double bit ax and crosscut saw; the driver, "caralog" wheels, eight-wheeled log wagons, and tramroads; the rafters, spoke poles, peavys, and jam spikes; and mill workers, improved feeding equipment. But long hours (12 to 14 a day) and low daily pay ($0.66 to $1.25) continued as large corporations began replacing small operators after 1800. Gradually, workers had to move to isolated company towns as the tramroads went deeper into the forests, and submit to the rigid discipline of industrialism. Many faced brutal bosses and exploitation at company stores. Some were held in peonage, especially blacks, who were the majority of the forest workers except in east Texas and western Louisiana. In the late 1880s workers around Pascagoula joined the Knights of Labor and struck for a 10-hour day, but these efforts failed. Labor shortages and spontaneous strikes in western Louisiana led to the formation in 1910 of the Brotherhood of Timber Workers (BTW). The union asked for a 10-hour day, a minimum wage, bimonthly paydays in United States currency, and the end to company-store and hospital-fee abuses. Confronted by organized employers (the Southern Lumber Operators Association), the BTW affiliated with the Industrial Workers of the World but lost their battle in the face of opposition and violence from employers, citizen organizations, and local police. In 1919 Bogalusa timber workers, organized biracially, were also crushed. But wage gains came with the passage of New Deal legislation, and World War II labor shortages brought women of both races into the forests and sawmills. American Federation of Labor and Congress of Industrial Organizations organizing drives after the war were disappointing. Meanwhile, new machines made the workers more insignificant and their economic position less viable. Subsequent gains resulted from increases in the minimum wage.

See also INDUSTRY: / Timber Industry

Merl E. Reed
Georgia State University

Ruth A. Allen, *East Texas Lumber Workers: An Economic and Social Picture, 1870–1950* (1961); James E. Fickle, *The New South and the "New Competition": A Case Study of Trade Association Developments in the Southern Pine Industry* (1980); Nollie Hickman, *Mississippi Harvest: Lumbering in the Longleaf Pine Belt, 1840–1915* (1962). ☆

TOBACCO WORKERS

The first tobacco workers were white indentured servants imported by the Virginia Company of London to work for up to seven years in return for their ocean passage. Tobacco proved so successful, however, that white servants were soon replaced by slaves, and slaves and tobacco spread first to Virginia, then into Kentucky and North Carolina. After the destruction of slavery, tobacco growing continued to spread, and staple-crop agriculture persisted in the South until after World War II.

A traditional and conservative social order with distinguishing attitudes, habits, values, and lifestyles emerged out of slavery, staple-crop agriculture, and the rural economy. After the Civil War, the tobacco culture transmitted rural culture. The tobacco field was a family—men, women, and children working together throughout the long growing season that stretched over almost a year. The tobacco field was a school, a place to learn skills for coping in a society where formal education was an unaffordable luxury and social mobility a distant dream for all except the largest tobacco farmers. Finally, it was a church, a place to inculcate traditional values and to integrate and harmonize these with the realities of inequality, injustice, and a caste system.

The Tobacco Workers' International Union (TWIU) started in 1895 and launched a boycott against the products of the industry giant, the American Tobacco Company. The union did not make a major impact on the industry, though, until signing a closed-shop agreement in December 1933 covering almost 4,600 laborers at the Brown and Williamson factories in Winston-Salem, N.C., Louisville, Ky., and Petersburg, Va. In the summer of 1937 the American Tobacco Company, Philip Morris, and Liggett and Myers signed contracts making the TWIU the bargaining agent for their factories in North Carolina and Virginia. By the beginning of World War II, the South's key tobacco companies were organized by the TWIU or other unions, except for 15,000 R. J. Reynolds employees. Unionization ef-

Assembly line work in a cigar factory, Louisville, Kentucky, 1931

forts among those workers, and other tobacco workers, would continue to be hampered by black-white tensions.

See also AGRICULTURE: / Tobacco Culture; INDUSTRY: / Tobacco Industry

Crandall Shiflett
Virginia Polytechnic Institute

Anthony J. Badger, *Prosperity Road: The New Deal, Tobacco and North Carolina* (1980); Federal Writers' Project, *These Are Our Lives* (1939); Herbert R. Northrup, *Quarterly Journal of Economics* (August 1942); Crandall Shiflett, *Patronage and Poverty in the Tobacco South: Louisa County, Virginia, 1860–1900* (1982). ☆

URBANIZATION

BLAINE A. BROWNELL

University of Alabama at Birmingham

CONSULTANT

☆ ☆ ☆ ☆ ☆ ☆ ☆ ☆ ☆ ☆ ☆ ☆ ☆ ☆ ☆

Overleaf: Street corner in New Orleans, 1940

URBANIZATION

|||||||||||||||||||||||||||||||||||||||||||||||||||||||||

Until the 20th century most historians of the United States considered cities mere by-products of national settlement or, at best, latecomers to the process. This seemed especially true for the South, the nation's most rural region. Towns and settlements were, however, footholds in a forbidding American wilderness and often precursors of agriculture. They grew up alongside the farm as necessary links in the patterns of regional and international trade, at first along the coast and the rivers and later across the sprawling interior. Such was also the case in the South, though the process of city building along the Chesapeake and the Tidewater was somewhat less pronounced because scores of rivers and thousands of tributaries penetrated the backcountry. Towns grew up everywhere, but few lasted long. In the early colonial era regional peculiarities did not overshadow the broad similarity of urbanization emerging across British North America.

Many southern towns still reflect the varied national legacies of their origins—the Spanish established St. Augustine in Florida and San Antonio in Texas, the French settled in New Orleans and Mobile, and the English founded Jamestown in 1607 and spread settlements inland. Each nation was attempting to exploit the opportunities of a new land and to forge commercial ties with Europe. In port cities such as Charleston and Savannah merchants clustered around the wharves with an eye on the ocean to which they had consigned their hopes and fortunes.

Throughout history cities have played a pervasive role in nurturing and transmitting culture, from high art to fads and fashions. Traditionally the sites of great institutions and large concentrations of population and resources, urban areas have been inherently more likely to encourage innovation and challenges to authority—a tendency that seemed to be especially pronounced along the frontiers of American settlement. Settlers were escaping from and clinging to an earlier cultural inheritance in the midst of a fresh but sometimes threatening landscape. The earliest southern cities were conduits of European culture, connected by paths of commerce to the Old World and the jumping off point for moves into the interior. They were centers of administrative authority and economic activity.

Antebellum Cities. Cities grew dramatically in the first decades of the 19th century as entrepreneurs, speculators, artisans, and common laborers sought opportunity in new places, usually further inland. As a result, fledgling towns dotted the southern landscape in Tennessee, Alabama, Mississippi, Louisiana, and Texas at the same time that the large plantations played a more prominent role in the region's self-image and its national reputation. The relationship between town and farm was very close, as a largely agricultural economy provided major commercial opportunities and towns competed for rural trade.

A civic elite emerged in antebellum cities and directed every aspect of urban development that mattered as the city strove for recognition and prosperity. Forty percent of Richmond's leadership elite served in posts in the city government, a quarter were stockholders in railroad or canal companies, and a third were involved in charity organizations. Control of the press in the community was the essential ingredient to this leadership group. Newspapers were the main medium for advertising, information, and boosterism. Prominent southern newspapers included the Richmond *Enquirer*, the Charleston *Mercury*, and the New Orleans *Bee*. Editors themselves were boosters. James A. Cowardin, editor of the Richmond *Daily Dispatch*, which was one of the nation's first penny presses, was on the Richmond Board of Trade, vice president of the Virginia Mechanics' Institute, president of a brokerage firm, and a member of the Virginia House of Delegates. Editors like Cowardin defended their cities from accusations by rival cities, as urban areas fought for advantages in the keen competition that led to either success and growth or eventual decline.

Antebellum cities took large steps in providing essential urban services. Major concerns of city governments were crime prevention; fire and police protection; installation of water systems; street lighting, paving, repair, and drainage; and the need for parks and city beautification. Private associations provided relief for the poor, although urban governments gradually became significant sources of financial support for it. Churches operated orphan asylums, and other groups ran houses for

widows or the elderly, and provided aid to the poor in general. Local governments established charity hospitals in some locations and almshouses almost everywhere. In locales such as Lexington, Ky., and Natchez, Miss., public education was a tradition by the time of the Civil War, but most city governments remained suspicious of public support for education. Lyceums and libraries encouraged adult education. Disease prevention was a major concern for urban areas throughout the nation, but especially in the South, where the climate made the region's people vulnerable to epidemics, such as the yellow fever plague that devastated Norfolk in 1855. Measures to encourage cleanliness proved to be the main weapon used by urban governments to prevent devastation from disease.

Antebellum cities were a part of the broader context of regional concerns. A considerable debate has taken place, for example, over whether or not southern towns were altogether inimical to chattel slavery, but, in any event, they surely appeared at least to undermine some of the more pronounced plantation features. Urban employers bargained for labor and were less likely than other southerners to inquire about a worker's status. The city provided slaves, and everyone else, a greater measure of anonymity and freedom from strict surveillance than rural areas. Cities attracted communities of free blacks and became magnets for freedmen after emancipation.

Impact of War. The Civil War devastated many southern urban areas. The business districts in Columbia and Charleston, S.C.; Fredericksburg, Petersburg, and Richmond, Va.; Selma, Ala.; and Atlanta, Ga., were all but destroyed. Even before the war the South's percentage of the nation's towns had been declining (in 1830 the 11 southern states that later became the Confederacy had 17.8 percent of the nation's towns; by 1860 the figure was 13.8 percent). The years of warfare spurred this decline. Many cities suffered because of the interruption in normal trade, damage to the surrounding farmlands, financial instability, disruption of public services, and loss of human life. For many cities, however, there were also benefits, such that the war was not the total disaster for urbanization that it has sometimes been portrayed. Cotton merchants in New Orleans and Memphis prospered after federal troops occupied those areas in 1862. Many cities escaped serious destruction, and some that were devastated, such as Atlanta, quickly recovered. The population of urban areas increased significantly during Reconstruction. Although older port cities such as New Orleans, Mobile, and Charleston did face a major recovery job after the war, the spread of the railroad brought the rise of new inland cities such as Atlanta, San Antonio, Houston, Dallas, and Birmingham. Older river towns like Memphis, Richmond, and Nashville continued to expand thanks to the expansion of the railroad system into their communities making them central locations for rail traffic. As before the war and as in other parts of the nation, the railroad was the key to success or failure of an urban area.

Expansion of Cities. Urban governments continued in the postbellum era the expansion of public services that had begun before the war. Advances were made in the growing cities in the installation of sewers, the paving of streets, the expansion of public edu-

cation, improved law enforcement and fire fighting, city beautification through parks, and the establishment of municipal-owned water companies and city-regulated private utilities. Again, as earlier, disease prevention was a central concern of the governments. Cholera devastated Nashville in 1873, while yellow fever had the same impact on Montgomery in the same year. Fighting diseases emptied city coffers and disrupted trade. New Orleans was most affected of all, though, as yellow fever epidemics hit the city in 1873 and 1878, when 3,977 died. Yellow fever hit Memphis in 1878 and killed 5,800 people, nearly half of them Irish. The well-off, including a large contingent of Germans who moved to St. Louis, fled the city.

The full impact of the Industrial Revolution, registered in the Northeast and Midwest in the last half of the 19th century, was felt in the South, but to a measurably lesser degree. The urban economy remained more commercial than industrial and more tied to agriculture. Major inland cities like Atlanta, Memphis, and Nashville did, to be sure, grow in this era, and New Orleans maintained its role as the region's dominant urban area. Birmingham emerged as a new industrial city and promoters created another new Alabama community, Anniston, as a planned industrial center. Boosterism and an urban-commercial ethos prevailed in all the region's larger cities, as they emphasized economic growth, new technology, strong local loyalty, and "progress." Chambers of commerce appeared in large and small towns. Downtown areas, which symbolized the concentration of urban power, people, and resources, appeared with new buildings and amenities.

Urban architecture at the turn of the

century was not, however, on the scale of the northern cities. Large office buildings did not dominate the skylines, but railroad stations, hotels, theaters, YMCAs, government office buildings, and churches did. Two- and three-story commercial buildings were erected after 1880 in business areas such as Second Avenue in Nashville and Commerce Street in Montgomery. Distinctive sections and neighborhoods within the cities, distinguishable by socioeconomic status and by racial composition, emerged. Central cities expanded through annexation and an increasing proliferation of retail and wholesale businesses. Growing suburbs surrounded a relatively dense central core, and urban patterns of trade and influence extended over a large area, perhaps even several counties.

These patterns were altogether like the urban configuration that appeared earlier in the North's largest cities, except that southern metropolises experienced decentralization at earlier stages of their development. At the beginning of the 20th century, in fact, some regional cities manifested arrangements that seemed almost preindustrial in character: a heavy concentration of business activity and upper-class residences near the city core, but with outlying shantytowns and a general mixture of populations and land uses throughout the central city.

Southern cities felt less of an impact in the late 19th century from foreign immigrants than their northern counterparts, but this should not lead to an underestimation of the importance of ethnic groups in southern cities. The Irish were a key part of the work force and the politics of Memphis, New Orleans, and Richmond. Merchants of Jewish ancestry were an important force

in business and politics in Atlanta and Montgomery. Near the end of the century, Italian immigrants flocked to New Orleans. To be sure, the percentage of foreign born in southern cities declined in this era, so that by 1900 only 3.4 percent of Richmond's population had been born on foreign soil, 4.6 percent of Charleston's, 6.3 percent of Savannah's, and 10 percent of New Orleans's. The proportion of foreign-born citizens declined in all major southern cities in the subsequent years. Between 1900 and 1940 the proportion of foreign residents in the populations of New Orleans and Norfolk dropped from 10.6 to 3 percent, and from 3.7 percent to 1.8 percent, respectively, and Houston (9.9 to 4) and Fort Worth (6.7 to 2) reflected a similar trend. In the Southwest, of course, a considerable number of foreign-born citizens were Mexican Americans. The impact of second- and third-generation members of ethnic groups remained significant, often greater than their numbers suggested.

The streetcar and the motor vehicle made their appearances before most southern urban areas had achieved the population densities characteristic of the largest 19th-century industrial cities. The first practical electric railway system, devised by Frank J. Sprague, was initiated in Richmond in 1888. By 1900 every large city in the South boasted a functioning streetcar system. Exclusive residential areas, such as Ghent in Norfolk and Annesdale Park in Memphis, were generally the first streetcar suburbs to appear in the South. Atlanta developer Joel Hurt pioneered that city's first residential suburb, Inman Park, in 1887 and also built the city's first electric street railway in 1889. Streetcars constituted the foundation of the urban transportation sys-

Alfred R. Waud, **Sunday in New Orleans—The French Market** *(1866)*

tem until about 1920, when they were challenged by the private passenger automobile and the motor bus; but they continued to transport the majority of passengers in and out of central business districts through the 1930s.

The transportation revolution initiated by the trolley was completed by the automobile. In 1920 motor vehicle registrations totaled approximately 20,000 in the Atlanta, New Orleans, and Memphis metropolitan areas, 16,000 in Birmingham, and 12,000 in Nashville. During the decade the increase in registrations ranged from about 192 percent in Memphis to 337 in Birmingham. Atlanta accounted for almost 20 percent of all the automobiles and motor trucks in Georgia in 1920, New Orleans contained a quarter of the registered vehicles in Louisiana, and Memphis and Nashville together accounted for almost a third of Tennessee's vehicle registration in 1920 and for more than a quarter by the end of the decade. Traffic congestion and problems of parking and

auto safety loomed larger as automobile registrations mounted, and some local leaders and businessmen began to question the motor vehicle's usefulness in the city even at this early date.

As elsewhere in the country the principal means of increasing city size was annexation of surrounding communities and territory. Significant population growth on the urban fringes was a major impetus for annexation in southern cities. Between 1900 and 1920 Birmingham increased its land area by almost seven times through the "Greater Birmingham" annexation of 1910. In 1909 Fort Worth doubled its land area by acquiring North Fort Worth, and doubled it again in 1922 with the addition of Arlington Heights, Riverside, and other outlying settlements. Atlanta more than doubled its geographic size in the first two decades of the century, and added even more territory during the 1920s. Knoxville's geographical size in 1920 was more than five and a half times what it had been 20 years earlier.

The first few years of the century witnessed a significant and growing differentiation between places of work and residence. Certainly, the skylines of 1940 bore little resemblance to those at the turn of the century. New office buildings—reverently identified as "skyscrapers"—hovered over major downtown intersections in the larger southern cities, and cast their shadows over the two- and three-story structures that characterized an earlier time. Together, these monuments to commercial and civic success formed impressive corridors in the heart of downtown, conveying a sense of both permanence and dynamism.

Commercial-Civic Elite. The greatest influence over economic and political affairs in the early 20th-century urban South was exerted by a commercial-civic elite composed of larger merchants, real estate agents, insurance brokers, bankers, contractors, and a variety of other people—attorneys, journalists, doctors, teachers, clergymen, and city officials—who were associated directly or indirectly with the business middle class. The social and economic interests of this elite group were wide ranging, but were concentrated primarily in the local area and specifically in the downtown business district. Perhaps the most important local associations they initiated were the chambers of commerce that took upon themselves the burdens of urban problems and tried to solve them. Besides their function as meeting places and discussion groups for the local elite, chambers usually maintained a lobby in the state legislature, dispatched members into surrounding counties and states to drum up business for the city, raised funds for national advertising drives, promoted

more "efficient" forms of government, and advocated comprehensive city planning. In the opinion of some observers, local chambers actually served as quasi-governments.

The commercial-civic elite was the most influential group in the southern city, but it did not preside over a monolithic community power structure. Its members did not agree on all matters of public policy, and they did not have anything resembling absolute control over public opinion and the electorate. Competing interest groups often forced commercial and civil organizations to back away from controversial issues, and many municipal governments were not powerful enough to impose specific business goals.

Clearly, though, the commercial-civic elite reigned supreme throughout the early 20th century, reaching its heyday in the business decade of the 1920s when its leadership was virtually unquestioned. The Depression was a genuine crisis for this group: the economy did not respond to any of the old, safe remedies, and enlightened free enterprise was unable to stem the tide of unemployment or even care successfully for its victims. But while the initiative may have passed to the national government in 1932 and 1933, the commercial-civic elite did not fade away. On the contrary, some of its members presided over the administration of government programs and actively solicited federal funds for civic projects.

Urban Change Since World War II. World War II was an important dividing line in southern history including the level of urbanization. The war not only brought a flood of GIs to southern ports and training centers, but ushered in probably the most dramatic period of social and demographic change in the region. The economic expansion in the immediate postwar era created new suburban communities and rising demands for more services. The major seaports of New Orleans, Galveston-Houston, Mobile, Charleston, Norfolk-Portsmouth, and Savannah gained increased trade and new shipyards through their strategic locations. Investments in Houston's chemical industry reached $600 million by the end of the war. Even inland cities could profit, as did Huntsville, Ala., where the construction of the Redstone Arsenal brought new prosperity and a final end of the Depression. Growth in such southern cities was often uncontrolled. Mobile, which had two major shipyards and an aluminum factory, grew from a 1940 population of 114,906 to a 1944 figure of 201,369. People from nearby rural areas flocked to the town and overwhelmed existing housing and municipal services. John Dos Passos visited Mobile in 1943 and wrote that it looked "trampled and battered like a city that's been taken by storm." The public schools could not cope with the burgeoning enrollments, and the police force struggled to handle higher levels of juvenile delinquency, robbery, racial conflict, and labor unrest that went with urban growth during the war.

Military installations and defense industries, such as Fort Benning in Columbus, Ga., Eglin Field in Florida, Fort Bragg in Fayetteville, N.C., and Lacklin Field in San Antonio, were vital to the economic growth of their areas. Many bases were established or greatly expanded during the war, and they retained their importance during the Cold War years. Powerful southern politicians, such as Mendel Rivers, who made Charleston into a booming military town, protected the interests of the cities they represented. The national space program proved to be an economic supplement to Houston, New Orleans, and other towns along the Gulf Coast, stretching to Florida.

Increased mobility also promoted economic development of the South's postwar cities. The expansion of the automobile industry, the building of the interstate highway system, and the growth of commercial aviation allowed major corporations to locate large factories in the region, transfer branch offices, and lure retirees to warmer climes. The tourist industry became a major factor. Since the late 1960s Houston, Dallas, Tampa, Shreveport, and Atlanta have built new air terminals to encourage the movement of goods and people.

The 20th century in general has continued to erode the differences between cities in the South and other regions, especially because of the new transportation and communications technologies that transformed all of urban America in this period. As the automobile stimulated new development on the urban fringe, the radio and later television brought national urban tastes and fashions in a most direct way to the urban South, and southern cities increasingly provided to surrounding rural areas the goods and fashions, the music and other entertainment made popular by these media. And air-conditioning may, as much as anything else, have helped pave the way for new migrations from the North and the influx of new businesses and industries that gave rise to the idea of the Sunbelt.

In the 1950s and 1960s the South confronted its legacy of racial injustice through bitter and often violent challenges to the structure and rationale of segregation. These conflicts took place in the major cities as well as in the small towns and reached an apogee in the Birmingham marches and bombings and the passage of the Civil Rights Act of 1964. The fall of segregation did not by any means erase the shadow of racism, but it did open the region for new growth and economic opportunities. By the 1970s blacks were playing an increasingly large role in the urban politics of major cities leading to the successful mayoral campaigns of Maynard Jackson (1973) and Andrew Young (1981) in Atlanta, Richard Arrington in Birmingham (1979), and Ernest "Dutch" Morial in New Orleans (1977). The success of black politicians has been followed by greater involvement by others traditionally left out of power, symbolized by the victories of Henry Cisneros in San Antonio (1981) and Kathy Whitmire in Houston (1981).

By the 1970s the Old South urban image had given way to that of the Sunbelt, a region generally defined as the southern half of the country from coast to coast. Here interstate highways, satellite relays, lower taxes, the relative absence of labor unions, a good climate, more land, and a "better quality of life" underwrote a shift in population from the Northeast and Midwest to the South and Southwest. Working-class whites fleeing Frostbelt economic problems have migrated south, and white-collar executives have come to the region as managers of branch offices or as part of the transfer of company headquarters.

The middle class is increasingly setting the tone not only for contemporary southern cities but for the region's culture as a whole. Post–World War II prosperity has strengthened the urban middle class, which is made up of professionals, white-collar workers,

business people, and blue-collar workers. Since the 1960s middle-class southerners, like other middle-class Americans, have left the cities for suburbs and a commuting lifestyle. These suburbs are much like those in the rest of the nation. The flight from urban areas has meant the loss of revenue sources for urban governments, and the failure of some suburban communities to provide needed schools, recreational areas, and services has strained the resources of nearby cities. The white middle class has recently shown a tendency to move back into southern cities in a gentrification of downtown neighborhoods in places such as Atlanta, Memphis, and Charlotte. The extent and long-range implications of this trend remain to be seen.

Southern cities have worked to create distinctive images. State and metropolitan convention bureaus vigorously promote the advantages of each southern city. Most stress the appeal of a good business climate and a more leisurely lifestyle and milder weather than in the North. Cities also promote themselves using images from the past—Memphis now attracts middle-class tourists by marketing the blues music that once was mainly for the poor, while Savannah and Charleston promote their historic-preservation projects as recreational sites.

Urban growth in the period since World War II has led to social, economic, and cultural changes in the South. The landscape has changed, with shopping malls, apartment complexes, subdivisions, and traffic loops merely the most obvious expression of the new look and expansive spirit. The development of a large urban middle class brought the appearance of major league sports. Viewing the matter in terms of civic pride, southern cities built new stadiums and arenas in order to lure professional teams south. By the 1980s there were major league baseball teams in Houston, Atlanta, and Arlington, Tex., and National Football League franchises in Dallas, Miami, Houston, Atlanta, Tampa, and New Orleans. The short-lived World Football League had clubs in eight southern states, and the now-defunct United States Football League established teams in Birmingham, Tampa Bay, Memphis, Jacksonville, Orlando, San Antonio, and Houston. Professional basketball teams play in Houston, New Orleans, San Antonio, Atlanta, and Norfolk–Hampton Roads, Va. Professional hockey is played in Atlanta and Houston. Dallas is the headquarters for World Championship Tennis and a soccer league. Golf tournaments and stock car races occur in dozens of southern cities.

The past two decades have witnessed an expansion of support for the arts in the urban South. Cities built theaters, concert halls, and exhibition centers. New Orleans completed the Rivergate International Exhibition Facility and the Theater for the Performing Arts in the 1970s and renovated its Municipal Auditorium. Shreveport built a new convention center, which opened in 1965. Houston saw the opening of the Jesse H. Jones Hall for the Performing Arts in 1966 and the Alley Theater in 1968. Southern urban leaders oversaw an architectural renaissance that reflected their confidence. Atlanta became the epitome of achitectural boosterism. A new airport, civic center, and the Peachtree Center (a downtown redevelopment project) became symbols of Atlanta's progressive spirit in the 1970s. John Portman's Regency-Hyatt House has become a symbol of symbols with futuristic elevators, a dangling cocktail lounge, and a revolving dome, which affords an excellent vantage from which to see what civic boosters have wrought. Other cities have encouraged a similar booster architecture of civic centers, luxury hotels, and domed stadiums, such as in Houston's Astrodome and New Orleans's Superdome.

Higher education expanded to meet the needs of the growing urban populations. Branch campuses of southern universities were opened in major cities such as Little Rock, Birmingham, New Orleans, San Antonio, Arlington, and Dallas. Small state colleges were upgraded to university status. Georgia State College in Atlanta, once a part of Georgia Tech's evening school, became Georgia State University. Southeastern College in Hammond, La., became Southeastern Louisiana University, and McNeese State College in Lake Charles became McNeese State University.

Regional Heritage and Cities. The question of the distinctiveness of southern cities has been a major concern of scholars studying southern urbanization. Southern cities were certainly always more like their counterparts—of comparable age and size—in other regions than they were like the surrounding hinterlands. They were generally affected by major new technologies at about the same time, if not precisely to the same degree, as cities in the North and West. And southern cities hardly had a monopoly on ethnic or racial prejudice, crime and violence, or strong religious inclinations and an orientation to family. But they could not escape the legacies of the region that contained them, and they reflected regional circumstances and tendencies that in some forms persist to this day.

Race—the often noted "key" to understanding southern history—had its urban dimension, and indeed regional cities cannot be comprehended without taking its effects into account. In the American South, ethnicity was overwhelmingly a matter of black or white, with one race in subjugation to the other. Innumerable threads of affection, nuance, and exception ran through this fabric, making it much more complex than it appears at first glance; but, still, the social division of the region into black and white, master and slave, merchant and common laborer determined the pattern. After emancipation blacks were pushed to the lowest rungs of the occupational ladder, and the reign of Jim Crow was firmly established in the statute books by the first decade of the 20th century. Blacks attended segregated schools in cities, lived in mostly segregated housing, were relegated to separate seating in theaters and streetcars, and were either segregated in parks and other public places or denied admittance altogether. Continual police harassment was periodically punctuated by drives to arrest "vagrants" (usually blacks without regular employment), and those arrested might well find themselves acting as conscripted city laborers. Black freedoms were further circumscribed by curfews instituted in black sections and by outbreaks of white vigilantism.

In cities, at least, though, blacks were more likely to find, in whatever period, relatively more opportunity for self-determination, no matter how constricted it might be. Greater opportunity in the urban centers of the North fueled the massive migration of southern blacks to New York, Chicago, Philadelphia, Cleveland, and Detroit in the late 19th and early 20th centuries. But blacks often migrated to southern cities first. As far back as the 1870s black neighborhoods with distinctive institutions such as Shermantown and Summer Hill in Atlanta and Black Bottom and Rocktown in Nashville had appeared on the fringe of southern cities near railroad tracks, industrial sites, and contaminated waterways. At the beginning of this century such black settlements were scattered—huddled next to railroad tracks, warehouses, and factories, along the rivers in Nashville and Memphis, and in alleyways, low-lying places, and even wooded areas along the city's fringe. The prevailing type of housing more closely resembled the small sharecroppers' cabins of the rural South—some divided into duplexes—than the congested tenements and older single-family homes that predominated in northern ghettoes. In most southern cities, especially New Orleans and Charleston, few census tracts contained populations that were less than 10 or 20 percent white or black. The racial heterogeneity in census districts was, however, misleading. Many blacks living in predominantly white areas were servants who occupied quarters behind their employers' homes, and clusters of black residences contiguous to white sections were like islands set apart. The pattern in all southern cities during the 20th century was one of advancing racial segregation and the increasing concentration of blacks in fewer, larger residential areas near the urban core.

The increasing racial segregation in the early 20th-century South opened the way for a new group of ambitious black entrepreneurs, who pursued the main chance with the vigor of their white counterparts and directed their efforts toward the black consumer. An older elite of clergymen, barbers, contractors, and house servants gave way to a newer elite of skilled laborers, larger merchants, doctors, lawyers, and other professional and business types. The new black elite advocated—as had most of their forebears—a philosophy of thrift, hard work, property ownership, material advancement, and even urban boosterism. Though oriented toward the city rather than the farm, these businessmen supported the goals of Booker T. Washington—especially as they were expressed by the National Negro Business League—and called for an end to ideological conflicts among national black spokesmen and organizations. They were not, however, passive accommodationists. Throughout the period black business and civic leaders protested the economic restrictions and legal sanctions applied to their race and lamented the conditions in their communities.

Indeed, most black residential areas were marked by poor housing, horrendous sanitation facilities, inadequate schools, police harassment rather than protection, and unpaved streets that turned to an impenetrable mire in heavy rains. But southern urban blacks contributed forcefully to the improvement of their communities in a number of ways, and their accomplishments are all the more impressive considering the obstacles cast in their way. As the 20th century advanced, black communities became larger and more complex, economically diverse, and socially organized. Black civic and service organizations proliferated, along with existing religious and fraternal groups, especially in those cities with a significant black middle class.

The impact of Afro-Americans on southern culture has been, of course, both substantial and abiding, and al-most impossible to measure with precision. The large black districts in the cities, with their distinct yet related subcultures, are a profound historical fact, comparable to the large communities of foreign immigrants in northern urban centers, and with perhaps even greater cultural influence. The culture of the urban South is thus a biracial project, though whites have not always been inclined to admit it. The relatively greater penchant among southerners for the institutions of family and church, for example, is certainly a shared cultural tendency.

Another aspect of 20th-century regional urban distinctiveness was the rural legacy of the South. It was etched in the urban landscape. Patches of open space, even close to downtown, were more common in southern cities, as were residential plots replete with chickens and pigs (though these were banished by public health ordinances in the 20th century). The old-time religion of the countryside was brought to town embodied by small churches, wandering gospel tents, and strictures against alcohol, gambling, Sabbath activities, and even public dancing.

A quick resort to violence among southern urban dwellers seemed very much a part of the regional heritage. The ancient doctrine of personal honor, once

Mule with wagon come to town, Columbus, Georgia, 1941

held high by a plantation aristocracy, somehow persisted among the lower classes of urban blacks and whites. If one can believe local newspaper reports, large numbers of men in both races and of all social classes habitually packed sidearms in city streets, and a profusion of weapons would appear on the slightest pretext. Reporters working the downtown sections considered a pencil, a bottle of whiskey, and a revolver standard equipment. Such reports appear to be confirmed by the relatively high murder rates in southern cities in the early 20th century. Memphis was titled the "murder capital of the world" in 1916, when 89 homicides per 100,000 people were recorded. Murder rates in Atlanta, Nashville, and New Orleans rose in the 1920s by 32 percent, 183 percent, and 44 percent, respectively. On the whole, homicide rates in major southern cities have substantially exceeded those in the North and Midwest. The most articulate and persuasive explanation for this phenomenon focuses on the southern "worldview" or on a "feudal agrarian myth" that demanded violence as a perverse cement of community.

The "rural" features of southern cities were not unique: urban America was largely populated by newcomers from the countryside. But the patterns of rusticity were perhaps more distinctive in the South; the region was, after all, largely rural and few migrants came from outside the South. Not surprisingly, some of these cultural tendencies were actually focused, enlarged, and formalized in cities, where larger audiences and better communications encouraged the recording and distribution of folktales, folksongs, and oral traditions. The twangy, plaintive music sung by rural whites and the rolling, mournful sounds of black blues found their ways into southern urban streets and alleyways and from there to a national and international audience. On the other hand, southern cities also fostered a prejudice toward the untutored and unsophisticated countryside, and recent rural newcomers were frequently the subjects of urban humor.

Ambivalence marked the historic role of southern cities as much as irony and tragedy seemed to characterize the history of the region as a whole. As cultural crucibles they provided greater focus for traditional, regional culture at the same time that they introduced new currents from the rest of the nation and the world. They boasted of their regional heritage and simultaneously claimed kinship with larger cities elsewhere. They celebrated the Lost Cause mythology while also calling for new technologies and joking about country bumpkins. In the final analysis southern cities were both southern and urban.

See also EDUCATION: Urbanization and Education; GEOGRAPHY: Towns and Villages; INDUSTRY: Sunbelt South; / Atlanta as Commercial Center; Grady, Henry W.; LANGUAGE: New Orleans English; Urban Speech; MYTHIC SOUTH: New South Myth

Blaine A. Brownell
University of Alabama
at Birmingham

Carl Abbott, *The New Urban America: Growth and Politics in Sunbelt Cities* (1981); Richard M. Bernard and Bradley R. Rice, eds., *Sunbelt Cities: Politics and Growth since World War II* (1983); Blaine A. Brownell, *The Urban Ethos in the South, 1920–1930* (1975), with David R. Goldfield, eds., *The City in Southern History: The Growth of Urban Civilization in the South* (1977); James C. Cobb, *South Atlantic Urban Stud-*

ies, vol. 1 (1977); Leonard Curry, *Journal of Southern History* (February 1974); David R. Goldfield, *Cotton Fields and Skyscrapers: Southern City and Region, 1607–1980* (1982), in *Perspectives on the American South*, vol. 3, ed. James C. Cobb and Charles Reagan Wilson (1985); David C. Perry and Alfred J. Watkins, eds., *The Rise of the Sunbelt Cities* (1977); Howard N. Rabinowitz, *Race Relations in the Urban South, 1865–1890* (1978); Leonard Reissman, *Journal of Social Issues* (February 1966); William Tabb and Larry Sawyers, eds., *Sunbelt/Snowbelt: Urban Development and Regional Restructuring* (1984); Rupert B. Vance and Nicholas J. Demerath, eds., *The Urban South* (1954); Richard C. Wade, *Slavery in the Cities: The South, 1820–1960* (1964). ☆

Segregation, Residential

||||||||||||||||||||||||||||||||||||||||||||||||||||||||||

Residential segregation has shaped the nature of southern urban life. At times, particularly during the antebellum period, this segregation has had an ethnic foundation. During the mid-19th century Nashville had its Germantown and Little Ireland, by the end of the century there was a pronounced Italian section in New Orleans, and even today there are such ethnic communities as San Antonio's Mexican American westside ghetto and Miami's Little Havana. There also has been economic segregation. On one end of the economic ladder were the factory districts of the mill towns and some of the larger cities, while at the other end were fashionable neighborhoods like Birmingham's South Highland and Atlanta's Buckhead. But the basic form of residential segregation has been racial. The extent of such segre-

gation has always varied from city to city, but southern cities in general have been more racially segregated than their northern counterparts. Although some blacks and whites could always be found living near each other, most southern blacks have historically lived among themselves in dispersed clusters that contained their own institutions and businesses.

Prior to the Civil War, however, segregation was less of a factor in southern residential life. The mass of urban slaves lived within the compounds of their owners, usually above the stable or kitchen, or in other outbuildings at the rear of the property. Yet, even then, the future pattern was already emerging. Some slaves were housed in barracks owned by industrial, commercial, or public employers. Others joined concentrations of free Negroes on the fringes of the antebellum city where they were freer from white surveillance.

In the years immediately after the war, some freedmen remained in the alley dwellings or shacks behind their former master's house and worked as domestics and handymen. This way of life persisted longest in older cities like Charleston and Savannah. In younger cities like Atlanta, Birmingham, and Houston, blacks flocked to the remnants of the old free black enclaves or to the remains of the freedmen camps set up earlier by the victorious Yankees. And in both types of cities new areas on the outskirts were thrown open to black settlement. Rows of shotgun or doublepen cottages spread across the least desirable locations—low-lying areas subject to flooding and epidemics and often adjacent to cemeteries, railroad yards, industrial plants, or other unhealthy sites. Such elemental city services as paved streets, lighting, and water supply were normally absent in these areas and remained so for many years to come. The houses themselves had only the most primitive sanitary facilities, were poorly constructed and therefore subject to frequent fires, and were better suited to rural than urban living. In 1877, for example, the Nashville Board of Health reported that the city's blacks "reside mainly in old stables, situated upon alleys in the midst of privy vaults, or in wooden shanties a remnant of war times, or in huts closely crowded together on the outskirts." Even if the buildings had been structurally sound and healthful, the severe overcrowding in each dwelling, where there was often more than one family per room, would still have made most of them unfit for human habitation.

As the century drew to a close, southern cities exhibited residential patterns more characteristic of preindustrial cities than of the typical city then emerging in the rapidly industrializing North. In the latter, the poor and unskilled tended to live close to downtown, while the middle- and upper classes took advantage of transportation breakthroughs that allowed them to flee the increasingly industrialized centers for newly accessible land on the periphery. In contrast, middle- and upper-class white southerners continued to live in large houses on spacious tree-lined streets near the core of cities that remained primarily commercial. When industry did develop in southern cities, it was normally along the railroad tracks on the edges of the city, areas to which blacks and other working-class people were drawn. Furthermore, while the influx of immigrants to northern cities increased, the South's antebellum immigrants were becoming assimilated and dispersed throughout the city. They were joined by a relatively

small number of eastern and southern European immigrants who, after some brief initial concentration, were integrated into the community. Such, of course, was not the case with blacks. Although typically found in scattered clusters, rather than the one or two large ghettoes that housed recent immigrants in northern cities and would house a later generation of blacks, southern blacks were segregated to an unprecedented degree within these smaller districts.

Poor white workers of native stock could sometimes be found mixed in among the blacks, together with small businessmen of foreign descent, widows, and others with limited mobility. But there was no question as to "where the niggers lived." Much of the resultant segregation was voluntary as blacks sought out their "own kind," or were attracted by the proliferating number of churches, schools, and places of entertainment established in these new areas. Still other blacks were attracted by the proximity of the unskilled and semiskilled jobs most commonly available for them. Black business streets often formed the spines of these neighborhoods. Here were the shops of black barbers, grocers, and undertakers, cheap hotels and bars, and eventually the offices of black doctors and lawyers. The major streets, as in the case of Atlanta's "Sweet Auburn," might also have the meeting hall of one or more fraternal orders, an office of the black-owned Atlanta Life Insurance Company, several churches, a theater, and perhaps some "high-class" clubs or restaurants. Blacks would still do much of their shopping in the white-owned clothing stores, pawn shops, and groceries on the street, or in the downtown establishments that provided segregated service, but for most southern urban blacks residential segregation clearly meant more than simply the absence of white neighbors—it was the foundation of the region's biracial society. As early as 1881 an Atlanta reporter could conclude that "far the largest proportion of Negroes are never really known to us. They are not employed in private homes nor in the business houses, but drift off to themselves, and are almost as far from the white people, so far as all practicable benefits of associations are concerned, as if the two races never met."

But this situation was not entirely voluntary. After all, an important degree of forced segregation especially affected middle-class blacks. Indeed, segregation in southern cities, to an even greater degree than in the North, was racial rather than economic, at least for blacks. Middle-class blacks were denied opportunities open to either their southern white counterparts or their black counterparts in the North, and they found themselves confined to the least attractive sections of the city with the poorest of their race and kept out of better neighborhoods they could afford to live in. Occasionally, such middle-class blacks might be found in neighborhoods or on blocks that were mostly white, but, as a rule, the whites were far below them in socioeconomic status.

Nevertheless, by the turn of the century enclaves of middle-class black housing emerged, like the one on Atlanta's west side that was built around what became the Atlanta University Center. Yet unlike in the North such neighborhoods were not the products of succession in which blacks moved into areas that once housed large numbers of whites. Instead, as was historically the case for southern blacks in general,

such neighborhoods were newly constructed for blacks (often by blacks) on either recently annexed land or land that was deemed unsuitable for whites. The fear of black expansion into white neighborhoods, however, led some cities to substitute de jure housing segregation for their existing de facto system. Baltimore led the way in 1910 with an ordinance requiring separate white and black neighborhoods. Then between 1911 and 1913 other cities, including Richmond and Atlanta, passed similar laws. Between 1913 and 1916 the laws spread westward to Louisville, St. Louis, New Orleans, and Oklahoma City. Such threats to middle-class black interests led the NAACP to challenge the Louisville law. Its efforts were rewarded in 1917 when the U.S. Supreme Court in *Buchanan* v. *Warley* declared legally enforced residential segregation unconstitutional. More laws were in fact passed after 1917, but in every case they were found to be unconstitutional. Yet restrictive covenants and other private arrangements remained in force, and, ironically, the degree of residential segregation increased significantly in both the North and South between 1910 and 1930. This was due partly to the migration of blacks, producing huge ghettoes in northern cities, but it was also due to the rapid growth of newer southern cities that lacked the region's old tradition of "backyard integration."

In the years following World War II, residential segregation continued to increase in southern cities at the same time that it began to decrease elsewhere in the country under the impact of rising black militancy and federal, state, and local antidiscrimination statutes. Few southern cities had the kind of large-scale ghettoes that dominated black life in the North, but a higher percentage of blacks continued to reside in the numerous smaller racial clusters that characterized southern urban life. This was the result of private action as well as municipal manipulation of transportation routes and the choice of sites for segregated public housing. Thus, by 1960 only 5.5 percent of the southern urban population lived in integrated neighborhoods, compared to 31.8 percent in the Northeast. Between 1964 and 1967 the percentage of southern urban blacks living in census tracts that were more than 75 percent black increased from 65 percent to 78 percent in Memphis, 79 percent to 90 percent in Shreveport, and 86 percent to 88 percent in Nashville.

In recent years there has been an increase in class segregation among southern blacks, a process that is historically more identified with northern cities. This change was due to a great surge in the number of middle-class blacks combined with the presence of new opportunities for better housing as whites moved to the suburbs. Such internal segregation continues, however, to be rarer than among whites. Racial discrimination is one obvious cause but so too is the relative homogeneity of the black occupational structure. The persistence of segregation also obscures differences in origins, compared to the past. The extent of neighborhood succession, that is, black migrants moving into once predominantly white areas, long the common road to segregation in the North, has now become more frequent in the South in the wake of more effective enforcement of fair housing legislation and the scarcity of unoccupied land for black housing. Furthermore, so-called displacement, in which whites replace blacks following

urban renewal or redevelopment, is also on the rise, though now the North is also moving in this direction. Then, too, the movement of middle- and upper-class whites to the suburbs and the consolidation of many black areas within the center of the city have produced a coring pattern more like that of the North, though as late as 1970, 14 percent of the South's metropolitan black population resided on the periphery, frequently in semirural areas, compared to 3 percent in the Northeast.

Patterns of racially determined residential segregation in northern and southern cities are now more similar than they have been at any time in the past, but, in the degree of segregation, its persistence within dispersed clusters, and the rural character of so much black urban housing, the regional uniqueness of southern housing patterns is still evident. The impact of these differences should continue to affect southern urban culture for years to come.

See also BLACK LIFE: Business, Black; Race Relations

Howard N. Rabinowitz
University of New Mexico

Ronald H. Bayor, *Georgia Historical Quarterly* (Winter 1979); Leonard P. Curry, *The Free Black in Urban America, 1800–1850* (1981); John Kellogg, *Geographical Review* (July 1977); Howard N. Rabinowitz, *Race Relations in the Urban South, 1865–1890* (1978); Roger Rice, *Journal of Southern History* (May 1968); Karl Taeuber and Alma F. Taeuber, *Negroes in Cities: Residential Segregation and Neighborhood Change* (1965); Richard C. Wade, *Slavery in the Cities: The South, 1820–1960* (1964). ☆

Urban Boosterism

||||||||||||||||||||||||||||||||||||||||

The southerner's penchant for, and enjoyment of, florid oratorical and literary expression attained its urban apogee in the person of the urban booster. Boosterism, as Sinclair Lewis noted, was a phenomenon of Main Street America. Few boosters, however, surpassed the evangelical fervor, continued popularity, and sense of purpose of the southerners.

The urban booster was an economic and political leader whose immediate objective was to promote a particular program and whose ultimate goal was to unite the citizenry behind his leadership. Surfacing in the late antebellum era, he was a product of the fierce urban competition for markets and internal improvements and of the rise of the penny press, which spread the gospel of progress to unanointed readers. The antebellum urban booster left two legacies to his postwar colleagues—an urban consciousness and huge debts. For the first time citizens were asked to think about "the city" as a distinctive entity possessing a personality and an image of its own. Future boosters utilized this consciousness to implement their projects.

The period between 1865 and 1930 was the golden era for the southern urban booster as he became enshrined along with Civil War heroes in the rhetorical pantheon that historian Paul M. Gaston referred to as the New South creed. The creed emphasized industrialization and urbanization while at the same time paying homage to Old South values. This combination of progressive rhetoric steeped in southern tradition suited the booster perfectly because it linked economic growth with political and social stability. Atlanta journalist Henry W. Grady became the major oracle of the creed, coaxing northern investments and southern stock subscriptions while also promoting white supremacy.

By 1900, despite Grady's proselytizing, southern economic development lagged further behind the North than it had in 1860. But failure was not part of the booster vocabulary and, if anything, boosters redoubled their efforts to obtain elusive growth. As part of the effort to improve their city's image, boosters embarked on extensive public works campaigns in the early decades of the 20th century, including street paving, electric lighting, and sewer and water services. They also avidly sought land accretions through annexation so that population and area figures would swell. Memphis political boss Edward H. Crump became so enraptured with census recordings of Memphis progress through population growth (primarily as a result of timely annexations) that he even recommended the 10-year federal census be taken every five years.

During the 1920s the "commercial-civic elite," as historian Blaine A. Brownell called the boosters of that decade, became more strident as their rhetoric became more hollow. The New South creed's neglect and even vilification of blacks and workers, as well as the evident failures of southern economic development, resulted in challenges to the booster ideal in the late 1920s when much of the South had lapsed into the depression that was soon to engulf the nation. Thomas Wolfe railed against the boosters' "dusty little pint-measure minds" and the conformity they enforced on a naive community slumping perceptibly toward bankruptcy. For Faulkner, the amoral Snopes clan embodied the precepts of booster acquisitiveness, and the Nashville Agrarians took their stand against false prophets and profits by restating the basic humanistic and rural qualities of southern culture.

Despite attacks by Wolfe, Faulkner, and the Agrarians, the boosters weathered the Depression and emerged from the war ready to evangelize a new generation of southern urban residents. In many respects, the religious metaphor is well-taken because boosters and evangelists, especially since 1945, have adopted similar techniques—measuring success in numbers and eschewing social issues. Boosters touted low wages and the absence of unions as regional benefactions, and they received industries appropriate to these attractions—low-wage, low-skill enterprises that exploited natural resources and took profits from the region.

If boosters were not successful during the immediate postwar years in generating quality development, they were successful in projecting positive urban images. Atlanta led the field with campaign slogans such as the "Atlanta Spirit," "Forward Atlanta," "A City too Busy to Hate," and "The International City" to attract growth and investment. More recently, boosters have sold history, as in New Orleans and Charleston, where preservation movements assume the proportions of big business, though the traditional temptation for monumental buildings such as luxury hotels and civic centers persists in these cities as well.

Ironically, when genuine prosperity finally washed over the region in the 1960s and 1970s, urban boosters were caught short as development tended to occur on the periphery while decay and population loss threatened urban vitality. Bankruptcy stalked new development in Atlanta, and deteriorated centers gnawed at Montgomery, Nashville, and Richmond. In spite of such problems southern urban boosters have continued to pursue growth in downtown redevelopment and historic preservation programs. Growing black and Hispanic constituencies have forced social issues on the shallow growth ethic, and contemporary boosters operate in a different political milieu from their predecessors who enjoyed the fruits of economic, political, and racial hegemony.

See also HISTORY AND MANNERS: Historic Preservation; INDUSTRY articles; MYTHIC SOUTH: New South Myth

David R. Goldfield
University of North Carolina
at Charlotte

Blaine A. Brownell, *The Urban Ethos in the South, 1920–1930* (1975); Charles Paul Garofalo, *Journal of Southern History* (May 1976); Paul M. Gaston, *The New South Creed: A Study in Southern Mythmaking* (1970); David R. Goldfield, *Urban Growth in the Age of Sectionalism: Virginia, 1847–1861* (1977); Harold H. Martin, *William Berry Hartsfield: Mayor of Atlanta* (1978); Merl E. Reed, *New Orleans and the Railroads: The Struggle for Commercial Empire* (1966); George B. Tindall, *South Atlantic Quarterly* (Autumn 1965). ☆

Urban Growth

For a century and a half urban growth in the South has held out the expectation of bringing social patterns and values into line with national norms. As the points of contact between agricultural hinterlands and the international economy, the cities of the 19th-century South were strongly drawn toward comparable centers of the North. During the years leading to the Civil War, trading towns of the Mississippi River and the Upper South were reluctant to share the venture of southern independence, with its destruction of internal commerce. In the 1880s and 1890s hopes for a New South were held most strongly by civic leaders in ambitious cities like Atlanta and Birmingham, who hoped to emulate northern industrial cities.

In the 20th century two generations of social scientists have waited for urban growth to undermine the cultural values and social patterns that have set the South apart from the rest of the United States. By the common analysis, the combined forces of industrialization, urbanization, and the expansion of a cosmopolitan middle class would help to close the cultural gap. In the words of sociologist Leonard Reissman, the emergence of large cities should move the South to "a level of modernity comparable to the nation as a whole."

There is no doubt that the South is rapidly attaining the same degree of urban development found in other parts of the country. In technical use, the term "urbanization" refers to the proportion of the population of a state, region, or nation living within urban areas. Table 1 compares the degree of urbanization in the South with that in the remainder of the United States. The surge of urban growth was especially pronounced in the three decades after 1940, with the differential closing at a slower pace during the 1970s.

Urbanization during the past generation has meant new economic roles and

influence for established centers and the emergence of new urban rivals. The 16 states of the "Census South" contained 10 metropolitan areas with more than 1 million residents in 1980, compared to 1 in 1940. Their combined metropolitan population of 18,542,000 was three and a half times the total for 1940. At mid-century, independent studies by Vance and Smith and by Duncan and his associates identified Atlanta and Dallas as the only southern cities to rank as high as the third level in the national urban system. By 1980, however, when a good measure of metropolitan importance was the volume of airline traffic, four southern airports ranked in the top 10 in passenger volume.

At the other end of the urban hierarchy, dozens of small southern cities have grown enough to earn recognition as metropolitan areas (defined as single or adjacent core cities with 50,000 residents along with the counties that have close economic ties to the core). The South counted 58 metropolitan areas in 1950 and 119 in 1980. Additions to the list during the 1970s include Victoria, Tex.; Alexandria, La.; Florence, Ala.; Hickory, N.C.; and Ocala and Braden-

Table 1. *Urbanization in South and Non-South*

	Urban-ization South	Urban-ization Non-South	Ratio South/Non-South
1900	18.0%	50.0%	.36
1940	36.7	65.7	.56
1950	44.0	65.8	.67
1960	57.7	74.4	.78
1970	64.4	77.2	.83
1980	66.9	77.1	.87

Source: U.S. Bureau of the Census, Population Reports *(1900, 1940, 1950, 1960, 1970, 1980).*

ton, Fla. Few parts of the South are now more than a two-hour drive from a metropolitan area.

Urbanization has drawn native southerners from the region's farms and small towns and mixed them with a substantial influx of newcomers. In 1979, for example, 8 percent of the southern population had migrated from outside the region in the past four years. Comparable figures for the Northeast and Midwest are 3–4 percent. In Florida and Texas annual in-migration has totaled in the hundreds of thousands.

The movement into southern cities has had an especially important impact on the region's black residents. The level of urbanization for blacks has closely paralleled that for whites, with 17.2 percent of southern blacks in urban places in 1900, 36.5 percent in 1940, and 67.4 percent in 1970. Because the rural South has been a region of extremely limited economic and educational opportunities for blacks, their urbanization has been a vital step in achieving the full benefits of citizenship. Moreover, the newcomers to the South now include significant numbers of blacks. Net in-migration of 14,000 blacks in the years 1970–75 marked the reversal of three generations of black flight. For 1975–80 the net inflow of blacks to the South totaled 195,000.

Many of the new southerners have been attracted by the changing economic base of southern cities. By the middle 1970s three-quarters of the major metropolitan centers in the region were dependent on tertiary activities (trade/finance/transportation) or quarternary activities (services/government/research). A comparison of the 10 largest urban centers in the South in 1940 and in 1980 shows some of the changes (Table 2). Over the 40 years the old river

ports and heavy industrial cities of Birmingham, Louisville, Memphis, and Wheeling have dropped off the list, while Baltimore and New Orleans have fallen several places. The replacement cities are three recreation/retirement cities—Miami, Tampa, and Fort Lauderdale—and the military center of San Antonio. Dallas, Houston, and Washington have also increased in relative importance. Another indicator of the emerging post-industrial economy is the list of medium-sized metropolitan areas (500,000 to 1,000,000) that grew by more than 25 percent during the 1970s. Austin and Raleigh-Durham are government and education centers, West Palm Beach and Orlando are recreation cities, and Tulsa is an energy boomtown.

The leading economic sectors in southern cities demand salaried experts and professionals. Military officers, aerospace engineers, tax accountants, medical researchers, university professors, petroleum geologists, and members of corporate publicity departments are members of the footloose middle

Table 2. *Largest Southern Metropolitan Areas (rank order)*

1940	1980
Baltimore	Washington
Washington	Dallas–Fort Worth
New Orleans	Houston
Houston	Baltimore
Atlanta	Atlanta
Birmingham	Miami
Louisville	Tampa–St. Petersburg
Dallas	New Orleans
Memphis	San Antonio
Wheeling	Fort Lauderdale–Hollywood

Source: U.S. Bureau of the Census, Population Reports (1940, 1980).

class. They expect to make their careers in a sequence of cities, and they are more dependent on the judgments of their professional peers than on the attitudes of their neighbors. They constitute not simply the white-collar class anticipated by social theory, but a modern mobile population with little attachment to regional traditions.

One of their impacts has been to homogenize the residential areas of southern cities. Families transferring from city to city tend to look for comparable communities. The taste of a minority of these mobile professionals runs to restored center city neighborhoods—Alexandria, Va., Inman Park in Atlanta, or the Fan District in Richmond. The majority choose suburbs that are indistinguishable from each other or from similar communities outside the South. The sprawl of Houston, the super suburb of Virginia Beach, northside Atlanta, and northside San Antonio offer essentially the same environment.

Indeed, it is arguable whether many of the largest southern cities retain their "southern" character. Baltimore and Washington, which were dominated by local elites with southern orientations as late as the 1930s, have been absorbed

The Miami Beach resort area, 1980s

within the megalopolis of the Northeast. Houston, Dallas, and Atlanta are high-rise cities, with new downtowns that rise like glass icebergs out of a sea of parking lots. Tampa and Fort Lauderdale serve a national market of vacationers and retirees who know little and care less about the mill towns and cotton crossroads of the historic South. Miami and San Antonio lie within the advancing frontier line of Latin America. If anything defines the uniqueness of the South, it is the patterns and problems of black-white relations. However, Hispanic Americans are the largest minority in metropolitan Miami and San Antonio (as well as in Austin and El Paso).

In the broadest view, urban development is pulling the South into a new regional alignment. Although the Sunbelt is a loosely defined concept, rates of population growth by states and metropolitan areas for the period 1940–80 show two regions of rapid growth in the United States. A Sunbelt-Southeast runs along the South Atlantic coast from Washington to Key West, and a Sunbelt-West angles from Louisiana, Texas, and Oklahoma across the Southwest and Rocky Mountain states to the Pacific. The nine southern states within these Sunbelt zones contain all 21 of the region's metropolitan areas that grew by at least 25 percent during the 1970s. They contain the 10 largest southern metropolitan areas and 24 of the 30 largest.

What remains of the Old South is half a dozen states on the western slope of the Appalachians and central Mississippi Valley. West Virginia, Kentucky, Tennessee, Arkansas, Mississippi, and Alabama have older cities and older manufacturing, a record of slower growth, and limited employment in government and high technology industry.

In summary, urban growth at the end of the 20th century is simultaneously reducing the distinctiveness of the South and drawing it into new regional configurations. The Sunbelt transcends the historic South and links its dynamic sectors to a new, larger region. For most residents, there are now more similarities than differences to life in Anaheim and Orlando, San Diego and Norfolk, Albuquerque, Austin, and Atlanta.

See also INDUSTRY articles

Carl Abbott
Portland State University

Carl Abbott, *The New Urban America: Growth and Politics in Sunbelt Cities* (1981); Blaine A. Brownell and David R. Goldfield, eds., *The City in Southern History: The Growth of Urban Civilization in the South* (1977); Ollinger Crenshaw, in *Historiography and Urbanization: Essays in American History in Honor of W. Stull Holt*, ed. Eric F. Goldman (1941); Otis D. Duncan et al., *Metropolis and Region* (1960); William H. Nichols, in *The American South in the 1960s*, ed. Avery Leiserson (1964); Leonard Reissman, *Journal of Social Issues* (January 1966); Rupert B. Vance and Nicholas J. Demerath, eds., *The Urban South* (1954). ☆

Urban Leadership

|||||||||||||||||||||||||||||||||||||||||||||||||||||

Though it was predominantly a rural, agricultural economy until recently, the South required urban centers that spawned their own leadership, frequently at odds with the leaders of agrarian society. During the colonial and antebellum periods the most important cities in the region were mostly coastal trade centers. Baltimore, Norfolk, Charleston, Savannah, Mobile, New Orleans, and other smaller cities provided outlets to northern and European markets for the grain, naval stores, tobacco, rice, and cotton exports produced by the plantation economy. During the colonial era many of the leading merchants and factors who dominated this trade were foreigners, usually Scotch, British, and French. By the 1820s, as the cotton trade expanded and came under the control of New York City, northerners took over the key urban functions of factoring and shipping the lucrative exports of the plantation economy.

Within the local power structure urban merchants and factors used their influence through commercial associations and city government to promote urban growth. Civic improvements in water supply, sanitation, police, and fire control were all subservient to the goal of enhancing the community's commercial prosperity. City governmental agencies were also used to regulate slaves and to guard against their revolt. Though they shared many of the aspirations for urban growth and industrial and commercial development with their counterparts in the North, the leaders of the southern middle class enjoyed less autonomy and less political and economic leverage within a society dominated by large slaveowning planters. Urban merchants and industrial entrepreneurs cooperated with planters in launching new railroads and industrial experiments. During the 1850s these efforts at economic development were linked to plans for sectional independence from the North.

Ultimately, the move toward urban development was contradicted by the commitment to the plantation economy and slavery. Slaveowners realized slave labor could be adapted to industrial work and urban labor markets only at the risk of losing full control over the slaves. Planters feared a large white working class in the cities that might oppose competition from slaves, and they did not wish to encourage the growth of an independent middle class with interests opposed to the slave regime. The strain between the urban middle class and planters became apparent during the secession crisis when urban representatives opposed secession for fear of severing commercial ties with the North. The dominance of the planter class became apparent when urban leaders ultimately capitulated and served the Confederate cause during the war.

During the war urban supply and manufacturing centers like Atlanta, Richmond, and Nashville experienced rapid growth and emerged as powerful components of the postwar economic order. Many entrepreneurs who gained experience during the war took their place in a growing cadre of urban middle class leaders in the New South era. Older seaports like Charleston, Mobile, and New Orleans suffered blockades during the war and continued to stagnate in the decades following it. Along the Piedmont, in northern Alabama, and elsewhere in the interior of the South, towns and cities experienced rapid growth as railroad centers or as textile, tobacco, and iron manufacturing centers. Few of the industrial and commercial leaders who were prominent in the rising cities of the New South came from the planter class. In cities like Atlanta and Nashville they were typically from the yeomanry and small-town merchant and professional classes. Most arrived in their cities after the war as

young men and rose to positions of wealth in wholesale commerce, railroads, manufacturing, banking, and insurance. Typically, they were Methodist, Presbyterian, or Baptist, and they celebrated their rise to riches as the reward of hard work and personal piety. By the 1880s representatives of this ascendant middle class "new man" articulated a regional vision of economic development, sectional reconciliation with the North, and interracial cooperation. Though they often paid homage to the Lost Cause of the Confederacy, those who proclaimed this New South creed recognized a departure from the Old South and offered the leadership of a young, progressive urban middle class as an alternative to the defeated planter class.

On the local level prominent merchants, manufacturers, and financiers used their influence through commercial associations, like the chamber of commerce, to direct public policy. Formal control of city government offices was typically held by smaller businessmen whose interests were confined to the local economy. City government continued to serve business interests in efforts to promote urban growth through bonds for railroads, lobbying for federal aid to harbor improvements, tax incentives to new industries, and improved city services. The most visible examples of urban enterprise were the industrial expositions held in Atlanta, Louisville, New Orleans, Nashville, and Charleston in the late 19th and early 20th centuries. Here the New South creed of economic development, national reconciliation, and black progress was displayed in lavish exhibits and reams of publicity. Linked to their vision of New South economic prosperity was a liberal social policy with special application to the black population of the postwar South.

Beginning in the 1880s with religious revivals and temperance campaigns, the reformers of the urban South sponsored a flurry of new private and government-sponsored charitable organizations. Reform moved toward efforts to improve sanitation and public health in the slums, expand and improve public education, and enforce temperance and sexual morality through government regulation. These reforms were linked to goals of economic progress through a healthy, educated, and generally upgraded work force. These policies of social uplift, which gained wide currency in the Progressive era, coincided with a growing tendency toward segregation in the work force, neighborhoods, and public facilities of southern cities. Segregation was approved, if not inspired, by business leaders as a means of assuring social stability in the crowded and competitive cities of the New South.

"Business progressivism," as historian George Tindall has labeled this conservative brand of reform, took firm hold in the early 20th century. Structural reforms in the manner of electing city government officials allowed for "at large" elections of councilmen and the introduction of commission and city manager forms of government. These reforms were intended to model government after the modern corporations and to reduce the influence of ward-level bosses and the poor black and white working-class voters who supported them. In several cities a southern brand of boss politics prevailed despite the efforts of business progressives to undermine their ward-level strength. Edward H. Crump in Memphis, Hilary Howse in Nashville, John Grace in Charleston, and Martin Behrman in New Orleans

represented the most durable of such urban bosses. The mobilization effort during World War I and the era of business prosperity that followed gave new strength to "business progressivism." Planning and zoning boards were attached to city government to give the commercial-civic elite additional control over the course of physical growth and residential segregation in their cities. Experts in business and planning expanded the powers of local government to cope with a variety of complex urban problems involving air pollution, traffic control, social welfare, and expanded urban services for the rapidly growing suburban population.

The Depression and the New Deal programs of the 1930s accelerated this growth of public authority as federal funds for highway, park, and airport construction, social welfare, and public housing poured into local agencies. World War II strengthened the federal partnership with southern cities, many of which were grateful recipients of government expenditures for aircraft, ships, weaponry, uniforms, and military bases. After the war a generation of returning veterans and businessmen eager to encourage further federal commitment to southern development began to take over the leadership of their cities. The war against fascism and the cold war against communism made the system of racial segregation a national embarrassment. Business leaders were hesitant, nonetheless, to dismantle the system on their own initiative. Many black business and professional leaders had thrived within a segregated society and were slow to push for desegregation.

A younger generation of college-educated blacks, many of them still in school, began in the 1950s to work through the NAACP and other local organizations to batter down the walls of segregation. Through the courts, public demonstrations, and civil disobedience they forced the leadership of southern cities to put an end to formal segregation in schools, public facilities, and to a lesser degree in the job market. Urban blacks also regained political power lost after Reconstruction and were able to extract concessions from white leaders. In cities like Atlanta black political power was sufficient to win key positions within city government. Whatever their formal positions within local government, however, the white business elites remain the most significant group within the power structure of major southern cities and are a force of growing importance within a region undergoing rapid urbanization.

See also BLACK LIFE: Business, Black; Politics, Black; INDUSTRY articles; MYTHIC SOUTH: New South Myth

Don H. Doyle
Vanderbilt University

Blaine A. Brownell, *The Urban Ethos in the South, 1920–1930* (1975), with David R. Goldfield, eds., *The City in Southern History: The Growth of Urban Civilization in the South* (1977); Eugene D. Genovese, *The Political Economy of Slavery* (1968); Floyd Hunter, *Community Power Succession: Atlanta's Policy-Makers Revisited* (1980). ☆

Urban Planning
||||||||||||||||||||||||||||||||||||||||

The South possesses a rich tradition of urban planning that extends back to the colonial era. Indeed, some of the most

innovative town plans of that period were located in the southern colonies. Williamsburg, the small but influential capital of colonial Virginia, introduced baroque civic design to the New World in a plan devised by Theodorick Bland. James Oglethorpe's Savannah plan of 1733 reflected the English philanthropist's commitment to a middle landscape ideal—a cautious blend of city and country. The town's spacious lots, orderly gridiron street pattern, and five squares that served as America's first public parks contrasted sharply with the more exploitative development overtaking northern cities at that time. Southern colonial urban planning also reflected a French cultural influence in the more formal design provided for New Orleans by Jean Baptiste Le Moyne, Sieur de Bienville, in 1722 focusing on the magnificent *place d'armes* dominated by St. Louis Cathedral.

Both the scale and quality of urban planning in the South declined in the 19th century reflecting a general American trend that emphasized rapid development as opposed to aesthetic layout. The gridiron marched relentlessly over the southern landscape, and paper towns sprang up and folded. Urban planning practice shifted to service delivery and transportation as southern cities participated increasingly in the national economy. The relatively slow rate of urbanization experienced by some southeastern cities such as Charleston and Savannah was a disguised blessing enabling those places to maintain their parks and ready access to the sea and to tree-lined thoroughfares, which later generations of Americans would appreciate greatly.

The aesthetic consciousness of southern urban planning evident in its colonial towns resurfaced in the 1890s as part of the national City Beautiful movement inspired by the 1893 Chicago Columbian Exposition. The movement fitted southern cities well by focusing on cosmetic rehabilitation rather than on more troubling spatial and racial concerns. Further, it was inexpensive and cities in a capital-poor region with a tradition of local government parsimony for services found an economical program that would enhance image at relatively little cost. The activities of the Charlotte Women's Club presenting awards for the best gardens and a similar group in Wilmington encouraging outdoor floral arrangements were typical of southern City Beautiful. Actually, the most innovative urban planning of the era occurred outside the region's cities in fashionable suburbs such as Joel Hurt's Druid Hills development near Atlanta, designed by John C. Olmsted, and Kingsport, Tenn., a planned industrial town creatively laid out by Earle S. Draper.

By the early 1920s, with the rise of a planning profession, planning's traditional physical concerns replaced the superficial activities of City Beautiful. Specifically, transportation and zoning came to characterize urban planning practice in the South, as elsewhere. The ubiquitous Harland Bartholomew, the nation's leading planning consultant at that time, traveled to several southern cities. He eschewed social questions and concentrated on physical planning—expanded road networks and zoning ordinances. Southern urban leaders welcomed the new planning tools as devices to reinforce and solidify traditional patterns of racial residential segregation.

The racial orientation of urban planning persisted after World War II with the rise of urban renewal as the major

planning strategy. While cities in other parts of the country evinced disregard for the integrity of black neighborhoods, southern cities were even more thorough in their planning policies, running highways through black districts and replacing demolished black housing with commercial structures to a greater extent than cities elsewhere. Ironically, the planning policies of more and better roads and fewer housing projects (as opposed to civic centers and office buildings) accelerated urban decline. By the 1970s new planning strategies evolved, not necessarily to reduce existing racial inequalities in the built environment, but to capitalize on national trends and legislation designed to conserve rather than to demolish. Cities directed planning resources toward downtown areas and neighborhoods emphasizing historic themes such as Underground Atlanta (which subsequently failed). The objective was to emphasize the southern city's cultural heritage, but the result was frequently a caricature of that past. Charleston and Savannah, perhaps the most authentic southern cities, were among the earliest and best-planned cities, and they are today the least troubled by the destructive forces of growth that other cities are scrambling, with mixed success, to ward off.

The planning profession is enmeshed in a southern dilemma that limits the effectiveness and influence of planners. The trend in professional planning nationally is a greater emphasis on social planning and accompanying measures to avoid or cope with economic decline. The commercial-civic elite, which still wields considerable power in southern cities, remains wedded to the growth ethic and tends to view planning as an interference with the urban land market. The success of historic preservation planning results in great part from its enhancement of downtown property values and the reconstitution (i.e., "whitening") of inner city residential neighborhoods and the investment opportunities such conservation implies.

David R. Goldfield
University of North Carolina
at Charlotte

Blaine A. Brownell, *Journal of Southern History* (August 1975); David R. Goldfield, *Cotton Fields and Skyscrapers: Southern City and Region, 1607–1980* (1982), *Journal of Southern History* (November 1976); Philip Morris, *Southern Living* (January 1978); Howard L. Preston, *Automobile Age Atlanta: The Making of a Southern Metropolis, 1900–1935* (1979); John W. Reps, *Tidewater Towns: City Planning in Colonial Virginia and Maryland* (1972); Dana F. White and Victor A. Kramer, eds., *Olmsted South: Old South Critic/New South Planner* (1979). ☆

Urban Politics

Throughout southern history the mercantile classes have formed the core of urban leadership. In colonial times the business elite dominated the governmental and economic institutions of the South's embryonic cities. For these leaders the key to urban growth was the economic development of regional hinterlands. In early Baltimore, for instance, city expansion depended upon a thriving grain and flour industry that drew directly from the wheat production of the nearby countryside. Enhancement of the local economy was therefore the primary aim of urban government in the southern colonies.

During the antebellum era the bond between the business elite and city government persisted. In New Orleans, the South's largest urban center, directors of local corporations often served simultaneously on the city council. In Richmond 40 percent of the local elite, mainly business and professional men, held governmental offices. Joseph R. Anderson, head of the Tredegar Iron Works, was typical. He became a bank director, an outspoken supporter of various railroad and canal enterprises, and a member of the Richmond city council.

Enlargement of the hinterlands remained important to urban leaders, but many directed greater concern toward developing a regional and national network of cities as well as increasing urban competition. The mercantile elite endorsed railroad subsidies and wharf improvements that would perhaps attract business away from other communities, but they also recognized the importance to urban growth of better fire and police protection, improved street lighting, drainage, and adequate health statutes. Although municipal services infrequently kept pace with local needs, few questioned their usefulness to urban boosterism. At issue in most urban political contests was the cost of municipal improvements, not their value. Voters commonly removed extravagant administrators from office.

The obligation to regulate urban slaves and free blacks won universal acceptance in the South, but other ethnic tensions periodically took political form. In 1836 differences among the French-speaking Creoles, the incoming Americans, and emigrants from Ireland and Germany prompted the city of New Orleans to divide into three separate municipalities. For 16 years three distinct governmental entities directed the affairs of the Crescent City while an inconsequential mayor and general council nominally presided. In 1852 inefficiency, disease, and natural disasters contributed to a reunification that solidified the American sections with the annexation of rapidly growing suburbs. Ethnic animosity, however, continued throughout the decade. In the New Orleans municipal elections of 1854, violent opposition to immigration led directly to the victory of the Know-Nothing party. This organization, with the backing of labor, controlled Crescent City government until the Union conquest in 1862.

Secession sentiment in southern cities was mixed. The commercial leaders in those cities with predominantly northern markets resisted separation. The elite in cities with import trade generally favored disunion. Support for the southern cause, nonetheless, was clearly present in all urban centers.

Urban politics in the Reconstruction South mirrored regional contests that pitted Republicans and their newly franchised black allies against former Confederates and other Conservative Democrats. In New Orleans the White League, a vigorous and ultimately successful foe of the Republican regime and its metropolitan police, helped to spawn a powerful political machine that dominated local affairs for nearly 75 years. A characteristic urban ring, the Regular Democratic Organization used election fraud, patronage, political favors, and violence to maintain control. Its leadership of largely first-generation Americans depended upon labor, new immigrants, and (until 1898) subordinate blacks for electoral support. Businessmen who received lucrative municipal franchises provided financial backing.

The Old Regulars' political opponents were more representative of the leadership in other southern communities. Deemed appropriately the commercial-civic elite by historian Blaine A. Brownell, its members included bankers, real estate entrepreneurs, insurance agents, merchants, and contractors as well as lawyers, journalists, teachers, doctors, and other middle-class, business-oriented professionals. In the Crescent City this group constituted a sporadic opposition that achieved its ends mainly through independent governmental boards. In Atlanta, Birmingham, and other cities the commercial-civic elite dominated municipal offices and generally influenced the disposition of city revenue, services, and regulations. Combining the New South creed with urban boosterism, local leaders sought new industry and greater business development within an atmosphere of municipal stability. Urban growth, often accomplished through annexation, was an acknowledged—though frequently contradictory—goal. The new suburbs, a major source of fresh problems, usually received fewer municipal services than did the central business districts and the industrial neighborhoods.

During the early 20th century the mixing of southern city councils and chambers of commerce intensified. In New Orleans the evolving Old Regulars under Major Martin Behrman and in Memphis the powerful machine of Edward H. Crump clearly inclined toward business interests. Business philosophy and the progressive impulse precipitated structural reform in numerous southern city governments. The city commissioner and the city manager forms of municipal administration, created in Dixie, found favor throughout the region. Governmental change, however, rarely altered political structure in the urban South. The New Orleans machine and the Crump organization continued to dominate the new commission councils in their towns.

During the 1920s the link between the commercial-civic elite and city hall raised urban boosterism to higher levels. The "Atlanta Spirit" became the regional model although Miami was perhaps the best example of city boom. City leaders used the automobile revolution and the new interest in municipal planning to promote programs for the economic growth of the central business district, the allocation of adequate land for commercial and industrial use, the improvement of local transportation networks, the separation of the races, and the controlled expansion of the periphery. Although these programs infrequently resolved municipal problems, they established patterns for future development.

During the Depression economic demands forced southern leaders to curtail municipal services and to engage in relief efforts. Many regional chief executives joined with their urban counterparts throughout the nation to plead for federal aid to the cities. After the election of Franklin D. Roosevelt, numerous southern mayors espoused New Deal programs. In Memphis local leaders welcomed cheap electricity from the Tennessee Valley Authority. New Orleans Mayor Robert S. Maestri often joked that the Works Progress Administration was a "money tree" for his community.

World War II brought new growth and added challenges to southern cities. After the conflict, aged political machines in New Orleans and Memphis faltered, and the commercial-civic elite

began to reassert itself. New-breed mayors such as De Lesseps S. Morrison of New Orleans, Robert King High of Miami, and William B. Hartsfield and Ivan Allen, Jr., of Atlanta took charge and advanced programs that were in line with commercial expansion and urban development. All facets of municipal administration, particularly building projects, were geared to the enhancement of the urban image in the South. Within this context of city maturation, the financial problems and political tensions of suburbanization began to appear. To cope with these difficulties, Miami and Nashville adopted metropolitan governments.

The civil rights movement contributed to the outward population shift when white southerners fled to the suburbs to escape integration. In Little Rock, New Orleans, and Birmingham resistance to desegregation had a debilitating effect upon the local economies. During these crises governmental and business leadership in the South was sorely lacking until harsh economic reality forced the commercial-civic elite to take a moderate stance on desegregation.

During the 1960s federal legislation on civil rights altered the political structure of the urban South forever and convinced white politicians to reassess their racial views. Candidates who did not address the needs of black voters had little chance for success. An expanding black electorate and white flight to the suburbs increased black political clout in the urban South. By the 1970s blacks commonly populated city councils throughout the region and many of the South's largest cities boasted their first black mayors. Although black governmental leaders often worked with and welcomed the support of the commercial-civic elite, they devoted greater attention to neighborhood needs. Many white governmental leaders also stressed historic preservation and rehabilitation of core areas as a means to offset the population decrease, and accompanying financial drains, of suburban flight. Over the past decade the commercial-civic elite has not surrendered its political power, but it has been forced to vie with other urban interest groups for the allocation of diminishing municipal resources. An increasingly diverse leadership in southern cities has begun to assess the value of economic growth against the importance of metropolitan cooperation, historic renovation, and neighborhood demands.

See also BLACK LIFE: Politics, Black; INDUSTRY: Civil Rights and Business; POLITICS articles

Edward F. Haas
Louisiana State Museum/
Tulane University

Carl Abbott, *The New Urban America: Growth and Politics in Sunbelt Cities* (1981); Blaine A. Brownell and David R. Goldfield, eds., *The City in Southern History: The Growth of Urban Civilization in the South* (1977); Edward F. Haas, *De Lesseps S. Morrison and the Image of Reform: New Orleans Politics, 1946–1961* (1974); Carl V. Harris, *Political Power in Birmingham, 1871–1921* (1977); Christopher Silver, *Journal of Urban History* (November 1983); Eugene J. Watts, *The Social Bases of City Politics: Atlanta, 1865–1903* (1978). ☆

Urban Poor

‖‖‖‖‖‖‖‖‖‖‖‖‖‖‖‖‖‖‖‖‖‖‖‖‖‖

Historian C. Vann Woodward depicted poverty as one of the burdens of southern history. Poverty, of course, is not a strictly southern phenomenon, but persistent and extensive poverty in the region is distinctive. Southern cities, as inextricable parts of their region, have shared this poverty. Generally, urban southerners have reflected the philosophy of other Americans with regard to poor relief, moving from first viewing poverty as a divine judgment requiring no intervention, to aid only for deserving poor, to work relief programs, to maintenance grants. Three elements have distinguished the southern urban poor and poor relief from poverty and welfare elsewhere: southern cities have generally lacked economic resources for an extensive welfare apparatus, the influence of evangelical sects has tended to limit public intervention, and an overwhelming proportion of blacks among the poor has encouraged official white neglect.

In the antebellum era poor relief tended to be seasonal and private—the needy received wood and food in the winter. The Norfolk Association for the Improvement of the Condition of the Poor typified the attitudes of southern private relief agencies by noting that "*sound discrimination . . .* is the first principle of this Association. It will give to none who will not exhibit evidence of improvement from the aid afforded." The poor, black and white, lived in the least desirable areas, and these locations exposed them to disease.

The decades after the Civil War witnessed an outpouring of literature on the poor and on the causes and relief of poverty. But the dominance of evangelical religion in the South, which emphasized the futility of human solutions to earthly problems, thwarted any investigative impulse in the South. The social gospel, which imbued Protestant churches in the North, was a relatively minor movement in the South. Regional culture reinforced the tendency to neglect and ignore urban poverty. In addition, because of the identification of urban blacks with poverty, the race issue restricted welfare discussions.

If the urban poor could not seek succor from official and even charitable agencies, self-help institutions provided some relief. This was especially so with the growing black community, which swelled with rural freedmen in the decades after the Civil War. The black churches, pooling the meager resources of their congregations, provided relief and burial services to needy families. The churches could do little about the poor's residential environment—typically rented wooden shacks on unpaved streets, devoid of urban services. The few public institutions devoted to poor relief, such as the poorhouse, were usually mismanaged and always underfunded. In New Orleans the poorhouse was administered by the head of the waterworks. In Atlanta the poorhouse consisted of two-room wooden "cottages" without ceiling or heat, where in the middle of winter children dressed "in rags and tatters." Moreover, wide differentials existed with respect to city donations to black and white charitable institutions (though expenditures in both were small). In Richmond in 1900, for example, city contributions to black charities amounted to $550, to white charities, $7,722, despite the greater prevalence of poverty in the black community.

As rural migration to southern cities quickened during the early decades of the 20th century, urban relief efforts failed to keep pace. Birmingham actually abolished its welfare department in the 1920s. The Depression quickly overburdened urban governments and only federal relief efforts relieved a dire situation.

The return of prosperity during and after World War II did not alter the southern philosophy of poor relief or the living conditions of the poor, who remained burdened not only by poverty but by poor housing, an unsanitary environment, and inadequate educational facilities, all of which reinforced that poverty. The poor resided within hailing distance of Houston's or Atlanta's gleaming skyscrapers. In San Antonio in 1970 nearly one out of every three families earned less than $3,000 a year (below the poverty level), and over 6 percent had incomes less than $1,000 a year—a figure that Robert Coles termed "almost incredible for an urban center." No southern city matched or exceeded the national average per capita urban expenditures for public welfare ($11.98), and San Antonio was exceptionally low at 45 cents per capita expenditure.

Race and poverty continued in tandem in southern cities. In Memphis, where blacks comprised 38 percent of the population, they represented 58 percent of all families with annual income less than $1,000 in 1949, and 71 percent of those families in 1969. By 1970 the black median family income in Memphis was only 56 percent of the white family income.

The Sunbelt prosperity of the 1970s did not effect a major transformation in either public poor relief or the decline of poverty. The trickle-down theory of economic development effected no noticeable improvements; in fact, the inflation generated by economic expansion tended to hurt low income groups. Though unemployment rates are lower in southern cities than in cities in the Northeast and Midwest, residents of southern slums are poorer, based on percapita income than slum dwellers in northeastern cities. While almost one-

half of the northeastern poor are unemployed, compared with only one-
quarter jobless in poor southern urban
neighborhoods, the numbers of those
working below a government-defined
living wage are significantly higher in
southern inner cities than in the North.

See also SOCIAL CLASS: Poverty

David R. Goldfield
University of North Carolina
at Charlotte

Blaine A. Brownell and David R. Goldfield,
eds., *The City in Southern History: The
Growth of Urban Civilization in the South*
(1977); J. Wayne Flynt, *Dixie's Forgotten
People: The South's Poor Whites* (1979); Carl
Grindstaff, *Social Problems* (Winter 1967);
John Kellogg, *Geographical Review* (July
1977); Peter A. Lupsha and William J.
Siembieda, in *The Rise of the Sunbelt Cities*,
ed. David C. Perry and Alfred J. Watkins
(1977); Howard N. Rabinowitz, *Race Relations in the Urban South, 1865–1890* (1978);
Edyth L. Ross, *Phylon* (Winter 1976). ☆

Urban Transportation

Cities in the South have undergone tremendous changes as a result of urban
transportation, but it was not until the
20th century and the advent of the automobile age that southerners experienced some of the same environmental
disruptions that occurred in places like
Boston and Philadelphia decades earlier.

Montgomery, Ala., and Richmond,
Va., were the first cities nationally to
boast the operation of an electric street
railway. But the unlikely appearance of

this new means of horizontal mobility in
the South did not effect dramatic
changes as in the North. Although
Atlanta, Birmingham, Memphis,
Nashville, Tampa, Jacksonville, New
Orleans, and Louisville all had streetcar
transit, their operations were small and
failed to help generate any significant
degree of decentralized housing, consumer services, or commercial activities. The increased mobility that
streetcars offered southerners certainly
resulted in suburban annexations: Atlanta had its Inman Park and Druid
Hills; Houston its Houston Heights and
Deer Park; Tampa its Tampa Heights;
and Memphis its Annesdale Park. But
by the conclusion of the 19th century,
the urban South was hardly comparable
to northern industrial cities where
streetcar patronage had helped create
the sprawling, fragmented metropolises
usually associated with late 19th-cen-
tury American urban life.

Failure of street railway systems to
influence decentralization in southern
cities was evident in their size and
shape. At the turn of the century, only
one city in the South—New Orleans—
could claim a population of over
100,000, and for every southerner living
in a city in the South with a population
of more than 25,000, approximately 15
others remained in smaller cities,
towns, or on the farm. Under the influence of street railway transportation
many of these provincial capitals retained circular shapes until well into the
20th century. Atlanta, for example, had
basically a circular shape enclosing an
11-square-mile area in 1900, but more
significantly the Georgia capital closely
resembled the size of Boston during the
mid-19th century. Thus, southern cities
entered the 20th century almost unin-
fluenced by the dominant means of

urban transportation of that era. In fact, at that time these relatively small American cities better fit the mold of a preindustrial walking city than that of a late 19th-century industrial metropolis.

Not until the first three decades of the 20th century did many cities in the South begin to outgrow their provinciality. Most of this growth occurred during the 1920s when the very symbol of that decade—the automobile—overtook the street railway as the most popular means of urban transportation. In Memphis between 1920 and 1930 automobile ownership increased by 192 percent; in Atlanta there were 215 percent more registered motor vehicles in 1930 than in 1920; and in Birmingham the figure climbed to as much as 337 percent.

Most of the changes automobile use brought to cities in the South were no different from those in other parts of the country. Businesses unable to survive in congested downtown locations sought refuge in the suburbs; traffic congestion tarnished the image of city fathers who promoted their cities as havens of business opportunity; and citizens of Atlanta, Birmingham, Charlotte, Nashville, and elsewhere found the amenities of suburban life more attractive than ever before.

Increased racial segregation was perhaps the one change private use of automobiles wrought in the urban South more dramatically than other places in the country. Writing about Los Angeles, the model automobile metropolis, one urban authority has claimed that the use of motor vehicles created a new land-use structure in which a measure of racial and class justice could be achieved. This was not the case in the urban South. Because whites were generally more affluent than blacks and could bet-

ter afford private automobiles as well as home mortgages, suburbanization outside southern cities was limited almost exclusively to whites. In fact, the automobile became the means by which whites achieved their desire for separate living. In terms of time and distance, whites and blacks residing in and around southern cities in 1930 were more segregated than ever before.

Ironically, although urban transportation aided the separate-but-equal doctrine in the urban South, it was through that same medium that blacks began to challenge white supremacy. Rosa Lee Parks's refusal to take a seat at the back of a Montgomery, Ala., bus in 1955 and the subsequent successful boycott of the Montgomery City Line buses by blacks not only brought Martin Luther King, Jr., to the attention of Americans as a civil rights activist but, more importantly, gave the civil rights movement credibility and momentum.

The Montgomery bus boycott ended segregation on Montgomery buses in 1956 and eventually led to integration on public transit conveyers in cities across the South. Decades earlier, however, the private use of automobiles in southern cities had established a pattern of racial segregation in suburban housing and educational facilities that integrated public transportation could not dent. Sometime in the 1960s the majority of urban white southerners shifted from central city areas to outlying suburbs. In 1974 the Southern Growth Policy Board's Commission on the Future of the South concluded that heavy reliance on the automobile has caused the urban regions of the South to be "less dense and more diffuse than the centralized cities that developed in other parts of the country in an earlier industrial age." Indeed it had, but perhaps the impact of the automobile on southern cities was even more significant to urban life there than commission members surmised.

See also HISTORY AND MANNERS: Automobile; Railroads

Howard L. Preston
Spartanburg, South Carolina

Rick Beard, in *Olmsted South: Old South Critic/New South Planner*, ed. Dana F. White and Victor A. Kramer (1979); Blaine A. Brownell, *Alabama Review* (April 1972), *American Quarterly* (March 1972), with David R. Goldfield, eds., *The City in Southern History: The Growth of Urban Civilization in the South* (1977); Howard L. Preston, *Automobile Age Atlanta: The Making of a Southern Metropolis, 1900–1935* (1979); Southern Growth Policy Board, *The Future of the South* (1974). ☆

ATLANTA
||||||||||||||||||||||||||

"Gate City of the South," "Capital of the New South," "A City too Busy to Hate," "Black Mecca," and "The World's Next Great City" are all slogans business leaders have coined to promote the growth of Atlanta over the last century and a quarter. Beginning with Atlanta *Constitution* editor Henry W. Grady, whose speeches in northern states in the 1880s carried the message that a reconciled South was a good place for investment, the Chamber of Commerce has actively promoted the potential of the city. The Cotton States and International Exposition of 1895 brought national attention for the somewhat modest imitation of the Chicago World's Fair. Later the Forward Atlanta campaigns of the 1920s and the 1960s utilized na-

tional periodicals to advertise the city's attractions for commerce and industry. The business promoters fared far better than Confederate Generals Joseph E. Johnston and John Bell Hood who defended Atlanta during the Civil War: they attracted the investment that has allowed the city not only to rebuild itself from its almost total destruction in 1864 but also to outpace the growth of other cities in the region.

In 1860 Atlanta had a population of slightly more than 10,000; a century later, its metropolitan total topped 1 million. Although this growth enabled the city to outdistance other southern contenders for economic leadership, such as Charleston, Birmingham, and even New Orleans, it still was not equal to the rate of northern rivals. The regional characteristic that did distinguish Atlanta (and other southern cities) well into the 20th century was its high proportion of black citizens, who, until the 1960s, were kept in careful check by the color line. In 1870, 45 percent of the population was black, a portion that declined to one third by 1900. Metropolitan growth in the last quarter of a century has maintained the overall ratio of blacks to whites at about 33 percent, but the lack of change in corporate limits helped to increase the black percentage in the city to 65 percent in 1980. The end of legal discrimination, coupled with increasing voter concentration in the last decade, led to the election of blacks to positions ranging from mayor (Maynard Jackson, 1973) to U.S. Congressman (Andrew Young, 1974). "A City too Busy to Hate," the Chamber of Commerce's slogan during desegregation in the 1960s, has become the "Black Mecca" of the 1970s.

Margaret Mitchell's *Gone with the Wind*, Stone Mountain's carving of the

Confederacy, Cyclorama's diorama of the battle of Atlanta, and calico-dressed black women at popular tourist restaurants represent for many the romantic image of the city as the "Capital of the Lost Cause." Yet, few, if any, traces of the Old South can be found in Atlanta. As the "Capital of the New South," its symbols are commercial: railroad stations, warehouses, hotels, and office buildings. In the late 19th century Atlanta pioneered one of the first skyscrapers in the Southeast (the Equitable Building, 1892, by Burnham and Root); in the late 20th century the city popularized the atrium hotel (the Regency-Hyatt House, 1967, by John Portman), the multiuse complex (Peachtree Center, 1967–81, also by John Portman), the suburban mall (Lenox Square, 1959), and the expressway. In fact, construction during the 1960s and 1970s erased many of the symbols of the original New South city, including the rail passenger stations, the Equitable Building, and the turn-of-the-century hotels.

Cultural life in Atlanta has grown with the city. In the 19th century several opera houses were built, the most famous being the DeGive Opera House, which, when it was used later as a movie theater, was the site of the world premiere of *Gone with the Wind*. In 1910 the city fathers succeeded in bringing the Metropolitan Opera of New York for a week's visit, an annual event, which, with an occasional hiatus caused by world wars and the Depression, continues today. The Woodruff Memorial Arts Center has evolved from an Arts Association chartered by families of leading boosters in 1903 into a place to see important regional works of art, the location of traveling exhibitions of national and international importance, and the site of Symphony Hall and a profes-

sional theater. University life commenced in Atlanta in 1867 with the founding of Atlanta University, the city's first black institution of higher education. Later, Atlanta's New South promoters financed the establishment of colleges as a means of enhancing the commercial vitality of a growing metropolis. Organized promotions brought, among others, Georgia Institute of Technology in 1888, Emory University in 1915, and Georgia State University in 1955. The population growth of the 1960s was matched by advances in both high and popular culture. The Atlanta Symphony (which was founded in 1944 as a youth orchestra) grew to maturity, while the construction of a stadium and coliseum allowed the city to attract professional sports teams, including the Braves (baseball), the Falcons (football), and the Hawks (basketball).

Atlanta continues to build on its original source of strength—its location in the national transportation network. Beginning in the 1840s when it was the terminus of the state-built railroad linking lines to Charleston and Savannah with an over-the-mountain route to Tennessee and the southern interior, Atlanta grew into the center of a southeastern railroad network. By 1920, 14 lines and four major systems connected through the "Gate City of the South." As auto and truck traffic have supplanted rail since World War II, Atlanta has benefited from the construction of the best interstate highway connections in the Southeast. The city also won over its nearby rivals to become the primary transfer point for air passenger service in the region. So many airline routes to southern cities have Atlanta connections that it is often said, "When you die and go to heaven, you must pass through Atlanta." A thriving convention trade and an uncommonly high number of offices of national corporations are the result of Atlanta's excellent air connections, leading business leaders to dream about being "The World's Next Great City."

See also EDUCATION: / Emory; Georgia Institute of Technology; INDUSTRY: / Atlanta as Commercial Center; Grady, Henry W.; MEDIA: / Atlanta *Constitution*; MYTHIC SOUTH: New South Myth

> Timothy J. Crimmins
> Georgia State University

Timothy J. Crimmins and Dana F. White, eds., "Urban Structure, Atlanta," a special issue of the *Atlanta Historical Journal* (Summer–Fall 1982); Franklin Garrett, *Yesterday's Atlanta* (1974); Andrew Hamer, *Urban Atlanta: Redefining the Role of the City* (1980). ☆

BIRMINGHAM

Cherokee, Choctaw, and Chickasaw tribesmen roamed Jones Valley before the first white settlers appeared in 1813 in the area that one day would be known as Birmingham. Furnaces and small ironworks were built in the area during the Civil War to provide armaments for the Confederate armies, but they were destroyed by Union forces.

When speculative entrepreneurs founded Birmingham in 1871, they predicted that it would become the "El Dorado of the iron masters" and the "manufacturing center of the habitable globe." Birmingham has never fulfilled that lofty prophecy, but the founders' vision was compelling enough to have attracted a number of major investors by 1880. Within two decades this cadre of New South industrialists, led by Henry

Fairchild De Bardeleben, had constructed 28 furnaces, had sunk numerous mines into the rich seams of coal and iron ore nearby, and had constructed railroads and villages throughout the mineral district, of which Birmingham became the center. Due primarily to the development of resources around Birmingham, coal production in Alabama increased from only 17,000 tons in 1872 to 8 million tons in 1900, and pig iron production leaped from just 11,000 tons to more than 1 million tons in the same period. Indeed, by 1898 Birmingham was the largest exporting point for pig iron in the United States, and the third largest in the world. It became known as the "Pittsburgh of the South."

The desires and needs of these early entrepreneurs, however, far outpaced the financial resources available in the capital-poor South. Consequently, investors from outside the district acquired and consolidated the holdings of many smaller and weaker companies. The largest of these new corporations was the Tennessee Coal, Iron and Railroad Company (TCI). Even though TCI inaugurated the production of competitive grade steel in 1899, it was plagued by financial problems, and by 1900 was almost wholly controlled by absentee owners in the North.

Northern control of Birmingham industry was further consolidated in 1907 when TCI was absorbed by the United States Steel Corporation. To insure that the competitive advantage offered by Birmingham's natural resources and cheap labor supply would not endanger the company's base operations at Pittsburgh, U.S. Steel instituted a series of discriminatory pricing systems for TCI products that remained in force until the late 1930s. Thus, Birmingham became one of the more prominent examples of the South's colonial status in the first half of the 20th century, because the city's economic fortunes were determined largely by policies made in Pittsburgh rather than by decisions made by local business leaders.

Birmingham's population grew from 38,415 to 132,685 between 1900 and 1920, and the place became known as "Magic City." By 1930 the population stood at 259,678. Birmingham's heavy industrial economy assured that its population would be more diverse than most southern cities. In addition to native whites, a significant number of first- and second-generation immigrants and an even larger proportion of blacks were attracted by the opportunities in the district. The competition for jobs among these groups was frequently enflamed by racial and cultural differences, and on occasion conflict would escalate into violence. Violence also inevitably accompanied the early, unsuccessful efforts by unions to organize workers at local mines and mills. Meantime, community leaders seeking to mitigate these conflicts could find little support among the industrialists, who wielded the most power but chose either to remain aloof from local affairs or to act solely to protect their economic interests. The city was especially hard hit by the Great Depression, but the increased demand for steel during World War II contributed to the emergence of Birmingham as a major southern industrial center by the 1950s. Today, a 55-foot-high cast-iron statue of Vulcan (the Roman god of fire), which is one of the largest iron statues in the world, stands atop Red Mountain, a symbol of the iron-and-steel-making legacy of the city below.

Birmingham was sometimes called the "Johannesburg of America" in the 1960s because of the racial conflict in the city. Eugene "Bull" Connor was re-elected police commissioner in 1957 and did little to discourage the white terrorism of blacks that had already appeared there. The spring of 1963 saw massive civil rights demonstrations and police violence against marchers. News photographs of blacks attacked by snarling dogs and angry police became a large part of the national image of the city. In September 1963 the bombing of the 16th Street Baptist Church, killing four young black girls, initially threatened the racial truce that had ended the demonstrations. Ultimately, however, the tragedy brought blacks and whites closer together. Racial peace appeared in the late 1960s, with the first blacks elected to the City Council in 1968. Richard Arrington became Birmingham's first black mayor in 1979.

In the early 1900s Birmingham's cultural and social life was dominated by a rigid adherence to Protestant moral standards (a city referendum in 1922 resulted in the closing of a public dance pavilion before the den of iniquity ever opened). That era ended long ago, though. Birmingham now supports a symphony orchestra, ballet companies, and theater groups. There are 65 public parks, a professional hockey team, and, until recently, a franchise in the United States Football League. The University of Alabama in Birmingham was established in 1964 as a branch campus of the University of Alabama, including schools of medicine, dentistry, and nursing. Other colleges include Birmingham Southern, Samford University, Miles College, Jefferson State Junior College, and Lawson State Community College.

Robert G. Corley
University of Alabama
at Birmingham

Ethel Armes, *The Story of Coal and Iron in Alabama* (1910); Carl V. Harris, *Political Power in Birmingham, 1871–1921* (1977); Marjorie L. White, *The Birmingham District: An Industrial History and Guide* (1981). ☆

CHARLESTON
||||||||||||||||||||||||||||||||||||

Charleston, founded in 1670, became wealthy and prosperous in the early 18th century through its commerce and the shipping of rice, indigo, and backcountry products. The city during its early period contained a mixture of nationalities and religious sects. Sephardic Jews, for example, established one of the largest Jewish communities in North America. Two main groups contributed most to the city's distinctive culture. One was composed of the wealthiest planters and merchants who set the tone for society. They were avid consumers of European culture as well as fashions. Their patronage of the theater helped to make Dock Street Theatre, opened in 1736, one of America'a first. Their enjoyment of fine music also led to the founding of the St. Cecilia Society, the earliest American organization sponsoring amateur and professional concerts. Charleston's elite played a large part in the establishment of a private subscription library in 1748 and the erection of private academies and schools. The wealthy also built elegant town houses, the most distinctive of which was the Charleston "single house," which faced not the street but its own side garden and whose width was that of a single room. The city's gentry, self-consciously aristocratic and proud of their social and cultural life, included some of the foremost proponents of a proslavery ideology, southern nationalism, and secession.

Although the wealthy were an important force in Charleston, the city was also a biracial society with a majority black population through much of its history. Most blacks were chattel slaves who as domestics, artisans, market workers, or laborers formed the backbone of the labor force. Less than 10 percent of Charleston's total population was composed of free blacks. Among them was a small but significant group of propertied tradesmen and artisans who created the fraternal and benevolent organizations, the Brown Fellowship and the Humane Brotherhood. But restrictions upon the rights of free blacks, especially after the abortive slave uprising engineered by Denmark Vesey in 1822, probably meant that free blacks maintained many ties with the slave community. A large West African slave trade, which lasted until 1808, helped blacks to maintain a distinctive cultural identity retaining elements from their African origin. Many black Charlestonians spoke Gullah, a dialect that combined African structures with African, Portuguese, and English words. The center of the distinctive black culture lay in religion. Blacks tended to favor the more evangelical sects such as the Methodist and Baptist churches—in the former they outnumbered whites by a margin of around eight to one, in the latter four to one. Charleston blacks founded their own church, Emmanuel African Methodist Episcopal, in 1815, but whites fearful of growing black autonomy suppressed it and forced blacks to rejoin churches with white members.

The Civil War, which began at Fort Sumter in the Charleston harbor, shattered the prosperity that had already begun to wane in Charleston. Through the late 19th century and into the 20th, white Charlestonians of the old elite clung to the symbols of their lost past— their antebellum houses and their cultural societies. Freedom brought black Charlestonians the ability to form separate churches and maintain their cultural identity, but poverty and discrimination continued to limit the roles they could play within the city. Industry slowly gained a foothold in postbellum Charleston, and the two world wars were the harbingers of new economic vitality and population growth. The 1984 population was 69,510.

In the modern period Charleston's culture has retained some of the influence of its elite and black populations but has increasingly become more like that of other Americans. The city has kept its older institutions but new ones have emerged as well so that today a list of Charleston's cultural centers proves formidable. Among the city's many museums are the Charleston Museum, recently relocated to modern quarters, and the Gibbs Art Museum. Charleston today also possesses semiprofessional ballet and theater companies, one of which performs at the historic Dock Street Theatre. Since 1977 the city has gained a richer cultural experience from the increased concentration upon the fine arts at the College of Charleston combined with the creation of the Spoleto Festival by Italian composer Gian Carlo Menotti. Named for its Italian birthplace, this annual summer event includes prominent as well as promising young musicians in areas ranging from opera to jazz.

See also EDUCATION: / Citadel; RECREATION: / Spoleto Festival U.S.A.; St. Cecilia Ball; SCIENCE AND MEDICINE: / Charleston Museum

Jane Turner Censer
The Frederick Law Olmsted Papers

Jack R. Censer
George Mason University

Frederick P. Bowes, *The Culture of Early Charleston* (1942); Erskine Clarke, *Wrestlin' Jacob: A Portrait of Religion in the Old South* (1979); Robert L. Harris, Jr., *South Carolina Historical Magazine* (October 1981); George C. Rogers, Jr., *Charleston in the Age of the Pinckneys* (1969). ☆

CHARLOTTE

Charlotte today is the regional focal point for a continuous network of urban communities in the Carolinas that number over 2 million people—and a far cry from the "trifling place" that visitor George Washington termed the community 200 years ago. At that time Charlotte was a small market town for vegetables, grains, and livestock and had achieved only brief fame as General Cornwallis's North Carolina headquarters. It sank back into relative obscurity until the early 1880s when a gold rush in Mecklenburg County, of which Charlotte is the county seat, revived the town.

By the 1850s cotton was king in Mecklenburg, and Charlotte, like so many other southern cities, developed processing and trade facilities for the region's agricultural products. Future growth of the city was problematic, though, because it did not enjoy the physical advantages of a waterline location so crucial to early 19th-century urban development. The city did occupy a strategic central point in the growing Piedmont agricultural region, and from the 1850s Charlotte became the major railroad center for the Carolinas.

The effective rail connections, as well as the contagious New South creed boosting industrial and urban development, encouraged local entrepreneurs like Daniel A. Tompkins to launch the "Cotton Mill Campaign" in the 1880s. A major objective of the campaign was to provide employment opportunities for rural whites increasingly impoverished by a depressed agriculture. The campaign attempted to alter the economic base of the Carolina Piedmont from predominantly staple agriculture to industry. Its success was seen by 1903, when one-half of the South's looms and spindles were located within a 100-mile radius of the city, most financed with indigenous capital. Charlotte typified southern urban growth of the era with its reliance on basic processing industry, though by the 1940s the city was primarily an administrative center. Charlotte, the "Queen City" (named for George III's wife in 1765), attained economic stability as it gained independence from King Cotton.

Charlotte's strategic rail connections attracted major highway systems beginning in the 1920s, when textile mills began deserting New England for the South. Two major interstate highways— 85 ("Textile Highway") and 77—intersect at Charlotte, making automobile pollution an increasing problem in the city. Despite the decline in the textile industry, Charlotte has avoided the economic problems of other Piedmont communities tied to the textile culture through a judicious policy of economic diversification as an administrative and financial center. The city managed to attract IBM and to add to its already-excellent transportation linkages a new airport in 1982.

The city also benefited from a relatively enlightened racial policy as evidenced by the pioneering Charlotte-Mecklenburg school busing plan. Charlotte's diversified economy, relatively high proportion of Yankees, and vibrant and prosperous inner-city neighborhoods make it something of an anomaly in southern urban culture. The future success of Charlotte, a medium-sized city of 331,000 residents in 1984, may very well depend upon the maintenance of its diverse economic base, its image as a city of neighborhoods, and its population diversity.

As Charlotte's economic base has shifted and expanded from an administrative hub for the Piedmont textile empire to the Southeast's major financial and high-tech center, its cultural profile has altered to complement the new demographic (high-salaried, high-skilled, high-educated) and economic trends of the 1980s. The Charlotte Symphony Orchestra attained professional status in 1981; the city's opera company and the recently expanded Mint Museum of Art enjoy a strong financial support from the growing professional population; Spirit Square, a converted church in downtown, has become the location for musical performances ranging from classical to jazz; and another church in the same area will become the Afro-American Cultural Center. Since 1972, the Creative Arts Department at the University of North Carolina at Charlotte has been a community focal point for dance, theater, voice, and fine arts education. The city's cultural centers have recruited actively from the North and even abroad for experienced personnel to direct these activities. There are no contemporary art galleries, however, and patron tastes rarely exceed the conventional in art and music.

David R. Goldfield
University of North Carolina at Charlotte

LeGette Blythe, *Charlotte and Mecklenburg County, North Carolina Today* (1967); James W. Clay, ed., *Atlas of Charlotte-Mecklenburg* (1981); Mary N. Kraft, *Charlotte, Spirit of the New South* (1980). ☆

DALLAS
|||||||||||||||||||||

In the beginning, Dallas had no special advantages in natural resources or geography to favor it over other frontier settlements in north central Texas. Its development has been due in large part to an aggressive civic spirit passed through generations. Somehow, writer Larry L. King has observed, "Dallas attracted men determined to build a great city: go-getters and can-doers, men of ambitious fevers." Each advantage they created became a springboard for other, more ambitious efforts.

The first settler was John Neely Bryan, who established a trading post on the east bank of the Trinity River in 1841 and laid out a townsite half a mile square near a good crossing on the river. Bryan apparently promoted his townsite widely. John B. Billingsley, who arrived at Dallas from Missouri in 1844, recorded in his journal: "We soon reached the place we had heard of so often; but the *town*, where was it? Two small log cabins—this was the town of Dallas; and two families of ten or twelve souls was its population." When Dallas County was created in 1846, Dallas was designated as the temporary county seat; in 1850 it was chosen permanent county seat over Hord's Ridge and Cedar Springs. During the Civil War the town became a Confederate administrative center, with quartermaster, commissary, transportation, and recruiting headquarters. Population reached 1,200 by 1872, and the *Texas Almanac* that year referred to Dallas as one of

three north Texas towns already "beginning to put on the airs of a city." In the early 1870s the Houston & Texas Central and Texas & Pacific railroads began operating into Dallas, thus assuring her economic future.

Beginning with the erection of the 15-story Praetorian Building in 1907, the Dallas skyline began to present an urban appearance. Thanks to the popular television program, *Dallas*, a prime-time soap opera about the oil-rich Ewing clan of Southfork Ranch, millions of Americans recognize the modern skyline. New buildings in the 1980s such as the 60-story Allied Bank Tower and the LTV Center, a 50-story skyscraper of stone, gave Dallas a new architectural significance.

"It is the Athens of the Southwest," *Fortune* noted in 1949, "the undisputed leader of finance, insurance, distribution, culture and fashion for this land of the super-Americans." The Chamber of Commerce likes to boast that "Dallas is neither typically Southern or Southwestern, but distinctly cosmopolitan in its outlook." The prevailing political mood is staunchly conservative. Municipal politics is oligarchic, dominated by populous, well-to-do, heavily Republican north Dallas. Blacks represent less than 30 percent of the city's population. Persons of Spanish origin—predominantly Mexican Americans—make up 12.3 percent. Lee Harvey Oswald's assassination of President John F. Kennedy on 22 November 1963 represented the greatest trauma in the city's modern era.

Community enterprises in the cultural field include the Dallas Symphony, the Dallas Civic Opera Company, Summer Musicals, the Dallas Ballet, the Dallas Theater Center, the Dallas Museum of Art, and the Shakespeare Festival. Among the principal institutions of higher education in Dallas County are Southern Methodist University, the University of Texas Health Science Center, Baylor University College of Dentistry, University of Dallas, Bishop College, Dallas Theological Seminary, University of Texas at Dallas, Dallas Baptist College, and Dallas County Community College District. Professional sports in the area are headed by "America's Team"—football's Dallas Cowboys—and include the Texas Rangers in baseball and the Dallas Mavericks in basketball.

Dallas has always been proud of its municipal competence and likes to think of itself as the "City That Works." Agitation by the Cleaner Dallas League (1902) for municipal sanitation, public parks, paved streets, and sidewalks led ultimately to a series of "city plans" and bond issues. Permissive zoning and intensive development, however, have created an office glut downtown, choked major freeways and roads, and caused commercial encroachment into the city's older residential neighborhoods. Its 1984 nonmetropolitan population figure was 974,000. Dallas is now split between residents who want a diverse but stable city and developers and others who prefer to live in a perpetual boom town—"Big D."

See also EDUCATION: / Southern Methodist University

Norman D. Brown
University of Texas
at Austin

Sam Acheson, *Dallas Yesterdays* (1977); A. C. Greene, *Dallas: The Deciding Years— A Historical Portrait* (1973); John W. Rogers, *The Lusty Texans of Dallas* (1951). ☆

HOUSTON
||||||||||||||||||||||||

Founded in 1836 by two brothers from New York, John and Augustus Allen, Houston is now the nation's fourth largest city with a 1984 population of about 1,706,000. Its metropolitan population recently surpassed 3 million. Houston is located in southeast Texas, about 50 miles from Galveston Bay. The city possesses a humid, semitropical climate, common to the Gulf Coast, which creates lush vegetation during the summer months. The catalyst for Houston's economy is energy, as the city calls itself the energy capital of the United States. Over one-quarter of the refining capacity of the United States and over one-half of the petrochemical capacity of the nation is located in Houston. In addition, over two-thirds of the world's oil tools are produced there. Although the city is 50 miles from Galveston Bay, the port of Houston is ranked among the top three in the country.

In 1900 Houston was a small city consisting of about 44,000 people within a nine-square-mile area. Southern in style and culture, the city called itself the Magnolia City in an attempt to accentuate these roots. But three factors in the 20th century combined to change its character and make it one of the fastest-growing urban areas in the United States. Galveston, its closest rival, was destroyed in 1900 by a hurricane and a flood, and one year later, oil was discovered in nearby Beaumont. With the assistance of the U.S. Army Corps of Engineers, the city dredged and widened Buffalo Bayou, creating the Houston Ship Channel, the shallow narrow waterway that connected the city to Galveston Bay. The result was a deep water port by 1914. The combination of oil and the safe port, plus the destruction of Galveston as a commercial rival, was the basis of Houston's economic boom in the 20th century.

In the 1920s refineries and petrochemical facilities were constructed along the Ship Channel, a process accelerated by the needs of the American military during World War II. The city's growth was also assisted by the mass introduction of air-conditioning after the war, as well as the acquisition of the National Aeronautics and Space Administration (and the title "Space City") in the late 1950s.

Another factor in Houston's rapid growth, and a major characteristic of the city, is a relatively conservative political climate and a concomitant belief in a free enterprise ideology, which has assisted business growth while limiting the size and functions of local government. As a result, the city is the nation's only major metropolis without zoning.

Spatially, the city is a sprawling— over 560 square miles—decentralized, automobile-based and freeway-linked urban region, with a low population density, which averages about 3,300 people per square mile. It is ethnically diverse, approximately 60 percent Caucasian, 25 percent black, and 15 percent Hispanic. A number of large economic and administrative activity centers give it a multicentered land-use pattern rather than the traditional central business district. Although facing a number of service-oriented problems, caused in part by rapid growth that has strained the city's ability to provide services, the city is an exciting and optimistic place in which to live.

Houston likes to call itself the "Third Coast," in reference to its artistic achievements, and supports major ballet, opera, symphony, and theater

companies. Numerous exhibits and performances occur regularly in parks, corporate plazas, churches, schools, and even shopping centers. The city's ultra-modern, skyscraper architecture, including landmark buildings by Philip Johnson, is world famous. Support of high culture has been a project of some of Houston's major families including the Cullens, the Hoggs, and the de Menils. There are over 25 colleges and universities in Houston, including Rice University, the University of Houston, and Texas Southern. The city contains a major national medical complex, the 230-acre Texas Medical Center, which was launched in 1943 and now includes 25 institutions. The Astrodome was the world's first domed stadium and is the home for professional baseball, football, and basketball. The mix of high culture and "urban cowboys" makes for an interesting and vital cultural scene.

See also EDUCATION: / Rice University

Barry J. Kaplan
Houston Research Services

Robert Haynes, *A Night of Violence: The Houston Riot of 1917* (1976); David G. McComb, *Houston: A History* (1981); Harold L. Platt, *City Building in the New South: The Growth of Public Services in Houston, Texas, 1830–1915*; Francisco Rosales and Barry J. Kaplan, *Houston: A Twentieth Century Urban Frontier* (1983); Marilyn M. Sibley, *The Port of Houston: A History* (1968). ☆

LITTLE ROCK

Quapaw Indian settlement, pioneer trading center, territorial capital, lazy Confederate outpost, western frontier of unreconstructed gentility, Little Rock has emerged in the second half of the 20th century as one of the bustling, dynamic cities of the Sunbelt South. It had a 1984 city population of 170,000.

Suffering under the peculiarly southern burdens of the crop-lien sharecropping system, a one-crop economy, a one-party political system, and widespread poverty, Arkansas experienced limited growth in the years before World War II, and Little Rock reflected the social complacency and the leisurely pace that characterized much of the southern region. Stimulated by their wartime experiences, however, Little Rock businessmen in the 1940s launched a program of planned growth and industrial development based on Little Rock's proximity to the state's wealth of such raw materials as timber, oil, gas, coal, and bauxite. Local leaders initiated a period of growth that altered dramatically the cultural and economic landscape of their city. By the mid-1970s Little Rock had become the major port on the Arkansas River, the chief market for the state's agricultural produce, the second largest manufacturing center in Arkansas, the site of a growing university complex, and the home of a flourishing arts community that includes symphony, theater, opera, and ballet.

In 1957 Little Rock became the focus of international attention in a struggle over the desegregation of Central High School. When Governor Orval Faubus used the Arkansas National Guard to block the entry into the school of nine black children, President Dwight Eisenhower responded by sending the 101st Airborne Division into the city to accomplish the federal court-ordered desegregation. The confrontation was but a temporary impediment to the desegregation process in Little Rock, which was completed within the next decade, but it was a major factor in modifying racial attitudes and practices of the city. The unfavorable publicity and consequent economic stagnation caused a widespread reassessment of racial attitudes and social values in Little Rock and contributed to the growth of a more liberal spirit in this traditionally moderate city.

Little Rock is a blend of both southern and western cultures. In the southern tradition Little Rock is noted for its hospitality to strangers, its neighborliness, and its regard for good manners and good cooks. Its population is approximately 25 percent black. The social hierarchy is not as rigid, however, as those of neighboring states, and it yields easily to the possessors of talent, ambition, and wealth. Little Rock's dramatic growth in the last 40 years and the influx of outsiders from all parts of the globe have given a cosmopolitan outlook and a progressive spirit to the city.

See also LAW: / Little Rock Crisis

> Elizabeth Jacoway
> University of Arkansas
> at Little Rock

Harry Ashmore, *Arkansas: A Bicentennial History* (1976); Leland DuVall, ed., *Arkansas: Colony and State* (1973). ☆

LOUISVILLE
||||||||||||||||||||||||||||||||||

Founded in May 1778, Louisville, Ky., first served as a base for George Rogers Clark's ambitious offensive against British-held fortresses in the Northwest during the American Revolution. Clark, a Virginia militia captain, located the settlement at the falls of the Ohio River, the only natural break in navigation on the Ohio-Mississippi River system, which stretches from Pittsburgh to New Orleans. Soon after Clark established his outpost, the settlers named their new home Louisville in honor of King Louis XVI of France, who pledged aid to the American cause. Two years later, the Virginia Legislature designated Louisville the county seat of its newly formed Jefferson County (part of Kentucky after statehood in 1792).

Louisville thrived as a commercial center after 1830 when the opening of the Louisville and Portland Canal stimulated river traffic by allowing steamboats to bypass the falls. According to the Census of 1850, one of every six of the county's almost 60,000 residents was a slave, but over 1,600 blacks lived in freedom. In 1850 Louisville was the nation's 10th largest city, having first attracted emigrants from France and Great Britain and then from Germany and Ireland. Still influenced by 19th-century demographics, the Falls City is perhaps unique among major southern communities because almost equal

Bridges over the Ohio River at Louisville, 1964

numbers of Baptists and Roman Catholics, the area's largest religious denominations, reside there.

Although Louisville was called a "western" town before the Civil War, the city emerged from the conflict as "The Gateway to the South." Most Louisvillians began the war as conservative Unionists, but federal violations of the civil rights of Kentuckians combined with congressional protection for blacks to intensify postwar anti-northern sentiment. At the same time, "Marse Henry" Watterson, the ebullient editor of the Louisville *Courier-Journal*, admonished southerners to follow his city's progressive example by welcoming industry and adopting a more subtle form of racism. Much later, in 1956, the River City, again led by an outspoken press, pioneered southern cities in the successful integration of public schools. In 1975, however, the implementation of court-ordered, countywide busing met with scattered white violence.

By the end of the 19th century Louisville became an important regional manufacturing center, with distilling, meat packing, farm implements, tobacco and wood products, and railroading as its economic mainstays. Subsequently, the Falls City added automobiles and trucks, major appliances, coatings, aluminum products, and chemicals to its industrial constellation. Beginning in the mid-1970s several older industries fell on hard times or built new plants elsewhere, prompting vigorous efforts by community leaders to halt further exodus and to nurture white-collar industries like insurance, banking and finance, law, corporate headquarters, and health care. The city is the center of sophisticated medical research exemplified by the artificial heart experiments conducted by the Humana Heart

Institute. Higher education is also important to Louisville's economy with two Catholic colleges, major Southern Baptist and Presbyterian seminaries, and the state-supported University of Louisville, a former municipal institution with schools of medicine (1837) and law (1846) that once drew many students from the South.

Louisville's 1984 city population was 290,000, but in the metropolitan area the figure was nearly 800,000. The city has a strong reputation for the performing arts. It has distinguished itself as a center of informal jazz education, producing well-known stylists like singer Helen Humes, trumpeter Jonah Jones, and guitarist Jimmy Raney. Beginning in 1949 the Louisville Orchestra achieved national recognition for its promotion and newly commissioned music and, more recently, the Actors Theater of Louisville, one of the nation's most successful regional companies, has earned international attention for its annual Festival of New American Plays. Louisville also boasts flourishing professional ballet and opera companies. Most of the city's arts groups perform in a $34.5 million complex that adjoins the Main Street preservation district, a unique collection of 19th-century commercial buildings, many with cast-iron fronts, for which imaginative uses have been found. Nearby, Princeton architect Michael Graves's pyramidal structure, Humana Tower, was completed in 1985. Louisville also has an art museum, a museum of science and history, and a zoo.

Sports are important to the city. In 1983 the Louisville Redbirds, a triple-A baseball team, drew over 1 million fans, an all-time minor league record. The University of Louisville men's basketball team, frequent contenders

for the NCAA major college championship, play in a renovated 19,000-seat Freedom Hall. The vintage Kentucky Derby, the first jewel in horse racing's triple crown, draws tens of thousands to Churchill Downs the first Saturday each May. The race is preceded by a week-long festival that has become a major attraction. The Falls City is the fourth largest convention center in the South, ranking behind only Houston, Atlanta, and Dallas. Louisville's Muhammed Ali established a unique record in boxing and is perhaps the city's best-known sports figure.

Because of its strategic river location and proximity to the North, Louisville early experienced greater economic and social diversity than most of the South. After the Civil War, however, the River City fully identified with Dixie, though sometimes preaching to the region about industrial and racial progress. Louisvillians are still confirmed southerners, despite the fact that their city's progressive image has paled before the Sunbelt's success at building a modern economy and achieving biracial accommodation.

See also MEDIA: / Louisville *Courier-Journal*; RECREATION: / Kentucky Derby

Thomas L. Owen
University of Louisville

Allen J. Share, *Cities in the Commonwealth: Two Centuries of Urban Life in Kentucky* (1982); Samuel W. Thomas, *Louisville since the Twenties* (1978), *Views of Louisville since 1766* (1971); Richard C. Wade, *The Urban Frontier: The Rise of Western Cities* (1959); George Yater, *Two Hundred Years at the Falls of the Ohio* (1979). ✫

MEMPHIS
||||||||||||||||||||||||||

In 1819 land speculators Andrew Jackson, John Overton, and James Winchester capitalized on the removal of the Chickasaw Indians by founding the city of Memphis on 5,000 acres they had purchased in the 1790s. In its infancy the "Bluff City" was a rough-and-tumble frontier town, a haven for the boisterous flatboatmen bound for New Orleans who "got lickered up" and cavorted in the local fleshpots. The arrival of the steamboat—and later the railroad—helped establish Memphis as a trade center, but of primary importance was the emergence of King Cotton in the Old Southwest. The city's overwhelming dependence upon the crop, as well as the system of labor that produced it, resulted in its reorientation as a southern city; it supported a thriving slave market in the antebellum years and enthusiastically cast its lot with the Confederacy after Fort Sumter.

Prior to the 1870s Memphis sported a heterogeneous population mix in which Germans and Irish figured prominently in the local cultural scene. After that decade's disastrous yellow fever epidemics, which resulted in financial ruin and the surrender of the city charter in favor of a state-administered taxing district, the foreign-born avoided the location. As a result, the arrival of the rural inhabitants—both black and white—fueled the city's population growth.

The steady infusion of native-born farm folk led H. L. Mencken to term Memphis the "most rural-minded city in the South" and the "buckle" of the Bible Belt—a reference to the fundamentalist religion that saturated the community. Memphis also became the economic and cultural center for Mid-South blacks. Robert R. Church, a rural transplant from nearby Holly Springs, Miss., reputed to be the South's first black millionaire, headed the region's largest black business community. His son, Robert E. Church, Jr., went into politics and became the nation's most powerful black Republican by the 1920s. For nearly the first half of the 20th century the city's government was dominated by another native of Holly Springs, Edward H. Crump. Boss Crump presided over a Democratic machine so powerful that he single-handedly ruled not only Memphis but Shelby County and exerted considerable statewide influence as well. The city's reputation and morale received a blow in 1968 when Martin Luther King, Jr., was assassinated there while assisting a garbage workers' strike.

A Crump contemporary, songwriter W. C. Handy, penned "The Memphis Blues" in 1909, and Beale Street, the main thoroughfare of the city's black community, gained the reputation as the birthplace of that distinctive musical form. Memphis later nurtured a host of blues and rock-and-roll performers including B. B. King, Isaac Hayes, Jerry Lee Lewis, and its "father" of rock and roll, Elvis Presley. The opening of Graceland, Presley's mansion, to the public and the restoration of Beale Street reflect the city's attempt in recent years to preserve its rich musical heritage. The Pink Palace Museum and Mud Island Museum emphasize the historic link between the "Bluff City" and the Mississippi River. With Memphis State University, Christian Brothers College, LeMoyne-Owen College, Rhodes (formerly Southwestern at Memphis), and the University of Tennessee Center for the Health Sciences, the city serves as the educational heart of the Mid-South. The 1984 Memphis population was 648,000.

See also MEDIA: / Memphis *Commercial Appeal*; MUSIC: / Beale Street; POLITICS: / Crump, E. H.

Roger Biles
Memphis State University

Gerald A. Capers, *The Biography of a River Town: Memphis, Its Heroic Age* (1966); Margaret McKee and Fred Chisenhall, *Beale Black and Blue: Life and Music on America's Main Street* (1981); Robert A. Sigafoos, *Cotton Row to Beale Street: A Business History of Memphis* (1979). ☆

MIAMI
‖‖‖‖‖‖‖‖‖‖‖‖

Miami is the central city in a southeast Florida metropolitan area with a 1980 population of 1.6 million. The city traces its origins to the 1890s, when urban boosters and land speculators, particularly railroad and hotel man Henry M. Flagler, began promoting tourism in southern Florida. By the 1920s Miami and the nearby suburbs of Miami Beach, Coral Gables, and Hialeah had begun to experience boom conditions. Building on its essential natural resources of seashore, sunshine, and subtropical climate, Miami emerged between 1920 and 1940 as one of the fastest-growing metropolitan areas in the nation. Art Deco buildings popular in that time gave Miami a distinctive look.

Military training activities and the location of several naval and air bases in the area stimulated the Miami economy during World War II. In postwar years the city's economy expanded consider-

ably as construction, light manufacturing, air transportation, and service activities crept up on a still-dominant tourism. The city's population grew rapidly as well, and the urban periphery was subdivided and built up by real estate developers. The rising affluence of Americans and the widespread adoption of air-conditioning in the 1950s strengthened Miami's place as a tourist and retirement haven, pushing the population of the Miami metropolitan area to 935,000 by 1960, almost twice the 1950 amount. Increasing numbers of Miami's newcomers were migrants from the Northeast and Midwest, a demographic development that made Miami more affluent, more Jewish, and more liberal on political and social issues than cities in the rest of the South.

Unlike many other southern cities Miami did not expand its boundaries through annexation after 1925. As a result, numerous small municipalities were incorporated during the 1930s and 1940s, and a rising proportion of Miami-area population resided in unincorporated territory. This fragmentation of local government led "good government" reformers to initiate a decade-long campaign for consolidated metropolitan government. With the beginning of Miami's "Metro" government in July of 1957, the area acquired the nation's first two-tier, or federated, metropolitan government.

The two decades since 1960 have brought dramatic change to Miami. The mass exodus of 800,000 Cubans to the United States between 1959 and 1980, most of whom settled in the Miami area, permanently altered the city's character and culture. As of 1980 Hispanics comprised 56 percent of the population in the city of Miami and over 35 percent in the entire metropolitan area. With

Miami's black community growing through the arrival of over 50,000 Haitian exiles in recent years, non-Hispanic whites have become a minority in the Miami area population—a 20-year demographic revolution without precedent in American history.

In the past decade, Miami has emerged as the business and cultural capital of the entire Caribbean basin. Miami was already a major center of international trade and banking by the end of the 1970s. Foreign investment poured into the city, along with the profits from a highly lucrative illegal drug trade. Latin American tourism now surpasses 2 million visitors annually, or about one-sixth of Miami's total tourist business. New skyscraper development in the central business district has transformed Miami's skyline, symbolizing the city's commanding position as the gateway to Latin America. Although Miami shares in the phenomenon of Sunbelt urban growth, the city has always been an anomaly in the American South. Indeed, the patterns of growth and change that have shaped 20th-century Miami demonstrate both the vitality and the cultural diversity of the region. The 1984 nonmetropolitan population figure for Miami was 373,000.

See also ETHNIC LIFE: Caribbean Influence; / Cubans; INDUSTRY: / Flagler, Henry M.

Raymond A. Mohl
Florida Atlantic University

Thomas D. Boswell and James R. Curtis, *The Cuban-American Experience: Culture, Images and Perspectives* (1984); William W. Jenna, Jr., *Metropolitan Miami: A Demographic Overview* (1972); David B. Longbrake and Woodrow W. Nichols, Jr., *Sunshine and Shadow in Metropolitan Miami* (1976); Raymond A. Mohl, *Sunbelt Cities: Politics and Growth since World War II* (1983); Helen Muir, *Miami, U.S.A.* (1953); Arva Parks, *Miami: The Magic City* (1981); Bruce Porter and Marvin Dunn, *The Miami Riot of 1980: Crossing the Bounds* (1984); William Wilbanks, *Murder in Miami: An Analysis of Homicide Patterns and Trends in Dade County (Miami), Florida, 1917–1983* (1984); Reinhold P. Wolff, *Miami: Economic Pattern of a Resort Area* (1945), *Miami Metro: The Road to Urban Unity* (1960). ☆

MOBILE
||||||||||||||||||||

Mobile, founded in 1702 by French naval officer Jean Baptiste Le Moyne, Sieur de Bienville, was named after the nearby Maubila Indians. It has been and continues to be a river-port city largely dependent for its prosperity and even its existence on the economic activity of the hinterland it serves. The Indian trade in colonial times, cotton before and after the Civil War, regional timber, and Birmingham's iron and coal have all flowed through Alabama's only port. Local industries include shipbuilding and chemical plants in addition to the port-related activities.

Mobile's economy boomed in the 1850s thanks to the cotton production of antebellum Black Belt plantations. The city grew rapidly before the war and many fine structures were built, some of which, with their New South cousins, survive to lend an air of southern charm to the modern city. After the defeat of the Confederacy, Mobile languished for several decades. It was almost a century until another war, World War II, brought a second boom, built not on cotton but on defense industries, principally shipbuilding. The city's wartime experience led to considerable expansion and economic growth. Many of the war workers stayed on after 1945 and became an integral part of the city, adopting many of the old town's values and much of its lifestyle for their own.

Alabama's largest city until the end of the 19th century, when Birmingham surpassed it, Mobile has not found the 20th century particularly congenial. A city of promise all too rarely fulfilled, it remains hopeful about the benefits of the Tennessee-Tombigbee Waterway project, coastal oil and natural gas, and a variety of other economic prospects. Its 1984 population was 205,000. Mobile is home to such southern rituals as the annual Azalea Trail, Junior Miss Pageant, and Senior Bowl all-star college football game. The city cultivates its real and imagined colonial and antebellum heritage, celebrating Mardi Gras, whose mother in North America it claims to be, but conscious of the greater success of its age-old rival river city, New Orleans. The University of South Alabama, Spring Hill College, and S. D. Bishop State Junior College are located in Mobile.

See also RECREATION: Mardi Gras

Michael Thomason
University of South Alabama

Harriet Amos, *Cotton City: Urban Development in Antebellum Mobile* (1985); Melton A. McLaurin and Michael Thomason, *Mobile: The Life and Times of a Great Southern City* (1981). ☆

MONTGOMERY
|||||||||||||||||||||||||||||||||||||

Located in the traditional plantation Black Belt, Montgomery sprawls away from a high red bluff overlooking an oxbow bend in the Alabama River, just below the fall line and the end of the Appalachians. It was both the "Cradle of the Confederacy" and the birthplace of the civil rights movement.

Hernando de Soto and his soldiers were the first white men to see the area near present-day Montgomery, stopping at the Indian village of Tawasa on 8 September 1540. For more than 200 years thereafter, Spain, France, and Great Britain struggled for empire there, but Americans finally gained the territory in 1814. Montgomery was founded in 1819 on the site of the Alibamo village of Econchata. The frontier village grew as a transportation center for cotton, and in 1846 the state capital was moved there from Tuscaloosa. Montgomery became a political center and a stronghold of the growing southern states' rights movement. The Deep South states selected Montgomery as the site for their secession convention, and they organized the Confederate States of America in Alabama's Capitol, where Jefferson Davis was inaugurated president on 18 February 1861. The Confederate capital was changed to Richmond later in 1861. After Confederate defeat and Reconstruction, recovery was slow, but Montgomery recovered faster than some other Old South cities because of its continuing importance in government, agriculture, transportation, and some light industry.

In 1917 World War I gave Montgomery another economic boost with the establishment of four military installations, the largest of which was Camp Sheridan. While stationed there, Lieutenant F. Scott Fitzgerald courted debutante Zelda Sayre at the Montgomery country club. On the plantation site where De Soto had camped and where the Wright brothers had run the nation's first civilian pilot-training school in 1910, the War Department established an aviation installation that became a permanent one, Maxwell Field, now one of the 10 oldest U.S. Air Force bases in the country. The Air Corps Tactical School moved there in 1931 and developed the strategic bombardment doctrine later employed in World War II. After that war, Air University, the U.S. Air Force's professional educational center, was placed at Maxwell Air Force Base. In the late 1920s Mayor William A. Gunter pioneered in building America's first planned municipal airport, which is now Gunter Air Force Station, the Air Force's data systems computer center.

In 1955 Montgomery again found itself in the vortex of change with the beginning of the Montgomery bus boycott. A painful 15-year period followed, including the 1961 Freedom Bus Riders' beatings, the Selma to Montgomery march of 1965, and eventually desegregation. In view of that period, the degree of racial accommodation now evident among Montgomery's residents, 40 percent of whom are black, is remarkable.

Cattle and soybeans long ago unseated King Cotton on Montgomery's old

State capitol, Montgomery, Alabama, constructed in 1851

plantation lands, and there is some light industry, insurance, banking, and finance. However, Montgomery's economic underpinning is government at all levels, involving both civilian and military positions. Nearly one out of five inhabitants is connected, either directly or indirectly, with the military. Politics remains a favorite sport in between Auburn-Alabama football games, and its chief practitioner was George C. Wallace, Jr., until his recent retirement. There are three public and two denominational institutions of higher learning—traditionally black Alabama State University, Auburn University at Montgomery, Troy State University at Montgomery, Methodist-affiliated Huntingdon College, and the Churches of Christ's Faulkner University—as well as the Air Force's colleges and schools of Air University. The 1984 Montgomery population numbered 185,000.

Montgomery high society maintains its complex circles and hierarchies of elitism, based on bloodlines from an older South. These circles have been revitalized by new people bringing in talent, energy, and new wealth. The new Alabama Shakespeare Festival Theater, the gift of multimillionaire contractor Winton M. Blount, Jr., along with the new Montgomery Museum of Art, promise to make Montgomery flourish as a cultural center. Meanwhile, the city's historic preservation group, the Landmarks Foundation of Montgomery, guards "The Cradle's" visible past, restoring its historic buildings and attracting many tourists. Folk culture has its shrine at Hank Williams's grave.

John Hawkins Napier III
Cameron Freeman Napier
Montgomery, Alabama

J. Wayne Flynt, *Montgomery: An Illustrated History* (1980); Beth Taylor Muskat and Mary Ann Neeley, *The Way It Was, 1850–1930* (1985); Cameron Freeman Napier, *The First White House of the Confederacy* (1978); John Hawkins Napier III, *Alabama Historical Quarterly* (Fall 1967); Clanton Ware Williams, *The Early History of Montgomery* (1979). ☆

NASHVILLE
||||||||||||||||||||||||||||||

Founded as Fort Nashborough in 1780 by North Carolinians under the leadership of James Robertson and John Donelson, this frontier outpost became a center for fur trading and land speculation. Nashville grew rapidly as the major port on the Cumberland River, northern terminus for the Natchez Trace, and trading center for a developing agricultural hinterland of cotton, grain, tobacco, and livestock. The city's bustling western economy thrust upward an ambitious and powerful group of land speculators, planters, politicians, and military leaders, the most notable of whom was Andrew Jackson, the first president elected from trans-Appalachia America. The rise of political leaders Felix Grundy, James K. Polk, and John Bell and the movement of the state capital to Nashville in 1843 reflected the growing importance of the city within Tennessee and the region.

As residents of a commercial city of more than 16,000 in 1860, standing between the heart of the plantation belt and the Midwest, Nashvillians were ambivalent toward secession. It was the first major Confederate city to fall to the Union invasion in February 1862. During federal occupation it flourished as a Union supply center for the western theater of war. Spared the wartime destruction and blockades suffered by other southern cities, Nashville became a major force in transforming the southern economy in the New South era. The Louisville & Nashville Railroad, Tennessee Coal and Iron, and dozens of aggressive commercial and manufacturing firms led the way.

During the late 19th century many of Nashville's colleges were founded, including Fisk University and Meharry Medical College, both for blacks, Vanderbilt University, and George Peabody College for Teachers. All were founded with the support of northern philanthropists intent on reconstructing the minds of southern youth. Along with numerous smaller denominational schools, these colleges bolstered the city's historic claim as the "Athens of the South." Simultaneously, the city became a publishing and administrative center for several major Protestant denominations, a trend that engendered another fanciful name, the "Protestant Vatican."

In the 20th century Nashville's economy shifted to insurance, banking, and brokerage. By the 1920s it boasted of being the "Wall Street of the South," led by the ill-fated financial empire of Caldwell and Company. Nashville's insurance companies, eager to appeal to the new flood of rural white migrants to

The Parthenon in Nashville, a replica of the temple in Athens, Greece, constructed in 1896

the cities of the South after World War I, sponsored radio programs with "old timey" music. The "Grand Ole Opry," begun in 1925, became the most famous of these radio shows and formed the nucleus of a nascent recording industry. World War II exposed millions of soldiers and civilians to southern country music, and postwar affluence, along with the continued rural migration to the cities, generated new markets for the music. Recording studios, song writers, musicians, and singers clustered on Nashville's Music Row. In the 1950s Broadcast Music Incorporated broke the New York monopoly on music copyrights and opened the door to a national market for country music. Business leaders in the Athens of the South, initially embarrassed by the image of hillbilly music, came to embrace "Music City, USA," with its flourishing recording and tourist industries, as a major asset. Nashville's 1984 nonmetropolitan population was 462,000.

See also EDUCATION: / Fisk University; Vanderbilt University; MEDIA: / Nashville *Tennessean*; MUSIC: / Grand Ole Opry

Don H. Doyle
Vanderbilt University

Don H. Doyle, *Nashville in the New South, 1880–1930* (1985); John Woolridge, ed., *History of Nashville, Tennessee* (1890). ☆

NATCHEZ
||||||||||||||||||||||||||

Natchez, one of the oldest settlements on the Mississippi River, was named for the Indian tribe that inhabited the vicinity. The French built a trading post there in 1714 and two years later erected Fort Rosalie; the settlement on the

bluffs passed into the hands of the English (1763) and the Spanish (1779) and in 1798 became a part of the United States with the creation of the Mississippi Territory. Although it was not incorporated until 1803, Natchez was for a time (1798–1802) the capital of the new territory and in 1817 became the first capital of the newly created state of Mississippi. By 1821, however, the legislature had begun the search for a more central location and moved the seat of government to Jackson that year.

During the steamboat era Natchez was an important cotton port, famous up and down the river for the taverns and gambling dives that flourished at Natchez-under-the-Hill, the landing. The city was also the southern terminus of the storied Natchez Trace, an Indian trail running in a southwesterly direction from Nashville that was cleared by General James Wilkinson as a military road in the early 1800s.

Natchez became a center of wealth and culture in the antebellum period, and many of the cotton barons who had extensive landholdings in the surrounding area or across the river in Louisiana built splendid homes for themselves in the city. It is these mansions and the

Longwood, at Natchez, built in 1850s

invitation to "Come to Natchez, Where the Old South Still Lives" that every year draws thousands to the Natchez Pilgrimage. Indeed, the Pilgrimage, founded by a local garden club in 1932, is the city's preeminent industry and for its citizens the focus of the social season—a time when descendants of the planter-barons and newcomers open their homes and when many don antebellum dress to attend balls and to appear in the "Confederate Pageant." An annual antiques symposium focuses attention on decorative arts in the South and the city.

Natchez today is especially noteworthy for its architecture, which ranges from the Spanish Provincial style of the late 18th century to the Greek Revival style of the antebellum period and the Oriental style of Longwood, with its bulbiform dome and its Moorish arches, said to be the largest octagonal house in America. Natchez stands alongside Charleston and Savannah as examples of cities that have dedicated themselves to the preservation of their historic architecture. Members of the Hare Krishna religious cult bought one of Natchez's old houses in the early 1980s, but they quickly adapted to the old city's ways. The county seat of Adams County, Natchez had a population of 22,015 in 1984.

See also ENVIRONMENT: / Natchez Trace; HISTORY AND MANNERS: / Pilgrimage

Charles East
Baton Rouge, Louisiana

Mary Wallace Crocker, *Historic Architecture in Mississippi* (1973); Joan W. Gandy and Thomas W. Gandy, *Norman's Natchez: An Early Photographer and His Town* (1978); D. Clayton James, *Antebellum Natchez* (1968); Mary W. Miller and Ronald W. Miller, *The Great Houses of Natchez*, photography by David Gleason (1986). ☆

NEW ORLEANS

New Orleans is a multiracial, multiethnic, largely Catholic city located on the fringes of the Bible Belt. Founded by Jean Baptiste Le Moyne, Sieur de Bienville, in 1718 as a French fortification near the mouth of the Mississippi River, the original city (now the French Quarter or Vieux Carré) was modeled after La Rochelle in France. This area originally was called the *place d'armes* but was renamed Jackson Square in 1849. The mosquito-infested, disease-ridden site combined with French neglect to retard growth and make New Orleans an economic liability for much of the French reign. Ceded to Spain in 1762–63, the city began to prosper as its new administrators spurred colonization by permitting British and American settlers into the region. Spain ceded back New Orleans and the rest of the Louisiana territory to France only to see Napoleon sell it to the United States in 1803. A 1788 fire leveled much of the city, but it was rebuilt using a distinctive mix of Spanish and French architecture. In modern times the city has been an enthusiastic supporter of historic preservation programs for buildings in the French Quarter.

The antebellum era was a golden age for New Orleans. By 1860 it was the largest city in the South (population 168,675) and the fifth largest city in the United States. The War of 1812 brought cooperation between Americans and Creoles against the British, and afterwards the city became an even more important trade center. It remained a predominantly French-speaking city throughout the period, although a large influx of Americans, bolstered by German and Irish immigration, made more heterogeneous an already cosmopolitan populace. The first Mardi Gras parade was in 1857, and it soon became a symbol of the New Orleans spirit. New Orleans was occupied by federal forces between 1862 and 1865, but its white majority later resisted Reconstruction by electing Democratic mayors who were determined not to share power with the freed blacks. In the Gilded Age the city stagnated economically, saw its race relations deteriorate, and succeeded only in adding another layer to its polyglot population through a large-scale Sicilian immigration. Sanitation problems promoted recurrent outbreaks of cholera and yellow fever. Within this troubled context New Orleans demonstrated its cultural vitality, though, by developing jazz as a popular musical form.

In the 20th century New Orleans possessed one of the South's rare urban political machines, which dominated the city from 1904 until its defeat by De Lesseps S. "Chep" Morrison in 1946. Although New Orleans lagged behind its more dynamic Sunbelt competitors after World War II (it ranked fifth among Old South cities with a population of 557,482 in 1980), oil and tourism bolstered a reinvigorated economy. Flood control programs helped the city become a major port in the early 20th century, and shipbuilding industries proliferated in the era during World War II. New Orleans now ranks as the nation's second busiest port. It became a center for National Aeronautics and Space Administration activities in the 1960s. The Voting Rights Act of 1965 transferred political power in the now majority-black city to "progressive" mayors like Moon Landrieu in 1970 and Ernest N.

"Dutch" Morial (the city's first black chief executive) in 1978. The 1984 population numbered 559,000.

New Orleans has been a unique cultural center in the American South. A cosmopolitan, Catholic background has made its cultural patterns distinctive through most of southern history. St. Louis Cathedral, completed in 1794, is the oldest one in the United States. The city was an early center of opera with its St. Charles Theater, and the Opera House Association now offers six operas annually. The French Quarter, Fat City, Bourbon Street, Basin Street, and Mardi Gras all evoke images of joyous entertainment and celebration. Storyville used to be a byword for vice and gambling.

In the contemporary era New Orleans has initiated new occasions for good times. The New Orleans Jazz and Heritage Festival is now held in April, a Spring Festival each April or May, the France-Louisiana Festival in July, and the New Orleans Food Festival in July or August (reflecting the importance of cuisine in defining the city's distinctive character). New Orleans has long encouraged sporting activities. It was a center of prizefighting and horse racing in the late 19th century, it now hosts the Sugar Bowl football classic on New Year's Day, and the Superdome is the home for the professional football Saints and the Pride, a women's basketball team. The Cotton Centennial Exposition was held in 1884–85 and the New Orleans World's Fair in 1984. The city, finally, is a medical center, with 22 hospitals, including the Louisiana State University and Tulane medical schools and the Ochsner Foundation Hospital.

See also ART AND ARCHITECTURE: French Architecture; Spanish Architecture; BLACK LIFE: / Mardi Gras Indians; Storyville; ED-

UCATION: / Tulane University; LANGUAGE: / New Orleans English; MEDIA: / New Orleans *Times-Picayune*; RECREATION: Mardi Gras

Arnold R. Hirsch
University of New Orleans

H. W. Gilmore, *American Sociological Review* (August 1944); Edward F. Haas, *De Lesseps S. Morrison and the Image of Reform: New Orleans Politics, 1946–1961* (1974); John Smith Kendall, *History of New Orleans*, 3 vols. (1922). ☆

RICHMOND

Founded at the falls of the James River in 1607, Richmond initially served as a crossroads for trade between the Tidewater plantations and the West. When it was incorporated as a town in 1742, Richmond possessed only 250 inhabitants, though its hinterland boasted the estates of some of Virginia's most prestigious families. The city's role as an administrative center—as Virginia's capital beginning in 1779, briefly as capital of the Confederacy, and throughout the 19th and 20th centuries as the nerve center of the state's business community—along with trade and manufacturing, made Richmond one of the South's wealthiest cities.

Old South Richmond was a unique blend of regional traits and features that were decidedly non-southern. The city's rigid gridiron layout adorned by densely packed-in brick town houses, its ethnic diversity, and its extensive industrial sector gave Richmond a look not unlike that of Philadelphia or Baltimore. As the manufacturing hub of the Old South, Richmond excelled in iron, tobacco, and flour processing. Yet the wide-spread use of slaves as factory laborers, carters, and domestics underscored the city's commitment to "the peculiar institution" and compelled whites to construct an elaborate and rigid system of social controls. The sheer size of Richmond's black community, which in 1860 numbered 14,275 (or 38 percent of the city's population), enabled it to develop an institutional life that flourished in the postwar era and supplied a counterbalance to Jim Crowism.

The process of rebuilding Richmond's ruins following the Civil War fostered visions of urban greatness that exceeded those of Old South entrepreneurs. Building upon the trade and manufacturing base formed in the antebellum era, city promoters vigorously backed canal, railroad, and, by the 20th century, highway connections to an enlarged hinterland. Between 1867 and 1914 Richmond annexed aggressively, thereby incorporating the streetcar suburbs that fanned out from the city center as well as the manufacturing rival of Manchester located on the south side of the James. Prior to 1900, however, city leaders were torn between promotion of urban growth and the desire to forestall change of any sort, and this dilemma was reflected in a marked tendency toward frugality in public expenditures for needed city improvements. Only in the late 1880s, when organized labor through the Knights of Labor temporarily seized the reins of local government, was there serious consideration of civic improvements.

After 1900, however, the vision of Richmond as a New South metropolis gained a broader following. To supply a political foundation for continuous expansion, Richmond experimented with governmental reform, adopting a modified commission government in 1912.

This gave way in 1917 to a strong mayoral form committed to progress through public planning for city development. Nevertheless, Richmond retained a bicameral city council (which proved to be a bastion of fiscal conservatism) until 1947, when it shifted to a nine-member, nonpartisan legislative body with a city manager as chief administrator. Spearheaded by downtown business leaders intent on making local government operate as a business, the new political structure proved more amenable to public backing of urban development initiatives, including expressway construction, urban renewal, provision of public housing, and, by the 1960s, development of a civic center complex.

The growing political power of the city's black community, stimulated by white flight to the suburbs during the 1950s and first evidenced in local elections in the 1960s, produced, in 1977, a black majority on the city council and appointment of Henry March as the city's first black mayor. As had been evident since statewide disenfranchisement of blacks in 1902, race was a pivotal issue in local affairs, but Richmond successfully avoided the violent confrontations that rocked other cities especially during the 1960s. Although the 1980 census revealed that the city's population continued a downward trend that had begun in the 1950s, revitalization of housing in inner-city neighborhoods such as the Fan, Jackson Ward, and Church Hill underscored the public and private commitment to preserve portions of Old Richmond as the basis for future growth. The 1984 city population was 219,000.

Ironically, even as the city failed to maintain demographic dominance within the metropolis during the 1960s and 1970s, Richmond retained and enhanced its function as a cultural center. During the past decade the city added museums, theaters, and performing arts companies to its already substantial and diversified cultural base. Indeed, the formation of Virginia Commonwealth University—through the merging of the Richmond Professional Institute and Medical College of Virginia—not only enlarged the educational and cultural opportunities in the city but supplied an impetus to revitalization of adjacent neighborhoods and enlargement of the downtown civic center. The recent creation of a Federated Arts District at the edge of the downtown shopping area underscores Richmond's determination to retain its hegemony over the cultural life of the metropolis and to increase activity in the city center. In higher education (Richmond boasts three universities and numerous professional schools), the performing arts, and in a variety of professional and amateur sports, Richmonders continue to look to the city's center, not to its mushrooming suburbs, for their cultural life.

See also MEDIA: / Richmond *Times-Dispatch*

Christopher Silver
Virginia Commonwealth University

Michael Chesson, *Richmond after the War, 1865–1890* (1981); Virginius Dabney, *Richmond: The Story of a City* (1976); David R. Goldfield, *Urban Growth in the Age of Sectionalism: Virginia, 1847–1861* (1977); Christopher Silver, "Greater Richmond and the Good City: Politics and Planning in a New South Metropolis, 1900–1976" (Ph.D. dissertation, University of North Carolina, 1981); Emory M. Thomas, *The Confederate State of Richmond: A Biography of the Capital* (1971). ☆

SAVANNAH
||||||||||||||||||||||||||||

Founded on a bluff overlooking the Savannah River, Savannah developed with deliberation and planning that has had continuing cultural importance since its establishment by James Oglethorpe in 1733. Influenced by the neighborhood developments of late 17th-century London, Oglethorpe envisioned and planned a city of symmetrical squares, gardens, and broad avenues. Even as the military purposes of the colony gave way to the rice and cotton economy of the 18th century, Savannah retained the charm of its origins. British occupation during the Revolution and repeated difficulties with epidemics such as yellow fever did, however, limit early growth.

Stereoscope view of Savannah harbor, 1870s

During the 19th century Savannah joined other southern cities in active boosterism in an effort to enlarge its trade and commercial activity. A modest success resulted, and Savannah emerged as an important cotton and timber port for the Georgia and South Carolina Piedmont. The building of the Central of Georgia Railroad to Macon contributed to this role, and on the eve of the Civil War Savannah's population of 22,292 was large by southern urban standards. During the war years General William Sherman targeted Savannah as his destination for the March to the Sea, and the city fell to Union forces in December 1864. The destruction was large but the city quickly recovered its prewar fortunes, extended rail lines, and expanded timber and cotton exporting. By 1880 the city could boast the same garden-like charm of its origin and a population of 30,709. In the late 19th and early 20th centuries Savannah joined the state of Georgia in a gradual diversification of economic patterns. The

slow transformation temporarily halted Savannah's growth, and the city's relative economic deprivation indirectly contributed to the preservation of its original buildings and plan. Cotton diminished in importance, but timber, particularly pulpwood and turpentine products, remained strong. This has continued into the 20th century as Savannah is now the leading foreign trade port between Baltimore and New Orleans, with primary emphasis on container shipping. Its 1984 population numbered 145,000.

Corresponding to commercial changes, the population of Savannah has experienced a slow but steady growth. Since Savannah is a seaport, immigration played a more important role in its growth than in the growth of most interior southern cities. An early Jewish community developed, and in 1860 the free population of Savannah and surrounding Chatham County was more than 25 percent foreign born. More significant is the continuing large black population. Although free whites outnumbered both slave and free black populations in 1860, Savannah's black population constituted a majority or near majority in the late 19th century and the early 20th. Large black populations (34 percent in 1970 and 36 percent in 1980) remain a part of the modern Savannah profile.

For all its growing commercial importance, Savannah's principal role in the South has been as a leader in the effort to preserve the region's past. Since 1839 the city has been home to the Georgia Historical Society, a most important center for the study of southern history. Telfair Academy of Arts and Sciences, founded in 1920, serves as a museum of the decorative arts, costumes, paintings, and sculpture. As the leading city of coastal Georgia, Savannah has a black land grant college, Savannah State, chartered in 1889, and a predominantly white senior college, Armstrong State. Both are part of the University System of Georgia and have merged many programs in recent years, reflecting a greater interracial cooperation. Although the original plans of Oglethorpe have remained, the city's early architecture sadly deteriorated in the late 19th and early 20th centuries. Since World War II, however, the original area of Savannah has been transformed through the Historic Savannah Foundation (founded in 1955). The restoration of old Savannah is one of the most complete for any American city. Today, visitors can see the restored architecture of William Jay, Charles Clusky, or W. G. Preston featuring wrought iron, gardens, and the Oglethorpe squares. Such domestic restoration has been accompanied by work on public buildings and commercial districts including the city hall, Factor's Walk, the Cotton Exchange Building, Telfair Academy, and a number of churches. The restored charm of Savannah has given the city an important

source of revenue through the hosting of small conventions. More importantly it has made Savannah an inspiration for the restoration of other cities and a continuing symbol of the beauty of urban planning in a southern setting.

Thomas F. Armstrong
Georgia College

Federal Writers' Project, WPA, *Savannah* (1937); Richard Haunton, "Savannah in the 1850s" (Ph.D. dissertation, Emory University, 1968); Mills Lane, *Savannah Revisited* (1969). ☆

TAMPA

The village of Tampa originated as a civilian settlement adjacent to Fort Brooke, an army post established in 1824 near Tampa Bay on Florida's Gulf Coast. Tampa grew slowly and prospered in the 1850s as a commercial center with a port that dominated the area's cattle trade to Cuba. The town's population of 900 overwhelmingly supported the Confederacy.

After several decades of decline, Tampa's population expanded by 760 percent during the 1880s with the arrival of the cigar industry. Spanish- and Cuban-born entrepreneurs who had fled war-torn Cuba were attracted to Tampa by its port and rail facilities and its proximity to Cuban sources of clear Havana tobacco, which was used to make luxury, hand-rolled cigars. The skilled labor force was composed of Cubans and Spaniards who were later joined by Italian immigrants. The local cigar industry started in the new town of Ybor City, which was annexed by Tampa in 1887.

By 1910 Tampa had become the capital of domestically produced clear Havana cigars, and 45 percent of its residents were first- or second-generation immigrants. Separated from both the native Anglo and black communities, the Latin population lived in Ybor City where mutual aid societies and foreign-language newspapers thrived. The cigar city continued to prosper through the 1920s when its population exceeded 100,000.

The Depression nearly destroyed Tampa's economy, which was based on a luxury product that never regained its former popularity. Moreover, the city's image was sullied by its reputation for political corruption, crime, and violence.

After World War II Tampa broadened its economic base by taking advantage of its location and the growth of the Sunbelt. Military expenditures at MacDill Field stimulated the economy, as did phosphate shipments that made Tampa one of the nation's busiest ports. The biggest boost came from new residents who helped Tampa more than double its population during the 1950s. Tampa's image as a progressive city was advanced by its success in achieving desegregation peacefully in the 1960s. The hundreds of new businesses included medium-sized manufacturing, but service industries predominated with banks and insurance companies locating regional headquarters in Tampa. By 1980 the city's population of 271,523 was at the hub of the third fastest-growing metropolitan area in the country. Its 1984 population had grown to 275,000.

Tampa's emergence as a leading Sunbelt city was marked by the creation of new educational and cultural institutions. The University of South Florida was created by the state legislature in 1956, and a public community college began operating in 1968. The city also has a private college, the University of Tampa (1931). Recently founded cultural institutions include an art museum, a performing arts center, and a museum of science and industry. Since opening in 1959, Busch Gardens has become one of Florida's busiest tourist attractions. Tampa has also gained prominence as the home of a professional football team, the Tampa Bay Buccaneers.

Although originally a southern city with a Latin flavor, Tampa has been "Americanized" and homogenized to the point where today neither its population nor its culture is distinctively southern.

See also ETHNIC LIFE: / Cubans; Spanish

Robert P. Ingalls
University of South Florida

Richard M. Bernard and Bradley R. Rice, eds., *Sunbelt Cities: Politics and Growth since World War II* (1983). ☆

VIOLENCE

RAYMOND D. GASTIL

New York, New York

CONSULTANT

☆ ☆ ☆ ☆ ☆ ☆ ☆ ☆ ☆ ☆ ☆ ☆ ☆

Overleaf: Reconstruction violence against blacks portrayed in the film **Birth of a Nation, 1915**

VIOLENCE, CRIME, AND PUNISHMENT

|||||||||||||||||||||||||||||||||||||||||||||||||||||||

Violence has been associated with the South since the time of the American Revolution. Connecticut soldiers threatened to leave the front if they were forced to serve alongside those from Virginia, because of the cruelty of the fights among the latter. The attitudes associated with slavery and the warped experiences of young males in this environment were often cited as causes of such cruelty and violence. Historian John Hope Franklin has demonstrated that the South was addicted to violence on every level of society well before the Civil War. Prime evidence for this was the duel, which became widely accepted among "gentlemen" in the South, whereas it died out soon after its introduction in the North. But the duel was only the most formalized means of defending an exaggerated sense of honor with violence. "Honorable" fights were common, and on lower social levels street fights and ambushes were accepted forms of behavior.

Journalist H. V. Redfield pointed out that the tendency to take the law into one's own hands for the sake of honor was reinforced by the weakness of law officers. Patterns thus developed tended to further weaken the state and to support anarchy, for once it became accepted that people had the right to kill for their own purposes, they then took this right to include actions against law officers and jurors who might be so courageous as to get in their way. The shootout superseded the law; because the punishments of the law were seldom visited on the murderer, those who felt wronged were often led to bypass it as well. However the process began, the result was a markedly lower regard for human life.

Border or mountain feuding, such as that of the Hatfields and McCoys, was an extreme form of the same tradition, and one bearing little connection to slavery. The immediate cause of many minor mountain wars was the Civil War and the hatreds it engendered in border states. The explosion of the James gang in the West, and the endemic violence of the next generation, had much the same origin. In fact, in the postwar period Kentucky became one of the most violent states in the nation. Exploding again in the labor wars of the 1930s, the coal-mining regions of Kentucky and West Virginia renewed that tradition. Harlan County was the violent center of a violent area.

Southern violence is of a particular kind. Stereotypically, verbal violence has been thought to characterize Mediterranean peoples, fistfighting and other types of physical assault are often associated with the Irish, whereas suicide—internalized violence—may be associated with Scandinavians, Japanese, and other relatively "controlled" peoples. Violence in the South has meant primarily lethal violence, or violence that is cruel and abrupt, designed to punish. This southern type of violence exists in the traditional southern states, but also in an expanding South. Southern attitudes toward violence appear, for example, among southern blacks residing in northern or border cities and among the rural southern white folk who make up a large proportion of the population in the West, particularly the Southwest.

The Study of Southern Violence. The first detailed study of comparative southern homicide rates was conducted by H. V. Redfield. Traveling widely in the South, Redfield in the 1870s compiled extensive files on homicide rates. He found that as one moved south through the counties of Indiana, Ohio, or Illinois, the incidence of homicide rose regularly. He demonstrated that the phenomenon was as characteristic of the Old South as of the New. For example, the homicide rate of South Carolina was 10 times greater than that of Massachusetts, and in the West, that of Texas was 10 times that of Minnesota. Redfield found that assaults on honor, or even political struggles, frequently resulted in murder, because of the almost universal practice of carrying weapons. The street duel, which was later portrayed on movie and television screens as a western phenomenon, was common in South Carolina in his day, as were organized night fights or mob killings— which at that time were not characteristically interracial.

In the 20th century a number of other scholars examined the differences between northern and southern homicide rates. In the early years of the century Frederick Hoffman pointed to the extreme rate in a city such as Memphis. No longer primarily a rural problem— nor solely a white concern—a high homicide rate had become characteristic of black populations, a fact that had not been true in Redfield's day. H. C.

Brearley's studies of homicide in the 1920s revealed that the seven states with highest homicide rates were southern. Studies by Lottier, Porterfield, Shannon, and Hackney reported statistics of an equivalent kind up to the 1970s. FBI statistics from 1983 show that, although regional differences are now less extreme, an important North-South differential remains.

Explanations of Southern Violence. On viewing discrepancies such as these, social scientists have often advanced explanations positing poverty, low educational levels, or the oppressive and racist nature of southern life. However, cultural anthropologists see cultural patterns that developed early and still persist in the South as conducive to high homicide rates.

Such a cultural hypothesis was tested in the 1970s by Raymond D. Gastil, a sociologist. Some of the data regarding homicide rates that Gastil examined are reported in Table 1. Because of the movement of people in and out of the South over the last hundred years and the mixing of regional populations, particularly in border states and large cities, the researcher formulated an "Index of Southernness" that attempted to measure the prevalence of certain aspects of southern culture as the observer moves north and west from states such as Mississippi, Alabama, and South Carolina. The result of this study was to reinforce the assumption that the cultural variable of "southernness" represented an important part of the explanation of regional variation.

This approach has had both critics and defenders. Other factors besides regional origin surely correlate with homicide, most notably youth, sex, and residence in a large city (or other special environment, such as the states of Ne-

Table 1. *Criminal Homicides per 100,000 Population by States*

State	White	Non-White	Total	State	White	Non-White	Total
Ga.	4.4	27.3	10.0	Mich.	1.8	20.4	3.6
Ala.	4.2	25.3	10.5	W.Va.	3.1	13.3*	3.6
S.C.	4.9	19.5	10.0	Hawaii	2.5*	3.9*	3.5
Va.	6.9	20.2	9.7	Ohio	1.9	21.3	3.5
Alaska	6.3	19.2*	9.3	N.Y.	1.8	18.7	3.3
Fla.	3.8	34.4	9.3	Ind.	1.8	22.6	3.0
N.C.	3.9	24.9	9.2	Kans.	2.2	18.7*	2.9
La.	3.1	19.1	8.3	S.D.	1.7*	33.3*	2.9*
Nev.	7.2	18.2*	8.1	Pa.	1.5	18.0	2.7
Miss.	2.5	15.5	8.0	N.J.	1.6	13.8	2.6
Tenn.	3.7	27.0	7.6	Wash.	2.2	12.8*	2.6
Tex.	4.3	30.7	7.6	Oreg.	2.0	27.0*	2.5
Ark.	3.7	21.7	7.5	Utah	1.8*	17.6*	2.1*
Ariz.	4.5	27.3	6.8	Conn.	1.2	18.0*	2.0
Ky.	4.5	27.1	6.1	Neb.	.87*	40.5*	1.9
N.M.	4.8	22.9*	6.1	Maine	1.8*	0.0*	1.8*
Okla.	4.0	23.2	5.8	Idaho	1.1*	30.0*	1.5*
Md.	2.5	21.3	5.6	Wis.	1.3	12.9*	1.5
Del.	2.3*	24.2*	5.4	R.I.	1.3*	4.8*	1.4*
Wyo.	4.3*	42.9*	5.2*	N.D.	1.0*	23.1	1.4*
Ill.	2.3	25.1	4.7	Mass.	1.1*	10.4*	1.3*
Mo.	2.8	22.9	4.6	Minn.	1.1*	16.7*	1.3*
Calif.	3.3	18.3	4.5	Iowa	0.9*	10.3*	1.0*
Colo.	3.0	32.1	3.9	N.H.	1.0*	0.0*	1.0*
Mont.	3.1*	25.0	3.9	Vt.	0.0*	0.0*	0.0*

*20 or fewer homicides

Source: Vital Statistics of the United States, 1964, *vol. 2, pt. B (1966)*.

vada or Alaska). After allowing for these factors, however, a considerable portion of the variance still appears to come from cultural tradition. The correlations are particularly dramatic for white homicide. Although these separate rates are not published by the FBI along with the other homicide statistics, it is possible to ascertain fairly correct racial statistics because in over 90 percent of recorded homicides, murderer and victim are of the same race.

The very high black homicide rates, often 10 times those of whites, would seem on the one hand to confirm the assumption of a southern "cause" of lethal violence, because of the overwhelming concentration of blacks in the South in the past. On the other hand, the high homicide rates have followed the black migration to large cities, North and South, and therefore have disguised the regional influence. There are many explanations for this particular intensification of the "subculture of violence"; in part, black homicide rates no doubt reflect specifically black experience rather than general southern history, experience that has been reinforced by modern conditions.

The rise of the Ku Klux Klan and its repeated revival; an exaggerated interest in violent sports, such as football, cockfighting, and dogfighting; and the tendency of southerners to regard war as a game, as manifested in the historically greater interest of the South in the military, are all indicative of the region's violent tendencies. This militant, anarchical element in the South is also illustrated by the history of the Texas Rangers, an irregular, border defense force that only gradually became a part of the state's own apparatus.

If the South's attitude toward murder in defense of "rights" or honor has been forgiving, its view of offenders once within the system has tended to be relatively harsh. As Henry Lundsgaarde points out, southerners tend to "publicly approve of the use of lethal violence to settle personal disputes and problems," and judicial officials in the region seem more predisposed "to recommend severe punishment for those wrongdoers who threaten the moral values, beliefs, and social mores of the general public than their counterparts in other parts of the country." Analysis of the latest statistics on the rate of incarceration by state produces a map closely resembling that produced by the attempt to construct the Index of Southernness described above. The South has also tended to be favorably inclined toward capital punishment; most of those facing the death sentence in the 1980s were in the South. In December 1983, for example, 65 percent of the nation's 1,202 individuals awaiting execution were in southern prisons.

Attitudes toward Violence. Attitude studies also confirm the difference between the South and the rest of the country. Southerners have a much more positive attitude toward gun ownership. They are more likely to believe in corporal punishment and more likely to have experienced it than people elsewhere in the country. In 1971 sociologist John Shelton Reed, perhaps the most perceptive student of southern violence today, conducted an attitude survey and noted that relatively more southerners than other Americans condone violence; the attitudes of these small subgroups of the sample were characterized as those of warriors, vigilantes, and anarchists.

John Shelton Reed views the culture of violence as a learned trait, and as such, one that is apt to be found in the best "socialized" southerners rather than the least. He points out that the South is not *simply* violent, but that it is violent in certain respects. In many crime categories the South is at or below national averages. If one breaks down homicide data, it is clear that the South is far ahead of the rest of the country in murders of lovers, spouses, or other family adults, as well as other murders

University of Alabama student, and later Alabama governor, George C. Wallace, bloodying a Tulane University opponent in a boxing match, 1939

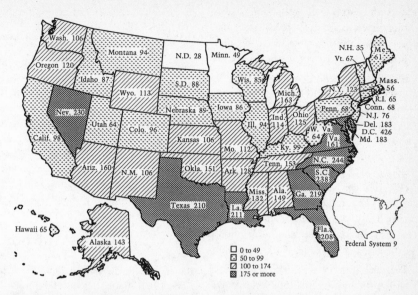

Rate of Sentenced Prisoners in State and Federal Institutions, by Jurisdiction, on December 31, 1980 (per 100,000 Resident Population)

Source: U.S. Department of Justice, Bureau of Justice Statistics, Prisoners in State and Federal Institutions on December 31, 1980 (1982).

resulting from arguments or disputes. But southerners are no more likely than people from other regions to kill their own children, to kill as the result of psychopathy, or to kill as an accompaniment to another crime. Southern homicide is not, in other words, random. This is the reason that a southerner is often astonished to find that the murder rate in his region is higher than in, for example, New York City. "Crime in the streets," including murder, is more common in New York. One is not very likely to be killed in the South as long as cultural rules are obeyed and situations that in the southern ethos "justify" killing are avoided.

Reed suggests that the concept of justifiable homicide is at the heart of the southern tendency to violence. One carries a gun or a knife because one might have to use it, and one uses it because the occasion merits it. Reed points out

that much of the literature and popular culture of the South revolves around violence, which is often viewed in a neutral or even laudatory way. Southern humor often involves violent incidents, but not, of course, incidents of psychopathic or "criminal" killings in the ordinary sense. For southerners, murder in defense of honor, after sufficient provocation, is more often tragic rather than simply wrong.

The South developed on the frontier and remained a frontier for a long time. It developed in fear—fear of the Indian, fear of the outsider, fear of the slave (or for the slave, fear of whites). To many southerners over a period of centuries the protection of the law was feeble at best. In this context the southerner developed or maintained ways of coping that were abandoned or never developed in the more densely settled and reliably governed North. The Civil War broke down what were often only poorly institutionalized regulatory measures, and once again the recourse was violence. To a significant extent a propensity for violence continues at two ends of the spectrum in the South. It is part of the life of the most socialized, a part of living the honorable life within society; while at the bottom of the social ladder, the life of the drifter, the outlaw, is an anarchical alternative that has always seemed more appealing to the young southerner than to people in other sections. Only in this latter sense can one perhaps speak of the "southernization" of America as a whole. There seems to be a resurgence of American reverence for a wild, interior frontier, for a purer naturalism; this too has its southern roots as surely as the mythical cowboy of the West.

See also HISTORY AND MANNERS: Frontier Heritage; Military Tradition; LAW: Criminal Justice; Criminal Law; Police Forces; RECREATION: Football

Raymond D. Gastil
Freedom House

Edward L. Ayers, *Vengeance and Justice: Crime and Punishment in the 19th-Century American South* (1984); H. C. Brearley, *Homicide in the United States* (1932); Dickson D. Bruce, Jr., *Violence and Culture in the Antebellum South* (1979); John Hope Franklin, *The Militant South, 1800–1861* (1956); Raymond D. Gastil, *American Sociological Review* (June 1971); Elliot Gorn, *American Historical Review* (February 1985); Sheldon Hackney, in *Violence in America: Historical and Comparative Perspectives*, ed. Hugh Davis Graham and Ted Robert Gurr (1969); Frederick Hoffman, *The Homicide Problem* (1925); Colin Loftin, Robert Hill, and Raymond D. Gastil, *Criminology* (May

1978); Stuart Lottier, *Journal of Criminal Law and Criminology* (June–July 1938); Henry P. Lundsgaarde, *Murder in Space City: A Cultural Analysis of Houston Homicide Patterns* (1977); Thomas Pettigrew and Rosaline Spier, *American Journal of Sociology* (May 1962); Austin Porterfield, *American Sociological Review* (August 1949); H. V. Redfield, *Homicide, North and South: Being a Comparative View of Crime Against the Person in Several Parts of the United States* (1880); John Shelton Reed, in *Perspectives on the American South*, vol. 1, ed. Merle Black and John Shelton Reed (1981), *Political Science Quarterly* (September 1971); Lyle Shannon, *Journal of Criminal Law and Criminology* (September–October 1954); U.S. Department of Justice, Federal Bureau of Investigation, *Uniform Crime Reports* (1983); Bertram Wyatt-Brown, *Southern Honor: Ethics and Behavior in the Old South* (1982). ☆

Civil Rights, Federal Enforcement

Prior to 1957 federal intervention to protect the legal rights of black southerners was infrequent at best. Beginning with the Little Rock crisis, the passage of the Civil Rights Act of 1957, and the creation of the U.S. Commission on Civil Rights, however, a new era of federal legal action in the South was born.

From 1957 through the late 1960s federal authorities faced three major and often intertwined legal questions concerning the South: how to ensure southern blacks' right to register and vote; how to secure the desegregation of southern schools and colleges; and how to protect civil rights activists from illegal and often violent harassment of their efforts. On all three fronts federal officials—in the White House, at the Department of Justice, and in the Federal Bureau of Investigation—acted cautiously and conservatively in all but a few instances. That caution of three successive presidential administrations—Eisenhower, Kennedy, and Johnson—was strongly condemned by civil rights movement participants and supporters. At the same time, most white southerners failed to appreciate that the degree of federal action and intervention was much lower than could well have been the case, given the formal powers available to the federal authorities.

Critics of these administrations consistently pointed out that federal authorities were making only the most limited use of certain powers at their disposal: the voting rights provisions of the 1957 and 1960 civil rights acts; the Reconstruction-era criminal statutes codified as 18 U.S.C. 241 and 242; the statute giving the president very expansive federal police powers in any circumstance where state authorities are unable or unwilling to protect constitutional rights (10 U.S.C. 333); and the provisions authorizing all FBI agents and U.S. marshals to make warrantless arrests for any violation of a federal statute that they witnessed (18 U.S.C. 3052, 3053).

The degree of federal restraint was not a matter of happenstance, nor, as some have surmised, was it simply a result of presidential inability to mobilize the resources and energies of the FBI, whose longtime director, J. Edgar Hoover, was accurately regarded as an extreme conservative in matters of race. Instead, in all three areas—schools, voting, and violence—limited federal intervention was based on a straightfor-

ward policy supported by all the presidents and attorneys general who were involved: that the racial transformation of southern society would proceed furthest, fastest, and with the fewest scars if federal authorities encouraged maximum voluntary compliance by southern officials and resorted to the coercive use of federal remedies and manpower as little as possible.

Throughout the 1957–64 period Justice Department officials seeking to eliminate racial discrimination from southern voter registration offices made persuasion their first and foremost tool. Only in counties or parishes where registrars rebuffed such approaches and continued to discriminate were federal civil suits brought. Similarly, even in such widely heralded federal-state confrontations as the integration of the University of Mississippi in 1962 and the University of Alabama in 1963, federal officials relied upon private conversations and negotiation and employed actual force only when all other means of obtaining obedience to the law had failed. Furthermore, even in instances where the very lives of civil rights activists were in danger, Justice Department officials moved with caution rather than alacrity. Many movement workers became deeply embittered at the lack of federal response to the shootings, burnings, and beatings that occurred throughout the Deep South between 1961 and 1965.

The summer of 1964 witnessed both a new assertion of federal power in the most violent of the southern states, Mississippi, and passage of the comprehensive Civil Rights Act. Prodded by the murder of three civil rights workers in June 1964, the Johnson Administration established a substantial FBI presence in the state. At the same time,

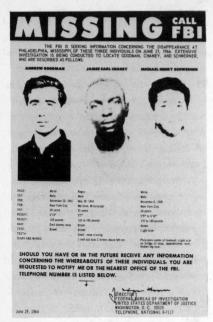

FBI poster seeking information on missing civil rights workers, Mississippi, 1964

passage of the new law gave the government a powerful new tool for combating racial discrimination, particularly in public accommodations. Even in relative "hot spots" such as St. Augustine, Fla., and Selma, Ala., federal officials favored persuasion and conciliation before adopting stronger actions.

Passage of the 1965 Voting Rights Act, which provided for the appointment of federal registration officials in unregenerate southern counties, led many movement activists to expect the kind of extensive federal intervention throughout the South that the movement had sought but previously failed to obtain. To their great disappointment, however, federal officials at the Justice Department again applied the principle they had followed in previous years: direct federal authority should be exerted only where state and local officials failed to show good-faith compliance. Thus, far fewer federal registrars were sent into the South than civil rights proponents requested. A movement initiative to win passage of new federal statutes to eliminate jury discrimination and to specifically forbid any physical harassment of civil rights workers also failed to succeed in 1965–66.

Many movement participants and sympathizers, looking back at the so-called Second Reconstruction years, argue that a more aggressive and forceful federal stance would have meant more racial progress, and at a lesser cost in dead, wounded, and emotionally scarred. Former federal officials, however—those men who served in the Justice Department hierarchy in the 1960s—believe that what many view as the South's tremendous racial progress since the late 1960s would not have occurred and that much of the previous bitterness would not have subsided had not the federal executive branch followed the moderate and restrained path that it did. Had federal authorities employed more heavily the coercive and punitive powers at their disposal, deep racial divisions might well have been further deepened and also prolonged. One's view of how sufficient the changes in southern race relations over the past 15 years have been will in large part determine whether one judges the federal law enforcement stance of the 1960s to have been intelligent or inadequate.

See also BLACK LIFE: Freedom Movement, Black; LAW: Civil Rights Movement; MEDIA: Civil Rights and Media

David J. Garrow
City College of New York
CUNY Graduate Center

Carl M. Brauer, *John F. Kennedy and the Second Reconstruction* (1977); Richard Maxwell Brown, in *Perspectives on the American South*, vol. 1, ed. Merle Black and John Shelton Reed (1981); Haywood Burns, in *Southern Justice*, ed. Leon Friedman (1965); Robert K. Carr, *Federal Protection of Civil Rights: Quest for a Sword* (1947); John Doar and Dorothy Landsberg, U.S. Congress, Senate, Select Committee to Study Governmental Operations with Respect to Intelligence Activities, *Hearings—Federal Bureau of Investigation*, vol. 6, 94th Cong., 1st sess. (1976); John T. Elliff, *Perspectives in American History*, vol. 5 (1971); Allan Lichtman, *Journal of Negro History* (October 1969); Neil R. McMillen, *Journal of Southern History* (August 1977); Burke Marshall, *Federalism and Civil Rights* (1964). ☆

Cockfighting

||||||||||||||||||||||||||||||||

Ritualized violence is an integral aspect of many sports, and the extreme of recreational violence can be found in the so-called blood sports. In these activities animals are pitted against each other, usually with fatal consequences for the loser, while spectators wager on the outcome. Cockfighting, dogfighting, and bearbaiting were brought to the United States by early settlers from the British Isles where such activities have a long tradition.

Cockfighting is the most common organized blood sport in America and may have as many as several hundred thousand devotees. Fights are regularly scheduled at hundreds of permanent arenas or "pits." Many cockpits are quite elaborate and may be equipped with refreshment stands, public address systems, and tiers of bleachers. There are three national publications for "cockers," as cockfighters call themselves, including the oldest, *Grit and Steel*, founded in 1899. They even have a lobbying group, the United Gamefowl Breeders Association.

Though cockfights occur throughout the country, a disproportionate number of fans are found in the rural South. A recent survey of cockers (Bryant and Capel, 1974) found that 54 percent of respondents resided in the Southeast or Southwest. Also, an examination of a recent issue of *The Gamecock*, a cockfighting magazine, revealed that two-thirds of the more than 200 advertisements originated from southern states. The 1973 film *Feathered Warrior* (Appalshop, Ben Zickafoose, with Gene DuBey and Bill Hatton) documented cockfighting in Appalachia.

In the South, most cockfighters are white, male, middle to lower-middle class, and from rural areas. There is, however, great diversity among cockfight fans. Women and children attend fights with surprising frequency. At some pits blacks regularly attend and participate on apparently equal terms with whites. A sociological study of cockfighters indicated that, as a group, they were not psychopathic, sadistic, or in other ways psychologically disturbed. On the contrary, the values of the individuals studied were not very different from those of comparison groups of non-cockers.

Both animal and human violence are associated with cockfighting. Before each match, pointed steel "gaffs" several inches long are attached to the legs of the cocks. Individual matches vary in length from a few seconds to over an hour, and usually the loser dies from injuries sustained during the match. Surprisingly, the fights are not as visually gruesome as one might expect. The steel gaffs inflict puncture wounds that bleed relatively little, and the birds' feathers tend to conceal blood. Cockfighting violence, nonetheless, is reflected in the vocabulary of the sport. "Bayonets" and "slashers" are types of gaffs, and a "butcher" is one of the hundreds of strains of gamecocks.

The general milieu of cockfights provides high potential for violence between the human participants. Drinking, though prohibited in most pits, regularly occurs surreptitiously. Gambling is an inextricable aspect of the sport, and, as in any competitive event, tempers can flare. Some spectators and cockers regularly carry concealed weapons. Despite the possibility of violence, serious disagreements between participants are relatively rare, probably due to strong norms against fighting at pits.

An elaborate structure governs how matches are conducted. The rules are published, and a referee in the pit at all times controls the fight and determines the winner according to the established regulations. (See Ruport, 1949, for sample sets of rules for conducting cockfights.) The referee's word is final in any dispute. Gambling between spectators at fights is informal and consists of accepting odds shouted by others just before each match begins. Bets are promptly paid after each match.

Because the sport is illegal in most areas, cockpits remain in a location only if local authorities look the other way. Police usually crack down on cockpits when there are complaints from the community. Thus, it is in the pit owner's best interest to avoid adverse publicity by preventing violence. Occasionally disputes do occur and fights break out. Disruptive individuals are immediately ejected and may be banned from future attendance.

Cockfighting is deeply rooted in southern culture. The mascot of the University of South Carolina, for example, is the "fighting gamecock." To those outside of the subculture, cockfighting may be synonymous with cruelty, violence, and brutality. To the cocker, however, it is a noble pastime that embodies the values of courage, stamina, and competition, and in many areas of the South, cockers proudly display bumper stickers and special license plates proclaiming their involvement in "the sport of kings."

Cockfighters invoke a variety of justifications for their sport. They link the names of many great Americans to cockfighting, including Washington, Lincoln, and Andrew Jackson. They claim that cockfighting is recreation that can involve the entire family and that the gamecock exemplifies the spirit of valor and bravery. They argue that, unlike the fowl raised in modern factory farms, their roosters have ample room and are treated very well. In addition, cockers argue that the natural aggression of gamecocks actually makes it cruel not to allow them to meet their destinies in the pit.

Few football fans would admit that violence is one of the reasons they attend games. The same is true of cockfighters. To a cocker the sport is not really about violence and death. It is about competition, camaraderie, and gambling.

See also RECREATION: Gambling

Harold A. Herzog, Jr.
Mars Hill College

C. D. Bryant and W. C. Capel, *Grit and Steel* (October 1974; April 1975); Charles R. Gunter, *Tennessee Folklore Society Bulletin* (December 1978); Harold A. Herzog,

Jr., and P. B. Cheek, *Southern Exposure* (Fall 1979); Charles H. McGaghy and Arthur G. Neal, *Journal of Popular Culture* (Winter 1974); A. Ruport, *The Art of Cockfighting: A Handbook for Beginners and Old Timers* (1949); G. R. Scott, *The History of Cockfighting* (1957); Eliot Wigginton and Margie Bennett, eds., *Foxfire 8* (1984). ☆

Crime, Attitudes Toward

||||||||||||||||||||||||||||||||||||||||||||||||||||||||||||||

The southern states lead the nation in both the number of violent offenses against persons and the number of people imprisoned for crimes of violence. Southerners generally believe that those who violate criminal laws should be severely punished. Available criminal justice statistics, however, do not provide a clearcut picture of the effects of punishment on the social order.

Southern beliefs concerning proper behavior in interpersonal relations have deep roots in the regional culture. The distinguished southern scholar H. C. Brearley was among the first to call attention to the complex relationship between southern propensities toward lethal violence and regional legacies of personal pride, slavery, racism, lynching, and a castelike social structure. Lynching of both blacks and whites greatly increased after the Civil War, and the practice of collective violence against racial, ethnic, and other minorities continues to this day. The tenacious support of southerners for the right to own and use firearms combines with frontier values of individualism and self-sufficiency to sustain a cultural milieu that admits to both graceful living and judicial self-help.

The available evidence on popular attitudes toward the punishment of crimes compels two conclusions: (1) southerners are more predisposed than others to approve publicly of the use of lethal violence to settle personal disputes and problems; and (2) southern judicial officials are more likely to recommend severe punishment for those wrongdoers who threaten the moral values, beliefs, and social mores of the general public than their counterparts in other parts of the country.

In determining punishment the value of any person's life may be assessed either in terms of his or her social status (the traditional Anglo-Saxon approach) or in terms of the particular characteristics of the offender's act (the modern legalistic approach). The legalistic approach to punishment nominally omits the elements of revenge, reciprocity (an eye for an eye), and restitution benefits. The social costs and benefits associated with any form of behavior are ultimately determined by a combination of public attitudes and values relating to the achievement of the common good. A brief overview of the Texas Penal Code, which shares many characteristics with the penal statutes of other southern states, may serve to illustrate these general points.

Texas homicide statutes define homicide as the destruction of the life of one human being by the act, agency, procurement, or culpable omission of another. Noncriminal homicide, which is not punishable by law, includes a variety of homicides that are classified as justifiable; e.g., killing in self-defense, killing to protect one's property or the property of third persons, or killing in the performance of public duty.

Criminal homicide is subdivided into five major statutory categories. Each one is associated with specific minimum and maximum punishments. Murder is punishable by a minimum prison sentence of five years, by life imprisonment, or by a maximum 99-year prison sentence; capital murder, which specifically applies to anyone who kills a public official, is punishable by life imprisonment or death by execution; voluntary manslaughter imposes a minimum sentence of two years and a maximum prison sentence of 20 years; involuntary manslaughter limits the maximum prison sentence to 10 years; and negligent homicide is treated as a misdemeanor punishable by a fine not to exceed $2,000, imprisonment for one year or less, or a combination of imprisonment and a fine. The individual who kills another citizen in the heat of a personal argument or lethally responds to an injury to pride or property is more likely to escape any official punishment than the person who kills a public official. The slayer who combines killing with a property offense is most likely to be punished with either death or consecutive 99-year life sentences.

Public attitudes imbedded in penal statutes and individual criminal court decisions further reveal their southern regional characteristics if one looks at the available national survey statistics. Survey data from the southern region in

Stereotypical redneck southerner, in the film Easy Rider, *1969*

the most recent compilation of public attitudes toward criminal justice suggest the following generalizations about popular attitudes: (1) southerners own more handguns than persons in other regions of the United States; (2) southerners do not believe that private gun ownership should be subject to legal prohibition; (3) southerners generally believe that the public display and availability of pornographic materials lead individuals to commit rape; (4) southerners favor severe punishment of individuals who either possess or use marijuana. The survey data allow the conclusion that southerners view the possession of both marijuana and pornographic materials as more threatening to life and liberty than either the ready availability of firearms or the continuation of legal statutes that make the private use of firearms permissible in a variety of situations normally prohibited in other cultural regions.

As a result of such attitudes the South has more prison inmates under lock and key than any other region in the United States. The 1979 rate of sentenced prisoners in both state and federal institutions was twice as large for the southern region as for any other region in the nation. An astounding 12 percent of southern prisoners died at the hands of fellow prisoners. As of 31 December 1979, the South had a total of 459 prisoners on death row or the equivalent of 81 percent of the total U.S. death-row population.

Comparative and national statistics reveal that southerners believe strongly that criminals should be punished severely. The statistics fail to reveal why southerners generally believe in this pure form of retributive justice. Forthright acknowledgment of the obvious fact that a disproportionate number of private citizens annually kill or seriously injure others without receiving any form of official punishment also suggests that any understanding or even explanation of popular attitudes toward criminal punishment must begin with an analysis of the regional cultural patterns of the violent South.

See also LAW: Criminal Justice; Criminal Law

Henry P. Lundsgaarde
University of Kansas

Mississippi Delta, 1968

H. C. Brearley, in *Culture in the South*, ed. W. T. Couch (1934); James Harmon Chadbourn, *Lynching and the Law* (1933); Timothy J. Flanagan, David J. van Alstyne, and Michael R. Gottfredson, eds., *Sourcebook of Criminal Justice Statistics-1981* (1982); Leon Friedman, ed., *Southern Justice* (1965); Raymond D. Gastil, *American Sociological Review* (June 1971), *Cultural Regions of the United States* (1975); Sheldon Hackney, *American Historical Review* (February 1969); Henry P. Lundsgaarde, *Murder in Space City: A Cultural Analysis of Houston Homicide Patterns* (1977); Arthur F. Raper, *The Tragedy of Lynching* (1933); Milton Rokeach, in *International Encyclopedia of the Social Sciences*, vol. 1, ed. David L. Sills (1968). ☆

Guns

||||||||||||

Since the early 1800s the image of southerners with firearms has served as a cliché for the nation and, indeed, the world. The firearm is certainly a secure cultural feature of the South, but that is true of rural groups in other geographical locations. Firearms, generalized violence, and "southernness" have, however, been historically linked in the popular and literary imagination and have served as negative features distorting overall perceptions of the southern reality. Since the 1960s the gun itself has taken on a larger meaning in the context of the American nation, and the traditional identification of southerners with guns has both reinforced stereotypes of regional violence and reaffirmed many southerners' interest in weapons.

The South has traditionally been portrayed as a gun-toting culture. In the last century northern and European travelers frequently remarked on the prevalence of guns and knives in the region. Today many non-southerners, especially urban dwellers, express surprise at gun racks in pickup trucks, the pro-gun-ownership bumper-sticker slogans, and the assertive attitudes of southerners about the right to carry firearms.

All studies agree that gun ownership and levels of gun usage are relatively high in the South. According to several recent studies, about 65 percent of southerners and about 44 percent of non-southerners own guns. National Opinion Research Center analyses of data for the 1970s compared nine regions, three of which included states generally defined as southern (South Atlantic, East South Central, and West South Central). Residents of Alabama, Kentucky, Mississippi, and Tennessee (the East South Central region) had the highest rate of gun ownership in the nation—74.9 percent of the populace owned guns. The lowest southern rate—57.8 percent—was in the region comprised of Texas, Arkansas, Louisiana, and Oklahoma (although the latter is not usually considered part of the South). The highest non-southern rate, 64.9 percent, found in the Mountain region (e.g., Nevada, Utah), was quite similar to the southern rates; but the lowest rate, 24.3 percent in New England, was markedly lower. Recent studies of college students have shown that far more southern students have fired guns than their northern counterparts, 81 percent and 56 percent, respectively. Of those southern males living in non-gun-owning households, estimates are that 91 percent had fired a gun. Whether the existence of such statistics, coupled with notably high rates of violent crime in the South, constitutes sufficient rationale for the widely held belief that a "southern subculture of violence" exists is problematical.

The belief in such a subculture flourished for many years. Persuasive arguments emanated from politicized campuses and newsrooms of the 1960s, and authors of popular and academic articles asserted that violence was an inherent quality of southerners' worldview. Only in the late 1970s and early 1980s did more balanced, critical views find their way into print. Academicians—not exclusively from the South—pointed out that the South's high rates of gun ownership and violent

crime may not be causally related; that is, owning firearms does not necessarily predispose southerners to violent solutions to personal problems. High rates of firearm ownership in the South, they contended, are primarily related to the preponderance of shoulder weapons, i.e., shotguns and rifles, found there among sportsmen. Most firearm-related violence is committed with handguns, a type of weapon whose ownership is, according to an authoritative source, "not very much more prevalent in the South than in other regions." Furthermore, weapon ownership in the South is highest in rural and small-town areas, yet violent crime is primarily an urban phenomenon: a connection between urban crime and regional patterns of weapons ownership has not been proven.

Although regionwide patterns of gun ownership do not provide solid evidence of the South's being a particularly violent milieu, gun ownership in the South has always had symbolic, ritual meaning. The presentation of a series of guns to young males serves as a rite of passage, especially among rurally oriented folk. This progression typically begins with the gift of a BB gun, then a .22 rifle, usually followed by a small-gauge shotgun, often a 20-gauge or, formerly, a 16-gauge. The BB gun is used to develop essential safety skills and to impart basic principles of ballistics. Its use is generally unsupervised, and generations of southern youths have hunted frogs and small birds and have annoyed dogs with these guns. Mock wars fought with BB guns range far and wide in rural southern areas. These are elaborate affairs complete with imaginative scenarios and peculiar etiquette—"don't aim for the face," for example, or "eye shots are unfair."

The next stage of firearm socialization

involves the use of the first "real-gun"— the .22 rifle. The first gun of this sort is often a solidly made, bolt-action or pump-action weapon purchased at a catalog store or perhaps handed down from a father, uncle, or grandfather. Use of this more deadly and usually quite accurate weapon is fraught with hazard, and numerous cautionary tales are passed from father to son as to appropriate contexts for its use. The .22 is a small-bore squirrel and rabbit gun that many adult hunters still prefer. Many young people (and young-at-heart adults) take to the woods in the autumn in search of squirrels in the tree tops. For some, the satisfaction of having brought down a moving, elusive "bushy-tail" transcends the deer-hunting mystique.

Young hunters often learn basic skills at fall dove hunts; one of a youth's first experiences in the field is to learn about frustration from trying his hand at shooting this evasive bird. Sometimes shooting over fields illegally baited with corn, the participants probably use more lead in a day than their gray-clad ancestors did during four years under the Stars and Bars. The number of doves actually shot is, however, almost secondary to the deals consummated, friendships made, and bonds established at these communal rituals. For dove hunting, youths often first receive a 20-gauge shotgun and later graduate to a 12-gauge when their upper-body strength and bulk allow them to master that weapon's recoil.

Once a young person has exhibited field-and-stream know-how and has not committed any major breach of safety or hunting etiquette, he will be lent, then given, a deer rifle of any of a wide variety of calibers. The favored 30–06 has recently declined in popularity because of the introduction and popularization of the more flat-shooting .243 and .270. For use in dense vegetation, "a brush gun," the .44 carbine or .223, often fills the bill. With this proliferation of calibers and weaponry, some hunting enthusiasts now have different guns specifically earmarked for certain types of game—often when one or two all-purpose guns would serve efficiently and much more economically. One wag joked to a gun enthusiast that while he had rifles for rabbit, squirrel, deer, and bear, he was deficient in firearms for hunting armadillos and aardvarks (the latter a nonnative species, and neither a game animal).

Handguns have been anecdotally linked to the South from antebellum times to the present. Recent data show that close to 40 percent of all southerners own handguns, a rate that is about 16 percentage points higher than in non-southern areas, with the exception of the Mountain region. Ownership rates have generally been found to be higher among white Protestant males than among others. Many handgun owners routinely carry revolvers or automatics in their glove compartments, briefcases, or, in the case of women, their handbags. For some southerners (and northern gun enthusiasts) the handgun possesses a certain aesthetic appeal. Most modern handguns are reliable, reasonably safe, and extremely durable. Although some gun enthusiasts claim to use handguns for hunting, their primary function is as a defensive or, frequently, offensive weapon. Some handgun aficionados prefer big-bore "macho" weaponry, such as the .357 and .44 magnums. Others, feeling the pull of tradition, prefer the old reliable .38, .45, or .32 calibers. When in the field or on the water, many outdoorsmen in the South routinely carry .22 magnum pistols in their boats or on their belts as a "kit gun." These are useful for dispatching snakes or other varmints, signaling for help in an emergency, and having "just in case."

Gun shows in the South are a major spectacle. People of all ages troop by long rows of tables covered by a dizzying array of weapons, uniforms, coins, knives, and survival gear. Men and boys dressed for the hunt examine the various weapons, make trades, buy and sell, and renew old friendships. As might be expected, survivalist tracts are much in evidence. The gun show, like the turkey shoot or gander pull of earlier times, is a social occasion that allows a renewal of ties with acquaintances, friends, relatives, and even symbolically with ancestors.

Many southerners possess and prominently display ancestral weaponry from "the war" and subsequent conflicts as well as hunting rifles and shotguns passed down for generations and kept in working order. The preservation and maintenance of these old .44s and .36s suggest that weapons have a totemic significance that transcends the merely decorative and functional. For many rural families in the past, the gun was probably one of the most expensive items they owned and therefore one of the most valuable (next to land) that could be passed on to heirs. The weapons serve as a vital link to ancestors—one of the remaining physical evidences of who they were and of who contemporary southerners are. The weapon links the southerner to a mythic golden age or, alternately, to a hardscrabble, but meaningful existence in the piney woods.

The pronounced cultural interest in weaponry evident in the South may stem from a perceived need for protection from varmints (both the four-legged and two-legged varieties), the enjoyment of hunting and the social constellation surrounding it, and a desire for a link with the past. Although this significant cultural symbolism has become entangled in the broader national debate over crime, attaching too much significance to the role of the gun in the South may be a mistake. The South has been a predominantly rural milieu and continues to hold certain rural values. In this context, to paraphrase Freud, sometimes a gun is just a gun.

See also RECREATION: Hunting

Fred Hawley
Louisiana State University
at Shreveport

Dickson D. Bruce, Jr., *Violence and Culture in the Antebellum South* (1979); Raymond D. Gastil, *Cultural Regions of the United States* (1975); Sheldon Hackney, *American Historical Review* (February 1969); Lee Kennett and James L. Anderson, *The Gun in America: The Origins of a National Dilemma* (1975); John Shelton Reed, *One South: An Ethnic Approach to Regional Culture* (1982); James D. Wright, Peter Rossi, and Kathleen Daly, *Under the Gun: Weapons, Crime, and Violence in America* (1983). ☆

Harlan County, Kentucky

IIIIIIIIIIIIIIIIIIIIIIIIIIIIIIIIIIIIIIIIIIIIIIIIIIIIIIIIIIIIIIIIII

The 1930s were a time of labor upheaval in the United States. There were strikes, picket lines, lockouts, riots, sit-down strikes, marches, protests, musterings of national guardsmen, and many charges of police brutality. Amid this labor unrest that was truly national in scope, one place caught the attention of the nation and much of the Western world. Previously almost unknown, it accumulated a huge literature in newspapers and magazines and generated a voluminous body of folk music. The place has since been known as "bloody Harlan."

The 1930 census revealed a population of 64,577, nearly all of which was dependent in one way or another on coal mining. John W. Hevener has published a careful study of the county's labor strife in the troubled decade, concluding that the struggle caused 11 deaths and 20 woundings. When viewed against the background of the region's grim history these casualties appear startlingly low—but bloody enough to justify the county's reputation. Harlan County earned its niche in the folklore of American labor violence. However, in considering Harlan's reputation for lawlessness and bloodshed, one can appreciate that the labor struggles mark only a brief and relatively minor facet of its turbulent history.

Harlan County lies between two great barrier walls—the long steep parallel ridges known as the Cumberland and Pine mountains. The area was settled sparsely and late. After the first settlers had built their cabins, forbidding hills kept out new waves of settlers and preserved intact the mores and culture, the ignorance and cunning, the crankiness and suspicion, the narrowness and prejudices, the loyalties and clannishness that marked the pioneer families. Sam Howard, a Revolutionary War veteran, was the county's first permanent settler. His and the 30 or 40 other backwoods families who followed around 1800 had been hardened by decades of warfare. As a people they had been seasoned by two centuries of scrabbling in the backwoods, clearing endless new ground,

fighting with the French, struggling over wilderness lands with the British, and countering almost incessant raids from both southern and northern Indians. It was inescapable that the people who stopped off at such places as the Poor Fork and Wallins Creek were a hardbitten, self-reliant lot who would be quick with knife and gun whenever it appeared to them that they were being "picked on."

The county was established by the legislature in 1819, and the county seat was "established" at Sam Howard's old place, which he called Mount Pleasant. By any standard meaningful to contemporary Americans this backwoods bailiwick was desperately poor. The people there fished, hunted until most of the game was exterminated, and gained such money as came into their hands by bartering ginseng, feathers, whiskey, brandy, hides, and saw logs to stock drovers and backwoods merchants. These settlers became remarkably interrelated, an important circumstance in a society that valued "blood kin."

The county was of the most rudimentary character, with a budget of $6,025.60 in 1857. Data on this period are hard to come by, but there is no reason to believe that the population was unusually violent in those years. During the Civil War, Harlan County residents were Unionists (except for a pro-southern enclave on Clover Fork) and formed strong home guard units to keep the peace. Unlike neighboring Letcher County, which split on the issue and fostered a little war within a big one, Harlan countians did little fighting among themselves. Instead, they relentlessly bushwacked Confederate forces that ventured into their midst between 1862 and 1864.

The struggle left many mountain

counties impoverished, divided, and hate filled so that numerous little "wars" followed Appomattox. In the half century after Lee surrendered, scarcely a county was without one of these vendettas that spread from valley to valley until practically the entire population was at peril. Breathitt County was wracked by one struggle after another, as were Clay, Letcher, Pike, Knott, and Bell. The dead were beyond count and included a circuit judge, a U.S. commissioner, a county attorney, a city marshall, a trustee of the State College of Kentucky, a physician, and a witness guarded by a company of state militiamen armed with a Gatling gun.

This bloody record reflected a lingering statewide frontier mentality that endorsed murder as a form of private justice. In that bloody period only Arkansas and Mississippi ranked with Kentucky in violent crime. It was the considered judgment of the *New York Times* (26 December 1878) that Kentucky was "the Corsica of North America," its people considerably less civilized than the Italian Mafia.

Harlan County did not escape these troubles. In April 1882 Wilse Howard won a few dollars from Bob Turner in a card game. Turner drew a gun and compelled Howard to return the money. Three days later Howard killed Turner from ambush. There is no credible tally of the deaths in the ensuing Howard-Turner War. It ended when the Turner faction caught the Howards in "Harlan Town," killed four of them, and wounded seven others.

The whirlwind industrialization of Harlan radically changed its society and economy. In the years from 1900 to 1920 the population increased from 9,838 to 31,546. Subsistence farmers left their hollows and river valleys to mine coal in "company towns." Their dependence on family or "clan" was abandoned for day wages and an erratic coal market. People who had lived all their lives amid "blood kin" and friends found themselves in small houses in communities that were totally dominated by the omnipresent power of coal and iron policemen. When the market for coal evaporated in recurrent depressions, famine and rebellion followed. The rebellions were repressed by a political system that grew directly out of the coal economy: the circuit judge, sheriff, and county chairmen of both political parties were in the coal business. That the men revolted in such uprisings as the "battle of the Evarts" and the "battle of Fork Ridge" is understandable. The only surprise lies in the small number of casualties.

Harlan was never as violent as its sister counties 70 miles away in West Virginia—"Bloody Mingo" and "Bloody Logan." In 1922 the Logan County War saw veritable armies of miners pitted against formations of deputy sheriffs and national guardsmen. Nonetheless it must be conceded that "Bloody Harlan" was not a gratuitous nickname. In 1916 a homicide rate of 0.8 per 100,000 persons was recorded in New Hampshire (a different kind of Appalachian state), and rural America as a whole reported 5.2. Harlan's rate was a horrendous 63.5. Perry reported 30.4. Harlan's neighbor to the south, Wise County, Va., came up with 39.3, and its eastern neighbor, Letcher, led the nation with 77.9—nearly 80 times that of New Hampshire.

See also SOCIAL CLASS: Appalachia, Exploitation of; Labor, Organized; / Coal Miners; Company Towns

Harry M. Caudill
Whitesburg, Kentucky

John W. Campbell, *The Southern High-lander and His Homeland* (1922); Joe Daniel Carr, *Filson Club History Quarterly* (April 1973); Mabel Green Condon, *A History of Harlan County* (1962); David A. Corbin, *Life, Work and Rebellion in the Coal Fields: Southern West Virginia Coal Miners, 1880–1922* (1981); Paul Frederick Cressy, *American Sociological Review* (June 1934); John W. Hevener, *Which Side Are You On?* (1978); G. C. Jones, *Growing Up Hard in Harlan County* (1985); Winthrop Lane, *Civil War in West Virginia* (1922); Howard W. Lee, *Blood-letting in Appalachia: The Story of West Virginia's Four Major Mines Wars and Other Thrilling Incidents of Its Coal Fields* (1969); Elmon Middleton, *Harlan County, Kentucky* (1934); George W. Titler, *Hell in Harlan* (1972). ☆

Honor

‖‖‖‖‖‖‖‖‖‖‖‖‖

Southerners of the antebellum era made it clear that they subscribed to an ethic of honor, but they never specified exactly what honor meant. In large part, this was because the meaning of honor depended on its immediate context, on who claimed and who acknowledged it. In fact, honor might be defined as a system of beliefs in which a person has exactly as much worth as others confer upon him. Antebellum northerners and most 20th-century Americans have some difficulty understanding the idea of honor, for it runs contrary to what has come to be a national article of faith: each person, regardless of race, class, sex, or religion, possesses equal intrinsic worth—regardless of what others think of him. Insult has little meaning to people who share such a faith, but if one takes honor seriously, insult from a respected person can cut to the quick.

Accordingly, much of the violence in the South from the 18th century to the present appears to have been sparked by insult, by challenges to honor. Southerners believed a man had to guard his reputation and his honor, by good manners and, if necessary, by violence. Insult literally could not be tolerated.

Women, although traditionally venerated in the South, could have no honor—only virtue. The ultimate protection of honor lay in physical courage, an attribute not considered to be within a woman's sphere. White men also refused to concede that black men could possess honor, although black southerners recognized honor among one another. Further, the honor of wealthy white men could not be damaged by men of lesser rank. Honor came into play only among equals. Contrary to stereotype, though, honor was not restricted to the southern aristocracy. Men of every class felt themselves to be honorable and could not tolerate affront and still enjoy the respect of their peers. The elite alone dueled, of course, but the duel was only the most refined manifestation of honorable conflict, the tip of the iceberg. Fighting, shooting, stabbing, feuding, and shotgun weddings were considered legitimate and inevitable results of honor confronting honor.

An emphasis on honor, concurrently with high homicide rates, prevailed in the 19th-century South, although the cult of honor became less formalized (and probably more dangerous in the process) after the Civil War. Duels faded away; shooting scrapes became more common. The concept of honor also spanned the subregions of the South, lowland and upland, slaveholding and nonslaveholding. It even persisted in southern cities, where volatile rural folkways combined with urban poverty and crowding to make southern cities peculiarly dangerous places to live.

The South was not alone in this culture of honor. In different variations, it has flourished for centuries in Mediterranean cultures such as those of Sicily and Greece. Cultures of honor also flourished among the aristocracy of 17th-century England and among the Scotch-Irish, both of whom exerted decisive influences on southern culture in its formative states. The idea of honor did not prosper among the Puritans, Quakers, or Congregationalists and seems to be at odds with the impersonal relations of a predominantly commercial society. Honor never sank deep roots in the North.

The South, on the other hand, from its very beginnings seemed designed to nurture honor. Slavery and the society it spawned provided the conditions in which the notion of honor could flourish. Honor thrives in a rural society of face-to-face contact, of a limited number of relationships, of one system of values. Honor depends upon a hierarchical society, where one is defined by who is above or below him. Honor grows well in a society where the rationalizing power of the state is weak; an adherence to honor makes the state, at best, irrelevant in settling personal disputes.

Honor found itself increasingly on the defensive in the 19th century, not only from the North and England, but also from within the South. Honor, necessarily a secular system of values, clashed with the ideals of Christian virtue. Evangelical southerners deplored and denounced the violence and pride honor condoned. In their eyes, people who let their actions be dictated by honor allowed themselves to become mere slaves of public opinion. The vast majority of southerners, of course, whatever their religious inclination, killed or assaulted no one, and even those who did resort to violence did so only once or twice in a lifetime—still enough to send many more southerners than northerners to jail and penitentiary for violent crimes, although southerners were notorious for not prosecuting crimes of violence.

Black southerners, once liberated from slavery, also adapted to southern codes of honor. White observers, particularly those from the North, were appalled that blacks fought and killed each other over the same apparently trivial provocations as white southerners. Indeed, the homicide rate of both races in the South exceeded that of both in the North. Southerners of both races, consciously or not, have held to their notions of honor far into the 20th century, even in northern cities. Those who find that high homicide rates today correlate with southern culture seem to be measuring the fallout of a culture of honor. Those who find a correlation with low literacy rates or poverty are describing the characteristics of a place in which honor can best survive in the present.

See also MYTHIC SOUTH: Militant South; Romanticism; / Hospitality

Edward L. Ayers
University of Virginia

Edward L. Ayers, *Vengeance and Justice: Crime and Punishment in the 19th-Century American South* (1984); Peter Berger, Brigitte Berger, and Hansfried Kellner, *The Homeless Mind: Modernization and Consciousness* (1973); Pierre Bordieu, in *Honor and Shame: The Values of Mediterranean Society*, ed. J. G. Peristiany (1965); Bertram

Wyatt-Brown, *Southern Honor: Ethics and Behavior in the Old South* (1982). ☆

Industrial Violence
||||||||||||||||||||||||||||||||||||||||||||||||||||||||

The United States has earned a reputation for having the most violent labor history of any industrial country, and the South followed the national pattern. The worst violence erupted during strikes, especially ones that involved employer efforts to destroy an existing union or to deny union recognition. In such disputes it is often difficult to determine which side initiated violence, but the results show that both employers (or their supporters) and strikers resorted to violence in the form of physical assaults, some of which were deadly. Company property was also occasionally destroyed, but workers often claimed this was done by employers themselves in an effort to discredit strikers or to encourage the intervention of troops. In any case, no union pursued violence as a systematic policy. Whether labor struggles turned violent was largely determined by the attitude of employers and their response to strike situations. If they hired strikebreakers and/or used armed guards to fight unionization, they created the conditions in which violence was most likely to occur.

Just as the South lagged behind the rest of the country in industrial development and the growth of organized labor, so too it experienced industrial violence somewhat later than other regions. After Reconstruction the first generation of industrialization in the South saw little labor-related violence despite the propensity of southerners to resort to mob violence in other areas of life. Although strikes disrupted textile mills, the South's leading industry, as early as the 1870s, southern textile workers never damaged mill property during this period, and they rarely harmed strikebreakers. The weakness of unions and the control exercised by employers, especially in company towns, help explain the general absence of violence. Moreover, the textile industry relied on a white labor force, which reduced the potential for industrial violence sparked by racial animosities. One of the few southern strikes with fatalities prior to 1910 came in 1894, when Alabama coal miners killed three black strikebreakers and a policeman.

The pace of industrial violence quickened after 1910. During a nationwide railroad strike in 1911–12, the introduction of strikebreakers led to a riot in New Orleans, La., that left six dead. In McComb, Miss., three black strikebreakers were killed, and the violence took the lives of several railway guards and a strikebreaker in Texas. Strikes by Louisiana lumberjacks and longshoremen affiliated with the Industrial Workers of the World resulted in picket-line violence in 1912 and 1913 that killed five strikers. During a 1919 strike by lumber workers affiliated with the American Federation of Labor, vigilantes in Bogalusa, La., killed four union men. Another national walkout by railway shopmen in 1922 resulted in the death of one striker and six black strikebreakers in violence that flared in seven southern states. The next wave of deaths came during the 1929 revolt of textile workers that took the lives of six strikers who were shot by police in a confrontation in Marion, N.C.

During the 1930s industrial violence reached new heights in the entire country. Spurred by union organizing drives and protective New Deal legislation, southern workers struck major industries, especially textiles, seeking recognition. Employers and their defenders responded with deadly force that cost the lives of over 20 strikers, including five shot by deputies in Honea Path, S.C., during the 1934 national textile strike. The decade's toll of strike-related fatalities in the South also included one strikebreaker, four company guards, and four local policemen. During this period antilabor violence was also costly to tenant farmers who organized the Sharecroppers Union of Alabama and the Southern Tenant Farmers' Union.

The record of fatalities in labor disputes shows that the bloodiest battles occurred on picket lines, where police often defended company interests by attacking strikers. Industrial violence did not result in the death of a single employer or company executive in the South. Although strikers sometimes initiated violence, especially in the period before 1929, they usually acted out of frustrated rage, and they failed to advance their cause by resorting to violence. Employers and their supporters used violent tactics to break strikes and intimidate workers, but management possessed so many legal weapons to fight unions that violence alone rarely determined the outcome of strikes.

Antilabor violence, however, made organizing both difficult and dangerous, especially when it was used systematically in southern communities dominated by antiunion industries. In Tampa, Fla., for example, vigilantes consistently employed threats, backed by periodic beatings and forced deportations, to stem the tide of trade unionism in the cigar industry from its establishment in the city during the 1880s to the 1930s when cigarworkers won union recognition. Similar tactics were used in other communities against

representatives of the Congress of Industrial Organizations (CIO) after creation of the organization in 1935. Gadsden, Ala., experienced a five-year reign of terror against CIO organizers and rubber workers who attempted to unionize the local Goodyear plant.

Industrial violence went largely unpunished, especially when its victims were trade unionists. Most community leaders and local police tolerated, or abetted, repression in the conviction that southern industrial growth and economic progress depended on preventing the development of unions. When arrests and indictments followed outbreaks of violence, they were usually directed against strikers as an additional method of hampering union activity.

New Deal legislation enhancing the right to organize and bargain collectively shifted labor battles from the streets to courtrooms, and industrial violence declined sharply in most parts of the country after 1937. Some southern cities followed this pattern. In Birmingham, Ala., for example, the violence that had plagued the city abruptly stopped when the Tennessee Coal, Iron and Railroad Company, the city's largest employer, recognized the steelworkers' union in 1937. Gadsden's campaign of threats, beatings, and destruction of union property ended during World War II when Goodyear workers, under the protection of the federal government, voted for a union.

In much of the South, however, industrial violence continued in defiance of the national trend. Between 1947 and 1962, 20 of the nation's 29 strike fatalities occurred in the 11 former Confederate states and Kentucky. The persistence of industrial violence in the South is difficult to explain, but lawlessness plagued labor disputes that pitted militant workers against staunch antiunion employers who dominated local communities and had the backing of police.

Since the 1960s most industrial violence in the South has been limited to sporadic property damage, except in isolated areas, such as Harlan County, Ky. Although resistance to unions remains strong, labor-management battles have become more institutionalized and less violent as they have increasingly taken the form of drawn-out legal disputes over union recognition and contract negotiations. When strikes do occur, they are now usually peaceful as in the rest of the country.

See also INDUSTRY: Industrialization, Resistance to; / Textile Industry; SOCIAL CLASS: Labor, Organized; / American Federation of Labor; Company Towns; Congress of Industrial Organizations; Longshoremen; Textile Workers

Robert P. Ingalls
University of South Florida

Hugh Davis Graham and Ted Robert Gurr, eds., *Violence in America: Historical and Comparative Perspectives* (1969); Melton A. McLaurin, *Paternalism and Protest: Southern Mill Workers and Organized Labor, 1875–1905* (1971); F. Ray Marshall, *Labor in the South* (1967); Charles H. Martin, *Journal of Southern History* (November 1981); Marc Miller, ed., *Working Lives* (1981). ☆

Literature and Song, Violence in Black

||||||||||||||||||||||||||||||||||||||||||||||||

Since the mid-19th century the physical and psychological violence of racial oppression has been a prominent concern in the literature of southern blacks. Prior to the 1930s writers were little more than descriptive in their treatment of the subject. This changed, however, in the late 1930s. Writers, to be sure, continued to support the crusade against lynching and other forms of anti-black violence in the South. The technique of their art, however, became more sophisticated. To a large extent, this was a result of the strong influence that the Harlem Renaissance of the 1920s continued to have on southern black literature in the 1930s.

The interracial violence in southern black life stimulated the creative imagination of southern black writers between the late 1930s and the early 1950s. It was a central theme in many poems and short stories; yet the fullest artistic treatment of the subject during this period was in novels of social realism, in problem novels, and in propaganda novels. In these works the lynching scene became a standard symbol of the intensity and pervasiveness of white-on-black violence and often functioned as a major structuring device. Patterns of imagery, narrative voice, thematic structure, character development, and other fictional techniques in the novels of this period reflected the violence that had become ingrained in southern society.

Richard Wright's *Native Son* (1940) is exemplary. Wright uses violence as the novel's primary imaginative idea. Although the novel is set in Chicago, its protagonist, Bigger Thomas, is a composite of various southern black youths for whom violence is the predominant fact of life. Wright demonstrates how the legacy of oppression affects the black psyche. Indeed, *Native Son* remains in the forefront of many southern black novels since the 1930s in which interracial violence undergirds the fictional art. Waters Turpin, William Attaway, George Wylie Henderson, and George W. Lee are among those southern black novelists in this period whose works have interracial violence at their core. Many of the period's novelists are known as members of the Richard Wright school or the protest school. Protest fiction dominated southern black literature until the 1950s.

Spearheaded by Ralph Ellison's *Invisible Man* in 1952, southern black writers began to concentrate more fully on intraracial violence as a manifestation of the legacy of racial oppression. Intraracial violence gave thematic focus to *Invisible Man*'s first chapter—the battle royal. Representative characterizations, symbolic actions, and generic themes of black life radiate from the intraracial violence of the battle royal. Intraracial violence helps define the novel's thematic structure as the protagonist, a black Everyman, searches for an authentic identity.

The concept of identity and the meaning of the racial past are major concerns in southern black novels published after World War II. Novelists frequently use the violence of the racial past as the context in which their protagonists examine, identify, and affirm their blackness. In their literary treatment of both the recent and the distant past, many contemporary writers use violence as the overriding metaphor for white resistance to any means blacks have used to participate more fully in southern life.

From Wright to Ellison, then, the emphasis on violence shifted from interracial to intraracial. Subsequently fiction writers during and after the 1960s shifted from primary to secondary emphasis on the violence associated with black life (past or present) in the South. Among contemporary writers this shift is evident in rather conventional treatments of a black past laden with violence, such as Margaret Walker's *Jubilee* (1966), as well as in more avant-garde treatments of the slave past, such as Ishmael Reed's *Flight to Canada* (1976). Ernest Gaines's *The Autobiography of Miss Jane Pittman* (1971) is representative of the secondary attention contemporary writers give to violence—interracial or intraracial, physical or psychological—as an index to southern black life. Through the development of a secondary character, Ned, rather than the novel's main character, Jane Pittman, Gaines chronicles the legacy of violence in southern black life from slavery to the 1960s.

The widespread white-on-black violence in the South of the 1960s is reflected primarily in the poetry of this period. The assassinations of civil rights leaders and other incidents of violence are the subjects of numerous poems. Some black poets of southern origin, chiefly Nikki Giovanni and Don L. Lee (Haki R. Mahubuti), became widely known for poems that advocate black-on-white violence as a defense against white oppression. Etheridge Knight became the most popular poet among a group of "prison poets," whose poems concern various kinds of violence affecting black life. During the 1960s poets were in the forefront of an influential group of writers—many of them southern—in whose works black-on-white violence is pervasive. These writers, whom social and literary critics label the Militant Black Writers, wrote as often of the urban North as of the South. The diminishing emphasis on violence in the fiction of southern blacks during the decade is in line with the philosophy of nonviolence that dominated the civil rights movement in the South.

The pervasive social violence of the 1960s did not, however, engender creativity in song as it did in other black arts and as it had done during the antebellum period. Southern blacks in general and vocal artists in particular adopted the slave songs as anthems. The lyrics of many of these songs were easily adaptable to contemporary situations, underscoring the historical continuity of the violence associated with living black in the South. Nina Simone was one of the few vocal artists who popularized songs generated by the physical and psychological violence of the period. Yet even the popularity of her "Mississippi Goddam," for instance, did not supersede that of earlier songs about interracial violence. "Strange Fruit," a song about lynchings in the South, which Billie Holiday had made famous a generation earlier, remained a standard among vocal artists ranging from classical to folk.

Rock, blues, jazz, folk, and popular singers continue to sing and to record songs about intraracial violence. Although several of them are contemporary products, the most popular are products of an earlier time. Since the late 19th century the Mississippi Delta has been the birthplace of numerous songs, especially in the blues, about intraracial violence in southern black life. The area still produces songs with a curious mixture of violence and heroism, such as the "bad men" songs. "Stagolee" (there are various spellings), the legendary prototype, has maintained its popularity since the late 19th century. Many of the songs from the Mississippi Delta have their genesis in the underworld life of gamblers and prostitutes. Others speak of intraracial violence precipitated by unrequited love, love triangles, and other forms of romantic passion. "Frankie and Johnnie," continually popular among contemporary singers, is representative of the type. Contemporary southern black songwriters (unlike the literary artists) seldom indicate in their works that intraracial violence among blacks in the South is a direct consequence of racial oppression.

Interracial violence in the South had been sharply curtailed by the 1970s. Among contemporary southern black songsters and literary artists, the violence of the past, not the present, receives attention. One notable exception is in blues songs, which continue to be written about love conflicts that precipitate intraracial violence. In the main, though, contemporary literature and song by and about southern blacks concentrate on the beauty and spiritual qualities of life among southern blacks.

See also BLACK LIFE: Freedom Movement, Black; Literature, Black; Music, Black; MUSIC: Blues; Jazz

J. Lee Greene
University of North Carolina
at Chapel Hill

Imamu Amiri Baraka (LeRoi Jones), *Blues People: Negro Music in White America* (1963); H. Rap Brown, *Die Nigger Die!* (1969); Charles A. Frye, ed., *Values in Conflict: Blacks and the American Ambivalence Toward Violence* (1980); Stephen E. Henderson, *Understanding the New Black Poetry: Black Speech and Black Music as Poetic Reference* (1973). ☆

Literature and Song, Violence in White

Violence has long occupied a significant place in white southern expressive forms of culture. In literature and popular culture white southern writers and performers have made use of violent motifs in order to describe and to come to grips with the region's history and experience. For many writers the South has served as a literary setting in which violence provides an undercurrent to everyday life. Others, however, have gone further, using the violence of southern experience as the key vehicle for conveying their sense of human nature and destiny.

Violence appeared prominently in southern writing with the beginnings of serious southern fiction during the antebellum period. Violence in many of these early works was intimately connected with larger questions of social virtue. This was especially true in the fiction of William Gilmore Simms, the most prominent writer in the antebellum South. Simms used violence in all his works as the main test of his characters' ability to lead lives of virtue and honor. For Simms, human beings were always vulnerable to the evil effects of human passions. He saw the greatest virtue in the man who could confront situations with courage and competence, while maintaining control of his own passions under the terrible stress that violent situations posed. In such tales of heroism as *The Partisan* (1835) Simms explored the character who could remain civilized even in the face of the awful disruptions of war. In such psychological works as *Martin Faber: The Story of a Criminal* (1833), Simms dramatized the tragedy of a man who, dominated by passion, lapsed into the excesses of violence.

Other writers from this period wrote much as Simms did. Such men as Nathaniel Beverley Tucker and William Alexander Caruthers wrote novels of southern chivalry that glorified the heroic characters of gentlemen in a violent world. Virginia-bred Edgar Allan Poe, in his tales of terror, explored the dark souls of individuals who, unable to control their passions, committed acts of unspeakable violence. Though few of Poe's works had a southern setting, their treatment of violence was quite consistent with southern ideas. And his verse-play *Politian* (1835) drew on an actual southern murder for its plot, which Poe chose not to set in the South.

The antebellum period also saw the rise of a significant school of "local color" writers, the southwestern humorists, who looked mainly at life on the southern frontier. Much of the humor in the works of writers such as Augustus Baldwin Longstreet derived from their presentation of the southern frontier as a place of virtual anarchy. Violence was a major manifestation of the lack of concern for social order that characterized the frontier folk in these works.

Violence continued to be important in post–Civil War southern writing. Although much southern literature between the end of the war and the early 20th century was within the bounds of the plantation tradition—glorifying a civilized stability in the Old South and minimizing its violence—at least a few writers stressed the importance of violence in southern life. The most prominent was the southern critic and racial liberal George Washington Cable. Recognizing the need for social change and decrying the effects of southern racism, Cable presented a South in which violence was endemic to social relations, in which men were quick to fight and tragically slow to reconcile social and political differences. From a quite different point of view, Thomas Dixon, Jr., spoke for the white South's fears of black aspirations. He used traditions of black savagery and violence in his most important work, *The Clansman* (1905), to argue the need for white supremacy and even for white violence to thwart black ambitions for equality.

But the most significant use of violence by postbellum southern writers came after 1930 in major works by novelists and poets of the Southern Literary Renaissance. Such writers as William Faulkner and Robert Penn Warren found in southern violence a key vehicle for addressing major social and moral issues. Thus, violence figures prominently in all of Faulkner's major novels. In such works as *Light in August* (1932) and *Absalom, Absalom!* (1936) violent episodes serve to underscore the problems of the South's history and society, and, more deeply, to explore the nature of human freedom and the consequences of human action in a vast, uncontrollable world. Faulkner's world was dense and violent, and he drew on southern historical and racial violence for its construction.

Robert Penn Warren, in both fiction and poetry, has looked directly to southern history for his sources, picking out individual violent episodes, and recreating them in ways that illuminate both southern history and more general questions of human nature and culture. Warren sees human beings as imperfect creatures in an uncontrollable world and has stressed the importance of original sin in any conception of human nature. His *All the King's Men* (1946), based on the career of Huey Long, describes a political setting filled with violence as Warren explores the meaning of human responsibility in a tormented world. In his long poem *Brother to Dragons* (1953, 1979), Warren focuses on the actual murder of a slave by the nephews of Thomas Jefferson in order to contrast his own pessimistic perspective with more optimistic views of human goodness and perfectibility.

Post–World War II southern writers have continued to use violence to structure their works. Especially significant in this regard is Flannery O'Connor, in whose fiction violence is a key to human nature and a force leading people to confront the demands of religious faith. In his novel *Deliverance* (1970), the poet James Dickey uses a series of brutal murders, set in the wilderness, to force his readers to come to grips with issues of human freedom and social order. The most controversial southern novel of the postwar years, William Styron's *The Confessions of Nat Turner* (1967), is based on the bloody slave rebellion of the 19th century. Through a "meditation" on historical violence, Styron explores the psychological dimensions of southern racism.

Other contemporary writers, though they have not made violence the symbolic focus of their works, have nevertheless maintained a southern literary tradition in which violence seems to underlie regional life. In works as disparate as Shirley Ann Grau's *The Hard Blue Sky* (1958), William Goyen's *Arcadio* (1983), and Barry Hannah's *Ray* (1980), one sees a South in which social relations are usually tense and filled with potential violence. Larry McMurtry's Texas novels similarly present a southern world where violence occurs easily. Violence thus remains an important element in southern writing; many of the key issues associated with violence have remained fairly constant since the antebellum period.

Violence has also been important in another major expressive form in the South, folk song and popular music. During the 19th century, violence was a key element in the plots of the traditional ballads that were current in southern plain-folk communities. These songs, many brought from the Old World but some originating in this country, present a harsh view of human nature and society and keep the human potential for violence clearly in the minds of their hearers. Among the more popular topics are tales of jealous murderers, of faithless and violent lovers, and of cruel betrayals. With the rise of the commercial country music industry in the 1920s, many of these traditional ballads were committed to records by such important early recording artists as Vernon Dalhart and Buell Kazee. A few early commercial songs, written for recording, also made use of structures and motifs from traditional songs—particularly from murder ballads.

In more recent years, most white southern song has focused on the difficulties of life and love, rather than on violence as such, but violence has continued to have a role in country music. This has been particularly true of the balladlike songs of such performers as Johnny Cash, Marty Robbins, and Johnny Horton. In addition, many of the prison songs so popular in country music evoke violent situations from southern life, and several successful pieces, including Kenny Rogers's "Coward of the County," proclaim an ethic in which a readiness to fight is taken as a necessary virtue. Violence has also entered into popular white southern music in some rather distinctive ways. During the Vietnam War era, for example, Merle Haggard gave voice to a violent intolerance familiar to southern tradition in his immensely popular "Fightin' Side of Me." Country music has remained faithful to the view that violence is a necessary part of human

life, a natural response to difficult situations. Such a view has long been important in expressive forms of white southern culture.

See also LITERATURE articles; MUSIC: Country Music

Dickson D. Bruce, Jr.
University of California, Irvine

Dickson D. Bruce, Jr., *Violence and Culture in the Antebellum South* (1979); John Hope Franklin, *The Militant South, 1800–1861* (1956); Sheldon Hackney, *American Historical Review* (February 1969); John Shelton Reed, *One South: An Ethnic Approach to Regional Culture* (1982); Jimmie N. Rogers, *The Country Music Message: All About Lovin' and Livin'* (1983). ☆

Mexican Americans, Violence toward

||||||||||||||||||||||||||||||||||||||||||||||||||||

Violence between Anglo-Americans and Mexicans or Mexican Americans has existed since their first contacts in the 1820s, and in the subsequent 160 years Mexican Americans have consistently been on the receiving end of that violence. Texas has continually been at the hub of violence as a meeting ground between the cultures of the southern and eastern United States and the Mexican Southwest. Violence resulted from the Anglo-Americans' conquest of Mexican territory, their taking of lands owned by Mexicans, and their economic subjugation of Mexican Americans. Although Anglo-American economic expansion has been the underlying cause for the ongoing conflict, the rationale for this domination and violence has relied heavily on particular American and southern cultural traditions as well as stereotypes of Mexicans to justify Anglo-American actions and assuage the resultant guilt.

Through the 1800s the mythic idea of Manifest Destiny strongly influenced Americans, and many adventurers coming from the southern and eastern United States felt it was their right to take and develop southwestern lands. They saw themselves as racially, culturally, spiritually, and technologically superior to the Mexicans. Southerners in particular could not understand or tolerate the Mexican's centralized government, authoritative Catholic religion, and undeveloped pastoral economy. Many eastern writers who had never been to Mexican territory wrote popular "dime novels" characterizing Mexicans as lazy, thieving, cowardly, and ignorant, but they were more complimentary of the "dark-eyed *senoritas*." These misinformed stereotypes, coupled with Manifest Destiny and the Mexican's mixed Indian-Spanish racial heritage, were used to create a convenient rationalization for capturing Mexican territory. This process culminated in the Texas War for Independence in the 1830s and the later war with Mexico in 1846, when the United States annexed Texas.

With the political and territorial conquest achieved, Anglo-Americans turned their attention to gaining private lands owned by the Mexican American inhabitants. Settlers and colonizers coming to the slave state of Texas were mostly from the southern United States. Their attitudes about blacks, as well as an economic class structure based on the inequality of races, set the pattern for relations with Mexican Americans.

Although Mexicans were not enslaved, they were a conquered and colonized people, and the southern psychology of discrimination and economic exploitation that had applied to blacks easily transferred to the Mexican American. Many Mexican Americans who were now U.S. citizens and supposedly protected by the Treaty of Guadalupe Hidalgo were forced off their property by land-hungry Americans. If land could not be had by legal means or trickery, then violence and intimidation would often be used by ranchers backed by local law officials, Texas Rangers, or the U.S. military. Frederick Law Olmsted, a northern traveler through Texas in 1853, told, for example, of Anglo-Americans forcing 20 Mexican families from their houses after the mere accusation that Mexicans were horse thieves.

Oral accounts until the early 1900s told of injured or slighted Anglo-Americans roaming the countryside killing any Mexican Americans they could find and then confiscating their property without repercussion from the law.

Many Mexican American *corridos*— ballads of south Texas in the late 1800s and early 1900s—dramatized such occurrences. The case of Gregorio Cortez was probably the most famous of these incidents, as were the *corridos* composed about him. Cortez, a Mexican American farmer, was sitting on his porch in Karnes County, Tex., in June of 1901, when an Anglo-Texan sheriff looking for a horse thief approached him. Existing stereotypes were that all Mexicans were horse thieves and potentially dangerous. A gun battle ensued in which the sheriff was shot, and Cortez was pursued over south Texas by several posses. During the chase many unsuspecting Mexican Americans, who happened to be in the wrong place at the wrong time, were killed by the posses ostensibly because they were members of Cortez's "gang." As it turned out most of the so-called accomplices were laborers walking to and from work through the brush country of the area. Cortez was later captured, but through his exploits he became the hero of many *corridos* and a symbol of resistance for Mexican Americans. After serving a prison term, he was acquitted and pardoned of the crime, which in effect was that of defending himself against Anglo-American economic control and stereotypes.

Since the days of Cortez, violence toward Mexican Americans has been covert but effective in perpetuating their economic subjugation and lower-class status. Stripped of their lands as a source of livelihood, Mexican Americans became a cheap labor pool used in building Texas agriculture and industry. Too often the rationale used by Texas businessmen and ranchers to justify this exploitation has gone back to the old stereotypes, that Mexicans are ignorant, irresponsible, lazy, and content with very little in life. When Mexican Americans have rebelled against these assumptions they have suffered violence and intimidation, the threat of deportation (even if they are American citizens), and economic reprisals.

From the early 1900s any Mexican American effort to unionize or strike in agriculture, mining, and industry, or to protect conditions, has been met with stiff resistance. Laborers were at the mercy of bad bosses, labor contractors, and immigration officials, and they were discriminated against in restaurants, businesses, and public places. As late as 1967 Mexican American efforts to protest and unionize met with violence in the Rio Grande Melon Strike when then governor John Connally sent Texas Rangers to the site.

Since the 1960s many changes have been made through the efforts of the Chicano movement, the Texas Farmworker Union, the United Farmworker Union, and especially through the rise of Mexican American political power. With more Mexican American public officials, the situation has improved, although violence and exploitation have not disappeared. Laborers are still intimidated, and police often shoot first and ask questions later when in the *barrios* (Mexican American neighborhoods). In small Texas towns unexplained killings still occur.

Anglo-American economic expansion in the Southwest has spawned much violence. The rationales—the American and southern cultural traditions and the stereotypes that perpetuate conflict and violence toward Mexican Americans— have been used and reused in different eras for basically the same purpose.

See also ETHNIC LIFE: / Mexicans

Dan W. Dickey
Austin, Texas

Frederick Law Olmsted, *Journey Through Texas* (1857); Américo Paredes, *With His Pistol in His Hand: A Border Ballad and Its Hero* (1958); Cecil Robinson, *With the Ears of Strangers: The Mexican in American Literature* (1963). ☆

Organized Crime

In both historical and fictional literature, the South has often been portrayed as a region characterized by crime and violence. The vigilante, the lyncher, the duelist, the race-rioter, and the frontier ruffian have played prominent roles in the region's history. Writers such as W. J. Cash and Sheldon Hackney have described the pervasiveness of violence in southern history, and many writers have concluded that crime and violence assume a distinctive pattern in the region's development. Despite the numerous accounts of a southern propensity for violence, one aspect of it that has received little attention is organized crime in the South.

The term *organized crime* lacks precise definition but is generally employed to describe the illegal enterprises and operations of those underworld organizations commonly called the Mafia, La Cosa Nostra, and the Mob. In the 20th century these organizations have dominated criminal activities such as gambling, prostitution, narcotics, bootlegging, and extortion. Centered in large metropolitan areas throughout the United States, these "families," as they are called, are headed by "bosses," or "godfathers." Each boss is a member of a national organized crime "commission," which dictates overall syndicate policy. Although most of these families are located in large cities in the Northeast, Midwest, and West, three have been assumed to operate from the southern cities of New Orleans, Miami, and Dallas.

According to the organized crime unit of the FBI, the first formal Mafia family in America was established in New Orleans during the Reconstruction era by Italian and Sicilian immigrants who used Mafia organizations in their native country as the basis for a Louisiana family. Recent scholarly studies have shown that this account is not supported by concrete evidence. The earliest publicity given to a Mafia organization in Louisiana came from widespread newspaper coverage of the 1890 assassination of New Orleans police chief David C. Hennessy. In 1891, 16 Italian and Sicilian residents of the city were tried and acquitted of the Hennessy murder. Inflamed by sensational newspaper accounts and stirred to action by anti-Italian remarks made by Mayor Joseph Shakespeare, a mob broke into the Orleans Parish prison and lynched 11 of the defendants. Many writers have described the Hennessy killing as the action of a Mafia vendetta, but an exhaustive study by Humbert Nelli uncovered no evidence to substantiate that version.

The first reliable evidence of organized crime in Louisiana came with the establishment of a slot machine empire in the state by New York mobster Frank Costello in 1935. Costello evidently made a deal with Senator Huey P. Long, whereby the state government would allow the machines in return for a share of the profits for the Long political machine. The Costello operation soon branched into "lotto" (the numbers game), bookmaking, and pinball machines. Shortly after the end of World War II, Costello, Meyer Lansky, the notorious financial wizard of the national syndicate, and Carlos Marcello, a Louisiana entrepreneur, opened two gambling casinos in Jefferson Parish. During the 1948–52 administration of Governor Earl K. Long, casino gambling, slot machines, pinball machines, handbook operations, and lotto flourished openly in the southern half of the state.

Since the early 1950s Carlos Marcello has been reputed to control organized crime in Louisiana and in neighboring states. According to such sources as the Metropolitan Crime Commission of Greater New Orleans and Senator Estes Kefauver's committee on organized crime, Marcello heads an organized criminal empire that takes in almost $1 billion annually from vice, theft, blackmail, extortion, robbery, and political graft. After intensive investigation by the Justice Department under Attorney General Robert Kennedy, Marcello in 1962 was forcibly deported to Guatemala because he had never become a naturalized citizen. Within a few months, Marcello returned to Louisiana and for many years has managed to evade the concerted efforts of law enforcement agencies to uncover concrete evidence of his criminal activities. He did serve a brief sentence in a federal penitentiary for assaulting an FBI agent in 1967, and in 1981 he was convicted of attempting to bribe a federal judge and of conspiracy to influence federal officials. He is currently serving a lengthy term in a federal penitentiary. Despite the many allegations about Marcello's Mafia family in Louisiana, virtually nothing is known about the organization, and little evidence has been produced to support those allegations.

In Florida, Santo Trafficante, Jr., reputedly took over leadership of a Mafia family after his father died in 1954. Originally headquartered in Tampa, the syndicate moved to Miami in the late 1960s. Trafficante reportedly served as the coordinator of Meyer Lansky's casino gambling and wide-open vice, which flourished in Havana during the 1952–59 regime of Cuban dictator Fulgencio Batista. When Fidel Castro came to power in 1959, he jailed Trafficante and closed down the mob's operations on the island. In retaliation, Trafficante,

along with Chicago Mafia boss Sam Giancana, conspired with the CIA in several futile attempts to assassinate Castro. Today, the Trafficante organization supposedly dominates the lucrative narcotics trade between Latin America and Florida and is currently engaged in a struggle with Latin American narcotics traffickers.

Little is known about the Dallas family of Joseph Civello. Some accounts depict it as an independent Mafia family; others describe it as the Texas arm of the Marcello empire. Civello allegedly controls illegal vice in Texas and serves as a conduit for communications among various Mafia families. Civello came most prominently into the news when he was identified as one of the 57 mobsters who attended the infamous Appalachian meeting at the upstate New York home of organized crime figure Joseph Barbera, Sr., on 14 November 1957.

Probably the best-known individual in the history of organized crime in the South was Jacob Rubenstein, better known as Jack Ruby. Born in Chicago in 1911, Ruby began his career in the Al Capone organization. He moved to Dallas in 1947, where he joined the Civello organization. Ruby operated several nightclubs, or "striptease joints," handled bookmaking operations and prostitution, and had close contacts with the Dallas police. In 1959 Ruby visited the Havana prison where Santo Trafficante was incarcerated, and he assisted in smuggling arms and supplies to anti-Castro guerrilla fighters in Cuba. Ruby had frequent contacts with close associates of Teamsters union boss Jimmy Hoffa, and he communicated with members of the Civello, Marcello, and Trafficante organizations. During the month prior to the assassination of President John F. Kennedy, he made numerous long-distance telephone calls to known mobsters. When Kennedy was assassinated, Ruby was seen at Dallas police headquarters, where Kennedy's accused assassin, Lee Harvey Oswald, was held in custody. On the morning of 24 November 1963 Ruby shot and killed Oswald in the basement of police headquarters. Convicted of the Oswald killing, Ruby spent the next three years in a Dallas jail. He died in January 1967.

In 1979 the Select Committee on Assassinations of the U.S. House of Representatives issued its final report on the Kennedy assassination, and it concluded that either Marcello or Trafficante may have conspired to kill the president. Kennedy's war on organized crime, his failure to eliminate Castro, and his sexual intimacy with Judith Exner, the girlfriend of Sam Giancana, provided possible motives. The committee found evidence that both Marcello and Trafficante had expressed the desire to be rid of Kennedy and that Lee Harvey Oswald's uncle, as well as several of the people with whom he associated during his stay in New Orleans in 1963, had connections with the Marcello family. The committee, however, could not furnish reliable proof of its speculations.

The subject of organized crime in the South has received scant attention from historians and other scholars. Much of the available material on the subject contains a considerable amount of sensationalism, speculation, and unfounded accusations. Because of its highly controversial nature, organized crime has attracted the attention of journalists and popular writers whose works lack documentation. The reports and studies of congressional committees and government agencies likewise fail to employ the proper techniques of historical inquiry. Much more research into the topic is necessary before an accurate and responsible history of organized crime in the South is possible.

See also ETHNIC LIFE: Caribbean Influence; / Italians

Michael L. Kurtz
Southeastern Louisiana University

G. Robert Blakely and Richard N. Billings, *The Plot to Kill the President* (1981); Michael L. Kurtz, *Louisiana History* (Fall 1983); Humbert S. Nelli, *The Business of Crime: Italians and Syndicate Crime in the United States* (1976); U.S. Congress, House of Representatives, *Investigation of the Assassination of President John F. Kennedy: Hearings Before the Select Committee on Assassinations of the U.S. House of Representatives* (1978–79); U.S. Congress, Senate, *Report on the Select Committee to Investigate Organized Crime in Interstate Commerce* (1951). ☆

Outlaw-Heroes

||||||||||||||||||||||||||||||||||||||||

Southern history and legend have been marked by a procession of outlaws whose illegal behavior in the service of some noble cause or ideal has elevated them to heroic status. Most southern outlaws, like the Harpe brothers who wantonly robbed and murdered across the frontier South, were notorious rather than heroic. But there have always been southern outlaws who fit E. J. Hobsbawm's definition of "social bandits": those who are forced to break the law to avenge a wrong or to defend their honor, family, or community from some oppressive power or circumstance. From the Regulators of colonial South

Carolina (1767–69), the first organized vigilantes in America, to Luke and Bo Duke of the "Dukes of Hazzard," "good old boy" lawbreakers in one of the most popular television programs of the 1980s, honorable outlaws have been celebrated in southern folklore, popular culture, and high arts. Other regions and nations have celebrated them as well.

Southerners have enshrined a wide range of outlaw-heroes in myth and legend. The outlaws' diversity reflects the complexity of a region that embraces the extremes of colonial Virginia and frontier Texas, black and white, planter and mountaineer, yeoman and slave. In 1676 Nathaniel Bacon achieved heroic status by leading an illegal armed rebellion against the legitimate but unresponsive government of Virginia. The South Carolina Regulators stepped outside the law with popular support to control the backcountry in the 1760s. A significant number of southern outlaw-heroes were spawned and found their justification in the events of the Civil War and Reconstruction. In the white southern mind and myth, and eventually in the mythology of other regions, southerners were driven into outlawry by rapacious Yankee armies, corrupt Radical Republican politicians, predatory carpetbaggers, and vindictive former slaves. Guerrilla fighter and bank robber Jesse James protected southern women and children in frontier Missouri from violent northern persecution during the war. For years afterward he protected them from usurious banks and railroads. Similarly, the Ku Klux Klan and other white vigilante/terrorist groups were active in the South during Reconstruction. Harriet Tubman and John Brown were outlaw-heroes to black southerners and abolitionists for their attempts to free slaves.

In the late 19th century the Hatfields and McCoys were two of the well-known feuding mountain clans who ignored points of law and fought over issues of honor and family loyalty. Morris Slater ("Railroad Bill"), the legendary black Robin Hood of Alabama, fought the law and stole for his poverty-stricken people until he was cut down in 1896. During the Depression of the 1930s in the Southwest, Bonnie Parker and Clyde Barrow, "Pretty Boy" Floyd, and other rural outlaws stole from the rich and gave to the poor in the tradition of Jesse James. Junior Johnson was a champion stock car racer in the 1960s who learned his driving skills while running moonshine in the hills of North Carolina, evading the meddling federal agents who put his daddy in jail. Johnson was compared to "Robin Hood or Jesse James" and was called the "last American hero" by Virginia-born writer Tom Wolfe. Since the early 1970s southern actor Burt Reynolds has appeared in a long series of popular movies with Dixie settings in which he has played lovable outlaws who fought corrupt sheriffs, transported illegal beer, and robbed the gas stations of a heartless oil corporation. In the early 1980s cousins Luke and Bo Duke broke the law each week in their stock car "General Lee" while untangling themselves and their down-home kin from the corrupt operations of the judiciary and police in their mythical southern county.

The outlaw-hero's marginal status has defined the limits of acceptable behavior within southern society. He has provided traditional southern culture with a safety valve: honorable models for rebellion. Moreover, southern outlaw-heroes have reflected and reconciled what W. J. Cash called the "social schizophrenia" of the southern character: intense individualism versus a deep sense of responsibility for others; "he-donism" versus "puritanism"; unre-strained violence versus a gentlemanly code of conduct; wanderlust versus a profound sense of place and tradition. Nowhere has this "split" psyche been more apparent than in the southern out-law-hero and nowhere have these con-tradictions been so well reconciled. The outlaw-hero is the single figure who can engage with impunity in explosive, il-legal behavior because it is justified by some noble purpose.

There has never been unanimity re-garding individual outlaw-heroes, es-pecially when race is involved. The knights of the Ku Klux Klan have always had both white and black detractors in the South. And the status of many outlaw-heroes has varied over time. Klansmen enjoyed less heroic status during the "Second Reconstruction" of the 1960s than they had in earlier eras. The outlaw-heroes of the southern black and Mexican American fit the standard southern pattern except that they were seen as mere badmen by the white cul-ture they fought. The 1831 slave revolt led by Nat Turner and the violent strug-gles of Gregorio Cortez with Texas law-men were justified in the eyes of their people on the familiar basis of resisting legal but oppressive forces: the cruelties of slavery in Virginia and the uneven hand of justice in the Rio Grande Val-ley. In some cases no justification was offered for black outlaw-heroes such as the bullying badmen in black folksongs: Stackolee, John Hardy, the Bully of the Town. Their tough defiance and ability to survive in a hostile white world were the stuff of black heroism with no need for moral justification.

There has been a fine line in southern culture between a rebellious hero cel-ebrated for his uninhibited vitality and the true outlaw-hero who is completely

beyond the law. Southern frontier heroes like Davy Crockett and Jim Bowie were widely celebrated in folklore and pop-ular southwestern humor for behavior that was often violent and illegal, but they were not generally considered out-laws. Although the southern gentleman who skirted the law to duel for his honor was sometimes seen as a heroic figure representing the best of his culture, this did not make him an outlaw. Heroic Confederate military figures such as Robert E. Lee and Stonewall Jackson were perhaps outlaws in the eyes of the North, but not to southerners. Confed-erate Partisan Rangers John Hunt Mor-gan, John Singleton Mosby, and William Clarke Quantrill owed their he-roic status to dashing guerrilla warfare behind enemy lines. However, only Jesse James and a few other southern guerrillas clearly crossed over the line to "outlaw-hero" status by robbing banks and railroads long after the war had ended.

Since the beginnings of commercial country music in the South in the 1920s, some of its most popular figures have celebrated rebellious, rambling behav-ior in their songs. Much of the popu-larity and heroic status of Jimmie Rodgers, Hank Williams, Johnny Cash, and Merle Haggard have derived from their legendary participation in this life-style. The same was true for southern rockabilly rebels Elvis Presley and Jerry Lee Lewis. In the 1970s Texans Willie Nelson and Waylon Jennings were mar-keted with great success as "outlaw" country musicians because of their spir-ited rebellion against straightlaced Nashville's musical and social norms. Yet none of these were traditional outlaw-heroes driven beyond the law. Rather they were rebel-heroes cele-brated for their ability to pursue an in-dependent lifestyle while maintaining, like the outlaw-hero, some allegiance to church, home, and mother. Ironically, all these country musicians have used the image of the free-spirited western cowboy to suggest their rugged independence. Despite country music's southern lineage, its performers have often rejected the "hillbilly" image in favor of western motifs that provide more positive and widely accepted images of heroism and rebellion.

A related regional borrowing occurred in the century following the Civil War when the western hero with his personal "code" that transcended the law began to bear a striking resemblance to the southern outlaw-hero with his code of honor. Western heroes of all kinds were fashioned out of real and fictional southerners with outlaw qualities: guerrilla-bandit Jesse James, cowboy-vigilante "The Virginian," farmhand-gunfighter Shane. When such western heroes took the law into their own hands they did it with the southern outlaw-hero's sense of honor and purpose—usually to aid a community besieged by savage forces.

There was a historical basis for this western adaptation of southern characters and traditions; Texas's cowboys and Missouri's outlaws were largely southern in origin and worldview. An equally important reason for this borrowing was the climate of the post–Civil War era. The relatively homogeneous South with its romantic myths of a gracious, agricultural past and noble Anglo-Saxon heroes (outlaws and otherwise), exerted a strong pull on a nation fearful of urbanization, industrialization, and immigration. The nation turned readily to western heroes who embodied traditional qualities of the southern outlaw-hero in a frontier setting free of urbanization and immigration, yet also free of controversial factors associated with the South such as slavery, aristocracy, and defeat.

Regardless of an outlaw-hero's morality as judged by outsiders, or the historical accuracy of the legends surrounding him, glorified "social bandits" like England's Robin Hood have long served significant psychological, sociological, and mythological functions for those who feel frustrated, victimized, and powerless. Southern outlaw-heroes who have demonstrated the continuing utility of the "social bandit" in this century by becoming heroes of national and international proportion include Jesse James, Bonnie and Clyde, Burt Reynolds's outlaw persona, and the fictitious Dukes of Hazzard. These southern outlaw-heroes have a universal appeal in a tumultuous century because they embody the comforting values of a traditional culture yet have the strength and courage to break the law and successfully rebel against the injustices of life.

See also BLACK LIFE: / Turner, Nat; FOLK-LIFE: / Murder Legends; Wagner, Kinnie; HISTORY AND MANNERS: / Crockett, Davy; MEDIA: / Reynolds, Burt; MUSIC: / Lewis, Jerry Lee; Nelson, Willie; Presley, Elvis; Rodgers, Jimmie; Williams, Hank; REC-REATION: / Johnson, Junior

George B. Ward
Texas State Historical Association

Roger D. Abrahams, *Deep Down In the Jungle: Negro Narrative Fiction from the Streets of Philadelphia* (1970); W. J. Cash, *The Mind of the South* (1941); David Brion Davis, *American Quarterly* (Summer 1954); Hugh Davis Graham and Ted Robert Gurr, eds., *Violence in America: Historical and Comparative Perspectives* (1969); E. J. Hobsbawm, *Primitive Rebels* (1965); John A.

Lomax and Alan Lomax, *Folksong U.S.A.* (1947); William A. Settle, Jr., *Jesse James Was His Name* (1966); Tom Wolfe, *The Kandy-Kolored Tangerine-Flake Streamline Baby* (1965). ☆

Political Violence

No other major section of the country can match the South's record of violence, political and otherwise. Southern political violence, like organized violence nationally, has featured repression by social and political elites of those who threatened (or were perceived to threaten) their control. The rare colonial insurrections—Bacon's Rebellion in Virginia (1675–76) and Culpepper's Rebellion in North Carolina (1677–78)—were in the main middle-class or upper-class revolts against ruling factions in their respective colonies and involved very little bloodshed. The Regulator movements of North and South Carolina in the 1760s and 1770s arose out of frontier conditions in the backcountry. The North Carolina movement sought to force the colonial authorities in the east to provide more responsible government in the west. The rebels were defeated on the battlefield of Alamance in 1771, after which six of their leaders were hanged. The South Carolina Regulators were vigilantes organized to suppress anarchy and force the colonial authorities in Charleston to bring government to the frontier. Neither movement aimed seriously to modify the structure of colonial government, much less to overthrow it.

In fact, many backcountry settlers felt a greater kinship with England after 1775 than with the eastern planters who led the movement for independence. Organized North Carolina Loyalists were decisively defeated at the battle of Moore's Creek Bridge in 1776, but partisan warfare raged between Whigs and Tories for several years in some interior districts of the Carolinas and Georgia.

Antebellum vigilantism, aimed at actual or suspected slave insurrections and their white instigators, had not been political, strictly speaking. But the goal of keeping the slaves in subjection, by force if necessary, and the day-to-day requirements of slave discipline conditioned southerners to the use of force as a regular instrument of policy. Even greater discord followed in the wake of southern secession in 1861. Unionist sentiment existed in varying measure throughout the South, reflected in active or passive opposition to the Confederacy. It was strongest in the border states and in the mountain areas of Virginia, North Carolina, Tennessee, Georgia, Alabama, and Arkansas. Opinion was not uniform in these regions, however, and warfare of family against family, even brother against brother, was not unknown. Such hostilities engendered bitterness that lasted for many years, sometimes in the form of blood feuds.

These wartime differences were translated after the war into political party divisions: former Unionists became Republicans, and ex-Confederates affiliated with the Conservative or Democratic party. Federal Reconstruction policy introduced the Republican party to the South in 1867 as the champion of Unionism, black freedom, and civil rights. Regional opposition to these goals drew heavily on prewar precedents.

It was but a short step from the militia musters and the slave patrols of the

1850s to Ku Klux Klans, and the so-called home guards, white leagues, and red-shirt clubs of the Reconstruction era. All were designed to enforce white supremacy. For more than a decade after 1865, therefore, white southerners of a certain age and disposition felt it their duty and privilege to continue the twin struggles against Unionism and for white supremacy, now joined as a crusade against the "Black Republican" party. The crusade took several forms. All were more or less inspired, organized, and led by the middle and upper classes, appearances sometimes to the contrary notwithstanding.

The most spectacular form of resistance, but the least effective in the long run, was the midnight raiding by the Ku Klux Klan and its kindred organizations. Formed in Tennessee in 1866, the Klan spread throughout the South in the spring of 1868 as congressional Reconstruction policies went into effect. It killed, flogged, and intimidated hosts of black and white Republicans in the areas where it flourished, but by 1872 it was put down by a combination of state and federal judicial and military action. The Klan helped to impeach and remove Governor William W. Holden of North Carolina, but it failed to end Reconstruction in any state.

Probably the most successful form of political violence was the urban riot. Seventy-eight have been counted for the years 1865 through 1876 in cities like Memphis and New Orleans and in villages like Camilla, Ga., and Clinton, Miss. Generally planned in advance, they often resulted in the death or banishment of Republican leaders of both races and the demoralization of their followers. Such riots occurred throughout the Reconstruction period and sporadically afterward, the last of them in Wilmington, N.C., in 1898 and Atlanta in 1906.

Closely related to the urban riots were the activities of the white league, red-shirt club, and other paramilitary groups that dispensed with the bizarre disguises of the Ku Klux Klan and operated in broad daylight. They rode about before elections, breaking up Republican meetings and intimidating Republican candidates and voters. Georgians pioneered this tactic in 1870, and it was repeated with increasing sophistication throughout the Deep South from 1874 to 1876. With the urban riots, it was largely responsible for bringing southern Reconstruction to a close by 1877.

From the 1870s to the 1890s southern Democrats controlled their respective states by means of honest electoral victories (where possible) and partial disfranchisement, fraud, and violence (where necessary). Republicans were permitted to vote and to elect candidates in the mountains and the black belts, but only as long as they did not threaten statewide Democratic control. In the 1890s, after a variety of agrarian insurgent movements, sometimes featuring coalitions with Republicans, Democrats began more systematically to disfranchise their opponents through constitutional or legislative action. Henceforth, the law would accomplish peacefully what riots and red shirt campaigns had done through threats and violence. The generation after 1890 saw the climax not only of black disfranchisement but of lynching and enforced racial segregation as well.

The violence of the second Ku Klux Klan in the 1920s was not primarily political, and except for such isolated events as the assassinations of Governor William Goebel of Kentucky in 1900 and Senator Huey P. Long of Louisiana in 1935, substantial political violence did not return until the advent of the civil rights movement, or Second Reconstruction, of the 1950s and 1960s. The civil rights laws of 1957–64, and especially the Voting Rights Act of 1965, helped return millions of black voters to the polls after the lapse of three generations.

The civil rights movement used non-violent protest as a means of winning public opinion throughout the country to peaceful change. Most of the violence that came was directed by whites against the desegregation of schools, businesses, and public facilities rather than the voting booth. It was not, therefore, specifically political until Martin Luther King, Jr., and his colleagues shifted their emphasis in 1964 to black voter registration. The killing of Michael Schwerner, Andrew Goodman, and James Chaney in the registration drive in Mississippi and other acts of violence in 1964 hastened congressional passage of the Voting Rights Act the following year.

In 1979 members of the Ku Klux Klan and the American Nazi party shot and killed five Communist Worker's party demonstrators at Greensboro, N.C. Unlike most of the political violence since the Civil War, this event had little or no direct racial bearing; the perpetrators and the victims were all white. The incident dramatized the enmity that developed after World War II between political fringe groups of the far left and right. The enmity was most volatile in the South, where violence-prone Klansmen and Nazis were most in evidence.

The reasons for the South's affinity for violence are not easy to pinpoint with assurance, but surely racial dissension has played a central role. So too, perhaps, has the region's rural, scattered population, which traditionally encouraged hunting, self-protection, private settlement of grievances, and attendant carrying of weapons. Politically, the South has experienced more bitter conflict, arising from deep racial and class divisions, than any other section of the country. Even when these conditions change and internal differences abate, old cultural patterns retain a life of their own.

See also BLACK LIFE: Freedom Movement, Black; / King, Martin Luther, Jr.; HISTORY AND MANNERS: Reconstruction; LAW: Civil Rights Movement; SOCIAL CLASS: Communism

Allen W. Trelease
University of North Carolina
at Greensboro

Richard Maxwell Brown, *Strain of Violence: Historical Studies of American Violence and Vigilantism* (1975); William Gillette, *Retreat from Reconstruction, 1869–1879* (1979); Hugh Davis Graham and Ted Robert Gurr, eds., *Violence in America: Historical and Comparative Perspectives* (1969); Steven F. Lawson, *Black Ballots: Voting Rights in the South, 1944–1969* (1976); Allen W. Trelease, *White Terror: The Ku Klux Klan Conspiracy and Southern Reconstruction* (1971); Wilcomb E. Washburn, *The Governor and the Rebel: A History of Bacon's Rebellion in Virginia* (1957); C. Vann Woodward, *The Strange Career of Jim Crow* (1955; 3d. rev. ed., 1974). ☆

Prisons

||||||||||||||||||

American penitentiaries developed in two distinct phases, and southern states participated in both. Virginia, Kentucky, Maryland, and Georgia built prisons before 1820, and between 1829 and 1842 new or newly reorganized institutions were established in Maryland, Tennessee, Georgia, Louisiana, Missouri, Mississippi, and Alabama. Only the Carolinas and Florida resisted the penitentiary before the Civil War.

Southerners fiercely debated the justice and utility of the penitentiary throughout the antebellum era. Some citizens and legislators argued that the institution constituted an essential part of any enlightened government, whereas other southerners warned that the penitentiary posed a real and direct threat to freedom and republican government. Advocates of the institution believed that the law would be more effective if punishment was less physically brutal; opponents of the institution believed that locking men up out of public sight to "reform" them was a farce and a dangerous precedent. They preferred that their states adhere to the older methods of punishment: fines, branding, imprisonment in local jails, or hanging. In the only two referenda on the penitentiary— in Alabama in 1834 and in North Carolina in 1846—southern voters expressed overwhelming opposition to the institution, but southern states nonetheless created one penitentiary after another. Virtually no reformers championed the cause of penal innovation; rather, obscure state legislators took it upon themselves to keep the South abreast of "progress" made in the rest of the Anglo-American world. The new institutions they created closely resembled one another and their northern counterparts.

Most of the prisoners in these antebellum southern prisons were white men, disproportionately from cities, and of immigrant background. Almost no women received penitentiary terms. After 1818 only Louisiana consistently sentenced slaves to prison. Most states of the Deep South incarcerated exceedingly few free blacks in their prisons, but Virginia and Maryland sent many free blacks to their penitentiaries. Neither state was happy with this situation, however, and both experimented with ways to avoid imprisoning free blacks— including selling them into slavery or leasing them to outside contractors.

Southern governments were not enthusiastic about spending money for any prisoners and always sought ways to make prisons pay for themselves. Pressure mounted for the inmates to be leased to businessmen to make shoes, pails, wagons, and other articles, and leasing was instituted in Alabama, Texas, Kentucky, Missouri, and Louisiana. Often free workers demanded that convict labor be kept out of competition with "honest workmen."

Antebellum southern prisons were not substantially different from northern prisons. Most people in both regions had little faith in reformation, and prison officials North and South dealt out harsh physical punishment, supplied poor food, spent most of their energies on financial matters, became entangled in political patronage, and let contractors or lessees assume real control of the prisons.

The similarity between northern and southern prisons, however, abruptly disappeared with the Civil War and emancipation. Virtually all southern prisons were destroyed or badly damaged in the war, and southern governments had few resources with which to rebuild them. Southerners had become accustomed to the idea of centralized state penal institutions, but they now confronted a radically different situation: postwar prisons would no longer be reserved primarily for white men. Four million exslaves were now liable for incarceration, and the number of defendants who received penitentiary sentences soon outstripped even ambitious attempts by state officials to build penitentiaries. Many southern states, often with reluctance, turned to leasing convicts to work outside the prison walls. More than 9 of 10 prisoners were black men, most of them in their early twenties, most of them convicted of the lesser degrees of larceny. Many of them died in prison, and nearly all were mistreated.

No single political group in the postwar South bore sole responsibility for inaugurating the convict-lease system—although the Democrats reaped most of its benefits. Black and white politicians, Republicans and Democrats, tolerated the system. Within 15 years after the Civil War all the ex-Confederate states allowed businessmen to submit bids for the labor of the state's felons.

In the late 1860s and early 1870s, a time of experimentation, leases ran for relatively short periods and convicts worked primarily as agricultural and railroad laborers. Railroad work on an expanded scale absorbed most of the penal labor of virtually every state in the 1870s. In the 1880s and 1890s convicts became increasingly concentrated in mining, especially in the states leasing the largest number of convicts: Alabama, Georgia, Florida, and Tennessee.

The lease system grew not only out of the inertia of the Old South but also the demands of the expanding capitalist system of Gilded Age America. On railroads and then in mines, the convict-lease system served as the only labor force capitalists investing in the South knew they could count on to penetrate swamps and primitive mines. Indeed, as businessmen and officeholders haggled over convict leases, widespread corruption grew up around the system.

Because the New South had so few industries, because those industries were concentrated in relatively small areas, because the products of those industries (especially coal) were so crucial to the growth of the southern economy, and because southern labor was relatively unorganized, convict labor undermined the wage scale and working conditions of entire southern industries. In the early 1890s, after 20 years of suffering at the hands of the convict-lease system, miners in Tennessee and Alabama launched large-scale revolts. Their opposition was joined with that from residents of communities where lessees established camps, cynical politicians of opposition parties, and people of conscience (such as Julia Tutwiler and George Washington Cable) who opposed the lease because it offended their sense of justice.

These protests helped bring the convict-lease system to a very gradual end. Although some southern states—Virginia, Texas, Tennessee, Kentucky, and Missouri—had long used manufacturing prisons in addition to the lease system, as late as 1890 the majority of southern convicts passed their sentences in convict camps run by absentee businessmen. Only three southern states (Mississippi, Tennessee, and Louisiana) completely abolished the convict-lease system before the turn of the century. Even those states that did end the lease system did not build new penitentiaries. Inmates were moved to state-run prison farms, which were considered more healthy and more secure

Convict labor chain gang, North Carolina, 1910

than scattered convict camps. Different classes of prisoners were separated from one another and death rates declined. Reformers continued to agitate for and gradually established juvenile reformatories, as well as prison schools, libraries, and commutation laws. Yet scandals continued to surface throughout the 20th century, highlighting the brutality and corruption of southern prisons.

The South today keeps a far higher percentage of its population in prison than any other part of the country. Although crime rates in the South generally fall below the national average, the region continues to build new prisons at a faster pace than the rest of the United States. The prisons already in operation are usually crowded far beyond their designed capacity. As has been the case since the first decade after the Civil War, blacks make up a disproportionately large percentage of the inmate population in the region and are sentenced for considerably longer terms than their white counterparts. Most southern states spend far less than the national average per convict; training

and rehabilitation programs, as well as prison employees, receive only about two-thirds as much funding in the South as in the nation as a whole.

Cultural predispositions lie behind the South's bleak penal history. Southerners have generally held a less optimistic view of human nature than many other Americans and thus have placed less faith in the state in general and "reformatory" institutions in particular. Southerners have tended to adhere to the stern retributive justice of the Old Testament rather than the more compassionate ideals of the New Testament. Southerners in political power long operated in a one-party system that allowed penal corruption and neglect to go unchallenged by other parties. The history of prisons in the South suggests that southern culture is intimately linked with the often tragic history of southern class and race relations.

See also LAW: Criminal Justice; Criminal Law

Edward L. Ayers
University of Virginia

Edward L. Ayers, *Vengeance and Justice: Crime and Punishment in the 19th-Century American South* (1984); *Southern Exposure* (Winter 1978) (special issue on prisons); Hilda Jane Zimmerman, "Penal Systems and Penal Reform in the South Since the Civil War" (Ph.D. dissertation, University of North Carolina at Chapel Hill, 1947). ☆

Race Riots

||||||||||||||||||||||||||||

In antebellum times, race riots were called "slave revolts" or "slave insurrections," but even then racial violence was not limited to the South. During the Civil War, draft and labor riots between the races broke out in several northern cities. The most dramatic took place in New York City in mid-July 1863. It raged for five days, and estimates of those killed ranged up to 1,200.

Referring to such violence as a "riot" is not only incomplete but often misleading. Some of the traumatic episodes in the South, as well as the North, were largely one-sided, white massacres of defenseless blacks with a macabre combination of carnage and carnival. *Webster's New Collegiate Dictionary* defines massacre as the killing of a number "of . . . human beings under circumstances of atrocity or cruelty." The terms *pogrom* or *race war* could logically be applied as well.

Beginning with Reconstruction and continuing until the turn of the 20th century, race riots stand out as phenomena of the New South, but they reflect features of the region that go back to the Old South and continue into the 20th century. One cause for racial violence was political; only in the South was the political system openly dependent upon white supremacy. States with black belts—contiguous counties with population ratios of 40 percent black or more—were in constant political turmoil. It was essentially a struggle among white men over who would rule: a white minority (Democrats) was trying to maintain dominance over another white minority (Republicans) who controlled the formidable black voting bloc.

Sometimes economic grievances, rather than partisan politics, led to race riots. This was true of the racial massacre that occurred at Memphis on 1 and 2 May 1866, when whites went on a rampage and tried to destroy the new black community. When peace was restored, two whites and 46 blacks had been slain. The racism of poor whites was far more virulent than that of the wealthier, more conservative white supremacists. After Appomattox, the poor whites found themselves in competition with blacks for the limited economic opportunities in the South. They were perfect tools for the race-baiting political demagogues, who often goaded them into open acts of passion and violence. Racism seemed the only thing poor whites had in common with the landlord and/ or planter-merchants.

On 30 July 1866 New Orleans was the scene of the first significant political race riot. Here a mob—supported by the police—assaulted a black suffrage convention. When the smoke cleared, 37 blacks and three of their white supporters had lost their lives. Then between 1868 and 1876, race riots erupted in Pine Bluff, Ark., in the state of Louisiana at Colfax, Opelousas, Coushatta, and again in New Orleans in 1874. Others broke out at Meridian, Vicksburg, and Yazoo City, Miss. In 1876 racial violence flared in South Carolina, a state with a population ratio that exceeded four blacks to each white. In the town of Hamburg an episode escalated into a pitched battle, as 200 whites imported heavy arms and munitions and massacred blacks. Hostilities persisted intermittently throughout the presidential election of 1876.

The compromise of 2 March 1877 and President Hayes's inauguration two days later marked the end of the Reconstruction era. Blacks continued to vote and to hold office, though, and political race riots continued. In 1883 the city of Danville, Va., was the scene of political violence. Here the Democrats exploited the passions of the poor whites with a cry for white supremacy and white solidarity and instigated an election-eve riot on "the color-line issue" to insure the triumph of their party in the legislature.

The Populist revolt of the 1890s presented the South with its greatest challenge since Reconstruction. In some places, the rise of the Populist party in the South divided the white vote to such an extent that the black vote became the balance of power. The revival of the race issue was the Bourbons's answer to this threat. Again the demagogues pulled out their "stock themes" and appealed to the passions of poor whites to do the dirty work of politics for the sake of party unity, white solidarity, and white supremacy. Political riots were to continue until total black disenfranchisement became a fait accompli.

In 1890 Mississippi invented the standard device for voiding the Constitution on a racial basis—an "understanding clause," which required interpretation of written material in addition to literacy as a prerequisite for voting. A modified version of the Mississippi formula was adopted in 1895 by South Carolina. Violence erupted when elitist white factions sought to enforce South Carolina's "grandfather clause,"

which made it illegal to vote if your grandfather had not voted, thus eliminating descendants of slaves.

The Phoenix riot of November 1898 occurred in the upcountry of South Carolina. At a crossroads country store in the Phoenix community in Greenwood County, and in neighboring communities, election-day riots resulted in the death of one white man and the execution of at least 12 blacks. Included among the wounded were three members of one of the most influential white families, the Tolberts (leading Republican and federal officeholders), who were forced to flee the violence.

The Wilmington, N.C., race riot in 1898 was a watershed; race riots after this were no longer distinctive southern events. During the first decade of the 20th century, riots broke out in the South at New Orleans in 1900 and at Atlanta in 1906. In the North riots occurred at New York in 1900; Springfield, Ohio, in 1904; Greenburg, Ind., in 1906; and Springfield, Ill., in 1908. The worst of these exploded in Atlanta without warning after the Atlanta *Journal* had for months carried on a "nigger-baiting" gubernatorial campaign with Hoke Smith and former Populist Tom Watson on one side and Clark Howell and the regular Democrats on the other. Anarchy reigned for four days.

Race riots in East St. Louis, Ill., and Houston, Tex., in 1917, were the prelude to the period dubbed the "Red Summer." James Weldon Johnson used that name to describe the race riots that bloodied the streets of more than 20 towns and cities—North and South—in the six-month period from April to early October 1919. The riots of the Red Summer first struck at Charleston, S.C., and were followed by those at Longview, Tex.; Washington, D.C.; Omaha, Neb.;

Knoxville, Tenn.; and Chester, Pa. The most violent ones occurred at Elaine, Ark., and in Chicago and could be classified as a pogrom and a race war, respectively. Finally, the Tulsa race riot of 1921 was the most serious of the post–World War I era. It had the ingredients of a race war, which propelled this conflict into a new dimension. The city's black community suffered a disaster.

The interim between the Tulsa riot and World War II marked a transitional era from the old-style to the new-style riot. The latter, observed August Meier and Elliot M. Rudwick, "first appeared in Harlem in 1935 and Detroit in 1943, where black attacks were mainly directed against white property rather than white people." They were more likely to occur in the North than in the South. The ghetto riots of the 1960s had no American precedent, and they profoundly shocked both white and black citizens. Beginning in 1964, urban riots swept the Chicago suburb of Dixmoor, Harlem in New York City, the Bedford-Stuyvesant section of Brooklyn, Rochester, Philadelphia, and the New Jersey cities of Jersey City, Elizabeth, and Paterson. "Burn, baby, burn!" was the exultant cry first heard in Watts, the black ghetto of Los Angeles. The following summer witnessed similar chaos in New York, in Cleveland's Hough section, and in Chicago. In 1967 still more violence occurred in Tampa, Cincinnati, and Atlanta, with the most serious riots in Detroit and Newark, where in six days of rioting, 26 were killed and 1,500 were injured, and damage reached $30 million. In April 1968 Dr. Martin Luther King, Jr., was assassinated in Memphis, and this tragedy triggered a new wave of burning and looting in more than a hundred cities.

Urban violence subsided after the riots triggered by the King assassination, yet many of the underlying causes remained at the end of the 1970s. The Miami riot of May 1980 and the renewal of the turbulence there in 1982 demonstrated that the elements that created ghetto riots still exist. Massive racial violence should no longer be viewed, though, as either a southern phenomenon or a northern urban problem, but as a distinct national one.

See also BLACK LIFE: Lynching; Race Relations; MYTHIC SOUTH: Racial Attitudes

H. Leon Prather
Tennessee State University

Scott Ellsworth, *Death in a Promised Land: The Tulsa Race Riot of 1921* (1982); H. Leon Prather, *We Have Taken a City: Wilmington Racial Massacre and Coup of 1898* (1984); Elliot M. Rudwick, *Race War at East St. Louis, July 2, 1917* (1972); William M. Tuttle, Jr., *Race Riot: Chicago in the Red Summer of 1919* (1974). ☆

Southwestern Violence

The roots of the apparently casual mayhem in the wild West can be found in the violence-prone ethic of Texas and the South, specifically in the history of the Scotch-Irish who immigrated to America in the 18th century. Conditioned to border war by generations of fighting first the English across the Tweed and then, as colonists in the province of Ulster, the turbulent Irish, by 1730 they were leaving for America by the thousands. Avoiding existing settlements, these Scotch-Irish headed immediately for the western, Indian frontier.

Independence of thought and action, which was a primary benefit of frontier life, was not without its costs. The threat of Indian hostilities existed for all whites living on the fringe of Anglo-American civilization. The settlers valued the virtues of strength, physical courage, and self-reliance; Augustus Baldwin Longstreet observed in 1833 that to be "the *very best* men in the county . . . in the Georgia vocabulary, means that they could flog any other two men in the county." Life on the Indian frontier was savage, and the frontiersman was familiar with violence.

With the crossing of the Sabine River, new circumstances combined to make frontier conditions even more violent for the Anglo-American pioneer. Texas was the place where western and southern violence overlapped. The brief but bloody revolt against Mexican sovereignty spawned border warfare that lasted for generations and mutual antagonism and mistrust that linger to the present day. In Texas, also, the frontiersman encountered for the first time Indians who were superbly skilled horsemen—Comanche and Kiowa warriors—who fought westward expansion to a standstill until the development of repeating firearms. Finally, the unsettled conditions of a newly won independence and a virtually nonexistent legal system drew like a magnet the derelicts and outlaws of the more developed states in the East. One long-time Texan observed that before 1836 fighting was no more common among the Anglo-American colonists in Texas than in the United States. With the inauguration of the "powder-stained Republic," however, turbulence prevailed in many places. Hundreds of American—mostly southern—soldiers of fortune flocked to the Texas army in 1836, and with its

disbanding after San Jacinto, its footloose men stayed on. During the 10 years prior to annexation to the United States, war spirit in Texas continued to run high: legal authority was minimal, bars to immigration were nonexistent, and all sorts of people left the United States for Texas. The western frontier developed too swiftly for its courts of justice.

Texans, like other frontiersmen, commonly settled differences with personal violence, whether by fighting, shooting, stabbing, or dueling. More than two-thirds of the indictments in the district courts of the Republic were for the crimes of assault and battery, affray, assault with intent to kill, or murder. About 60 percent of the assault and battery cases resulted in convictions, but sentences were light—ordinarily 5 or 10 dollars and costs. Prosecutors in trials for more serious offenses encountered great difficulty in obtaining convictions because juries tended to give serious consideration to pleas of self-defense or "unbearable provocation." Only two men, in fact, were executed for murder in the Republic. A Texas doctor wrote that "the killing of a fellow was looked upon with greater leniency than theft," a crime of rare occurrence and harsh punishment on the frontier. Homicide, moreover, was most often a crime without malice. Hot-tempered, armed men, on a sudden and often trivial irritation, killed their fellow men. Personal honor was a thing of great value, and in a raw new land no recourse to the courts existed. The very presence of armed, reckless men, imbued with such an ethic, made any quarrel a potential homicide.

While the middle and lower classes did away with each other in street brawls, barroom shootings, and knife fights, the gentry followed the prescribed form of manslaughter for their class, the formal duel. During the period of the Republic alone, Texas witnessed "affairs of honor" between many officers of the army, including one in which the principals were its general-in-chief, Albert Sidney Johnston, and its acting commander, Felix Huston. Soldiers were not alone in resorting to the "code duello." Numerous Texas senators and representatives exchanged shots on the field of honor, and a fight between President Mirabeau B. Lamar and a member of his cabinet was barely averted.

This heritage of organized and personal violence naturally produced a corps of proficient, if ill-disciplined, soldiers. Ten years of brutal raiding and counterraiding from San Antonio to the Rio Grande followed the Texas Revolution's apparent end at San Jacinto, and as scouts, escorts, and mounted infantry, the Texas Rangers serving under Zachary Taylor and Winfield Scott in Mexico took a full measure of revenge for the Texan dead at the Alamo and Goliad. So ruthlessly efficient was Colonel John Coffee Hays's ranger regiment that General Taylor reportedly said of them, they "are the damndest troops in the world; we can't do without them in a fight, and we can't do anything with them out of a fight." As atrocities attributed to the Texas troops multiplied, the exasperated Taylor sent home all companies but one, Ben McCulloch's spy company, whose daring and precise reconnaissance activities discovered and reported Santa Anna's secret movement toward Taylor's army in February of 1847 just in time to allow the American general to assume a strong defensive position at Buena Vista and thus salvage the United States war effort in northern Mexico.

Not surprisingly, Texas soldiers carried the same ardent martial spirit into the Civil War. As Jefferson Davis observed upon the arrival of the leading elements of the Texas brigade at Richmond in 1861, "the soldiers of the other states have their military reputations to gain, but the sons of the defenders of the Alamo have theirs to uphold." The Texas Brigade of the Army of Northern Virginia, for example, amassed one of the most glorious combat records of any Civil War unit, North or South. They were equally notorious as foragers. Recruited primarily from counties on or near the Indian frontier, this brigade displayed almost superhuman courage and élan at Gaines Mill, Sharpsburg, Gettysburg, Chickamauga, and at the Wilderness, where its decimated regiments are credited with checking the assault of a full Union corps. Despite terrible losses—one of its regiments sustained the highest percentage of casualties of any Civil War unit in a single day at Sharpsburg—the Texas Brigade maintained its formation to Appomattox, with Lee vowing to call upon it "so long as a man remains to wave its flag."

Undoubtedly much of the violence experienced on the frontier was the result of the restlessness engendered by successive wars. The Texas Revolution, the Mexican War, and the Civil War all produced men who had tasted action and could not return to the discipline of the settled world. Jesse James looms largest among this group, but he is only one of scores who continued the war well beyond the passing of the armies.

Many cowboys were also southerners dispossessed by the late war. Among the classic protagonists of western literature are Shane, whose "folks came out of Mississippi and settled in Arkansas," and the model for later cowboys of

American fiction, the Virginian of Shiloh Ranch. Like his predecessors on the American frontier, the cowboy valued independence, self-reliance, hard work, austerity in manners and possessions, honesty, bravery, and a rugged stoicism born of life in nature. Like the long rifle and bowie knife of earlier frontiersmen, however, his six-gun was his most enduring icon, and in both legend and fact he was too often quick to react to a real or supposed affront with violence.

Along with the heroic Shane and the Virginian, western fiction also presents the evil Major Tetley of *The Oxbow Incident*, who, dressed in a Confederate uniform and cowboy boots, leads a murderous lynch mob. He represents an undesirable side effect of the frontier imperative of self-reliance and the quest for order—vigilantism and lynch law. Although in the older states of the Deep South both practices flourished well into the 1930s and beyond, long after the development of formal courts of law, it was on the frontier that mob violence, in the name of law and order, took root in America. Nowhere was lynch justice more swift or certain than on the frontier.

Perhaps the most notorious example of vigilante usurpation occurred in east Texas between 1839 and 1844. The so-called Regulator-Moderator War had its background in the influx of lawless characters into the Neutral Ground between the Mexican province of Texas and the state of Louisiana in the first three decades of the 19th century. After 1806 Mexican law forbade the settlement of any lands within 20 leagues of the border of the United States, yet by 1836 the east Texas borderlands had a greater combined population than all other areas of the new Republic combined.

These uninvited citizens, largely refugees from justice in the "old states," had become so accustomed to administering their own affairs and giving summary punishment to criminals that they were unwilling to accept the courts of the Texas Republic.

When a killing resulted from a quarrel over fraudulent land certificates, Texas courts acquitted the accused killer. The former defendant quickly organized a posse of 30 "Regulators" to deal with continuing violence. Although their stated purpose was the suppression of crime, this band burned homes and intimidated personal enemies until a rival faction of "Moderators" arose to oppose them. The first act of the Moderators, the murder of the leader of the Regulators, was met with bloody reprisal, and their already inferior numbers were soon further reduced by Regulator guns and ropes. So powerful did these vigilantes become that they openly defied the courts of Shelby County and contemplated overturning the government of the Texas Republic and declaring their new leader dictator.

Regulator excesses, however, strengthened the Moderators' position, and open warfare broke out once again. East Texas experienced a reign of terror while fields went uncultivated, men were shot from ambush, and prisoners were hung without trial. Only when President Sam Houston ordered 600 Texas militiamen into the region to arrest the leaders of the two factions were peace and order restored.

Statehood strengthened civil government in Texas, but it could not erase the effect of generations of summary frontier justice. Too often mixed with vigilantism was an equally malevolent racism, a curious phenomenon on the American frontier. In some ways the frontier was the freest of places, in which a man was judged on the quality of his work and such virtues as honesty, bravery, and shrewdness. The southern frontier was, however, also heir to the Old South's legacy of black slavery. Anglo-Texans never forgot the Alamo and Goliad or forgave the nation that martyred Crockett, Travis, Bowie, and Fannin. Germans, a numerous, prosperous, aloof, and Unionist minority in central Texas, were viewed with great suspicion by their Anglo-Texan neighbors, a prejudice that culminated in the slaughter of German prisoners of war by Confederate irregulars following the battle of the Nueces in 1862. Indians most of all, especially the fiercely imperialistic Comanches, were regarded as a race of savages whose very existence was a bar to the progress of civilization, and raid and counterraid between these mutually antagonistic cultures escalated into a war of attrition, which the Native American could not hope to win. Finally, when an Anglo-Texan was brought before the bar of justice in Langtry, charged with the murder of a Chinese laborer on the Southern Pacific Railroad, Judge Roy Bean freed him, asserting that "nowhere in his lawbook could he find a rule against killing Chinese."

The courage and honor, the militarism and violence of the 19th-century frontiersman, soldier, and cowboy remain part of present-day Texas culture. Texas A&M University provided more general grade officers to the Allied cause in World War II than any other officer-training academy, and Texans received a higher per capita share of Congressional Medals of Honor in Vietnam than servicemen of any other state. Cowboys and would-be cowboys still carry rifles in the gun racks of their pickup trucks, and for recreation the good old boys still enjoy a good free-for-all at the local honky-tonk on a Saturday night. Here, culturally and geographically, the South and the West meet and are one. The only difference, a Texas Ranger once observed, is that to the east of a certain imaginary line running down the middle of the state, roadhouse brawls take place in the parking lot; to the west they are conducted indoors—a vestige, one may suppose, of the southern heritage of order and decorum juxtaposed with the western tradition of experiencing life "with the bark on."

See also GEOGRAPHY: Southwest

Thomas W. Cutrer
University of Texas at Austin

Dickson D. Bruce, Jr., *Violence and Culture in the Antebellum South* (1979); Marcus Cunliff, *Soldiers and Civilians: The Martial Spirit in America, 1775–1865* (1968); John Hope Franklin, *The Militant South, 1800–1861* (1956); Joe B. Frantz, in *Violence in America: Historical and Comparative Perspectives*, ed. Hugh Davis Graham and Ted Robert Gurr (1969); Elliot Gorn, *American Historical Review* (February 1985); William Ransom Hogan, *The Texas Republic: A Social and Economic History* (1946, 1969); Jack K. Williams, *Dueling in the Old South: Vignettes of Social History* (1980). ☆

"BONNIE AND CLYDE"

Bonnie Parker (1910–1934) and
Clyde Barrow (1909–1934). Outlaws.

On the morning of 23 May 1934 six law officers fired more than 160 shots at a car driving down a road near Arcadia, La. Fifty shots hit the car's passenger and driver—Bonnie Parker and Clyde Barrow, better known as "Bonnie and

Clyde." The fatal ambush was the culmination of months in pursuit of the notorious outlaws, who had killed at least 12 people since April of 1932.

Bonnie Parker was high-spirited and intelligent. Her family moved from Rowena, Tex., to Dallas when her father died in 1914. There, she met Clyde Barrow, the quick-tempered, uneducated son of desperately poor parents. By the time they met, Barrow had already been involved in petty crimes. Bonnie's criminal association with him began when she smuggled a gun into a Texas prison where he was being held, thus allowing him to escape.

Often with various other gang members, Bonnie and Clyde drove for miles along the back roads of Texas, Oklahoma, Missouri, Arkansas, and Louisiana. They lived mostly in stolen cars, and they survived on the spoils of their victims. Panic and criminal incompetence characterized Barrow's escapades and often resulted in purposeless killings.

When news spread that Texas Ranger Frank Hamer and his men had killed Bonnie and Clyde, crowds gathered at the scene, tearing off parts of the car, hacking away locks of Bonnie's hair, taking whatever they could that had belonged to the infamous pair. One determined souvenir seeker even tried to amputate Clyde's trigger finger. The desire to possess anything with which Bonnie and Clyde had been associated was compulsive, and it has continued. The death car itself sold at auction in 1973 for $175,000.

For two years, Barrow's gang terrorized residents in and around Texas and, in doing so, sparked the phenomenal growth of a legend. The image of a tiny, cigar-smoking woman and a daring gangster together, living dangerously

and outrunning poorly organized pursuers, evoked great excitement. Bonnie's devotion to Clyde and Clyde's successful rise from the anonymity of dire poverty further incited the romanticization of their exploits; and books and movies, such as *Bonnie and Clyde* (1967), have sustained their memory. Many of their contemporaries cheered the outlaws' deaths, but, in a decade when Americans needed heroes, countless others sympathized with and celebrated the careers of Bonnie and Clyde.

Jessica Foy
Cooperstown Graduate Programs
Cooperstown, New York

John Treherne, *The Strange History of Bonnie and Clyde* (1985). ☆

CAPITAL PUNISHMENT
|||||||||||||||||||||||||||||||||||||||||||||||||||||||||||

Few social issues attract as much public attention as capital punishment. Arguments against capital punishment commonly focus on execution as an amoral or unjust form of legalized homicide. Arguments for the death penalty range from the biblical "an eye for an eye" principle of revenge to the plausible but scientifically unproven theory that capital punishment deters would-be offenders from extreme forms of criminal behavior. While the pros and cons of capital punishment undoubtedly will continue to be debated by both private citizens and public officials in all 50 states, southern states lead the nation in the number of death sentences and executions. Official criminal justice statistics reveal that 3,830 death-row inmates in U.S. state prisons were executed between the years 1930 and

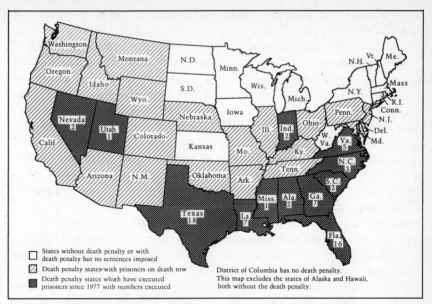

The Death Penalty in the United States, 1977 to October 1986

Source: Adapted from **Southern Changes** *(August 1987).*

1981. Sixty percent (2,307) of these executions occurred in the South. By comparison, the Northeast accounted for only 16 percent (608), the West for 13 percent (511), and the North Central states for 11 percent (404) of the total number of state-authorized executions.

The 1972 U.S. Supreme Court decision in *Furman* v. *Georgia* resulted in a temporary national moratorium on executions. In response to this landmark decision, which found Georgia's death penalty law to be unconstitutional on grounds that it violated Eighth Amendment protections against "cruel and unusual punishment," individual legislatures revised state criminal statutes to comply with evolving constitutional guidelines. Five additional death penalty cases, all from southern states, were considered by the U.S. Supreme Court in 1976. The temporary national moratorium on capital punishment was finally broken by the widely publicized Utah execution by firing squad of Gary Gilmore in 1977.

Although national public opinion polls do not show significant regional differences in public attitudes toward the death penalty, official statistics as of 31 December 1983 indicate that 777 death-row inmates, or 65 percent of the total number of prisoners (1,202) awaiting execution, were incarcerated in southern correctional institutions (U.S. Department of Justice, 1984). By the end of 1983, 38 states had death penalty statutes. With the sole exception of West Virginia, which abolished its death penalty laws in 1965, all southern states allow capital punishment.

Henry P. Lundsgaarde
University of Kentucky

Edward J. Brown, Timothy J. Flanagan, Maureen McLeod, eds., *Sourcebook of Criminal Justice Statistics* (1984); U.S. Department of Justice, *Capital Punishment 1983: Bulletin* (1984). ☆

CHAIN GANG
||||||||||||||||||||||||||||||||||

The profit motive and a desire to eliminate tax burdens dominated post–Civil War southern discussions of criminal punishment. The region was impoverished by the war and yet had now to deal judicially with free black as well as white offenders. Convict lease to private contractors and corporations became a standard alternative to government maintenance throughout the southern states. Because convict labor was most profitable when used for large-scale work projects such as levee repair, railroad building, and road construction, the chain gang was closely associated with the lease system. By 1886 it was the chief form of convict labor in eight southern states, and it persisted in these states long after its abolition in the North and West.

Unlike antebellum chattels, chain-gang crews cost lessees little if anything—an 1867 Georgia railroad lease stipulated a $25 annual fee per inmate—and convicts were infinitely expendable since those who died were quickly replaced. Men, women, and often children sentenced for crimes ranging from the theft of a keg of nails and vagrancy to premeditated murder worked as gangs under armed guard, joined together by a long squad chain attached to ankle irons. Escape was further impeded by stride or hobble chains that allowed a span of about eight inches between leg irons. Throughout its history, a disproportionate number of those sentenced to this form of labor were black: 846 out of 952 in an 1878 survey;

2,113 out of 2,221 in Georgia, 1902.

Whether moving the sand and earth required to shore up levees in the Delta mud or "chipping" turpentine in Florida swamps, crews of convicts worked from 10 to 14 hours per day. They were transported to work camps in mule-drawn boxcars or windowless cages with tiers of plank beds on either side. Once at a campsite, these portable cages served as permanent housing when tents or rough-hewn cell houses were not set up. Food, typically fatback, corn bread, and cowpeas, was rationed, often spoiled, and in summer swarmed with flies. Sanitation in the work camps was not even rudimentary. Convicts lacked wash basins, towels, and soap; they slept, secured by a logging chain, in their work clothes, on bare vermin-infested mattresses. No attempt was made to isolate tubercular or syphilitic prisoners.

Medical care was unknown, and entire gangs fell prey to diseases such as meningitis. Shackle poison (an infection caused by the constant friction of ankle irons), malnutrition, overwork, beatings, or self-inflicted mutilations, such as hamstringing, claimed others. Those who tried to escape or who failed to work hard or fast enough were often punished by confinement to a coffinlike sweatbox, flogging, or the riveting of 20 to 50 pound iron weights to leg shackles. At the height of the lease system, the death rate was so appalling (45 percent of the prisoners working the Greenwood to Augusta railroad died annually in the period 1877–79) that leading critics such as the editor of the New Orleans *Daily Picayune* argued that imposing the death sentence on any convict with a term in excess of six years was more humane and expedient.

The hostility of free labor, especially when convict crews were brought in as strikebreakers, led to the abolition of the private lease system in most southern states by the turn of the century. The chain gang, however, did not disappear. Used by state or county officials primarily as road crews, gangs actually became more important, and more visible, with the advent of the automobile. Reformist activity increased in the 1920s, and exposés of abuses culminated in the 1932 Warner Brothers' release of Robert Burns's *I Am a Fugitive from a Chain Gang*—"A gruesome experience" according to *Variety*, "and dynamite for the state of Georgia." Subsequently the use of chain gangs was greatly reduced, although even in the early 1960s small details were still in evidence. Georgia was the last southern state to completely abolish the practice.

Although images of the chain gang in literature (Richard Wright's *Black Boy*) and film (Stuart Rosenberg's film *Cool Hand Luke*) are vivid reminders of the institution, its most enduring legacy is musical. Tunes range from the mournful "holler," a "strange wailing chant" unintelligible to white "walking bosses," to blues lyrics directly inspired by the experience of gang work—such as "Chain Gang Blues" by Ma Rainey and

Kokomo Arnold, "Levee Camp Blues" by Robert Pete Williams, and George "Bullet" Williams's "Escaped Convict Blues," with its evocation of tracking hounds. Particularly important is the work song. Supplying a meter for manual labor that required coordination of axes, hoes, and hammers, work songs also provided a partial outlet for frustration and anger. Along with the harsh nonmechanized work that sustained them, the songs have now largely disappeared.

Elizabeth M. Makowski
University of Mississippi

Edward L. Ayers, *Vengeance and Justice: Crime and Punishment in the 19th-Century American South* (1984); Bruce Jackson, *Wake Up Dead Man: Afro-American Worksongs from Texas Prisons* (1972); Daniel A. Novak, *The Wheel of Servitude: Black Forced Labor after Slavery* (1978); Paul Oliver, *Blues Fell This Morning* (1960); J. C. Powell, *The American Siberia* (1891); Carl Sifakis, ed., *Encyclopedia of American Crime* (1982); Jesse F. Steiner and Roy M. Brown, *The North Carolina Chain Gang* (1927); Walter Wilson, *Forced Labor in the United States* (1933). ☆

CONVICT LEASING

Convict leasing provided southern employers with cheap, manageable, and readily available workers for two generations before the last remnants of the system disappeared in the 1930s. Although the practice of hiring out or leasing convicts originated in the pre–Civil War penal systems of Alabama, Kentucky, and Louisiana, the system was not adopted by all southern states until the 1870s.

Convicts working on a road, Oglethorpe County, Georgia, 1941

Prior to emancipation, most southern black offenders were slaves and were punished by their masters as permitted or required by the state slave codes. Thus, penal facilities in the prewar South were largely for "whites only." Some of these offenders were turned over to private contractors, typically textile manufacturers. But, as free persons after 1865, black offenders constituted a sudden and sizable addition to southern prison populations, which the economically depressed states found difficult to handle. The solution was convict leasing on a vast, biracial scale.

The zenith of the brutal and exploitative system lasted from about 1880 to 1910. During those years convict leasing was in reality a legal postwar form of slavery for white and black prisoners alike, although blacks far outnumbered whites (especially in the Deep South) and received much harsher treatment.

Depending on where they had been convicted, postwar southern convicts were leased to cotton, rice, sugarcane, and tobacco planters; levee builders; coal mines; timber companies; and railroad construction firms. Prisoners of both races and sexes, sometimes no more than eight or nine years of age, suffered from overwork, physical abuse, meager diets, and little or no medical care. Death and injury rates were appalling. As the most despised element in the population, convicts had few spokesmen or defenders. Several states had established "penitentiary rings" supported by politicians who favored leasing because it relieved their states of responsibility for maintaining convicts and because the system brought "easy" revenues to public treasuries at no sacrifice to voting taxpayers. Beginning in the 1890s, however, coalitions

of political opponents, labor interests, and humanitarian reformers were able to abolish leasing gradually state by state.

Convict leasing should not be considered identical to state or county "chain gangs," which continued to exist in the post–World War II South. "Chaingang" prisoners were also badly treated, but they were under the custody of public authorities rather than the more insensitive, inhumane, and publicly unsupervised private contractors of the lease system.

See also LAW: / Black Codes; Slave Codes

Mark T. Carleton
Louisiana State University

Mark T. Carleton, *Politics and Punishment: The History of the Louisiana State Penal System* (1971); Dan T. Carter, "Convict Lease" (M.A. thesis, University of Wisconsin, 1964); Hilda Jane Zimmerman, "Penal Systems and Penal Reform in the South Since the Civil War" (Ph.D. dissertation, University of North Carolina at Chapel Hill, 1947). ☆

COPELAND, JAMES
(1823–1857) Outlaw.

The name of no other outlaw in southern Mississippi and Alabama is more shrouded in mystique and controversy than that of James Copeland, who was hanged 30 October 1857 on the banks of the Leaf River near Augusta in Perry County, Miss. Indeed, Copeland was a household word from Mobile Bay to Lake Pontchartrain not only because his clan had terrorized folks in that region during the flush times of the 1830s and 1840s but also because he dictated his memoirs to a highly literate young sheriff, J. R. S. Pitts. Published first in 1858 with later editions in 1874 and 1909, *The Confession of James Copeland* created a furor that still persists amid the piney woods and coastal counties.

Tales about Copeland, born in Jackson County on the Mississippi Gulf Coast, are still spun. His brutal life of larceny, arson, and murder captivated the imagination of generations who either admired him as a latter-day Robin Hood or scorned him as a contemptible desperado. His errant ways began as a lad of 12 with the theft of a pocket knife, followed shortly thereafter by grand larceny and the burning of the local courthouse, assisted by an older accomplice, Gale H. Wages, whose clan he soon joined—a clan eventually bearing the name Copeland.

Though the clan operated mainly in south Mississippi and Alabama, Copeland's criminal path took him as far east as the Chattahoochee River, as far west as the Rio Grande, and as far north as the Wabash. In his *Confession* he related crimes committed in the company of his mentor Wages and one Charles McGrath, a quintessential fraudulent frontier preacher. Copeland, who credits himself with only two murders, stole anything readily converted to cash, but he specialized in the theft of horses and slaves. Before the trio split up to avoid capture, Wages supposedly buried their savings of $30,000 in gold in the Catahoula Swamp in southwestern Mississippi. The gold coins are still sought by treasure hunters.

Hoping to escape the grasp of Mississippi officials who had indicted him for murder, Copeland surrendered to Alabama authorities to serve a term for larceny. However, deputies of Sheriff Pitts awaited his release, and after four more years in custody, James Cope-

land—in the words of Pitts—"expiated his blood stained career on the scaffold" before a massive October crowd in 1857.

John D. W. Guice
University of Southern Mississippi

J. R. S. Pitts, *Life and Confession of the Noted Outlaw James Copeland* (1980). ☆

CORTEZ, GREGORIO
(1875–1916) Outlaw.

Gregorio Cortez was a legendary figure from the Texas-Mexico border. In 1901 Cortez became a fugitive from the law after he killed a sheriff who attempted to arrest him for allegedly having stolen a horse. Details pertaining to the actual shooting are clouded, but significant misunderstanding clearly occurred because of language problems.

For 10 days Cortez managed to elude hundreds of men who chased him throughout the rough country of the Rio Grande region. Finally he was captured and tried in court. He was acquitted of murdering the sheriff but was convicted of killing a member of the posse that sought to capture him. Cortez was pardoned in 1913 and died in 1916 under mysterious circumstances.

The importance of Gregorio Cortez lies in what his story reveals about Mexican American–Anglo-American relations along the United States–Mexican border in the early 1900s. This was a time of marked racial friction influenced by border tensions between Mexico and the United States. The dominant society saw Cortez as a killer and fugitive, but people of Mexican background viewed him as a folk hero who had defied oppressive Anglo lawmen.

Popularized by border balladeers at the time, Cortez's story became the subject of Américo Paredes's *With His Pistol in His Hand: A Border Ballad and Its Hero* (1958). In the early 1980s Jack Young directed the film *The Ballad of Gregorio Cortez*, which played before a national television audience and in theaters across the United States.

Oscar J. Martinez
University of Texas at El Paso

DUELING

Dueling was introduced in America by French and British officers during the Revolution. The practice was outlawed throughout the North after the Alexander Hamilton–Aaron Burr duel in 1804. The death of Hamilton shocked the North, which had already all but abolished the practice. In the South dueling became a criminal offense, with stiff penalties if the duel resulted in a death. Opposition to the practice was one of the few respectable social causes in the antebellum South. Despite statutes, antidueling societies, and public disapproval of the practice, dueling remained an important part of southern culture until the Civil War.

Many southern politicians and editors either engaged in duels or received or issued challenges. A list of such men reads like a "who's who" of the antebellum South, and includes Andrew Jackson, William Clingman, William Yancey, Henry Clay, Cassius M. Clay, Henry Wise, Thomas Hart Benton, Sam Houston, William Crawford, Jefferson Davis, Judah P. Benjamin, John Randolph, George McCuffie, William Graves, Louis T. Wigfall, and Albert

Sidney Johnston. Duels were not, however, limited to political and social leaders. Parvenus often used the duel as a vehicle for social advancement. Although it was not considered proper for a true gentleman to accept a challenge from a social inferior, such lines were often unclear, particularly in the Southwest.

Most duels were fought with pistols, although occasionally rifles were used. In New Orleans, swords remained the weapon of choice among some duelists. Duelists were supposed to follow elaborate rules, which were described in John Lyde Wilson's *The Code of Honor* (1838), but duels did not always proceed according to those rules. Indeed, before the publication of Wilson's book most duelists, especially those not living in Charleston or New Orleans, likely knew little of the prescribed rules. The rules of dueling required that a challenge be sent, with an opportunity for the offending party to make amends and avoid a conflict. Nevertheless, spontaneous fights between gentlemen, with knives or canes as weapons, were considered by many a form of dueling. When Congressman Preston Brooks beat Charles Sumner with a cane until the Massachusetts senator was insensible, it was considered the equivalent of a duel by Brooks's Charleston constituents. Northerners, on the other hand, considered this act particularly barbaric because Sumner was seated, with his back to Brooks, when the attack began. Similarly, when Alexander H. Stephens, while unarmed, was attacked and knifed by a political rival, southerners considered the event within the bounds of political behavior.

The duel was one aspect of antebellum southern fascination with chivalry. Most duels were fought over alleged or perceived insults. The cause of a duel could be personal, social, professional, or political. Duels were often fought over the honor of one's family, and particularly of women in the family. Social pressure, a desire to prove one's masculinity, or hotheadedness alone drove innumerable southern men to the field of honor.

Paul Finkelman
University of Texas at Austin

John Hope Franklin, *The Militant South, 1800–1861* (1956); Bertram Wyatt-Brown, *Southern Honor: Ethics and Behavior in the Old South* (1982). ☆

FILIBUSTERS

"Filibusters," in the 19th-century meaning of the word, were individuals who led, enlisted in, or helped outfit private military expeditions designed to invade foreign lands. The term came into vogue during the years between the Mexican and Civil wars, when thousands of Americans defied proscriptive clauses in the American Neutrality Act of April 1818 and participated in expeditions to such regions as the Mexican Yucatán, Spanish Cuba, Central America, and Ecuador. This form of filibustering has continued to the present. In 1981 a group of American adventurers drew considerable public notice when they were charged by the FBI with plotting an armed invasion of the island of Dominica, for the purpose of overthrowing its government. Two more times within five years after that, federal agents foiled plots conceived in Louisiana and Mississippi to overthrow a foreign government, the last a 1986

attempt to seize Surinam in Central America.

The United States was by no means the only country to spawn such expeditions in the 19th century, nor was there anything uniquely southern about filibustering. The famous plot of Aaron Burr (1805–7), for instance, occurred during the Jefferson Administration, before the rise of sectional consciousness in the South. It would be misleading, moreover, to simplify even the pre–Civil War expeditions as purely southern endeavors. Men of all regions enlisted in filibuster ranks, for a variety of personal and ideological reasons, including mere adventurism and an ethnocentric belief—sometimes called Manifest Destiny—that Americans had a God-given mission to impose their republican institutions upon peoples presumed to be less fortunate. New York City and California were two of the country's flagrant centers of filibuster activity. On the other hand, many people could be found throughout the United States who opposed filibustering. Several scholars have suggested that filibustering was an expression of antebellum American romanticism.

Nevertheless, when James Stirling, an English visitor to the United States, informed his countrymen in 1857 that filibustering was "essentially a thing of the South" (*Letters from the Slave States*), he was hardly the victim of a far-fetched delusion. Filibustering found its strongest popular support in the Deep South; in several instances federal authorities found it virtually impossible to prosecute blatant violations of the Neutrality Act in the Gulf states because of the force of public opinion. More significantly, several expeditions either began with, or developed, a southern, sectional orientation. Certainly this was the case with former governor John A. Quitman's Cuba conspiracy from 1853 to 1855. Southern governors, congressmen, newspapermen, and even judges and preachers helped Quitman assemble ships, arms, and men to invade Cuba, because they wanted to prevent Spain from "Africanizing" (abolishing slavery in) Cuba and they shared Quitman's belief that new slave states would provide security from the American antislavery movement. The most successful filibuster of the age, a native Tennessean named William Walker, who invaded Nicaragua and became its president in 1856, won widespread southern support when he reestablished slavery in his conquest.

Several commentators, therefore, have presented filibustering as a southern cultural trait. The noted historian John Hope Franklin, for instance, interpreted filibuster expeditions as an element within the general category of southern militarism and violence. However, given northern participation in the filibuster movement, the idea of filibustering as peculiarly southern is a fusion of myth and reality.

Robert E. May
Purdue University

Charles H. Brown, *Agents of Manifest Destiny: The Lives and Times of the Filibusters* (1980); Robert E. May, *The Southern Dream of a Caribbean Empire, 1854–1861* (1973); Edward S. Wallace, *Destiny and Glory* (1957). ☆

HATFIELDS AND McCOYS
||||||||||||||||||||||||||||||||||||||||||||||||||||||||||||||

The Hatfield-McCoy feud, the most famous southern Appalachian vendetta, was one manifestation of general late 19th-century American violence— bloody labor troubles, western lawlessness, and political assassination. It was also part of the cultural milieu of the isolated Tug River Valley along the West Virginia–Kentucky border, an area known for widespread illiteracy, fundamentalist churches, and disrespect for law. Exaggerated family and clan loyalties and acute sensitivity to affronts often mixed with the consumption of moonshine whiskey to produce explosive situations.

Numerous incidents, such as a dispute over ownership of a razorback hog, a romance between "Devil Anse" Hatfield's son Johnse and Randolph McCoy's daughter Rose Anna, and a deadly election altercation, were behind the Hatfield-McCoy feud. Home-guard and bushwhacking activities by the two families during the Civil War had also set the stage for conflict.

Several bloody events in the 1880s drew national attention to the feud: the killing of Ellison Hatfield, a brother of "Devil Anse," at an election in 1882

Devil Anse Hatfield, Kentucky fighter, 1880s

and the retaliatory murder of three sons of Randolph McCoy by enraged Hatfields; the battle of Grapevine Creek, a pitched battle on the Jug Fork River; and a merciless raid on New Year's night 1888 in which Hatfields burned McCoy's house and killed two more of his children. The feud was elevated to an interstate battle when West Virginia Governor Willis Wilson refused to extradite Hatfield partisans indicted in Pike County, Ky., for the 1882 murders and when he instituted habeas corpus proceedings for return of nine who were seized later by Kentucky authorities in raids into West Virginia. The sensational journalism of large city newspapers provided the nation with gory and sometimes fabricated accounts that did much to encrust the feud with myth and legend.

The hanging of one Hatfield partisan and the sentencing of others to prison terms following an April 1897 trial in Pike County signaled an end to the feud. By then many of the participants, including "Devil Anse," who had become a symbol of the bloodthirsty mountaineer, were weary of the killing. The entry of industry and improved transportation broke the bonds of isolation and fostered a new society that had far less patience with violent feuds. The Hatfields and the McCoys turned to peaceful pursuits, and both families produced important business, industrial, and political leaders for the New South.

Otis K. Rice
West Virginia Institute
of Technology

Virgil C. Jones, *The Hatfields and the McCoys* (1948); Otis K. Rice, *The Hatfields and the McCoys* (1978). ☆

JAMES BROTHERS

Alexander Franklin James (1843–1915) and
Jesse Woodson James (1847–1882). Outlaws.

Noted outlaws Frank James and Jesse James were born and raised on a western Missouri farm, sons of a prosperous, slaveowning family that had moved from Kentucky in 1842. Like many Missourians, they were southern in origin and outlook. Before and during the Civil War, violence over slavery and secession divided Missouri and consumed the James family. In the absence of regular Confederate troops in Missouri during the war, organizations of pro-southern guerrillas formed to respond to the harsh treatment of southern sympathizers by Union troops and Kansas guerrilla raiders. In 1862 Confederate private Frank James joined guerrilla leader William Clarke Quantrill. Seventeen-year-old Jesse rode with William "Bloody Bill" Anderson's guerrilla band in 1864 after Union militia reportedly attempted to hang Jesse's stepfather, harassed his pregnant mother, and gave him a severe whipping. Both brothers were deeply involved in violent irregular warfare. In this crucible of blood and fire America's best-known outlaws were created.

After the war many guerrillas resumed normal lives though they were denied amnesty and the right to vote. The James brothers, however, did not settle down. Their family had been banished from Missouri, and according to legend, when Jesse attempted to surrender in 1865, he was shot by federal troops. By 1866 Frank and Jesse James had begun their long careers as bank and train robbers. Supporters argued that their treatment during and after the war forced them outside the law and justified their actions. This notion was reinforced when Pinkerton detectives hired by the railroads threw an explosive device into their parents' home, killing their nine-year-old half brother and blowing their mother's arm off.

When the James brothers were involved in an 1869 bank robbery and murder, newspaperman John N. Edwards began an influential 20-year crusade to idealize their lives as guerrillas and outlaws. He portrayed them as dashing southern gentlemen who protected women and children from northern persecution during the war and defended helpless victims of northern banks and railroads afterwards. Many people of southern background agreed that the James brothers were knights of the South's Lost Cause and frontier Robin Hoods.

As people in all regions felt the pinch of big business in the post–Civil War decades, the James brothers were praised nationally in folklore and popular culture as bold western outlaw-heroes who robbed the rich and gave to the poor. This widespread romantic portrayal of the James brothers played a significant role in bringing qualities of the southern gentleman to the western hero. Like later fictional western heroes such as the Virginian and Shane, the James brothers of legend lived on the wild frontier but upheld the chivalrous code of their southern background: they protected the weak and righted wrongs with a fierce sense of honor, pride, and style.

Despite the romantic image of the James brothers, Governor Thomas Crittenden felt they had given Missouri a bad name. In 1881 he offered a $10,000 reward of railroad money for their capture. On 3 April 1882 gang member Robert Ford betrayed Jesse James with a deadly shot from behind while visiting

Jesse and his family in their home. Ford was sentenced to hang for murder, but the governor gave him a full pardon. The manner of Jesse's death was the final step in his ascent to the rank of hero. Frank James surrendered his pistol six months later and was tried but acquitted of several crimes.

The James brothers were outlaws for a remarkable 16 years. Thanks to local and public support for their role in the Civil War and their attacks on banks and railroads, they were never apprehended and never convicted of any crimes. A century after the end of their outlaw careers, Frank and Jesse are still celebrated in movies, songs, and novels as heroes of the Lost Cause and Robin Hoods of the West.

George B. Ward
Texas State Historical Association

David Brion Davis, *American Quarterly* (Summer 1954); John Newman Edwards, *Noted Guerrillas, or The Warfare of the Border* (1877); William A. Settle, Jr., *Jesse James Was His Name* (1966). ☆

KNIGHTS OF THE GOLDEN CIRCLE (KGC)

The Knights of the Golden Circle (KGC) was a secret antebellum organization promoted by George W. L. Bickley, a Virginia-born editor, adventurer, and doctor of eclectic medicine. He hoped to create a great slave empire encompassing the West Indies, the southern United States, Mexico, Central America, and part of South America—hence the name Golden Circle. But his main goal was annexation of Mexico, whose relations with the United States were strained in the late 1850s.

Hounded by creditors, "General"

Bickley, self-styled "President and Commander-in-Chief of the KGC American Legion," left his Cincinnati base in 1860, toured the East and the South, and promoted a filibustering expedition into Mexico. He received his chief support in Texas, where at least 32 "castles" (lodges) were established under local leadership. Bickley had limited newspaper support elsewhere in the South, and there were rumors that linked prominent southern politicos to the KGC (Jefferson Davis, William L. Yancey, John B. Floyd, John C. Breckinridge), but these were probably fabrications.

Bickley's attempted invasion of Mexico was ineptly handled; he failed to secure the support of Governor Sam Houston, who had seemed interested; and he failed to show up at the appointed time with a large force he claimed he was collecting in New Orleans. In April a number of his disgusted supporters met in New Orleans and expelled Bickley. He retaliated by calling for a convention in Raleigh in May, at which time he was reinstated.

Once more Bickley turned his attention to Mexico. This time he was sidetracked by the 1860 campaign. With Lincoln's election Bickley became an ardent advocate of southern secession and supported it in Tennessee and Kentucky.

The "General" served a stint as a Confederate surgeon, deserted, and for a short time lived with a backwoods woman at Shelbyville, Tenn. In July 1863 Bickley was arrested in Indiana for spying and consequently was imprisoned until October 1865, although nothing was proved. He died a broken man in August 1867.

The KGC was a prime antebellum example of the South's aggressiveness and expansionism. Nevertheless, it was a militancy that failed to achieve its goals. The Republicans in the 1864 campaign tried to link antiwar Democrats to the treasonable plots of the KGC, but, in fact, no "castles" were established in the North. The KGC gained a widespread but unfounded reputation for popularity and it embittered relations between the North and South.

Ernest M. Lander, Jr.
Clemson University

Ollinger Crenshaw, *American Historical Review* (October 1941); Roy S. Dunn, *Southwestern Historical Quarterly* (April 1967); Robert E. May, *The Southern Dream of a Caribbean Empire, 1854–1861* (1973). ☆

KU KLUX KLAN, CULTURE OF

Desperate, Dreadful, Desolate, Doleful, Dismal, Deadly, and Dark are the seven days of the Klan Kalendar, and the organization's actual malevolence—past and present—is impossible to ignore. But it would also be a mistake to dismiss the cultural implications of the Hooded Empire in southern society.

Characteristic of most Klansmen are an overwhelming ignorance and a complete alienation from society and its institutions. In the Klan's earlier incarnations thousands of otherwise solid citizens were members, but most Klansmen in the 1980s are powerless people on the fringes of society and the economy. They seem to be filled with hate and anger, going through life manipulated by their employers, by the finance company, by the landlord, by demagogic politicians, and finally by smooth-talking Klan salesmen.

Having been ignored for so long, many of these Klan recruits are attracted by the aroma of power that surrounds the leaders such as the dominant 1960s personality, Robert Shelton, and his 1970s successor, Bill Wilkinson. It must be power, the prospective Klansman reasons, because the Grand Wizards can get on the television talk shows; they can go to city hall and attract half the police and all the press in town; and they have big cars and bodyguards and can even wear a suit that does not look as if it had been bought that morning. Once he joins, the new Klansman gets on the evening news himself, just by standing on the street corner in his robe.

In addition to power, the social side of the Klan, the sense of belonging to something, is a compelling attraction. Many Klansmen have belonged to nothing else. Surprisingly few of them, considering the Klan's lip service to Christianity, even attend church. For such people, the Klavern fills an important though unarticulated role. Frequently, Klan gatherings and rallies have an atmosphere that, for all its perverse weirdness, can be compared to a country camp meeting. There may be music and speeches, children playing in the grass, mama and daddy dressed in their robes, grandma sitting in her folding lawn chair, and plenty of fish and beer.

Increasingly, in the 1980s version of the KKK, women and children are drawn into the fold. The "youth corps" units run by the larger Klan organizations are an unabashed effort to remind the younger generation of the Klan's special place in white southern history while simultaneously insuring that the ranks will continue to be filled in the coming years. Likewise, the role of women in the Invisible Empire is now both social and functional. Whereas the Klans of yesteryear had their auxil- iaries, who sewed robes and prepared food for the men, the female Klan member today is likely to take up her semiautomatic rifle and put on her camouflage uniform for exercises at the local paramilitary camp.

The KKK adapts to societal changes while trying to hold fast to an idealized white southern view of race, religion, and history.

Randall Williams
Southern Changes
Montgomery, Alabama

Anne Braden, *Southern Exposure* (No. 2, 1980); Lenwood G. Davis and Janet L. Sims-Wood, *The Ku Klux Klan: A Bibliography* (1984); Patsy Sims, *The Klan* (1979). ☆

KU KLUX KLAN, HISTORY OF
||||||||||||||||||||||||||||||||||||||||||

After devoting several decades to the study of southern history, Ulrich B.

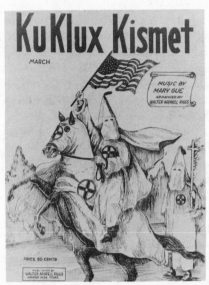

Cover for the music to a Ku Klux Klan song

Phillips ventured one of his few generalizations about southern character. The acid test of a true southerner, he declared in a now-famous essay, was his or her insistence that the South, despite the presence of a sizable black population, "remain a white man's country." No organization so exemplified this credo and carried it to its logical, and often violent, extreme as the Ku Klux Klan.

Begun in May and June of 1866 in the hinterland of postbellum Tennessee, at Pulaski, by six former Confederates eager for amusement and diversion, the Klan soon lost its innocence as its organizers progressed from playing jokes on each other to tricking and frightening blacks. As news of the Klan spread, new groups or "dens" were formed, first in Tennessee and then throughout the South. Despite its official 1867 "prescript" supporting the Constitution of the United States, the Klan's favorite modus operandi became intimidation and violence against those, specifically the freedmen and their white allies, who threatened to upset the carefully crafted southern hierarchical society that placed the white male socially, economically, and politically supreme. Particularly horrifying to Klansmen was any idea of racial equality or so-called black domination. Thus, blacks were whipped for crimes ranging from insolence and voting Republican to making a good crop and becoming prosperous. Others were lynched for alleged rapes and for violating racial norms. Although the Klan was active in only one-quarter of southern counties, it received initial encouragement from the conservative press and the educated elements of society, who eventually became disgusted with the Klan's excesses and withdrew their support by 1870. The combination of the call for disbandment of the Klan by Imperial Wizard Nathan Bedford Forrest in 1869 and the passage and enforcement of the federal Ku Klux Klan Acts in 1870 and 1871 signaled an end to much of the Klan's power, although sporadic outbreaks of violence against blacks continued.

The 19th-century South was largely a closed society, suspicious of anything that threatened its canons of political, religious, and social orthodoxy. To this tradition, the South at the turn of the century joined with much of the North in adding an unhealthy portion of American nativism and its concomitant distrust of Catholics, Jews, and blacks. Thus fertile ground was prepared for the Klan's revival in the wake of D. W. Griffith's sympathetic and successful 1915 movie, *Birth of a Nation*, based on Thomas Dixon, Jr.'s, novel, *The Clansman*. When former preacher, salesman, and history teacher William J. Simmons's reorganization of the Klan in Georgia in 1915 united with the salesmanship of Edward Young Clarke and Elizabeth Tyler, the response was nationwide. The resurgent Klan, numbering at its height over 2 million members, transcended the boundaries of the old Confederacy in its appeal to native-born Americans who feared and distrusted anything they perceived as foreign or inimical to community morality. Also nationwide was the violence that has characterized the Klan from its inception, although most atrocities were still committed in the South. Mob psychology, the anonymity of the hooded costumes, oaths of secrecy imposed by the Klan, and the fears of certain groups conspired to sanction crimes that an individual alone might otherwise never have contemplated. As during Reconstruction, revelations of such excesses destroyed the comparatively widespread support enjoyed by the Klan, and membership declined sharply.

The Klan was never again able to command a membership equal to that of the 1920s. During the push for civil rights by blacks in the 1960s, however, membership in the South rose in response to the perceived threat to accustomed social patterns, and the Klan once more made its influence felt through a reign of terror. Consumed with hatred and fear of social change, Klan members relied on the South's honored tradition of violence for resolving any disagreement—from individual dispute to sectional conflict. Their methods became increasingly sophisticated and deadly. Klansmen added bombing and arson to their familiar repertoire of beating, tarring and feathering, and lynching. Such excesses again brought a backlash from the larger community. It could tolerate and even encourage what it viewed as violence necessary to preserve cultural patterns, but there was a critical line between necessary and wanton violence that the Klan could not overstep without loss of community support. Deprived of this approval and of new issues on which to capitalize, the Klan remains weakened and fragmented by power struggles among its leaders, who are almost as likely to recruit members in New England as in the Deep South.

Mary E. Stovall
Greenville, Mississippi

David M. Chalmers, *Hooded Americanism: The History of the Ku Klux Klan* (1965); John Moffatt Mecklin, *The Ku Klux Klan: A Study of the American Mind* (1924); Allen W. Trelease, *White Terror: The Ku Klux Klan Conspiracy and Southern Reconstruction* (1971). ☆

MOB VIOLENCE

Throughout their history Americans have resorted to mob violence in the form of physical assaults, extralegal executions, and riots. Whether spontaneously organized or formally constituted into a more permanent movement, numerous groups have taken the law into their own hands, primarily for the conservative purpose of protecting the existing order against real or imagined threats.

During the 18th century the first vigilante movements appeared on the southern frontier, where law enforcement was ineffective. In 1767 local citizens formed the South Carolina Regulators, who mounted a two-year campaign to rid the area of outlaws through mock trials followed by whippings and/or banishment. "Lynch law," the popular term for this practice, originated in western Virginia in 1780, when settlers—led by Colonel Charles Lynch—dispensed private justice. The practice of "regulating" undesirables through lynch law became a national phenomenon that spread westward with the frontier. Some of the worst outbreaks occurred in Texas, which had more vigilante movements than any other state.

After 1830 collective violence also erupted in well-established communities as a means of summary punishment in both the North and the South. In addition to flogging and sometimes killing whites suspected of opposing slavery, southern mobs occasionally attacked transgressors of local morality, such as five gamblers who were hanged by Vicksburg, Miss., vigilantes in 1835. With the close of the frontier, lynching became increasingly a southern phenomenon, which was used, along with race riots, largely to enforce white supremacy. Although most victims of lynch law were black, mob violence also took the lives of whites, such as immigrants, radicals, and union organizers, who were considered outsiders and a threat. In 1891 a mob executed 11 Italians accused of killing the police chief of New Orleans, La. Anti-Semitism figured in the 1915 lynching of Leo Frank in Atlanta. Industrial violence claimed the life of an Arkansas union leader who was lynched in 1923.

Corporal punishment, often in the form of a flogging and/or the application of tar and feathers, was the most common vigilante method of regulating behavior in the South. Frequently administered by well-organized groups such as the Ku Klux Klan, this type of mob violence claimed thousands of victims from the 1890s through the 1930s. The targets were usually whites whose "offenses" ranged from the violation of local moral codes to support for unpopular causes, such as unions and communism.

People of all classes, including the elite, engaged in mob violence, and many members of the southern press and police endorsed or tolerated vigilantism. As a result, few participants were ever punished. After World War II, mob violence generally declined as changing southern attitudes, outside pressures, and the forces of modernization undermined local support for mob action. During the 1950s and 1960s, however, violence was directed at blacks and whites involved in the civil rights movement. Although infrequent today, collective violence remains a threat as demonstrated by the 1979 killing of five communists by vigilantes in Greensboro, N.C.

See also LAW: / Frank, Leo, Case

Robert P. Ingalls
University of South Florida

Richard Maxwell Brown, *Strain of Violence: Historical Studies of American Violence and Vigilantism* (1975). ☆

NIGHTRIDERS
||||||||||||||||||||||||||||||||||||||

If Reconstruction brought a twinkle of progressive thought to the South, it also bred fiery resentment and rabid emotions. Slavery had been demolished, and, overnight, former plantation owners were without labor. A depressed, war-weary southern economy now had an even larger labor force in which poor whites competed for jobs with newly freed blacks. Out of this climate hatred sprouted, and in southern communities throughout the region nightriders and Klansmen rose up in efforts to intimidate blacks psychologially and physically.

In *Night Riders in Black Folk History*, Gladys-Marie Fry discusses the function of the nightrider or "Ku Klux" in controlling blacks before and after the Civil War. This form of intimidation was used before the Civil War to discourage unauthorized movement, to guard against slave insurrections, and, after the war, to repeatedly let blacks know their behavioral boundaries. Black oral history is rich with stories of evil white men joining together to incite the fears of black families and entire towns. Nightrider incidents are stored in the minds of elderly blacks, and although many do not recall the chronological specifics of the events, they well remember acts of intimidation, often having heard tales from older family or community members.

Nightriders were not unique to Reconstruction. Although the practice flourished then, black folk history shows that nightriding existed throughout slavery. The Reconstruction Ku Klux Klan was probably a modern version of the antebellum patrol system. The patrols or "paterollers" set out to check the passes of the slaves, to maintain curfew, and to physically abuse rule breakers. Folklorist William Lynwood Montell writes that slaveowners in the Kettle Creek area of Tennessee relied on the patrol system because they had trouble keeping slaves on the plantation.

Though the stereotype of a masked, robed Klansman was in many cases a true image, many nightriders often traveled without the disguise of a white garment. In the Cumberland plateau community of Free Hill, Tenn., not one resident remembers a Ku Klux disguise or mask; rather, as one resident explained, "these were people that they knew, they knew from down in town." The absence of a mask or hood, however, did not mean that there was no attempt to disguise. Groups of men always came at night and assumed the community would flee out of fear. For them, night itself was some disguise, and there was little risk of recognition.

Tom Rankin
Southern Arts Federation
Atlanta, Georgia

Gladys-Marie Fry, *Night Riders in Black Folk History* (1975); William Lynwood Montell, *The Saga of Coe Ridge: A Study in Oral History* (1970); Elizabeth Peterson and Tom Rankin, *Free Hill: A Sound Portrait of a Rural Afro-American Community* (Tennessee Folklore Society recording, 1985). ☆

ORANGEBURG MASSACRE

Violence against blacks in the South erupted on 8 February 1968 when a fusillade of gunfire by state highway patrolmen killed three students and wounded 27 others on the campus of South Carolina State College at Orangeburg. The killings, known in civil rights circles as the "Orangeburg massacre," attracted little national attention at the time, being incorrectly reported by the Associated Press as "an exchange of gunfire." The shooting occurred on the third night of confrontations that had begun when students at the predominantly black college protested the segregation policy of the town's only bowling alley, five blocks from the campus.

The Orangeburg massacre was the first time students on an American college campus had been slain by law enforcement officers. The episode preceded by more than two years an event that became a cause célèbre— the slaying of four white Kent State University students by National Guardsmen in May 1970. A few days later in that same month, Jackson, Miss., city police and state highway patrolmen opened fire on protesting black students at Jackson State University (then Jackson State College), killing two students. A President's Commission on Campus Unrest investigated the Kent State and Jackson State shootings, but its historical section failed to mention the killings two years earlier at Orangeburg.

Jack Bass
University of South Carolina

Jack Nelson and Jack Bass, *The Orangeburg Massacre* (1970). ☆

PARCHMAN
|||||||||||||||||||||||||||||||||

The intervention of convict lease stalemated the penitentiary movement in the postbellum South. Because convicts, most of whom were black, were leased, southern states stopped maintaining existing prisons, and penitentiaries became "mere shells of buildings, depositories for the old, the sick and the most dangerous." The state of Mississippi outlawed convict lease (though not the equally infamous chain gang) by constitutional amendment in 1890 and sought institutional alternatives for using convict labor that would not jeopardize the interests of free labor. Legislators authorized the purchase of several tracts of land on which penal farms were erected to provide convicts with "healthful agricultural labor" and the state with significant profit.

The largest of these farms was established at the turn of the century on some 13,000 acres purchased from a Sunflower County planter, James Parchman. When folksong collector John A. Lomax visited Parchman in the 1930s, more than 2,000 inmates tilled 17,000 acres of rich Delta land, channeling

Camp B, Parchman Penitentiary, Mississippi, 1975

large sums into the state treasury. Lomax found his blues and ballad recording hindered by the length of convict work days and noted that part of the farm's profit came from the "economies" practiced: labor from 4:00 a.m. until dark and a total lack of mechanization.

In 1968 a regional prison report outlined conditions at Parchman and penitentiaries in Arkansas and Louisiana, concluding that "the three states put together could not out of presently available funds and facilities provide the components of one prison which would meet minimum national standards." Parchman's brutality and corruption were not unique. Angola in Louisiana was also infamous, but by the 1960s Parchman had become legendary. Beatings were routinely administered for infractions ranging from failure to address an officer properly to attempted escape. Inmates employed as armed guards— 170 out of a total force of 210 guards as late as 1968—abused and often killed fellow prisoners.

In 1971 documented instances of brutality against several hundred incarcerated civil rights workers led to sweeping changes. Within three years, the trusty system was abolished; inadequate, segregated facilities were abandoned; and vocational training was implemented.

Today most of Parchman's 21,000 acres of cotton land are leased to local farmers, and many of its 12,000 prisoners participate in external rehabilitation programs. A stadium, a new $3 million hospital, and apartments for family and conjugal visiting are maintained. Traditional black and white uniforms have been replaced with denim trousers and work shirts. Still, the aura of fear and the reality of punishment remain. Said B. B. King of his childhood visit to his uncle, a fellow bluesman and former Parchman inmate Bukka White: "After that . . . I knew I wanted to stay far away from the place."

Elizabeth M. Makowski
University of Mississippi

L. C. Dorsey, *Cold Steel* (1982); William Ferris, *The New Journal* (25 January 1973); Marvin Hutson, "Mississippi's State Penal System" (M.A. thesis, University of Mississippi, 1939); John A. Lomax, *Adventures of a Ballad Hunter* (1947); Roy Reed, *New York Times* (27 January 1973); Dunbar Rowland, *Mississippi* (1907); Southern Regional Council, *The Delta Prisons: Punishment for Profit* (1968). ☆

PEONAGE

Peonage, a Latin American labor system that entered the United States through Mexican land acquisitions, relies on debt to bind laborers to the land. In 1867 Congress passed a law (14 Stat. 546) that prohibited peonage both in territories recently acquired from Mexico and throughout the United States. The law lay dormant until 1901, when U.S. attorney Fred Cubberly uncovered it and brought a case against Samuel T. Clyatt for using laborers in his turpentine operation to work off debts. During the statute's dormancy, the intricate farm labor system that developed in the South blurred the distinctions between law and custom. State legislatures enacted enticement laws, emigrant agent restrictions, contract laws, vagrancy statutes, the criminal surety system, and convict labor laws, while planters used both laws and rural customs to keep laborers, in most cases black sharecroppers, from leaving their employ. Such labor laws,

like discrimination and disfranchisement statutes, became more severe in the 1890s and the first decade of the 20th century.

As the *Clyatt* case (*Clyatt* v. *United States*, 197 U.S. 207) progressed through appeals that ultimately decided the constitutionality of the law, the extent of peonage in the South became more apparent. In Alabama, Judge Thomas G. Jones, experimenting with light sentences and publicity in 1903, dramatized how pervasive peonage had become. In 1906 Booker T. Washington joined with local whites in Alabama and brought another precedent-setting case that exposed, through the plight of Alonzo Bailey, the tight legal framework that trapped men who took cash advances under "false pretenses" and left their jobs before completing the contract. The case also showed the draconian nature of southern rural labor laws. The basic "false pretenses" law had been on the books since 1885, but laborers had won a series of Alabama cases, for employers had been unable to establish the intent of laborers who left their jobs. In 1903 Alabama tightened its law, as did Georgia; Florida followed in 1907. Under the amended law, a laborer's taking the money and failing either to pay it back or work it out was "prima facie evidence of the intent to injure or defraud his employer." A 1907 rule of evidence prohibited the laborer from taking the witness stand to explain his intent. After two appeals, in 1911 the Supreme Court struck down the law (*Bailey* v. *Alabama*, 211 U.S. 452; *Bailey* v. *Alabama*, 219 U.S. 219). Yet other states, particularly Florida and Georgia, persisted with similar laws until the 1940s. The Supreme Court also ruled against the widespread practice of allowing planters to pay off fines of laborers who were facing jail sentences and then working them as criminals (*United States* v. *Reynolds*, 235 U.S. 133). This series of cases successfully unraveled much of the legal net that caught vulnerable farm workers and sucked them into the vortex of peonage. Still, peonage continued outside the law.

Most peonage cases originated in the old cotton belt that ran from South Carolina through the Black Belt of Georgia and Alabama and into the Mississippi and Arkansas deltas. During the first decade of the century many immigrants who were transported to the South became the focus of a series of cases and glaring publicity lasting several years. While successful court cases made southerners aware of the law, peonage continued as evinced in numerous complaints and prosecutions. The vast complaint file in the National Archives suggests not only the extent of involuntary servitude but also the helplessness of barely literate workers who tried to escape. Local law enforcement officials either ignored such conditions or actively supported planters. Most rural laborers did not understand the workings of the law and were caught up in the customary relationship of landlord and tenant; relatively few questioned their conditions. In some cases planters did not understand the law either. Court cases and complaints revealed clearly the bottom rung of the southern rural labor system and showed the confusion in distinguishing freedom from bondage.

Complaints and cases declined during the 1930s, although a landmark Arkansas case in 1936 used an 1866 statute (14 Stat. 50) outlawing slave kidnapping to prosecute lawman Paul Peacher and thus extend federal juris-

diction over any kind of involuntary servitude—not just that which involved debt. In recent years most peonage complaints have come from migrant laborers, and several successful prosecutions have revealed the vulnerability of such agricultural workers. Thus, in a larger sense, peonage has represented continuity with the South's slave past.

See also LAW: / Black Codes

Pete Daniel
Smithsonian Institution

William Cohen, *Journal of Southern History* (February 1976); Pete Daniel, *The Shadow of Slavery: Peonage in the South, 1901–1969* (1972); Daniel A. Novak, *The Wheel of Servitude: Black Forced Labor After Slavery* (1978). ☆

REDFIELD, H. V.
(1845–1881) Journalist.

Redfield's *Homicide, North and South* was the most careful and extensive study of the differences in regional homicide rates produced in the 19th century. Although the work of a little-known amateur, it is an outstanding example of the American social science of the period.

Horace Victor Eugene Redfield was born about 1845 in Erie County, N.Y., into a family with Vermont origins. However, after his father's early death, he accompanied his mother to the South and in 1860 was residing in Jasper, Marion County, Tenn. A journalist in adult life, he wrote no other known book. Redfield died in 1881 in Washington, D.C., where he had been based for several years as correspondent for the Cincinnati *Commercial*. In the preface to *Homicide* he emphasized his southern upbringing and claimed to have spent most of his life in the South. The author went out of his way to praise southern life and the treatment he had received there. He realized that many would view his work as an attack on the South, but he wished that it could be viewed as friendly criticism that might lead to reform.

Redfield began his book by noting that the rural rates for homicide in England, New England, and the Upper Midwest were very similar, but that rates for the South were much higher than for any civilized country in at least the previous two centuries. He tried to document this remarkable fact and inquire into its causes. He traveled widely throughout the country, collecting data from official sources where it was available (primarily in the North) and developing complete newspaper files where this was possible. He compared rates in the late 1860s and 1870s for "old states" North and South and for frontier states, finding that South Carolina's were as many times greater than New England's as Texas's rates were greater than Minnesota's. In both cases he estimated well over 10 times as many murders per 100,000 population in the South as in the North. He pointed out that Texas was populated largely from the Old South and Minnesota from the North. By comparing homicide rates and population origins in Ohio, Indiana, and Illinois, he demonstrated that the line between North and South ran through these states, whereas Iowa more clearly belonged to the North.

Redfield saw several patterns in southern homicide. Drunken brawls might not be too different from those in the North, yet they more often led to murders, both because of the attitudes of those involved and the general practice of carrying weapons. Murder often occurred to redress insult to personal honor or because of a tough's desire to show off. Groups, whether gangs or clans, often attacked rival groups out of animosity or for political ends. Feuds as such played less of a part in his analysis than one might expect, given his familiarity with Kentucky.

Although very close to the Civil War, he could not see the war as a major cause of southern patterns that greatly antedated it. He saw the most general cause of southern violence as a lack of regard for human life. He thought an exaggerated sense of honor contributed to the high rates of homicide, as did the unnecessary carrying of weapons, particularly concealed weapons. In many rural areas he pointed out that a lone law officer was often powerless or afraid to intervene. Even if caught, the murderer would seldom be convicted or would be given a light sentence. Redfield cited many cases illustrating the difficulty of getting convictions in the South. Convictions were seldom achieved for several reasons: the jurors did not take killing as seriously as in the North; they would be more likely to accept the reasons justifying the killing than would northern jurors; the jurors knew they might themselves later be involved in murder and would not want to meet a juror related to a person they had helped convict; they feared imminent retaliation by relatives of the murderer should they convict.

A great deal has changed since Redfield's study. In his time, for instance, he found whites more involved in murder than blacks. (This may have been because of the availability of weapons, or simply because he did not have sufficient information on black homicide.)

Redfield may well have contributed to the amelioration of the situation as he found it, but lethal violence still casts a shadow over southern culture and thus the nation as a whole.

Raymond D. Gastil
Freedom House

New York Times (18 November 1881); H. V. Redfield, *Homicide, North and South: Being a Comparative View of Crime against the Person in Several Parts of the United States* (1880); J. H. Redfield, *Genealogical History of the Redfield Family* (1860). ☆

TEXAS RANGERS

When the first English-speaking colonists moved into Mexican Texas, they brought their own customs, social values, laws, and officials. Among these were the Rangers.

Since the beginnings of the Anglos' westward drive—in the case of Texas settlers, generally through the South—armed, mounted men ranged the line of advancing homesteaders to protect them from Indians and outlaws. These men were usually civilians locally paid, armed with their own guns, and not in uniform.

Rangers may have had their origin hundreds of years ago in English estates in the role of protectors of their employers' lands, patrolling or ranging at will. Once across an ocean and on the southern frontier, they came to deal with whatever trouble could not be appropriately solved by local police, sheriffs, or the army. Rangers were never intended as a substitute for either the police or the army. They were volunteer, but, unlike local lawmen, they were willing to pursue their foe as far as was

necessary and were much more mobile than regular army detachments. They would fight on their opponents' terms and settle trouble as they saw it without the delays of formal legal process.

When Stephen F. Austin's Texas colony was threatened by Indian attacks in 1823, he called out a company of rangers for protection. They were not the first such men in the field, but they were probably the first officially called Rangers.

For over 40 years Ranger units in Texas were temporary, raised when necessary and dismissed when not needed. They were called "Rangers," "spies," "volunteer companies," "Corps of Rangers," and "Ranging Companies." Later the term Texas Rangers was commonly used, as in 1866 legislative finance bills.

The duties of the Rangers varied with the times. First, they opposed small groups of hostile Indians. When the Republic of Texas was established in 1836, sporadic conflict between Mexico and Texas continued. The Rangers then faced two enemies, Indians and Mexicans. For a dozen years Rangers were irregular fighting units, riding as scouts, guerrillas, and cavalry support for regular troops. Some groups became virtual border guards on the Rio Grande between Texas and Mexico. Others ranged the northwest frontier of Texas in pursuit of Indians. In time, the Indians were driven from Texas, and the Rio Grande—with exceptions—became a stable, recognized international border.

The next Ranger opponent was the outlaw. Rangers turned to the role of peace officers, serving somewhat as a state police force, though never that in name. They regulated cattle rustling, fence cutting, mob violence—any breach of the law that was too widespread or too violent for local officers.

Of debatable efficiency against Indians, Rangers were demonstrably effective against outlaws. They established a lasting reputation for quick striking power over a vast area. To the Anglo businessman and settler, the Ranger meant courage, peacekeeping, and frontier resourcefulness. To his opponents, he represented unhesitating violence, unrelenting pursuit, and a willingness to use any means, including firepower, to enforce the law.

Over the years, Rangers established a standard of personal bravery that became the basis of myth. The story maintaining that only one Ranger was necessary to quell any riot was certainly myth, but individual acts of courage supported the belief that it just might be true. The Rangers have also attracted considerable criticism. They have been accused of brutality, racism, and illegal arrest. In recent years, Mexican Americans have been especially critical of the Rangers, seeing them as an authoritarian force used against minorities. Rangers have been called strikebreakers and paid assassins. But they have more supporters than critics, as their continued service indicates. The most common feeling is that "as long as there is a state of Texas, there will be Rangers."

Established as a permanent service in 1874, the Rangers were authorized by the Texas Legislature to enlist 450 men. Temporary enlistments in earlier years had risen as high as a thousand. The number of Rangers has since varied from a low of about 20 in 1900 to 94 in 1982.

For many years the Texas Rangers served the state directly under the governor and an adjutant general. In 1935 the service became a division of the Texas Department of Public Safety.

Today they are charged with suppressing riots and insurrections, apprehending fugitives, assisting peace officers anywhere in the state, and dealing with major crime on their own initiative.

John L. Davis
Institute of Texas Cultures

John L. Davis, *The Texas Rangers, Their First 150 Years* (1975); James B. Gillett, *Six Years with the Texas Rangers* (1921); Walter Prescott Webb, ed., *The Handbook of Texas* (1952), *The Texas Rangers* (1935). ☆

WILMINGTON RACE RIOT

At the entrance of the Cape Fear River, about 30 miles from the east coast of North Carolina, rests the port city of Wilmington. On the morning of 10 November 1898—two days after a statewide election in which terrorized blacks had largely refrained from voting—an armed and angry mob of about 500 white men gathered in front of the headquarters of the Wilmington Light Infantry. From there, in military order and led by Colonel Alfred M. Waddell, they marched to the office of the black newspaper. They forced the door open, broke windows, destroyed furniture, and then burned the building down.

Thus began one of the worst massacres of the Progressive era. In 1898 Wilmington was, ironically, perhaps the most racially tolerant post-Reconstruction southern city. Blacks figured prominently in the city's political and economic life, occupying high positions in government and holding jobs as restaurant owners, barbers, and artisans. The collector of customs at the port of Wilmington, one of the city auditors, the coroner, 30 percent of the aldermen, clerks, firemen, policemen, and justices of the peace were all black. Conspicuous also were black lawyers, a black voting majority, and Alex Manly's black-run newspaper, the Wilmington *Record.*

At the same time, masses of poor whites and blacks lived in abject poverty. Many Democrats were poor, lower-class whites, who scolded employers for giving blacks preference in hiring.

In the 1894 state election the Fusionist forces, a coalition of Populists and Republicans with their black allies, triumphed. Two years later they elected Wilmington's Daniel Russell as the first Republican governor since Reconstruction. In March of 1897 they altered Wilmington's charter, which enabled the Republicans to usurp control of the city government from an office-holding Democratic clique. The old politicians (city bosses) unsuccessfully challenged the victorious allies in the courts.

For a period of months prior to the riot, the "Secret Nine"—a cabal of minor Democrats—clandestinely planned to overthrow the new government. The Wilmington race riot was preceded by a statewide supremacy crusade, which the resurgent Democrats launched to regain political ascendency in 1898. It was abetted by a propaganda campaign, and armed vigilantes terrorized the black population.

During mid-October the Democrats resurrected an Alex Manly editorial that had appeared in the Wilmington *Record*

on 18 August. It refuted claims that black men were raping white women and committing other crimes and stated that black men "were sufficiently attractive for white girls of culture and refinement to fall in love with them." Printed out of context and headlined daily in the local papers the article was a catalyst for the riot that exploded on 10 November.

Manly escaped days before a large mob, led by ex-congressman Alfred M. Waddell, burned his press. The wounding of William Mayo (white) roused the whites to a frenzy. A massacre ensued, but no whites were slain, and only three were injured. The large number of blacks killed can never be known.

The Democrats subsequently overthrew the legally elected Republican government and unanimously elected Waddell mayor. The next day, amidst jeering crowds, a militia with "fixed bayonets" banished prominent white Republican and black leaders. After two days the blacks who had hidden in the woods came out to find their property, businesses, artisan trades, municipal jobs, and even the traditionally black-occupied menial vocations taken over by the self-appointed new administration and its supportive clan.

H. Leon Prather
Tennessee State University

H. Leon Prather, *We Have Taken a City: Wilmington Racial Massacre and Coup of 1898* (1984). ☆

WOMEN'S LIFE

CAROL RUTH BERKIN

Baruch College, City University of New York

CONSULTANT

☆ ☆ ☆ ☆ ☆ ☆ ☆ ☆ ☆ ☆

Overleaf: Doris Ulmann photograph of a young woman, Brasstown, North Carolina, 1930s

WOMEN'S LIFE
||||||||||||||||||||||||||||||||||||||||||||||||||||||||||||

"Who was the southern lady?" a serious scholar asked her colleagues. But few historians thought it a serious question. Everyone, of course, knew the answer. In a sea of historical uncertainties, the southern woman has been a cherished constant. Everyone knows her and can call her by name. If she is white, she is Miss Scarlett; if she is black, she is mammy. In either persona, the southern woman radiates mystery, but a comfortable, predictable mystery. Scholars have plumbed, measured, and charted her depths as a cultural figure, and they have learned to recognize her white soul and her black one. They can consign her to the novelists and poets who write, after all, about eternal verities.

Or can they? Since the serious study of American women began in the 1970s, the southern woman has become a troublesome figure. If she is white, she simply will not stay on her pedestal. She keeps stepping down to work in the tobacco fields of 17th-century Maryland; to run taverns and printing presses in 18th-century Carolina; to fight for abolition, and to speak out against slavery; to criticize the very chivalric code that purports to honor her in the antebellum era. In the New South she organizes mission schools, fights for unions in the mill towns, and demands suffrage at the height of her Victorian respectability. In the modern era she organizes anti-lynching leagues, runs Works Progress Administration agencies, joins in civil rights struggles, and creates political organizations to defeat or defend controversial social legislation like the Equal Rights Amendment.

If she is black, she removes her mammy's apron and her mammy's smile and becomes a member of a vital slave culture, a tobacco and cotton field worker, a midwife, a religious leader among her people. She is not content to be the linchpin of the planter's "domestic patriarchy," but is sometimes a fierce opponent of the peculiar institution. In the New South she resists agricultural oppression, is a union supporter when she is allowed access to a union, and risks her job in a domestic worker's strike. In the 20th century she becomes a segregation fighter, a college educator, and a Democratic party keynote speaker.

Who was the southern woman—and who is she? One cannot be certain anymore. Whoever she is, historians now realize that she is central to the understanding of southern culture—its reality as well as its myths. For, if chivalry became the southern code of behavior, its object and raison d'être was the southern white woman. If slavery became its "peculiar institution," the representative of its most benign aspects was the black mammy and the symbol of its darkest side was the black concubine. If strong family ties came to bind southerner to southerner across the miles and decades, the southern woman was the heart of each family. Everything from the delights of southern hospitality to the modern advantages of cheap southern labor leads one to explore the experiences of the southern woman. Finally, she is also central to understanding American women, for southern women are as distinctive in women's past as the South is in our nation's past.

Women in the Colonial South. Family has always seemed the centripetal force in southern culture. Yet, among white southerners at least, family has undergone more dramatic changes than most southern institutions. So too have the roles women have played in these families.

While patriarchal, nuclear families migrated to 17th-century New England, the Chesapeake colonies filled with kinless, unmarried men. Planters preferred to import young males to work the tobacco fields, and thus they created a society with roughly six men to every woman. For decades, family life of any sort eluded many of these men. Southern males thought of this sexual imbalance as a "paradise for women," but many women may have disagreed. Relentless pressures pushed young, native-born women into the role of wife and mother as early as 16 or 17 years old.

The Chesapeake environment shaped family life and structure also. While the average New England couple lived to raise a large family and become grandparents, a southern couple learned to expect death and disaster. Disease was the villain. Half of all marriages were ended by malaria or related diseases after seven years. The young husband or wife was then left to care for two or three small children. Not surprisingly, remarriage, with the rearing of a new family, was common. Thus, southerners created a unique family structure, with

large temporary households made up of stepmothers or fathers, half brothers and sisters. A vocabulary of impermanence developed as children referred to their father's "now-wife" and stepmothers spoke of raising "sons-in-law" rather than sons of their own blood.

Where early and sudden death was a norm, southern women found themselves with greater legal and economic responsibilities than their northern counterparts. For, in a society where adult kin of either sex were rare, isolated farms were more common than towns, and sons were usually minors at their fathers' deaths, husbands tended to entrust their estates to their wives. Many southern women inherited an entire estate, despite the certainty that they would remarry. As relatively young women, they took on the responsibilities of managing their own fortunes and the fortunes of their children. Ironically, a husband's death left southern women with greater familial and social power than long life provided other American women.

The southern white woman's life cycle was different from her New England sister's, yet in their daily household routine all colonial women had much in common. When needed, the southern wife toiled in the fields. But most of her day was spent in domestic duties. She tended gardens, kept a dairy and poultry, baked, preserved foods, sewed, mended, cleaned her home (if a free moment for such a luxury presented itself), fed the family and household servants, and cared for infants and young toddlers alike.

Farm boundaries were a woman's life boundaries in most cases. Yet some women seemed to escape between the cracks in this still fluid, underpopulated, labor-scarce society. Widows ran farms, opened taverns, and kept small shops. Women took their neighbors to court, suing for default on debts or for libel. And, in a society where government would not, and perhaps could not, allocate funds for relief and welfare functions, women left by chance or by choice outside the protection of a male guardian were granted legal rights and social approval to seek economic independence.

By the 18th century the Chesapeake's "demographic disaster" had ended. Perhaps immunities to local diseases developed, or planters learned to locate their families away from the malarial environments. A native-born population came to outnumber immigrants, and their longer life span made the development of a patriarchal, nuclear family possible. Even the sexual imbalance slowly righted itself. Southern women began to marry later, in their early twenties, and to husbands more their own ages. The "American" colonial family had arrived in the South: father, mother, and seven or eight children.

In this family, women's role as surrogate patriarch diminished. Adult sons inherited directly from fathers and were assigned to manage the inheritance of minor siblings. Longer-lived fathers were now able to direct their children's lives, pulling on the key strings of property and dowry. The patriarch was ascendent; the southern wife was eclipsed.

Yet new emphasis on tasks within the home accompanied this shift to a stable nuclear family. Most importantly, across the colonies, a new attitude toward child rearing evolved. Its causes varied—religious imperatives prompting it in the Quaker and Puritan worlds, economic prosperity promoting it in the South. The results were the same: the family became child-centered, and the woman's central role became that of mother. Class was the key to this new emphasis on child care, for only white mothers with household servants could spare the time for children beyond the toddler phase. Beginning as an elite ideal, the nurturant mother was to become "nature's" and "God's" true woman in later decades.

During the early 18th century the marital and familial experiences of women North and South seemed to converge. In truth, however, the regions were on quite different trajectories. The southern family was moving toward its fullest expression of patriarchy in the 19th century; the northern family was undergoing subtle but significant modifications that weakened its patriarchal core. The growth of the black slave system was, of course, central to the intensification of patriarchy in the South. Southern planters chose to describe the plantation as a single social unit, incorporating slave labor and personal household into one dependency. The planter's authority over the slave and his authority over his wife and children were parts of the whole cloth of his authority over the plantation family. The power over the slave seemed to prepare the way for greater authority with other dependents. At the same time, the need for sexual protection of his wife and other white females of his household came to vindicate his quest for absolute power over the slave.

The rapid increase of slaves in the colonial South dramatically transformed the lives of black women also. Until the 18th century black women's demographic and mortality patterns had paralleled those of their white counterparts. Now, however, in the black population as well as the white, native-born men and women constituted a majority in most of the southern colonies, and by 1740 the sex ratio had begun to even out. For some blacks trapped in slavery, the rise of great plantations provided one small but significant advantage: in slave quarters, population density meant the opportunity to forge tight communities, develop a minority culture, and elaborate a kinship network. Yet for many blacks, isolated or in twos and threes on small farms, family life remained impossible.

The structure of marriage and family were, perforce, different for slaves than for their masters. Patriarchy was not a viable model. Black males could not assert authority over a dependent wife, for both male and female were themselves dependents. Secondly, marriage did not mean the transition for a woman from a father's guardianship and home to a husband's care and household. Indeed, the absence of a physical relocation bespoke the absence of the psychological and legal transference. A slave woman remained on her home plantation even after marriage, for her role as laborer superseded her role as wife.

Slaves did not attempt to emulate the white family structure. The extended family, more than the nuclear family, fit the needs of men and women who might be separated by sale, lease, or transfer to other slave quarters. Like the nuclear family, the extended family had its psychic benefits and costs to all members. Thus far no one has examined them.

The Impact of the American Revolution. The American Revolution, like the Civil War, left different legacies to the North and South. When the war ended and the architects of the Republic had set its cornerstone of republican government in place, women's role in the new nation was examined by northern intellectuals. But the war, fought longer and more fiercely in the South, had devastated much of the region. Renovation, not innovation, was the southern planter's agenda. Thus, "Republican Motherhood," the new idealization of women in northern society, did not take hold in the South as firmly as it did in other regions.

For northern ideologues, Republican Motherhood included an acknowledged role for women in American political life, not as citizens but as the primary educators of future male citizens. Thus, a woman performed a *civic* duty as she performed a familial duty. Republican Motherhood was a rendition of the preindependence trend toward a child-centered family. This emphasis on women as socializing agents did lead to a new and positive evaluation of women's intellectual and moral capacities. It also produced an educational revolution for women in the New England and middle states. Formal schooling for young women flourished there. From Republican Motherhood came a justification for greater participation in public affairs and a greater sense of self-esteem for women. From the women's academies and schools came a knowledge of society, a vocabulary to criticize it, and a shared female experience. The results were soon evident in the reform movements of the 1830s and 1840s.

In the South, however, the reestablishment and entrenchment of the planter patriarchy kept the roles of wife and mother private ones for women. Southern women might have been responsible for their children's morals and values, but their endeavors remained a service within the family rather than a civic function. Indeed, southern male intellectuals and educators did not publicly challenge the notion of female intellectual inferiority until the 1840s.

Their hesitant call for formal education of women came 50 years after Benjamin Rush and Susannah Rowson outlined the moral and intellectual potential of the Republican Mother. On the eve of the Civil War, southern women had the highest rate of illiteracy among adult white women in the nation. And black slave women were barred from literacy by law.

Had the idea of the Republican Mother taken root in southern consciousness, southern social and economic realities in the early 19th century would have diffused its impact. White southern women of all classes lived in greater isolation than their northern sisters and had less access to the company of other women. The creation of female voluntary and reform associations, a logical extension of Republican Motherhood, required an urban setting that did not exist in the mainly rural South. In addition, southern women of both races continued to marry earlier, die younger, and bear more children than northerners did. White southern women entered adult roles too quickly to allow the hiatus of the female academy. Finally, southern women did not find the opportunity for participation and leadership within the churches that northern women rushed to accept in the early 19th century. Southern men remained in control of the evangelical churches, church participation remained a family function, and separate women's organizations did not develop within the church.

The Southern Lady. The 1830s did produce a new southern female paradigm—the southern lady. She was, in theory if not in fact, virtuous, modest, pious, and submissive. As a wife, she was "queen of the home"; as a mother, she was devotion and self-denial personified. His-

torian Anne Firor Scott aptly says that for this model of southern femininity, "life was one long act of devotion."

The southern lady was the logical companion to the idealized southern patriarch, who was himself the kind and protective, stern but just father to both his white and black families. The southern lady's enduring and open respect for, and submission to, her husband was firm evidence of the benign nature of the southern way of life and its peculiar institution. If the pressure of a life on the pedestal was strongest among the elite, the image of a self-sacrificing and devoted wife and mother took firm hold among the ordinary white folk as well.

Even as the pedestal was constructed, however, deep internal fault lines showed themselves. Among the elite class, marriage was prompted as much by a father's consideration of land and slaves and a young girl's fear of spinsterhood as by admiration for a new husband. Reality rather than romance waltzed many a southern belle down the aisle. Daily life on the pedestal was far from romantic or inspirational. All white wives, rich or poor, worked for their daily bread. Plantation mistresses supervised slaves, rationed supplies for the black work force, and acted as medical expert for the white and black community. Poorer women worked in the fields when their labor was needed. The majority of white women spun and sewed, gardened, supervised hog butcherings, made their own lard soap and even their yeast. Urban women were drafted into producing goods or providing services for their husband's shop or trade. Acts of "devotion" were made in the physical rather than the spiritual realm.

Had people been listening, they would have heard southern ladies protesting their lives. Plantation mistresses resented the lack of control over their own sexual lives and reproductive systems, and they objected to their husbands' sexual behavior. Many hated slavery, if not for its immorality and injustice, then for the burden it placed upon them as plantation mistresses. They were exhausted by their duties as arbiters of so many complex and tension-filled interracial and intraracial relationships. They resented their lack of education and the intellectual and physical isolation of their lives. Their discontent challenged the cherished image of boundless maternal devotion.

It is not hard to locate the sources of their discontent. In the South Carolina of 1856, 40.4 percent of all white women were married before their 20th birthday, often to men 10 years their senior. This pattern marked a return to 17th-century models. And, although southern men applauded the fertility of their wives, shouting "well done" to women who bore six children in nine years, southern wives were not cheered by this praise. Two decades of childbearing meant 10 or 11 children. Or, put more graphically, during 180 months of married life, a Louisiana woman was pregnant 90 months and was nursing 70. While Harvard doctors like Horatio Storer bemoaned the decreasing size of New England Protestant families, southern women continued to spend their married lives in reproduction.

Opposition to the sexual double standard, to the morality of specific social institutions, to inequality of male and female education, and to lack of control over fertility was a common theme among American women, North and South. In the North, however, women's reform societies worked to combat such manifestations of the double standard as prostitution. Southern ladies could not

use similar methods to promote reform. No existing women's organizations could be called upon to lead campaigns on women's issues. Southern women who wished to be activists made their ways north. Thus, female leadership was drained from the region, as it would be again a century later. Finally, southern plantation patriarchy had so successfully circumscribed women's lives that public protest or reform activity lacked any legitimacy or apparent logic. What, after all, was the point of a reform organization when prostitution or concubinage was not a social but a family affair?

Relations between slave women and slave men were, of course, determined by different rules. Yet historians disagree on the sexual politics of the slave community. They know that husband and wife remained part of an extended network of kin and fictive kin and that work roles were less differentiated because both sexes worked in the fields. In their roles as slaves, men and women enjoyed—or suffered—a rough equality, and they were both dependents of the master or mistress, with no economic ties binding them to each other. Some historians argue, however, that a sexual division of labor was established *within* the slave quarters, where male and female roles were sharply defined.

The Civil War and the New South. The Civil War changed the circumstances of southern women's lives much as the American Revolution had altered the lives of northern women. Military defeat and the dismantling of the slave system weakened the patriarchal power of the planter-husband over his wife. The change was most apparent on mundane levels. Immediately following the war, with many of their men dead or disabled and the economy destroyed, white women were often forced into independence.

For many, the role proved permanent, for the war had created a second southern "demographic disaster." One quarter of a million white men had died in the Civil War. Many who had survived moved west, seeking new land and a new start. By 1870 North Carolina had 25,000 more women than men; Georgia had 36,000 more. Among blacks a similar demographic disaster had occurred. Black female-headed households, now visible as public units rather than private plantation arrangements, were common in the postwar era. Disease and poverty, not the battlefield, took black male lives. For example, in New Orleans, black widows constituted 81 percent of the female heads of households.

Industrialization and urbanization began to transform women's lives also. First, the shift from plantation slavery to systems of sharecropping or tenant farming affected white and black rural women dramatically. Blacks, acting as a family unit, resisted the older work patterns of slavery. A sexual division of labor was the freed black's goal, with women out of the fields and in charge of domestic production. White landowners railed against what they called "female loaferism," but for black men and women this effort to keep one family member's labor outside the grasp of the white landlord and exclusive to the family represented a measure of control over their economic lives.

Often, the desire to free black women from fieldwork could not be fulfilled. As late as 1920, 90 percent of the black women in tenant families did some field work, either with their husbands or for wages off the family farm. Sixty-five per-

cent of the women in black landowning families also did field work.

White tenant farm women shared much in common with these black women. In 1920, 40 percent of all white landowning women worked in the fields and 67 percent of all white tenant women. In all, a far greater percentage of white women worked in the field than did those in other regions of the country.

For women of both races, the crossover into male work was as old as colonial society, North or South. Male crossover to domestic chores or child care was far less common, however. Thus, rural black and white women carried a double duty.

In other basic ways region and class created a uniformity of experience that overshadowed race. Rural women of both races continued to marry young, to have many children, and to spend most of their adult lives in mothering. Like their colonial ancestors, these postwar southern women served as midwives and healers to their communities. And, while farm women in the Midwest reaped the benefits of mechanization and the newest household technologies, southern rural women continued to perform household tasks with primitive tools. A preindustrial women's culture thus remained alive in the South long after Sears and Roebuck catalogs had transformed other regions.

Many of these southern farm women became active participants in agricultural reform movements. In the 1880s and 1890s women were a significant proportion of Alliance and Populist organizations. Although these movements failed, rural women had an experience that set them apart from both northern women and their urban southern sisters Populist women activists were effective within an organization controlled by men. They were not viewed as isolated eccentrics by their communities. In the New England states this sense of support from men was an urban, not a rural, phenomenon.

In the South, as in New England, the rise of the mill town and factory created a new set of circumstances for women. In the mills and mill-town life, the consequences of sexual divisions of labor within the family and in production became more starkly visible, perhaps because their vocabularies and measurements seem more familiar to the modern eye.

Between 1880 and 1920 southern mill-town development would recapitulate for southern working women the experiences of New England female factory workers before the Civil War. The first southern mill workers were farm daughters, most easily spared from the family farm. Female-headed farm families, highly vulnerable to the ups and downs of the cash-crop economy, were the next source of mill labor. By 1890, 40 percent of the workers in the four leading southern textile states were women or girls.

The agricultural depression after 1900 drew male-headed farm families to the mill towns. These new male workers drove women out of the mills. At the same time, the simple production techniques in the textile factories made child labor profitable. Thus, new family work patterns were established: fathers and children went to the mills, while mothers worked at home. Here, women tended gardens, performed unpaid but essential domestic tasks, and helped to meet living costs by taking in boarders. In these families, female labor became private or "hidden" labor.

By 1920 changes in production and the enforcement of early minimum-wage laws forced another shift in work patterns. Children, paid at a minimum wage, were no longer desirable employees. Married women reentered the mill, where they soon became victims of wage and job discrimination—paid less than males for identical labor and barred from supervisory positions. In this discrimination—as in the double duty of housework and paid work—southern white Protestant women were joined to their northern, ethnic Catholic and Jewish sisters, and like them, they had fewer babies after the first generation in the mill. In their willingness to participate in strikes and to become labor activists, bold southern women matched the careers of northern activists.

The names of Florence Reece, Ella May Wiggins, and Aunt Molly Jackson are familiar to southern workers. Their battles for equal pay, for union rights, and for better working conditions for men and women are legendary. Yet even in activism, a sexual division was evident. Women, one scholar observed, led strikes; men led unions.

Remarkable differences between the experiences of northern and southern working-class women remain. These are largely unexplored. For example, northern industry quickly became urban industry; southern mill production remained rural. Northern urban working-class women thus may have had more job choices (e.g., home piecework versus factory work), a more vigorous and diverse labor-reform movement, and stronger support networks.

Black women made their way to New South towns and cities during this era also. In an urban setting the consequences of racial divisions of labor become more sharply defined. Black women were forced to take domestic jobs, keeping house for white families at rates as low as $3 a week in 1935. The black mammy may have been an imaginary figure before the Civil War, but after it, she definitely existed. She cared for white children, ran white homes, and dominated white kitchens while white mothers worked for wages outside the home or joined the growing numbers of middle-class women's organizations and volunteer societies.

In the South, race cut the same deep chasms through labor solidarity that ethnicity and religion cut in the North. Black women workers in New South factories were often temporary workers; white women held year-round jobs. During layoffs, these black women survived by working as maids in their white co-workers' homes. Thus, women workers met each other both as members of a working class and across a color line, as employee and employer. Not until the 1940s, when women began to work in offices and education, did black and white women share the same relationship to production.

Change came in the New South in another major area—educational opportunity for southern women. Public school systems were established in the region, and as students, black and white females received the benefits—uneven though they were—of literacy. But the shift of education out of the home and into a public institution had a second significance for women. A maternal function was taken over by the state, and women were drafted to perform that function in the new, public sphere. Thus, a role previously assigned to all married women became an occupation for a small number of women. Teaching provided these women with a respectable and, in the black community, prestigious profession. It also offered some measure of economic independence.

Young Florida cowgirls posing in Jacksonville studio, c. 1930s

Teacher training became the raison d'être for women's colleges and normal schools. Again, the revolution in education in the South recalled the earlier development in education in the North. The significance of higher education for women was similar, creating for southern women those "bonds of womanhood"—shared experiences based on gender—that historians have described for early 19th-century New England women. These were the first close ties that did not grow out of family relationships. Finally, higher education provided women with the intellectual tools to examine and criticize their society.

For many southern women, the most dramatic break with antebellum traditions was their entry into public life. Many factors set the stage for this new visibility: the rise of towns and cities, helping to create a critical mass for collective activity; the entrance of women into the paid work force; improved education; the decline of male participation in and control over religious organizations; and the creation of leisure time for elite white women who traded the responsibilities of the slave system for the less demanding relationship of household servant and mistress.

Without doubt, the first conduit for women into public life was the church.

In the aftermath of the Civil War, southern women joined forces to rebuild church buildings and raise emergency funds. By the 1890s female mission societies, especially within the Methodist church, had grown into a major arm of the evangelical order. The Methodist Women's Board of Foreign Missions, for example, owned $200,000 worth of property and ran 10 boarding schools, 31 day schools, and a hospital. From such church-based organizations, southern women, like their northern sisters in the early 19th century, gained training in organization and leadership, self-confidence, and a legitimate public role.

The notion of women as morally superior to men—once a cornerstone of the southern lady's pedestal—was revived, but in a new context and for a new purpose. This time, women, not men, elaborated the ideology. Women's maternal concern and their moral sensitivity, argued activists, propelled them into such projects as the crusade against alcohol, aid for the poor, improvement of working conditions for women, and abolition of child labor. In the South, as in the North, "social housekeeping" moved women's sphere out of the private home and into public and political life.

But southern white women who came to social housekeeping, and later to Progressivism, followed a different timetable from northern women because they responded to very different circumstances. The Civil War defeat, which generated or at least allowed major economic and demographic changes in the South, also demanded a period of basic economic and social recovery. While New England women mounted reform movements in the 1870s and 1880s, southern women were engaged in rebuilding and survival.

A more basic difference, however, lay not in chronology, but in the breadth and reach of social housekeeping, North and South. Northern women operated within the context of a society open to change, but southern reform-minded women struggled within a conservative political and social environment. The energies of southern women were divided by race, despite a shared ideology of "social housekeeping" and the creation of similar organizations. Only occasionally did black and white reformers work together on a project such as school improvement.

Not surprisingly, the women's suffrage movement came late to the South and was less successful there than in any other region. The demand for women's suffrage came at a time when southern political leaders were restricting rather than expanding voting rights in their states, for class and racial ends. Suffragists' support of a federal amendment raised the spectre of new federal "intervention," sincerely or simply rhetorically feared. Finally, in the South women's suffrage was linked with race issues—historically with abolition, more recently with growing black political hopes. Thus, like many of the reforms of the Victorian and Progressive eras, suffrage was filtered through a uniquely southern history and experience.

The American feminist movement, never strong in the South, dissipated after the suffrage victory. Social housekeeping, however, continued to motivate some southern activist women during the 1920s and 1930s. Women could still unite over issues of child welfare, educational reform, and working conditions for women. Often their goals put them on a collision course with southern industrialists. Demands for shorter work days and a ban on night work for women, for example, made the Southern Council on Women and Children in Industry challenge unregulated capitalism in the South and made this women's council a classic Progressive organization.

In the South, as in the North, women's labor reform brought middle-class and working-class women into an uneasy alliance. Too often middle-class women spoke for, rather than with, the working-class beneficiaries of the reform effort. The sharp edges of class frequently severed ties of gender in the northern industrial centers, where vigorous union movements often vied with women's reform organizations for women workers' loyalties. Ironically, in the South such a contest between class and gender rarely occurred because the union movement was too weak to bid effectively for working women's loyalty. Thus, southern experiments in cross-class cooperation such as the Southern Summer School for Women Workers sustained a sense of sisterhood longer than northern organizations such as the Women's Trade Union League.

During the 1920s black and white women activists did come together for a major reform effort. Led by Jessie Daniel Ames, these women launched an antilynching campaign. Ames's vision may have been marred by racial stereotyping, but her "revolt against chivalry" had serious feminist implications. It struck at the remaining underpinnings of southern patriarchy by challenging the myth that racial dominance protected white women's purity and virtue. It challenged sexual stereotypes of black and white women and raised basic questions about sexual and social relations. Such questions went unanswered, yet they were raised again in the 1960s and 1970s.

The Modern South. Today, southern women's lives follow more closely the American mainstream. Yet regional and subregional variations remain. In the rural South, especially in the Mississippi Delta and in the predominantly Catholic areas of Louisiana, rates of fertility and infant mortality are higher than the national norms. From the old cotton belt of the Southeast through the Black Belt of Alabama, larger families and greater risk of infant death are a black phenomenon. In eastern Kentucky, white "hillbilly" women share these conditions. Poverty, not race, is the apparent villain.

The search for work has played havoc with sex ratios in the modern South. Job-seeking Appalachian women, barred from coal mines and timbering, have left a male majority in many of their counties. On the other hand, in the inner Coastal Plain and the Delta, women have remained behind while men have migrated to northern and southern cities. Changes in southern women's rates of employment have paralleled national trends over the last several decades. According to the 1980 census, 50 percent of married women with a husband present were employed. In the 13 southern states in 1980 the percentage of employed married women living with employed husbands ranged from a high of 49 percent in North Carolina to a low of 28 percent in West Virginia. Perhaps more striking are the data on employment of all mothers. In 1980, 58 percent of all females in North Carolina aged 16 or older with children aged 6 or younger worked outside the home, as did the majority of such mothers in seven other southern states. For mothers with children between the ages of 6 and 17, the percentage employed ranged from 70 percent in North Carolina to 46 percent in West Virginia, the only southern state in which a majority of mothers of children aged 17 or younger were not employed.

With higher employment rates have come more varied job opportunities for southern women; but income differentials between women and men, often called the "earnings gap", remain discouraging. As of 1981 the state with the largest earnings gap in the nation was Louisiana, with women's median income being only 50 percent of men's median income. The smallest gap in the South (and the fifth smallest in the nation) was in Tennessee, where women's median income was 64 percent of men's. Interestingly, among the 15 states with the smallest gap in 1981 were 7 southern states. Economic conditions, changing attitudes about men's and women's roles, and higher divorce rates, among other factors, have dramatically affected southern women's experiences in recent decades.

In the foreseeable future, marriage and employment will continue to be linked since over 90 percent of American women marry at some point in their

Country storekeeper, Reganton, Mississippi, 1975

lives. However, divorce rates in the South and and West are higher than in other parts of the country. The crude divorce rate (i.e., the number of divorces and annulments per 1,000 population per year) for the East South Central census division, consisting of Alabama, Mississippi, Tennessee, and Kentucky, has for several decades ranked the fourth highest among the nine census divisions, and Texas and Arkansas are in the nation's so-called divorce belt.

In the South, as elsewhere, female heads of households with children but with no husband present face particularly pressing financial problems, especially black women. According to 1980 census data, in seven southern states 35 percent or more of the single-parent households headed by women had a 1979 income below the poverty level. In 10 southern states 50 percent or more of these households below the poverty level were black. Such figures point to some of the most glaring problems facing southern women.

For blacks and whites, kinship networks remain strong. Thus southern women still operate within a matrix of kin as well as gender, class, or race. Indeed, many black women remain members of, or heads of, extended families, a pattern consistent in southern black culture since the colonial era.

Finally, southern society remains politically and religiously conservative. Whether the southern woman supports or opposes that conservatism, it shapes her political, social, and ideological options.

The choice—to defend or attempt to change their region's conservatism—has been a pressing problem since 1950. Indeed, what distinguishes the modern southern woman from her 19th-century ancestors may be her active role in shaping her own ideologies. This marks an independence from northern women as well as from southern men. During the civil rights movement, for example, young black and white women took as their role models not northern women but middle-aged southern black women. The Fannie Lou Hamers of the rural and small-town South inspired their activism.

Common goals did not necessarily produce common experiences for black and white women, however: for black women, kinship and family and church ties may have provided needed emotional support; for white women activists, commitment to the movement meant a sharp and painful wrenching away from traditional support systems and often led to an awakening of feminist consciousness. As abolition work had led the Grimké sisters to women's rights, SNCC work often led southern college women to feminism. Southern black women, however, have remained more committed to racial than to gender issues.

A number of southern feminist leaders, such as Texas's Liz Carpenter, Sarah Weddington, and Frances Farenthold, have left the southern battlefield to lead national feminist organizations. Today the southern battlefield remains an active one. The attack on traditional southern segregation patterns, followed in the 1970s by the creation of state commissions on women's equality and by ERA ratification drives, led conservative white women to political activism. Thus, the modern feminist movement has become a significant intrasectional women's struggle.

Extremist organizations such as the Ku Klux Klan, John Birch Society, and the National States Rights Party campaign against the ERA. Antifeminist Phyllis Schlafly is not a southern woman, yet her strongest support comes from women of the South. There, antifeminism is also strongly supported by fundamentalist churches. For many southern black women, of course, the church had provided similar support for civil rights activity. Thus, reformist or conservative, southern women's public activities continue to be centered in the church.

To some observers, the battle against the ERA, and its implication of revised sex and gender roles, seems to be a symbolic crusade. By opposing the ERA, southern women—and men—had an opportunity to register their distress at the forces of change still at work upon their region.

This conflict over change, the conflicting values it reflects, the intraregional variations of fertility, wealth, and demographics all suggest that no easily identifiable "southern woman" exists. Yet the dual idealization of the past—southern lady and black mammy—were never representative either. Class, race, occupation, rural or urban environment, and age have always worked their variations and transformations on any common theme. The powerful images of "Miss Scarlett" and "Mammy" were based on the power of the elite planter class who created these ideals. They were able to maintain an illusion of uniformity. The modern South lacks the agency to perform such an ideological sleight of hand.

See also BLACK LIFE: Family, Black; Race Relations; EDUCATION: Teachers; FOLKLIFE: Childbirth; Family Folklore; Weddings; / Quilting, Afro-American; Quilting, Anglo-American; HISTORY AND MANNERS:

Beauty, Cult of; Debutantes; Cookbooks; Fashion; Manners; Patriotic Societies; Sexuality; / United Daughters of the Confederacy

Carol Ruth Berkin
Baruch College
City University of New York

Mary Frances Berry and John Blassingame, *Long Memory: The Black Experience in America* (1982); Catherine Clinton, *The Plantation Mistress: Woman's World in the Old South* (1982), *Journal of the Early Republic* (Spring 1982); Ronald D. Eller, *Miners, Millhands, and Mountaineers: Industrialization of the Appalachian South, 1880–1930* (1982); Mari Evans, ed., *Black Women Writers, 1950–1980* (1985); Sara Evans, *Personal Politics: The Roots of Women's Liberation in the Civil Rights Movement and the New Left* (1979); Jean Friedman, *The Enclosed Garden: Women and Community in the Evangelical South, 1830–1900* (1985); Norval D. Glenn and Beth Ann Shelton, *Journal of Marriage and the Family* (August 1985); Herbert G. Gutman, *The Black Family in Slavery and Freedom, 1750–1925* (1976); Margaret J. Hagood, *Mothers of the South: Portraiture of the White Tenant Farm Woman* (1939); Jacquelyn Dowd Hall, *Revolt Against Chivalry: Jesse Daniel Ames and the Women's Campaign against Lynching* (1979); Joanne V. Hawks and Sheila L. Skemp, eds., *Sex, Race, and the Role of Women in the South* (1983); Anne Goodwyn Jones, *Tomorrow Is Another Day: The Woman Writer in the South, 1859–1936* (1981); Jacqueline Jones, *Labor of Love, Labor of Sorrow: Black Women, Work, and the Family from Slavery to the Present* (1985); Kathy Kahn, *Hillbilly Women* (1972); Thelma Kandel, *What Women Earn* (1981); Suzanne Lebsock, *The Free Women of Petersburg: States and Culture in a Southern Town, 1784–1860* (1983); Mary Beth Norton, *Liberty's Daughters: The Revolutionary Experience of American Women* (1980); Anne Firor Scott, *The Southern Lady: From Pedestal to Politics, 1830–1930* (1970), *Journal of American History* (March, 1974); Kathryn L. Seidel, *The Southern Belle in the American Novel* (1985); *Southern Exposure*, (Winter 1976); Julia Cherry Spruill, *Women's Life and Work in the Southern Colonies* (1938); Thad W. Tate and David L. Ammerman, eds., *The Chesapeake in the Seventeenth Century: Essays on Anglo-American Society* (1979); U.S. Bureau of the Census, *Current Population Reports*, Series P-20, no. 380 (1983), *General Social and Economic Characteristics, 1980* (by state) (1981). ☆

Appalachian Women

||||||||||||||||||||||||||||||||||||||||||||||||||||

For women of Appalachia geography is the common denominator; other factors point to diversity. The formative experience for Appalachian women was the frontier process when westward-moving pioneers staked their claims in the region, which includes 13 states or portions thereof. As a group, Appalachian women have frequently fallen victim to caricature. In terms of class, ethnicity, education, vocation, and aspiration, they embody disparate personae contradicting popular images shaped by cartoon characters like Daisy Mae Yokum of Dogpatch, U.S.A., or Aunt Loweezy, wife to moonshining mountaineer Snuffy Smith.

Generally, the Appalachian region has been characterized by a patriarchal family structure and dominated by white, Anglo-Saxon Protestants. Nonetheless, as early as the late 18th century and certainly by the 19th a class system operated, and different ethnic and racial groups coexisted, among them Caucasians, Negroes, and Indians, as well as the mysterious Melungeons. Decades of relative isolation and economic retardation left the region and its people a preindustrial society that began to give way to the modernizing effects of industrialization only in the 20th century. Class structure became even more clearly defined, urban areas increased in number and size, the traditional family lost ground, and cultural pluralism became apparent. The experiences of Appalachian women have been influenced by all these developments.

During the antebellum period Appalachian females seem to have been less fettered by geographical isolation, social conventions, and the patriarchal family than during later decades of the century. Generalizations are dangerous, however, for considerable difference existed between the lives of women in isolated areas and those in small villages and towns—differences intensified by class. Furthermore, reports of early travelers failed to distinguish clearly between Appalachian traits and those of Americans elsewhere, whereas local colorists of the late 19th century labeled Appalachians "peculiar people." Some evidence indicates that Appalachian women of this earlier period asserted themselves at religious and political meetings. Certainly, through their labor on the farms and in the homes, they made a vital contribution to family survival in a preindustrial economy. Some managed to escape the traditional constraints of familial existence by keeping boardinghouses and teaching. Only a minuscule number supervised slaves, for the institution of slavery was far less significant in the mountains than elsewhere in the South. Although an independent spirit is frequently ascribed to Appalachians, the region did not completely avoid the influence of the planter-dominated South with its code of chivalry; and mountain women were not totally removed from the influence

of the "southern lady"—an ideal that transcended class lines and challenged topographical barriers.

The turbulent years of Civil War and Reconstruction dealt harshly with Union supporters as well as with Confederate sympathizers in Appalachia. The genuine deprivation of people torn by their own factionalism and plagued by foraging parties from both armies helped shape the national image of Appalachians as needy and the southern mountains as a legitimate missionary field. Judged by northeastern standards, Appalachians seemed poor, but their land harbored tremendous wealth. New South advocates, some of them native mountaineers, in league with northern investors soon began the irreversible alteration of the mountains and their people. Substantial numbers of poor but proud highland peasants became mill operatives, miners, and coke drawers.

In the early decades of the 20th century scores of Appalachian women moved into the textile factories throughout the Blue Ridge and the Piedmont and exchanged the old, rural, patriarchal family system for the new village paternalism of mill owners. As southern labor stirred, these females, some of them mere girls, led strikes like those in 1929 at Elizabethton, Tenn., and Marion, N.C. A few working-class women were directly influenced by agencies like the Southern Summer School for Women Workers, the Highlander Folk Schools, and the Industrial Department of the Young Women's Christian Association, in turn affecting the lives of other female factory workers. Middle- and upper-class women in Appalachian towns led the work of civic organizations like the YWCA.

New cultural elements had also been introduced into the region during the late 19th and early 20th centuries as coal operators actively recruited "new" immigrants. Substantial numbers of Italian and Hungarian females as well as members of other ethnic groups, mostly Catholics, followed their men into the hollows of West Virginia, southwest Virginia, eastern Kentucky, and northeastern Tennessee. Coal operators also increased the black population as they imported workers from the Deep South after World War I had virtually halted immigration.

During this transition various humanitarian and religious efforts were directed toward the reformation of Appalachia. In the forefront were female outsiders, mostly teachers and nurses, known in the mountain vernacular as "fotched-on" women. Truly outstanding among them was Mary Breckinridge, who hailed from the Kentucky Bluegrass. She established the Frontier Nursing Service in 1925 and devoted the next 40 years to prenatal and postpartum treatment of mothers and infants in eastern Kentucky, meanwhile building a general practice of family medicine.

During the 20th century, portions of the Appalachian region have suffered the boom-bust cycle of the coal industry; other areas with a more diversified economy have enjoyed relative prosperity. Pockets of rural and urban poverty still exist in the region despite massive federal aid programs, and displaced Appalachians can be found in the ghettos of northern and midwestern cities. Nonetheless, women of Appalachia in general have more reason now than ever before to expect a fair share of the nation's goods and services and the opportunity to enjoy a full life. While some have remained trapped at the lowest economic levels, others from humble

origins have moved into comfortable middle-class status. Indeed, there are "rags-to-riches" sagas like those of Mother Maybelle and the Carter Sisters, Dolly Parton, and Loretta Lynn. The few women miners have received considerable attention during the last decade. In a less flamboyant way, other young women have written their own success stories by leaving the hillside farms and coal camps for industrial assembly lines, secretarial positions, and college and university campuses; among them was Juanita Morris Kreps, secretary of commerce during the Carter administration.

A broad spectrum of opinion on feminist issues can be found among mountain females. An attempt to create a network during the 1970s culminated in the establishment of the short-lived Council of Appalachian Women, which purchased the rights to the *Magazine of Appalachian Women* (*MAW*) and briefly published a journal entitled *Appalachian Women*.

See also ENVIRONMENT: / Appalachian Mountains; Blue Ridge; ETHNIC LIFE: Mountain Culture / Appalachians; FOLK-LIFE: / "Hillbilly" Image; INDUSTRY: Industrialization in Appalachia; / Mining; LITERATURE: Appalachian Literature; MUSIC: / Carter Family; MYTHIC SOUTH: Appalachian Culture; New South Myth; / Appalachian Myth; SCIENCE AND MEDICINE: / Breckinridge, Mary; SOCIAL CLASS: Poverty / Coal Miners; Highlander Folk School

Margaret Ripley Wolfe
East Tennessee State University

Carol Crowe-Carraco, *The Register of the Kentucky Historical Society* (July 1978); Ronald D. Eller, *Appalachian Journal* (Winter 1979); Sidney Saylor Farr, *Appalachian*

Women: An Annotated Bibliography (1981); Kathy Kahn, *Hillbilly Women* (1973); Henry D. Shapiro, *Appalachia on Our Mind: The Southern Mountains and Mountaineers in the American Consciousness, 1870–1920* (1978); Southern Summer School Papers, American Labor Education Service Collection, Cornell University, Ithaca, N.Y.; *Time* (3 January 1977); David E. Whisnant, *All That Is Native and Fine: The Politics of Culture in an American Region* (1983). ☆

Belles and Ladies

|||||||||||||||||||||||||||||||||||||||||||||||

Southern lore has it that the belle is a privileged white girl at the glamorous and exciting period between being a daughter and becoming a wife. She is the fragile, dewy, just-opened bloom of the southern female: flirtatious but sexually innocent, bright but not deep, beautiful as a statue or painting or porcelain but, like each, risky to touch. A form of popular art, she entertains but does not challenge her audience. Instead, she attracts them—the more gentlemen callers the better—and finally allows herself to be chosen by one.

Then she becomes a lady, and a lady she will remain until she dies—unless of course she does something beyond the pale. As a lady she drops the flirtatiousness of the belle and stops chattering; she has won her man. Now she has a different job: satisfying her husband, raising his children, meeting the demands of the family's social position, and sustaining the ideals of the South. Her strength in manners and morals is contingent, however, upon her submission to their sources—God, the patriarchal church, her husband—and upon her staying out of public life, where she

might interfere in their formulation. But in her domestic realm she can achieve great if sometimes grotesque power. As a slave mistress, for example, she was capable of enormous cruelty as well as deeply felt kindness; she was a premier manager yet also a slave to the patriarch. Melanie Wilkes was a great, good lady; Marie St. Clare a cruel and narcissistic one; and Scarlett O'Hara, that perpetual adolescent, never made it much past the belle.

Such a description can never satisfy, of course, for it is wrenched out of history, where the attributes of southern womanhood change over time, and it reflects only one out of the immense variety of attitudes about the southern woman. What has changed less than the southern woman's attributes and her reception, however, is her ontology. As the allusion to fiction suggests, southern womanhood exists as more than a historical prescription, job, role, or even source of identity. In fact, to see it as an actual identity is to literalize southern womanhood's function as a symbolic construct within southern ideology, and thus to perpetuate that ideology. Southern girls who assume the roles of belle and lady take on an entire history of the meaning of the South—its class, race, and gender systems, and its past and future. As belle and lady, a woman "becomes" the traditional South; as gentleman and scholar, a man enters into a complex relation *to* the South. He may be idolatrous worshipper, lord and master, dashed and demoralized failure; in any case, he acts as subject to her object, as knower to her known. The gender roles thus work together to prevent change and to obscure reality both between human beings and within the South's conception of itself. Where they fail to work, as is increasingly the case

in our time, where southerners of both sexes rebel against the belle (or worse, ignore her), the chance for change finds its place.

Southern men have toasted and celebrated southern womanhood since the South began to think of itself as a region, probably before the American Revolution. The lady, with her grace and hospitality, seemed the flower of a uniquely southern civilization, the embodiment of all it prized most deeply. In truth, southern womanhood has much in common with the ideas of the British Victorian lady and of American true womanhood. All deny to women authentic selfhood; all enjoin that women suffer and be still; all show women sexually pure, pious, deferent to external authority, and content with their place in the home. Yet southern womanhood differs in several ways from other 19th-century images of womanhood. The southern lady has been from the start at the core of a patriotic impulse; the identity of the South is contingent in part upon the persistence of its tradition of the lady. Secondly, the ideal of southern womanhood seems to have lasted longer than the other ideals, even to the present. Thirdly, southern womanhood has from the beginning been inextricably linked to racial attitudes. Its very genesis, some say, lay in the minds of guilty slaveholders who sought an image they could revere without sacrificing the gains of racial slavery. And finally, the class—aristocratic—that the image of the lady represents has deeper ideological roots in the South than elsewhere in the United States.

Thus, when Lucian Lamar Knight once again, in 1920, toasted the southern woman's "silent influence," "eternal vigil," and "gentle spirit"; when he claimed that the "blood royal of the an-

My Southern Rose.

A belle of the South

cient line" still lives in her daughters, his language suggested her primary ideological functions: to unify the South in its difference; to sustain the desire for British class structure; to protect the racial purity of legitimate white patriarchal inheritance; to provide a container for the conscience that would perpetuate ideals without danger of contact with reality; and thus to keep actual women elevated into perpetual silence and passivity.

Historians speculate variously about the origins and historical function of the concept of southern womanhood in southern ideology. In the knot of region, race, sex, and class, some find one thread clearer than others. In general, they agree that the function of southern womanhood has been to justify the perpetuation of the hegemony of the male sex, the upper and middle classes, and the white race.

Anne Firor Scott sees the base of the pedestal in racial slavery: "Because they owned slaves and thus maintained a traditional landowning aristocracy,

southerners tenaciously held on to the patriarchal family structure. . . . Any tendency on the part of any of the members of the system to assert themselves against the master threatened the whole, and therefore slavery itself." Thus, Scott continues, it was "no accident that the most articulate spokesmen for slavery were also eloquent exponents of the subordinate role of women." The threat of violence takes a surprisingly strong role in even the most sophisticated proslavery arguments for women's subordination, as Kent Leslie's work on George Fitzhugh, Chancellor Harper, and Thomas R. Dew shows. Thus, when Louisa McCord argued against women's emancipation, she claimed that, without the protection of the pedestal, women would be intolerably vulnerable to male physical superiority. The argument can still be heard in the South today. W. J. Cash, also, found racial supremacy at the origin of the image. Woman alone could perpetuate white superiority, because of what Cash calls her "remoteness from the males of the inferior group," a remoteness not paralleled in the relationships between white men and black women. "The [white] woman must be compensated, the revolting suspicion in the male that he might be slipping into bestiality got rid of, by glorifying her," argues Cash. Lillian Smith, too, in *Killers of the Dream* (1949), sees the origin of southern womanhood in this "race-sex-sin spiral": "The more trails the white man made to back-yard cabins, the higher he raised his white wife on her pedestal, when he returned to the big house. The higher the pedestal, the less he enjoyed her whom he put there, for statues are after all only nice things to look at."

Insecurities of a more class-related sort led southerners to create the lady,

according to William R. Taylor. Despairing at southern social and economic decline and fearing "social dissolution" (particularly in the forms of an open society and a dismembered family), southerners "grasped for symbols of stability and order to stem their feelings of drift and uncertainty and to quiet their uneasiness about the inequities within Southern society." But southern men, Taylor argues, could not associate feeling, introspection, or moral awareness with masculinity. The popular plantation novels solved this problem "without robbing the Southern gentleman of his manhood. The Southern answer to this question lay in the cult of chivalry—in having the Cavalier kneel down before the altar of femininity and familial benevolence."

Yet ultimately, as Sara Evans points out, "it made no sense to place women in charge of piety and morality and then deny them access to the public sphere where immorality held sway." Certain pre-Civil War southern men, Taylor says, "began regretting the moral autonomy which they had assigned to women" and returned full circle, to insist upon a rigid gender, race, and class hierarchy that made woman, slave, and yeoman subject to the Cavalier.

A suggestion that class takes precedence over race and gender in grounding southern womanhood can be found in the incidence of the "lady" in literature by black women. Linda Brent's slave master, for example, promises her he will make her into a "lady" in exchange for sex; clearly the idea was not, even then, limited to white women. And in Zora Neale Hurston's novel *Their Eyes Were Watching God* (1937), Janie becomes a lady, ornamental and silent, within an all-black community, as a sign of class elevation. If a black woman can become a southern lady, then something other than racial exclusion is going on. But can a white lower-class woman climb into ladyhood? Eudora Welty seems to see the lady as a construct that preserves class immobility when she makes it clear in *The Optimist's Daughter* (1972) that Fay's lower-class origins prevent her from attaining the sort of consciousness that makes a "real" lady, that is, a lady in mind and in spirit.

Yet another argument finds the origin of southern womanhood in Western civilization's patriarchal tradition, antedating and then reinforcing racial slavery and class structure. Bertram Wyatt-Brown locates the source of southern womanhood in the South's retention of the ancient code of honor, the system of "patriarchy and womanly subordination." Public reputation, not private guilt, motivates behavior in this system; hence the "enforcement of gender and family conventions [is] community business" rather than personal choice. Men of all classes agreed upon female subordination and docility as a norm. And women participated willingly in their subordination, Wyatt-Brown argues, because southern womanhood meant not simply self-sacrifice and silence, but sacrifice for family honor, in which women took pride, and courage, in accepting fate without complaint. Thus did the patriarchal system of honor simultaneously subordinate its women and reward them for their acquiescence. John Ruoff also argues for the primacy of patriarchy over slavery as the source for southern womanhood. Southern settlers brought with them from England a belief in patriarchal values, says Ruoff. These values made the man the source of family authority, the family the source of societal order and stability, and the planter class the source of authority

within society. Then, as early as the 17th century, a native southern aristocracy developed an "ethos of leisure and consumption" that "stipulated that women should perform an essentially ornamental function in society." The development of the master-slave relationship thus reinforced and was reinforced by the prior notion that the husband held absolute authority in the home.

Sara Evans also points to Europe for the myths about women that southern colonists brought along with their patriarchal social and familial assumptions. Those basic myths polarized women into the "virgin, pure and untouchable, and the prostitute, dangerously sexual." The clustering of images—goodness and light with virginity, evil and darkness with sexuality—seemed to be reified and therefore confirmed when white planters owned black slave women. Race and sex thus fused to create in the "white lady" the southern version of the 19th-century's cult of true womanhood.

Whatever the relative importance of class, race, and patriarchy, it is the peculiar relation of patriarchal attitudes toward women with the development of a hierarchical slave society that produced, in the early 19th century, both the South's most intense period of self-definition and the refinement of the images of the lady as the slaveholder's ideal—and the dominant ideal of the South.

How have women fared through all this construction of ideology? Most have, of course, literalized the symbol; it would be nearly impossible not to. Thus, for most southern women "southern womanhood" has become a very practical and personal concern, a way to be—to reject, to revise, or to adopt.

The rare ones have rejected the necessity even to pretend to conform, have radically criticized their society, and have often left the South, in body if not in mind. The Charleston Grimké sisters moved North—Sarah in 1821 and Angelina in 1820—and, from that "refuge," at times addressing the southern white women at home, directly attacked the "assumptions upon which southern society based its image of women," including, of course, slavery. In fact, Sarah's *Letters on the Equality of the Sexes* were, according to Anne Firor Scott, the "earliest systematic expression in America of the whole set of ideas constituting the ideology of 'women's rights.' " Sara Evans has shown that the 1960s feminist revival found its roots, too, in the South. Once again southern white women—this time in the civil rights movement—saw the connection between racial and sexual oppression, thus providing the initial impulse toward contemporary feminism. Shirley Abbott, in *Womenfolks* (1983), offers herself as a contemporary explanation of why southern girls leave home.

At the opposite extreme from outright rebellion, some women have determined to shape themselves entirely into the ideal. "We owe it to our husbands, children, and friends," wrote Caroline Merrick to a friend in 1859, "to represent as nearly as possible the ideal which they hold so dear." At the extreme, such women blanked out their perceptions and repressed their feelings until they lost, almost entirely, a sense of self. Educated, on the other hand, into the belief that they were perfection itself, some real southern women found it hard to admit and harder to rectify such "besetting sins [as] a roving mind and an impetuous spirit."

More typically, though, southern women neither left home nor attained perfection. Instead, they made for themselves a public persona, a mask of sorts that coexisted with but did not always correspond to an inner self. Such self-division produced guilt both about what they felt was the wolf within and about the inevitable hypocrisy involved in concealing it. In the South the conflict between image and reality took its purest form in the years before the Civil War. Although the ideology depicted them as passive, submissive, and dependent symbols of leisure, these women found that actual experience involved long days of hard active work making administrative decisions that determined how the household ran.

Whereas the image had her needing the economic protection of her husband, reality found her chafing, as did Mary Boykin Chesnut, at her economic dependence. Whereas the ideal southern woman was chaste as a cake of ice, many women felt a natural physical attraction to their husbands and even possessed a "humor so earthy as to contradict the romantic tradition of universal refinement among Southern ladies," says Bell Wiley. Whereas the woman presumably lived in ignorance of it, miscegenation aroused anguish in many. Whereas the ideal woman was a repository of culture and the arts, her actual ignorance of worldly reality (which the image called innocence) was maintained by the low quality of education available for women in the South. The ideal woman, however, remained a pious Protestant, and in fact evidence of any widespread (if private) religious skepticism is rare. Thus each element of the image—leisure, passivity, dependence, sexual purity, submission, ignorance (with the possible exception of piety)—failed to correspond to the reality of women's lives, and for women to undertake to match the ideal must have required creativity and persistence.

The history of woman's specific accommodations to and revisions of the belle and the lady is complicated, fascinating, and ongoing. Anne Firor Scott, Jacquelyn Dowd Hall, and Suzanne Lebsock have notably pieced out parts of that story, a story too long to tell here except in the most generalized way. It seems that most southern women have in their daily lives worked around these conflicts with the ideology of southern womanhood. They have done so in the interests of values and desires that can be called "women's culture" and that subvert, at times, the values of the dominant culture. On the other hand, the fate of the belle in literature, as Kathryn L. Seidel untangles it, has been less hopeful. The belle has moved from the "madonna" of the antebellum period to the narcissistic and masochistic "Magdalen" of, for instance, Faulkner's Temple Drake. These are for Seidel two sides of the same person; they represent the psychosexual distortions inherent in the image itself.

Has southern womanhood died—co-opted by television and trashy passion novels—or metamorphosed into some sort of Sunbelt Total Woman? Long-held images of southern womanhood have not disappeared any more than have the systems that produced them. Perhaps in a place like Sunbelt Atlanta, though, the southern woman has finally found a suitable arena for her skills at manipulating the images.

See also BLACK LIFE: Freedom Movement, Black; Miscegenation; Race Relations; / Hurston, Zora Neale; HISTORY AND MANNERS: Sexuality; LITERATURE: Sex Roles in Literature; / Faulkner, William; Welty, Eudora; MYTHIC SOUTH: Family; Racial Attitudes; Romanticism; / Cash, W. J.

Anne Goodwyn Jones
University of Florida

Irving H. Bartlett and Glenn Cambor, *Women's Studies*, vol. 2 (1974); Linda Brent, *Incidents in the Life of a Slave Girl* (1973); W. J. Cash, *The Mind of the South* (1941); Phyllis Fraley, *Atlanta Magazine* (October 1984); Jacquelyn Dowd Hall, *Revolt Against Chivalry: Jesse Daniel Ames and the Women's Campaign Against Lynching* (1979); Anne Goodwyn Jones, *Tomorrow Is Another Day: The Woman Writer in the South, 1859–1936* (1981); Suzanne Lebsock, *The Free Women of Petersburg* (1983); Michael O'Brien, *All Clever Men Who Make Their Way* (1982); John C. Ruoff, "Southern Womanhood, 1865–1920: An Intellectual and Cultural Study" (Ph.D. dissertation, University of Illinois, 1976); Anne Firor Scott, *The Southern Lady: From Pedestal to Politics, 1830–1930* (1970); Kathryn L. Seidel, *The Southern Belle in the American Novel* (1986); William R. Taylor, *Cavalier and Yankee: The Old South and American National Character* (1961); Bertram Wyatt-Brown, *Southern Honor: Ethics and Behavior in the Old South* (1982). ☆

Blues-singing Women

In his classic collection of essays, *The Souls of Black Folk* (1903), W. E. B. Du Bois, a northern, black intellectual, expressed the meaning of "sorrow songs" to black people: "They that walked in darkness sang songs in the olden days—sorrow songs—for they were weary at heart. They came out of the South unknown to me, and yet I knew them as of me and mine." In the sorrow songs Du Bois heard "the voices of the past," preserved from generation to generation through oral tradition.

The origins of the blues are in the sorrow songs of the slaves. Both musical forms describe the daily experience of human oppression, while also maintaining a breath of hope that someday, somewhere, human beings will be judged by their souls, their minds, and their acts, rather than their racial background. At the same time, the blues express personal themes and dilemmas that are practically universal. Women who sing the blues sing primarily about love, infidelity, sex, and passion, as they occur in everyday situations and as they are altered by death, liquor, superstition, migration, natural disasters, and loneliness.

Unlike the sorrow songs, which portray the shared oppression of the slave community, the blues portray idiosyncratic and specific experiences in the lives of individuals. This thematic change reflects the social history of southern blacks. In antebellum times slaves sang of their despair, hope, and protest primarily in their work songs and spirituals. After emancipation, black sharecroppers who worked small plots of land sang about the trials and hardships of their individual lives. Early blues developed in the late 19th-century South, as a form of leisure entertainment, a way of communication, and a form of autobiography. In the early blues or "country blues," an individual lament combined with an affirmation of self, representing the black experience in general through an individual life.

By the turn of the century the rural blues were familiar to southerners, black and white, but until a number of black women recorded the "classic blues" during the 1920s most Ameri-

cans were unfamiliar with the music. The most successful classic blues singers were southern black women, and their themes are written predominantly from a woman's point of view. In their study *Negro Workaday Songs* (1926), Howard W. Odum and Guy B. Johnson noted that "among the blues singers who have gained more or less national recognition, there is scarcely a man's name to be found." Among the more famous women who recorded classic blues are Ma Hunter, Bertha "Chippie" Hill, and Memphis Minnie. Lesser known recording artists include Sara Martin, Lizzie Miles, Trixie Smith, Ada Brown, Eliza Brown, Cleo Gibson, Edmonia and Catherine Henderson, Mary Mack, Ann Cook, Mary Johnson, Lottie Beamon, Lucille Bogan, Georgia White, and Lillian Glinn. These blues-singing women were extremely popular during the 1920s and early 1930s, until the Depression ended the era of classic blues. Born in the late 19th century or the early 20th, a majority of them enjoyed a decade of success and afterward were sadly forgotten. They died poor and unrecognized.

According to historian Bill C. Malone, Americans were gradually introduced to the blues between 1914 and 1920, a period when numerous southern blacks were migrating to the North. Many blues lyrics are a direct response to northern urban life, and blues women who moved to the North were also likely to alter the instrumental style of their music. The blues were not recorded until Mamie Smith (a northern cabaret singer who was probably the first black singer to record a solo performance) sang "Crazy Blues" for Okeh Records in 1920. The record sold well, demonstrating that there was a market for blues music, particularly among black listeners. Following this, Lucille Hegamin ("The Georgia Peach"), Rosa Henderson, and Edith Wilson recorded smooth, refined, professionalized versions of the blues (including "St. Louis Blues" and "He May Be Your Man, But He Comes to See Me Sometimes") in a style influenced by both vaudeville and ragtime.

Ma Rainey and Bessie Smith are primarily responsible for recording and popularizing more authentic southern blues, and for inspiring the numerous southern women who recorded "classic blues" during the 1920s. Rainey, often called "Mother of the Blues," provided the link between country and classic blues. Like traditional male blues artists, she spent most of her career on the road, attracting large audiences across the South and, less frequently, among southerners who had migrated to the North, particularly in Chicago. According to author and music critic Le Roi Jones (Amiri Baraka), "Ma Rainey's singing can be placed squarely between the harsher, more spontaneous country styles and the smoother, theatrical styles of later blues singers." Born and raised in Columbus, Ga., she retained a rapport with southern audiences. Accompanied by a traditional jug band, she sang country blues including "Counting the Blues," "Jelly Bean Blues," "See See Rider," "Corn Field Blues," "Moonshine Blues," and "Bo-Weevil Blues."

The influence of Ma Rainey upon Bessie Smith is well documented. Often called "Empress of the Blues" or "Queen of the Blues," Smith is probably the best of the recorded classic blues singers. Her life story has become a legend. Born in Chattanooga, Tenn., in 1898 to a large, poor family, Smith enjoyed a decade of success and affluence beginning in 1923. At first, she recorded a number of songs previously sung by others, including "Gulf Coast Blues," "Aggravatin' Papa," and "T'Aint Nobody's Business If I Do." During her career, she recorded over 180 songs, among them "Mama's Got the Blues," "Lady Luck Blues," "See If I'll Care," "Kitchen Man," "Black Mountain Blues," "Nobody Knows You When You're Down and Out," "Nashville Woman Blues," "I Ain't Gonna Play No Second Fiddle," and "Safety Mama." Backed by professional jazz musicians, Smith enjoyed brief success performing for northern urban audiences, yet she was most popular among southerners, black and white. Like other classic blues artists, her success ended during the Depression. She died a tragic and unnecessary death in an automobile accident in 1937.

Although numerous southern women sang and recorded the blues during the 1920s, few are remembered today. A small number continued to record during the 1940s and 1950s, but blues-singing women were never again as popular as they had been during the classic era. A contemporary blues style is exhibited in the recordings of Big Mama Thornton. Backed by electric guitar, she projects a strong, vibrant voice in a style influenced by rock and roll and rhythm and blues. Born and raised in Alabama, Thornton recorded during the early 1950s and 1960s, appealing to audiences in both the United States and Europe. At the same time, countless women who had once sung and performed the traditional or classic blues remained unrecognized. For example, Mary McClain Smith, who is Bessie Smith's half sister and who sings in the classic blues style, was known as "Diamond Teeth Mary" in her heyday. She had performed mostly on the road, traveling by train or bus, spending her money as soon as she earned it. After a career spanning 32 years, performing with Nat King Cole, Duke Ellington, Billie Holiday, and Fats Waller, among others, she retired poor and was never recorded. She lived in obscurity, depending upon social security alone for income, until recently, when she was rediscovered by the Florida Folklife Center.

Whether or not they were recorded, blues-singing women have greatly influenced southern and American music. In the South, blues and white folk music have influenced and enriched one another. Blues themes about love, infidelity, sex, and passion frequently appear in the lyrics of female country stars such as Loretta Lynn, Dolly Parton, and Tammy Wynette, as well as lesser known country artists Alice Garrard and Hazel Dickens. In addition to influencing country lyrics, women who sang classic blues have affected the lyrics and recording styles of rock singers Janis Joplin and Bonnie Raitt. Blues-singing women are also a major influence upon jazz, particularly represented in the delicate voice and music of Billie Holiday. Her recording of "Strange Fruit," for example, clearly illustrates her kinship to the classic blues. By describing the brutality of a lynching, this haunting tune protests the inhumanity of a racist society, as did the sorrow songs of the slaves. An idiosyncratic response to an isolated event becomes representative of the black experience in general.

See also BLACK LIFE: Music, Black; MUSIC: Blues; / Smith, Bessie

Ruth A. Banes
University of South Florida

Chris Albertson, *Bessie* (1972), liner notes for *Bessie Smith: The World's Greatest Blues Singer*, Columbia Records (GP-33, CV 1040); *Blues Classics by Memphis Minnie*, Blues Classics 1, Arhoolie Records (BC-1); W. E. B. Du Bois, *The Souls of Black Folk* (1903); Peter B. Gallager, St. Petersburg *Times* (6 August 1982); Alberta Hunter, *Amtrak Blues*, Columbia Records (JC-36430); Le Roi Jones, *Blues People* (1963); *Memphis Minnie, vol. 2, Early Recordings with "Kansas Joe" McCoy*, Blues Classics 13, Arhoolie Records (BC-13); Bill C. Malone, *Southern Music/American Music* (1979); Paul Oliver, *Bessie Smith* (1971), *The Story of the Blues* (1969); Harry Oster, *Living Country Blues* (1969); Tony Russell, *Blacks, Whites, and Blues* (1970); *Sippie: Sippie Wallace with Jim Dapogny's Chicago Blues Band*, Arhoolie Records (F-1032); *Bessie Smith: The World's Greatest Blues Singer*, Columbia Records (GP-33, CV-1040); Derrick-Stewart Baxter, *Ma Rainey and the Classic Blues Singers* (1970); Chris Strachwitz, liner notes for *Big Mama Thornton in Europe*, Arhoolie Records (F-1028), liner notes for *When Women Sang the Blues*, Blues Classics 26, Arhoolie Records (BC-26); *Big Mama Thornton in Europe*, Arhoolie Records (F-1028); *Big Mama Thornton, vol. 2, With the Chicago Blues Band*, Arhoolie Records (F-1032); *When Women Sang the Blues*, Blues Classics 26, Arhoolie Records (BC-26). ☆

Child-raising Customs

||||||||||||||||||||||||||||||||||||||||||||||||||||||

Like other aspects of southern culture, child-raising customs have been distinctly shaped by rural ways of life and by the conditions of a biracial society. These customs have guided parents in rearing their offspring from infancy to preadolescence, and include habits of nurturing, methods of discipline, values regarding work and play, and means of incorporating a child into the family.

Evidence of these customs is sketchy before the mid-18th century when parents, increasingly literate and intent on leavening folkways with new, Lockeian notions of the importance of early childhood, began to record their methods and expectations. Southern parents in general did not subscribe to the ideas of a child's propensity for evil and ruination that were common in the North. In a century of high infant mortality a healthy child was a boon if not a rarity. Newborns were kept warm, dressed in loosely fitting smocks, and affectionately handled. The vast majority of southern women nursed their own children. But among the elite, breast-feeding was seen as possibly harmful to the mother, and women who could afford to do so made use of wet nurses immediately. It appears that mothers typically were anxious during weaning (usually at 12 to 18 months) and teething periods.

The relatively secular, practical attitude of southern parents also guided them in matters of discipline and work. Women had primary responsibility for child care, but fathers were not uninvolved in bestowing affection and dispensing punishment. At the age of six or seven, boys began to be dressed in long pants rather than the shift worn by both sexes, and parents typically encouraged male children to explore the outdoors, to learn early to ride and hunt, or, in poorer families, to trap and fish. Girls were kept closer to home, but parents clearly valued high-spirited, even boisterous, children of both sexes. Observers agree that southern children were undisciplined and unsupervised compared to children in the North, and evidence suggests that the absence of any systematic attempt to "break the will" of children in the name of duty to God or parents was distinctly southern.

Even though physical punishment was used freely, parents also enjoyed their children with equal vigor, having them perform for visitors by singing, reciting, or shooting. In wealthier families this time of free-ranging play lasted until about age 10, when boys began to learn male duties from their fathers and girls took up female chores and skills such as cooking and embroidery. In poorer homes, white and black, work began as soon as children were able to contribute to the sustenance of the family.

As with discipline, a youngster's sense of belonging to a family was comparatively free from elaborate religious values and heavy emphasis on individual conscience. Southern children were raised into their niche by associating duty and deference with kin. By the late 18th century, with longer life spans permitting contact between three generations, southern children were routinely reared by aunts and grandparents and thus taught that the social world, dispersed by rural distances, was inseparable from the world of family.

These basic patterns of child rearing persisted into the 19th century, although some important shifts occurred. In general, the nurturing of infants among whites kept to established customs, except that elite women were more inclined to breast-feed their own infants, at least in the first few weeks after birth. Afterwards, slave women were used as nurses. Elite mothers also became somewhat more reliant on advice books and physicians. Two significant changes did occur in child-rearing beliefs. First, parents began to attribute a special domain to childhood in which offspring were romanticized as pure and even exemplary. The "little strangers" at birth became in three or four years little angels whose tender natures needed constant tending by all-loving mothers. Second, children were reared into gender differences earlier and more deliberately after the 1820s. Fathers took over the discipline of both sexes until age six or seven, after which time they placed particular emphasis on removing their sons from the maternal world. Especially in the planter class, boys were somewhat separated from girls by the age of 10 and taught to behave in an honorable, "manly" way, while girls had to cast off tomboy ways and assume a mildness of temper deemed feminine.

Children's autonomy was further tempered by teaching them of their forefathers and the importance of family reputation and blood ties. Reprimand or approval was applied in the name of ancestors and continuing family tradition, and the significance of such was supported by unique patterns of cousin intermarriage and preservation of family lore. As sectional differences heightened by the 1850s, the children of slaveowners grew more anxious about the "racial purity" of their ancestry, and tensions grew between the slaveowners and their so-called black family of slaves.

Black children under slavery also were raised with a sense of belonging to two families. More than romantic rhetoric, this contrast between the black family in the quarters and a distant but powerful white paternalism accounted for distinct customs in black child rearing. Although most slave children lived in nuclear families, the constant work demanded of parents kept them apart from offspring who were looked after collectively by women too old for planting and chopping. Older children often took care of those immediately younger, and thus were the dispensers of discipline

and values long before they became parents themselves. A child's life under slavery, although perhaps initially as carefree as a white child's, changed sharply about age 10, when boys were put into long pants and both sexes were put to adult work. Black parents, looking toward this trying time, raised their children to be circumspect about life in the quarters and attentive to the strengths of religion. A child was taught that white playmates became masters and that parents, powerful in the quarters, might themselves be punished as children.

The Civil War, the end of slavery, and the penetration of industrial modernity altered child-raising customs but did not completely transform their powerful tradition. Hospital births, improved nutrition, and standardized medical advice by the 1890s began to characterize infant care for families who could afford them. In these families, children were disciplined with less use of corporal punishment. They were less often idealized as angels and seen more as young individuals who would become productive adults. Wealthier white children saw somewhat less of poor black children, and the advent of public education even in many rural areas placed important tasks of child raising under agencies with general standards for self-expression, discipline, reward, and the sense of gender differences.

Many continuities with the past remained, however. Black nurses were much employed in the raising of upper-class white children, and vestiges of white paternalistic "family feeling" persisted. Rural life and its rhythms still informed childhood. Elite children were reared to appreciate the land as the only source of virtue and well-being in the face of urbanization. Well into the 20th century the sense of family membership and ancestry remained a strong factor in the upbringing of these children and was made even sharper by frequent parental emphasis on Old South lore and the cataclysm of war.

For poor, especially black, children childhood remained a time of rural adventure soon encroached upon by work in the fields and work in the homes of whites. Manifold kin connections spread the rearing of children in segregated black communities where an abstract sense of the South was overshadowed by the immediacies of work and racial identity. Here mothers were the dominant child raisers in all aspects of discipline and family continuity, and the church, rather than formal schooling, was for many children the chief force in learning social values and spiritual aspiration. The local church, too, provided such institutional help as day care and food distribution in both ordinary and hard times.

See also BLACK LIFE: Family, Black; FOLK-LIFE: Family Folklore; SOCIAL CLASS: Poverty

Steven M. Stowe
New York University

Dottie Abbott, ed., *Mississippi Writers: Reflections of Childhood and Youth*, 2 vols. (1985–86); James Agee and Walker Evans, *Let Us Now Praise Famous Men* (1941); Eugene D. Genovese, *Roll, Jordan, Roll: The World the Slaves Made* (1976); Chris Mayfield, ed., *Growing Up Southern: Southern Exposure Looks at Childhood, Then and Now* (1981); Anne Moody, *Coming of Age in Mississippi* (1968); William A. Percy, *Lanterns on the Levee* (1941); Daniel Blake Smith, *Inside the Great House: Planter Family Life in Eighteenth-Century Chesapeake Society* (1980); Steven M. Stowe, *Intimacy and*

Power in the Old South: Ritual in the Lives of the Planters (1987); Bertram Wyatt-Brown, *Southern Honor: Ethics and Behavior in the Old South* (1982). ☆

Children's Games

||||||||||||||||||||||||||||||||||||||||||||||||

Children's play was rarely mentioned by observers of the Old South. Sources that do exist suggest that southern children had active play lives and that games occupied a major portion of their time. Assumptions about social roles, human nature, and conduct were expressed in their play. Many old and popular southern games are remnants of significant events in history and common cultural traditions of the region.

Literature on white middle-class children's games may be found in novels, diaries, and artistic prints. Eighteenth-century prints show a number of games, and below each picture is a statement of the moral lesson the game teaches, reflecting the dominant cultural values. Informal ball games included stoolball, cricket, fives, tip-cat, and baseball. Hop-scotch, leap-frog, and hide-and-seek, all common to American children today, and imitative games such as playing house are also identified in the prints. Board games included chess, foxand-geese, and checks, which is similar to checkers.

L. Minor Blackford, in *Mine Eyes Have Seen the Glory*, recorded typical games of the Blackford children of Virginia in the mid-1850s. Examples included Anthony over, hickeme dickeme, blindman's buff, prisoner's base, pull-over-the-bat, kite flying, bull-in-the-pen, cutting jacks, stilt walking, knock, and catch out. The boys often played soldier, perhaps resulting from their awareness of the Mexican War. Additional outdoor play included snowballing, hunting, gymnastics, wrestling, swimming, and skating.

The relationship of play to Old South values was often clear as in the case of representational play or playacting, in which children created small, real-life dramas or imitated everyday life. The dramatic elements of this play, such as in "playing" soldier, were analogous to social roles in antebellum society. Among the more affluent families of the Old South, games emphasized effort and skill, teaching children that outcomes of situations depended on the amount and quality of effort one expended.

Many historical and contemporary games of black children, on the other hand, are most notable for exhibiting an attitude of resistance and assertiveness on the part of the players. Older game songs that date from the days of slavery express an anger against slave masters. The following example of an old game song demonstrates resistance:

Way go, Lily
Way go, Lily
I'm going to rule my ruler

Children's Games, *a painting by southern primitive painter Theora Hamblett, 1972*

I'm going to rule my ruler
I'm going to rule him with a hickory
I'm going to rule him with a hickory

This song probably originated during slavery and is rarely heard now except in Charleston and Savannah. Blacks have used creative song games in "talking bad" to their oppressors since coming from Africa, allowing them to say what they needed to say without being perceived as a threat.

Another common Afro-American children's game song, played by forming a ring, is "Little Sally Walker." One of a cycle of ring games with African roots, its lyrics encourage a child to "rise":

Little Sally Walker
Sitting in a saucer
Crying and a-weeping
Over all she has done

Rise Sally Rise
Wipe out your eyes
Fly to the east, Sally . . .

Contemporary games of black children show an inherited oral tradition and simultaneously engage in nonverbal behavior that involves body movement and gestures similar to playacting. Clapping games are popular and are primarily nonverbal. Most of the games are rhythmical and allow for improvisation.

Older game songs common along the Georgia and South Carolina coasts have been recorded by Bessie Jones and Bess Lomax Hawes in *Step It Down.* Jones is a black woman born in an area famed for its rich Gullah culture. The book reflects her efforts to preserve remnants of southern tradition and the African heritage. Many of these older game songs may still be heard in black communities and are often taught within organized play times in an effort to preserve cultural traditions. The renewed interest in the preservation of the multiethnic origins of America has stimulated educators to consider traditional games as an instrument for teaching about cultural uniqueness and historical events.

There is limited documentation of games indigenous to the South in the 20th century, and it is likely that southern children's play has become very much like that of other children in the United States. Changes in game preferences of American children were examined by Sutton-Smith and Rosenberg (1961), who compared four studies on games over a 60-year period from 1896 to 1959. They found that formalized games, such as party games, ring games, acting games, singing games, and dialogue games were becoming less important while imitative games and chasing games continued their popularity. This shift away from formalized games is especially significant in relation to the South, where games have been traditionally more decorous and formal than elsewhere in the country.

The uniquely southern aspects of children's games that remain represent traces of ethnic diversity within the dominant American culture and are most likely found within the poorer regions as well as among the larger minority groups. Awakened desire to cultivate multicultural heritage is acting as a stimulus to preserve some traditionally southern children's games as a unique folk art.

See also BLACK LIFE: African Influences; Slave Culture

> Rachel D. Robertson
> Arizona State University

L. Minor Blackford, *Mine Eyes Have Seen the Glory* (1954); Ruth F. Bogdanoff and Elaine T. Dolch, *Young Children* (January 1979); Dickson D. Bruce, Jr., *Southern Folklore Quarterly* (1977); Jane Carson, *Colonial Virginians at Play* (1965); Bessie Jones and Bess Lomax Hawes, *Step it Down: Games, Plays, Songs, and Stories from the Afro-American Heritage* (1972); B. Sutton-Smith and Bruce G. Rosenberg, *Journal of American Folklore* (January–March 1961). ☆

Clubs and Voluntary Organizations

||||||||||||||||||||||||||||||||||||||||||||||||||||||||

Somewhat slower than northern women to form clubs and associations, southern women did not participate in social and public affairs through organized groups until after the Civil War and Reconstruction. The loss of one-fourth of the region's males and the accompanying poverty of the late 19th century forced women into the work force and brought increased independence. Release from the burdens of directing large plantation households and supervising the physical care of slaves added to the leisure time of women of means at the same time that the wives of professional and middle-class townsmen also gained added freedom from domestic duties. Moreover, as public colleges stressing industrial and commercial curricula were founded, more southern daughters entered professional fields. Finally, the increasing urbanization of the South facilitated the organization of groups in which women could express their growing sense of social usefulness, self-reliance, and initiative.

Southern women first banded together to further the foreign and home mission work of their churches. Anne Firor Scott has concluded that "the public life of nearly every Southern woman leader for forty years began in a church society." Methodist women formed the Board of Home Missions in 1882, and Baptist women formed the Women's Missionary Union in 1888. The church "circle" was the most accessible and approved institution outside the home through which women were able both to initiate reform through city missions and settlement houses and also to lay the foundation for the interracial cooperation that would come in the 20th century. Concurrently, the Women's Christian Temperance Union (WCTU), organized in the South after Frances Willard visited the region in the 1880s, developed under state leaders such as Caroline Merrick in Louisiana, Belle Kearney in Mississippi, Julia Tutwiler in Alabama, and Rebecca Felton in Georgia. The puritannical foundations of the temperance movement provided a base for allied work of the WCTU in its crusade for the abolition of the convict-lease system, the establishment of industrial schools for girls and homes for youthful offenders, and other reforms.

In the late 1880s and 1890s southern women were drawn into the club movement. Between 1894 and 1907 federations of various cultural and self-improvement groups were formed in every southern state and by 1910 all were members of the General Federation of Women's Clubs (GFWC). Although the initial goal was self-edification, the federated clubs became, in the words of Mrs. Percy Pennybacker, a Texas matron who headed the national GFWC in 1913–14, a "recruiting station in which the unaccustomed women shall be trained to find themselves . . . and [assume] widening responsibilities in the world's work." As a major tool of social change in the South, women's clubs promoted statewide library and adult education programs, guardianship laws for divorced women, marital blood tests, sanitary milk supplies, child labor laws, protective legislation for women, and myriad other reforms. In their "alternative universities" clubwomen kept abreast of current events, mobilized public opinion, and, most importantly, promoted the woman suffrage movement. In the 1920s and 1930s club representatives formed Joint Legislative Councils in most southern states to lobby their club agendas at the statehouse.

Excluded from the GFWC, black women formed their own Southern Association of Colored Women's Clubs after Margaret Murray Washington began the Tuskegee Woman's Club in 1895. Unlike white women, black clubwomen were especially concerned with issues of importance to poor women, working mothers, and tenant wives. Their work was best represented by the community betterment and social service programs of the Atlanta Neighborhood Union initiated by Lugenia Burns Hope in 1908. Also important to southern black women were the mutual aid societies created to provide medical care and burial assistance. Some persisted well into the 20th century.

From the time in 1851 when Ann Pamela Cunningham of South Carolina began the first woman's patriotic society in the United States, the Mount Vernon Ladies' Association, southern white women have responded to organizations commemorating the past. The unique history of the South fostered a high level of interest in genealogy and an attraction to the Colonial Dames of America, the Daughters of the American Revolution

(DAR) (its first southern chapter was founded in North Carolina in 1898), and especially the United Daughters of the Confederacy (UDC), founded by Nashville women in 1894 from numerous existing cemetery memorial societies and soldier relief associations. The UDC, like the DAR, was socially glamorous, perpetuating social hierarchies as it strove to glorify the southern war effort, particularly through the creation of libraries on the Confederate past. In recent years, as it has declined in membership, the UDC has shifted its focus to historical preservation.

Reflecting their natural gregariousness and their quest for the "bonds of sisterhood," southern college women founded in the post–Civil War years a number of Greek-letter sororities. Such collegiate groups and related literary societies have remained popular in southern universities. Many women have "graduated" to high-society organizations that flourish in southern towns and cities, best represented by the Junior League and other benefit groups, whose principal functions are to raise funds for community arts and social services. For other women, principally those in small towns, social activities center around the meeting hall of the Order of Eastern Star and other auxiliaries to male fraternal orders.

Academic and professional women in the South created associations patterned after northern organizations. In 1903 the Southern Association of College Women (SACW) was formed in Knoxville and under the strong direction of Elizabeth Avery Colton devoted its energies to raising the standards of institutions of higher education for the region's young women. In 1921 SACW merged with the American Association of University Women. Delta Kappa Gamma, founded in 1929 by Annie Webb Blanton and a charter group of Texas teachers, grew beyond its early southern chapters into an international society for women educators. Altrusa International, begun in Nashville in 1917 as a service club for business and professional women, is one of many such groups that serve to coordinate the leadership and community service of women professionals. Another is Pilot International, founded in 1919 by a Kentuckian, Lena Madesin Phillips.

Rural women in the South, both black and white, are still active in home demonstration clubs organized before World War I by the extension departments of land-grant colleges. They are unique among women's organizations in that from the outset they have had professional leadership salaried through federal and state funds. Organized rural women have devoted their attention almost exclusively to home improvement and rural community development, often working with the American Farm Bureau to stress citizenship, safety, and home and community beautification. Urban women, too, through ubiquitous garden clubs promote memorial plantings, highway beautification, pilgrimages, and the restoration of historic homes and buildings.

Both the economic straits of southern state governments and the general political conservatism of the region's electorate have led women to form associations to institute social change. One of the earliest was the New Orleans Anti-Tuberculosis League formed by Kate Gordon in 1906. Early 20th-century women created societies for village improvement, modern roads, public schoolhouse improvement, and child labor abolition. Reflecting southern emphasis upon maternal responsibilities, the National Congress of Mothers (later the PTA) was founded by a Georgia woman, Alice M. Birney, in 1897, and the National Congress of Colored Parents and Teachers was begun in Atlanta by Selena Sloan Butler in 1926. In 1930 Jessie Daniel Ames of Texas formed the Association of Southern Women for the Prevention of Lynching (ASWPL), which eventually united 40,000 churchwomen to confront the issues of race, lynching, and interracial sex before it met its goals and ceased to exist. The ASWPL is the most distinctive women's voluntary association in southern history.

With the enfranchisement of women in 1920, the eligibility of women to hold public office, and the increasing access of southern women to professions once the exclusive enclave of men, the club and voluntary association work of southern women has declined. Many women have turned from volunteer work to paid jobs. Moreover, women have had less need to pursue education through cultural and literary organizations. As other agencies have arisen to meet society's needs, the federated clubs and reformist associations are no longer major agents for social change. Nonetheless, there is scarcely any southern town or city where women of both races do not still join together in numerous social, professional, and civic organizations.

See also AGRICULTURE: / Agricultural Extension Services; BLACK LIFE: Fraternal Orders, Black; EDUCATION: Fraternities and Sororities; HISTORY AND MANNERS: Historical Preservation; / United Daughters of the Confederacy; Pilgrimage; POLITICS: / Felton, Rebecca; RELIGION: Missionary Activities; SCIENCE AND MEDICINE: Health, Public

Martha H. Swain
Texas Woman's University

Sharon Harley and Rosalyn Terborg-Penn, eds., *The Afro-American Woman: Struggles and Images* (1978); Gerda Lerner, *Journal of Negro History* (April 1974); John Patrick McDowell, *The Social Gospel in the South: The Woman's Home Mission Movement in the Methodist Episcopal Church, South, 1886–1939* (1982); Margaret Nell Price, "The Development of Leadership by Southern Women Through Clubs and Organizations" (M.A. thesis, University of North Carolina, Chapel Hill, 1945); Anne Firor Scott, *The Southern Lady: From Pedestal to Politics, 1830–1930* (1970). ☆

Education of Women

Until recently, the chivalric image of the southern lady supported the hierarchy of race, class, and sex that defined the region's socioeconomic structures. The education of southern white women could proceed only if it did not tamper with that ideal. Translated into social consequences, chivalry blighted educational opportunities for southern white women. From the revolutionary era until recent decades, the South consistently lagged behind other regions of the country in implementing educational reforms for its female population. On the eve of the Civil War, despite the widespread popularity of female academies, the rate of illiteracy among adult white women was highest in the South. Not until World War II did regional differences in female education begin to narrow.

For the majority of southern black women formal education did not begin until the Civil War destroyed the institution of slavery. Black females then took their place beside black males in the schools founded for the freed people by northern missionary societies, the

Freedmen's Bureau, and the newly visible black churches. Many of these private schools, specializing in primary instruction, were superseded by segregated public school systems at the end of Reconstruction. After 1877 black private schools increasingly emphasized either an industrial arts or a liberal arts curriculum. Ironically, in the arena of education, the interplay between racism and sexism resulted in what Gerda Lerner termed the "sex loophole in race discrimination": educational achievements did not readily translate into wider economic opportunities for black males but were profitable for black females. The path to upward social mobility for black families turned upon the higher education of their daughters. Educated black women became the mainstay of the teacher corps in the region's segregated public schools.

Throughout the colonial period the education of young white children was both a private family concern, largely the privilege of the middle and upper classes. Only in the large urban coastal settlements of the South did one find formal, private schools often called "adventure schools." Generally, southern mothers, like their northern counterparts, tended to the early education of their young sons and daughters. The upper classes employed tutors for their sons once formal instruction began in earnest. A few planters' daughters shared in the classical training made available to their brothers; for the most part, though, female education remained both superficial and ornamental, designed to make them more attractive in the marriage market. Thus, while sons of the upper classes learned Greek, Latin, ancient and modern history, mathematics, and the sciences, their sisters were instructed in the fine arts of conversational French, music, dancing, painting and drawing, fancy needlework, moral training, scripture reading, and the bare rudiments of writing and arithmetic.

Cultural attitudes toward women's education remained surprisingly uniform across the northern, middle, and southern colonies. Intellectual accomplishments were not appropriate for females. A woman's mental and physical capacities supposedly could not "endure" the rigors of a classical training. Higher education "taxed" a woman's brain, defeminizing her and thus rendering her unfit for her role as wife and mother.

In the aftermath of the American Revolution these beliefs increasingly came under attack by American intellectuals. Men such as Benjamin Rush argued that the success of the republican experiment in government depended upon a well-educated citizenry. Because women were responsible for supervising the education of their male as well as female offspring, it became necessary after the Revolution to upgrade women's education, shifting from "style to substance" and, of necessity, from the home to the female academy.

The academy or seminary movement caught fire in the northern and middle states first and then spread to the South. Some scholars contend that planters, their economy disrupted by the Revolution, first attended to economic recovery before investing in their daughters' education. The other interpretation favors a more cultural/ideological explanation: it stresses an emerging plantation culture firmly grounded in patriarchy. This view suggests that although southern elites came to embrace the female academy movement by the second decade of the 19th century, the education of southern women remained more limited than that of their northern and western counterparts. Southern academies remained committed to the ideal of "fitting women for their roles in the plantation culture: a well-read elite serving as wives and mothers to the master class." Although the education of southern white women remained heavily influenced by moral training and scripture reading, definite gains had been made in the quality of women's education. By the late antebellum period plantation daughters also received some of the educational training heretofore reserved for their brothers.

Female academies and seminaries served the interests of the middle and upper classes. Together, the costs of boarding and tuition made academy life a privilege of the well-to-do. During the antebellum period northern and western states moved to combat this inherent class bias by investing in state-supported primary, secondary, and normal schools. Once again, the South lagged behind. Although most southern states created paper systems of free primary schools for whites just before the Civil War, education scholars generally attribute the beginning of free state-supported public education for all southern children to the reforms initiated by Reconstruction governments.

Coeducation was the rule for white boys and girls at the primary level in urban areas. In the secondary institutions that gained popularity in post-Reconstruction southern cities the sexes remained segregated. Southern white girls eagerly availed themselves of public education, especially at the secondary level. Enrollment in female high schools generally surpassed that of male high schools. By World War I, however, high schools were an accepted part of the states' systems of instruction, and coeducation was the norm.

Women seeking education beyond the secondary level had two choices: matriculation at a normal school with its emphasis on teacher training, or enrollment at a women's college offering a liberal arts curriculum. Although the first women's college with degree-granting privileges was founded in Macon, Ga., in 1836, women's colleges came of age in post–Civil War America. Those colleges that existed prior to the war really provided only a seminary education. Northern and western states were first in establishing normal schools and women's colleges on a large scale. Slower to respond to demands for female higher education, six southern states reported no normal schools as late as 1872. White women's colleges were founded in the South during the last two decades of the 19th century: Sophie Newcomb (1887), Goucher (1888), Agnes Scott (1889), and Randolph-Macon (1893) led the way. Black women took advantage of either the private black colleges such as Fisk University or the few state-supported normal and industrial schools such as Florida Agricultural, Mechanical and Normal College.

Judging by entrance requirements, age of admission, standardization of curriculum, and library and laboratory facilities, women's colleges initially were below the standards set for men's colleges. Northern states made the first serious efforts to rectify that situation. The U.S. Commissioner of Education divided institutions of higher learning into A and B divisions those that offered the classic four-year liberal arts curriculum and those that did not. As late as 1907 between 68 and 75 percent of the women's colleges in division B were located in the South. On the eve of World War I only 6 of the 140 institutions in the South calling themselves women's colleges were regarded as such by the Southern Association of College Women.

The push for coeducation at the collegiate level paralleled the development of women's colleges in the South. Although Trinity College of Duke University accepted three sisters into the 1874 freshman class, coeducation first became policy at Duke in 1896. Almost as soon as women gained entrance to the men's colleges, a backlash occurred. Arguments advanced to discourage female admission to male institutes centered on the notion that women would lower the standards of men's colleges and thus drive away large numbers of male students and faculty. Yet beneath that nagging belief in female inferiority lay the unacknowledged fact that women were in actuality competing successfully with male students for the academic honors offered by the colleges.

The beginning of the 20th century saw the concept of the coordinate college advanced by male educators as a compromise between separate women's colleges and coeducation, although in the South the movement did not gain broad support until the period between the world wars. Under the coordinate college plan women would benefit from their association with men's colleges. The large endowments made to male institutes encouraged distinguished faculties and superior library and laboratory facilities. Women enjoyed these privileges under the coordinate college program, but at the same time they remained "protected" in their separate classes and social organizations.

The period between the two world wars also witnessed a steady increase in the matriculation of southern white women on college campuses. By the end of World War II regional differences in women's education at all levels had diminished sharply. During the 1970s and 1980s, due to the contemporary women's movement, women's higher education shifted again in favor of coeducation. Many of the coordinate colleges have merged with their male institutions, while many separate women's colleges have opened their doors to men or become part of the expanding state college and university systems.

In the study of women's education the focus has been on regions other than the South. To date, no systematic work on southern women's education exists. Scattered evidence suggests that education is a double-edged sword in the hands of southern women, white and black. Black women teachers in the late 19th and early 20th centuries founded schools and colleges that provided an alternative to the inferior segregated schools of the region. Those black institutions contributed vital social ser-

Teacher at Bethune-Cookman College, Daytona Beach, Florida, 1940s

vices to the local black community. And, as scholars are discovering, the schools often became centers for organized community efforts to promote social change. There is also the recent example of the participation of young southern white college women in the civil rights movement and later in the feminist movement. Young white women from women's colleges first supported black students who challenged segregation and race discrimination. The events of the early 1960s carried those women forward to question the very bedrock of southern society—the patriarchial, racist, and class-based assumptions implicit in the ideal of southern womanhood.

See also BLACK LIFE: Education, Black; Freedom Movement, Black; EDUCATION articles

Kathleen C. Berkeley
University of North Carolina
at Wilmington

Isabella Margaret Elizabeth Blandin, *History of Higher Education of Women in the South Prior to 1860* (1909); Dianne Puthoff Brandstadter, "Developing the Coordinate College for Women at Duke University: The Career of Alice Mary Baldwin, 1924–1947" (Ph.D. dissertation, Duke University, 1977); Catherine Clinton, *The Plantation Mistress: Woman's World in the Old South* (1982); Florence Davis, "The Education of Southern Girls from 1750–1860" (Ph.D. dissertation, University of Chicago, 1952); Sara Evans, *Personal Politics: The Roots of Women's Liberation in the Civil Rights Movement and the New Left* (1979); Gerda Lerner, *The Majority Finds Its Past: Placing Women in History* (1979); Mary Beth Norton, *Liberty's Daughters: The Revolutionary Experience of American Women* (1980); Thomas Woody, *A History of Women's Education in the United States*, 2 vols. (1929). ☆

Elderly
||||||||||||||||||||

In recent years the South has become a haven for elderly Americans. According to the U.S. census, by 1970 the region led the nation in the number of residents over age 65, and more than 6 million aged individuals lived below the Mason-Dixon line. As of 1980 the median age of Floridians, 34.7 years, was the highest in the nation; and Florida's proportion of residents aged 65 or older, 34.7 percent, was higher than any other state's.

The growing elderly population in the South is a modern development. Traditionally, both the Northeast and North Central states have had far larger concentrations of elderly persons. In the 19th century, in fact, the South was noted for its young population. Two factors explained this historic condition. First, in contrast to other regions, the South experienced extremely high mortality rates, even among its adult members. One was far more likely to grow old in the North than in the South. Second, many of the southern states were relatively "new" and rural. They attracted the young and mobile, leaving the old to die in the cities of the East Coast.

The South of the 19th century, therefore, provided little in the way of special services for its aged population. Unlike the North, there were relatively few old-age homes or other provisions for those over 65. The status of the old in southern society remained tied—as it traditionally had been in America—to the ownership of property and control of kin.

In the last two decades much of this has changed. Nationwide, demographic trends associated with birthrates, infant mortality, and longevity have led to a higher proportion than ever before of persons aged 65 and over in the population—approximately 11 percent in 1980. Migration of the elderly to the Sunbelt has transformed both the nature of southern old age and the communities in which they live. Although an overwhelming proportion (24.7 percent) of all migrants head for Florida, every southern state has been affected by their numbers. According to census data, the southern states with the highest proportion of elderly residents in 1980 were Florida (17.3 percent), Arkansas (13.6 percent), and West Virginia (12.2 percent). The states with the lowest proportion included Georgia (9.4 percent), South Carolina (9.2 percent), and Virginia (7.5 percent). In Florida a striking 87 percent of the residents aged 65 or over lived in urban areas, as did 26 percent of the elderly in Texas. In most other southern states, however, only a slightly higher percentage were urban rather than rural residents; and in Mississippi, West Virginia, and North Carolina, the majority of the elderly lived in rural areas.

On the whole, these elderly individuals are better educated and wealthier than the natives; yet they come to the region without the traditional status granted by land, occupation, and family. As a result, for the first time the region is developing social services to meet the needs of elderly persons. In places like the peninsula of Florida, the Ozark Mountains, and the Texas hill country the effect is undeniable. In new communities, older cities, and even rural areas, southern culture is being transformed by the politics, recreational demands, and medical and housing needs of their older citizens. Clearly, the growth in attention to the elderly's

needs will continue. The future of the South will be one in which the elderly will play an ever larger and more significant role.

Respect for the elderly has long been a southern value, communicated through folklore, literature, and song. "When an old man dies, a library burns," is an old folk saying suggesting the value of the elderly in a rural, peasant, oral culture. Historian C. Vann Woodward has pointed out that while a Hemingway character with a grandfather is "inconceivable," a Faulkner hero without one is also. Welty, Warren, O'Connor, McCullers, and other leading regional writers have filled their stories with old people. Southern whites are respectful, yet the elderly are also portrayed, at times, as a burden, symbols of a noble past that has not been equaled in later times. Faulkner's heroes, for example, are sometimes haunted by their grandparents, as is Gail Hightower in *Light in August*, who confuses his own identity with that of his heroic Confederate ancestor. The image of the snuff-dipping, corncob-puffing granny in the Appalachian and rural white South is also not always favorable, but even this figure is a feisty creature, admirable in tough times.

Elderly blacks have been frequently

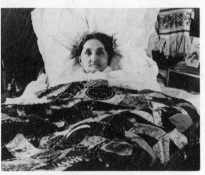

Georgia woman and her patchwork "crazy quilt," 1890s

portrayed, by whites as well as blacks, as repositories of wisdom. From Uncle Tom in Harriet Beecher Stowe's 19th-century novel, to Uncle Remus, to Faulkner's Dilsey in the *Sound and the Fury*, to Ernest J. Gaines's Miss Jane Pittman, elderly Afro-Americans have generally been seen as patient, experienced, sober, warm, and perhaps above all, spiritual, as though profiting from their suffering. In contemporary times they are also seen as assertive, willing to speak up eloquently against injustice.

The elderly have been valued in the regional folk culture as a source of specific knowledge and skills and as the embodiment of southern tradition, which had to be orally passed on to survive. Howard W. Odum, in *The Way of the South* (1947), saw grandparents as a key force in inculcating family and regional traditions. "You tell me that I must forget," says one imaginary grandmother to her grandchildren. "But I say unto you, you must remember."

See also FOLKLIFE: Family Folklore; GE-OGRAPHY: Population

Carole Haber
University of North Carolina
at Charlotte

Forrest J. Berghorn, Donna E. Shafer et al., *Dynamics of Aging: Original Essays on the Process and Experience of Growing Old* (1980); Charles F. Longino and Jeanne C. Biggar, *The Gerontologist* (June 1981); Daniel Scott Smith, Mark Friedberger, and Michel Dahlin, *Sociology and Social Research* (April 1979); U.S. Bureau of the Census, *Historical Statistics of the United States* (1975); U.S. Senate Special Committee on Aging, *America in Transition: An Aging Society*, 1984–85 ed. (1985). ☆

Family, Modernization of

Although industrialization in the North tended to erode the importance of the family in social life, throughout most of the 19th and well into the 20th century the South resisted those changes that tended to diminish the importance of kinship. In the South more than any other region, the family was at the center of social life, remaining the chief forum for socialization, education, and community.

Industrial development in the South was tied to agriculture. The traditional closeness of the southern agrarian family, its regional persistence, and the clearly defined roles of men and women inhibited economic change. Urbanization rubbed against the grain of deeply rooted agrarianism and conflicted with localist, communal values, a source of strength for so many southern families. A strong anticapitalist, antiindustrial ideology existed in the South, as portrayed in literature from the proslavery writers, Populists, and southern Agrarians (*I'll Take My Stand*) to William Faulkner. Much of this distrust grew out of the desire for personal freedom, but some was the consequence of the nature of the South's industry, which primarily benefitted investors from outside the region.

The nuclear family was the norm in the South long before industrialization. Relatives and boarders augmented this basic unit, especially among the affluent, but it nevertheless prevailed. Although the typical farm family in the South was large and primarily an economic unit, during the 19th century the family increasingly became an emotional and spiritual refuge as well. Per-

Mother, family, and servant in a stitchery by Ethel Mohamed, Belzoni, Mississippi, photographed in 1978

haps the first American family type to be dominated by the emotional intensity associated with modern-day families was that of the wealthy planter. In many plantation families, children were their parents' chief source of pride and satisfaction. In these families, childhood was a time to play, to learn formally from a tutor or private school teacher, and a time to discover one's surroundings.

The offspring of poorer rural families enjoyed fewer of these luxuries and received less concentrated attention from their parents, who had little leisure time. Hardships of making a living from modest farms constricted childhood. At young ages, children were expected to take a hand in the running of the farm; the family members always worked together. But because of the seasonal rhythms of farm life—the rainy days when one could not work in the fields, Sundays, and holidays—the family had playtime together. Thus, close bonds developed, and members of the poorest families demonstrated strong feelings of affection for one another. Children have long been prized among all black and white rural southerners and still today more attention is given to them than in other areas. Fewer children than elsewhere are in day-care arrangements, and more preschoolers are watched by

parents or nearby relations, partly for economic reasons and partly for cultural ones.

Historians and sociologists see a standard pattern to industrialization's impact on the family. In the North, for example, as fathers increasingly left home for the workplace, a mother's chief role was to raise children, leading to a deeper attachment between mother and child. As the family became less producer oriented and more consumer oriented, family size decreased.

In the South these developments occurred very slowly, and southern families resisted some of the trends that seemed to characterize the North. Where allegiance to family, community, and patriarchy were strongest, the encroachments of modernization were least likely to be felt. Unlike antebellum New England, where the labors of the youthful Lowell girls were legendary, many southern fathers defied mill owners who sought to hire young women. They felt the work was unsuitable for southern ladies—whether rich or poor—and feared such employment would destroy the harmony of the family. The "Waltham" system, where dormitories and matrons assured the highest morals and guarded the working girls' reputations, failed in the South. When forced by poverty to send his daughters to the mills, the white father was too proud to allow them to leave the patriarchal nest, and, in addition, wanted to retain economic control of their labor. Contracts were made between the mill and the father for working children. Families continued to live together, and although the father may not have worked in the mill, he received the family wage.

In resisting the redistribution of family authority that accompanied industrialization in the North, the southern family also sought to maintain the sharp divisions between males and females that often characterized family responsibilities in the South. The man's role as the unchallenged patriarch, the strong, respected provider, was supported by key elements of southern culture. The woman's inner strength and purity, her social and spiritual superiority, and her political and economic inferiority were also seen as important components of the southern way of life, components to be preserved. This southern romanticism continued to hold sway throughout the 19th century and beyond, slowing down industrialization and urbanization.

When urbanization and industrialization finally developed in the South after World War II, the changes that occurred closely paralleled the transformations that had been occurring in the North for decades. The role of women changed, and Anne Firor Scott suggests that the movement of women into the world of gainful employment was born of necessity and of changing economic conditions. It is possible to argue that when the factories needed cheap labor, it became acceptable for women to work in mills; when businesses needed secretaries, when children needed teachers, whenever economic imperative existed, mores and social barriers gave way.

Once in the work force, women were more readily able to enter public life, though again this development was painfully slow. Correspondingly, the man became less of a patriarch and more of a partner. Post–World War II social and economic change in the South also lessened the importance of the family as an economic unit and a source of emotional satisfaction. Consequently,

divorce has become a reality among families, even in rural areas and small towns.

Industrialization also accelerated southern geographic mobility, which now more closely resembles patterns in the North. Southern families traditionally maintained a strong sense of place. They tended to remain in the same region over long periods of time, which meant that families in a southern community had more extensive kinship and social ties than those in the North. Furthermore, southern men and women tended to put a high premium on holding their families together. Offspring often remained within reach of the family circle throughout their adult lives, even attending the same church, and divorce among whites was much rarer in the South than in the North. Although most families did not want to move or split up for the sake of industrial jobs, and mobility was much lower than in other regions, many southerners, both black and white, sought employment and educational opportunities in the North during the early 20th century.

See also BLACK LIFE: Family, Black; FOLKLIFE: Family Folklore; INDUSTRY: Industrialization and Social Change; Industrialization, Resistance to

Orville Vernon Burton
University of Illinois

Carol K. Bleser, ed., *The Hammonds of Redcliffe* (1981); Orville Vernon Burton, *In My Father's House Are Many Mansions: Family and Community in Edgefield, South Carolina* (1985); James C. Cobb, *Industrialization and Southern Society, 1877–1984* (1985); Carl N. Degler, *At Odds: Women and the Family in America from the Revolution to the Present* (1980); Margaret J. Hagood, *Mothers of the South: Portraiture of the White*

Tenant Farm Women (1939); Daniel Blake Smith, *Inside the Great House: Planter Family Life in Eighteenth-Century Chesapeake Society* (1980). ☆

Family Dynasties
||||||||||||||||||||||||||||||||||||||||||||||||

When considering the ultimate expression of power in the American South, one thinks of the planter patriarch holding sway over a large plantation worked by gangs of slaves. With one hand the great planter marries off his children to other leading planters in order to augment his landed empire, and with the other hand he serves at the county court or the statehouse to reinforce his political power base.

This image is not without historical foundation, but it is largely the product of a tendency to generalize from a particular moment in the life of the South. For, indeed, there was a golden age of planters in the middle decades of the 18th century, a time when significant parts of the plantation South—especially the Chesapeake and the Carolina Low Country—were governed by a few landed families. These elite members of the southern gentry sat atop the power structure (from the county courts and parish vestries to the lower houses of assembly) setting the tone for virtually all phases of social, economic, and political life. The influence of this elite group of planters was reinforced by ties of blood or marriage that had been first established in the last quarter of the 17th century. In the decades before the Revolution, for example, no less than 70 percent of the 110 leaders of the House of Burgesses were drawn from families resident in Virginia before 1690.

How did these few great planter families manage to extend their influence over the generations? Sons and daughters were carefully, strategically, placed on lands accumulated for them by the economic success and political power of their fathers. This small, homogeneous elite of perhaps no more than 100 wealthy families—English by descent, Anglican in faith, linked to one another by ties of kinship and bonds of economic interest—monopolized political power in 18th-century Virginia. For example, seven members of the Carter family, the richest of all the Virginia clans in the 18th century, owned a total of 170,000 acres of land and 2,300 slaves scattered over seven counties.

The historical prominence of leading planter families such as the Carters, the Byrds, and the Lees should not obscure the relative brevity of their dominance of southern history. In fact, this golden age of great family dynasties flourished only between the early years of the unpredictable, dangerous settlement on the frontier and the 19th-century emergence of a much more diverse, middle-class society.

Younger sons of the English gentry arriving in Virginia in the early years of the 17th century fully expected to establish strong and prosperous family and kin groups. Their power base was to be grounded in the great fortunes they believed would be extracted from gold, precious metals, and (by the 1620s) tobacco. Although a few of these men became wealthy tobacco barons in the early years, most of them failed in finding fortunes and building family lines to perpetuate their status and power.

Most ambitions were stifled by the overwheming odds against survival in the disease-ridden early South. An endemic malarial environment in the Chesapeake and parts of the Carolina Tidewater created an oppressively high mortality rate that stunted family size, produced a society of orphans and step-parents, and virtually precluded the development of an elderly generation. Perhaps most significant, the high death rates thwarted any tendency toward strong patriarchal authority. Few men who expected to build powerful, multigenerational family dynasties could hope to succeed in an environment where men generally did not live long enough even to see their grandchildren, let alone to nurture and direct their careers. Instead, most gentlemen in this Hobbesian world struggled simply to survive—abruptly finishing their lives with nothing accumulated, nothing permanent to pass on to their heirs. Not until the final decade of the 17th century, when life expectancies gradually lengthened and slave importations increased dramatically, did a few leading families begin to build the large tobacco plantations and powerful family dynasties that would prevail in the 18th-century South.

At the other end of this golden age of southern planters, essentially after 1790, the picture is more difficult to assess. Prominent southern family lines continued well into the 19th century; indeed, scholars consider the antebellum era as the flush time for self-consciously paternalistic planters, men such as George Fitzhugh who intoned the virtues and obligations of the patriarch watching out for all his "people." Some historians, such as Eugene D. Genovese, believe that the paternalism of southern slaveholders reached something of a climax (both politically and ideologically) during the antebellum

era. One can surely detect in the writings of these influential planter families an increasing self-consciousness about their patriarchal role—perhaps an indication itself of the minority position they held. They laid great stress on family and kin loyalty, strategically planned marital alliances, a deep attachment to the land, and complete control in managing the slaves, servants, kin, and various hangers-on, who comprised the great planters' "people."

By the 19th century, though, southern society had changed—perhaps not dramatically, for most of it was still based on a staple-crop economy—but clearly the practice of deference to a few leading planters had begun to decline and in some places to disappear altogether. Great wealth was no longer the only road to political power, as scores of middle-class lawyers, teachers, and middling planters found their way into the political arena of the antebellum South.

Clearly, the spread of slaveholding was instrumental in democratizing political leadership among whites in the antebellum South. Slave-based plantations, once the preserve of a relatively few wealthy tobacco and rice planters in the early South, became a much more widely diffused system of labor by the mid-19th century, as cotton spread throughout the Lower South. In some of the most heavily populated slave states (South Carolina, Mississippi, Alabama, Georgia) between one-third and one-half of all white families held slaves in 1860. Most families owned a modest four to six slaves, but, more importantly, at least half the white families in the Deep South had a direct material interest in the protection and perpetuation of slavery. Hence, the number of legitimate spokesmen for slaveholding interests grew rapidly in the 19th century. Wealthy landed families continued to exert political influence; but that influence was increasingly outweighed by an expanding pool of slaveholding lawyers and merchants (particularly the former), who by mid-century controlled the county court in every southern state. By 1850 political power in the South carried a discernibly middle-class connotation.

In the postbellum South the disintegration of family dynasties, especially in the political arena, was even more conspicuous. With the growth of urban centers in the New South, political life became an increasingly diverse affair. Recent studies show that most urban officeholders in the South during the late 19th and early 20th centuries came from new families, not from heirs of old notable families.

More significant was the gradual deterioration of the planters' social and economic hegemony in the New South. According to C. Vann Woodward, the essential drama of the New South was "the story of the decay and decline of the aristocracy, the suffering and betrayal of the poor white, and the rise and transformation of a middle class." As hundreds of textile mills, railroads, and banking institutions emerged in the postwar South, economic power passed from the hands of landowners to manufacturers and merchants. Although some scholars see important family continuity between the elite planter class that prevailed in the antebellum South and the industrialists who dominated the New South, most historians detect an unmistakable fragmentation in planter hegemony during the postwar transformation of the southern economy.

See also AGRICULTURE: Plantations; HISTORY AND MANNERS: Colonial Heritage;

MYTHIC SOUTH: / Fitzhugh, George; Plantation Myth; SCIENCE AND MEDICINE: Disease, Endemic; SOCIAL CLASS: Politics and Class

Daniel Blake Smith
University of Kentucky

Eugene D. Genovese, *Roll, Jordan, Roll: The World the Slaves Made* (1976), *The World the Slaveholders Made* (1971); David Jordan, in *The Chesapeake in the Seventeenth Century: Essays on Anglo-American Society and Politics*, ed. Thad W. Tate and David L. Ammerman, (1979); Aubrey Land, *Journal of Economic History* (November 1965); Daniel Blake Smith, *Inside the Great House: Planter Family Life in Eighteenth-Century Chesapeake Society* (1980); Charles S. Sydnor, *Gentlemen Freeholders: Political Practices in Washington's Virginia* (1952); C. Vann Woodward, *Origins of the New South, 1877–1913* (1951). ☆

Feminism and Antifeminism

The South is historically the region of the United States most resistant to changes in the role of women. Of the 10 states that failed to ratify the Nineteenth Amendment by 1920, only one was north of the Mason-Dixon line. More recently, southern legislatures were crucial to the defeat of the proposed Equal Rights Amendment (ERA), as 9 of the 15 states that did not ratify it were former Confederate states. Only Texas and Tennessee approved the amendment, and Tennessee later voted to rescind. Since the 1890s, however, southerners have also played an active role in the women's rights movement. The modern feminist movement, which began in the 1960s and continues today, has made its presence felt in the region, but since the mid-1970s has encountered a powerful antifeminist challenge.

Both the more radical "women's liberation" branch of the feminist movement and the more moderate "women's rights" branch have been active in the South. In the late 1960s women's liberation groups sprang up in many urban centers and university communities. By the early 1970s both the National Organization for Women (NOW) and the National Women's Political Caucus (NWPC) had chapters in every southern state, joining older established women's organizations including the League of Women Voters, the Business and Professional Women's League, and the American Association of University Women as advocates of women's rights. Several southern women rose to positions of prominence in feminist organizations: Liz Carpenter helped organize the NWPC and was a cochairperson of ERAmerica from 1976 to 1979; Frances Farenthold chaired the NWPC from 1973 to 1975; and Sarah Weddington successfully argued *Roe* v. *Wade* (1973) (in which the Supreme Court liberalized abortion laws), and, as an aide to President Jimmy Carter, promoted feminist goals. As first lady, Rosalynn Carter was an enthusiastic advocate of the ERA.

Until 1972, in the South as in the rest of the nation, there seemed to be considerable support for feminist goals and little active opposition. Between 1971 and 1973 all southern states created commissions on the status of women. Both Texas (1972) and Virginia (1971) added equal rights amendments to their state constitutions. In the U.S. Senate Sam Ervin of North Carolina fought to modify or defeat the ERA with little support from his fellow southerners. When Congress voted overwhelmingly in 1972

to submit the amendment to the states, only two southern senators (Ervin and Mississippi's John Stennis) and nine southern congressmen voted against it. Both Texas and Tennessee ratified within two weeks.

The decisive victory of the ERA in Congress and its warm reception in the states (14 ratified within a month) awakened latent antifeminist sentiment; opponents of ratification began to mobilize in the South and throughout the nation. In its 1972 platform the American party denounced "this insidious socialistic plan to destroy the home," as did other right-wing groups active in the South, including the National States' Rights party, the Ku Klux Klan, and the John Birch Society. In the mid-1970s "New Right" groups, including the Conservative Caucus and the National Conservative Political Action Committee, became involved in the ERA controversy in the South, and, through the use of sophisticated direct-mailing techniques, mobilized hundreds of thousands of southerners to write letters to their legislators opposing ratification.

Phyllis Schlafly of Illinois, working through the Eagle Forum and the National Committee to Stop ERA (founded 1972), became the most visible leader of the opposition to the amendment. Along with her native Midwest, the South provided Schlafly her greatest following. She became a cult heroine to her supporters, political and religious conservatives who, sharing her conviction that women were most fulfilled through marriage and motherhood, opposed feminist reforms that they perceived as diminishing these roles and weakening the traditional American family. In the South large numbers of ERA opponents were religious fundamentalists who rejected the whole concept of sexual equality as contrary to

biblical teachings. The close cooperation between fundamentalist churches
and Stop ERA and other opponents of
ratification was a distinctive feature of
the ERA controversy in the South.

The antiratification forces in the
South faced off against state coalitions
composed of state and local chapters of
organizations that had endorsed ERA at
the national level. In contrast to rank
and file Stop ERA activists, these organizations were more often composed
of professional women and upper middle-class housewives with greater experience in lobbying. However, the very
diversity of the pro-ERA forces, together
with the fact that most supporters were
involved in other causes, meant that the
state coalitions were often loosely coordinated and at a disadvantage against
their opponents who pursued with religious intensity the single goal of stopping the ERA.

A majority of southerners favored ratification of the ERA (Gallup 1978), important regional newspapers endorsed
the amendment, and prominent southern politicians—e.g., James Hunt
(N.C.), Reuben Askew (Fla.), James B.
Edwards (S.C.), and President Jimmy
Carter—actively supported ratification,
but no other southern state ratified after
1972. The reactions of southern state
legislators varied from Mississippi (a
state eventually written off by ERA supporters), where the amendment never
emerged from committee, to North Carolina and Florida, where the ERA succeeded in the house only to be narrowly
defeated in the senate. There was also
considerable support for ratification
among state legislators in South Carolina and Virginia. As proponents
searched for the last three states (of the
38 necessary for ratification), they felt
frustrated by narrow losses and the skill-

ful political maneuvering of their opponents; Liz Carpenter charged that "a
handful of wilful and mischievous men"
in Florida, North Carolina, and South
Carolina were blocking the ERA.

The most important reason, however,
that additional states failed to ratify was
that opponents were successful both in
raising doubts about the potential effects
of ratification and in linking the ERA to
such controversial issues as abortion
and gay rights. In the South opponents
appealed effectively to the southern
penchant for chivalry and religious conservatism as well as to the regional antipathy toward expansion of federal
power. While proponents argued in vain
that the ERA would protect women
against discrimination in laws affecting
domestic relations, employment, government benefits, and education, opponents insisted American women
would lose their right to be supported
by their husbands, be driven into the
work force, and have to turn over their
children to state-run child-care facilities. Fundamentalist ministers throughout the South testified that the
amendment represented a direct rejection of God's will. Senator Ervin, whose
minority report to the Senate was widely
distributed by Stop ERA, lent his authority to the charges that ERA would
require sexual integration of prisons,
dormitories, and restrooms and compel
the military to draft women and use them
in combat. This last point proved to be
particularly damaging, as many southern legislators proved to be as passionate about the maintenance of a strong
defense free of female encumbrances as
about the protection of womanhood. The
proponents' response, that Congress
could draft women even without the
ERA, was not particularly reassuring.

Some southern legislators saw the

ERA, with its Section II providing for federal enforcement, as yet another infringement upon the rights of states, and insisted that state governments could adequately guarantee equality for women. Still chafing over Supreme Court decisions on school prayer and integration, many southerners feared the outcome of the inevitable court battles over interpretation of the ERA. Others were upset by previous congressional action to protect the rights of blacks and women, and, dismayed by what they perceived as a welter of changes forced upon the South from without, saw a vote against ratification of the ERA as an opportunity to register an objection to rapid social change over which they seemed to have no control.

Having been stirred to action by the ERA controversy, antifeminists went on to form the "Pro-Family Movement" to promote and defend their concept of the family and to repeal feminist-inspired laws and court rulings. By 1977, the year of the United States Conference for International Women's Year (IWY), there were two strong social reform movements in the United States with conflicting ideological perspectives on women and the family. Feminists and antifeminists battled at state conferences leading up to the IWY convention over the election of delegates to the national convention and the right to speak for American women. Most successful in the South and in the heavily Mormon Southwest, the profamily forces elected all of the delegates from Mississippi and a few from Alabama, Georgia, Louisiana, and Texas. But these delegates, together with the delegates from southwestern states, accounted for a scant 20 percent of the total attending the Houston convention. At congressional hearings called by their champion, Senator

Jesse Helms of North Carolina, profamily spokesmen testified that their point of view had been deliberately stifled. In Houston feminists celebrated the unity of women of all ages, races, and regions in support of a broad platform of feminist demands, including passage of the ERA; a major federal role in developing childcare programs; gay rights; access to abortion, family planning, and sex education; and a host of issues anathema to the profamily movement. Across town, Schlafly led representatives of Stop ERA, the Eagle Forum, Conservative Caucus, National Right to Life, the Mormon Club, the DAR, and the John Birch Society in a counterconvention attended by 11,000 people. She denounced the IWY conference as a symbol of degeneracy financed by five million federal dollars.

Between 1977 and 1982 feminists gained an extension of the deadline for ratification of the ERA but no new states. Meanwhile, opposition to the amendment and to feminism in general was one of the key issues uniting an increasingly powerful political movement. The Pro-Family Movement helped solve the New Right's search for a constituency by drawing many previously nonpolitical conservatives into political activity. By 1980 the Pro-Family Movement had merged with the New Right to form an effective coalition that influenced the Republican party to drop its support for the ERA and adopt an antiabortion plank. They claimed credit for Reagan's decisive victory over Jimmy Carter, whose party platform endorsed federally funded abortions and the withholding of campaign funds from Democratic candidates who failed to support the ERA. Certainly, the resurgence of antifeminism and social conservatism was only one reason for

Carter's defeat, but it helps to explain why Reagan carried the traditionally Democratic South, save only Carter's native Georgia.

When the deadline for ratification of the ERA passed in June 1982, the amendment was immediately reintroduced. Feminists vowed to change their tactics from the defensive to the offensive, to stop trying to persuade "negative politicians" and to elect legislators supportive of their goals. Taking lessons from the New Right, NOW formed its own political action committee (NOWPAC) and claimed to have elected 61 percent of their candidates in the 1982 congressional elections. However, feminists still expend much of their energy defending previous accomplishments against antifeminist opponents who celebrate the defeat of the ERA as the beginning of their effort to restructure America in keeping with "Pro-Family" values.

Marjorie Spruill Wheeler
University of Southern Mississippi

Janet K. Boles, *The Politics of the Equal Rights Amendment: Conflict and the Decision Process* (1979); David W. Brady and Kent L. Tedin, *Social Science Quarterly* (March 1976); Ann Fears Crawford and Crystal S. Ragsdale, *Women in Texas: Their Lives, Their Experiences, Their Accomplishments* (1982); Sara Evans, *Personal Politics: The Roots of Women's Liberation in the Civil Rights Movement and the New Left* (1979); Carol Felsenthal, *The Sweetheart of the Silent Majority: The Biography of Phyllis Schlafly* (1981); Marcia Fram, *National Catholic Reporter* (16 July 1982, 30 July 1982); Nancy Gager, ed., *Women's Rights Almanac* (1974); Susan Harding, *Feminist Studies* (Spring 1981); Jane DeHart Mathews and Donald Mathews, *Organization of American Historians Newsletter* (November 1982);

Subject files, Schlesinger Library, Radcliffe College, Cambridge, Mass. ☆

Genealogy
|||||||||||||||||||||||||

In recent years genealogy has been called "roots mania," referring to Alex Haley's engrossing saga of tracing the origins of a black southern family. Haley's *Roots*, published in 1976, and the television miniseries based on it provided a stimulus for genealogical research as a fulfilling hobby, especially in the South. The North Carolina Department of Archives and History, for instance, reported a 76 percent increase in researchers in its archival services branch between 1974 (9,506 researchers) and 1984 (16,780 researchers). Although not all of these researchers were looking for family data, an estimate was that about two-thirds of them were.

The study of family history is frequently a serious pursuit, both as an intellectual activity and as a profession. The annual Institute of Genealogy and Historical Research offered by the Samford University Library at Birmingham, Ala., has conducted well-attended institutes in genealogy for more than 20 years. Professional genealogists frequently are called upon in the courts to prove or disprove the validity of claims of kinship in the settlement of estates, the Howard Hughes estate in Texas being a recent example. Contemporary group life in the South is marked by the presence of numerous genealogical societies, patriotic organizations, lineage and hereditary groups, to say nothing of the many family associations that hold regular reunions. Patriotic societies based on lineage have long been popular in the southern states. In 1983 the 11 states of the Confederacy accounted for more than one-third of the membership of the National Society, Daughters of the American Revolution, boasting 77,276 members out of the total of 209,624. Among the well-known lineage organizations of southern origin are the Order of the First Families of Virginia, the German Society of New Orleans, Huguenot Descendants of the Founders of Manakin Town in the Colony of Virginia, the Descendants of the Jersey Settlers in Adams County, Miss., and the United Daughters of the Confederacy. These prestigious organizations spawned an ongoing interest in the dynastic families of the South, and the goal of much genealogical research in the 19th century was to prove a relationship to the early immigrants who established themselves in this country before the American Revolution.

The paths of early migration led from the eastern seaboard westward through the South. Today southern research institutions are called upon to provide documentary evidence for descendants of these early migrants as well as those who later settled and remained in the South. Vital records such as wills, marriage bonds, and deeds as well as court records, tax lists, and land records in southern courthouses have been searched, researched, and even removed by zealous genealogists. Through the efforts of the various states and aided by the Church of Jesus Christ of Latter Day Saints, many county records have been microfilmed, and the film is available to researchers in the various state archives departments. Indeed, interest in preservation of records is characteristic of the region: the two earliest state archives departments in the na-

tion were established in Alabama and Mississippi, in 1901 and 1902 respectively.

In the Bible Belt an early acquaintance with the "begats" of the Old Testament contributed to a sense of the importance of family lineages. Pioneer churches provided a means for reinforcing family ties. As the frontier moved southward and westward, these religious ties were strengthened. Churches as well as cemeteries recorded the progress of families from the seaboard states as they moved, generation after generation, slowly and steadily toward the West. The custom developed of having annual reunions at rural churches and cemeteries with the annual cemetery cleaning a feature of the occasion. Family groups, those who had moved on and their children and their children's children, returned and still return to these events.

In addition to church homecomings, reunions of individual family groups or clans bring together several generations. Some reunions are structured organizations with officers, publications, and well-planned meetings. Others are less formal get-togethers planned by round-robin correspondence and telephone calls. A small but well-known group of the descendants of Jefferson Davis meet semiannually on the Davis Plantation in Wilkinson County, Miss. In West Feliciana, La., every 50 years the descendants of Alexander and Anne Stirling meet at the home place, Wakefield Plantation. Most such reunions, however, are conducted annually, often at the rural churches where the family worshipped or at family homes.

Genealogies of American Indians have been compiled since the late 19th century when the southern tribes sought to obtain compensation from the United

States for lands that had been their ancestral tribal possessions. The Indian Claims Commission was established to review these claims, and, as it was necessary to prove one's descent from a tribal member, the Indian Claims Commission amassed a store of information on Indian families. This information was augmented by files built up by lawyers who represented the claimants. Due in large part to 20th-century tribal renewal movements, researchers are seeking out the files of these lawyers in order to preserve permanently the information they contain.

An interest in black genealogy is assuming noticeable proportions with the encouragement of studies in black history, the observation of Black History Month, and the stimulus of Alex Haley's *Roots*. Black genealogy is practically all southern based, and blacks wishing to probe into pre–Civil War lineages will need to search church records where baptisms of slaves were listed, cemetery records, recorded manumissions in legislative proceedings and court records, wills in which slaves were involved, estate inventories, lists of slave sales, plantation journals, tax rolls, passports issued (usually by governor or secretary of state) for travel across state and territorial lines (usually by governor or secretary of state), and diaries of plantation mistresses. Military records also provide a rich field for black genealogical research, as blacks have participated in military organizations since the Revolution.

Slaves were first listed by name in the Slave Schedules of the 1850 and 1860 federal censuses. After the Civil War the records of the Freedmen's Bureau documented the families of thousands of blacks, and the 1870 federal census listed black families.

What a boon it would be to black genealogists if every community had numbered among its citizens a black man such as William Johnson, a free man of color and a resident of Natchez. His diary meticulously detailing life in Natchez and mentioning names of slaves and their masters was edited by William Ranson Hogan and Edwin Adams Davis and published by the Louisiana State University Press in 1951.

In addition to the vital records found in county courthouses and archives, newspapers are a valuable source for genealogists. Not only do they provide information on births, deaths, estate settlements, real estate transactions, and marriages, but they furnish valuable social commentary to flesh out statistical material pertaining to families. Reflecting as they do the thoughts and opinions of many minds, newspapers are a cultural catalog of the times. Nowhere is the interest in recording family data more apparent than in the southern country newspaper. Here the genealogist may possibly find records of great-grandfather's birth, his marriage, where he spent his vacation, who came to visit him, the property he bought and sold, his children, his death, and numerous other details of his existence. Newspapers are even more important when local and county records have been lost or destroyed.

A number of union lists are helpful in locating newspaper files, such as Clarence Brigham's *History and Bibliography of American Newspapers, 1690–1820*; Gregory's *American Newspapers, 1821–1926*; and the Library of Congress *Newspapers on Microfilm* (several editions). The formation of a vast data base of newspaper holdings is currently under way. This is the United States Newspaper Project, an undertaking conceived by the Council of Learned Societies, planned by the

National Endowment for the Humanities (which is providing matching funds to the states for its implementation), and assisted by the Library of Congress. At the completion of this project, which is being conducted in three phases, all extant newspapers published since September 1690 will be produced in microform, identified in the computer network and made available through interlibrary loan services. The southern regional data entries will be made through SOLINET, the Southeastern Library Network affiliated with OCLC, the Online Computer Center in Dublin, Ohio.

A person conducting genealogical research of southern families will find various compilations and indexes indispensable, such as Earl Gregg Swem's *Virginia Historical Index* (1934 and 1936). The colonial records of Georgia, North and South Carolina, and Virginia have been published and are available in most research libraries.

Important genealogical records are offered in micrographic format, such as North Carolina deeds and wills on microfilm and an index to 170,000 North Carolina marriage bonds on microfiche, both produced by North Carolina Division of Archives and History. The South Carolina Department of Archives and History has indexed and microfilmed the will transcripts of South Carolina, 1782–1868.

The following list contains a guide to research in the South:

Alabama — M. F. Webb, *National Genealogical Society Quarterly* 57 (1969)

Arkansas — Tom W. Dillard and Valerie Thwing, *Researching Arkansas History: A Beginner's Guide* (1980)

Florida — Diane C. Robie, *Searching in Florida: A Reference Guide to Public and Private Records* (1982)

Georgia — Robert Scott Davis, Jr., *Research in Georgia: With a Special Emphasis upon the Georgia Department of Archives and History* (1981)

Kentucky — Beverly West Hathaway, *Inventory of County Records of Kentucky* (n.d.); George K. Schweitzer, *Kentucky Genealogical Research* (1981)

Louisiana — Donald J. Herbert, *Church and Civil Records,* 31 vols. (n.d.)

Mississippi — Mississippi Genealogical Society, *Cemetery and Bible Records,* 19 vols. (n.d.); *Genealogical Research: Methods and Sources,* vol. 2 (1983)

North Carolina — Helen Leary, F. M. and Maurice R. Stirewalt, *North Carolina Research Genealogy and Local History* (1980)

South Carolina — Brent H. Holcomb, *A Brief Guide to South Carolina Genealogical Research and Records* (1979)

Tennessee — George K. Schweitzer, *Tennessee Genealogical Research* (n.d.)

Texas — G. Winfrey, *Stripes* 9 (1969)

Virginia — Donald J. Martin, *Journal of Genealogy* (February 1979)

See also BLACK LIFE: Family, Black; Genealogy, Black; FOLKLIFE: Cemeteries;

Family Folklore; HISTORY AND MANNERS: Patriotic Societies; MEDIA: Newspapers, Country; / *Roots* ☆

Madel Morgan
Mississippi Department of History and Archives

Healers, Women

|||||||||||||||||||||||||||||||||||||||||||

Women in the South have a long tradition of helping family and friends maintain and restore health. Healing traditions were brought to the South with the early settlers, and they evolved as ideas and procedures were incorporated from European medical practice, African traditions, and American Indian traditions. The passing of remedies and techniques for care of the sick through generations of women is found in many cultures. Distinctive southern healing characteristics stem from the types of rural areas in which folk medicine practices have predominated and from the healers' use of indigenous plants and animals. Because modern techniques for controlling infectious diseases were adopted later in the South than in the North and because many rural southern areas have had shortages of medical personnel, folk healing practices have been particularly important throughout the region.

A mainstay of southern healing has been the use of readily available ingredients. Traditionally, many rural women raised herbs and medicinal plants such as comfrey, ginger, and catnip, along with their flowers and vegetables. They also made use of wild plants and trees, such as cottonwood leaves and fever grass. Household staples—eggs, baking soda, sugar, and whiskey—were also important to the care of the infirm. Teas and syrup were the vehicle for many medicines; other agents were directly applied as poultices to sores, sprains, and pains.

Knowledge and advice about health and healing came also from purveyors of patent medicines, who traveled from town to town attracting a following through shows and testimonials of cures. Mail-order almanacs and manuals were also sources of new information.

The role of women in healing and nursing was strongly supported by tradition. In years when infectious diseases like smallpox, typhoid, and malaria caused much illness and death, women spent long hours alleviating the sickness and suffering. Death was a commonplace occurrence, but religious beliefs and the belief in a joyous afterlife helped to ease the pain associated with death. Before the 20th century medicine was not a well-established profession based on scientific principles. Until the reform of medical education around 1910 almost anyone could claim competence and practice medicine. Mistrust of and disdain for doctors were widespread, as were social movements to restore the art of healing to the domestic sphere. Health-reform movements flourished throughout the country in the mid-19th century because of the failure of medical professionals to cure and because women sought a way to improve the quality of life in a confusing world undergoing major transitions. They were especially prevalent in the South because faith in self-treatment and the home healing arts was in harmony with tradition.

Many health-reform sects such as

the Thomsonians, the homeopaths, and the hydropaths prescribed specific remedies and formulas. These prescriptions were added to the already rich base of healing knowledge in the South. Magical cures, formulas for healthful living, medicinal cures derived from local plants and animals, and professional health care coexisted with minimal conflict. Of the many remedies known in the South, some work well and some have proven to be useless or dangerous. Behind them are generations of women who grew and gathered plants, raised animals, treated injuries, prepared barks, herbs, and plants for treatments, applied poultices, and administered medicines. Many of these beliefs and practices, which point out the self-sufficiency and independence of southern women and their families, are preserved in the *Foxfire* books.

Midwifery was another special preserve of women. With the exception of such areas as Appalachia and the Ozarks, southern midwifery was an occupation dominated largely by black women who passed their skills and knowledge down to their mature daughters or nieces. Although the practices of midwives were allegedly a cause of childbed mortality rates higher than those of the North, more recent investigations suggest that other factors, especially nutrition, were responsible.

In the 1920s programs to train midwives in obstetrics were supported in southern states by welfare. Midwives met in the county health departments, and under the supervision of public health nurses learned how to keep germs away during births, fill out birth certificates, and care for the equipment they used. By the 1970s nearly all traditional midwives were retired from practice, although nurse-midwifery training programs continue today.

Nurse-midwifery has increased greatly in importance since Mary Breckinridge began the Frontier Nursing Service in the 1920s. By the 1960s teams of medically supervised nurse-midwives from the University of Mississippi worked in locations throughout the South where infant deaths were disproportionately high. These nurse-midwives have demonstrated that they reduce infant deaths and provide high-quality care that women appreciate.

In recent years the number and availability of physicians and other health professionals have increased, but there is also a greater acceptance of women as healers in roles outside the family. Many southern women became nurses and other health professionals in the 1970s while enrollments of women in medical schools dramatically increased. These changes reflect an increasing involvement of women in healing roles beyond the home and an accompanying belief that women can share economic responsibility without neglecting their traditional roles in healing and caring for their own sick.

See also EDUCATION: / *Foxfire*; ENVIRONMENT: Plant Uses; FOLKLIFE: Folk Medicine; SCIENCE AND MEDICINE: Health, Public; Health, Rural; Self-dosage; / Breckinridge, Mary; Disease, Endemic; Disease, Epidemic

Molly C. Dougherty
University of Florida

Mary Breckenridge, *Wide Neighborhoods: A Story of the Frontier Nursing Service* (1952); Marie Campbell, *Folks Do Get Born* (1946); Alex Freeman, *Kentucky Folklore Record* (October 1974); Paul F. Gillespie, ed., *Foxfire 7* (1982); Guenter Risse, et al., *Medicine without Doctors: Home Health Care in American History* (1977); Sharon A. Sharp, *Women's Studies International Forum* (October 1986); Karen Shelley and Raymond Evans, in *Appalachia/America: Proceedings of the 1980 Appalachian Studies Conference*, ed. Wilson Somerville (1981); Jack Solomon and Olivia Solomon, compilers, *Cracklin' Bread and Asfidity: Folk Recipes and Remedies* (1979); Wilbur Watson, ed., *Black Folk Medicine: The Therapeutic Significance of Faith and Trust* (1984). ☆

Household

||||||||||||||||||||||||||||

Mint juleps on the veranda, a kettle full of collard greens with cornbread in the oven—whatever the caste or class, from top to bottom of the social ladder, the South is known for its warm and open hospitality. Perhaps this open-door policy developed during the colonial era because taverns for guests were few and far between. Travelers often spent the night in the home of a stranger, as plantations and farmhouses were the only source of shelter in the sparsely settled southern region. By the antebellum era southerners were so well known for their hospitality that this generosity had become proverbial. One southerner described a Sea Island planter so fond of his dinner guests that he insisted they move into his home, whereupon the couple stayed through the births of two children. Although most instances of hospitality in the Old South were not so extreme (indeed this tale tells as much about the art of southern storytelling as it does about hospitality), custom and circumstances combined to make many southern households almost perpetual

guesthouses throughout most of the 19th century.

Southern homemakers frequently complained that the virtual parade of family, friends, and strangers would "turn the house into a tavern." Many women, isolated on estates far from town, with infrequent chance for escape, welcomed the company. Most often, though, the wives of wealthier planters, those residing on elaborate estates with lavish reputations, found the tasks associated with hospitality burdensome. Indeed, these plantation mistresses often coped with a crowd of a dozen at breakfast and a score or more for Sunday dinners.

Family members, of course, were universally welcomed into southern homes. For a variety of reasons, kinship ties in the South were strong and extended. During the antebellum era, marriages between cousins occurred with some frequency among whites. Second and even third cousins were frequently childhood playmates and later friends for life, among blacks as well as whites. It was a point of great pride to most southerners that family would never be turned away. As a result "poor relations" became familiar fixtures in the homes of the more prosperous of the clan. The household was a body of persons loosely interconnected by blood and marriage. The head of the household was obviously the all-powerful patriarch, but his wife had great influence on family affairs.

Southern homes of the middle and upper classes always maintained servants. Domestic service in the postbellum period was almost entirely a black occupation. Those of limited means might not have a live-in staff, but it was a mark of financial ease to hire a cook-housekeeper to come into the home daily. During the holidays or at times when guests were expected for longer visits, southern homemakers would often draw on the family of their hired help, binding white households and black families into generational patterns of master-servant relations, which were often hangovers from the slavery era as well. Black mothers often had aspirations that their children should escape the domestic thrall of "workin' for Massa," through education or by migration north. But the majority of southern blacks spent much of their lives "workin' for the man" (a catch-all phrase for whites), and black women encouraged offspring to take advantage of the paternalism built into the southern system of household help.

This paternalism had many drawbacks, some identical to the problems encountered during slavery. Servants were underpaid and subject to long hours and numerous deprivations. If a woman lived in the house of her employer, she was often given basement or attic quarters—the smallest or most unhealthy in the residence. Even if a woman wanted to return home to her family at night, many white employers insisted that their servants live in. Many black cooks bemoaned the fact that they were rarely able to cook for their own families and were sometimes limited to alternate Sundays off. If a cook or a maid did return home, she was privy to "the servant's pan"—leftovers from the white family's table. White homemakers varied in disposition, but most kept close watch over this donation— allegedly to prevent being taken advantage of, although it was obviously the black family who suffered extortion. As late as 1935 the weekly wage for women household servants in the South was $3 a week. Without the servant's pan, many black children would have starved

on the combined wages of their parents, who remain underpaid in domestic service occupations even today.

Black women servants complained bitterly of false accusations of stealing—being searched by employers and suffering other humiliations even after years of loyal service—and of being subject to sexual harassment by the husbands in white households. It was not always simple to put a stop to these advances by male employers, for complaint to the white mistress could result in dismissal. And the black woman who called attention to a white man's sexual aggression was branded herself as the cause of the misconduct.

Despite her exploitation and marginal rewards, the black woman was able, in many cases, to wield enormous influence within the white household. In those homes where white women were unwilling or unable to manage, magisterial black women often dominated the household. In those homes where men were widowed and children motherless, black women often filled surrogate maternal roles: Carson McCullers's *Mem-*

Domestic servant tending a child, Atlanta, Georgia, 1939

ber of the Wedding vividly reflects this touching relationship. Scores of southern novelists have sentimentally explored this subject in their work.

Only recently have authors such as Ann Petry in *The Country Place* and William Melvin Kelley in *dem* delved into the subject with a less nostalgic view. These two works are set in the North, where most black novelists live and work in modern America; however, even novelists remaining in the South, such as Louisianian Walker Percy, have begun to alter this early saccharine portrayal. Elgin Buell (*Lancelot*) provides sharp and bitter insight. The master's right-hand man may be daily subject to his employer's demands, but he is acknowledged by the ill-fated Lancelot as perhaps the most intelligent and trustworthy member of the household: the two men act out their roles of master and servant, but the black is playing on white guilt and generosity to insure his escape from the South.

Some may wonder whether in the modern South the traditional virtues of paternalism, hospitality, and a conspicuously languid style can endure. In some cases, the visitor from the North may wonder if this effusive affability is merely for show or genuine. Southern custom has always maintained that what meets the eye is more important than what does not. Thus, a dazzling display of gracious generosity may remain a vital symbol of southern heritage.

See also AGRICULTURE: Plantations; HISTORY AND MANNERS: Sexuality

Catherine Clinton
Harvard University

Jane Carson, *Plantation Housekeeping in Colonial Virginia* (1975); Catherine Clinton,

The Plantation Mistress: Woman's World in the Old South (1982); Angela Davis, *Women, Race and Class* (1981); Florence King, *Southern Ladies and Gentlemen* (1976); Anne Firor Scott, *The Southern Lady: From Pedestal to Politics, 1830–1930* (1970). ☆

Indian Women
|||||||||||||||||||||||||||||||||||||||||

When Europeans first came into contact with Indians in what is today the southeastern United States, native women enjoyed considerable autonomy and personal freedom. Although it would be misleading to apply the term "equality" to the relationship between the sexes in these societies, women certainly were not subservient to men (nor men to women). Men and women merely had different responsibilities, which were equally important to community welfare.

The division of labor in these societies was fundamentally gender based: men hunted and women farmed. Restrictions on pregnant and menstruating women further separated male and female spheres. Yet because southeastern Indians depended on agriculture for subsistence, women had a major economic role. Their contribution was reflected in rituals such as the Green Corn Ceremony, in which women presented the new crop. Domestic chores performed by women included preparing food, gathering wood, carrying water, constructing utensils and furnishings for their houses, and caring for children. These responsibilities stemmed from the matrilineal kinship system and the matrilocal residence pattern, both of which were widespread in the Southeast: men lived in the houses of their wives and mothers, and children were considered to be related to mothers and not fathers. Women regulated their own behavior in most tribes, but their role in political decision making varied among southern tribes. Most influential were Cherokee women, who could speak in council and to whom a specified political position, that of War Women, was ascribed. More commonly, foreign affairs were left to men, whereas matrilineal clans resolved internal controversies.

European contact dramatically altered the status of southern Indian women. In the 18th century the deerskin trade, essential to many southern colonial economies, gave male hunters a disproportionate share of economic power. In the 19th century the U.S. government's "civilization" program and the efforts of missionary societies began to revolutionize Indian sexual roles. Men took up the plow and became dominant economically, politically, and domestically, while women became subservient. Some remnants of traditional female autonomy remained, however. The southern Indians who organized formal governments, for example, attempted to protect property rights of married women and ultimately pointed the way for similar laws adopted by southern states. In 1892 the *Albany Law Journal*, citing the Choctaws in particular, pointed out that the model for such progressive state legislation came from southern Indians.

See also ETHNIC LIFE articles on Indian tribes

Theda Perdue
Clemson University

E. Merton Coulter, *Georgia Historical Quarterly* (March 1927); Rayna Green, *Signs* (Winter 1980); Charles Hudson, *The Southeastern Indians* (1976); Ben Harris McClary, *Tennessee Historical Quarterly* (March 1962); Theda Perdue, *Furman Studies* (December 1980). ☆

Land, Women on the (I)
||||||||||||||||||||||||||||||||||||||||||||||||||||||||

Like Margaret Mitchell's famed fictional heroine, Scarlett O'Hara, southern women have always had a special attachment to the land. Women of all classes and color, not merely ladies of the planter class, have by preference or necessity been part of the agricultural heritage of the Old South. The romanticization of this association is the mythical facade of southern culture, but the bonds between women and the land formed a foundation for the development of a plantation economy.

Men brought women to the New World as the tamers of the wilderness, a frontier that promised as much danger as it did reward for those who pioneered the interior. Women were needed as settlers of these initial colonies, which many men were content simply to explore. The Earl of Southampton, concerned with the failing Virginia Company, argued "that the plantation can never flourish till families be planted and the respect of wives and children fix the people on the soil." The earliest settlers of the South had great trials with which to contend. Not only did they face an increasingly hostile native population, but the climate of the region was arduous and unhealthy, especially for women who repeatedly hazarded pregnancy. The codification and refinement of chattel slavery further hampered the colonial population, by demoting blacks to a deteriorating status within society and forcing whites to stand guard against those within as well as outside the community.

Although white women might not have been the initiators of southwestward expansion of settlement and the development of a planter aristocracy, they fully participated in the building of the Old South. Judith Giton Manigault, a Huguenot refugee, for example, fled her native France, settling with her husband in Charleston in 1685. Her early years in Carolina were brutal: "I have been six months without tasting bread, working like a ground slave; and I have even passed three and four years without having food when I wanted it." She perhaps savored her family's successes even more due to the harshness of her early struggles.

Life on the seaboard was relatively easy compared with the daily challenges of the frontier. As a young bride, Sally Buchanan, the wife of a pioneer settler of Davidson County, Tenn., lived at a fort near the Cumberland River. She and the other women of the settlement had to be guarded when they went outside the walls of the stockade to tend to the livestock, to do the wash, and to cultivate gardens. Families were crowded into close, uncomfortable quarters for safety. Women had little time to contemplate domesticity when trying to care for their families in these cramped and congested conditions. When the fort was attacked on 30 September 1792 Buchanan was nine months pregnant with her first child. While men fought off the attack from the four guardhouses and women and children cowered under beds, Buchanan kept her husband and his 16 comrades supplied with whiskey and bullets throughout the nightlong battle. Her heroism is celebrated in Cumberland folklore, but her role reflected the demands the southern frontier could and did place upon women.

No matter what the size of the property or the location of the land, white women's contributions to their husband's estates were enormous. Whether her husband's farm was large or small, was planted by slaves, hired hands, or family, or was confined to one plantation or to several, the southern matron was a figure of formidable industry and talent, fulfilling designated and vital responsiblities. Women were not only in charge of the food, shelter, and clothing of all those on the estate; they were also saddled with teaching and doctoring in the absence of professionals. While supplying their families with innumerable services as wives and mothers, black and white women on the plantation were presented with additional burdens associated with slavery. While females of the master and slave classes fulfilled traditional roles as nurturers, they were additionally assigned numerous chores to keep the plantation running.

The white mistress was beset by a veritable barrage of extra duties, not merely supervisory tasks, but work essential to production. Southern matrons grew herbs, blended medicines, planted gardens, spun cloth, knitted socks, sewed clothes, slaughtered pigs, processed and cured meat, plucked chickens, scoured copper utensils, preserved vegetables, churned butter, dipped candles, wove rugs, and performed numerous other harsh and unromantic chores. In addition to this relentless routine, women were often charged with the management of the entire plantation during a husband's absence. Order, efficiency, ability to negotiate, and dispatch in business dealings were expected of the model southern housewife.

Black women were afforded no such power on the plantation; yet their work roles were even more demanding. Slave women were dynamic figures within the black family, working side by side with men in the fields while providing care and affection for their families as well. Black mothers supplied models of strength and endurance for their offspring. Because many men were promoted as artisans on the plantation, field workers were often women. Although the system monopolized and exploited black women's labor, many were able to leave behind testimony to their talents and abilities. Baskets woven in accordance with tribal tradition and gourds decorated with patterns handed down from generation to generation demonstrate survival of African influences. Quilts such as Harriet Powers's masterpiece hanging in the Boston Museum of Fine Arts reflect biblical stories, and other needlework shows how black women were able to weave together the various strands of their lives, despite the obstacles.

The Civil War marked the beginning of a new era for women on the land. The passing of the Old South and the attempt to create a new order marked a traumatic and challenging time for southern women. Both black and white women were tied to the land, although in very different terms following Appomattox. The defeat of the Confederacy brought about the abolition of slavery, but the patterns of exploitation of black women's labor continued. And the crop-lien system incorporated white families into systems of labor expropriation that had previously been restricted by race rather than by class. Many members of the

prewar planter class were severely reduced in status. Landownership became a burden to many formerly wealthy whites who faltered in the face of steep taxes and the falling price of cotton. Smaller farmers were especially hard pressed, and rural families were constantly on the move to find better land. Blacks who tried to escape the land, to settle in towns and cities, were often driven back into rural areas by economic necessity. The attempts of freedpeople to achieve autonomy in the postwar South were rejected by the majority of whites, who were dead set against black landowning. Women, struggling to rebuild their war-torn communities, hoping to put the war behind them, and longing to build a new life for their families, were caught in the crossfire.

Women of the Old South were born into a folk culture so rich that modernism held little allure. Although many southern women, especially former slaves, were quick to abandon the shackles of the past, the majority continued their deep and abiding love of the land. The women of the rural South preserve their heritage today, cherishing what enriches and endures. Land provides southern women a vehicle for self-discovery, as author Alice Walker suggests in her essay "In Search of Our Mother's Gardens."

See also AGRICULTURE: Plantations; BLACK LIFE: Family, Black; Landowning, Black; Slave Culture; FOLKLIFE: / Needlework; HISTORY AND MANNERS: Frontier Heritage

Catherine Clinton
Harvard University

Catherine Clinton, *The Plantation Mistress: Woman's World in the Old South* (1982);

Jean Friedman, *The Enclosed Garden: Women and Community in the Evangelical South, 1830–1900* (1985); Jacqueline Jones, *Labor of Love, Labor of Sorrow: Black Women, Work, and the Family from Slavery to the Present* (1985); Anne Firor Scott, *The Southern Lady: From Pedestal to Politics, 1830–1930* (1970); Julia Cherry Spruill, *Women's Life and Work in the Southern Colonies* (1938). ☆

Land, Women on the (II)

||||||||||||||||||||||||||||||||||||||||||||||||||||||||||||

The Civil War ended one struggle over life and labor in the South and set off another over the nature of the new social order. Women played a vital role in that struggle. After emancipation, for example, black women helped resist gang labor by withdrawing from the fields and devoting their time to caring for their homes and children. But they had to chop and pick cotton again as members of sharecropper families or earn meager wages as farm and domestic workers. Black women's work, though altered, remained necessary to family survival.

Freedmen and the South's yeoman farmers alike were ensnared by the crop-lien system. Furnishing merchants insisted that farmers plant cash crops like cotton and tobacco, and yeoman self-sufficiency was gradually undermined. Tenancy increased, and owners of small farms retained a tenuous hold on the land. Women proved especially vulnerable in the cash-crop economy. Landlords favored families that could muster a large male work force. Tenant widows led insecure lives unless they had sons who could plant, cultivate, and harvest the crops. Daughters were among the most expendable of farm

workers. Thus, in the South's Piedmont during the 1870s, women made up the first wave of migrants from farms to the region's fledgling factories.

Farm women, however, were not simply victims of regional social and economic change. In the late 19th century rural southern women were linchpins in the agrarian revolt that exploded in the countryside. Plummeting crop prices, merchant abuse, railroad rate differentials, and government indifference to farm people's plight set the stage for radical reform efforts. Female members of the Southern Farmers' Alliance encouraged the brethren, rallied other women to the cause, and relished the unprecedented opportunity to discuss important economic, social, and political issues. Women were needed on the front lines at the Alliance hall and at home. Within the context of the reform movement, women's domestic tasks were endowed with political significance, for they lessened their families' dependence on merchants. "It won't do," one Texas Alliance sister observed, "for poor farmers to live at home and board at the store." When the Populist party offered farmers a political solution to their economic problems, women continued to support the revolt. Deprived of the vote, rural southern women nonetheless acted on Mary Elizabeth Lease's pithy admonition to "raise less corn and more hell." They used their pens and voices to back the Populists in the reform press and from lecture platforms.

As the 20th century dawned, southern farmers faced both advances and setbacks. Landowners enjoyed prosperity while tenants saw things go from bad to worse. Cotton prices rebounded; credit became more accessible for some farmers; farm bankruptcies declined. The very conditions that favored landowners, however, worked to tenants' disadvantage, for higher land values undercut their chances to climb the agricultural ladder, and the crop-lien system continued to limit their options.

Most southern women remained rooted to the land, but the contours of their lives differed greatly according to their economic circumstances. Wives of prosperous white landowners, like antebellum plantation mistresses, managed their households and often hired black women to relieve them of such backbreaking tasks as the weekly wash. Fieldwork, moreover, was outside their realm of duties.

Middling and tenant farm women of both races mastered and juggled myriad tasks that required physical endurance and skill. They bore and reared the largest families in the nation: 6 children were typical, but 12 or 13 were not uncommon. Repeated pregnancies and the demands of a large farm family often made these farm women old before their time, yet their children were a source of joy and pride. Well into the 20th century poor southern farm women enjoyed few of the household conveniences that were lightening the labors (if not necessarily shortening the workweek) of urban women. With the help of their children, they toted pails of water from a well to the house and cut firewood to heat cookstoves. They supplied the family larder by gardening, preserving fruits and vegtables, raising chickens and gathering eggs, and milking cows and churning butter. Sometimes farm women augmented family finances by bartering or selling surplus produce.

The demands of cash-crop agriculture, furthermore, meant that the wives and daughters of tenants and small-farm owners often had to divide their time between the kitchen and the fields. Although field work was an additional burden, many women preferred the camaraderie of the tobacco barn to the isolation of the house, or the sense of accomplishment at the end of a chopped cotton row to the endless rounds of housework. Many, in fact, took pride in their field prowess and enjoyed the relative fluidity of men's and women's work roles. As one Piedmont North Carolina farm woman testified: "We done men's work. We done women's work. You name it and we done it."

The early 20th century spawned another attempt at agricultural reform in the South. This time the impetus came from agrarian progressives at state and federal departments of agriculture and land-grant colleges. While farm demonstration agents promoted crop rotation, diversification, and soil fertilization, home demonstration agents promoted domestic science and efficient housekeeping. Home economics extension agents, often rural schoolteachers, organized clubs to teach new ways of cooking, sewing, canning, and home decorating and encouraged women to market their produce and handiwork. In addition, professional rural social work-

Two children with a cantaloupe, Mississippi Delta, 1936

ers tried to ameliorate the condition of poor farm women who suffered from inadequate health care and the nutritional deficiencies inherent in a meat, meal, and molasses diet.

Such efforts at reform from the top down, however, could not solve the agricultural problems of the South, where the depression of the 1920s and 1930s took its severest toll. Powerful images of southern tenant farm women entered the national imagination through Depression-era documentary photography. Again, as in the Populist years, farm women joined forces against displacement—through organizations like the Southern Tenant Farmers' Union and the Alabama Sharecroppers Union—and took advantage of the opportunities offered by the Farm Security Administration to gain or hold on to their land.

But New Deal farm policies that encouraged landowners to cut crop production and to mechanize pushed even more farmers off the land and into the cities or the migrant stream. After 1940 the South's farm population declined precipitously. Thousands of southern women, especially blacks and Appalachian mountaineers, joined the post–World War II migration to the North. Severing ties to the land was a heartwrenching experience for many.

Yet the southern population remained one of the most rural in the country. For many women who remained on the land, the next four decades brought enormous changes: electricity, better transportation, and improved communications eroded differences between rural and urban women and their homes. For other rural women, however, the early 20th century seemed little different from the 19th. On the whole, rural women's participation in subsistence farming has declined during the last several decades.

Rural women have adapted their traditional roles to the needs of modern agriculture and thereby have reshaped their ties to the land.

See also AGRICULTURE: Garden Patch; Plantations; Sharecropping and Tenancy; / Agricultural Extension Services; Farm Security Administration; BLACK LIFE: Migration, Black; HISTORY AND MANNERS: Great Depression; New Deal; Populism; INDUSTRY: Industrialization and Change; SOCIAL CLASS: Tenant Farmers; / Farmers' Alliance; Sharecroppers Union; Southern Tenant Farmers' Union

> Lu Ann Jones
> University of North Carolina
> at Chapel Hill

Margaret J. Hagood, *Mothers of the South: Portraiture of the White Tenant Farm Woman* (1939); Dolores Elizabeth Janiewski, "From Field to Factory: Race, Class, Sex, and the Woman Worker in Durham, 1880–1940" (Ph.D. dissertation, Duke University, 1979); Julie Roy Jeffrey, *Feminist Studies* (Fall 1975); Joan M. Jensen, *With These Hands: Women Working on the Land* (1981); Kathy Kahn, *Hillbilly Women* (1972); Marc S. Miller, ed., *Working Lives: The Southern Exposure History of Labor in the South* (1981). ☆

Maiden Aunt
||||||||||||||||||||||||||||||||||

She is a favorite character of fiction and stereotype, but a person who in fact touched the lives of most southerners— the maiden aunt. The demand for marriageable women exceeded the supply during the colonial era, but by the time of the American Revolution the spinster (single women at home were often drafted to the female task of spinning, the origin of the term) was a folkloric figure in southern states. The never-wed woman in southern culture was not only dependent upon men, like her married counterpart, but she was denied the status accorded to matrons and mothers. She was forced to live out her life on the fringes of society, a perpetually lone figure in a culture of tightly knit couples and children. Within the home (usually that of a brother or sister), however, she was often a cherished and fond member of the family circle. Indeed, the maiden aunt became both influential and indispensable.

It was assumed, because of social pressures to marry, that most unmarried women had been rejected, passed over, or never given any opportunity to snare a husband. This promoted several unattractive images of old maids. One antebellum girl described them as "forlorn damsels who made the midnight air echo with their plaintive bewailings, for only bats and owls return their melancholy strains." In southern society the "old" maid ranged anywhere from age 18 to 80. A girl might feel spinsterish if younger sisters married before she did, if she was not married by age 21, or simply if all her friends had "deserted" her for husbands.

Southern women, as a rule, married very young—younger than their northern counterparts and much younger than men. Shortly after puberty, black women often selected a mate, whom they married by folk custom though not by law. Historians of the slave community have found teenaged brides common on the plantation. Studies of planters have confirmed that white women also commonly wed as schoolgirls. In the Old South the average age of marriage for white women was 20, and that of black women was slightly lower. Thus, women who remained unmarried in the South were classified as spinsters at a much earlier age than elsewhere.

The Civil War, of course, greatly reduced the supply of young men to marry. Many southern daughters during the second half of the century were thus demographically deprived of husbands. Strikingly, the Reconstruction era was the first period since early colonial days when interracial sexual relations and even marriage were accepted to any notable extent. However, a large number of the single white women—and especially those of the upper and middle classes—remained unattached, many becoming leaders in shaping new educational and employment opportunities for women. Gradually, career opportunities for females expanded, and the stigma associated with women who lived alone lessened.

Nevertheless, throughout most of the 19th century and well into the 20th, southern society attempted to shelter and confine single women. Those who failed to marry were more often forced by custom or circumstance to spend their time and energy with "other women's families." Spinsters clearly served surrogate roles with the family—single daughters or maiden aunts might be welcome as an extra pair of hands or as substitute mothers—but they were also social outcasts, denied the status a woman could achieve only through her role as matriarch. Few parents, even those of enormous wealth, would bequeath money to an unmarried daughter.

Only in modern times have single women in the South received any of the family resources. Traditionally, a woman was expected to inherit through her dowry. If she did not marry she could only rely on the charity of parents or siblings. Brothers and sisters eagerly provided these spinsters with homes in exchange for valuable domestic services. Maiden aunts were teachers and nurses, confidants and disciplinarians. Indeed, their whole lives were bound up with the strenuous chores of child rearing, but, like servants, the children they tended were not their own.

"Aunt adoption" was a particularly southern phenomenon. Women often singled out a niece for special affection and in many cases quite lavish consideration. This cultivation of a favorite by aunts was traditional and certainly not limited to unmarried or childless females. It was not uncommon for a southern mother to "donate" one of her several daughters to the family of a beloved brother or sister who had no children, or even merely no *female* offspring. This would reduce the burden of the natural parents (costs for living expenses and dower) while maintaining family ties and offering emotional, and sometimes financial, benefits for the adopted child.

Upon occasion a pregnant mother would secure a promise from a favorite sister that if she did not survive the ordeal of childbirth, the surviving sister would look after the orphaned children; in some cases women wanted their husbands to marry these spinsters. With death in childbirth uncommonly high in the South until the 20th century (nearly double that of the North), unmarried women sometimes literally inherited an entire family through marriage to the spouse of a dead sibling. These cases were extreme, yet they reflect the pivotal importance to southern women of the maiden aunt, despite her never-married, childless status.

The stereotypes of these women were most often unflattering exaggerations. Many fictional portraits of maiden aunts painted them as dizzy and foolish, the proverbial "Aunt Pittypat" character of *Gone with the Wind*. A more sympathetic portrayal has been developed by several southern authors who have characterized sturdy, proud females channeling their energies and talents into their nephews and nieces and leading challenging and fulfilling lives: variants on the theme established in one of Faulkner's early novels, *Sartoris*, with the spirited and understanding Miss Jenny. Many of these characters, especially those created by women novelists such as Ellen Glasgow, possess a feminist component: they chose not to enter the ranks of women trapped and trampled by husbands.

Another significant variant for the never-married woman was the portrait of a lady of questionable character. There were women in southern society and southern fiction who chose to lead lives unhampered by spouses but who refused to deny themselves sexual companionship. For some, their reckless behavior at a younger age had supposedly robbed them of their reputation for virtue, leading to a devaluation on the marriage market. Others purportedly were predisposed to this character defect—loose and immoral without hope of redemption. In either case, perpetual singlehood was their fate. This semitragic figure was most poignantly revealed in Tennessee Williams's Blanche DuBois, the fading belle of *Streetcar Named Desire*.

The plays, films, and novels of the South depict lone women in their variety and complexity, but these myriad roles cannot match the mark these women have made in the great drama of real life. Their impact has been enormous and their contributions monumentally enriching to southern culture.

See also BLACK LIFE: Miscegenation; Slave Culture; FOLKLIFE: Childbirth; Family Folklore; HISTORY AND MANNERS: Civil War; Reconstruction; Sexuality; LAW: Family Law; RELIGION: Missionary Activities

Catherine Clinton
Harvard College

Josephine Carson, *Silent Voices: The Southern Negro Woman Today* (1969); Catherine Clinton, *The Plantation Mistress: Woman's World in the Old South* (1982); Maria Fletcher, "The Southern Heroine in the Fiction of Representative Southern Women Writers" (Ph.D. dissertation, Louisiana State University, 1963); Anne Goodwyn Jones, *Tomorrow Is Another Day: The Woman Writer in the South, 1859–1936* (1981); John C. Ruoff, "Southern Womanhood, 1865–1920: An Intellectual and Cultural Study," (Ph.D. dissertation, University of Illinois, 1976); Lillian Smith, *Killers of the Dream* (1949); Julia Cherry Spruill, *Women's Life and Work in the Southern Colonies* (1938); Alice Walker, *In Love and Trouble: Stories of Black Women* (1973). ☆

Marriage and Courtship
||||||||||||||||||||||||||||||||||||||||||||||||||||||||

Southern courtship and marriage were most distinctive in the colonial period; the past three centuries have all but erased peculiarly southern patterns. Because 17th-century migration to the southern colonies, unlike that to the North, was predominantly male, women were a particularly valuable commodity. Indeed, an early governor of Virginia would explain that from "the want of wives have sprung up the greatest of hindrances of the encrease of the plantation." In the early decades of settlement, the sexual imbalance and the absence of kin gave white women a great deal of freedom in the choice of a marriage partner. Married typically in her mid-twenties to a somewhat older man and widowed within a decade, an immigrant woman became even more desirable when in the possession of her deceased husband's property. Second-generation women, still outnumbered by men, married earlier than their mothers, probably in their mid- to late-teens; like their mothers, many were pregnant on their wedding day.

Only in the early decades of the 18th century did the population stabilize; then, the demographic pattern that persisted into the 19th century was established: white women in their early twenties (expected to be virgins) married men several years older. Although they almost never chose their children's mates, pre-revolutionary era parents retained a very effective veto in the form of the marriage settlement they were expected to provide (and might withhold). Once a young man and young woman had selected each other, their fathers would enter into negotiations to determine each child's marriage portion. For affluent families, as in the North, such arrangements were crucial to their power and prestige. Young people were trained by their parents in how to make a prudent choice; as one traveler noted, courtship was "the principal business in Virginia."

If, in the years before the American Revolution, material considerations outweighed emotional ones in the selection of a mate, later the balance would be tipped in the other direction. As southerners, like their northern counterparts, came increasingly to expect that their earthly happiness would come from love, and as changes in the economy and custom diminished the importance of the parental settlement, young people became freer to follow the promptings of their own hearts. To be sure, most chose mates from a similar background and of comparable economic standing, but the most important factor was that elusive quality known as "character." Men wanted wives who would be cheerful and affectionate, and women hoped for husbands who would prove kind and even tempered. As a result, southerners tended to find their mates among friends, neighbors, and even cousins, not because of any particular social ideology or strategy, but because in a region that was sparsely settled those who were already known were those who could best be trusted.

In the antebellum period, men and women met and courted at parties, barbecues, church meetings, and other social gatherings. A young man might pay court to a young woman by visiting her at home, or, if separated by great distance, by writing her love letters, to which she would carefully respond. Alexis de Tocqueville noted that American women were especially free before marriage and were more constrained after. The selection of a husband was the most important choice a woman would ever make; consequently, some women played the belle, flirting outrageously and rejecting suitors capriciously (or so it seemed to the men), as if to prolong their final moments of freedom and to assert their greatest power over the opposite sex. Though most couples anticipated intimacy and affection, some women seem to have retreated in the face of so momentous a choice. Once a couple had engaged themselves, they would, out of love and respect, seek the approval of the young woman's father.

The marriage ceremony usually took place in the bride's parents' home, in the presence of family and close friends.

Marriage for whites was an institution sanctioned by law, religion, and custom. Slave marriages, however, were protected by custom only. Nonetheless, by the 19th century, most slaves entered into enduring unions, marriages in the eyes of the slave community, if not the law and the church. As with whites, demographic patterns shaped the nature of marriage in the colonial period. Because planters at first preferred to import male Africans, creating sex ratios as high as two to one, and because most slaves were scattered in small groups on small plantations, opportunities to create stable and lasting unions were severely limited. As a result of the similar imbalance in white sex ratios in the 17th century, some African and Afro-American women may have served as white men's concubines or common-law wives. Others became the partners of older slave men, who often lived on other plantations. By the middle of the 18th century importation of slaves began to decline, and the slave population increased naturally. By that time most slave women were marrying in their late teens, slave men perhaps several years older. Larger plantations afforded some couples opportunity to marry and move into their own cabins on the home plantation. Many, however, had to find mates "abroad" on other farms; in that case, a woman and her children would live in their own cabin on her home plantation, and her husband would be allowed to visit on weekends or perhaps some nights.

The postrevolutionary expansion of the South and the establishment of large cotton and sugar plantations created a different pattern of slave marriage. Increasing numbers of slaves could hope to find mates on their own plantations. Moreover, the federal prohibition of slave imports after 1808 gave masters added incentive to encourage slave fertility. By her early twenties, the typical slave woman had entered into a union that would endure, usually, until death or the master severed it. That slaves themselves regarded such unions as binding is given ample testimony by the great number of couples who took advantage of emancipation to register their marriages, thus obtaining civil sanction for their unions and official legitimacy for their children.

Slave marriages were always contingent upon the approval of the master. Sometimes he performed the ceremony, reading an edited version of the standard Christian marriage service. At other times, the slaves might follow their own customs, such as jumping over the broomstick, with a respected slave officiating. Some masters allowed their slaves great latitude or even feted favored slaves; others cruelly mocked the slaves' behaviors. Often masters complied with their slaves' wishes, recognizing that a contented labor force was in their own best interest. Others, however, intent upon encouraging slave reproduction, would select or purchase particular slave men as husbands for particular slave women. At other times, a slave whose mate had been sold away would likewise be forced to acquire a new mate. There are even scattered but largely unsubstantiated references to slave breeding, using selected slave men as "studs."

Scholars have not yet examined post–Civil War southern courtship and marriage with as much care as they have devoted to the antebellum period. Patterns for the majority of whites do not appear to have been different from those in the North, for in the decades preceding the Civil War the main differences were those related to a lower social density: a greater tendency toward marriage between cousins, friendly involvement of family and friends in courtship, and perhaps less

Catholic wedding, Louisville, Kentucky, c. 1950

privacy for courting couples. Time has probably erased such differences. For blacks, emancipation eliminated the restrictions of slavery, allowing them to participate in civil and religious marriage ceremonies as a prelude to enduring unions.

As of 1970, the average age of first marriage for a southern white man was 22.8 and for a female, 20.0; the corresponding age for southern black men and women were almost exactly the same: 22.9 and 20.0 respectively. All groups were marrying several months younger than the national average for their gender and race.

See also FOLKLIFE: Family Folklore; Weddings

Jan Lewis
Rutgers University, Newark

John Blassingame, *The Slave Community: Plantation Life in the Antebellum South* (1972); Lois Green Carr and Lorena Walsh, *William and Mary Quarterly* (October 1977); Jane Turner Censer, *North Carolina Planters and Their Children, 1800–1860* (1984); Herbert G. Gutman, *The Black Family in Slavery and Freedom, 1750–1925* (1976); Allan Kulikoff, *Law, Society, and Politics in Early Maryland* (1977); Jan Lewis, *The Pursuit of Happiness: Family and Values in Jefferson's Virginia* (1983); National Center for Health Statistics, *Monthly Vital Statistics Report*, vol. 32, no. 13 (21 September 1984); Ellen Rothman, *Hands and Hearts: A History of Courtship in America* (1985). ☆

Marriage and Divorce Laws

Chivalry—the romantic ideal of male-female relationships—was as much a legal doctrine as a social prescription in the antebellum South. No statute or code used the term, but its underlying assumptions about the weakness of women and the protective authority of men ran through southern domestic law. From the first colonial statutes and case law on marriage and divorce, women were accorded an inferior status. "Reform" of this status—liberalization of divorce law, passage of married women's property acts, and adoption of equal rights amendments—neither arose from nor carried forward any general program of equality for men and women under the law.

Marriage and divorce law in the colonial South mixed ecclesiastical and civil procedures. Marriage made a single woman into a *femme covert*, whose legal person and property are merged with her husband's. Coverture originated in English common law and was widely adopted in all the colonies. The wife lost the right to sue and be sued, to use or manage the common property, and to arrange for her children's estates without the consent of her husband, unless arrangements were made prior to marriage or the courts intervened upon a suit of equity. At her husband's death, a wife possessed a life interest in a part of the common property (dower). Divorce was uncommon. Where they functioned, church courts could order an annulment (a declaration that the marriage had never been valid) or a separation with division of property but without the right to remarry. This, again, was the English practice, as well as being common in Roman Catholic countries. A third form of divorce, by specific legislative decree, was not adopted in the colonial South, though it was quite common in New England.

The demography of the early southern settlements, marked by early death for women from childbirth, epidemic diseases, and overwork, ironically countered, in a limited way, the detriments imposed upon women by the law. The value of wives and mothers, particularly in frontier communities, was a matter of supply and demand, not legal formulas. Southern colonial women were administrators of estates, heirs, heads of families, and substantial property holders. As *femmes sole*, they ran businesses, sued, and were sued. In the absence of other forms of divorce, these women obtained redress by petitioning the local courts.

During the revolutionary era divorce laws were liberalized (partly in response to the expansion of women's educational opportunities) to the extent that women with grievances against their spouses gained access to courts under general divorce laws. But postrevolutionary chivalric ideals of personal conduct (and of offenses justifying divorce) were everywhere apparent. An Alabama code provision of 1852 spelled these out: "The legal responsibilities of a wife are to live in the home established by her husband; to perform the domestic chores (cleaning, cooking, washing, etc.) necessary to help maintain that home; to care for her husband and children. The legal responsibilities of a husband are to provide a home for his wife and children; to support, protect and maintain his wife and children." In cases of conflict, the rights of the husband remained paramount, so long as he provided for the family. Indeed, it was neither a crime nor grounds for divorce for a man to force his wife against her will to engage in sexual relations.

Southern states introduced divorce by legislative decree at the end of the 18th century. In 1839 the Maryland legislature passed the first general divorce law in the South (much like the general

incorporation acts promulgated in the same era), and it was soon copied by other southern general assemblies. The Virginia statute of 1853 was typical—allowing divorce in cases of adultery, impotency, felony, abandonment (of three years or more in duration), prostitution, and cohabitation. When women appealed disputed lower court divorce rulings to supreme courts, judges counted the submissiveness of the wife-plaintiff in her favor. The court protected the wife, the weaker partner, from the erring husband, under the unwritten law of chivalry. Divorce remained relatively uncommon in the pre–Civil War era, though the rate steadily increased and would continue to increase throughout the next century and a half. Marital separation by consent or necessity was far more common.

The most notorious of the marital separations explicitly sanctioned by the law involved slave families. Masters might encourage, or even officiate at, slave marriages (which had little or no legal sanction), but married slave women had no legal remedy for dissolution of their marriage by sale, gift, or devise. Slave women were chattel, and whether they were trusted members of the family circle, field hands, or breeding stock, chivalry played no part in their lives.

The mid-19th century did bring genuine reform in the legal status of free southern married women. For a decade before the Civil War, and then with added vigor in the years of Reconstruction, southern state legislatures enacted married women's property acts. As in their contemporaneous northern counterparts, these laws allowed married women to dispose of their own property, including that property obtained during marriage. Such property, after divorce or widowhood, remained theirs. Although these laws were never absolute guarantees of entitlement (in some of them wife did not have sole possession of wages and rents even if they were earned only by her), they did elevate the legal status of the *femme covert*. In practice, such women often already managed family and business finances. The new laws protected a part of the family assets against a husband's creditors, no mean advantage in the boom-and-bust economy of the antebellum South and in the hard times following the Civil War. At the same time, proponents of these bills in legislatures rarely showed any sympathy for more sweeping reform of domestic law. Women were still protected by men. Political rights, as well as recognition of women as heads of households or as independent participants in the marketplace, did not immediately follow upon the married women's property acts. Georgia, for example, officially. recognized women as heads of households in 1982.

Over the past century southern legislators and courts have redressed some of the inequities of domestic law, while retaining the prerogatives of chivalric protectors of wives and mothers. Women's participation in public affairs has not destroyed such prejudices, though the oppressive weight of discrimination in the law has lessened. Divorce laws in 8 of the 13 southern states no longer require proof of fault or immorality. Recognition in divorce settlements of nonmonetary contribution to family life in the form of homemaking and child rearing is now standard practice in Arkansas, Florida, Kentucky, Maryland, Mississippi, and Virginia, as it is in almost all the northern states. Nevertheless, local courts throughout much of the South continue to regard themselves as the protectors of traditional roles in the family. State equal rights amendments (in the few southern states that have them) have not brought an end to this latter-day expression of chivalry, despite husbands' suits claiming reverse discrimination.

Although a historical and sentimental tie can thus be discerned between chivalric attitudes among southern lawmakers and judges and the simultaneous protection and debasement of women under the law, it is not so clear that this relationship is purely southern. Women were denied equal access to education, professional occupations, wealth, political activity, and public expression in the North, under rationales very similar to those given in the South. Married women's property laws had a very similar economic (rather than egalitarian) basis in North and South. The post–Civil War movement to prohibit, or at least curtail, divorce had its origins in New England and New York, not the South. Indeed, the South was an innovator in liberalizing some domestic and economic restrictions upon married women. To be sure, southern women were not so well organized, vocal, or successful in the drive for autonomy as their northern sisters—allowing southern lawmakers the chance to loosen domestic restrictions without fear of militancy among the recipients of their largesse. Perhaps for this reason—a mixture of tacit consent and continuing disorganization—southern women are still waging the legal fight against chivalry.

See also BLACK LIFE: Family, Black; HISTORY AND MANNERS: Sexuality; LAW: Family Law

N. E. H. Hull
University of Georgia

Barbara A. Babcock et al., *Sex Discrimination and the Law: Causes and Remedies* (1975); Jane Turner Censer, *American Journal of Legal History* (January 1981); Carl N. Degler, *At Odds: Women and the Family in America from the Revolution to the Present* (1980); Doris J. Freed and Henry H. Foster, Jr., *Family Law Quarterly* (Winter 1981); George E. Howard, *A History of Matrimonial Institutions*, 2 vols. (1904); Leo Kanowitz, *Sex Roles in Law and Society* (1973); Paul M. Kurtz, *Family Law Quarterly* (Summer 1977); Suzanne Lebsock, *Journal of Southern History* (May 1977); Peggy A. Rabkin, *Fathers to Daughters: The Legal Foundations of Female Emancipation* (1980); Max Rheinstein, *Marriage Stability, Divorce, and the Law* (1972). ☆

Matriarchy, Myth of

||||||||||||||||||||||||||||||||||||||||||||||||||||||

A matriarch is a woman who maintains the authority to make major decisions and to control the property as well as the political environment of the family. In some traditional African societies, like the Ashanti, lineage was traced through the female; however, her power was limited by male members of her line. Similar lineage patterns could be found in North America among Indians such as the Cherokee. Nonetheless, truly matriarchal societies have been rare throughout world history.

During the colonial period in the United States, slavery was found everywhere. Not all enslaved Africans came from matriarchal or even matrilineal societies, but many of them were familiar with these family patterns. Typically, African women were socialized to be self-reliant, to be the center of family activity, and to contribute to family income or food production. Once enslaved, African women were valued by their masters for their labor and as producers of additional slaves. Healthy family development was not a priority among slaveowners, so black family survival was always precarious. In some communities, such as the Maryland plantation where Frederick Douglass was born, mothers were not allowed to take care of their own children, because the value of their labor was preferred; child rearing was left to older women, like Douglass's grandmother.

Despite the challenges, family life among slaves managed to continue in various forms. By the early 19th century most slaves lived in the South, many of them working on plantations. Family survival often depended upon slave mothers, who were usually allowed to provide care for their young children. Moreover, in some slave communities, like the Cedar Vale plantation in Virginia, family life was encouraged. Slave parents lived together with their offspring and perhaps other kin, who made up an extended family. Members other than parents helped to care for children; grandmothers, in particular, played an important role in child rearing. Extended families are common in traditional African societies. Slavery in the New World accommodated well to this familial arrangement, which promoted family survival for generations after slavery. Following Emancipation, black women often found work as live-in domestic servants. Grandmothers who were at home cared for the children of their daughters, who worked and lived elsewhere.

Extended familial organization was only one of the similarities between Africans and Indians during the slavery era. As a result of similar worldviews,

Africans and Indians could relate well in the New World environment that Europeans often found alien. Although slavery fostered self-reliant mothers and female-centered families, Europeans dominated North America by the 17th century and attempted to discredit non-European culture, promoting a negative view of African women. In modern times, this negative view has been misinterpreted as black matriarchy.

Black women, who have been victims of the heritage of slavery and economic exploitation, have, nevertheless, been blamed for causing family disruption and deterioration. The 1965 U.S. Labor Department report, *The Negro Family: The Case for National Action*, strengthened the myth of black matriarchy. This document, referred to as the "Moynihan Report," was built upon earlier theories of black family development put forth by black sociologist E. Franklin Frazier. Frazier blamed slavery for destroying the African patriarchal family, which he believed to be the common form of family authority. The conclusions of the Moynihan study, on the other hand, led to indictments of black women for usurping authority in the family by dominating black men in employment, achieving higher educational levels, and making family decisions. One of the suggested solutions to the problem of so-called black matriarchy was for black men to throw off female control and to reorganize families along patriarchal lines. Patriarchy was deemed the panacea for all the ills created by dominant black women. This solution seemed natural in a society where Western values embrace the traditional values of patriarchy.

In Western societies income and education are prerequisites for achieving authority and power outside, as well as

Woman washing clothes by hand, Vicksburg, Mississippi, 1968

inside, the home. Curiously, the myth of black matriarchy never has taken into consideration that black women have not attained power in American society; they consistently remain at the bottom of income scales that compare men and women by race. Black status in the U.S. economy has been determined by racism and sexism, not by black female ascendency as the authority figure in the home or the community. When necessary, black women have been forced to become the foundation for family survival.

Nevertheless, female-headed households have not been the dominant structure in black families since emancipation. The growing rate of single-parent households in the late 20th century is high among blacks, but it is not exclusive to black families. In 1970, 29.3 percent of black families and 7.8 percent of white families were headed by women. In 1982 the respective figures were 47.2 percent and 15.3 percent. The increasing divorce rate in

American society has promoted this situation among women, and the death rate for black men, always the highest among men and women, blacks and whites, contributes to the high number of black female heads of families, many of whom face poverty. As of 1983 over one-third of all single-parent, female-headed families lived below the poverty level, and of these 56.2 percent were black. In five southern states in 1980, 70 percent or more of the single-parent, female-headed families below the poverty level were black. Recently the needs of such families have received increasing attention, particularly from black leaders.

Self-reliance and willingness to assume family responsibilities are values learned by black females early in life. These values, which can be found in rural and urban communities, across regional lines, and among the educated and noneducated, are essential to family and personal survival in a society that has historically placed little value on the quality of black life.

See also BLACK LIFE: Family, Black

Rosalyn Terborg-Penn
Columbia, Maryland

Agnes Ahosua Aidoo, in *The Black Woman Cross-Culturally*, ed. Filomina C. Steady (1981); John Blassingame, *The Slave Community: Plantation Life in the Antebellum South* (1972); Frederick Douglass, *Narrative of the Life of Frederick Douglass* (1963); E. Franklin Frazier, *The Negro Family in the United States* (1939); Herbert G. Gutman, *The Black Family in Slavery and in Freedom, 1750–1925* (1979); Bernice Reagon Johnson, *Feminist Studies* (Spring 1982); U.S. Bureau of the Census, *Current Population Reports*, Series P-20, no. 380 (1983), *General Social and Economic Characteristics, 1980* (by state) (1981); U.S. Department of Labor, *The Negro Family: The Case for National Action* (1965). ☆

Mexican Women

Mexicans living in the South have traditionally resided in Texas, and the historical and contemporary experiences of *las Tejanas*—the Mexican women of Texas—offer a unique perspective on life in the westernmost realm of the South. Beginning in 1659 with the founding of El Paso del Norte, Mexican pioneers attempted to carve out a prosperous province called *Tejas* despite hostile American Indians and apparent neglect from the colonial government in Mexico City. Mexican women on the frontier performed various tasks in addition to nurturing children and maintaining a home. They cleaned the mission sacristy, made candles, tended the sick, and taught domestic arts (such as cooking and knitting) to the small numbers of American Indian women living at the mission. In addition, they worked alongside their fathers or husbands feeding livestock and tending crops. Under the Spanish and Mexican legal systems, women possessed community property rights and owned land in their own name.

Because of Indian raids, a shortage of colonists, and indifference from the colonial government, *Tejas* was a struggling outpost. In 1820 the Mexican government decided to take action; it invited Anglo settlers to Texas. At first Anglo and Mexican pioneers enjoyed cordial relations. *Tejanos* offered help and hospitality to the new arrivals. However, as the Anglo population swelled, cultural differences, misunderstandings, and prejudice eroded the goodwill between Anglos and Mexicans. From 1830 onward the new arrivals viewed Mexicans as inferior beings. Expedition reports, diaries, and journalistic accounts characterized Mexicans as lazy, greasy, dumb, superstitious, sneaky, and morally degenerate. Mexican women, in particular, were deemed sensual, wanton creatures—a stereotype that has survived to the present. As Texas pioneer Susan Magoffin recorded in her diary, "The women go around with their arms and neck bare—perhaps their bosoms exposed (and they are none of the prettiest or whitest)."

These pejorative observations held tragic implications. After the Texas Revolution and the United States–Mexican War, Anglos took over property they coveted, and Mexicans had no legal recourse. For instance, in 1830 Doña Patricia de Leon was one of the wealthiest women in the Southwest. She and her husband owned large, prosperous landholdings in south Texas worth over $500,000. Although Doña de Leon had been a principal financial supporter of the Texas Revolution, she and her family fled the state in 1836. Eight years later she returned in poverty to her home in Victoria. Moreover, the only woman ever executed in the history of Texas was of Mexican descent. Convicted of murder based on circumstantial evidence, Chepita Rodriguez was executed in 1863.

From 1836 to the 1950s Texas was a segregated state with segregated schools, restaurants, theaters, and jobs. Mexicans were relegated to the lowest occupational levels with little opportunity for advancement. Whether in urban or rural areas, several members of a family labored to put food on the table.

As farm workers, Mexicans have usually been paid as a family unit rather than as individuals. During the early decades of the 20th century, a rural *Tejana* had few occupational choices outside of laboring in the fields with her husband and children. Sometimes unmarried daughters worked as clerks in stores that catered to Mexican clientele, but more often women worked as domestic servants for Anglo landowners. Urban women faced similar circumstances. They were typically employed by laundries, garment factories, canneries, and packing houses. Moreover, stores that served Hispanics hired *Mexicanas* as sales clerks and office help. They also served as maids in private homes, hotels, and businesses.

The economic participation of Mexican women was not overlooked in their communities. During the early 1900s Spanish-language newspapers, such as *El Cronista del Valle* of Brownsville, editorialized that the industrial employment of *Tejanas* posed a threat to the family. Newspapers argued that factory labor would turn women into "robots with no emotion or sense of home responsibilities." Although this blanket prohibition against female employment was an extreme in Mexican communities, most Hispanic families did accept the notion that, while unmarried daughters could work for wages, wives were to stay within the confines of the home unless financially desperate. Many mothers, however, supplemented their families' incomes by taking in sewing, laundry, and boarders.

In addition to home and work duties, many 20th-century *Tejanas* have been involved in labor and political struggles. Examples of trade-union activism include the El Paso Laundry Strike of 1919, the San Antonio Pecan Shellers'

Strike of 1938, and the recent two-year dispute at Farah, one of the largest clothing manufacturers in the state. These women have also been involved in various political and community activities. Groups of *Tejanas* raised funds for Ricardo Flores Magon and the *Partido Liberal Mexicano* during the era of the Mexican Revolution (1910–26). Magon, one of the first proponents of political and economic equality for Mexican women, enjoyed considerable popularity among Hispanic women. In 1911 Magon supporters Andrea and Teresa Villarreal published the first feminist newspaper in Texas, *La Mujer Moderna*. *Tejanas* also helped organize *El Primer Congreso Mexicanista*, held on 11–12 September 1911 in Laredo. Addressing a number of civil rights issues, the Congress protested lynchings of Mexicans and called for an end to inferior, segregated schools. The education of women was also an important issue. As Soledad Pena declared, "the best way . . . is to educate woman; to instruct her, and to encourage and to give her due respect." Pena and other women involved in the meetings founded the *Liga Feminist Mexicanista*.

In addition, *Tejanas* have participated in *mutualistas* and patriotic societies. *Mutualistas* provided insurance and charitable services to their members and to residents of the local Mexican community. Some organizations became involved in trade-union activities. For example, *Mexicana* labor organizer Sara Estela Ramirez worked for *La Sociedad de Obreros, Igualdad y Progreso*. During the 1970s *La Raza Unida*, an incipient Hispanic political party, actively recruited women both as precinct workers and candidates. Mexican women have also made inroads in the Democratic party, as well as in nonpartisan civic

groups such as the League of United Latin American Citizens. *Tejanas*, however, are still clustered in the lower socioeconomic brackets. According to the 1980 census, the median income of Mexican women in Texas averaged $7,750. (The figures for Anglo and black women reached $10,586 and $8,503, respectively.) In fact, their average earnings were 43.7 percent of those garnered by Anglo males. These economic disparities can be explained, in part, by the low levels of education characteristic of Mexican-American women. Fifty-five percent of *Tejanas* in the labor force have eight years or less of formal education while only 4 percent have attained college degrees. Although not a panacea, an expansion of educational opportunities for Hispanic women holds exciting possibilities for the future.

From the frontier period to the present, *Tejanas* have displayed remarkable resiliency and resourcefulness. Whether establishing a settlement in a hostile land or working in the factories and fields, they have been survivors and innovators. As political organizers, labor activists, teachers, blue-collar workers, and as wives and mothers, *Tejanas* have been important, creative forces shaping Texas and southern history.

See also ETHNIC LIFE: / Mexicans; HISTORY AND MANNERS: Mexican War; SOCIAL CLASS: Labor, Organized

Vicki L. Ruiz
University of California, Davis

Martha P. Cotera, *Diosa y Hembra: The History and Heritage of Chicanas in the U.S.* (1976); Arnoldo De Leon, *They Called Them Greasers: Anglo Attitudes toward Mexicans in*

Texas, 1821–1900 (1983); Mario T. Garcia, *Proceedings of the National Association for Chicano Studies* (1979); Magdalena Mora and Adelaida R. Del Castillo, eds., *Mexican Women in the United States: Struggles Past and Present* (1980); Vicki L. Ruiz, *Southwest Institute for Research on Women, Working Paper No. 19* (1984); Paul S. Taylor, *Mexican Labor in the United States*, 2 vols. (1930–32). ☆

Politics, Women in

The South has added distinctive connotations to the definition of women's "proper sphere" in the United States. An examination of southern politics confirms that, even though constrained by powerful cultural, legal, social, economic, and psychological forces, women have steadily moved from a predominantly private family role into public political activities.

The culture of the Old South, although never monolithic, generally restricted women to a narrow orbit circumscribed by the ascendant symbol of "the lady." Inspired by a variety of literary and historical sources, as well as by practical considerations, the complex image of "the lady" magnified the prevalent 19th-century national "cult of true womanhood," which prescribed piety, purity, submissiveness, and domesticity as preeminent female virtues and consigned women to the special province of the home. Southern shibboleths about women created an elaborate rationale dedicated to the defense of the peculiar institution of slavery and infatuated with the medieval code of chivalry. Submissiveness translated into inferiority, polemics superseded reason, myth obscured reality, and idealization became repression.

Disfranchised and denied orthodox political influence, women developed unconventional methods to challenge the male-dominated system. In time southern women proved particularly ingenious in their devices, but few opportunities existed in the society before 1860. In South Carolina, the Grimké sisters represented the dilemma of antebellum dissenters, who frequently took the path of imposed or self-imposed exile.

After 1865 southerners were compelled by education, industrialization, and urbanization to reconsider women's proper place. Voluntary associations, often affiliated with the authoritative institution of the church, enabled southern women to gain confidence as administrators and public speakers. From the 1870s they participated openly if not powerfully in state political organizations.

The campaign for women's suffrage and the crusade against lynching epitomized the strengths and weaknesses of the political efforts of southern women. To avoid the abusive epithet "short-haired women," they painstakingly displayed ladylike demeanor and selectively deferred to tradition in their appearances and actions. Racism, states' rights, and pragmatic elitism compromised both the Southern States Woman Suffrage Conference created in 1913 by Kate Gordon of New Orleans and the Association of Southern Women for the Prevention of Lynching launched in 1930 under the leadership of Jessie Daniel Ames of Texas. Torn between the desire for change and the perceived need for social control, southern reformers acquiesced in the dogma of white supremacy. The failure, except for ephemeral and fragile coalitions, to transcend the race question prevented the achievement of gender solidarity. Although Arkansas, Tennessee, and Texas among the former Confederate states secured partial women's suffrage through legislative enactment and also ratified the Nineteenth Amendment, only the dreaded federal intervention brought full citizenship in 1920. Many veterans of the suffrage wars competed successfully for state political positions, but inexperience and prolonged socialization impeded the acquisition of real power. Toleration, not equality, most accurately described the condition of southern women.

The political culture after 1920 accentuated three southern phenomena: women as appointed male successors, women as male proxies, and women as mirrors of male political authority. Occasionally a successor has established her own political identity, but most women appointed to office have exerted marginal influence. Appointed U.S. senators, Rebecca Felton of Georgia, Hattie Caraway of Arkansas, Rose Long of Louisiana, and Dixie Graves of Alabama upheld the accepted image of southern women. Caraway won two complete terms in the elections of 1932 and 1938, but the precedents she set in the Senate had limited significance. The classification of "gracious southern lady" has survived in the career of Representative Corinne "Lindy" Boggs of Louisiana, who initially triumphed in 1973 in a special election for her missing husband's congressional seat.

Two dramatic examples typify the southern woman as male proxy. Elected governor in Texas in 1924 and 1932 as a substitute for her disqualified husband, Miriam "Ma" Ferguson unabashedly offered voters two Fergusons

for the price of one. Lurleen Wallace's brief administration as nominal governor of Alabama caricatured women in politics. Exploited by her ineligible husband, Governor George C. Wallace, who emerged victorious in her name in 1966, she stoically endured subordination until her death in 1968.

An exceptional model of women who are mirrors of male political authority, Rosalynn Carter attracted unusually intense scrutiny during her husband's presidency. All presidents' wives derive prestige from their relationships, but Carter's southern background marked her as "the steel magnolia," a superficial but telling delineation that popularly symbolized the contradictory impact of southern culture on women in politics.

In the era of the Second Reconstruction after World War II, organized attacks on race and sex discrimination reappeared. Awareness of racism stimulated consciousness of sexism, and again the South figured prominently in the battle. Women activists in student and civil rights groups publicized the common injustices, but the struggles allied women temporarily rather than permanently and expectations of fairness and equality remained unmet.

Southern women have played a part in their own victimization by their equivocal attitudes. Both enthralled by and at odds with the stereotypical claims of their peculiar morality and virtue, they tailored their arguments to gain maximum advantage. Conflicting demands for liberation and the preservation of special protection negated each other.

Alteration, not transformation, has distinguished the political status of southern women. Evolutionary and revolutionary, conservative and radical, conformist and iconoclastic, pragmatic and idealistic, racist and egalitarian, their causes have embodied many of the paradoxes of the regional heritage that have influenced contemporary cultural patterns. Ambivalent about women's roles, the South sanctions sexual politics and the illusion of change, while the southern cultural tradition continues to inhibit genuine participation by women in its politics.

See also BLACK LIFE: / Hamer, Fannie Lou; POLITICS: / Felton, Rebecca

Betty Brandon
University of South Alabama

Sara Evans, *Personal Politics: The Roots of Women's Liberation in the Civil Rights Movement and the New Left* (1979); Jacquelyn Dowd Hall, *Revolt Against Chivalry: Jessie Daniel Ames and the Women's Campaign against Lynching* (1979); Sharon Harley and Rosalyn Terborg-Penn, eds., *The Afro-American Woman: Struggles and Images* (1978); Julie Roy Jeffrey, *Feminist Studies* (Fall 1975); Gerda Lerner, *The Majority Finds Its Past: Placing Women in History* (1979); Anne Firor Scott, *The Southern Lady: From Pedestal to Politics, 1830–1930* (1970); A. Elizabeth Taylor, *The Woman Suffrage Movement in Tennessee* (1957). ☆

Race Relations and Women

||||||||||||||||||||||||||||||||||||||||||||||||||||||||||||||||||

Antebellum plantation society made manifest the South's dual caste system based on race and sex. During the era of slavery white women and black women and men occupied an overtly subordinate position compared to white men, but the forms and functions of ra-

cial and sexual oppression differed in each case. Blacks of both sexes served as the primary labor force within a staple-crop economy, and slave women, as childbearers and nurturers, were integral to the reproduction and sustenance of that labor force. In contrast, white women had primary responsibility for household management and bore the heirs who would eventually oversee the geographical expansion and increasing politicization of the region's "peculiar institution." Thus, although their inferior legal and social position derived from physical characteristics that differentiated them from white men, blacks and white women held statuses that were not strictly analogous. Certainly, white women's class prerogatives and material advantages derived from the exploitation of slaves, both male and female. For these reasons, relations between women of the two races, whether conducted in white households or in the public arena, were fraught with tension.

Together with their menfolk, black women helped to create a distinctive Afro-American culture that rejected the white (male) middle-class values of aggressive individualism and personal ambition. A cooperative ethos informed the slaves' religious beliefs, kin relations, and day-to-day resistance to bondage. Despite this sense of racial separateness, however, black people never lost sight of the goal of equality, defined first as freedom from slavery and then, after emancipation, as full legal rights and economic opportunity. The black scholar-activist W. E. B. Du Bois termed this double consciousness "twoness." For black women, twoness meant that their relations with white women would be problematic in both cultural and political terms. Moreover, conflict between the two groups of women was exacerbated by the South's social divisions of labor, which dictated that the most arduous and disagreeable household chores were labeled not so much women's work as black women's work. Well into the 20th century, black women scorned white women as lazy and condemned the time-honored tradition that allowed one group of women to play a direct role in the economic exploitation of another.

White women brought quite different perspectives to bear on the issue of race relations. Individual white women throughout southern history have represented a wide spectrum of attitudes. In the 19th century Sarah and Angelina Grimké, daughters of a Charleston slaveholder, devoted much of their adult lives to the abolitionist cause in the North, and the two sisters showed special sensitivity to the plight of slave women. During the civil rights revolution, Anne Braden, Lillian Smith, and Virginia Durr joined the struggle initiated by blacks against disfranchisement and segregation. In contrast, vengeful slave mistresses quick to unleash their anger on slave women and white housewives who, in the 1960s, clawed the faces of black freedom riders or sprayed peaceful civil rights demonstrators with insecticides demonstrated the ways in which the white supremacist imperative could turn woman against woman.

Nevertheless, exclusive attention to these extreme forms of behavior obscures the complexity of women's roles in race relations. For example, the female relatives of a Birmingham Ku Klux Klan member who bombed a black church in that city and killed four black girls in 1963 cooperated in the 14-year investigation that led to his conviction and imprisonment for life. Their clandestine activities as FBI informants

sprang from feelings that were not altogether clear—either personal dislike for the man's tyrannical nature, their own sympathy and concern for the victims, or a combination of these motives. Upper middle-class white women figure prominently in accounts of racial liberalism in the South, but perhaps only because their public pronouncements have been better documented than more modest challenges to the racial caste system carried out by their less well-to-do sisters. In fact, it would be exceedingly difficult to correlate white women's sense of racial egalitarianism with their class standing; privileged white women, in their roles as employers, landlords, and voter registrars, often upheld the tenets of racial inequality.

Indeed, a focus on nonelite white and black women after slavery reveals an irony in the history of southern race relations—that these two groups exhibited mutual suspicion and hostility toward one another despite their very similar material condition. For example, tenant farm wives from the late 19th century through the 1930s followed the same daily and seasonal household routines. They lived in similarly dilapidated cabins (in some cases the same dwelling alternately housed black and white families) and reared equal numbers of children with little in the way of cash or modern conveniences. These women took pride in their large families and in their ability to work in the fields "like a man." Their domestic responsibilities, combined with petty trade activities, set them apart from their husbands, who labored exclusively in the realm of the larger commercial economy.

Nevertheless, female tenants of the two races had few occasions to explore these common bonds. In the late 1930s

tutional structure, their prayerful presence and domestic support for a largely itinerant ministry were critical to a sense of successful mission.

The nature of evangelical religion also encouraged the gathering together of women and their families for religious services. Out of this gathering rapidly grew societies of women working together to pursue certain spiritual goals, missionary work, religious education of children, and various aid societies. Joint religious activities have been central to the organized social life of southern white women since that time.

Where Afro-Americans, slave or free, were Christian, they tended to follow the same pattern as white evangelicals. Black women were not permitted to take roles of institutional leadership but had the same freedom of religious expression as did the whites, although the circumscribed nature of their social lives did not permit them to form as extensive a network of female societies. In the folk religion of the South, on the other hand, some black women held positions of power. On the plantations they often acted as spiritual leaders—prophetesses or witches—called upon for assistance by blacks and whites alike. Black women often took the lead in organized voodoo activities, particularly in New Orleans, where the two Marie Laveaus, mother and daughter, were widely celebrated priestesses during a 50-year period in the middle of the 19th century.

The continued dominance of evangelical Protestantism after the Civil War and the failure of people with strikingly different religious orientations to migrate into the South tended to reinforce patterns established earlier. Institutional religious leadership would go to the men; the women would find their role in the ladies' auxiliary. As the South became increasingly middle class, the women sought ways in which they could spend their increased leisure time in projects allowing them to use their intelligence and energy in the service of others. The church organizations provided that opportunity.

The women in the largest white denominations organized their activities along similar lines. Baptist, Methodist, and Presbyterian women all developed missionary societies. The task of these organizations was to develop support, both financial and spiritual, for foreign missionaries. Although women were barred from the clergy of these major religious groups, they were encouraged to become foreign missionaries. Many unmarried women went abroad under the auspices of the missionary societies. Wives were also commissioned along with their husbands in missionary activities—not as clergy, but as nurses, teachers, social service workers, and, above all, witnesses to Christ's saving grace. There was probably no role available to southern women that so enabled them to use their courage, intelligence, initiative, and resourcefulness, as that of spinster missionary. One of the most widely known religious figures among Southern Baptists is Charlotte "Lottie" Moon, a genuine cultural heroine, who served as a missionary in China for many years and whose exemplary life is used by Baptists to symbolize the entire missionary enterprise.

Unlike the Baptist women who focused almost exclusively on foreign missions, the Methodists began to look closer to home as well for fields of service. As Methodist women began to seek and be denied positions of leadership in the denomination, they developed progressive societies to address the evils in the culture around them. They organized social settlements and a variety of services for poor and working women. It was Methodist women's organizations that represented the social gospel movement in the South. These women also formed a vanguard in the struggle to establish some basis for racial cooperation.

Even before the Civil War the evangelical denominations provided education for their women. These women, after all, managed the homes in which the next generation of evangelicals would be raised. After the war, in both white and black denominational schools and colleges, women were given an education that sometimes led them to reject the principle on which the education was based. Many of those black and white women who challenged the religious, social, and political status quo got their inspiration from the very tradition they opposed.

In recent years, as women have increasingly insisted that they be allowed to provide ministerial leadership in their churches, the South continues to lag behind the rest of the nation in ordaining women. The largest number of female clergy to be found in the South is in the growing Pentecostal movement.

Whereas women have been influential in founding new religious movements in other parts of the United States, rarely, if ever, has a woman been instrumental in the formation of such a movement in the South. The religious homogeneity of the region, as well as the patriarchal emphasis of the culture, has tended to restrict religious innovation of any kind. Southern women have channeled their spiritual energies into the traditional religious structure. Those who have been unable to fit into the cultural mold have either left the region or turned inward upon themselves and nurtured their spiritual lives. The stifling of southern women's spiritual insights has led some of these women to seek self-fulfillment in areas outside the life of the churches, an enterprise that only today is meeting with any degree of success.

See also BLACK LIFE: Religion, Black; FOLKLIFE: Voodoo; RELIGION articles

> Thomas R. Frazier
> Baruch College,
> City University of New York

Jean E. Friedman, *The Enclosed Garden: Women and Community in the Evangelical South, 1830–1900* (1985); Samuel S. Hill, *The South and the North in American Religion* (1980); Donald Mathews, *Religion in the Old South* (1977); Albert J. Raboteau, *Slave Religion: The "Invisible Institution" in the Antebellum South* (1978); Anne Firor Scott, *The Southern Lady: From Pedestal to Politics, 1830–1930* (1970); Noreen Dunn Tatum, *Crown of Service: A Story of Woman's Work in the Methodist Episcopal Church, South, from 1878–1940* (1960). ☆

Suffrage and Antisuffrage

||||||||||||||||||||||||||||||||||||||||||||||||||||||||||||||||

Prior to the Civil War the South showed little interest in woman's enfranchisement. During Reconstruction the issue was raised in several constitutional conventions, but in no state were women granted the right to vote. After Reconstruction woman suffrage became associated with the South's desire to reduce the importance of the black male vote. A widely discussed proposal was the enfranchisement of women with educational and/or property qualifications.

This extension of the franchise would include black as well as white women. Fewer black women would be able to meet these requirements, so the proportion of white voters would be increased. The strength of the Negro vote would be diluted, and white control of southern politics would be assured.

Proposals to enfranchise women meeting certain qualifications were introduced in constitutional conventions in Mississippi (1890), South Carolina (1895), and Alabama (1901). None of these proposals was adopted, however. Involving women in politics was contrary to southern cultural traditions, and southern men were unwilling to use this strategem even for the purpose of coping with the vexing race issue.

In 1892 the National American Woman Suffrage Association established a special committee on southern work. This committee was composed of southern women and was chaired by Laura Clay of Kentucky. It endeavored to influence public opinion through the distribution of literature and the sponsoring of lectures. Due largely to its efforts, suffrage organizations were formed in all the southern states before the end of the decade.

When crusading for the ballot, southern women followed the guidelines of the National American Woman Suffrage Association. They conducted their agitation with dignity and restraint. They avoided the militant tactics advocated by Alice Paul's National Woman's party. The National Woman's party organized branches in the southern states, but its following there was small. It conducted no militant agitation in the area, but some southern women participated in such activities in the nation's capital. The oldest of the White House pickets and suffrage prisoners, for example, was a southern woman, 73-year-old Mary C. Nolan of Jacksonville, Fla.

The suffragists assured the public that enfranchisement would enable women to be better wives, mothers, citizens, and taxpayers. They would use their votes for the general betterment of society. The antisuffragists countered by arguing that enfranchisement would constitute a threat to the home and the family. Participation in politics would coarsen women and cause them to lose their femininity. It would also cause them to neglect their household duties and would lead to quarrels between husbands and wives.

The "antis" did little organizing in the South and can hardly be considered to have had a movement there. Their strength lay in their appeal to traditional prejudices and to generally established values. They were endeavoring to maintain the status quo while the suffragists were working for change.

The suffragists established lobbies in state capitals. Bills to enfranchise women were introduced in state legislatures, but they were seldom passed. In only three states were significant gains made. In Arkansas in 1917 the legislature passed a law permitting women to vote in primary elections. The following year Texas passed a similar law. In 1919 Tennessee granted women the right to vote for presidential electors and also the right to vote in municipal elections. No southern state, however, allowed full enfranchisement.

When the federal woman suffrage amendment was submitted to the states for ratification, it encountered its strongest opposition in the South. Many southerners considered suffrage a state, not a federal, matter and feared that ratification would mean federal control of elections. Others held that the enfran-

Suffragists in early 20th-century Kentucky

chisement of black women would reopen the entire issue of the Negro's role in politics. Some predicted that it would usher in another era of Reconstruction.

In June 1919 Texas became the first state in the South to ratify the Susan B. Anthony Amendment. A few weeks later, Arkansas followed. Kentucky ratified in January 1920. In July 1919 Georgia became the first state in the Union to reject the proposed amendment. Georgia's example was soon followed by Alabama, South Carolina, Virginia, Mississippi, and Louisiana.

Thirty-five states had ratified by August 1920. The approval of only one more was needed. The governor of Tennessee submitted the question to a special session of the legislature. A bitter controversy ensued. Those opposing ratification called the proposed amendment a peril to the South and urged its

rejection. Those in favor maintained that eventual ratification was a certainty and that Tennessee's refusal could only delay it. After much emotional debate and political maneuvering, both houses of the legislature approved, and on 26 August 1920 the Nineteenth Amendment became part of the U.S. Constitution.

Two southern states refused to accept woman suffrage as the supreme law of the land. Mississippi and Georgia did not allow women to vote in the general election of 1920, claiming that the Nineteenth Amendment had been ratified too late to permit women to comply with state election laws. Georgia's leading suffragist, Mary Latimer McLendon of Atlanta, telegraphed the secretary of state in Washington and asked his opinion in regard to her eligibility to vote. Her effort was in vain, however, because the secretary refused to become involved.

During the months that followed, Mississippi and Georgia yielded, and woman suffrage prevailed throughout the South. Women voted and held office. The fears of the "antis" were not realized, however. Women did not lose their femininity, nor did they neglect their homes for politics. Only a few aspired to political careers.

The South's strong opposition to woman suffrage was due to its basic conservatism, its devotion to the ideal of the patriarchal family, and its fear of federal interference in elections. Having no alternative, the South accepted enfranchisement, but remained conservative in its attitude toward women and the family. The advent of woman suffrage apparently resulted in no appreciable change in the fundamental nature of southern culture.

See also POLITICS: Voting

A. Elizabeth Taylor
Texas Woman's University

Clement Eaton, *Georgia Review* (Summer 1974); Paul E. Fuller, *Laura Clay and the Woman's Rights Movement* (1975); Kenneth R. Johnson, *Journal of Southern History* (August 1972); Anne Firor Scott, *The Southern Lady: From Pedestal to Politics, 1830–1930* (1970); A. Elizabeth Taylor, *Journal of Mississippi History* (February 1968), *South Carolina Historical Magazine* (April 1976; October 1979), *The Woman Suffrage Movement in Tennessee* (1957). ☆

Workers' Wives

||||||||||||||||||||||||||||||||||||||||||

Although attention has been given to upper-class southern women (e.g. the "southern belle") and slave women (e.g., the "black mammy"), the wife of the southern worker has been neglected. Not bound by the restrictions of racism or the social demands to appear "ladylike," the worker's wife has been a significant contributor to southern history and society.

On the southern colonial farm, work was divided along gender lines. In addition to cooking, cleaning, and rearing children, women had responsibility for small animals, the dairy, gardening, and the orchard. Men cared for large animals, planted and harvested crops, and did general field work. But, in times of need, for example during harvest season, sex roles on the colonial farm merged as children and wife helped the husband bring in the crops.

The preindustrial work patterns continued into the antebellum South. As Frank L. Owsley noted in *Plain Folk of the Old South*, the wife of the yeoman farmer "hoed the corn, cooked the dinner or plied the loom, or even came out and took up the ax and cut the wood with which to cook the dinner." The Civil War revealed both her productivity and her endurance; after her husband went off to fight, often with her encouragement, she took over the farms and shops, and women provided the bulk of the urban labor force.

As scholars have recently discovered, southern women have had a more active and important role in southern politics than has been traditionally assumed. The Women's Christian Temperance Union (WCTU), antilynching crusades, and the progressive reform movements of the 19th and 20th centuries involved wives of southern workers, as well as middle- and upper-class women. But their role as political activists dates back even further. Workers' wives, for example, were politically active in the

1600s in Bacon's Rebellion in Virginia, and women such as Harriet Tubman were later involved in resistance to the slave system.

The industrialization of the South transformed to some extent the economic and social functions of women as well as men. In order to support their families, both husband and wife left farms and took factory jobs. In Alabama, while the number of men drawn into industry between 1885 and 1895 increased 31 percent, that of women increased 75 percent. In 1890 women constituted 40 percent of the work force in the four largest southern textile plants. But their political activity did not change. Women, particularly wives of workers, were active in protesting child labor, and, like Ella May Wiggins of the Gastonia strike, they were heavily involved in southern industrial struggles.

Nowhere was the importance and influence of workers' wives more vividly revealed than in the southern coalfields. By law and superstition (a mine would supposedly explode if a woman entered it), women were prohibited from industrial work, that is, working in the coal mines. And because southern coal towns were usually in isolated, rural areas, women were not able to find employment in other industries as did miners' wives in northern coalfields. They

Rural married couple, Batesville, Mississippi, 1968

hardly submitted, however, to the life of Victorian domesticity.

In the era before unions (1880–1933) men worked in the mines 10–14 hours a day, 6 days a week. Hence, their wives essentially controlled the domestic economy and ran the family. To assist the husband in supporting the family, wives continued their preindustrial roles of caring for the family garden, taking in boarders, and doing the laundry of company officials and single miners. And it was the wife who dealt with the daily frustration of keeping the house clean and sanitary in a town filled with coal dust and grime because the company refused to install sanitary facilities such as running water and sewers.

In the company towns that predominated in the southern coalfields, the home was hardly a "separate sphere" sheltering women from the cruelties of the competitive, "public" world, as was said to have been the case in northern urban areas. With her husband down in the coal mines, a wife dealt with the company store and had direct, day-to-day contact with company officials. Consequently, she most keenly and intensely felt the coal company's abuse of power, especially its exploitation in the form of low wages, monopolistic prices, and the lack of sanitary facilities.

Women expressed their anger toward the coal operators in a number of ways. One was in song; Florence Reece, who wrote the classic labor song, "Which Side Are You On?" after company police had driven her husband out of their company town, was but one of a multitude of female, coalfield troubadors, a list that also includes the likes of Aunt Molly Jackson, Sarah Gunning, and more recently Hazel Dickens.

Women expressed their desire for improved living and working conditions in the coalfields, as well as their anger, by becoming major advocates for union-ization. The exploits of the legendary union organizer Mother Jones are well known. But Ralph Chaplin, (author of "Solidarity Forever") captured Jones's appeal when he wrote, after hearing her speak: "She might have been any coal miner's wife filled with righteous fury." The miner's wife helped offset the rigors of labor strife by planting larger gardens and canning more food. With wages stopped, the usual source of food and clothing (the company store) cut off, and shelter denied (miners were thrown out of company houses during strikes), min-ers could not have succeeded in any coal strike without this extensive prepara-tion.

Miners' wives formed auxiliaries to the United Mine Workers of America to promote the union cause. These orga-nizations, sometimes denigrated as sep-arate, sexist, and unequal, nevertheless increased social awareness and cama-raderie among coalfield women and pro-vided needed moral and financial support for organizing the southern coal-fields. And wives of miners fought, often violently, for the union. After witnessing a gun battle during a coal strike in West Virginia in 1912 a San Francisco jour-nalist reported, "In West Virginia women fight side-by-side with the men." Indeed, the wife's hostility to the com-pany and her role in strikes were so important that coal company officials often took elaborate measures to try to co-opt them into the company-town sys-tem.

As the Academy Award-winning movie *Harlan County, USA* revealed, wives of miners still play a significant role in the unionization of the coalfields. The relative ease with which women have entered the coal mines as workers suggests that the coalfields may be a less "macho" culture than once assumed. Wives of workers in other southern in-dustries and occupations have faced ob-stacles similar to those faced by miners' wives and have made similar contribu-tions.

See also INDUSTRY: Industrialization and Change; / Mining; SOCIAL CLASS: Labor, Organized; / Coal Miners; Company Towns; Textile Workers

David A. Corbin
Washington, D.C.

David A. Corbin, *Life, Work, and Rebellion in the Coal Fields: Southern West Virginia Miners, 1880–1922* (1981); Margaret J. Ha-good, *Mothers of the South: Portraiture of the White Tenant Farm Woman* (1939); Anne Firor Scott, *The Southern Lady: From Ped-estal to Politics, 1830–1930* (1970); Julia Cherry Spruill, *Women's Life and Work in the Southern Colonies* (1938). ☆

Working Women

||||||||||||||||||||||||||||||||||||||||||||

From the colonial period to the present the work performed by southern women has varied according to race and class. Upper- and middle-class white women rarely worked in the public sphere be-fore the 20th century; white working-class women and black women, before and after emancipation from slavery, worked for many generations in agri-cultural labor and became the South's first industrial workers. Changes in the patterns of women's work in the South resulted from industrialization, the de-cline of agricultural labor, and in-creased urbanization. Southern women have a long history of working to support themselves and their families and of struggling to gain fundamental rights within their workplaces. In 1985 southern women, like women throughout the United States, continued to resist occupational segregation in the lowest-paid sectors of the economy and sought to maintain their jobs in a rapidly changing economy.

Women's work in the southern colonies was performed by slaves, indentured servants, and free white women. Like men's work, women's labor was home based and geared toward life in an economy dependent on agricultural production. The work performed by women in the southern colonies varied widely according to class and race. In Virginia, for example, Indian women built houses, farmed, and provided the principal means of production. As white women came into the colonies in greater numbers, they managed households on plantations or smaller farms. Provided with limited education and training, white southern women in colonial towns worked as retail dealers, monopolized the millinery and dressmaking trades, and sold foodstuffs and liquor.

In the early 17th century most southern domestic workers were female white indentured servants. Later in the century these workers were replaced by black slave women who performed myriad skilled and unskilled jobs in antebellum southern society. Slave women worked as children's nurses, cooks, seamstresses, housekeepers, midwives, dairy maids, and agricultural laborers. Forced to spend most of their time working for others, slave women were only occasionally allowed to garden and raise poultry for consumption by their own families or for sale to their masters. During the period between 1775 and 1812 slave women were

trained as skilled spinners and weavers, and their labor changed the South from a region that imported all manufactured goods to one in which home manufacturing was widespread.

Work for women in the early 19th-century South continued to be defined by an agricultural, slave-based economy. Slave women worked in agriculture and domestic service. Wealthy white women, dependent on slave labor, administered large plantations or ran large homes in southern cities. Wives of yeoman farmers managed much smaller farms, with the help of their children. The dominance of staple-crop agricultural production affected the lives of all southern women, regardless of their social or economic status.

After the Civil War exslave women responded to freedom by refusing to work in white homes and for the first time demanding the right to work for their own families. Within a few years, however, economic imperatives compelled large numbers of black women to perform domestic work for white southerners, although day work replaced the live-in arrangement reminiscent of slavery. In the decades after the Civil War, increasing numbers of black and white southern farm families lost their land, mortgaged future cotton or tobacco crops to obtain money for supplies, and struggled for survival in a cashless, debt-dominated economy. Gradually, the women in these families, those most easily spared from agricultural labor, began to work as spinners and weavers in newly built southern cotton mills. Female mill workers, and frequently their children, became the region's first industrial workers and provided farm families with cash wages, which were increasingly necessary for survival. Urban and commercial development was slow in the South in the late 19th century, and only a few women from southern middle-class families had the opportunities to work in urban areas as teachers and clerical workers.

In the 20th century the occupational distribution of women workers varied dramatically between the North and the South. In 1910, 83 percent of the southern female work force was in agriculture and domestic service, compared to 33 percent in the North. As late as 1950 manufacturing employed fewer than 18 percent of the region's women workers but 34 percent of those in the North. In the 1920s, with the onset of agricultural depression in the region, farm tenancy increased for both white and black women. White women had the option of industrial work more frequently than black women, who were usually denied manufacturing jobs, except for seasonal handwork in the tobacco industry. The large number of southern women in agriculture and domestic service constituted a reserve pool of workers waiting to "move up" to manufacturing work. This labor surplus reduced the job security of female industrial workers and increased the leverage manufacturers had over them.

The margin of survival for southern women workers was always much thinner than for their northern sisters. Before 1940 southern wages were substantially lower than the national average, while the cost of living in the South was only 5 percent lower than in other regions. In 1946 southerners made up 25 percent of the nation's population but received only 8 percent of the national income. Because wage rates were low for all workers, southern families often depended on the wages of two or more family members, and women's wages were more critical to the family

economy than in the North. Southern women working in cotton textiles, for example, typically provided 30–40 percent of the family income.

The biracial composition of the female work force in the South and rigid occupational segregation by race have affected both black and white women workers. Sixty percent of the southern female work force was black in 1910, and the figure was 40 percent as late as 1940. White women workers feared being replaced by black workers as managers repeatedly threatened to hire black workers in the place of white employees. Black women migrated north and west to obtain the industrial work denied them within the region or moved into urban areas within the South to toil as domestic workers for an increasingly prosperous white middle class. Only with the civil rights movement of the 1960s did black southern women gain access to work in the textile industry, the South's largest employer, and to clerical positions. This racial shift within southern industry was also important because of its impact on unions. Black women, many of whom had gained organizing experience in the civil rights movement, often proved to be more willing supporters of unions and more active union members than their white counterparts.

Black domestic workers were among the first southern women to participate in organized resistance to existing working conditions. Their locally organized and self-financed efforts were modest in scale, rarely involving an entire community or municipal area. In 1880, for example, black washerwomen in Atlanta organized an association in a black church, and a year later 3,000 washerwomen, cooks, servants, and childnurses struck for higher wages. For each

Student training in mechanics at Bethune-Cookman College, Daytona Beach, Florida, 1940s

publicized protest of this type there were no doubt hundreds of similar, even smaller efforts of which no record has survived.

The history of southern women and unions began with the response of black and white women workers, including homemakers and farmers' wives, to the Knights of Labor. Women who had been active in the Grange and Populist movements responded to the Knights and joined locals in communities across the South. In 1889 over 50 women's local assemblies were already in the region—10 of which had been organized by black women—and southern women's locals comprised 30 percent of the Knights' women's assemblies in the United States. After the demise of the Knights in 1890, American Federation of Labor (AFL) craft unions concentrated on organizing male workers and ignored the needs and concerns of female workers, who turned to middle-class reform groups for support.

Throughout the 1920s the plight of women workers in the South drew the attention of the Young Women's Chris-

tian Association, the National Women's Trade Union League, and the Southern Summer School. These groups emphasized the importance of organizing all the workers within a given industry, focused on the needs of the thousands of southern female workers, and offered direct assistance to striking southern workers. These efforts provided a crucial transitional form of organizing, which transcended the limited goals of the AFL and later encouraged the emergence of the Congress of Industrial Organizations (CIO) in the South.

In 1937 the clothing unions joined with the Textile Workers' Organizing Committee to launch the CIO's first major campaign in the South. Female organizers, especially native southerners, were now hired to work throughout the region. After World War II the CIO launched "Operation Dixie," a far more intensive effort to organize southern workers than the union drives of the 1930s. As the CIO focused on the textile industry, in which women made up over 50 percent of the work force, organizers emphasized union benefits for women workers. The drive brought 400,000 new members into southern locals, over half of them women.

Southern women workers faced strike defeats and declining union membership during the 1950s and 1960s. After the civil rights movement and the opening of industrial jobs for black southerners, however, new efforts in southern union-organizing drives have come increasingly from black women. Long denied access to jobs in the industrial sector, black women in the 1980s hold over 50 percent of the operative positions in many southern plants.

By 1989 the southern female work force reflected national trends more than regional differences. A total of 48 percent of all southern women work outside the home, compared to 50 percent nationally. Among black women, representing 18 percent of the southern female work force in 1980, 52 percent held paid jobs. Southern women are still the lowest-paid workers; in 1980, 65 percent of southern female workers were employed in either manufacturing, clerical, or service occupations. Contemporary southern working women have had to deal with the adverse consequences of deep recessions in the region's basic industries—textiles, tobacco, furniture, and steel—and simultaneously to confront the rapid job shifts resulting from the development and use of new technologies in the clerical and service sectors.

See also AGRICULTURE: Sharecropping and Tenancy; / Grange; BLACK LIFE: Freedom Movement, Black; Slave Culture; Workers, Black; EDUCATION: Teachers; INDUSTRY: Industrialization and Change; / Textile Industry; SOCIAL CLASS: Labor, Organized; Tenant Farmers; / American Federation of Labor; Congress of Industrial Organizations; Knights of Labor; Textile Workers; Tobacco Workers

> Mary Frederickson
> University of Alabama
> at Birmingham

Mary Frederickson, *Women, Work and Protest: A Century of Women's Labor History* (1985); Margaret J. Hagood, *Mothers of the South: Portraiture of the White Tenant Farm Woman* (1939; 1977); Dolores Elizabeth Janiewski, *Sisterhood Denied: Race, Gender, and Class in a New South Community* (1985); Jacqueline Jones, *Labor of Love, Labor of Sorrow: Black Women, Work and the Family from Slavery to the Present* (1985); Alice Kessler-Harris, *Out to Work: A History of Wage-Earning Women in the United States* (1982); Tobi Lippin, ed.,

Southern Exposure (Winter 1981); Julia Cherry Spruill, *Women's Life and Work in the Southern Colonies* (1972). ☆

AMES, JESSIE DANIEL
(1883–1972) Social reformer.

Jessie Daniel Ames, born 2 November 1883, had moved three times in Texas by the time she was a teenager. Her father, a stern Victorian eccentric, migrated from Indiana to Palestine, Tex., where he worked as railroad station master, and in 1893 the Daniels moved to Georgetown, Tex., the site of Southwestern University, from which Ames later graduated.

The brutal Indian Wars and vigilantism of the period created a violent atmosphere, which strongly affected the sensitive young Jessie. A strong-willed child, she had resisted the perfect table manners expected of her and often was sent to the kitchen. In the Daniel kitchen young Jessie heard about a lynching nearby in Tyler, an event she remembered for years and that influenced her lifelong efforts to abolish lynching.

In June 1905 Jessie Daniel married a handsome army surgeon, Roger Post Ames, who later died in Guatemala. In 1914 she rose to prominence in Texas as an advocate of southern progressivism and women's suffrage. Unlike most suffragists in the early 1920s, she understood the grave injustice against blacks in this country. She served as a vital link between feminism and the 20th-century struggle for black civil rights.

In 1924 she became field secretary of Will Alexander's Atlanta-based Commission on Interracial Cooperation. She immediately began organizing against lynching in Texas, Arkansas, and Oklahoma. Alexander brought her to Atlanta in 1929 as Director of Women's Work for the Commission, and in 1930 she began "Southern Women for the Prevention of Lynching," which in nine years had 40,000 members. Alerted by friendly law officers and her contacts in the press when a lynching threatened, Ames contacted women in that county who had pledged to work against violence. Her work was not always appreciated. Opposition came from women as well as men. "The Women's National Association for the Preservation of the White Race" claimed that Ames's women "were defending criminal Negro men at the expense of innocent white girls."

Ames did not support the federal antilynching law in 1940 as being practical. She said the bill would pass the House and southern senators would then defeat it. She was soon at odds with her boss, Dr. Alexander, as well as her old allies in the NAACP.

From May 1939 to May 1940 in the South, for the first time since records had been kept, not a single lynching occurred. World War II, however, dealt a death blow to Southern Women for the Prevention of Lynching, just as it did to the attempt to abolish the hated poll tax in the South. The alliance between women and victimized blacks, which Ames hoped for, was postponed.

In 1943 Southern Women for the Prevention of Lynching was absorbed by the newly formed Southern Regional Council, as was the Interracial Commission. Ames wanted to work for the new agency but found her services were not needed.

In the foothills of the Blue Ridge Mountains Ames set about to rebuild her life. Elected superintendent of Christian Social Relations for the Western North Carolina Conference of the Methodist Church, she welcomed the opportunity "to get back into public life and be remembered." She later returned to Texas, and was honored in the 1970s as a pioneer who combined feminism with civil rights activism. Jessie Daniel Ames died on 21 February 1972 at the age of 88.

See also BLACK LIFE: / Commission on Interracial Cooperation; SOCIAL CLASS: / Southern Regional Council

> Marie S. Jemison
> Birmingham, Alabama

Jessie Daniel Ames Papers, Texas Historical Society, Dallas, Texas State Library, Austin, and Southern Historical Collection, University of North Carolina, Chapel Hill; Association of Southern Women for the Prevention of Lynching and the Commission on Interracial Cooperation Papers, Trevor Arnett Library, Atlanta University; Jacquelyn Dowd Hall, *Revolt Against Chivalry: Jessie Daniel Ames and the Women's Campaign Against Lynching* (1979). ☆

ATKINSON, TI-GRACE
(b. 1939) Feminist.

Ti-Grace Atkinson captured public attention between 1966 and 1972 as one of the most articulate and radical speakers for the women's movement in the United States. She was a protégé of Betty Friedan, who promoted her in the National Organization for Women (NOW) because her "lady-like blond image would counter-act the man-eating specter." Yet Atkinson, who was described by the media as "softly sexy," "tall," and "elegantly feline," came to stand for all that Friedan saw as most damaging to the movement: total separation from men, advocacy of abortion on demand, and the destruction of marriage and the family.

Atkinson was born in 1939 to an established Baton Rouge family. Had she remained at home, she might have become simply the family eccentric, an acceptable, though not desirable, role for southern women of her class. But she was one of those southerners whom Roy Reed described as born afire and who spend their days looking elsewhere for something to ease the burning. Although Atkinson virtually disowned and never discussed her southern upbringing, she always insisted that interviewers record her name as the Cajun "Ti-Grace."

Married at 17, Atkinson went to Philadelphia. By the time she was divorced five years later, she had taken a B.F.A. at the University of Pennsylvania and was establishing a career as an art critic, writing for *Art News* and acting as the founding director of the Philadelphia Institute for Contemporary Art. Then, Simone de Beauvoir's *The Second Sex* converted her to a new philosophy. In 1966 Atkinson joined the nascent NOW, where her appearance, manners, and genteel Republican connections were put to use in national fund-raising.

A year later, Atkinson moved to New York City to pursue graduate study in political philosophy at Columbia University. As president of the local NOW chapter, she generated conflict within the group with her demands for changes not only in the organization's goals and programs but also in its internal structure. Failing to achieve her aims within NOW, she resigned in 1968 to start The October 17th Movement, later modestly renamed the Feminists. Acting on her

fierce drives for constant purification, Atkinson and a small group of 15 to 20 women created a mechanically egalitarian group, within which women were to separate totally from men. Although frequently cited as a lesbian, Atkinson was in fact an advocate of celibacy. It was, she acknowledged, a model for which most women were not ready.

Atkinson's distinctive position in the women's movement was characterized by her exceptional intelligence, her uncompromising radicalism, and a willingness to follow any position to its logical conclusion. She took the Mafia as a model of resistance, living outside the law, and formed an alliance with reputed mobster Joseph Colombo's Italian-American Civil Rights League. This affiliation was widely attacked, and on 6 August 1971 Atkinson divorced herself from the rest of the women's movement.

Despite this breach, in November 1971 she helped organize the Feminist party, which attempted to get the major political parties to incorporate feminist positions into their 1972 platforms. After publication in 1974 of *Amazon Odyssey*, a collection of her speeches and other writings from 1967 to 1972, Atkinson faded from public view. She continues to live in New York City.

Jordy Bell
Croton-on-Hudson, New York

Ti-Grace Atkinson, *Amazon Odyssey: Collection of Writings* (1974); Maren Lockwood Carden, *The New Feminist Movement* (1974); Betty Friedan, *New York Times Magazine* (4 March 1973); Martha Weinman Lear, *New York Times Magazine* (10 March 1968); *Newsweek* (23 March 1970). ☆

BAKER, ELLA JO

|||||||||||||||||||||||||||||||||||||||||||||||

(b. 1903) Civil rights activist.

Ella Jo Baker, the daughter of Georgianna and Blake Baker, was born in 1903 in Norfolk. When she was seven, Baker's family moved to Littleton, N.C., to live with her maternal grandparents, who owned a plantation where they had previously worked as slaves. The absence of adequate public school for blacks in rural North Carolina and her mother's concern that she be properly educated resulted in Baker's attending Shaw University in Raleigh. There, she received both her high school and college education. Following her graduation in 1927, she moved to New York City to live with a cousin, where she worked as a waitress and, later, in a factory.

The product of a southern environment in which caring and sharing were facts of life, and of a family in which her grandfather regularly mortgaged his property in order to help neighbors, Baker soon became involved in various community groups. In 1932 she became the National Director of the Young Negroes Cooperative League and the office manager of the *Negro National News*. Six years later, she began her active career with the National Association for the Advancement of Colored People (NAACP), working initially as a field secretary in the South. In 1943 she was appointed National Director of the Branches for the NAACP. In both capacities Baker spent long periods in southern black communities, where her southern roots served her well. Her success in recruiting southern blacks to join what was considered a radical organization in the 1930s and 1940s may be attributed, in part, to her being a native of the region and, therefore, best able to approach southern people. Baker, who neither married nor had children of her own, left active service in the NAACP in 1946 in order to raise a niece. A short while later she reactivated her involvement with the NAACP, becoming president of the New York City chapter of the NAACP in 1954.

In 1957 Baker went south again, this time to work with the Southern Christian Leadership Conference (SCLC), a newly formed civil rights organization. The student sit-in movement of the 1960s protested the refusal of public restaurants in the South to serve blacks and resulted in Baker's involvement in still another civil rights group. As the coordinator of the 1960 Nonviolent Resistance to Segregation Leadership Conference, which brought together over 300 student sit-in leaders and resulted in the formation of the Student Nonviolent Coordinating Committee (SNCC), Baker is credited with playing a major role in SNCC's founding. Severing a formal relationship with SCLC, she worked with the Southern Conference Educational Fund. In recognition of her contribution to improving the quality of life of southern blacks and to the founding of the Mississippi Freedom Democratic party, Ella Baker was asked to deliver the keynote address at its 1964 convention in Jackson, Miss.

Currently, Ella Baker resides in New York City where she serves as an advisor to a number of community groups. Prior to the recent release of the film *Fundi: The Story of Ella Baker*, few people outside of the civil rights movement in the South knew about Baker's long career as a civil rights activist. She is probably less well known than many other civil rights workers because she was a woman surrounded by southern men, primarily ministers, who generally perceived women as supporters rather than as leaders in the movement, and because of her own firm belief in group-centered rather than individual-centered leadership.

See also BLACK LIFE: / National Association for the Advancement of Colored People; Southern Christian Leadership Conference; Student Nonviolent Coordinating Committee

Sharon Harley
University of Maryland

Ellen Cantarow and Susan Gushee O'Malley, *Moving the Mountain: Women Working for Social Change* (1980); Clayborne Carson, *In Struggle: SNCC and the Black Awakening of the 1960s* (1981), Transcript of a Recorded Interview with Miss Ella Baker, 19 June 1968, The Civil Rights Documentation Project, Moorland Spingarn Research Center, Howard University, Washington, D.C. ☆

Tallulah Bankhead, Alabama-born actress

BANKHEAD, TALLULAH

(1902–1968) Actress.

Born in Huntsville, Ala., 31 January 1902, Tallulah Bankhead, actress and legend, dazzled outraged audiences in a career spanning 50 years, 51 plays, 18 films, numerous radio and television appearances, lectures, and nightclub extravaganzas. Her name, like her image, evoked contradictions. Bankhead stood for a respected Alabama family engaged in national and state Democratic politics. Tallulah remained conscious of her southern heritage and family position while transforming her given name into a synonym for flamboyance and excess.

Bankhead was a well-mannered belle who expected to be treated as a lady, yet she threw temper tantrums, drank to excess, and used drugs. To say her

speech was scatological is an understatement. Married once to actor John Emery, from 1937 to 1941, she was first seduced by and then seduced untold numbers of men and women. Nevertheless, she prudishly rejected plays that Tennessee Williams wrote with her in mind because the language and the conjunction of sex and religion were objectionable.

Although her career was chronicled and celebrated, it was not always illustrious. From the moment she arrived in New York in 1917 at the age of 15, Tallulah discovered that it was more difficult to find satisfactory roles than it was to exploit her beauty and boldness to gain notoriety as a flapper in the postwar era. The vivacious rebel captivated London, where she lived from 1923 to 1931. Although the social, political, and artistic elite there pursued her, working-class young women constituted the fanatical cult that made Bankhead's mediocre plays box-office successes.

Bankhead's attempt to repeat her London triumphs in Hollywood in the early 1930s resulted in six forgettable films with such titles as *Tarnished Lady* and *My Sin*. The studios foolishly promoted this child/woman as a femme fatale à la Dietrich while criticizing her offscreen antics as offensive. Hollywood failed to provide the desired critical and financial success, and the role of Scarlett O'Hara went to a younger woman.

Not until the 1940s did Tallulah win acclaim and awards for her performances in two plays and one film: in *The Little Foxes*, as Regina Giddens; in *The Skin of Our Teeth*, playing Sabina; and in Alfred Hitchcock's *Lifeboat*. A two-year stint, beginning in 1950, as the mistress of ceremonies of *The Big Show* on NBC radio completed what 30 years of performance and press coverage had begun. Her first name, husky voice, and the word "Dahling," an appellation for both intimates and strangers, were recognized as the unofficial trademarks of a major personality known nationally and internationally.

During the last 20 years of her life, Tallulah Bankhead increasingly exploited, and was victimized by, the tension between being a legend and being a professional actress. The Tallulah personna had always been inclined to dominate any character she attempted to represent. In her later years she fell back on self-caricature, disrupting serious performances with a camp version of "Tallulah, Dahling," incited by a new cult following composed primarily of gays. Thus, when she finally attempted to render Tallulah-inspired protagonists in Tennessee Williams's *A Streetcar Named Desire* and *The Milktrain Doesn't Stop Here Anymore*, it was too late. The legend had eclipsed the actress and woman.

Ida Jeter
Saint Mary's College of California

Tallulah Bankhead, *Tallulah* (1952); Brendan Gill, *Tallulah* (1972); Lee Israel, *Miss Tallulah Bankhead* (1972). ☆

CARTER, LILLIAN
‖‖‖‖‖‖‖‖‖‖‖‖‖‖‖‖‖‖‖‖‖‖‖‖‖‖‖‖‖‖‖‖‖‖‖‖‖
(1898–1983) Public figure.

Born in Richland, Ga., on 15 August 1898, Lillian Jackson Carter was the daughter of James Jackson, a Richland postmaster from whom she inherited an active interest in social justice and liberal politics. She remembers, for example, her father bringing meals from the local hotel, which served whites only, to blacks who waited at the post office.

In 1923 Jackson married James Earl Carter. The Carters had four children: James Earl, Jr.; Gloria; Ruth; and William Alton. A trained nurse, Lillian Carter worked in a Plains, Ga., hospital during the 1920s and 1930s, helped with the Carter family business, served as housemother to an Auburn University fraternity during the 1950s, later managed a nursing home, and served in the Peace Corps in India from 1966 to 1968. In 1978 she and Gloria Carter Spann published *Away from Home: Letters to My Family*.

Devotion to family characterized Lillian Carter. She never disguised her ambitions for Jimmy Carter nor her pride in his accomplishments. She campaigned for his elections, from the Georgia Legislature to the presidency. She had earlier helped in her husband's race for the state legislature. When James Earl Carter died in 1953, she was offered his legislative seat but declined. She later claimed that she might have accepted had she not been so grief stricken.

A staunch supporter of civil rights, Lillian Carter stood firmly with the national Democratic party throughout the 1960s. In 1964 she served as cochairman of President Lyndon Johnson's Americus, Ga., campaign office and suffered harrassment for her leadership. In explaining her actions, Lillian stated: "I just couldn't stand to see a Negro mistreated." In 1977 the Synagogue Council of America awarded her its Covenant of Peace award, and in 1980 she was named honorary chairman of the Peace Corps National Advisory Council. Religious but not puritanical, Lillian Carter preferred small-town life, hated to dress up, liked bourbon, and admitted that the only luxury she wanted was "a good-looking car." She died of cancer in Americus-Sumter County hospital at the age of 85.

Julia Kirk Blackwelder
University of North Carolina
at Charlotte

Good Housekeeping (April 1977); *Ms.* (October 1976); *New York Times*, 1977–80; *Redbook* (October 1976), *Time* (3 January, 28 February 1976); *Who's Who of American Women*, 12th ed. (1981–82). ☆

CARTER, ROSALYNN
||||||||||||||||||||||||||||||||||||||||||||||||||||||

(b. 1927) Former first lady of the United States.

Like First Lady Eleanor Roosevelt, Rosalynn Smith Carter played a major role in national affairs during her tenure in the White House. Since then, she has acted as a partner in many of former President Jimmy Carter's political and business endeavors, and she has strongly promoted mental health and women's rights issues. Her autobiography, *First Lady from Plains* (1984), has been warmly received by political analysts and literary critics.

Rosalynn Carter, First Lady of the United States, 1977–81

Born in Plains, Ga., 18 August 1927, Rosalynn Smith enjoyed a relatively carefree childhood until her father died of leukemia when she was 13. The following years were lean ones for her family; her mother, Allie Smith, was forced to make ends meet by taking in sewing and selling extra eggs and butter from the family's farm. Rosalynn helped her mother by working part-time after school in a beauty salon. After her graduation from Plains High School as valedictorian of her class, Rosalynn Smith entered Georgia Southwestern College, a two-year college in Americus, Ga. In 1944 while visiting her best friend, Ruth Carter, Rosalynn spied and admired a picture of Ruth's brother Jimmy, a U.S. Naval Academy student. The couple married two years later. Ambitious and intelligent, she viewed her husband's naval career as her ticket out of Plains. Jimmy Carter's career took the young couple as far as Hawaii before his father died in 1953, when he resigned his commission to return to Plains to take over the family peanut business. Although she opposed his decision to return to Plains, Rosalynn Carter soon plunged into keeping books for the business, raising her family, and, eventually, taking accounting courses.

Politics has been the lifeblood of the Carter family. Rosalynn Carter's first taste of public life occurred in the early 1960s during her husband's membership on the local schoolboard. His liberal political stances often brought threats to her family and the peanut business from area residents. In Jimmy Carter's 1962 bid for the Georgia state senate Rosalynn Carter handled all of his campaign correspondence. By 1970, when Carter was elected governor of Georgia, she had gained experience and, thereby, a reputation as a "steel magnolia"—a warm, gracious woman who was also politically astute. Eager to move beyond the boundaries of the governor's mansion, she worked with the Georgia Governor's Commission to Improve Service for the Mentally and Emotionally Handicapped, as a volunteer at the Georgia Regional Hospital in Atlanta, and as honorary chairman of the Georgia Special Olympics; over the next four years she helped establish 134 day-care centers for the mentally retarded.

From 1973 to 1976 Rosalynn Carter campaigned independently in 96 cities and 36 states in Governor Carter's bid for the presidency. Once the Carters reached the White House, the new first lady took an active interest in national policy making, attending Cabinet meetings, holding weekly working lunches with President Carter, heading a diplomatic mission to South America, and attending the Camp David Mideast Peace Summit. She continued to pursue mental health reform on a national level while serving on the President's Commission on Mental Health and on the Board of Directors of the National Association of Mental Health. Her support of the Equal Rights Amendment won her a merit award from the National Organization for Women.

Rosalynn Carter again took to the campaign trail in President Carter's re-election drive of 1980. His defeat was particularly devastating for her; after two decades of public service she initially found it difficult to adjust to private life. Since her return to Plains she has renewed her focus on mental health and women's rights. Numerous speaking engagements and promotions of her autobiography have allowed Rosalynn Carter to talk publicly and candidly about her life as first lady and to raise social and political issues of concern to her.

Elizabeth McGehee
Salem College

Patricia A. Avery, *U.S. News and World Report* (25 June 1984); Rosalynn Carter, *First Lady from Plains* (1984); Charles Moritz, ed., *Current Biography* (1978); *Who's Who in America*, 11th ed. (1980–81). ☆

CHESNUT, MARY BOYKIN
(1823–1886) Diarist and author.

Mary Boykin Miller Chesnut was born 31 March 1823 in Stateboro, S.C., eldest child of Mary Boykin and Stephen Decatur Miller, who had served as U.S. congressman and senator and in 1826 was elected governor of South Carolina, as a proponent of nullification. Educated first at home and in Camden schools, Mary Miller was sent at 13 to a French boarding school in Charleston, where she remained for two years broken by a six-month stay on her father's cotton plantation in frontier Mississippi. In 1838 Miller died and Mary returned to Camden. On 23 April 1840 she married James Chesnut, Jr. (1815–85), only surviving son of one of South Carolina's largest landowners.

Chesnut spent most of the next 20 years in Camden and at Mulberry, her husband's family plantation. When James was elected to the Senate in 1858, his wife accompanied him to Washington where friendships were begun with many politicians who would become the leading figures of the Confederacy, among them Varina and Jefferson Davis. Following Lincoln's election, James Chesnut returned to South Carolina to participate in the drafting of an ordinance of secession and subsequently served in the Provisional Congress of the Confederate States of America. He served as aide to General P. G. T. Beauregard and President Jefferson Davis, and he achieved the rank of general. During the war, Mary accompanied her husband to Charleston, Montgomery, Columbia, and Richmond, her drawing room always serving as a salon for the Confederate elite. From February 1861 to July 1865 she recorded her experiences in a series of diaries, which became the principal source materials for her famous portrait of the Confederacy.

Following the war, the Chesnuts returned to Camden and worked unsuccessfully to extricate themselves from heavy debts. After a first abortive attempt in the 1870s to smooth the diaries into publishable form, Mary Chesnut tried her hand at fiction. She completed but never published three novels, then in the early 1880s expanded and extensively revised her diaries into the book now known as *Mary Chesnut's Civil War* (first published in truncated and poorly

edited versions in 1905 and 1949 as *A Diary From Dixie*).

Although unfinished at the time of her death on 22 November 1886, *Mary Chesnut's Civil War* is generally acknowledged today as the finest literary work of the Confederacy. Spiced by the author's sharp intelligence, irreverent wit, and keen sense of irony and metaphorical vision, it uses a diary format to evoke a full, accurate picture of the South in civil war. Chesnut's book, valued as a rich historical source, owes much of its fascination to its juxtaposition of the loves and griefs of individuals against vast social upheaval and much of its power to the contrasts and continuities drawn between the antebellum world and a war-torn country.

Elisabeth Muhlenfeld
Florida State University

Elisabeth Muhlenfeld, *Mary Boykin Chesnut: A Biography* (1981); C. Vann Woodward, ed., *Mary Chesnut's Civil War* (1981), with Elisabeth Muhlenfeld, eds., *The Private Mary Chesnut: The Unpublished Civil War Diaries* (1985). ☆

CHOPIN, KATE
(1851–1904) Writer.

Although Katherine O'Flaherty Chopin was a native of St. Louis (born 8 February 1851) and spent barely 14 years in Louisiana, her fiction is identified with the South. At 19, Kate O'Flaherty married Oscar Chopin, a young cotton broker, and moved with him to New Orleans and later to his family home in Cloutierville, La., near the Red River. After Oscar died in 1882, she returned with their six children to St. Louis; but when, eight years later, she began to write, it was the Creoles and 'Cadians of her Louisiana experiences that animated her fiction.

Distinctly unsentimental in her approach, she often relied on popular period motifs, such as the conflict of the Yankee businessman and the Creole, a theme that informs her first novel, *At Fault* (1890), and several of her short stories. These vivid and economical tales, richly flavored with local dialect, provide penetrating views of the heterogeneous culture of south Louisiana. Many of them were collected in *Bayou Folk* (1894) and *A Night in Acadie* (1897). Chopin's second novel, *The Awakening* (1899), also strongly evokes the region, but is primarily a lyrical, stunning study of a young woman whose deep personal discontents lead to adultery and suicide. Praised for its craft and damned for its content, the novel was a scandal, and Chopin, always sensitive to her critics, gradually lost confidence in her gift and soon ceased to write.

Chopin died of a brain hemorrhage after a strenuous day at the St. Louis World's Fair, where she had been a regular visitor. She was remembered only as one of the southern local colorists of the 1890s until *The Awakening* was rediscovered in the 1970s as an early masterpiece of American realism and a superb rendering of female experience.

Barbara C. Ewell
Loyola University

Barbara C. Ewell, *Kate Chopin* (1986); Per Seyersted, *Kate Chopin: A Critical Biography* (1969); Peggy Skaggs, *Kate Chopin* (1985); Marlene Springer, *Edith Wharton and Kate Chopin: A Reference Guide* (1976). ☆

DURR, VIRGINIA
(b. 1903) Social reformer.

Born on 6 August 1903, Virginia Foster Durr spent childhood summers on her grandmother's plantation in Union Springs, Ala., where antebellum customs were preserved virtually intact. Her father had been destined to inherit the mantle of the slave-owning aristocracy; instead he was reduced to genteel poverty, first as a Presbyterian minister, then as an insurance salesman in Birmingham. Although an inheritance from her grandmother eventually allowed the family to pursue a fashionable social life in Birmingham, they were never altogether secure. "You see," she recalls, "we lived in this half way stage between being benevolent despots . . . and trying to make a living . . . and the poorer we got, the more snobbish we became." By the time she reached adolescence, Virginia Foster had absorbed the lessons of ladyhood: the sexual inhibitions, aristocratic pretensions, and racial taboos that went along with good manners and noblesse oblige.

The events of the 1920s and 1930s, however, exposed what Durr calls "the contradictions, the total contradictions" in her parents' world and set her on a profoundly different path. In 1920 she went North for two years of college at Wellesley where, for the first time, she met black students as equals. In 1926 she married a young lawyer named Clifford Judkins Durr; a year later their first daughter was born. Working for the Red Cross and the Junior League during the Depression, Virginia saw Birmingham's unemployed iron ore and steel workers "literally starving to death" because the city fathers refused to provide adequate relief.

Meanwhile, Virginia Durr's sister Josephine had married Hugo Black, who was elected to the U.S. Senate in 1920 and appointed to the Supreme Court in 1936. Black's recommendation helped Clifford secure a job in Washington, where he became assistant general counsel of the Reconstruction Finance Corporation and then a member of the Federal Communications Commission (FCC). In Washington, the Durrs joined a lively circle of like-minded young southerners. She had four more children during these years and reveled in the excitement of the early New Deal. Attending the La Follette Committee hearings on antilabor violence in Birmingham, her compassion for the poor turned to outrage at the Tennessee Coal and Iron Company, the U.S. Steel subsidiary that dominated her hometown. After the death of her only son, she became increasingly involved in politics in her own right, first in the Woman's National Democratic Committee and then in the Southern Conference for Human Welfare (SCHW).

Virginia Durr was a founding member of the SCHW and director of its Washington Committee, the most vital of its local organizations. The committee raised funds, united the capital's southern contingent for action on issues affecting the South, and conducted a vigorous congressional lobbying campaign. As executive vice-president of the National Committee to Abolish the Poll Tax, she helped lay the groundwork for eliminating a major device by which blacks and poor whites were barred from the polls.

The postwar years brought a swing to the right and the beginning of the Cold War. In the 1948 presidential campaign Virginia Durr left the Democratic party to serve on Henry Wallace's platform committee and to run for governor of

Virginia on the Progressive party ticket. Clifford refused reappointment to the FCC because of his objections to President Harry Truman's loyalty program. Smeared as a "Communist sympathizer," he soon gave up his effort to practice law in the capital and moved to Denver to take a job with the Farmers Union. When Virginia Durr signed a petition critical of the Korean War, Clifford was forced to leave that job, too. Reluctantly, the Durrs moved back to Alabama, where Clifford established a law practice in Montgomery and Virginia worked as his secretary.

Living with Clifford's parents in Montgomery, then moving to their own home in Wetumpka, the Durrs struggled to overcome their isolation and integrate themselves into the community they had left two decades before. In 1954, however, Virginia was pulled back into the political limelight when she was subpoenaed to appear at Senate Internal Security Commission hearings, presided over by Mississippi's James Eastland, on Communist influence in the Southern Conference Education Fund (an offshoot of the SCHW). A year later the civil rights movement began in earnest when Rosa Parks, a friend of the Durrs and a longtime stalwart of the NAACP, set the Montgomery bus boycott in motion. "It was a terrifically thrilling period," Virginia Durr recalls. "I wouldn't have missed it for anything." Clifford took civil rights cases. Virginia joined Dorothy Tilley's "Fellowship of the Concerned" and published articles on the movement. The Durr home became a mecca for lawyers, journalists, and civil rights workers. In the late 1960s Virginia brought her political experience to bear once more in the Alabama National Democratic party, founded in opposition to the George

Wallace-controlled regular Democrats.

Rosa Parks, Virginia Durr once observed, is "a remarkable woman . . . really what you would call the perfect Southern lady." And so, to be sure, is Virginia Foster Durr. Peeling away ladyhood's repressive conventions, she has kept its informing spirit: gracious, generous, and attuned to the nuance of individual lives even as she pursued justice and gloried in the rough and tumble of a political fight. In that sense she is part of a little-known tradition—the southern lady as radical, embodying the past while fighting for a different future.

See also SOCIAL CLASS: / Southern Conference for Human Welfare

> Jacquelyn Dowd Hall
> University of North Carolina
> at Chapel Hill

Hollinger F. Barnard, ed., *Outside the Magic Circle: The Autobiography of Virginia Foster Durr* (1985); Virginia Durr Papers, Schlesinger Library, Radcliffe College; Tom Gardner, *Southern Exposure* (Spring 1981); Sue Thrasher and Jacquelyn Dowd Hall, Southern Oral History Program, University of North Carolina, Chapel Hill, 1975. ☆

EDELMAN, MARIAN WRIGHT

(b. 1939) Civil rights lawyer.

Marian Wright Edelman is founder and president of the Washington, D.C.-based Children's Defense Fund. Born 6 June 1939 to a Bennettsville, S.C., Baptist minister and his wife (who also raised her four brothers, her sister and 14 foster children), Edelman in 1983 was named by *Ladies' Home Journal* one of the "100 most influential women in America." In 1985 she received a MacArthur Foundation award of $228,000 which she promptly devoted to her Children's Defense Fund to make the needs of children—especially poor children—a top priority on America's agenda. She is a voice for children who cannot vote, lobby, or speak out for themselves. Edelman is concerned with every aspect of childhood health and education, infant mortality, teenage pregnancy, and child abuse. Her work graphically details the effect of poverty on the minds and future of America's children.

Awards and accolades for Marian Wright Edelman have cascaded in a steady stream since her undergraduate days at Spelman College in Atlanta, where a Merrill Scholarship afforded her a year's study at the Universities of Paris and Geneva. She now serves as chair of Spelman's Board of Trustees.

In the intervening years, she has fulfilled her early promise as one of *Mademoiselle* magazine's "four most exciting young women in America" (1965) and as *Vogue*'s "Outstanding Young Woman of America (1965–66)." During those years, many pieces of civil rights legislation were forged under the force of her determination and penchant for detail. Her brilliant congressional testimony, her lobbying for and drafting of legislation, and her highly focused intellect and energy led former Vice President Walter Mondale to call Marian Wright Edelman "the smartest woman I have ever met."

Marian Wright grew up in a close-knit southern family, for whom civil rights represented an American ideal. Her father's final days in 1954 were spent with a radio at his side, listening to news of the school desegregation decision (*Brown* v. *Board of Education*) being argued before the Supreme Court.

His last words to Marian, a week before the decision came down, were, "Don't let anything get between you and your education."

Edelman graduated from Spelman as valedictorian in 1960, won a John Hay Whitney Fellowhip to Yale University Law School, received her LL.B. in 1963, and joined the NAACP Legal and Education Defense Fund as staff attorney in New York. From 1964 to 1968 she served as director of the Fund's Jackson, Miss., office, where in 1965 she became the first black woman admitted to the Mississippi Bar.

In Mississippi during the thick of the civil rights movement, she organized Head Start programs throughout the state for the Child Development Group of Mississippi (CDGM) and developed a keen awareness of the effect of poverty and hunger on the lives of young children. Her advocacy drew national attention to children suffering from hunger and malnutrition in America. As a Field Foundation Fellow and partner in the Washington research project of the Southern Center for Public Policy, she became a principal architect of and successful lobbyist for the Food Stamp Act of 1970. That year she became an honorary fellow at the University of Pennsylvania Law School and won the Louise Waterman Wise Award. In 1971 *Time* magazine named her one of 200 outstanding young American leaders. From 1971 to May 1973 she served as director of the Center for Law and Education at Harvard University—a position she left to form the Children's Defense Fund.

Edelman's research on the plight of children in America is quoted in the major media, cited by congressional committees, and used in state and federal programming. She is the author of three books, *Children Out of School in America* (1974), *School Suspensions: Are They Helping Children?* (1975), and *Portrait of Inequality: Black and White Children in America* (1980), all published by the Children's Defense Fund, as well as numerous articles and scholarly papers.

Mary Lynn Kotz
Washington, D.C.

Harry A. Ploski and James Williams, eds., *The Negro Almanac* (1983); *Psychology Today* (June 1975); *Who's Who in America* (43d ed., 1984–85); *Who's Who in Black America* (4th ed., 1985). ☆

FAMILY REUNIONS

"Next week be the fourth of July and us plan a big family reunion outdoors here at my house," says Celie, the main character in Alice Walker's *The Color Purple*. On the day of the reunion family members analyze the custom this way: " 'Why us always have family reunion on July 4th,' say Henrietta, mouth poke out, full of complaint. 'It so hot.' " . . . " 'White people busy celebrating they independence from England July 4th,' say Harpo, 'so most black folks don't have to work. Us can spend the day celebrating each other.' " Among the other attendees are two women who sip lemonade and make potato salad, noting that barbecue was a favorite food for them even while they were in Africa. The reunion day is especially joyful for the two women, who had been thought lost until their appearance at the reunion, where they are joyfully reunited with Celie and the other family members.

Southern family reunions are characteristic of extended and elaborated

Dinner on the grounds, Houston, Mississippi, 1967

families, who plan the occasions around celebration, abundant good food, shared reunion responsibilities, simple recreational activities, and, above all, talk.

Although summer is the most popular season and the Fourth of July a popular date for family reunions for both black and white southern families, family reunions can happen at any time. Some families have them annually, others have them on a schedule best described as "every so often," and still others have them only once or twice in a generation's lifetime, depending on some member's initiative in getting the reunion organized.

Like the indefinite date for family reunions, there is an inexactness as to who constitutes "family" for each gathering. Some families invite only the descendants of a given couple and those descendants' spouses and children. Others invite the eldest couple's brothers and sisters and their children plus in-laws and some of the in-laws' relatives. Some gather households that have only a vague bond of kinship—those who are

"like family" because of strong friendships. There is inevitably a logic of kinship and affection to each family reunion, and such a party is hard indeed to crash.

The impetus for a family reunion, if it is not an annually scheduled event, may be a late-decade birthday party for one family member, a holiday, a wedding anniversary, or the celebration of an achievement such as paying off a home mortgage. Sometimes a family holds a reunion for a homecoming of one of its members, as in the case of Eudora Welty's novel *Losing Battles*, which is a family reunion story focused around the day a son and husband return from a stay at Parchman, the Mississippi state prison.

Families often gather in someone's home, though summer picnic versions are commonly held in state or city parks. Motels, hotels, or restaurants host them, as do club houses or community centers, but by far the most popular settings after homes are churches. "Dinner-on-the-grounds" in the churchyard, with food burdening tablecloth-covered makeshift tables set on sawhorses, is a happy memory of family reunions in the minds of many southerners.

The occasion for catching up on the relatives' news and gossip, perhaps for transacting a little family business, for settling or even stirring up family disputes, and for generally getting in touch again, a family reunion in the South usually has no program. There might be an occasional game or swim or boat ride, but the main activities are conversation and eating. The time span may be overnight or even several days, but it is most frequently only over one meal.

The food might be barbecue with baked beans and coleslaw or fried fish with hush puppies, fried potatoes, and a salad. A restaurant meal might be ordered, but in a great many cases family reunion food is a large and generous potluck dinner where each participating household brings versions of its best offerings of food and drink—fried chicken, ham, meat casseroles, rice dishes, cooked garden vegetables, fresh raw vegetables, potato salad, gelatin salad, seafood salad, homemade rolls and breads, cakes, pies, cookies, jams, preserves, pickles, watermelons, iced tea, and lemonade. A time for eating, conversing, and sharing each other's company, a southern family reunion is a special occasion for reaffirming family ties.

Gayle Graham Yates
University of Minnesota

Alice Walker, *The Color Purple* (1982); Eudora Welty, *Losing Battles* (1970). ☆

GIBSON, ALTHEA

(b. 1927) Tennis player.

Althea Gibson was the first black tennis player to win a major national tournament. She dominated women's tennis in 1957 and 1958 and was later elected to the National Lawn Tennis Hall of Fame (1971) and the Women's Sports Hall of Fame (1980).

Gibson was born in Silver, N.C., on 25 August 1927. Her parents, Daniel and Annie Washington Gibson, sharecropped cotton and corn. Seeking a better living, the family moved to New York City when Althea was three years old. When she was a schoolgirl, Gibson's success in city paddle tennis tournaments caught the attention of sponsors, who financed her tennis lessons. Her backers also arranged for Gibson to at-

tend high school in Wilmington, N.C., where she competed on the black tennis circuit. From 1947 to 1956 Gibson won 10 straight national singles championships in competitions for black women sponsored by the American Tennis Association.

In 1953 Gibson graduated from Florida Agricultural and Mechanical University in Tallahassee and thereafter began her rapid rise in the U.S. Lawn Tennis Association. Her first invitations to important USLTA tournaments received nationwide comment because her participation integrated the previously all-white women's competitions.

Gibson became internationally known in 1956, when she won tennis titles in France, Great Britain, and Italy. The next year she was ranked as the number one woman tennis player in the United States. In 1957 and 1958 Gibson won the women's singles and doubles events at Wimbledon, England, as well as the women's singles championships in the United States. The Associated Press named her outstanding woman athlete for those years.

Gibson's autobiography, *I Always Wanted to Be Somebody*, was published in 1958. In it she recalled her father's fondness for the small, "three-store town" in South Carolina that he and his family left to go north. He always wanted to return there "and raise chickens on the old farm place." Gibson herself hesitantly returned south to attend high school, having heard stories of the terrible brutalities under Jim Crow segregation. Looking back on the experience, she wrote that "it wasn't a Ku Klux Klan nightmare like I'd been afraid it might be," but she "hated every minute of it" and determined "that I was never going to live any place in the South, at least not as long as those laws were in existence." Gibson won the women's professional singles championship in 1960 but subsequently focused on golf and toured as a professional golfer. She married William Darben in 1965. In 1975 Gibson became athletic commissioner of the state of New Jersey.

Lynn Weiner
Roosevelt University

Althea Gibson, *I Always Wanted to Be Somebody* (1958); *Who's Who of American Women, 1983–84* (1983). ☆

GRIMKÉ SISTERS
Sarah Grimké (1793–1874) and
Angelina Grimké (1805–1879).
Abolitionists.

The Grimké sisters, Sarah and Angelina, were unique in the American antislavery movement. They were southerners, women, and members of a family known to own slaves. Sarah was born in 1793 and Angelina in 1805, the last of 11 Grimké children. Sarah virtually adopted her new baby sister, and they remained close throughout their lives. The Grimké family belonged to Charleston's elite upper class, whose children were reared in luxury and served by many slaves. They were city dwellers, but their large plantation in upper South Carolina and its numerous slaves were an important source of family wealth. The sisters' education in a select girls' academy stressing the social graces was slight and superficial. They were expected to marry well, bear children, and become successful matrons. However, the sisters lost interest in conventional life as each grew into adulthood.

Religion led them both to reject slavery. Though the Grimké family church was St. Philip's Episcopal, each sister, in her early twenties, experienced conversion in revivals of other churches. Sarah in time became a member of the Society of Friends, Angelina an enthusiastic Presbyterian. Sarah came to know Friends during her father's final illness. In 1821, following his death, she moved to Philadelphia and joined the Friends' Society. She accepted their firm tenet opposing slavery as a sin and eventually won her sister to the Quaker faith and the antislavery conviction. After her efforts failed to convert family and friends, Angelina left Charleston to make her home with Sarah in Philadelphia.

In early 1853 the more activist Angelina began to make contact with the antislavery movement. After William Lloyd Garrison published a letter of hers in the *Liberator*, Angelina began to write her first tract, *Appeal to the Christian Women of the South*. The American Anti-Slavery Society rushed it into print. The society then urged her to aid the cause by addressing women's groups in "parlor meetings"; Sarah went with her and remained at her side.

They were the only women asked to the "Convention of the Seventy," which met in October of 1836, for the training of new agents to spread abolitionism. Theodore Weld, whom Angelina later married, was the leader in the sessions and gave the sisters special training for their coming lecture tours. They went from this convention to their crowded "parlor meetings," held in churches, and they accepted invitations from other localities. They were swept into preparations for a forthcoming "Convention of American Anti-Slavery Women," held in March of 1837. When it ended, the Grimkés had come to know most of the abolitionist leaders in the East, men and women, and were themselves regarded as belonging to the circle of female leaders. The Grimkés arrived in Boston in May of 1837 and began their historic antislavery crusade. They also increasingly spoke out in favor of women's rights, despite criticism from antislavery leaders.

The spring months of 1838 saw Angelina Grimké's greatest triumphs. Twice in a crowded Massachusetts legislative hall she addressed a committee of the legislature, a sensational occasion headlined in the press. Also, Boston's antislavery women rented the Odeon Theater, and for five meetings, one a week, Angelina addressed an overflowing hall on abolition of slavery. In Philadelphia, she calmly addressed a mass meeting of a Convention of American Anti-Slavery Women with a threatening mob outside.

Angelina and Weld were married the day before the convention. When the sessions ended, Sarah accompanied them to their new home, and she stayed with them for the remainder of her life. Angelina fully expected to return to her work for the antislavery cause, but did not do so. She and Sarah assisted Weld on his best-known tract, *American Slavery as It Is* (1839). Three children were born between 1839 and 1844, two boys and a girl.

In the late 1850s both sisters taught in the Eagleswood School, which Weld headed. Later the family lived near Boston, where Weld and Angelina continued to teach. When war came in 1861, Angelina Grimké, at the age of 56, returned to part-time public life. Garrison had persuaded Weld to lecture again, this time in aid of the war effort. Angelina now rejoined her old friends in forming an organization, "Loyal Women of the Republic," and once again she was speaking for freedom of the slaves. Sarah was over 70 when the end of the war brought full emancipation. She died in 1874. Angelina suffered two strokes, the first in 1875, and was ill until her death in 1879.

Katherine Du Pre Lumpkin
Chapel Hill, North Carolina

Gerda Lerner, *The Grimké Sisters from South Carolina: Rebels against Slavery* (1967); Katherine Du Pre Lumpkin, *The Emancipation of Angelina Grimké* (1974); Weld-Grimké Collection, Clements Library, University of Michigan, Ann Arbor. ☆

JACKSON, AUNT MOLLY

(1880–1960) Labor activist and composer.

Aunt Molly Jackson is known for writing over 100 songs about the lives and struggles of Kentucky coal miners and their families. She was born Mary Magdalene Garland in Clay County, Ky., to Oliver and Deborah Robinson Garland in 1880. Her father was a coal miner, minister, and labor organizer. By the age of five Mary Garland was assisting her father at union meetings, leading picket lines, and composing songs. At 14 she married Jim Stewart, a coal miner. Within four years she had borne two children and completed training in nursing and midwifery—a career she would follow for the next 30 years.

Jim Stewart was killed in a mine rockfall in 1917. While married to her second husband, a miner named Bill Jackson, "Molly" Jackson was given the nickname "pistol packin' mama." She carried a gun for protection while traveling through the hills as a midwife and while riding to her husband's still, hidden deep in the mountains. Her husband's brother drafted a song about her that was later made into a popular hit.

During the early years of the Depression, while campaigning throughout Appalachia for the rights of coal miners, Jackson became widely known as "Aunt Molly." In 1931 she was "discovered" by a delegation (which included Theodore Dreiser and John Dos Passos) that visited Harlan County to investigate reports about starvation and the denial of civil liberties. Jackson, who had been blacklisted by the mine operators, was persuaded to come north and tour the country to raise funds for the miners. She first appeared before 21,000 people in New York City and eventually visited 38 states. Her impassioned speeches and songs widely publicized the labor struggles in Kentucky while raising thousands of dollars, which she sent south.

Aunt Molly Jackson was divorced from Bill Jackson in 1931. She later married Gustavos Stamos and settled in New York City by 1936. There she continued to eke out a living as a composer, working as a labor activist on behalf of industrial workers. She died in Sacramento, Ca., in 1960.

Aunt Molly Jackson's best-known songs include "Harlan County Blues," "Kentucky Miner's Wife's Hungry, Ragged Blues," and "I Am a Union Woman." Like other women composers of the South, including Florence Reece ("Which Side Are You On?"), Ella May Wiggins ("Mill Mother's Lament"), and Sarah Ogan Gunning ("I Am a Girl of Constant Sorrow"), Jackson is credited with boosting the morale of striking workers while bringing nationwide attention to the living and working conditions in the South. Jackson also contributed to the growing interest in American folk music, especially through her influence on the American composer Elie Siegmeister.

Lynn Weiner
Roosevelt University

Philip S. Foner, *Women and the American Labor Movement*, 2 vols. (1979–80); John Greenway, *American Folksongs of Protest* (1953); Edward Jablonski, *Encyclopedia of American Music* (1981); *New York Times* (3 September 1960). ☆

JOHNSON, LADY BIRD

(b. 1912) Former first lady of the United States and conservation advocate.

Claudia Alta Taylor Johnson was born on 22 December 1912 near Karnack, a small east Texas town. Her parents were Thomas Jefferson Taylor, a landowner and country storekeeper, and Minnie Lee Pattillo, both Alabama natives. Lady Bird, so named by a nursemaid, was the youngest of three children and the only daughter. When she was five her mother died and her Aunt Effie Pattillo, a genteel Alabamian, moved to "The Brick House," the family home in Karnack, to care for her. Lady Bird Taylor was educated in local public schools, graduating from Marshall High School in 1928. She attended St. Mary's Episcopal School for Girls in Dallas and then received two bachelor degrees (liberal arts and journalism) from the University of Texas at Austin. In 1934 she married Lyndon Baines Johnson, the secretary of a Texas congressman, after a two-month courtship. Washington, D.C., was home for the Johnsons almost continuously from 1934 until 1969. They had two daughters, Lynda Bird on 19

March 1944 and Luci Baines on 2 July 1947.

Lady Bird Johnson emerged as a public figure when her husband became vice president in 1961. As the nation's "second lady" she earned a reputation as a gracious hostess who skillfully combined superb good taste with down-home southern hospitality. Her role as national hostess and decorator was enlarged when she became first lady in November 1963. As a political helpmate she made a special appeal to the Deep South, which she traversed in a whistle-stop tour during her husband's campaign in 1964. Aware of the importance of her position, she began to record on tape aspects of her personal and public life; one-seventh of the resulting transcript has been published in the 800-page *A White House Diary* (1970). The journal is a testament to Lady Bird Johnson's keen sense of family, devotion to the principles espoused by her husband, and commitment to her own special concerns—national beautification, conservation, education, and children.

Lady Bird Johnson attributes her love of land, nature, and nation to her early years of growing up in the east Texas piney woods and Alabama cotton lands and to her later life in the Texas hill country, where the ancestral Johnson family home is located. For her First Lady's Committee for a More Beautiful Capital she tapped prominent architects, conservationists, and philanthropists who landscaped Washington with seasonal plantings and groves, refurbished memorials, and improved parks and school yards in the inner city. The Highway Beautification Act of 1965 translated into public policy her programs for control of billboards, the screening of junkyards, and highway plantings. Following the retirement of

President Johnson in 1969 and his death in 1973, Lady Bird Johnson has devoted her time to her daughters and seven grandchildren and to her extensive holdings in the Texas television and other media, begun in the 1940s with the purchase of station KTBC in Austin. She has continued to focus her public work on roadside beautification, conservation, and the arts.

In 1982 more than 100 historians who rated first ladies on the basis of their leadership, intelligence, value to country, and independence ranked Lady Bird Johnson third, following Eleanor Roosevelt and Abigail Adams.

See also POLITICS: / Johnson, Lyndon Baines

Martha H. Swain
Texas Woman's University

Elizabeth Carpenter, *Ruffles and Flourishes: The Warm and Tender Story of a Simple Girl Who Found Adventure in the White House* (1970); Lady Bird Johnson Papers, Lyndon Baines Johnson Library, Austin, Tex.; Lady Bird Johnson, *Texas—A Roadside View* (1980), *A White House Diary* (1970); Ruth Montgomery, *Mrs. LBJ* (1965); Marie Smith, *The President's Lady: An Intimate Biography of Mrs. Lyndon B. Johnson* (1964). ☆

JORDAN, BARBARA
‖‖‖
(b. 1936) Lawyer and politician.

Barbara Charline Jordan holds the Lyndon B. Johnson Centennial Chair in National Policy, LBJ School of Public Affairs, the University of Texas at Austin. She first came to national prominence in November 1972 when she was elected to the U.S. House of Representatives from the 18th Congressional District in Houston, Tex. She and Andrew

Young, who was elected that same year from Atlanta, Ga., were the first two blacks from the Deep South to win national office since the turn of the century.

Born 21 February 1936, the youngest of three daughters, to the Ben Jordans in Houston, Barbara Jordan grew up in a devoutly religious environment. Her parents and grandparents were lifelong members of the Good Hope Baptist Church in Houston's predominantly black Fifth Ward. As a child, she was a bright student with a natural flair for speaking. Her high school teachers encouraged her to develop her talent by participating in various oratorical contests. Although the Houston school system was segregated, the precocious youngster took many honors in citywide matches. She graduated magna cum laude from Texas Southern University and earned her law degree at Boston University in 1959.

Returning to Houston, the fledgling barrister worked three years before

Barbara Jordan, U.S. representative from Texas and educator, 1980s

being able to open her law office, but the lure of politics was already beckoning her. She became active in the local Democratic party. In 1966, following redistricting, Barbara Jordan was elected to the Texas Senate, the first woman to win a seat in the upper chamber of that legislature. During her six years in the senate, she earned the admiration of her white male colleagues for her ability to get along well with others and to influence the passage of such legislation as the Texas Fair Employment Practices Commission, improvement of the Workmen's Compensation Act, and the state's first minimum wage law. In 1972 Barbara Jordan made history when the senate unanimously elected her president pro tempore. On 10 June 1972, in the traditional "Governor for a Day" ceremonies, she became the first black woman governor in U.S. history.

In 1971 her supporters in the state senate carved out a new congressional district to include a majority mixture of blacks and Hispanics. In November 1972 that electorate gave her a sweeping victory as their representative to Congress from the 18th District. She was assigned to the important House Judiciary Committee. In the wake of the scandals growing out of the Watergate break-in on 17 June 1972, the Senate Select Committee on Presidential Campaigning, under the chairmanship of Sam Ervin of North Carolina, began holding hearings in May of 1973. One year later, on 9 May 1974, the House Judiciary Committee under Peter Rodino opened impeachment hearings against President Richard Nixon.

During the House hearings, Barbara Jordan became a household name throughout America. As *Time* magazine said, "She voiced one of the most cogent and impassioned defenses of the Constitutional principles that emerged from the Nixon impeachment hearings." Opinion polls soon listed her as among the 10 most influential members of Congress, and Democratic party leaders chose her, along with Senator John Glenn, to give a keynote address to its 1976 national convention.

Always realistic, Barbara Jordan firmly resisted all efforts to draft her as a candidate for the vice-presidential nomination that year. She believed the country was not ready for such a development, although it was slowly inching toward the goal of equality in race relations. For personal reasons, Jordan retired from politics in 1978. She accepted a position as professor at the University of Texas. In 1982 she was one of the 100 professors honored with chairs established in commemoration of the centennial year of the institution. Barbara Jordan has left a legacy of great accomplishments in public service, both legislatively and personally. She resides today in Austin, Tex.

Ethel L. Payne
Washington, D.C.

Ira B. Bryant, *Barbara Charline Jordan: From the Ghetto to the Capitol* (1977); *Ebony* (February 1975); *Houston Post* (21 July 1976). ☆

LYNN, LORETTA

(b. 1937) Entertainer.

Country music is an essential accompaniment to contemporary images of the South and is the source for an emergent regional mythology. Loretta Lynn is a rural southerner who celebrates the traditional values of the South through her original compositions and her authentic folk style. She has created and portrayed the "coal miner's daughter," a popular myth of the working-class southern woman that may become as pervasive as the myth of the antebellum southern belle, Scarlett O'Hara.

Born in the small community of Butcher Holler, Ky., 14 April 1937, Loretta Lynn is the second of eight children born to Clara Butcher and Ted Webb. When she was 13, she married Mooney Lynn, a soldier who had recently returned from World War II. The first of her six children was born when she was 14, and she was a grandmother by 28. Loretta Lynn had been married over 10 years before she began singing for audiences other than her family. She was successful almost immediately after the release of her first record, "I'm a Honky Tonk Girl" (1960), which was her own composition. Neither the small recording company, Zero, nor the Lynns could finance promotion of "I'm a Honky Tonk Girl," so Loretta and Mooney mailed copies of the record, along with a short letter of explanation, to disc jockeys across the nation. When they realized that the record was a hit, the Lynns sold their home in Washington state and drove to Nashville in a 1955 Ford to sign a contract.

Since then, Loretta Lynn has released over 60 singles and 50 albums for Decca and MCA, including many of her own compositions. Based upon *Billboard*'s year-end charts of hit songs, her most successful singles have been "Success" (1962), "Wine, Women, and Song" (1964), "Blue Kentucky Girl" (1965), "Happy Birthday" (1965), "You Ain't Woman Enough" (1966), "Dear Uncle Sam" (1966), "If You're Not Gone Too Long" (1967), "Fist City" (1968), "You've Just Stepped In (From Stepping

Out on Me)" (1968), "Woman of the World—Leave My World Alone" (1969), "That's a No, No" (1969), "You Want to Give Me a Lift" (1970), "I Know How" (1970), "I Wanna Be Free" (1971), "You're Looking at Country" (1971), "One's On the Way" (1972), "Rated X" (1973), "Hey, Loretta" (1974), "She's Got You" (1977), and "Out of My Head and Into My Bed" (1978). Loretta Lynn has won a number of awards, including a Grammy, 12 nominations and three awards from the Country Music Association for top female artist, two awards from *Record World*, three from *Billboard*, and four from *Cash Box*. In 1961 she received an award as "The Most Promising Female Artist" and by 1972 she had become the first woman to be honored as the Country Music Association's "Entertainer of the Year." In 1980 the album soundtrack of the film *Coal Miner's Daughter*, which featured Loretta's hit songs sung by actress Sissy Spacek, was named "Album of the Year" by the Country Music Association.

Loretta Lynn is popular regionally, nationally, and internationally. She received an honorable mention in the 1973 Gallup Poll list of the world's 10 most admired women. In addition to creating southern regional mythology, Loretta Lynn's lyrics and life history reflect the social history of working-class southern women and reinforce the American values of individualism, patriotism, and freedom. She embodies the American "rags to riches" story within a southern setting.

Ruth A. Banes
University of South Florida

Ruth A. Banes, *Canadian Review of American Studies* (Fall 1985); Dorothy A. Horst-man, *Stars of Country Music*, ed. Bill C. Malone and Judith McCulloh (1975); Loretta Lynn with George Vecsey, *Coal Miner's Daughter* (1976); Vertical file on "Loretta Lynn," Country Music Foundation Library and Media Center, Nashville, Tenn. ☆

MARTIN, MARIA
||||||||||||||||||||||||||||||||||||||||||
(1796–1863) Painter and naturalist.

Maria Martin collaborated with John James Audubon in the production of *Birds of America*. Born in Charleston, S.C., the youngest of four daughters, little is known of her early life, although she appears to have been self-educated. Two events shaped her life: first, the marriage in 1816 of her sister, Harriet, to the Reverend John Bachman, amateur naturalist and Lutheran pastor of St. John's Church in Charleston, and second, a long friendship with Audubon.

After her marriage, Harriet Martin Bachman, who bore 13 children, secured the help of her sister, and by 1827 Maria Martin was living in the airy, verandaed Bachman home. After Harriet became a semiinvalid, her sister assumed the tasks of running the large house, including organizing and managing slaves. One of John Bachman's guests, John James Audubon, who visited Charleston in 1831, helped her develop her artistic talents.

Audubon taught Maria Martin to paint from life, and her natural but underdeveloped talent was sharpened until her skills as a painter of exquisite flowers, insects, butterflies, and landscapes became substantial. The flamboyant and often difficult Audubon began a collaboration with Martin in which she contributed backgrounds for the Audubon paintings. Audubon's vagueness in his attributions makes it unclear precisely which plates in the "Elephant folio" edition of *Birds of America* and in the Octavo edition published later contain her work. Audubon's *Ornithological Biography* credits her with 11 of the engravings in *Birds of America*, but she probably did more. Approximately 30 of the Octavo plates can be attributed to her. Audubon named "Maria's Woodpecker" (*picus martinae*) after her and he clearly considered her work superior.

In 1842 Audubon began illustrations for *The Vivaporous Quadrupeds of North America* for which Bachman would write the text. When John Bachman's eyesight failed, Maria Martin became what he called his "amanuensis." She measured and described specimens sent to them, took down Bachman's dictation, and edited it. "She corrects, criticises, abuses and praises," wrote Bachman. In 1846 Harriet Bachman died, and two years later John Bachman and Maria Martin married. From then until 1856, when she was incapacitated with paralysis of the right arm and subsequent failing health, Maria and John Bachman continued their work. Strong supporters of secession, the Bachman family fled to Columbia to avoid the fighting in the countryside, and soon after the Christmas of 1863 Maria Martin died there. She was buried in Ebenezer Church.

Martin's work was not publicly recognized, nor was the extent of her contributions to the understanding of southern flora and fauna realized, because of the circumstances of her life as a white southern woman. She combined within her character the elements of the southern lady, as set forth by tradition and contemporary mores, and an internal strength of will. She was supportive, dutiful, and reportedly good-tempered and amiable. Prevented from the public exercise of her talents and dependent upon others for her livelihood, Maria Martin's artistic abilities could only be pursued after the demands of her roles as housekeeper, aunt, and wife had been fulfilled. Despite these barriers, much knowledge of the natural environment of the antebellum South came from Maria Martin and her colleagues in Charleston.

See also ENVIRONMENT: / Audubon, John James

> Marion Roydhouse
> University of Delaware

C. L. Bachman, ed., *John Bachman D.D.* (1888); Annie Roulhac Coffin, *New York Historical Society Quarterly* (January 1965); Howard Corning, ed., *Letters of John James Audubon, 1826–1840* (1930). ☆

MITCHELL, MARTHA
(1918–1976) Public figure.

Martha Elizabeth Beall Jennings Mitchell, a well-known and controversial figure in recent American politics, was born in Pine Bluff, Ark. Her mother, Arie Ferguson Beall, was the daughter of a prominent South Carolina and Arkansas business leader. Her father, George Virgil Beall, was a cotton broker who suffered financial reverses after the stock market crash of 1929 and deserted his wife and daughter. Because Arie Beall was busy as an elocution teacher and very active in local affairs, Martha Mitchell was reared by her black nurse, Mary Byas Walker, from whom she received constant love and attention.

Mitchell briefly attended Stephens College in Columbia, Mo., transferred to the University of Arkansas, and graduated from the University of Miami in 1942. After teaching school and serving as a Red Cross volunteer, she worked at the Pine Bluff Arsenal. In mid-1945 she was transferred to Washington, D.C., an event she later regretted: "I would have been all right if I'd never left the South."

She married Clyde Jennings, Jr., of Lynchburg, Va., in 1946 and bore a son, Clyde Jay Jennings, in 1947. The marriage ended in divorce after 11 years. In 1957 she married John Newton Mitchell, a successful Wall Street lawyer. After living in New York City and Darien, Conn., the Mitchells purchased a large mansion in Rye, N.Y. Martha Mitchell was a gracious and charming hostess who maintained a southern gentility and femininity in her dress and hairstyle. A daughter, Martha Elizabeth Mitchell, was born in 1961. In 1969 John Mitchell became presidential campaign manager for Richard M. Nixon. He was appointed attorney general upon Nixon's election.

Because she was open and frank about happenings in Washington, Martha Mitchell soon became a media celebrity much loved by Middle America for her forthright comments and genuine good humor. Following her husband's resignation as attorney general in 1972 to head the Committee for the Re-Election of the President, the Watergate burglary occurred. Martha Mitchell later claimed that she was drugged and forcibly prevented from speaking out concerning the involvement of high-ranking Nixon Administration officials in the affair. There followed a growing estrangement from her husband during which she resorted to liquor and drugs to allay her fears. She died of cancer in 1976. Her spontaneity, sense of humanity, and heroic efforts to alert the country to the

danger of political repression were reflected in an anonymous floral tribute at her funeral in Pine Bluff that read: "Martha Was Right."

Dorothy D. DeMoss
Texas Woman's University

Winzola McLendon, *Martha: The Biography of Martha Mitchell* (1979); Jonas Robitscher, *Journal of Psychohistory* (Winter 1979); Helen Thomas, *Dateline: White House* (1975). ☆

MOBLEY, MARY ANN

(b. 1939) Beauty queen and actress.

Mary Ann Mobley was born 17 February 1939 in Brandon, Miss., and grew up in a small town where her social life centered around church, school, and family. A childhood dream was to be a missionary. She had years of piano, dance, and voice lessons and won an academic award, the Carrier Scholarship, to the University of Mississippi. At the university she became involved in beauty contests. In 1956 Bing Crosby selected her the most beautiful among 40 contestants in the Ole Miss Parade of Beauties, and the following year actor Fred McMurray, the contest judge, ranked her among the top five beauties. Her first national beauty title was National College Football Queen of 1957. In 1959 she reached the pinnacle of the beauty contest world, winning the Miss America Pageant.

Southerners tend to take their beauty queens seriously and to see them as models. Mary Ann Mobley translated her beauty pageant fame into a career as an actress. Her Broadway debut was as an ingenue in the play *Nowhere to Go But Up*, a role she landed shortly

Mary Ann Mobley, a Miss America from Mississippi, 1959

after finishing her year as Miss America. She has appeared in off-Broadway productions of *Oklahoma*, *The King and I*, *Hello, Dolly*, and *Cabaret*. She went to Hollywood in the early 1960s, appearing with another Mississippian, Elvis Presley, in *Girl Happy*. Other movies followed; she was named one of the ten stars of the future by the United Theater Owners of America and received a Golden Globe Award as the International Female Star of Tomorrow from the Hollywood Foreign Press in 1965.

Most recently, Mary Ann Mobley has appeared on television, ranging from frequent appearances on talk shows and game shows to a starring role in *Different Strokes*, where she plays the surrogate mother of two black children. Married to actor Gary Collins and mother of a daughter, Clancy, Mobley has been active in humanitarian causes such as the March of Dimes, United Cerebral Palsy Association, Exceptional Children's Foundation for the Mentally Retarded, and World Vision's feeding and medical centers around the world. A 1985 trip to Nairobi to shoot a documentary film on hunger in the Third World helped to dramatize that horror.

Brenda West
University of Mississippi

Jane Ardmore, *View Magazine* (8–14 February 1986); Mary Ann Mobley Collins file, Alumni Association, University of Mississippi. ☆

NEWCOMB, JOSEPHINE
(1816–1901) Philanthropist.

Josephine Louise Newcomb was the founder of H. Sophie Newcomb Memorial College, the first degree-granting college for women established within a previously all male major university. Born in Baltimore, Md., 31 October 1816, she was the daughter of Alexander Le Monnier, a prominent Baltimore businessman. Orphaned in 1831, Josephine Louise moved to New Orleans to live with her only sister. While summering in Louisville, Ky., she met and married Warren Newcomb, a successful businessman who lived in New Orleans most of the summer because his wholesale business was located there.

In 1866 Warren Newcomb died, leaving to his wife and a daughter, Harriott Sophie, born to the couple in 1855, an estate valued at between $500,000 and $850,000. Under her own direction Josephine Newcomb's inheritance increased to over $4 million by her death in 1901. In 1870, at age 15, Harriott Sophie died of diphtheria. Devastated by the loss of her child, Newcomb began to search for a suitable memorial to her daughter. An Episcopalian, she donated generously to the support of her church. A native southerner, she gave to numerous causes to assist the recovery of the war-torn South. She contributed to the library of Washington and Lee University. She founded a school for sewing girls and supported a Confederate orphans' home, both in Charleston, as well as a school for deaf children in New York. In 1886, at the behest of Ida Richardson, a wealthy New Orleans woman, and Colonel William Preston Johnson, president of the recently established Tulane University of Louisiana, Newcomb agreed to found a college for women as a memorial to her daughter.

Although coeducational colleges and independent women's colleges existed, the H. Sophie Newcomb Memorial College was a unique experiment, the design of which influenced Barnard at Columbia, Radcliffe at Harvard, and the Women's College of Western Reserve. Part of, and yet separate from, Tulane University, the college had a separate administration and faculty, empowered to formulate its own academic policy. The college's stated aim to offer a liberal arts education for women equal to that available for men represented a departure in the history of female education in the South. In an age when higher education for women was viewed with indifference, Josephine Louise Newcomb initiated significant change in the patterns of women's education.

See also EDUCATION: / Tulane University

Sylvia R. Frey
Tulane University

Brandt V. B. Dixon, *A Brief History of H. Sophie Newcomb Memorial College, 1887–*
1919 (1928); John P. Dyer, *Tulane: The Biography of a University, 1834–1965* (1966). ☆

PARKS, ROSA
||||||||||||||||||||||||||||||||||||||
(b. 1913) Civil rights activist.

The burden of 100 years of discrimination added to the weariness of a difficult day was just too much for the gentle black woman that early December day in 1955. Asked to give up her seat on a crowded Montgomery, Ala., bus to allow whites to sit down, Rosa Parks, once dubbed the civil rights movement's "most mannerly rebel," flatly refused.

Recalling that a year earlier a black teenager, Claudette Colvin, had been removed in handcuffs, kicking and screaming, for a similar offense, she felt sure the authorities would not repeat such a disgraceful performance. She was wrong. Summoned by the bus driver, the police arrested her and placed her in a cell with two other black women, one of whom would not speak to her. The other had attacked a man with an ax.

Born 14 February 1913 in Tuskegee, Ala., Parks was one of two children, and the only daughter, of Leona Curlee. Her mother was born on a tenant farm in Montgomery County. Raised in Montgomery, Parks attended Alabama State College, then worked as a clerk and an insurance saleswoman before becoming a tailor's assistant at the Montgomery Fair Department Store, where she was employed when the bus incident occurred. A former secretary of the Montgomery chapter of the NAACP, Parks also served as a "stewardess" (an assistant at communion services) at that city's African Methodist Episcopal Church.

"Rosa Parks was just the right person at the right time," civil rights activist E. D. Nixon later remarked. Nixon, an old friend of Parks and former president of the Alabama NAACP, paid her bail and asked if she would be willing to serve as a test case to challenge the legality of Montgomery's segregation ordinances. After receiving the support of her husband Raymond, a barber at Maxwell Air Force Base, and her mother, she agreed and thereby stepped into history as the "mother of the civil rights revolution."

The real challenge to white supremacy came not from judicial action, however, but from the leadership of Martin Luther King, Jr., the 26-year-old pastor of the Dexter Avenue Baptist Church, who launched the year-long boycott of the bus system in Montgomery's black Protestant churches. The bus boycott, with its attendant violence on the part of the police and the white community and its hundreds of arrests, was the crucible from which King emerged as a nationally known leader.

After a 381-day boycott the bus company capitulated and ended segregation on the city's public transporation network. On 13 November 1956 the U.S. Supreme Court ruled that bus segregation was unconstitutional.

Fired from her job as a result of her notoriety, Parks worked as a volunteer for the Montgomery Improvement Association, which was formed to coordinate the bus boycott. In 1957 she moved to Detroit, where she is still employed by Representative John Conyers of Michigan. Parks's husband Raymond, whom she married in 1932, died in 1977. The couple had no children.

The catalyst that sparked the militant phase of the modern civil rights movement, Parks has often expressed embarrassment at the adulation she has received as the symbol of black resistance to injustice. Honored at the White House by President Jimmy Carter in February 1979, along with other notable elderly blacks including Jesse Owens and the Reverend Martin Luther King, Sr., she was also awarded the Martin Luther King, Jr., Nonviolent Peace Prize in Atlanta in January 1980. Detroit has named a street and a school after her. Rosa Parks embodies the idea of the individual who is willing to stand up and be counted.

Helen C. Camp
New York City

Ebony (November 1980); *Los Angeles Times* (15 January 1980); *New York Times* (6 December 1955; 5 April 1978; 14 February, 24 February, 25 November 1979; 15 January 1980; 5 June 1982); *Southern Exposure* (Spring 1981). ☆

PARTON, DOLLY
||||||||||||||||||||||||||||||||||||||||||||||
(b. 1946) Entertainer.

Dolly Parton is often described as a contemporary "Cinderella," a fairy-tale princess, or a country gypsy—a platinum blonde heroine who escapes poverty in the foothills of the Great Smoky Mountains, achieves fame and fortune in Nashville and later Hollywood, and lives happily ever after. More realistically, she is a talented and creative artist and businesswoman.

Dolly Parton was born 19 January 1946 in Locust Ridge in Sevier County, Tenn., the fourth of 12 children, to Avie Lee Owens and Randy Parton. Her grandfather Owens was a minister, and

Dolly Parton, country music singer and actress, 1987

her early life with family and community centered around religion and the church. She learned to love storytelling, music, and singing, as well as to adhere to a rigid Christian moral code. Her mother sang the traditional folksongs she had learned from a harmonica-playing grandmother Owens. By the time she was five years old Parton was imagining lyrics and tunes, and when she was seven she had written her first song. An exceptionally intelligent child, Dolly Parton used the rich southern folk environment surrounding her to create poetry and music.

She began her singing career as a child on the Cas Walker Radio Show, broadcast from Knoxville, and she released her first record, "Puppy Love," in her early teens. At 18, after she graduated from high school, she moved to Nashville, and, despite a difficult beginning, which she describes in her song "Down on Music Row" (1973), she became a popular recording and television partner for country artist Porter Wagoner. Together, they recorded 13 albums and won awards for "Vocal Duo of the Year" in 1968, 1970, and 1971.

In 1967 Dolly Parton released her first solo album, and since then, she has recorded over 30 albums for Monument and RCA. She has written and recorded hundreds of her own compositions, which are usually autobiographical songs, work songs, or sentimental, moralistic ballads, often sung in a traditional country style reminiscent of the Carter Family, an authentic southern folk group that was among the first to record country music during the early 20th century.

Based upon *Billboard*'s year-end hit charts, her most successful singles have been "Mule Skinner Blues" (1970), "Joshua" (1971), "Jolene" (1974), "I Will Always Love You" (1974), "The Seeker" (1975), "All I Can Do" (1976), "Here You Come Again" (1978), "Heartbreaker" (1978), "Two Doors Down" (1978), "You're the Only One" (1979), "Baby, I'm Burning" (1979), "Starting Over Again" (1980), and "But You Know I Love You" (1981). She was "Female Vocalist of the Year" in 1975 and 1976 and was the Country Music Association's "Entertainer of the Year" in 1978. In 1980 *Billboard* listed her among the top female artists in country music and *Dolly, Dolly, Dolly* and *Nine to Five* among the top albums.

Dolly Parton achieved celebrity status by appealing to both country and pop music audiences and by entering the fields of television, film, and freelance writing. She has been featured in numerous periodicals and has appeared on the cover of *Playboy* (1978), *The Saturday Evening Post* (1979), *Parade* (1980), and *Rolling Stone* (1980). In 1976 she became the first woman in country music history to acquire her own syndicated television show, and she has since starred in three films, *Nine to Five* (1981), *The Best Little Whorehouse in*

Texas (1982), and *Rhinestone* (1984). She published a book of poems titled *Just the Way I Am* (edited by Susan P. Shultz, 1979) and is also writing a novel, *Wild Flowers*, for Bantam Books. Parton and Herchend Enterprises in 1986 opened Dollywood, a theme park based on Parton's life and located at Pigeon Forge, Tenn.

Dolly Parton has demonstrated the strength of a southern cultural and musical background, and she retains a loyalty to her homeplace and her people. The lyrics she writes in songs like "Jolene," "My Tennessee Mountain Home," and "Coat of Many Colors" portray strong women who hail from the working-class South. Moreover, in film, television, and music, Parton herself is a country woman with stamina, intelligence, independence, and a sense of humor. She has popularized the idea that mountain women in particular are not the stereotypical hillbillies viewed in comic strips or popular situation comedies, but rather complex, intelligent, articulate, and loving. Dolly Parton's music and personality will have a lasting impact upon popular images of women in the South.

Ruth A. Banes
University of South Florida

Chet Flippo, *Rolling Stone* (December 1980); Alanna Nash, *Dolly* (1978); *Playboy* (October 1978); Vertical files on "Dolly Parton," Country Music Foundation Library and Media Center, Nashville, Tennessee. ☆

PETERKIN, JULIA MOOD
‖‖‖
(1880–1961) Writer.

Julia Mood Peterkin was a southern writer best known for her sympathetic portrayals of black folklife in the South

Carolina Low Country, where she was born 31 October 1880. Her novel *Scarlet Sister Mary* won the Pulitzer Prize for literature in 1929.

Early reviewers focused on her depiction of black culture rather than on her literary techniques. Black intellectuals in particular, such as Countee Cullen, Langston Hughes, Paul Robeson, and Walter White, praised her avoidance of the racist stereotypes common at the time among white writers, North and South. W. E. B. Du Bois said of her, "She is a Southern white woman, but she has the eye and the ear to see beauty and know truth."

Scholars continue to find in her delineation of the worldview of a black community and in her depiction of its creole language, Gullah, a near-native sensitivity and richness of texture. She may, in fact, be regarded as a native speaker of the language. Raised by a Gullah-speaking nurse after the death of her mother, she wrote, "I learned to speak Gullah before I learned to speak English."

Folklorists have praised Peterkin's "primary knowledge" of Afro-American folk culture. Her explanation was that "I have lived among the Negroes. I like them. They are my friends, and I have learned so much from them."

The literary establishment, after its initial enthusiasm, ignored her writings for more than a generation. Not until the late 1970s were the literary aspects of her work—its scope and themes, characterization and narrative techniques—examined. Now literary scholars rank her fiction high, and recognize that she, like Joyce and Faulkner, was more interested in individual human beings in timeless and universal struggles than in local color. Although many of the incidents in her books she had personally witnessed on her plantation, Lang Syne (near Orangeburg, S.C.), the physical setting—Sandy Island, Heaven's Gate Church, and "Blue Brook" (Brookgreen) plantation—is often the Waccamaw region of Georgetown County, her summer home.

Peterkin's narrative technique grew out of the southern storytelling tradition (with the Gullah necessarily simplified to accommodate the limitations of her readers). She did not attempt, as did Hemingway, Dos Passos, Faulkner, and many of her other contemporaries, to borrow experimental styles from such modern European masters as Joyce. Unlike those of most writers, her male and female characters are equally well drawn and credible. Her vivid characterization owes much more to reality and the burdens of the immoderate past than to literary influences. There are no literary counterparts to her God-haunted, courageous, and compassionate black heroes and heroines—Scarlet Sister Mary, Black April, Cricket, Maum Hannah, and Killdee Pinesett, whom a modern critic calls "one of the most moving, one of the most admirable characters in modern fiction."

Among her most important works are the mythic *Green Thursday* (1924), a story-cycle like *Go Down Moses* and *Dubliners*; her classical tragedy *Black April* (1927), which has been called "perhaps her most powerful work of fiction"; her feminist comedy *Scarlet Sister Mary* (1928), whose sexually demanding heroine not merely endures but prevails over all men and circumstances; her lyrical but disappointing *Bright Skin* (1932); and her magisterial work of nonfiction, *Roll, Jordan, Roll* (1933).

See also LANGUAGE: Gullah

Charles Joyner
University of South Carolina,
Coastal Campus

Thomas H. Landess, *Julia Peterkin* (1976); Noel Polk, in *South Carolina Women Writers*, ed. James B. Meriwether (1979). ☆

PRINGLE, ELIZABETH ALLSTON
(1845–1921) Plantation mistress.

Elizabeth Allston Pringle exemplified the resourcefulness of elite southern women during and after the Civil War. She was born 29 May 1845 near Pawley's Island, S.C., to Robert Allston, a successful rice planter and future governor of the state, and Adele Petigru Allston. In her memoir, *Chronicles of Chicora Wood*, Pringle devoted no fewer than 100 pages to her family background, demonstrating the concern with lineage and heritage characteristic of wealthy 19th-century southerners.

Initially taught at home by a governess, Pringle was sent at age nine to join her sister at a small, select Charleston boarding school, which "finished off" young ladies by teaching them the fine arts and French, as well as basic subjects. The Allstons displayed considerable ambivalence about the education of their daughters, insisting that the girls study at home during the summer, yet acknowledging that by age 16 "balls, receptions, and dinners" made it "impossible" for a young girl to "keep her mind on her studies." Elizabeth Pringle was too young to attend social events before the Civil War, but she recalled her sister's gowns and beaus and parties with keen interest.

The war, of course, was a central experience in Pringle's life. Through her youthful eyes, the excitement of seeing the men march off with banners waving was a dominant early impression. But she also recalled her father's death, the steady reduction in food and clothing, the looting of the family residence, and tense confrontations with the now-free blacks on the family's various plantations. Clearly Elizabeth Allston derived much of her later strength and independence from watching her mother cope with these trying circumstances and from facing up to them herself.

In the fall of 1865 Elizabeth Allston's mother decided to support herself by opening a school in Charleston. Initially afraid to teach, her daughter was ashamed of her weakness. "Am I really just a butterfly?" she asked herself. "Is my love of pleasure the strongest thing about me? What an awful thought." After three months of teaching, she was ecstatic about her work and confident in her abilities.

In 1868 she accompanied her family back to Chicora Wood, where she married John Julius Pringle two years later. Her memoir is characteristically discreet on the subject of their relationship, but the marriage appears to have been a happy one until Pringle's untimely death in 1876. In a bold move, Elizabeth Pringle acquired her husband's plantation and elected to run it herself, growing rice, fruit, and raising livestock. When her mother died in 1896, she took over Chicora Wood as well. Thus, she became a substantial rice planter, a rare venture for a woman to undertake alone.

Elizabeth Allston Pringle pursued this occupation with vigor. She became deeply involved in agricultural techniques and in the often frustrating management of her workers. While she enjoyed years of prosperity, she succumbed to failure early in the 20th century, when severe weather and competition from other regions ruined many Low Country rice planters. But she voiced no regrets. "I have so loved the freedom and simplicity of the life, in spite of its trials and isolation," she asserted, noting too "the exhilaration of making a good income myself." In the last two decades before her death in 1921, she turned to writing, and her gracefully penned recollections add much to the understanding of southern womanhood and southern life during the important transitional period in which she lived.

Laura L. Becker
University of Miami

Patience Pennington, *A Woman Rice Planter* (1961); Elizabeth A. Pringle, *Chronicles of Chicora Wood* (1922). ☆

REECE, FLORENCE

(1907–1986) Writer and social activist.

Florence Reece is the author of several poems, short stories, and songs. A coal miner's daughter from Sharp's Chapel, Tenn., she is best known for her struggle song "Which Side Are You On?," written to rally support for the 1930 United Mine Workers' strike in Harlan County, Ky. No political ideologue, Reece wrote her song out of a sense of desperation when her husband, Sam, was blacklisted, beaten, and driven from their home because of his activities as a union organizer among his fellow miners. As she watched her children and others in the community suffer hunger and deprivation, Reece attempted to deal with her anger by writing these lyrics on the back of a calendar, reflecting the centuries-old southern folk tradition of articulating and simplifying complex personal and social problems through songs and storytelling. Along the picket lines across the South, her simple statement, rising out of a great frustration with the unfair exploitation of laborers and identifying the need for solidarity among all workers, quickly became a familiar chant sung to the tune of the old hymn, "I Am Going to Land On That Shore":

> If you go to Harlan County
> There is no neutral there.
> You will either be a union man,
> Or a thug for J. H. Blair.
>
> Which side are you on?
> Which side are you on?

Reece's militant assertion that the poor and the powerless "had to be for themselves, or against themselves" is the message that made "Which Side Are You On?" as meaningful to civil rights workers in Harlem during the 1960s as to the miners of Harlan County during the 1930s.

Reece, who came from the same impoverished section of Tennessee as Roy Acuff, continued to write prose and verse, finding her voice in the traditional themes of country and western music—motherhood, home, and country. In 1981 she published a collection of her work, *Against the Current*, which shows her abiding concern with social commentary and the problems of her people:

> If you take away their food stamps,
> And all their other means,
> What're you going to feed them on?
> They can't live on jelly beans.

Barbara L. Bellows
Middlebury College

John W. Hevener, *A New Deal for Harlan: The Roosevelt Policies in a Kentucky Coal*

Field, 1931–1939 (1978), *Which Side Are You On?: The Harlan County Miners, 1931–39* (1978); Loyal Jones, *Appalachian Journal* (Fall 1984). ☆

SMITH, LILLIAN

(1897–1966) Writer and social critic.

Internationally acclaimed as author of the controversial novel *Strange Fruit* (1944) and the autobiographical critique of southern culture *Killers of the Dream* (1949, rev. 1961), Lillian Eugenia Smith was the most outspoken white southern writer in areas of economic, racial, and sexual discrimination during the 1930s and 1940s. When other southern liberals—Ralph McGill, Hodding Carter, Virginius Dabney, and Jonathan Daniels—were charting a cautious course on racial change, Smith boldly and persistently called for an end to racial segregation. Furthermore, her work for social justice continued throughout her life. In 1955 she wrote *Now Is the Time* urging support for the Supreme Court's decision on school desegregation. Her last published book, *Our Faces, Our Words* (1964), reflects her personal knowledge and experience with the young black and white civil rights activists of the 1950s and 1960s.

Lillian Smith was born 12 December 1897, the seventh of nine children of Anne Hester Simpson and Calvin Warren Smith, and grew up in Jasper, Fla., where her father was a prominent business and civic leader. Some of the richness of that childhood is portrayed in *Memory of a Large Christmas* (1962). Her life as daughter of upper-class whites in the small-town Deep South ended rather abruptly when her father lost his turpentine mills in 1915 and moved the family to their summer home near Clayton, Ga. Financially on her own, Smith attended the nearby Piedmont College one year, was principal of a two-room mountain school, and helped her parents manage a hotel before she was able to pursue her interest in music. During the school terms of 1916–17 and 1919–22 she studied piano at Peabody Conservatory in Baltimore, spending summers working in the family's summer lodge and teaching music at Laurel Falls Camp for Girls, opened by her father in 1920.

In the fall of 1922 Smith accepted a three-year position as director of music at Virginia School in Huchow, China. But her ambitions for a career in music ended when her parents' ill health necessitated her return to direct Laurel Falls Camp. Under her direction from 1925 through 1948, the camp became an outstanding innovative educational institution, known for its instruction in the arts, music, theater, and modern psychology. It was also a laboratory for many of the ideas informing Smith's analysis of southern culture, especially her understanding of the effects of child-rearing practices on adult racial and sexual relationships.

Through the camp Smith also met Paula Snelling and began the lifelong relationship that encouraged and sustained her writing career. From 1936 to 1946 Smith and Snelling coedited a magazine, first called *Pseudopodia*, then *North Georgia Review*, and finally *South Today*, which quickly achieved acclaim as a forum for liberal opinion in the region.

A record-breaking best-seller, *Strange Fruit* was translated into 15 languages, banned for obscenity in Boston, and produced as a Broadway play. But *Killers of the Dream*, an even more insightful exploration of the interrelation-

ship of race, class, and gender in southern society, brought strong criticism from more moderate southerners. Though widely reviewed, none of her subsequent works achieved the popularity or financial success of her first novel.

Her more philosophical works, *The Journey* (1954) and *One Hour* (1959), demonstrate the extent to which Smith's concerns extended beyond race relations to encompass all aspects of human relationships in the modern world. In *The Journey* she wrote, "I went in search of an image of the human being I could be proud of." *One Hour*, Smith's response to the McCarthy era, is a complex psychological novel about the inevitable destruction unleashed in a commuity when the reality and power of the irrational are unacknowledged in human life.

Two collections of her work have been published posthumously: *From the Mountain* (1972), a selection of pieces from the magazine, edited by Helen White and Redding Sugg; and *The Winner Names the Age* (1978), selected speeches and essays, edited by Michelle Cliff with an introduction by Paula Snelling.

See also MEDIA: / Carter, Hodding; Dabney, Virginius; Daniels, Jonathan; McGill, Ralph

Margaret Rose Gladney
University of Alabama

Louise Blackwell and Frances Clay, *Lillian Smith* (1971); Margaret Rose Gladney, *Southern Studies* (Fall 1983); Fred Hobson, *Tell about the South: The Southern Rage to Explain* (1983); Jo Ann Robinson, in *Notable American Women: The Modern Period*, ed. Barbara Sicherman and Carl Hurd Green (1980). ✩

WALKER, MAGGIE LENA
|||||||||||||||||||||||||||||||||||||||||||||||||||||||||
(1867–1934) Banker.

Walker, born 15 July 1867 in Richmond, Va., founded the Saint Luke Penny Savings Bank in Richmond in 1903, becoming the first woman bank president in the United States. Before her death she helped to reorganize it as the present-day Consolidated Bank and Trust Company, the oldest continuously existing black bank in the country. The bank, like most of Walker's activities, was the outgrowth of the Independent Order of Saint Luke, which she served as Right Worthy Grand Secretary for 35 years. Under her leadership this female-founded but previously male-run mutual benefit association established a juvenile department, an educational loan fund for young people, a department store, and a weekly newspaper. Growing to include 80,000 members in 2,010 Councils and Circles in 28 states, the order demonstrated a special commitment to expanding the economic opportunities within the community in the face of racism and sexism. It sought to develop interdependence among black women as a positive response to their problems and a step toward collective well-being.

Walker believed that black women had a "special duty and incentive to organize." And her work as a founder or leading supporter of the Richmond Council of Colored Women, the Virginia State Federation of Colored Women, the National Association of Wage Earners, the International Council of Women of the Darker Races, the National Training School for Girls, and the Virginia Industrial School for Colored Girls was a positive representation of that belief. Additionally, Walker and others of the Saint Luke women were instrumental in political activities of the black community including the struggle for women's suffrage, voter registration campaigns after the passage of the Nineteenth Amendment, and the formation of the Virginia Lily-Black Republican party, which nominated Walker for State Superintendent of Public Instruction in 1921. Throughout the 1920s Walker handled the finances of the National League of Republican Colored Women.

As a contributor to the ideological perspectives and political strategies of the black community, Walker symbolizes the growing belief in the early 20th century in economic development and self-help. All of her activities were motivated by a profound belief in the necessity to create an independent, self-sustaining community. Walker also helped direct the NAACP, the National Urban League, and the Negro Organization Society of Virginia.

Throughout her life and career this daughter of a washerwoman developed a distinct understanding of what it meant to be wife, mother, businesswoman, and female activist. It was this perspective that shaped her struggle to expand notions within the black community of the proper role of women and within the larger society of the proper place of blacks.

Elsa Barkley Brown
Emory University

Wendell P. Dabney, *Maggie Walker and the I.O. of Saint Luke: The Woman and Her Work* (1927); Sadie Iola Daniel, in *Women Builders*, ed. S. Daniel (1931); Maggie Lena Walker Papers, Maggie Walker National Historic Site, Richmond, Va. ☆

INDEX OF CONTRIBUTORS

||||||||||||||||||||||||||||||||||||||||||||||||||||||||||||||||||||||||||||||||||||||||||||||||||||||

Index

|||||||||||||||||||||||||

Boldfaced page numbers refer to main articles

Italicized page numbers refer to illustrations

Abolitionism, 527–28

Absalom, Absalom! (Faulkner), 26, 93, 371

Aerospace, **132–34**, 168

African Methodist Episcopal (AME) church, **81–82**, 247

Agee, James, 223, 240, 251

Agrarians, Vanderbilt, 168

Agricultural Adjustment Administration (AAA), 251–52, 276

Agriculture, 133; farmers' organizations, 202, 219, 258–59; migrant workers, **229–33,***231*; scientific agriculture, 122, 126, **134–36**, 166, 168–69, 188–89; women and, 480–82, 506. *See also* Sharecroppers and tenants

Air-conditioning, 289

Alabama: absentee landownership, 209; aerospace industry, 133; alcoholism, 139; child labor, 266–67; divorce law, 489; frontier religion, 37; genealogical records, 471; gun ownership, 358; homicide rate, 347; Marxist perspective on, 226; peonage, 412; Sharecroppers Union, 270–71

Alcohol and alcoholism, 107–8, **136–39**

Alexander, Will, 512–13

Allen, Young J., 49

All the King's Men (Warren), 45, 46, 371

American Association for the Advancement of Science (AAAS), 155

American Colonization Society, 108

American Farm Bureau Federation (AFBF), 232

American Federation of Labor (AFL), 203, 220, **252–53,**, 270, 511

Ames, Jessie Daniel, 431, 453, **512–13**

Amish, 5

Anesthesia, 183–84

Anglican church, 16–17, 35, 56, 244

Animals, blood sports and, **353–55**

Anniston, Ala., 285

Annual Worker Plan, 232

Appalachia and Appalachians: exploitation of, **208–11**; poverty, 206–7; religion, **14–16**; women, **434–37**

Appalachian Regional Commission, 209

Architecture: religion and, 10–11, **16–18,** *18*; urban, 285–86, 288, 291

Aristocracy, **211–13**. *See also* Planter elite

Arkansas: blue laws, 84–85; elderly population, 458; genealogical records, 471; gun ownership, 358; homicide rate, 347; women's voting rights, 504

Arminianism, 72

Asbestos workers, 217

Asbury, Francis, **82–83**

Assemblies of God, 55

Association of Southern Women for the Prevention of Lynching, 453, 513

Atkinson, Ti-Grace, **513–14**

Atlanta, Ga., **316–18**; aerospace industry, 133; annexations, 287; architecture, 291; aviation, commercial, 133; black community, 292; boosterism, 291, 300; Civil War and, 285; growth of, 301; homicide rate, 294; patent medicine industry, 165; planning of, 308; politics, 310; poverty, 313; race riots, 388; railroads and, 285; segregation, 295, 296, 297; socialism, 247; transportation, 286, 287, 314, 315

Audubon, John James, 533–34

Aunt adoption, 484

Austin, Stephen F., 415

Automobiles, 167–68, 287, 315–16

Aviation, commercial, 132, 133–34

Bachman, John, 533, 534

Bacon, Nathaniel, 378

Baker, Ella Jo, 27, **515–16**

Bakker, Jim, 21, 92

Baltimore, Md., 112, 297, 303, 309

Bankhead, Tallulah, *516*, **516–17**

Bankhead-Jones Farm Tenancy Act of 1937, 204

Baptism, 3; as rite of initiation, 6–8, 9

Baptists, 7, 8, 10, 12; Antimission, 37, 67–69; Appalachian religion and, 14, 16; Arminianism, 72; Calvinism and, 23; church architecture, 17; class tensions and, 198, 244, 245; frontier religion and, 35–36, 37; fundamentalism and, 39–40; Landmark, 69; missionary activities, 48–49; modernism and, 51, 52; National, **103–4;** restorationism, 5, 66, 67–69; sacred places, 112; Separate, 35, 198; Southern Baptist Convention, **114–45**

sports and, 290–91; transportation, 286–87, **314–16**; World War II and, 288–89
Urban riots, 382
Utopian settlements, 113

Vanderbilt University, 51
Vigilantism, 392, 408–9
Violence, **345–50**; alcoholism and, 137; anti-Semitism, 41; attitudes toward violence, 348–50; in cities, 293–94; 382; civil rights enforcement, **350–53**, *352*; cockfighting, **353–55**; dueling, 345, 391, **400–1**; explanations for, 346–48; filibustering, **401–2**; gun ownership and, 357, 358; honor and, 345, 363, 364; industrial violence, 203, 362, **365–67**; in literature and music (black), **367–69**; in literature and music (white), **369–72**; Mexican Americans and, **372–74**; mob violence, **408–9**; political, **381–83**, 387–88; race riots, **387–89**, 410, 416–17; in southwest, **389–93**; studies of, 346, 413–14. *See also* Crime and punishment; Ku Klux Klan; Lynching; Mountain feuding
Virginia: absentee landownership, 208, 209; church architecture, 16; divorce law, 489; elderly population, 458; family dynasties, 462; frontier religion and, 35; genealogical records, 471; homicide rate, 347; prohibition, 88; religious idealism, 79–80
Voodoo, 164
Voting rights, 388; suffrage movement, 430, 496–97, **503–6**, *505*

Wage rates, 510
Waldensians, 31
Walker, Alice, 47, 479, 524
Walker, Maggie Lena, **545**
Walker, William, 402
Wallace, George C., 206, *348*
Wallace, Lurleen, 497
War Labor Board (WLB), 219
War on Poverty, 240–41
Warren, Robert Penn, 45, 46, 371
Washington, Booker T., 170, 228, 412
Washington, D.C., 139, 302, 303
Watergate scandal, 531–32, 535
Watson, Thomas E., 259
Welfare, 238–39, 240–41, 284, 312–13
Welty, Eudora, 223, 440, 525
West Virginia, 345; absentee landownership, 208, 209; elderly population, 458; homicide rate, 347
"Which Side Are You On?" (Reece), 542–43
Whiskey, 137
White-collar workers, 221, 222, 229

Whites, poor, 196, 197, 237; Civil War and, 199; literary portrayals of, 198, **223–25**, 233–34; tenancy and, 250
Whitsitt, William, 51
Wiener, Jonathan, 226
Williamsburg, Va., 307
Wilmington, N.C., 49, 308; race riot of 1898, 388, **416–17**
Winchell, Alexander, 51
Wise Blood (O'Connor), 83–84, 104
Wolfe, Thomas, 299–300
Women, **421–34**; agriculture and, 480–82, 506; of Appalachia, **434–37**; belles and ladies, **437–42**, *438*; civil rights movement and, 27, 499; Civil War, impact of, 426–27; clubs and voluntary organizations, **450–53**, 502; coal miners and, 255–56; colonial era, 422–24, 509; education for, 424–25, 429, **453–57**, 503, 536–37; frontier life, 477–78; healers, **472–74**; Indian women, **476–77**; industrialization and, 428, 507; Ku Klux Klan and, 406; labor movement and, 428, 431, 435, 508, 510–11; the land, attachment to, **477–82**; maiden aunts, **482–85**; Mexican women, **493–96**; motherhood, 423, 424; on plantations, 478–79; in politics, **496–98**, 506–7; populism and, 427–28, 480; religion and, 57, 100–1, 429–30, **501–3**; Revolutionary War and, **424–25**; sex and reproduction, 426; sharecropping and tenancy, 249, 427, 480–82, 499–500; social housekeeping, 430–31; "southern lady" stereotype, 425–26; southern womanhood, concept of, 437–42; suffrage movement, 430, 496–97, **503–6**, *505;* virtue and, 363; workers' wives, **506–8**, *507;* working women, 269, 277, 279, 431–32, 460, 461, **508–12**. *See also* Black women; Family; Feminism
Women's Christian Temperance Union (WCTU), 451
Woodrow, James, 51, 163
Woodward, C. Vann, 237, 254, 464
World War I, 65
World War II, 130, 205–7, 219, 231, 288–89
Wright, Richard, 47, 367–68
Wright brothers, 132
Wyatt-Brown, Bertram, 440

Ybor City, Fla., 341–42
Yellow fever, 122, 128, 148, 154, 177, 188
Yeoman farmers, 196, 197, 199, 200; Owsley thesis on, **268–69**
Young, Stark, 168

Zion, South as, **79–81**

Picture Credits

||||||||||||||||||||||||||||||||||||||||||

Religion

1 Photographic Archives, University of Louisville (Kentucky)

4 William Ferris Collection, Archives and Special Collections, University of Mississippi Library, Oxford

6 Jack Delano, Library of Congress (LC-USF-34-46523-D), Washington, D.C.

12 Tom Rankin, photographer, Atlanta, Georgia

18 William Ferris Collection, Archives and Special Collections, University of Mississippi Library, Oxford

33 William Ferris Collection, Archives and Special Collections, University of Mississippi Library, Oxford

42 Waco Jewry Collection, The Texas Collection, Baylor University, Waco, Texas

55 William Ferris Collection, Archives and Special Collections, University of Mississippi Library, Oxford

62 William Ferris Collection, Archives and Special Collections, University of Mississippi Library, Oxford

87 Al Clayton, photographer, Peachtree Publishers, Atlanta, Georgia

92 Thomas Road Baptist Church, Lynchburg, Virginia

95 Billy Graham Evangelistic Association, Minneapolis, Minnesota

99 Ann Rayburn Paper Americana Collection, Archives and Special Collections, University of Mississippi Library, Oxford

109 Ann Rayburn Paper Americana Collection, Archives and Special Collections, University of Mississippi Library, Oxford

111 Oral Roberts University,Tulsa, Oklahoma

114 National Archives, Washington, D.C.

Science and Medicine

117 Jane Moseley, photographer, Center for Southern Folklore, Memphis, Tennessee

132 Wolff, Gretter, Cusick, Hill Collection, Kentucky Historical Society, Frankfort

133 National Aeronautics and Space Administration, Houston, Texas

136 Film Stills Archives, Museum of Modern Art, New York, New York

149 Photographic Archives, University of Louisville (Kentucky)

165 Marion Post Wolcott, Library of Congress (LC-USF-34-50583-D), Washington, D.C.

171 Frances Benjamin Johnston, Library of Congress (LC-J694-302), Washington, D.C.

175 Picture Files, The Texas Collection, Baylor University, Waco, Texas

177 National Archives, Washington, D.C.

189 Virginia State Library and Archives (45.9232), Richmond

Social Class

193 Dorothea Lange, Library of Congress (LC-USF-34-9599C), Washington, D.C.

203 Film Stills Archives, Museum of Modern Art, New York, New York

206 Esther Bubley, Library of Congress (LC-USW-3-38103E), Washington, D.C.

220 Jack Delano, Library of Congress (LC-USF-33-20926-M2), Washington, D.C.

229 Frank Collection, Mississippi Valley Collection, Memphis (Tennessee) State University Library

231 Marion Post Wolcott, Library of Congress (LC-USF-34-51178E), Washington, D.C.

242 William Ferris Collection, Archives and Special Collections, University of Mississippi Library, Oxford

277 Lewis Hine, Albin O. Kuhn Library and Gallery, University of Maryland, Baltimore County

278 Jack Delano, Library of Congress (LC-USF-34-43995D), Washington, D.C.

280 Photographic Archives, University of Louisville (Kentucky)

Urbanization

281 Marion Post Wolcott, Library of Congress (LC-USF-34-57018-D), Washington, D.C.

287 Historic New Orleans Collection (1951.68), New Orleans, Louisiana

293 Jack Delano, Library of Congress (LC-USF-33-20850-M5), Washington, D.C.
303 Metropolitan Dade County, Florida
327 Filson Club, Louisville, Kentucky
333 Ann Rayburn Paper Americana Collection, Archives and Special Collections, University of Mississippi Library, Oxford
334 Nashville (Tennessee) Area Chamber of Commerce
335 Natchez (Mississippi) Pilgrimage Garden Club
340 Charles East Collection, Baton Rouge, Louisiana

Violence

343 Film Stills Archives, Museum of Modern Art, New York, New York
348 University of Alabama Library, Tuscaloosa
352 Mississippi Department of Archives and History, Jackson
356 Film Stills Archives, Museum of Modern Art, New York, New York
357 William Ferris Collection, Archives and Special Collections, University of Mississippi Library, Oxford
386 Jack Delano, Library of Congress (LC-USF-33-20863-M3), Washington, D.C.
397 Photographer not given, Library of Congress (LC-USF-344-7541-2B), Washington, D.C.
402 West Virginia Department of Archives and History, Charleston
406 Texas Sheet Music Collection, The Texas Collection, Baylor University, Waco, Texas
411 William Ferris Collection, Archives and Special Collections, University of Mississippi Library, Oxford

Women's Life

419 Doris Ulmann, Art Department, Berea College, Berea, Kentucky

429 Florida State Archives, Tallahassee
432 William Ferris Collection, Archives and Special Collections, University of Mississippi Library, Oxford
438 Ann Rayburn Paper Americana Collection, Archives and Special Collections, University of Mississippi Library, Oxford
449 Jane Moseley, photographer, Center for Southern Folklore, Memphis, Tennessee
456 Gordon Parks, Library of Congress (LC-USW-3-17125C), Washington, D.C.
458 Georgia Department of Archives and History, Atlanta
460 Jane Moseley, photographer, Center for Southern Folklore, Memphis, Tennessee
475 Marion Post Wolcott, Library of Congress (LC-USF-34-51738D), Washington, D.C.
481 Marion Post Wolcott, Library of Congress [LC-USF-34-9610C], Washington, D.C.
487 Photographic Archives, University of Louisville (Kentucky)
492 William Ferris Collection, Archives and Special Collections, University of Mississippi Library, Oxford
505 Photographic Archives, University of Louisville (Kentucky)
507 William Ferris Collection, Archives and Special Collections, University of Mississippi Library, Oxford
511 Gordon Parks, Library of Congress (LC-USW-3-14883C), Washington, D.C.
516 Theater Collection, New York Public Library
518 Carter Presidential Library, Atlanta, Georgia
525 William Ferris Collection, Archives and Special Collections, University of Mississippi Library, Oxford
531 News and Information Service, University of Texas at Austin
536 Alumni Association, University of Mississippi, Oxford
539 Columbia Records, New York, New York